THE GOLDEN AGE OF ROCK
Volume One
1963 – 1968

NICK HAMLYN

THE GOLDEN AGE OF ROCK Volume One 1963-1968

Copyright © 2021 Nick Hamlyn

Published by PPR Publishing,
19 Kingswell Road, Northampton NN2 6QB.

www.pprpublishing.co.uk

All rights reserved.

A CIP catalogue record for this book
is available from the British Library

ISBN 978 1 9164347 6 9

Edition 1.1

Printed and bound in Great Britain by IngramSpark

CONTENTS

Introduction	1
1963	3
1964	15
1965	31
1966	76
1967	124
1968	218
Index	319
About the Author	325

THE GOLDEN AGE OF ROCK Volume One 1963-1968

THE GOLDEN AGE OF ROCK 1963-1976: INTRODUCTION

"We were living in a time that was tremendously exciting, musically. What we didn't know, then, was that it was a one-off, that things would never be quite like this again. There'd never be another time when the pop music scene was so intensely creative and the mainstream audience was so open to new ideas."
Pete Atkin, quoted in *Loose Canon – The Extraordinary Songs of Clive James & Pete Atkin* by Ian Shircore (RedDoor 2016)

I was eleven years old when I first heard the name of the Beatles, attached to a record being played as a new release on Radio Luxembourg. The radio station's reception in the UK was distinctly variable in 1962, but it was nevertheless the station of choice for a fledgling teenager interested in hearing the music that was in the charts or destined to be. The BBC Light Programme, which provided the only alternative, seemed generally to be far more interested in providing employment for an assortment of light orchestras, playing music that sounded to be decades old. The new release in question was called *Love Me Do*, and I remember that I did not think much of it.

The following January, a second Beatles record appeared. This one was called *Please Please Me* and it had everything – a driving rhythm, powered by electric guitars and crisp drumming, an instantly memorable melody, and a hook chorus line – the kind of thing that people later referred to as an 'ear worm'. I was won over and, when the record climbed to number one in the pop chart presented every week by an excited Alan Freeman (and this *was* on the BBC Light programme, the unmissable *Pick Of The Pops*), I was not at all surprised.

The Beatles became enormously popular – the most popular artists of their generation and time. If that were all we could say about the group, then the Beatles would simply take their place in a long line of popular artists, stretching from Enrico Caruso through to Adele and Ed Sheeran – artists for whom their existing or eventual fate is to just act as a focus for fan nostalgia. As it happens, this process does seem to be taking a long time in the case of the Beatles. Remarkably, for a group that broke up in 1970, they have achieved the second highest cumulative album sales of any artist in the 21st century so far. (The highest, for anyone who might be wondering, is Eminem.) The Beatles, however, were also innovative, remaining so for virtually their entire career. Having hit on a successful formula to make people buy their records, they could have merely carried on repeating it until the public found something else to follow. Early interviews with the Beatles make it clear that the members of the group had no expectation of being able to sustain a high level of popularity for more than two or three years. From album to album, however, and from single to single, the Beatles introduced modest novelties, never being content to do no more than repeat something that had worked before, for the sake of a guaranteed positive response. But it came anyway and by this means, the Beatles created a musical climate in which their successive record releases seemed to inspire the whole of the popular music world to take the Beatles sound and approach as a starting point for what they wanted to achieve themselves. In a very real sense, other artists would wait for each new Beatles record to appear, to tell them how they should now be sounding.

Of course, there were many other innovative and important musicians during the sixties and afterwards. But it was the Beatles who created a climate in which experimentation and innovation were equated with commercial success – particularly and most crucially, as far as the record companies were concerned. For this reason, the music of the Beatle years, and a little beyond, was encouraged and allowed to be experimental and imaginative to a degree that had not been the case previously and has not been the case since. Every year from 1963, rock and pop music was growing in stature, was making more and more impact on contemporary culture generally. It was a period when every month seemed to produce music that was new, music that was important. It was a period of immense creativity, a period during which rock music became taken seriously, became worthy of being treated as an art form.

It is important to stress that from the earliest days of rock 'n' roll in the fifties, the music was most definitely *not* considered to be anything remotely like an art form. Frank Sinatra famously stated, "Rock 'n' roll. The most brutal, ugly, desperate, vicious form of expression it has been my misfortune to hear". BBC radio presenter Steve Race said much the same thing, albeit in a more measured British tone. "Viewed as a social phenomenon, the current craze for Rock-and-Roll material is one of the most terrifying things ever to have happened to popular music… Musically speaking, of course, the whole thing is laughable." These were opinions shared by virtually the whole of the music establishment, by anyone who was not a teenager. In 1963, serious writing about rock music did not exist – the primary concern of the specialist music papers was the stars' favourite colour and their taste in girls (female performers being a very tiny minority). Just a few years later, at least one respected writer was comparing the Beatles' songwriting to that of Schubert.

Then, towards the end of 1976, a rock music style known as punk arrived (ignoring a sixties American genre also known as punk), played and followed by people who rather liked the idea of music that was "vicious", who did not want rock music to be treated as an art form. They viewed anyone who did, as being pretentious or worse. Punk was greeted with enthusiasm by the music press of the time, which spotted a way of boosting its flagging circulations by attracting a new generation of readers and accorded the music an importance that was much greater than mere record sales should have allowed. By this means, punk – a genre that did not value musical expertise – effectively put a brake on the idea that rock should continue to develop and make a significant renewed artistic statement from year to year. Some of the groups and solo artists that had based their careers on the old aesthetic achieved some of their biggest successes *after* the arrival of punk. Albums like *The Wall* and *The Final Cut* (both by Pink Floyd), *The Game* and *A Kind Of Magic* (Queen), *Duke*, *Abacab*, and *Three Sides Live* (Genesis), *Double Fantasy* (John Lennon), *Tug Of War* and *Give My Regards To Broad Street* (Paul McCartney), and *The River* and *Born In The USA* (Bruce Springsteen) sold in far greater quantities than anything produced by the likes of the Sex Pistols, the Clash, or Sham 69, but were somehow sidelined in terms of their perceived influence. There are some incredible records made by new artists since 1976, but they seem like the work of isolated adventurers, swimming against a tide of general pop mediocrity, rather than being part of a sustained artistic movement.

As the pages in this book are turned, the panorama of new album releases in both the US and the UK, presented in chronological order, is gradually revealed, just as it actually was for open-minded music fans living through those years. No attempt has been made to include every album to be released, but it is hoped that every album relevant to telling the story of the music's development is here, even if, in some cases, the record's ultimate musical worth is dubious. Several of the albums are jazz, or folk, or other genres that are not exactly 'rock', if by that we mean music with a forceful beat played by electric guitars, but all of them have proved to be influential and they played a part in determining the course followed by the music that was rock. However one chooses to define the term, one of the essential characteristics of rock, from its beginnings as a hybrid combining country with rhythm and blues, has always been its fondness for incorporating elements borrowed from other kinds of music. The *Golden Age Of Rock* cannot be properly explored without including those other kinds. The records themselves – certainly the best of them – explain exactly why the years 1963 to 1976 can be considered 'golden'. Volume One begins the story in March 1963 with the release of the first album by the Beatles, *Please Please Me*. It ends in December 1968, with Volumes 2 and 3 carrying on the story from that point. Volume 3 concludes with *Damned*, the first UK punk album, released in February 1977. While every effort has been made to establish the correct release dates for the various records, occasionally it has been necessary to make an educated guess. In a few cases, the precise day in the month is known for record releases, but so many do not have this information available, that it was decided to simply use the month for all of them. The album sleeves shown are the American versions in the case of albums by American artists or issued first in the US ; otherwise they are the UK versions.

My grateful thanks to the people who read the book in advance of its publication and made helpful suggestions for its improvement. They are Liz Hamlyn, Mike Richards, Dave Skinner, Cliff Steele, Richard Tomalin, and Phil Walker.

Nick Hamlyn,   Northampton UK,   January 2021

1963

THE BEATLES   PLEASE PLEASE ME

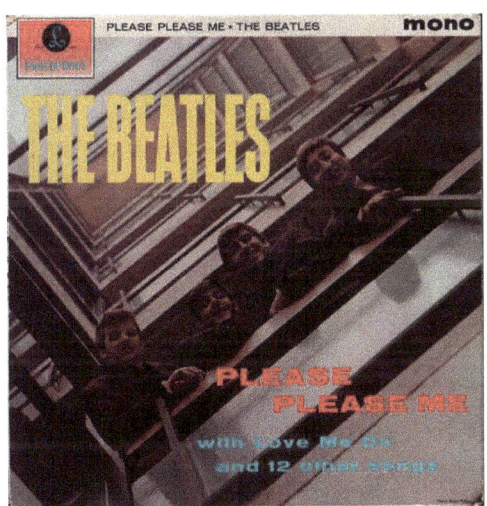

UK release   March 1963   Parlophone   PMC 1202 mono
              April 1963   Parlophone   PCS 3042 stereo
US release as INTRODUCING THE BEATLES   January 1964   Vee-Jay
              VJLP 1062 mono / VSLPS 1062 stereo
Two versions – omitting tracks 6 and 7 or omitting tracks 8 and 9

1. I Saw Her Standing There (McCartney/Lennon)
2. Misery (McCartney/Lennon)
3. Anna (Go To Him) (Arthur Alexander)
4. Chains (Gerry Goffin/Carole King)
5. Boys (Luther Dixon/Wes Farrell)
6. Ask Me Why (McCartney/Lennon)
7. Please Please Me (McCartney/Lennon)
8. Love Me Do (McCartney/Lennon)
9. P.S. I Love You (McCartney/Lennon)
10. Baby It's You (Mack David/Barney Williams/Burt Bacharach)
11. Do You Want To Know A Secret (McCartney/Lennon)
12. A Taste Of Honey (Bobby Scott/Ric Marlow)
13. There's A Place (McCartney/Lennon)
14. Twist And Shout (Phil Medley/Bert Berns (Russell))

John Lennon: guitar, harmonica, vocals / George Harrison: guitar, vocals /
Paul McCartney: bass guitar, vocals / Ringo Starr: drums, percussion (8,9),
vocals / Andy White: drums (8,9) / George Martin: producer, keyboards

Paul McCartney's "1,2,3,4!" count-in launches both the first LP by the year's most exciting new arrival and, as far as pop music was concerned, the sixties. (The event was celebrated, with a slightly different emphasis, in Philip Larkin's notorious poem, *Annus Mirabilis*.) The count-in is missing from the US version of the record, when it finally appeared in the next year – for that country, pop music's sixties would not begin until later on. The Beatles had achieved two single chart hits in the UK, *Love Me Do* and *Please Please Me*, the second of which had reached number one on every listing apart from that published in the trade magazine, *Record Retailer*. With other groups from Liverpool starting to follow behind, 'Merseybeat' was introduced as a name for what was received as a thrilling rebirth of a rock 'n' roll music that had almost faded away. Parlophone was keen to keep the momentum going and included both singles, together with their B-sides, on the LP. It also issued an EP in July, comprising the last four tracks and named after the final one, *Twist And Shout*. This became a UK singles chart hit in its own right, reaching number 2. It is likely that many young fans bought both the EP and the LP, little caring that the songs were duplicated. The sheer energy and rhythmic precision of *I Saw Her Standing There*, capped with powerful harmonised vocals and a sparkling George Harrison guitar solo, make the listener take notice as soon as the LP starts. They prove how the many, many hours of performing in clubs in Hamburg had turned the Beatles into the most convincing rock 'n' roll band since Buddy Holly and the Crickets first stormed into the charts on both sides of the Atlantic some six years previously. The song is one of eight written by Lennon and McCartney themselves (credited, as never again, the other way round). Claims made that the songwriters were drawing on a pool of dozens of completed songs were not true, but, given the impressive variety and distinctiveness of these eight, this hardly matters. The remaining six tracks are not the rock 'n' roll covers that might have been expected, but instead draw on early soul music, particularly female vocal groups, the Shirelles and the Cookies. The inclusion too of a theatre tune, *A Taste of Honey,* without in any way weakening the rocking impact of the album overall, is an indication that, right from the start, the Beatles were determined to avoid being seen as predictable. The album is brought to a conclusion by an extraordinarily powerful rendering of an old Isley Brothers hit, totally transforming *Twist And Shout* from soul into beat. Brian Poole and the Tremeloes, the group that Decca had chosen to sign in preference to the Beatles, were inspired to record a cover version of this cover version. They were unable to match the Beatles' drive and aggression, but gained their own first chart hit just through the association. In the UK, the LP dominated the charts for most of the rest of the year, only surrendering the top position when a new Beatles album was released to take its place. A stereo version was issued, but very much as an afterthought, since few teenagers possessed the equipment to play such a thing. Having been recorded on a two-track machine, the vocals were on one track and the instruments on the other. The stereo LP simply placed these tracks on either side, without any further attempt being made to create a proper mix. This did not matter very much at the time, since as Parlophone expected, the stereo record sold hardly at all.

THE BEACH BOYS   SURFIN' USA

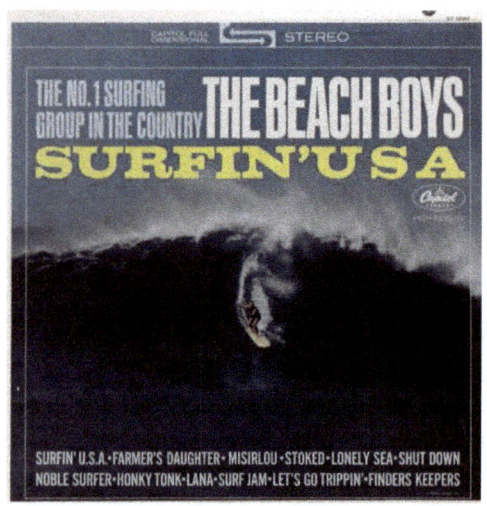

US release   March 1963   Capitol   (S)T 1890
UK release   August 1965   Capitol T/ST 1 890

1. Surfin' USA (Chuck Berry/Brian Wilson)
2. Farmer's Daughter (Brian Wilson/Mike Love)
3. Misirlou (Fred Wise/Milton Leeds/Nick Roubanis/Bob Russell)
4. Stoked (Brian Wilson)
5. Lonely Sea (Brian Wilson/Gary Usher)
6. Shut Down (Brian Wilson/Roger Christian)

7. Noble Surfer (Brian Wilson/Mike Love)
8. Honky Tonk (Bill Doggett/Billy Butler/Clifford Scott/Shep Shepard)
9. Lana (Brian Wilson)
10. Surf Jam (Carl Wilson)
11. Let's Go Trippin' (Dick Dale)
12. Finders Keepers (Brian Wilson/Mike Love)

Mike Love: vocals, saxophone / Carl Wilson: vocals, guitar / David Marks: vocals, guitar / Brian Wilson: vocals, bass guitar, keyboards, producer / Dennis Wilson: vocals, drums / Frank DeVito: drums (1) / Nick Venet: executive producer

Like the Beach Boys' first album, *Surfin' Safari,* issued the previous October, this LP established a pattern, whereby the group's latest hit was surrounded by hastily recorded filler in a similar style, in order to gain maximum commercial advantage from the single. Five of the tracks here are nondescript instrumentals, delivered by a group already best known for its striking close-harmony vocal interplay. By modern standards, or even the standards of the early sixties in the UK, the album also provides extremely short measure, at less than twenty-five minutes altogether. In the circumstances, the six new complete songs created by Brian Wilson, with whoever he chose to write the lyrics, are remarkably strong as far as their melodies are concerned. The beauty of one of them was recognised seventeen years later when Fleetwood Mac delivered a captivating version of *Farmer's Daughter* on the *Fleetwood Mac Live* album. *Surfin' USA,* the hit, was a very thinly disguised adaptation of one of Chuck Berry's favourite blues structures (the one he used on *Sweet Little Sixteen*). Indeed, Berry was eventually given full credit for the song, after his publisher threatened court action. Wilson's other songs don't stray very far away from rhythm and blues chords either, even if the harmony vocals are closer to barbershop, with Brian Wilson's own falsetto singing a key element. The Beach Boys chose to align themselves with a pop music style, surf music, that was never likely to be more than a transitory phenomenon. Partly for this reason, there is no sense on this LP that the listener is in the presence of artists likely to be around long enough to make a serious impact on popular music. The contrast in this respect with the British album (*Please Please Me*) released just a few days earlier is striking. (Although, as we know now, Brian Wilson went on to defy such expectations.) Perhaps Capitol thought this too, because the company did not even bother to release the album in the UK at the time of its first appearance in America. At least, however, the stereo version means what it says, with Capitol's four track recording facilities allowing music that is properly mixed for the format. The Beach Boys made two more albums like this during the remainder of 1963 and another in early 1964. Each had a hit single together with a couple of other memorable songs. Putting all these together into just one record would have created a great LP, but sadly, this was not how Capitol or the Beach Boys worked during the sixties.

THELONIOUS MONK   MONK'S DREAM

```
US release    March 1963    Columbia    CS 8765 / CL 1965
UK release    March 1963    CBS         (S)BPG 62135

1. Monk's Dream (Monk)
2. Body And Soul (Edward Heyman/Robert Sour/Frank Eyton / Johnny Green)
3. Bright Mississippi (Monk)
4. Five Spot Blues (Monk)

5. Bolivar Blues (Monk)
6. Just A Gigolo (Julius Brammer/Irving Caesar/Leonello Casucci)
7. Bye-Ya (Monk)
8. Sweet And Lovely (Gus Arnheim/Harry Tobias/Jules LeMare)

Thelonious Monk: piano / Charlie Rouse: tenor saxophone / John Ore: bass /
Frankie Dunlop: drums / Teo Macero: producer
```

Thelonious Monk was a pianist, playing the modern jazz style characteristic of the late fifties and a little after, known as 'hard bop'. Monk had been one of the young upstarts inventing a new style of jazz in the early forties, while taking part in jam sessions at a Harlem club by the name of Minton's Playhouse. It was a style, christened 'bebop' after the sound made by Dizzy Gillespie's trumpet, that caused as much of a musical revolution as did the development of rock 'n' roll a decade later. Monk played alongside fellow revolutionaries Dizzy Gillespie, Charlie Parker, and guitarist Charlie Christian, who sadly did not live long enough to see the end results of his endeavours. These musicians delighted in playing music that was fast and twisting and difficult, in order to throw off any rivals without the skills to keep up. Monk's own playing was unusual and immediately recognisable, described by one unsympathetic critic as being like an "elephant on the keyboard". Certainly, Monk was often heavy handed and he liked to strike adjacent keys as he played, creating a deliberately harsh sound. His music was not avant garde, but neither was it in any way easy listening, stretching ideas of acceptable tonality to the limit. *Monk's Dream* was the first album that Monk made for the major label, Columbia, after three years without recording anything at all. Nearly all the pieces chosen were ones that the pianist had recorded before, but now they fairly crackle with the energy of a performer who is absolutely relishing his return to the studio. Charlie Rouse is a good choice as musical partner, since his playing on tenor saxophone has much of the angular phrasing and abrasiveness of Monk himself. One of his predecessors in the Monk group was John Coltrane and Rouse does well to come close to the master saxophonist's invention and expertise. He does even better by managing this without sounding like a Coltrane clone. The interlocked pairing of Ore and Dunlop, meanwhile, does everything that a rhythm section should, driving the music along and making sure that the soloists shine. Through the sixties, Thelonious Monk seemed content to draw on his past achievements, creating ever more skilfully wrought interpretations of his favourite compositions, rather than attempting to compose very much that was new. The increased confidence of his playing, however, together with a level of critical support that he had not previously experienced, produced albums that serve his art particularly well. Several other albums made by the pianist through the sixties are as fine as this, most notably *Criss Cross*, which appeared later the same year. *Monk's Dream* is the one that captured the jazz enthusiasts' imagination, however, becoming the best selling record of Monk's career.

JAMES BROWN   LIVE AT THE APOLLO

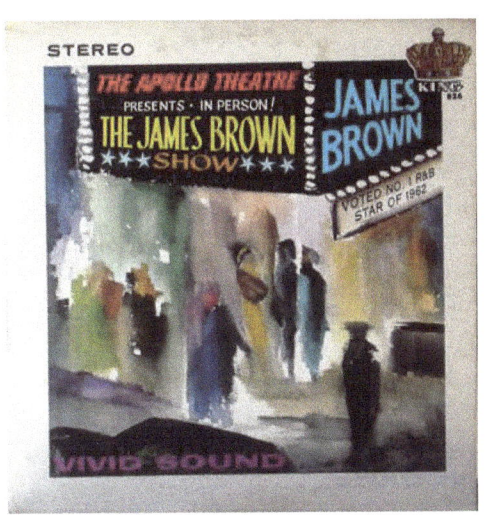

James Brown helped to invent soul during the fifties, with his first record, *Please Please Please,* becoming a huge R&B chart hit in 1956. Several hits later, Brown felt that a live recording of his dynamic stage show would do much to push his career further. Since Syd Nathan, the boss of King records, was reluctant to agree to the plan, Brown decided to finance a recording himself. During October 1962, the singer was scheduled to deliver a series of concerts at the Apollo Theatre in Harlem, New York – thirty of them, spread over six days. He selected the last of the series to be recorded, expecting that the momentum built up by then would deliver something particularly special. Brown was right and, hearing the result, with rapturous music dominated by an eleven minute version of the hit song, *Lost Someone,* performed as if it was a sermon in a revivalist church, Nathan agreed to release the record. It was an instant hit on the black music radio stations in the US, which, encouraged by the enthusiastic listener response, began playing the entire album, as if it was a single. The record proceeded to climb to number two in the National Album Chart, remaining in a high position for well over a year. The sleeve notes proclaimed, "This is without a doubt one of the most exciting albums ever recorded in a live performance" and, for once, an apparently exaggerated claim could be heard to be well justified.

```
US release     May 1963      King K 826      mono
UK release     May 1963      London HA 8184 mono

1. I'll Go Crazy (James Brown)
2. Try Me (James Brown)
3. Think (Lowman Pauling)
4. I Don't Mind (James Brown)
5. Lost Someone (James Brown/Bobby Byrd/LLoyd Stallworth)

6. Please Please Please Medley (James Brown/Johnny Terry/ others)
7. Night Train (Oscar Washington/Lewis Simpkins/Jimmy Forrest)

James Brown: vocals , producer / Bobby Byrd: vocals, organ / Bobby Bennett: vocals / Lloyd Stallworth: vocals / Louis Hamblin: trumpet / Teddy Washington: trumpet / Mack Johnson: trumpet / St.Clair Pinckney: tenor saxophone / Al Clark: tenor and baritone saxophone / Clifford Macmillan: tenor saxophone / Dickie Wells: trombone / Lucas Gonder: organ / Les Buie: guitar / Hubert Perry: bass guitar / Clayton Fillyau: drums / Sam Latham: drums
```

BOB DYLAN   THE FREEWHEELIN'

```
US release     May 1963      Columbia     CS 8786 / CL 1986
UK release     May 1963      CBS          (S)BPG 62193

1.  Blowin' In The Wind (Dylan)
2.  Girl From The North Country (Dylan)
3.  Masters Of War (Dylan)
4.  Down The Highway (Dylan)
5.  Bob Dylan's Blues (Dylan)
6.  A Hard Rain's A-Gonna Fall (Dylan)

7.  Don't Think Twice, It's All Right (Dylan)
8.  Bob Dylan's Dream (Dylan)
9.  Oxford Town (Dylan)
10. Talking World War III Blues (Dylan)
11. Corrina, Corrina (Trad. Arr. Dylan)
12. Honey, Just Allow Me One More Chance (Dylan/Henry Thomas)
13. I Shall Be Free (Dylan)

Bob Dylan: vocals, guitar, harmonica / Howie Collins: guitar (11) / Bruce Langhorne: guitar (11) / Leonard Gaskin: bass (11) / Herb Lovelle: drums (11) / John Hammond: producer / Tom Wilson: producer
```

Bob Dylan's second album lacks the energy of the first, released in March 1962, when the folk singer sounded excited to be making a record at all. This time, the album was recorded during eight sessions stretching over a year, so perhaps it felt more like a job of work to be done. Unlike previously, the emphasis is on Dylan's songwriting, although many of his compositions comprise new sets of words fitted to traditional melodies. *Masters Of War*, for example, is a re-casting of *Nottamun Town*; *Blowin' In The Wind* takes the spiritual *No More Auction Block* as its starting point; while *A Hard Rain's A-Gonna Fall* is based on *Lord Randall*. The songs that start each side of the record continue to make the biggest impression. *Blowin' In The Wind* is arguably the most famous Bob Dylan song of all. Peter, Paul and Mary released their own version of it in June 1963 and took it to number two in the National charts. Subsequently, the song was covered by a very large number of other artists, became the rallying call of the sixties counter-culture, and has been adopted as a hymn in many Catholic and Protestant church services. *Don't Think Twice, It's All Right* has proved to be almost as successful, again with numerous cover versions, including big-selling hit singles by Peter, Paul and Mary and the Four Seasons (in disguise, as 'The Wonder Who'). These songs, together with several of their companions on *Freewheelin'*, launched Bob Dylan as an influence on the course of music during the Golden Age, second only to the Beatles. The fact that Dylan's singing voice is an acquired taste – hardly a singing voice at all in conventional terms – and his guitar and harmonica playing no better than rudimentary, became irrelevant when set next to the power of his best songs.

CHARLES MINGUS
THE BLACK SAINT AND THE SINNER LADY

During the forties, Charles Mingus played bass with a number of bands, including those led by Louis Armstrong, Lionel Hampton, and Duke Ellington. He played with Charlie Parker at the saxophonist's acclaimed Massey Hall concert in Toronto in 1953 and began making albums of his own with a variety of different line-ups. Some of his albums from the late fifties were received as jazz masterpieces, particularly *Pithecanthropus Erectus* in 1956 and *Mingus Ah Um* in 1959. Mingus himself, however, regarded *The Black Saint And The Sinner Lady* as his finest achievement. Writing in the album's sleevenotes, he suggests, "throw all other records of mine away except maybe one other". Scored for an eleven-piece band, the music

comprises a single work, broken down for the purposes of recording into four related sections. The functional titles suggest that Mingus' intention was for the music to be performed as a ballet, although this was never achieved in reality. There is a certain amount of space for a few soloists to show what they can do, but mostly this is a densely packed work-out for the entire band. Partly based on the blues and partly employing modal structures in the manner of Miles Davis' innovative *Kind Of Blue* album from four years previously, the music has a rough, abrasive character that both marks it as distinct from any jazz record made in the fifties and ensures that it retains its impact half a century later. When rock and folk musicians began to respond to influences from the world of jazz, as the sixties unfolded, Charles Mingus was one of the main figures involved. Perhaps some of the simpler pieces he played in the fifties were most responsible for this, with Mingus' own bass playing dominating the music more than it does here. But it is *The Black Saint And The Sinner Lady* that is primarily responsible for Mingus being considered the most important jazz composer after Duke Ellington.

US release	May 1963	Impulse A(S)-35
UK release	May 1963	Philips 841 973 BY (Dutch record issued in US sleeve)

1. Track A – Solo Dancer
2. Track B – Duet Solo Dancers
3. Track C – Group Dancers
4. Mode D – Trio and Group Dancers / Mode E – Single Solos and Group Dance / Mode F – Group and Solo Dance

All compositions by Charles Mingus

Charles Mingus: bass, piano / Rolf Ericson: trumpet / Richard Williams: trumpet / Quentin Jackson: trombone / Don Butterfield: bass trombone, tuba / Jerome Richardson: soprano and baritone saxophones, flute / Dick Hafer: tenor saxophone, flute / Charlie Mariano: alto saxophone / Jaki Byard: piano, marimba / Jay Berliner: guitar / Dannie Richmond: drums / Bob Hammer: co-arranger on track 4 / Bob Thiele: producer

BENJAMIN BRITTEN   WAR REQUIEM

UK release	May 1963	Decca SET/MET 252-3
US release	May 1963	London A/OSA 1255

1. Requiem Aeternum
2. Dies Irae
3. Offertorium
4. Sanctus
5. Agnus Dei
6. Libera Me

Music composed by Benjamin Britten; words taken from the traditional Latin Mass for the Dead and from poems by Wilfred Owen.

Benjamin Britten: conductor / Dietrich Fischer-Dieskau: baritone / Galina Vishnevskaya: soprano / Peter Pears: tenor / London Symphony Orchestra / Highgate School Choir, directed by Edward Chapman / London Symphony Orchestra Chorus / Bach Choir / David Willcocks: chorus master / Melos Ensemble / Simon Preston: organ/ John Culshaw: producer

1963 seems to be late – nearly two decades late – for the recording of a work commemorating the Second World War, but the music was composed the previous year for the consecration of the new Coventry Cathedral, built to replace the medieval one that had been destroyed by bombing. Benjamin Britten was responsible for major classical works like his opera, *Peter Grimes,* the moving *Serenade* and *Nocturne,* written for his secret partner, Peter Pears, and the popular *Young Person's Guide to the Orchestra.* In 1963, his claim to the title of most eminent living British composer was unassailable. As it happens, a remarkable musical statement on the War had already appeared – Krzysztof Penderecki's astonishingly moving *Threnody to the Victims of Hiroshima,* from 1960. Britten makes no attempt to adopt the modern compositional procedures of Penderecki and there is nothing in his work that could not have been delivered over half a century earlier by Gustav Mahler, whose *Symphony of a Thousand* provides the most obvious reference point. There is nothing overtly mournful or angry in the music either, so that although the work undoubtedly has considerable grandeur and, in purely musical terms, goes a long way to justify the acclaim it has received, nevertheless, as a serious commentary on warfare, it is something of a missed opportunity. *War Requiem* is constructed as a church mass and is primarily a choral work, with space for a few solo singing performances too. Occasional words and phrases emerge to indicate that the lyrics are indeed war-related, but as is the norm with this kind of classical singing, the performers are mainly concerned with getting the notes right and do not place a very high premium on trying to deliver a coherent message. Even though they are singing in English, it is not often possible to make sense of the words. Britten's *War Requiem* made little impact on the music fans and musicians inspired by the other albums discussed in these pages, and Britten was clearly not interested in their music either, nor even the older popular music of the war-time period. It is claimed that the album sold 200,000 copies during the months following its release. Curiously, none of these sales can have taken place in general record shops, since the double LP conspicuously failed to enter the album charts. One suspects the firm promotional hand of Decca at work here, the company still smarting from its missed chance of signing the group already achieving the biggest record sales of the year, and determined to demonstrate a compensating success. For this critic, *War Requiem* is eclipsed artistically by another Benjamin Britten work, composed in 1963 and issued on record the following year. The *Cello Symphony,* with a virtuoso performance in the central role by Mstislav Rostropovich, achieves the masterpiece status – frequently taking the listener's breath away – that the *War Requiem* desperately tries to reach, but is unable to grasp.

THE SHADOWS   GREATEST HITS

UK release   June 1963   Columbia 33SX 1522   mono only
Not issued in the US

1. Apache (Jerry Lordan)
2. Man Of Mystery (Michael Carr)
3. The Stranger (Bill Crompton/Morgan Jones)
4. F.B.I. (Peter Gormley)
5. Midnight (Bruce Welch/Hank Marvin)
6. The Frightened City (Norrie Paramor)
7. Kon-Tiki (Michael Carr)
8. 36-24-36 (The Shadows)
9. The Savage (Norrie Paramor)
10. Peace Pipe (Norrie Paramor)
11. Wonderful Land (Jerry Lordan)
12. Stars Fell On Stockton (The Shadows)
13. Guitar Tango (Georges Liferman/Norman Maine)
14. The Boys (Brian Bennett/Bruce Welch/Hank Marvin)
15. Dance On! (Elaine Murtagh/Ray Adams/Valerie Murtagh)

Hank Marvin: lead guitar / Bruce Welch: rhythm guitar / Jet Harris: bass guitar (1-12) / Brian Locking: bass guitar (13-15) / Tony Meehan: drums (1-10) / Brian Bennett: drums (11-15) / Cliff Richard: bongos (1) / members of Norrie Paramor Orchestra (11,13) / Norrie Paramor: producer

The Shadows were formed as the backing group for Cliff Richard and quickly established themselves as the most technically accomplished set of musicians working in British rock 'n' roll. They began making records on their own and were successful as soon as they decided to abandon vocals and create classy instrumentals dominated by the sound of Hank Marvin's fluent lead guitar, usually enhanced by the use of echo. *Apache* became the first of several number one hits in the summer of 1960. The group's instrumental sound proved to be enormously influential on other groups working in both the UK and Europe. The Spotnicks from Sweden achieved a number of hits, while the Outlaws, who included in their membership Chas Hodges (later successful as half of Chas and Dave) and Ritchie Blackmore (founder member of Deep Purple), made several singles and an LP, though with limited chart success. Even the Beatles recorded a guitar instrumental, the appropriately titled *Cry For A Shadow*, as one of the tracks made in Germany in 1961 (with the unique songwriting credit, Harrison/ Lennon). Only America, which had its own instrumental group, the Ventures, resisted the Shadows' appeal. When the *Greatest Hits* album was compiled and released, the music of the Beatles and the other Merseybeat groups to follow in their wake was in full sway. The Shadows' music managed to avoid seeming outmoded partly because there were so many big-selling singles that were still fondly remembered, but more crucially because the Shadows had always played music that was a little more robust than the pop music surrounding them in the charts of the early sixties. Both Tony Meehan and Brian Bennett were particularly skilled drummers, easily capable of creating driving rhythms to propel the guitars. The Shadows released several hit albums during the sixties, but it is inevitably the hit singles that have provided the group's greatest legacy.

DAVE BRUBECK QUARTET   AT CARNEGIE HALL

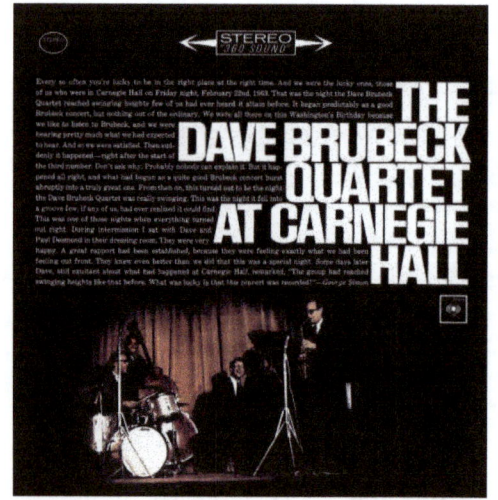

US release   June 1963   Columbia C2S 826 / C2L 26
UK release   June 1963   CBS (S)BPG 62155 / 62156

1. St Louis Blues (W.C.Handy)
2. Bossa Nova USA (Brubeck)
3. For All We Know (J.Fred Coots/Sam M.Lewis)
4. Pennies From Heaven (Arthur Johnston/Johnny Burke)
5. Southern Scene (Briar Bush) (Brubeck)
6. Three To Get Ready (Brubeck)
7. Eleven-Four (Paul Desmond)
8. King For A Day (Dave and Iola Brubeck)
9. Castilian Drums (Brubeck)
10. It's A Raggy Waltz (Brubeck)
11. Blue Rondo À La Turk (Brubeck)
12. Take Five (Paul Desmond)

Dave Brubeck: piano / Paul Desmond: alto saxophone / Eugene Wright: bass / Joe Morello: drums / Teo Macero: producer

When the Dave Brubeck Quartet arrived on the jazz scene during the fifties, it was already blessed with a significant asset to distinguish itself from the competition. This was the instantly recognisable playing of alto saxophonist Paul Desmond, who possessed a caressingly sweet tone on his instrument, such as had only previously been achieved by the Duke Ellington sideman, Johnny Hodges. To clinch the matter, Brubeck hit upon a further musical characteristic to make his group stand out and proceeded to compose and perform a number of pieces in an assortment of unusual time signatures. The music played at Carnegie Hall includes a couple of waltzes, remarkable enough for jazz. But there is also a performance delivered with eleven beats in the bar (*Eleven-Four*) and another with five beats in the bar. The latter piece, *Take Five*, had been released as a single two years earlier and managed the extraordinary feat, for any kind of jazz record in the early sixties, of becoming a chart hit, both in the US and the UK. The group played the five-four tempo with such easy confidence, that only a listener deciding to count the beats would have realised what was being achieved. Although a few jazz bands had previously played at New York's most prestigious venue, to be performing there in the early sixties was still a major recognition of an artist's status. Fortunately, Brubeck and his fellow musicians rose to the occasion admirably and delivered some of their most inspired playing. It led one critic, writing for AllMusic, to conclude that the recorded result is "one of the great live jazz albums of the 1960s". To capture it all, the music had to be released on a double album, and even then one track (*It's A Raggy Waltz*) had to be moved out of its true place in the running order so that the tracks could be accommodated within the length of LP sides. Double albums were a seldom used format at the time, although Columbia/CBS soon decided to make the two records available separately.

CLIFF RICHARD   CLIFF'S HIT ALBUM

UK release   July 1963   Columbia 33SX 1512 mono only
Not issued in the US

1. Move It (Ian Samwell)
2. Living Doll (Lionel Bart)
3. Travellin' Light (Roy C.Bennett/Sid Tepper)
4. A Voice In The Wilderness (Norrie Paramor/Bunny Lewis)
5. Fall In Love With You (Ian Samwell)
6. Please Don't Tease (Bruce Welch/Peter Chester)
7. Nine Times Out Of Ten (Otis Blackwell/Waldense Hall)
8. I Love You (Bruce Welch)
9. Theme For A Dream (Mort Garson/Earl Shuman)
10. A Girl Like You (Jerry Lordan)
11. When The Girl In Your Arms (Roy C.Bennett/Sid Tepper)
12. The Young Ones (Roy C.Bennett/Sid Tepper)
13. I'm Looking Out The Window (Don Raye/John Jacob Niles)
14. Do You Wanna Dance (Bobby Freeman)

Cliff Richard: vocals / Ernie Shear: lead guitar (1) / Ian Samwell: rhythm guitar (1) / Frank Clarke: bass (1) / Terry Smart: drums (1) / Hank Marvin: guitar, vocals (2-10,12,14) / Bruce Welch: guitar, vocals (2-10,12,14) / Jet Harris: bass guitar (2-10,12,14) / Tony Meehan: drums (2-10,12) / Brian Bennett: drums (14) / members of Norrie Paramor Orchestra (11-13) / Mike Sammes Singers (9,11) / Norrie Paramor: producer

Cliff Richard and the Shadows were essentially the UK equivalent of Buddy Holly and the Crickets. Like the Americans, Cliff moved fairly speedily from driving rock 'n' roll to a gentler form of guitar-driven pop music and he was hugely successful performing this in the UK and virtually every other country in the world, apart from the US. Cliff's greatest hits compilation followed closely behind that of his backing group, the Shadows, but more than their record, it sounds like a tribute to an era that was already over. The LP finishes on an upbeat mood, but even the rockin' *Do You Wanna Dance* seems to be looking back to the musical world that was being overturned by the Beatles. There are, to be sure, many fine moments to be found during the course of this hit parade. Most of them occur as soon as Hank Marvin is allowed to deliver a solo, for he has the knack of finding a refreshing counter-melody to set against Cliff's sung verses. The two songs on side two where the Shadows are not used find Cliff Richard straying dangerously close to easy-listening territory, even if the singer does have a voice with enough emotional depth to make a ballad work. At the other extreme, *Move It*, recorded before Cliff Richard had managed to put the Shadows together, is one of the two most successful British attempts to match the innovation and excitement of the best American rock 'n' roll (the other being *Shakin' All Over* by Johnny Kidd and the Pirates). Arguably, however, the most durable track is not this one, but the teen anthem, *The Young Ones*. With the Shadows still in the driving seat, the added strings have the effect of giving the song a compelling yearning quality. It is a more restrained version of the celebration of youth made just a few years later, the Who's *My Generation*, tailored for what seems like a less rebellious kind of teenager. Cliff Richard had already made a sufficiently big impact during the five years before his *Hit Album* was released to enable him to weather, not just the revolution brought about by the Beatles, but the succession of musical changes that followed. As of 2020, he had released nearly 150 singles and some seventy-five albums, not including compilations like this one. Remarkably, without ever becoming fashionable again, as he was when the records making up *Cliff's Hit Album* were in the charts, he has managed to become the third biggest selling singles artist in the UK, with only the Beatles and Elvis Presley beating him.

JOHN COLTRANE   IMPRESSIONS

At the end of 1960 and through 1961, John Coltrane was producing some startlingly innovative music, as he found imaginative ways to extend the modal approach to improvisation that he had helped Miles Davis to codify on the landmark *Kind Of Blue* album. Tracks like *My Favourite Things, India,* and *Impressions,* together with the whole of the *Africa/Brass* album were thrilling new departures, sounding like nobody else in jazz. As though temporarily exhausted, the music that Coltrane delivered immediately afterwards was altogether more conservative. He played with Duke Ellington, being careful not to

| US release | July 1963 | Impulse A(S)-42 |
| UK release | July 1963 | HMV CSD 1509 / CLP 1695 |

1. India
2. Up 'Gainst The Wall
3. Impressions
4. After The Rain

All compositions by John Coltrane

John Coltrane: soprano and tenor saxophones / Eric Dolphy: bass clarinet (1,3) / McCoy Tyner: piano / Reggie Workman: bass (1) / Jimmy Garrison: bass (2-4) / Elvinm Jones: drums (1-3) / Roy Haynes: drums (4) / Bob Thiele: producer.

upset the older musician's sensibilities, and he even recorded an album of low-key ballads with a torch singer (Johnny Hartman), music that steered perilously close to easy-listening. A further set of studio recordings made in 1963 were passed over in favour of an album focusing on two lengthy live performances from 1961 and 1962 and named after one of them, *Impressions*. The 2018 release of the ignored studio recordings as the album *Both Directions At Once* makes it clear that the Impulse record company made the right decision. The unreleased tracks cannot be so easily accused of playing it safe, but neither are they strong enough to restore the momentum of Coltrane's music. On the *Impressions* title track, Coltrane delivers a fast-flowing stream-of-consciousness performance on tenor saxophone for a quarter of an hour, over a rhythm section (just bass and drums for the most part, since Tyner is silent once the theme has been played) that oscillates between two chords, like an unfinished blues. Imagine replacing the saxophone with an electric guitar, and what we have here is the live music of Cream or the Jimi Hendrix Experience, played several years early. *Both Directions At Once* includes several attempts to create a more concise studio rendering of *Impressions*, but they entirely fail to reproduce the flames of the blazing live version. *India* is almost as long, with just a single root chord throughout, but this time Coltrane, on soprano saxophone, shares the solo space with Eric Dolphy, a player who is well able to withstand the comparison. As it happens, Dolphy was present during *Impressions* too, but only plays a handful of notes during the closing moments. The two studio tracks, short enough to have been released as singles, are sufficiently distinctive to provide respite from the live marathons – especially the caressing *After The Rain*, which allows McCoy Tyner his only significant outing on the album, providing a lush underlay with playing that, appropriately enough, is entirely impressionistic. In retrospect, it is clear that the *Impressions* album was something of a stop-gap release to allow Coltrane to rediscover his muse (and was entirely successful in this respect). The impact it made at the time was considerable, however. It allowed jazz enthusiasts to experience the thrill of hearing how a master innovator was able to continue his experiments with modal improvisation, proving how flexible and inspirational the format could be.

ELVIS PRESLEY   GOLDEN RECORDS VOL 3

| US release | August 1963 | RCA Victor LPM/LSP-2765 |
| UK release | March 1964 | RCA Victor SF/RD 7630 |

1. It's Now Or Never (Eduardo Aaron Schroeder/Wally Gold)
2. Stuck On You (Aaron Schroeder/J.Leslie McFarland)
3. Fame And Fortune (Ben Weisman/Fred Wise)
4. I Gotta Know (Matt Williams/Paul Evans)
5. Surrender (Doc Pomus/Mort Shuman)
6. I Feel So Bad (Chuck Willis)
7. Are You Lonesome Tonight? (Lou Handman/Roy Turk)
8. Marie's The Name (His Latest Flame) (Pomus/Shuman)
9. Little Sister (Pomus/Shuman)
10. Good Luck Charm (Schroeder/Gold)
11. Anything That's Part Of You (Don Robertson)
12. She's Not You (Doc Pomus/Jerry Leiber/Mike Stoller)

Elvis Presley: vocals, guitar / Scotty Moore: guitar / Hank Garland: guitar, bass guitar / Tiny Timbrell: guitar / Neal Matthews: guitar / Harold Bradley: guitar / Jerry Kennedy: guitar / Floyd Cramer: piano, organ / Gordon Stoker: piano / Dudley Brooks: piano / Bob Moore: bass, bass guitar / Ray Siegel: bass / Meyer Rubin: bass/ D.J. Fontana: drums / Buddy Harman: drums / Hal Blaine: drums / Boots Randolph: tenor saxophone / Jimmie Haskell: accordion / The Jordanaires: vocals / Millie Kirkham: vocals / Steve Sholes, Joseph Lilley, Chet Atkins, Urban Thielmann, Jeff Alexander, Hans J. Salter: producer.

Although Elvis Presley was one of the major developers of rock 'n' roll, and certainly the genre's first superstar, he very quickly allowed himself to be diverted into performing music that was not propelled by a strong beat and had little sense at all of excitement or aggression. The majority of the music on this third compilation of his hits is so far removed from the style that made the singer's name that, in the UK, RCA had to think carefully before releasing the record at all. This, despite the fact that six of the tracks on the LP had been UK number one hits. The success of the Beatles had changed the sound of popular music, had changed the rules governing what was likely to be successful. After *The Devil In Disguise*, which became a number one hit in the summer of 1963, Elvis had only one more UK number one during the sixties, and most of his singles failed to even enter the top ten. It was a similar story in the US. At least *Golden Records Vol.3* contains a number of songs that are still fondly remembered. When Volume 4 of the series was issued in 1968, *The Devil In Disguise* was the only true golden hit to be included. It was not the army that emasculated Elvis, as the vibrant recordings he made on his return to civilian life and issued on the LP *Elvis Is Back* make clear. It is Colonel Parker who gets the blame, for forcing Elvis to perform in a series of lacklustre films and to make music to match, but, equally, Elvis himself seemed to make very little effort to regain control of his own music. There are flashes through the sixties of what Elvis could still achieve musically, such as his masterful rendering of a Bob Dylan song, *Tomorrow Is A Long Time*, recorded in 1966, during one of the few sessions not devoted to putting together a film soundtrack. It suddenly becomes clear that Elvis could have maintained an excellent career through the sixties as a country-rock artist. Indeed, this is a direction hinted at too by both *Little Sister* and *She's Not You* on the *Golden Records Vol.3* album. Just once, Elvis attempted to bite back. During the recording session for the *Easy Come, Easy Go* soundtrack, which also took place in 1966, when Elvis was required to add his vocals to previously recorded backing tracks of distinctly doubtful quality, he is alleged to have complained to one of the studio engineers, "What are you supposed to do with shit like this?" The track he was referring to may well have been *Yoga Is As Yoga Does* which gets this critic's vote as the worst song that Elvis ever committed to vinyl.

THE FOUR SEASONS   GOLDEN HITS

The vocal group music known as doo-wop developed out of vocal quartet gospel, which in turn had derived from the songs of the barbershop quartets. The often highly stylised harmony singing, with doleful bass singers contrasting with ecstatic falsetto leads, and somehow avoiding a comic effect, was a major ingredient within fifties rock 'n' roll. As the decade drew to a close, doo-wop evolved into the harmony soul singing of people like the Shirelles and the Miracles and lost its more bizarre vocal sounds. Only the Four Seasons – hardly a soul group – retained the style without making the harmonies smoother and with the falsetto and bass extremes kept intact. Vee-Jay, a company suffering financial difficulties despite having the US rights to the first Beatles LP, rushed the production of a greatest hits compilation for the group. By August, the Four Seasons had enjoyed five big hits (three of which, *Sherry*, *Big Girls Don't Cry*, and *Walk Like A Man*, were successful in the UK too). To fill out the album, Vee-Jay had to use several songs that were not hits at all. During the next four years, the group had many more hits, although by that time it had signed to a different record company. Vee-Jay went bankrupt in 1966. A double LP, *Edizione D'Oro*, was issued by Philips in 1968 and includes all the Four Seasons' Sixties hits, including such small marvels as *Rag Doll*, *Dawn (Go Away)*, *Let's Hang On*, and *I've Got You Under My Skin*. Because it could, Vee-Jay issued a double LP comprising the Four Seasons *Golden Hits* and *Introducing The Beatles*, placed back to back, under the title, *The Beatles vs The Four Seasons*. In truth, however, the two groups had little in common, beyond the fact that both wrote many of their own songs. In the long term, the Four Seasons were not interested in taking a similar musical journey to that of the more successful British group and neither did their doo-wop derived music lend itself to experimentation. Nevertheless, during the seventies, the Four Seasons enjoyed a revival when they became influenced by the nascent disco movement. *Golden Hits* is an interesting, if flawed, memento of a group that had a unique sound in the sixties, and it represents the Four Seasons at the correct chronological period when the group was making its first impact, even if the contemporary listener is better served by *Edizione D'Oro*.

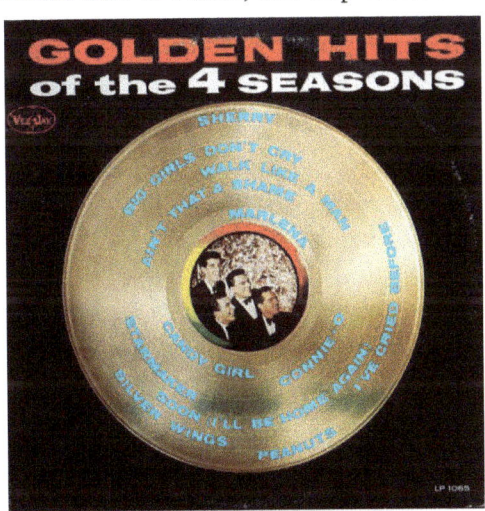

US release   August 1963   Vee-Jay   SR/ LR 1065
Not released in UK

1. Sherry (Bob Gaudio)
2. I've Cried Before (Bob Gaudio)
3. Marlena (Bob Gaudio)
4. Soon (I'll Be Home Again) (Bob Crewe/Bob Gaudio)
5. Ain't That A Shame (Fats Domino/Dave Bartholomew)
6. Walk Like A Man (Bob Crewe/Bob Gaudio)

7. Connie-O (Bob Crewe/Bob Gaudio)
8. Big Girls Don't Cry (Bob Crewe/Bob Gaudio)
9. Starmaker (Bob Crewe)
10. Candy Girl (Larry Santos)
11. Silver Wings (Bob Crewe)
12. Peanuts (Joe Cook)

Frankie Valli: vocals / Bob Gaudio: vocals, keyboards / Tommy DeVito: vocals, guitar / Nick Massi: vocals, vocal arrangements, bass guitar / Charlie Calello: orchestral arrangements, conductor / Sid Bass: orchestral arrangements / Bob Crewe: producer

THE SEARCHERS   MEET THE SEARCHERS

UK release   August 1963   Pye NPL 18086   mono only
Not issued in the US. MEET THE SEARCHERS/NEEDLES AND PINS (Kapp KS-3363/KL-1363), April 1964, has five of these tracks.

1. Sweets For My Sweet (Doc Pomus/Mort Shuman)
2. Alright (Jerry Ross/Lester Vanador)
3. Love Potion No.9 (Jerry Leiber/Mike Stoller)
4. Farmer John (Don Sugarcane Harris/Dewey Terry)
5. Stand By Me (Ben E King/Jerry Leiber/Mike Stoller)
6. Money (Janie Bradford/Berry Gordy)
7. Da Doo Ron Ron (Phil Spector/Jeff Barry/Ellie Greenwich)
8. Ain't Gonna Kiss Ya (James Marcus Smith)
9. Since You Broke My Heart (Don and Phil Everly)
10. Tricky Dicky (Jerry Leiber/Mike Stoller)
11. Where Have All The Flowers Gone (Pete Seeger)
12. Twist And Shout (Phil Medley/Bert Berns)

Mike Pender: guitar, vocals / John McNally: guitar, vocals / Tony Jackson: bass guitar, vocals / Chris Curtis: drums, vocals / Tony Hatch: producer

Encouraged by the success of the Beatles, manager Brian Epstein went back to the Liverpool clubs and signed the groups he liked best – Gerry and the Pacemakers, Billy J Kramer and the Dakotas, and the Fourmost – but he missed the Searchers, who were arguably the second most talented Merseybeat group. What they lacked was in-house songwriting ability, but they managed to cover a much wider area than their contemporaries when looking for suitable cover material. They had a lighter sound than the other groups, in which John McNally's fondness for upper register chords to strum on his rhythm guitar predominated. When tackling songs associated with the much tougher sounding Beatles, this did the Searchers no favours. Their ultra-light readings of *Money* and *Twist And Shout* are positively feeble when heard next to the better-known versions. On other occasions, however, the Searchers' sound gives them a very distinctive edge. They are able to do great things with Everly Brothers material and, covering a song by Pete Seeger, they effectively invented folk rock, even if they are never given any credit for it. Like many groups at this time, the Searchers put most effort into the recording of sparkling, distinguished singles and they were rewarded with several big chart hits. Tony Jackson and Chris Curtis both decided to seek solo success along the way (though neither managed it), but two versions of the group – the result of a big falling-out between Mike Pender and John McNally – still perform today on the nostalgia circuit.

BILL EVANS   CONVERSATIONS WITH MYSELF

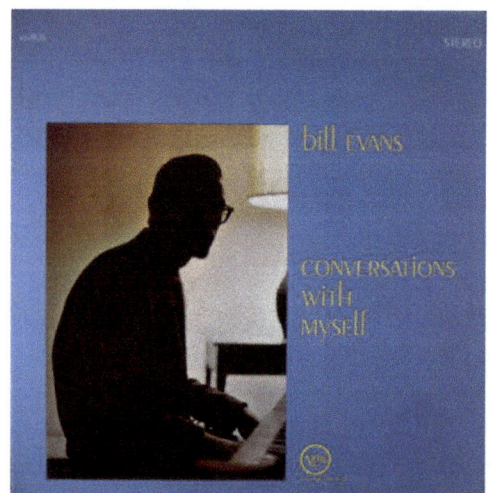

US release   September 1963   Verve V6/V-8526
UK release   September 1963   Verve VLP 9054

1. Round About Midnight (Thelonious Monk/Cootie Williams)
2. How About You? (Burton Lane/Ralph Freed)
3. Theme From Spartacus (Alex North)
4. Blue Monk (Thelonious Monk)
5. Stella By Starlight (Victor Young/Ned Washington)
6. Hey There (Richard Adler/Jerry Ross)
7. NYC's No Lark (Bill Evans)
8. Just You, Just Me (Jesse Greer/Raymond Klages)

Bill Evans: piano / Creed Taylor: producer

Although Bill Evans includes his own versions of a couple of pieces by Thelonious Monk on this album, his delicate, precise piano playing is at the opposite end of the style spectrum to Monk's. Evans was a member of Miles Davis's band for a little over a year at the end of the fifties, and was the main pianist on the ground-breaking *Kind Of Blue* album. Subsequently, he formed his own trio, but *Conversations With Myself* has Evans as the only musician, playing to his internal metronome rather than an actual rhythm section. It cannot exactly be described as a solo album, however, since Evans uses overdubbing to create three versions of himself playing simultaneously on each track. The technique was pioneered by guitarist Les Paul during the late forties and had become commonplace in rock and pop recordings. Jazz musicians, however, were generally suspicious of what they regarded as studio trickery, taking the attitude that a recording should be a true representation of what a musician could achieve in live performance. The only jazz musician to use overdubbing prior to Bill Evans was another pianist, Lennie Tristano, who used the technique on his self-titled album issued in 1956. Bill Evans proves that studio recording techniques can be valuable for the creation of music that is both intellectually and emotionally satisfying, even when that music is jazz.

PETE SEEGER   WE SHALL OVERCOME

```
US release        October 1963    Columbia   CS 8901/CL 2101
UK release        October 1963    CBS        (S)BPG 62209

1.  If You Miss Me At The Back Of The Bus (Pete Seeger)
2.  Keep Your Eyes On The Prize (Traditional)
3.  I Ain't Scared Of Your Jail (Pete Seeger)
4.  Oh Freedom (Traditional)
5.  What Did You Learn In School Today (Tom Paxton)
6.  Little Boxes (Malvina Reynolds)
7.  Who Killed Norma Jean? (Norman Roston/Pete Seeger)
8.  Who Killed Davey Moore? (Bob Dylan)
9.  A Hard Rain's A-Gonna Fall (Bob Dylan)
10. Mail Myself To You (Woody Guthrie)
11. Guantanamera (Joseito Fernandez/José Marti/Julian Orbon)
12. Tshotsholosa (Todd Matshikiza/Pat Williams)
13. We Shall Overcome (Charles Tindley and others)

Pete Seeger: vocals, 12-string guitar, banjo / Harold Leventhal: producer
```

They let Dave Brubeck play at Carnegie Hall, but a Pete Seeger concert was potentially more controversial. Seeger had been a member of the Weavers folk group during the fifties. The group had been extremely popular, but liked to include political material of a distinctly socialist stripe, in amongst the gentle melodies of the rest of its repertoire. During the McCarthy era, the approach inevitably got the group into trouble and it found itself banned from the mainstream media and concert venues. In 1963, the group, though still proscribed by American television, staged a successful reunion concert, also at Carnegie Hall. Now, Pete Seeger, the group's unofficial leader and focus, was playing at the venue on his own. He is a confident, if unspectacular solo performer. He lets the songs speak for themselves, which they very much succeed in doing. They include his best known performance, *Little Boxes*, which manages to wrap a deliberate social message inside a lyric and a melody with all the charm of a children's song. There are the essential pieces of Bob Dylan songwriting. *A Hard Rain's A-Gonna Fall*, composed as a response to the Cuban Missile Crisis, is lifted directly from Dylan's recently released second album. The bilingual *Guantanamera*, an expression of Cuban patriotism, was a big success for one-hit-wonder group, the Sandpipers, three years after this, but Seeger's rendering of the song, underscored by the rich chords of his twelve-string guitar, achieves a stark magnificence that was missed by the group's more pop-slanted version. And there is the title track of the album. *We Shall Overcome*, which began life as a spiritual, before being tinkered with over the years by a variety of interpreters, stands as the ultimate sixties protest song, a rallying call even more compelling than Dylan's *Blowing In The Wind*. To hear a Carnegie Hall audience, joining in the singing of a strident call for freedom, is to experience again what must have felt, certainly for Pete Seeger himself, like a truly historic moment.

THE BEATLES   WITH THE BEATLES

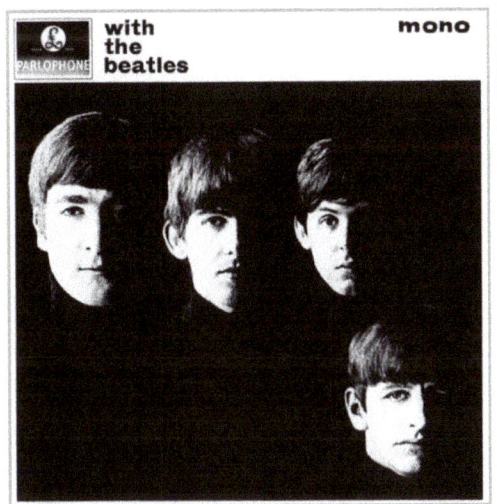

```
UK release   November 1963   Parlophone   PCS 3045 / PMC 1206
US release   MEET THE BEATLES   January 1964   Capitol   (S)T 2047
THE BEATLES' SECOND ALBUM   April 1964   Capitol   (S)T 2080
These have all the UK LP tracks, together with tracks from singles and EPs

1.  It Won't Be Long (Lennon/McCartney)
2.  All I've Got To Do (Lennon/McCartney)
3.  All My Loving (Lennon/McCartney)
4.  Don't Bother Me (Harrison)
5.  Little Child (Lennon/McCartney)
6.  Till There Was You (Meredith Wilson)
7.  Please Mister Postman (Georgia Dobbins/William Garrett/
        Freddie Gorman/Brian Holland /Robert Bateman)
8.  Roll Over Beethoven (Chuck Berry)
9.  Hold Me Tight (Lennon/McCartney)
10. You Really Got A Hold On Me (Smokey Robinson)
11. I Wanna Be Your Man (Lennon/McCartney)
12. Devil In Her Heart (Richard Drapkin)
13. Not A Second Time (Lennon/McCartney)
14. Money (Janie Bradford/Berry Gordy)

John Lennon: vocals, guitar, harmonica, percussion / George Harrison: vocals, guitar / Paul McCartney: vocals, bass guitar, piano, percussion / Ringo Starr: vocals, drums, percussion / George Martin: producer, piano, organ
```

There is a confidence about the performances collected on the second album made by the Beatles, the kind you acquire when you know that you have just achieved a run of three number one singles. There is the first song to be fully composed by George Harrison, together with seven new Lennon and McCartney songs, any of which could have become a hit single in its own right. The cover versions include a Chuck Berry classic that demonstrates how the Beatles' take on rock 'n' roll succeeded in making the music sound less rough, more modern, but without losing any of the drive of the earlier style. There are also some newly definitive versions of some Tamla Motown material, most notably including a song, *Money*, whose sheer power easily renders irrelevant both Barrett Strong's original and the various other covers of the song by assorted Merseybeat rivals. It is noticeable, in contrast to the albums issued by America's foremost group, the Beach Boys, that there is nothing on *With*

The Beatles that could be described as 'filler'. EMI's American company, Capitol, finally agreed to issuing a Beatles album in its country, although it insisted on trying to extract extra commercial value out of the music by splitting it into two albums, adding already released single sides to make up the numbers. It was a policy that the company followed on every Beatles album, prior to *Sgt Pepper's Lonely Hearts Club Band,* resulting in a larger number of Beatles albums being issued in the US than in the UK. It had the unfortunate side-effect of reducing the impact of the individual albums, as well as obscuring the line of development that could, for UK listeners, be heard to be taking place from album to album. On this occasion too, the policy created an anomaly, whereby the third album released by the Beatles in the US was given the confusing title of *Second Album.* Advance orders for *With The Beatles* in the UK amounted to 270,000 copies, making it the biggest-ever selling UK album, even before it was released. A week after the release date, sales reached half a million, qualifying the LP for inclusion as a hit in the singles charts. It continued to sell steadily and by 1965, it had become the first million selling LP record in the UK.

PHIL SPECTOR   A CHRISTMAS GIFT FOR YOU FROM PHILLES RECORDS

| US release | November 1963 | Philles | PHLP-4005 | mono only |
| UK release | November 1963 | London | HA-U 8141 | |

1. White Christmas (Irving Berlin)
2. Frosty The Snowman (Walter Rollins/Steve Nelson)
3. The Bells Of St Mary (A Emmett Adams/Douglas Furber)
4. Santa Claus Is Coming To Town (Haven Gillespie/J Fred Coots)
5. Sleigh Ride (Leroy Anderson/Mitchell Parish)
6. Marshmallow World (Carl Sigman/Peter De Rose)
7. I Saw Mommy Kissing Santa Claus (Tommie Connor)
8. Rudolph The Red-Nosed Reindeer (Johnny Marks)
9. Winter Wonderland (Dick Smith/Felix Bernard)
10. Parade Of The Wooden Soldiers (Leon Jessel)
11. Christmas (Baby Please Come Home) (Ellie Greenwich/Jeff Barry/Phil Spector)
12. Here Comes Santa Claus (Gene Autry/Oakley Haldeman)
13. Silent Night (Traditional)

Darlene Love: vocals (1,6,9,11) / The Ronettes (Veronica Bennett, Estelle Bennett, Nedra Talley): vocals (2,5,7) / Bob B Soxx & the Blue Jeans (Bobby Sheen, Darlene Love, Fanita James): vocals (3,12) / The Crystals (Dolores LaLa Brooks, Barbara Alston, Dolores DeevDee Kenniebrew, Patsy Wright): vocals (4,8,10) / Jack Nitzsche: arranger, percussion / Bill Pitman: guitar / Irv Rubins: guitar / Nino Tempo: guitar / Tom Tedesco: guitar / Al Delory: piano / Don Randl: piano / Leon Russell: piano / Jay Migliori: tenor saxophone / Lou Blackburn: trombone / Roy Caton: trumpet; Steve Douglas: tenor saxophone / Jimmy Bond: bass / Ray Pohlman: bass guitar / Hal Blaine: drums / Johnny Vidor Strings / Frank Kapp: percussion / Sonny Bono: percussion / Phil Spector: vocals (13), producer

The former singer and guitarist with the Teddy Bears used his proceeds from writing the 1958 hit, *To Know Him Is To Love Him*, to set up his own Philles record label and to start work as a producer. By the end of 1963, he had achieved three big hits with the Crystals (*He's A Rebel, Da Doo Ron Ron,* and *Then He Kissed Me*) and one with the Ronettes (*Be My Baby*). Phil Spector had conceived a distinctive approach to making records that became known as the 'wall of sound'. The musicians listed above are not a collective personnel for the tracks on the album – they all play throughout. Spector liked to use multiple instruments playing the same parts, in order to create a dense soundscape that threatened to engulf the singers delivering the melody. He did not like clarity, on the grounds that this would reduce the impact of the dense recording, and individual instrumental sounds were not intended to be heard. For this reason, he insisted that all his productions should be in glorious mono. The wall of sound seems to suit a collection of Christmas songs particularly well, as Spector oversees his favourite artists, singing a selection of classic, though almost entirely non-religious, seasonal fayre. *A Christmas Gift For You* has acquired the status of the definitive Christmas album and continues to sell well every year. In 1963, however, it was not particularly successful – it reached number 13 in the US album chart, but failed to sell much at all in the UK. The album's fortunes changed when it was reissued in 1972 on the Apple label, no doubt by way of a thank you from some of the Beatles for Spector having produced the album *Let It Be* and many records by John Lennon and George Harrison (for which he did not insist on applying his trademark method). It has been reissued several times since then.

THE KINGSMEN   IN PERSON FEATURING LOUIE LOUIE

The reason why an obscure rockin' doo-wop tune, recorded by the otherwise unheralded Richard Berry and the Pharoahs in 1958, should have become one of the most iconic rock 'n' roll songs of all, is somewhat mysterious. *Louie Louie* is based on the simplest of riffs, repeated over and over throughout the song, with a skeletal melody, that never moves away from the root chord, placed over the top. The Kingsmen were not the first group to cover the song, but they were the one to achieve the hit. Their playing has a rough and ready quality, good enough to deliver the song without any attempt at subtlety, as befitted a group working as a bar band. While the Merseybeat groups responded to the fact that they all felt themselves to be in competition by trying hard to play better than the rest, for the Kingsmen, 'good enough' would do.

```
US release      December 1963   Wand    WAND 657
UK release      December 1963   Pye     NPL 28050

1.  Louie Louie (Richard Berry)
2.  The Waiting (Don Gallucci/Lynn Easton)
3.  Mojo Workout (Julian Bright)
4.  Fever (Jerry Leiber/Mike Stoller)
5.  Money (Janie Bradford/Berry Gordy)
6.  Bent    Scepter (Don Gallucci)

7.  Long Tall Texan (Henry Strzelecki)
8.  You Can't Sit Down (Cornell Muldrow/Dee Clark)
9.  Twist And Shout (Phil Medley/Bert Berns)
10. J.A.J. (Dave Lewis)
11. Night Train (Jimmy Forrest/Lewis Simpkins/Oscar Washington)
12. Mashed Potatoes (Dessie Rozier)

Jack Ely: vocals (1) / Lynn Easton: vocals, saxophone / Mike
Mitchell: guitar / Don Gallucci: organ / Norm Sundholm: bass guitar
/ Bob Nordby: bass guitar (1) / Gary Abbot: drums / Jerry Dennon:
producer
```

This is emphasised by the one-take recording including the singer making an obvious mistake, when he enters too soon after the end of the guitar solo. The decision to use the take anyway, without bothering to get the group to play again, is, in this context, an inspired one on the part of the producer. Perturbed by the growing influence of youth culture, the American establishment seized on the Kingsmen's record as a suitable test case for its disquiet. Singer Jack Ely had chosen to deliver the lyrics – perfectly intelligible when sung by Richard Berry – in such a slurred manner that hardly a single word could be understood. The FBI embarked on a lengthy investigation to try and prove that the Kingsmen were guilty of obscenity, but was forced to abandon the case without making a charge. Meanwhile, the controversy helped to send the record to the number two position in the US chart and to eventually sell a million copies. The fact that the song was patently easy to play inspired a huge number of further cover versions to be recorded, although sadly for Richard Berry, he had already sold the publishing rights for a small cash sum. A fascinating tribute album to the song, including Berry, the Kingmen, some seventeen other versions, and five near-relations, was issued by Ace Records in 2002 as *Love That Louie: The Louie Louie Files*. Not that it matters, but there are eleven other tracks on the Kingsmen's album. These were recorded during a live performance and sound exactly like a bar band of the period might be expected to sound. The members of the audience are much more interested in talking amongst themselves than in listening to the music.

GERRY & THE PACEMAKERS   YOU'LL NEVER WALK ALONE EP

```
UK release    December 1963    Columbia    SEG 8295
Not released in US

1. You'll Never Walk Alone (Richard Rodgers/Oscar Hammerstein)
2. Jambalaya (Hank Williams)
3. Chills (Gerry Goffin/Jack Keller)
4. A Shot Of Rhythm And Blues (Terry Thompson)

Gerry Marsden: vocals, guitar / Les Maguire: piano /
Les Chadwick: bass guitar / Freddie Marsden: drums /
George Martin: producer
```

Gerry and the Pacemakers were the second Merseybeat group to achieve big success and were managed, like the Beatles, by Brian Epstein and produced by George Martin. They achieved their first hit with a song rejected by the Beatles, *How Do You Do It?*, and their second with a song called *I Like It*. The album that followed was called *How Do You Like It?* and yet it found no room for either hit amongst its collection of rock 'n' roll covers. There is considerable irony in the fact that the group's third number one single was a version of a sing-along ballad from the musical *Carousel*, because in a later documentary about the rise of the Beatles, Gerry Marsden had some very unkind remarks to make about the success of Cliff Richard and the Shadows, who he saw as being responsible for diluting the impact of rock 'n' roll with soft songs like *Living Doll*. Regardless, the fact that he achieved a big hit with *You'll Never Walk Alone* was responsible for its adoption as an anthem by fans of the Liverpool Football Club, which it still is some sixty years later.

1964

THE HOLLIES   STAY WITH THE HOLLIES

UK release   January 1964   Parlophone   PCS 3054 / PMC 1220
US release as **HERE I GO AGAIN**, with 5 tracks replaced by 2 issued as singles   June 1964   Imperial   LP 12265 / LP 9265

1. Talking 'Bout You (Chuck Berry)
2. Mr Moonlight (Roy Lee Johnson)
3. You Better Move On (Arthur Alexander)
4. Lucille (Al Collins/Little Richard)
5. Baby Don't Cry (Tony Hiller/Prerry Ford)
6. Memphis (Chuck Berry)
7. Stay (Maurice Williams)
8. Rockin' Robin (Jimmie Thomas)
9. Whatcha Gonna Do 'Bout It? (Gregory Carroll/Doris Payne)
10. Do You Love Me (Berry Gordy)
11. It's Only Make Believe (Conway Twitty/Jack Nance)
12. What Kind Of Girl Are You (Ray Charles)
13. Little Lover (Graham Nash/Allan Clarke)
14. Candy Man (Fred Neil/Beverly Ross)

Allan Clarke: vocals, harmonica / Graham Nash: vocals, guitar / Tony Hicks: guitar, vocals / Eric Haydock: bass guitar / Bobby Elliott: drums / Don Rathbone: drums (13) / Ron Richards: producer

The Hollies were presented as a Merseybeat group, but in fact they came from Manchester. *Stay* was the group's third single and the first of many top ten hits achieved through the Sixties. It turns a rather subdued song by doo-wop group, Maurice Williams and the Zodiacs, into a very exciting and dynamic beat performance. The Hollies' sound is very close to that of the Beatles, with two or three-part harmony vocals layered over well-played guitars and a crisp beat, and they draw on a similar mixture of soul and rock 'n' roll originals for their set-list. Only one song is written by members of the group and this is one of the weakest tracks on the album, although subsequent events proved that it nevertheless served as a good starting point from which Graham Nash and Allan Clarke could develop. The weakest track of all is the Hollies' version of *Do You Love Me*, a Motown song already taken to the top of the UK charts by Brian Poole and the Tremeloes. This cover tries a little too hard to better the hit by turning up the tempo too far. Overall, however, the Hollies perform their material with distinction and *Stay With The Hollies* is a fine debut.

GEORGIE FAME   RHYTHM AND BLUES AT THE FLAMINGO

UK release   January 1964   Columbia   33SX 1599   mono only
Not issued in US

1. Night Train (Jimmy Forrest/Oscar Washington/Lewis Simpkins)
2. Let The Good Times Roll (Sam Theard/Fleecie Moore)
3. Do The Dog (Rufus Thomas)
4. Eso Beso (Joe Sherman/Noel Sherman)
5. Work Song (Nat Adderley/Oscar Brown Jr)
6. Parchman Farm (Bukka White/Mose Allison)
7. You Can't Sit Down (Dee Clark/Phil Upchurch/Cornell Muldrow)
8. Humpty Dumpty (Eric Morris)
9. Shop Around (Berry Gordy/Smokey Robinson)
10. Baby Please Don't Go (Big Joe Williams)

Georgie Fame: vocals, organ / Big Jim Sullivan: guitar / Michael Eve: tenor saxophone / Johnny Marshall: baritone saxophone / Boots Slade: bass guitar / Red Reece: drums / Tommy Thomas: percussion / Johnny Gunnell: announcements / Ian Samwell: producer

The Flamingo was a club in London's Wardour Street. It opened as a jazz venue at the beginning of the fifties, but by 1963-4, its music policy had expanded to include rhythm and blues and ska, becoming a fashionable centre for the burgeoning mod culture in the process. Georgie Fame combined all of these music forms into his own sound, giving his songs an urbane gloss, quite different to the earthier rock 'n' roll influence that underpinned Merseybeat. His jazzy interpretations were delivered by his distinctive smoky voice, over a rich-toned Hammond organ placed centre-stage in his band. The style was immediately influential on several other performers adopting it wholesale, including Graham Bond, Zoot Money, John Mayall, and the Peddlers. Fame did not write any of his material, but chose it carefully from a variety of jazz and soul originals, together with a cover of a recent Jamaican hit, *Humpty Dumpty*. He was surprisingly lax with his songwriting credits, however, apparently believing that Mose Allison was responsible for *Work Song* and that Sonny Boy Williamson wrote *Baby Please Don't Go*. Columbia judged correctly that a live recording, especially one as full of club atmosphere as this one, would show off Fame's talents particularly well and released the LP in advance of any singles. The album sold well enough to establish Georgie Fame's name, but it did not manage to enter the charts.

THE ROLLING STONES EP

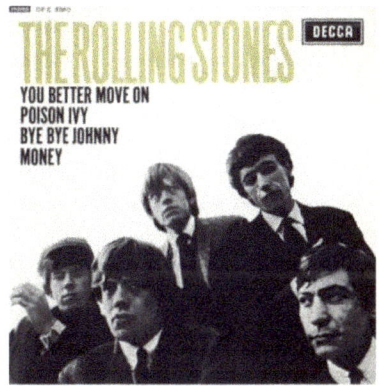

UK release January 1964 Decca DFE 8560
Not issued in US

1. Bye Bye Johnny (Chuck Berry)
2. Money (Janie Bradford/Berry Gordy)
3. You Better Move On (Arthur Alexander)
4. Poison Ivy (Jerry Leiber/Mike Stoller)

Mick Jagger: vocals, percussion / Brian Jones: guitar, vocals, harmonica, percussion / Keith Richards: guitar, vocals / Bill Wyman: bass guitar, vocals / Charlie Watts: drums / Andrew Loog Oldham: producer / Eric Easton: producer / Rolling Stones: producer

With the first two singles by the Rolling Stones having become modest UK hits, neither of them cracking the top ten, Decca did not feel confident in allowing the group to record a whole album. Instead the record company settled for this four track EP. This had been a popular format in the UK since the mid fifties, being viewed as a kind of mini-LP. The Stones seized on the chance to display their R&B influences, delivering robust performances of four of their favourite songs. The music is raw and exciting, with Bill Wyman's urgent bass lines being particularly impressive. The record reached number one in the EP chart.

BOB DYLAN THE TIMES THEY ARE A-CHANGIN'

US release   January 1964   Columbia CS 8905 / CL 2105
UK release   January 1964   CBS (S)BPG 62251

1. The Times They Are A-Changin'
2. Ballad Of Hollis Brown
3. With God On Our Side
4. One Too Many Mornings
5. North Country Blues
6. Only A Pawn In Their Game
7. Boots Of Spanish Leather
8. When The Ship Comes In
9. The Lonesome Death Of Hattie Carroll
10. Restless Farewell

All compositions by Bob Dylan

Bob Dylan: vocals, guitar, harmonica / Tom Wilson: producer

Bob Dylan's third album is a darker, bleaker affair than its predecessor, requiring more work from the listener to appreciate what is on offer. Dylan is railing against injustice generally and his lyrics are still the primary focus, since his melodies and his means of delivering them continue to be extremely basic. The title track, of course, is an anthemic call to action more explicit than *Blowin' In The Wind,* and taking its place as perhaps Dylan's strongest song to date. It was enough to make the album a chart success, although not quite at the level of *Freewheelin'*.

BEATLEMANIA

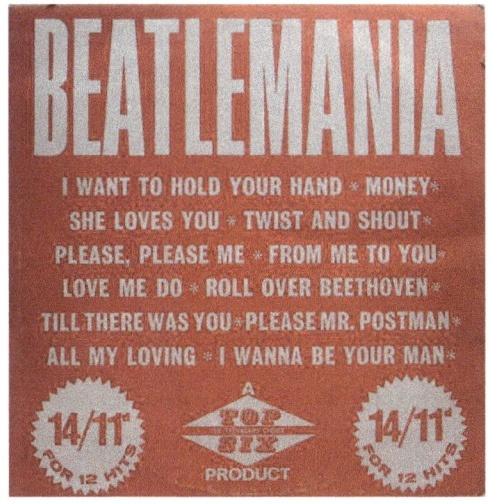

UK release   February 1964   Top Six   TSL 1
Not released in US

1. I Want To Hold Your Hand (John Lennon/Paul McCartney)
2. Roll Over Beethoven (Chuck Berry)
3. From Me To You (John Lennon/Paul McCartney)
4. Till There Was You (Meredith Willson)
5. Please Mr Postman (Dobbins/Garrett/Gorman/Holland/Bateman)
6. Twist And Shout (Phil Medley/Bert Russell)
7. All My Loving (John Lennon/Paul McCartney)
8. She Loves You (John Lennon/Paul McCartney)
9. I Wanna Be Your Man (John Lennon/Paul McCartney)
10. Love Me Do (John Lennon/Paul McCartney)
11. Please Please Me (John Lennon/Paul McCartney)
12. Money (Janie Bradford/Berry Gordy)

Johnny Harris: arranger / Jimmy Nicol: drums / other musicians possibly members of Nicol's group, the Shubdubs: Tony Allen: vocals / Roger Coulam: keyboards / Bob Garner: bass guitar

In 1954 in the UK, brothers David and Jacques Levy had the idea of starting a record label to issue cheaply produced sound-alike recordings of current hits. Their Embassy label signed a deal with the Woolworths chain of shops to sell the records. It was a concept that inspired several other entrepreneurs to do the same, and the Top Six label was one of the most successful of these during the early sixties. The enormous success of the Beatles encouraged Top Six to try an entire album of Beatles covers and although the result does not really sound as much like the Beatles as the record company must have hoped, the album still managed to enter the lower reaches of the charts. It clearly helped, of course, that the selling price was less than half that of the other albums on the market. Although uncredited, it transpired that the drummer was Jimmy Nicol, who became an obvious choice to replace Ringo Starr with the Beatles during two weeks of an international tour in June, when Starr was too ill to perform. Nicol must have hoped that he would manage to become successful on the back of this, although this did not happen.

STAN GETZ & JOAO GILBERTO   GETZ/GILBERTO

US release	March 1964	Verve	V6/V-8545
UK release	March 1964	Verve	VLP 9065

1. The Girl From Ipanema (Antonio Carlos Jobim/Norman Gimbel/Vinicius deMoraes)
2. Doralice (Antonio Almeida/Dorival Caymmi)
3. P'ra Machucar Meu Coraçao (To Hurt My Heart) (Ary Barroso)
4. Desafinado (Antonio Carlos Jobim/Newton Mendonca)
5. Corcovado (Antonio Carlos Jobim/Gene Lees)
6. So Danço Samba (Antonio Carlos Jobim/Vinicius deMoraes)
7. O Grande Amor (Antonio Carlos Jobim/Vinicius deMoraes)
8. Vivo Sonhando (Antonio Carlos Jobim)

Stan Getz: tenor saxophone / Joao Gilberto: guitar, vocals / Astrud Gilberto: vocals (1,5) / Antonio Carlos Jobim: piano / Sebastiao Neto: bass / Milton Banana: drums / Creed Taylor: producer

Soft-toned tenor saxophonist, Stan Getz, recorded several collaborations with Latin-American musicians during the sixties. The most successful, both musically and commercially, was this one, made with Brazilian singer and guitarist, Joao Gilberto. All the tracks are songs, delivered in Portuguese by Gilberto's gentle voice, over lightly played bossa nova rhythms. Drummer Milton Banana is able to keep the beat as steady as a drum machine, one that was programmed to be as minimalist as possible, and he is never in any danger of breaking into a sweat. The late-night, easy listening atmosphere that is the result suits Stan Getz's own playing perfectly, as he includes substantial solos as part of every song in the same relaxed manner as his accompanists. Two tracks feature singing by Joao Gilberto's wife, Astrud, participating in her first recording session. *The Girl From Ipanema* was severely edited to enable it to be released as a single, which proceeded to become a big international hit. As indeed was the parent album, which sold two million copies – remarkable for a jazz record – and it received a clutch of Grammy Awards.

THE DAVE CLARK FIVE   GLAD ALL OVER

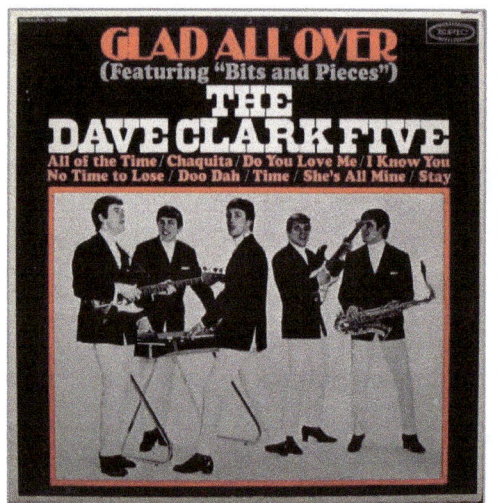

US release   March 1964   Epic   BN 26093 / LN 24093
Not released in UK

1. Glad All Over (Dave Clark/Mike Smith)
2. All Of The Time (Dave Clark/Mike Smith)
3. Stay (Maurice Williams)
4. Chaquita (Dave Clark/Mike Smith)
5. Do You Love Me (Berry Gordy)
6. Bits And Pieces (Dave Clark/Mike Smith)
7. I Know You (Dave Clark/Lenny Davidson)
8. No Time To Lose (Dave Clark/Mike Smith)
9. Doo Dah (Dave Clark/Ron Ryan)
10. Time (Dave Clark/Lenny Davidson)
11. She's All Mine (Dave Clark)

Mike Smith: vocals, organ / Lenny Davidson: guitar, vocals / Denis Payton: tenor saxophone, vocals / Rick Huxley: bass guitar, vocals / Dave Clark: drums, vocals, producer

Dave Clark was often considered to be the epitome of the dull-witted drummer, as he sat behind his drum-kit, bashing out the simplest of beats, with a fixed smile on his face. But he was, in reality, the most astute member of any band of the time. Acting as manager, he produced the recordings, most of them being written by himself in collaboration with other members, then kept control by merely licensing them to the record company for a limited time. Columbia (Epic in the US) was the third label to be involved and was presumably happy enough with the arrangement when the hits started. *Glad All Over* was the third Columbia single for the Dave Clark Five and it reached number one in the UK in January 1964, displacing the Beatles' *I Want To Hold Your Hand*. Something had to, but the music press made a big issue of it, promoting the Dave Clark Five (rather hastily as it turned out) as successor to the Beatles. The record was a big hit in the US too, making it the first non-Beatles British beat chart success. Dave Clark decided from the start to concentrate on the American market and the group became a much more successful act in that country. The first album, including the two definitive Dave Clark Five single hits, *Glad All Over* and *Bits And Pieces*, was not even issued in the UK. Instead, the less impressive *Session With The Dave Clark Five* was released in April, becoming the second US album by the group, in June.

THE ROLLING STONES

So confident were they of it being successful, that the Rolling Stones did not even put their name on the front cover of their first UK album. The group had been started in London by Brian Jones, using regular attenders at the Ealing Jazz Club, where British blues pioneer Alexis Korner played regularly. Charlie Watts had been Korner's drummer for a while

```
UK release      April 1964       Decca LK 4605
US release      May 1964  London  PS 375 / LL 3375 as
ENGLAND'S NEWEST HITMAKERS.  Not Fade Away instead of Mona

1. Route 66 (Bobby Troup)
2. I Just Want To Make Love To You (Willie Dixon)
3. Honest I Do (Jimmy Reed)
4. Mona (I Need You Baby) (Bo Diddley)
5. Now I've Got A Witness (Rolling Stones)
6. Little By Little (Rolling Stones/Phil Spector)

7. I'm A King Bee (James Moore)
8. Carol (Chuck Berry)
9. Tell Me (You're Coming Back) (Mick Jagger/Keith Richards)
10. Can I Get A Witness (Brian & Eddie Holland/Lamont Dozier)
11. You Can Make It If You Try (Ted Jarrett)
12. Walking The Dog (Rufus Thomas)

Mick Jagger: vocals, harmonica, percussion / Brian Jones: guitar,
harmonica, percussion, vocals / Keith Richards: guitar, vocals / Bill
Wyman: bass guitar, vocals / Charlie Watts: drums / Ian Stewart:
keyboards (5,9,10,11) / Gene Pitney: piano (6) / Phil Spector:
percussion (6) / Andrew Loog Oldham, Eric Easton, Rolling Stones:
producer
```

and some of the others had jammed with Korner on occasion. Andrew Loog Oldham, who became the band's manager, despite being no older than they were, decided to promote the Stones as darker alter egos of the Beatles, with non-matching, more casual clothes and longer hair. The group appeared on ITV's pop music show, *Thank Your Lucky Stars*, where host Brian Matthews told a shocked audience that one of the group had not had a haircut for 'three months'! The group's intention to play with an earthier, more blues-based sound than the Beatles was rather belied by the first single, a distinctly poppy version of a lesser known Chuck Berry song, *Come On*, issued in June 1963 and just failing to enter the top twenty. It was followed by a version of a Beatles song, *I Wanna Be Your Man*, given to the group by John Lennon and Paul McCartney, who came to the studio to play the song through for them. The Stones did a good job in making the song sound harder and much more energetic than the Beatles' own recording. The album had a harder sound too than either Beatles LP, even if the blues was a little diluted by the inclusion of soul and rock 'n' roll covers. It is clearly the work, however, of a group that is supremely confident in its abilities – a confidence that is underscored by the decision to open the LP with *Route 66*, a reinterpretation of a song previously associated with Nat King Cole, turning it into a rock music classic that from that moment was only ever associated with the Rolling Stones. Andrew Oldham and Eric Easton, who handled the legal matters, since Oldham was not yet twenty-one, are listed as producers on the record sleeve. In practice, neither man spent much time in the studio and the Rolling Stones were left to produce the record themselves. With Phil Spector as a studio guest, however, it is hard to imagine that he did not lend some of his expertise to the proceedings. The group had yet to achieve a number one hit at the time the album was released, but the album itself rushed to the top of the LP charts and remained in the chart for a year.

DUSTY SPRINGFIELD   A GIRL CALLED DUSTY

```
UK release     April 1964         Philips    (S)BL 7594
US release     8 tracks on STAY AWHILE / I ONLY WANT TO BE WITH YOU
               June 1964    Philips PHS 600-133 / PHM 200-133
               3 tracks on DUSTY  Oct 1964  Philips  PHS 600-156 / PHM  200-156
Both albums completed with UK tracks issued on singles and EPs

1. Mama Said (Luther Dixon/Willie Denson)
2. You Don't Own Me (John Madara/David White)
3. Do Re Mi (Earl King)
4. When The Lovelight Starts Shining Through His Eyes (Lamont Dozier
                                       /Brian and Eddie Holland)
5. My Colouring Book (Fred Ebb/John Kander)
6. Mockingbird (Charlie and Inez Foxx)

7. Twenty-Four Hours From Tulsa (Burt Bacharach/Hal David)
8. Nothing (Frank Augustus/Bob Elgin/Clarence Lewis Jr)
9. Anyone Who Had A Heart (Burt Bacharach/Hal David)
10. Will You Love Me Tomorrow (Gerry Goffin/Carole King)
11. Wishin' And Hopin' (Burt Bacharach/Hal David)
12. Don't You Know (Ray Charles)

Dusty Springfield: vocals / Ivor Raymonde: orchestra director / The
Breakaways (Margot Quantrell, Barbara Moore, Betty Prescott, Jean Ryder):
vocals / Johnny Franz: producer
```

As lead singer with the country-folk trio, the Springfields, the woman christened Mary O'Brien scored a couple of top ten hits before announcing her decision to go solo. Fans of the group were apprehensive, but in fact the result was something of a revelation. Dusty Springfield was discovered as having a far more soulful voice than was ever apparent on the Springfields' recordings and she used it to perform some very appropriate material to remarkable effect. Arguably, by the time she released the album, she had already put her strongest performances on two hit singles and two EPs, so that the two American albums that overlap with *A Girl Called Dusty*, but include those performances, emerge as stronger releases. Nevertheless, it is easy to hear in these songs the talent and emotional depth that led to Dusty Springfield acquiring a reputation as Britain's finest female singer of the period. *A Girl Called Dusty* climbed to number six in the album charts.

ERIC DOLPHY   OUT TO LUNCH

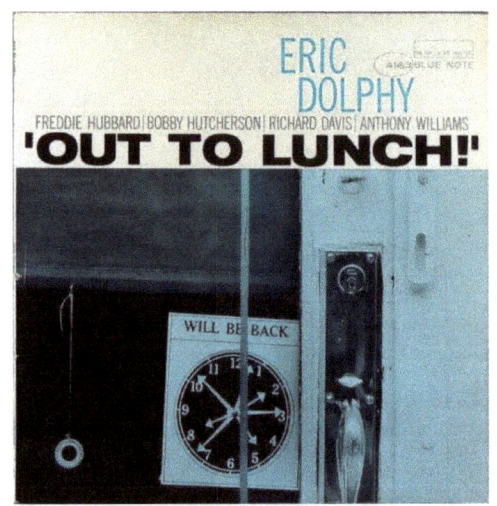

US release   May 1964   Blue Note   BST 84163 / BLP 4163
Not released in UK

1. Hat And Beard
2. Something Sweet, Something Tender
3. Gazzelloni
4. Out To Lunch
5. Straight Up And Down

All compositions by Eric Dolphy

Eric Dolphy: alto saxophone, flute, bass clarinet / Freddie Hubbard: trumpet / Bobby Hutcherson: vibraphone / Richard Davis: bass / Tony Williams: drums / Alfred Lion: producer

Alfred Lion's Blue Note record company was the most highly respected jazz label of the forties, fifties, and sixties and Eric Dolphy's *Out To Lunch* is widely considered to be one of the finest albums to be issued by it. Dolphy had, for a short time, been a member of John Coltrane's group and had been accorded the status of one of the prime movers of the jazz avant garde. The music is actually much more structured than this description would imply. The five tracks on the album are not lengthy modal improvisations in the John Coltrane manner, but are fully worked-out compositions, albeit delivered in a casual manner to make them sound more off-the-cuff than they really are, with the solo work fully integrated into the pre-planned parts. Dolphy's own solo playing, on all three of his instruments, is the most avant garde aspect of the music, as he produces tumbling lines, sometimes jagged and sometimes mellifluous, but always surprising and always magnificent. The contribution made by eighteen-year-old drummer, Tony Williams, is crucial too, as he finds ways of continually defying the listener's expectations, yet without ever losing the beat. It is the same technique he was applying to the music of Miles Davis's band at this time. The music of *Out To Lunch* has much in common with the work of Charles Mingus, with whom Eric Dolphy played several times, including a European tour immediately prior to the release of this album. At the end of June, Dolphy collapsed on stage in Berlin and was taken to hospital, where the doctor in charge made the assumption that a black jazz musician would be suffering a drug overdose and left him to recover naturally. In fact Dolphy was an undiagnosed diabetic and had fallen into a diabetic coma, from which he never recovered.

BUFFY SAINTE MARIE   IT'S MY WAY!

US release   May 1964   Vanguard   VRS / VSD7 9142
UK release   May 1964   Fontana   TFL 6040

1. Now That The Buffalo's Gone
2. The Old Man's Lament
3. Ananias
4. Mayoo Sto Hoon
5. Cod'ine
6. Cripple Creek (Traditional)
7. The Universal Soldier
8. Babe In Arms
9. He Lived Alone In Town
10. You're Gonna Need Somebody On Your Bond (Traditional)
11. The Incest Song
12. Eyes Of Amber
13. It's My Way

All compositions by Buffy Sainte Marie except where stated

Buffy Sainte Marie: vocals, guitar, mouth bow / Art Davis: bass (1) / Patrick Sky: guitar (9)/ Maynard Solomon: producer

Now That The Buffalo's Gone is a protest song, a lament for the treatment of the Native American people. It has the grandeur and the authority of an ancient folk song, but is in reality newly conceived by Buffy Sainte Marie, a singer who is herself of Native American descent. The song establishes the singer's credentials as a folk singer to be taken very seriously, while her distinctive voice, with an unusual combination of quavering and strength, immediately marks her as different from pure-toned singers like Joan Baez and Judy Collins (who did not, for the most part, write their own material). *Mayoo Sto Hoon* has lyrics in a Native American language, while *Cripple Creek* is accompanied by the traditional instrument shown on the album cover, the mouth bow. Two other songs on Buffy Sainte Marie's first album particularly forced the folk world to pay attention, her condemnation of the addictive pain-killer codeine, available on medical prescription, *Cod'ine*, and her highly effective anti-war song, *The Universal Soldier*, being taken up by several other performers.

THE GOLDEN AGE OF ROCK Volume One 1963-1968

VARIOUS ARTISTS   RHYTHM AND BLUES / RHYTHM & BLUES ALL STARS

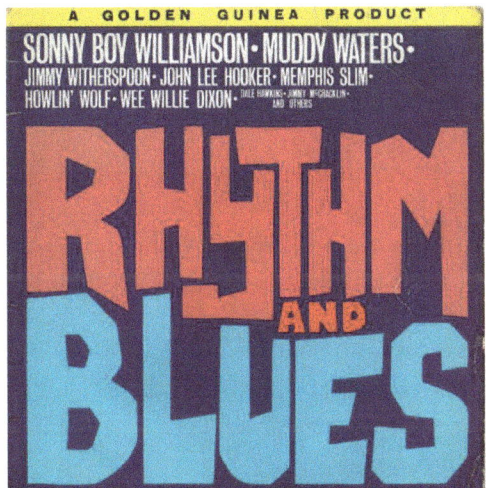

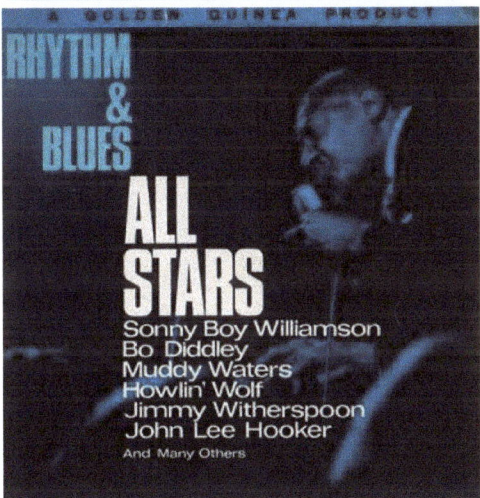

UK release   c.May 1964   Pye Golden Guinea   GGL 0280 / GGL 0293
Not released in US

1. Sonny Boy Williamson – Don't Start Me To Talkin' (Sonny Boy Williamson)
2. Little Walter – Juke (Walter Jacobs)
3. Jimmy Witherspoon – When The Lights Go Out (Willie Dixon)
4. Willie Dixon – Walking The Blues (Jack Dupree/Teddy McRae)
5. Memphis Slim – I Guess I'm A Fool (Memphis Slim)
6. Jimmy Rogers – That's All Right (Jimmy Rogers)
7. Jimmy McCracklin – New Orleans Beat (Everybody Rock) (Walter Jacobs)

8. Luther Dixon – The Feeling Of Love (Luther Dixon)
9. Howlin' Wolf – How Many More Years (Howlin' Wolf)
10. John Lee Hooker – Leave My Wife Alone (John Lee Hooker)
11. The Coronets – Nadine (Alan Freed)
12. Larry Williams – My Baby's Got Soul (M.Bookman)
13. Dale Hawkins – See You Soon Baboon (Eleanor Broadwater/Stanley Lewis)
14. Muddy Waters – You Need Love (Willie Dixon)

1. Sonny Boy Williamson – Fattening Frogs For Snakes (Sonny Boy Williamson)
2. Little Walter – My Babe (Willie Dixon)
3. Elmore James – The Sun Is Shining (Elmore James)
4. Lowell Fulson – Reconsider Baby (Lowell Fulson)
5. Jimmy Witherspoon – It Ain't No Secret (Willie Dixon)
6. Buddy Guy – First Time I Met The Blues (Little Brother Montgomery)
7. Howlin' Wolf – Smokestack Lightnin' (Howlin' Wolf)

8. Bo Diddley – Road Runner (Bo Diddley)
9. John Lee Hooker – Walkin' The Boogie (John Lee Hooker)
10. Memphis Slim – Mother Earth (Memphis Slim)
11. Jimmy Rogers – The World's In A Tangle (Jimmy Rogers)
12. Washboard Sam – Diggin' My Potatoes (Washboard Sam)
13. Otis Rush – So Many Roads (Paul Marshall)
14. Muddy Waters – Got My Mojo Working (Muddy Waters)

The success of the Rolling Stones, who were happy to acknowledge their love of the blues, encouraged Pye Records to release this pair of compilation albums, of songs by the most highly regarded Chicago blues performers, on its bargain-priced Golden Guinea label. Most of this music was recorded in the fifties and includes several undisputed classics by the men who defined the sound and style of contemporary electric urban blues. The *Rhythm & Blues All Stars* album is the superior collection if only because *Rhythm And Blues* chooses to interpret its brief rather more widely and includes several tracks that are not Chicago blues at all (and one, the Dale Hawkins song, that is out-and-out rock 'n' roll by an artist who would have seen Elvis Presley, not Robert Johnson, as his inspiration). This compilation is made essential, however, by its inclusion of the Muddy Waters/Willie Dixon song, *You Need Love,* that was turned into the iconic Led Zeppelin piece, *Whole Lotta Love.* Whoever designed the cover of the *Rhythm And Blues* LP, however, was clearly feeling confused by a British rock 'n' roll singer called Wee Willie Harris, because there is nothing remotely 'wee' about the imposing figure of Willie Dixon.

THE IMPRESSIONS   KEEP ON PUSHING

US release   June 1964   ABC-Paramount   ABC(S)-493
Not released in UK

1. Keep On Pushing (Curtis Mayfield)
2. I've Been Trying (Curtis Mayfield)
3. I Ain't Supposed To (Curtis Mayfield/Jerry Butler)
4. Dedicate My Song To You (Curtis Mayfield/Alice Beard)
5. Long Long Winter (Curtis Mayfield)
6. Somebody Help Me (Curtis Mayfield)

7. Amen (Traditional)
8. I Thank Heaven (Curtis Mayfield)
9. Talking About My Baby (Curtis Mayfield)
10. Don't Let It Hide (Curtis Mayfield)
11. I Love You (Yeah) (Curtis Mayfield)
12. I Made A Mistake (Curtis Mayfield)

Curtis Mayfield: vocals, guitar, producer / Fred Cash: vocals / Samuel Gooden: vocals / Johnny Pate: arranger

The Impressions, a vocal group led by Curtis Mayfield, achieved a number of hit singles and albums in the US through the sixties. *Keep On Pushing* was the most successful of these, reaching number 8 in the album chart, although like all the group's records, it failed to attract the attention of UK record buyers. Mayfield's high voice has an attractive fragility that works extremely well within the gentle soul music that the Impressions perform. Even on a rallying cry like the title track, the fact that Mayfield sounds as though he is struggling to do anything as energetic as pushing makes the message all the more effective. Although it shares the singing group format, the Impressions' version of soul music lacks the insistent dance beat of Motown and does not, therefore, sound very much like it. Curtis Mayfield was to exert a more far-reaching influence with the music he produced in the seventies, but his sixties music remains remarkably compelling. It is interesting to note that *Keep On Pushing* is one of the handful of albums shown on the front cover picture of Bob Dylan's *Bringing It All Back Home.*

ALEXIS KORNER'S BLUES INCORPORATED   RED HOT FROM ALEX

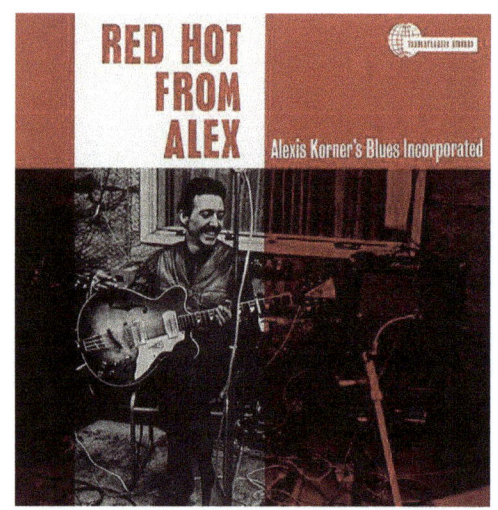

UK release	June 1964	Transatlantic	TRA 117
US release	1974	Just Sunshine	JSS-13

1. Woke Up This Morning (B.B.King/Jules Taub)
2. Skippin' (Alexis Korner)
3. Herbie's Tune (Alexis Korner)
4. Stormy Monday (T-Bone Walker)
5. It's Happening (Graham Bond)
6. Roberta (Alexis Korner)
7. Jones (Duke Ellington/Pauline Reddon)
8. Cabbage Greens (Alexis Korner)
9. Back At The Chicken Shack (Jimmy Smith)
10. Haitian Fight Song (Charles Mingus)

Alexis Korner: guitar / Herbie Goins: vocals / Dave Castle: alto saxophone, flute / Art Themen: tenor saxophone / Dick Heckstall-Smith: tenor saxophone / Ron Edgeworth: keyboards / Danny Thompson: bass / Barry Howten: drums / Nathan Joseph: producer

Alexis Korner joined Chris Barber's jazz band as a guitarist in 1949 and recorded as half of a duo with harmonica player Cyril Davies and as a member of Ken Colyer's Skiffle Group. In 1961, Korner and Davies formed Blues Incorporated to play the blues music that they both loved. The personnel changed frequently, but included many musicians who went on to find considerable fame, including members of the Rolling Stones, Cream, and Pentangle. Korner, though enthusiastic and knowledgeable, was not a particularly skilful guitarist, and he did not play solos in the manner of electric guitar heroes like B.B.King or Otis Rush. As a result, his band has a rather different sound to that of the various British blues groups that followed after him. He favours the playing of saxophonists in the lead role, giving Blues Incorporated a pronounced jazz flavour and causing Cyril Davies to leave the band in 1962. (He died of heart failure two years later, just short of his thirty-second birthday). Alexis Korner's influence was enormous, but his record sales were minimal. *Red Hot From Alex* is one of several albums to be issued and ignored through the sixties, but it gained considerable belated interest when it was reissued in 1969 at a budget price and repackaged to show Korner's later image, as a blues veteran with a Jimi Hendrix haircut. By this time, his vital contribution to the development of British blues-rock was being acknowledged and he was getting increasing exposure as a radio broadcaster.

THE BEATLES   LONG TALL SALLY EP

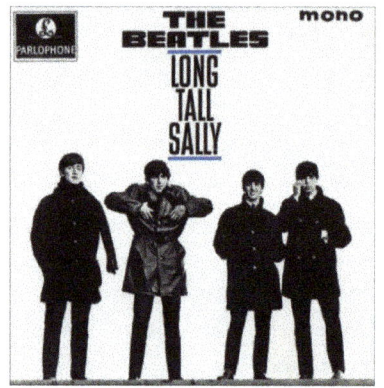

UK release   June 1964   Parlophone   GEP 8913
Not released in US

1. Long Tall Sally (Enotris Johnson/ Robert Blackwell/ Little Richard)
2. I Call Your Name (John Lennon/Paul McCartney)
3. Slow Down (Larry Williams)
4. Matchbox (Carl Perkins)

John Lennon: vocals, guitar / George Harrison: guitar / Paul McCartney: vocals, bass guitar / Ringo Starr: drums, percussion, vocals / George Martin: piano, producer

With the Beatles first film and accompanying records just about to be launched, Parlophone decided that the world could never have too much of its favourite group and released an EP containing four exclusive tracks. The record presents three authoritative covers of rock 'n' roll songs, alongside just one Lennon/ McCartney original. With Beatlemania at its height, these performances have no difficulty in persuading the listener that these old songs are being brought up to date and improved, even if the Beatles themselves would simply have been enjoying the R&B repertoire inspiring their early years. The EP effortlessly reached number one in the EP chart – doubtless it would have done the same if allowed into the singles chart.

THE BEATLES   A HARD DAY'S NIGHT

The first side of the Beatles' third album comprises a soundtrack to the group's 1964 film, *A Hard Day's Night,* in which they performed a number of new songs. The album is completed by other songs written by the Lennon/McCartney team at around the same time, but not used in the film. The album is the first (and indeed the only Beatles LP) to be made up entirely of songs written by John Lennon and Paul McCartney. The nature of the project means that, as on *Please Please Me,* the songs from two single releases are included. Musically, the album treads little new ground, but it does emphasise the Beatles' enormous skill in presenting a set of varied and memorable songs, without a single track that could be described as merely filling up space. Most of the songs are enhanced by the sound of George Harrison's newly acquired 12-string electric guitar. It is a sound that was soon borrowed by other groups, but for a brief period it gave the Beatles another distinctive advantage. In the US, an agreement with the film's distributor meant that United Artists were given the rights to the soundtrack songs, but not the other material, which ended up being scattered over three or four different albums. The soundtrack album is then completed by several instrumental versions of Beatle songs, played by an orchestra assembled by George Martin.

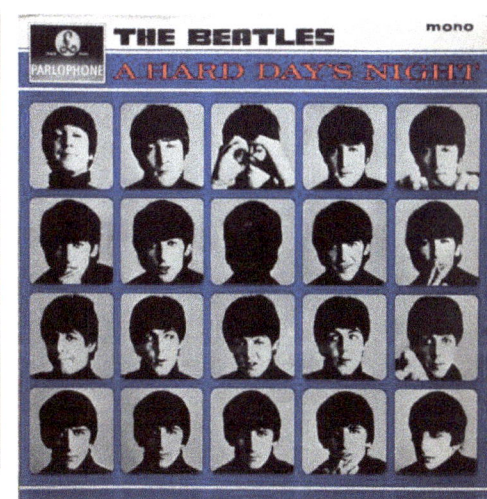

```
UK release   July 1964   Parlophone    PCS 3058 / PMC 1230
US release   July 1964   United Artists  UAS 6366 / UAL 3366
  5 tracks omitted and replaced by 4 instrumentals played by George
Martin and his Orchestra. 3 of the missing tracks were included on
SOMETHING NEW   July 1964  Capitol (S)T 2108, on which 5 of the tracks
already issued on the United Artists LP were repeated. I'll Be Back was
included on BEATLES '65   December 1964   Capitol (S)T 2228; You
Can't Do That had already been included on THE BEATLES' SECOND
ALBUM; Can't Buy Me Love had to wait until the 1970 LP HEY JUDE.
```

1. A Hard Day's Night
2. I Should Have Known Better
3. If I Fell
4. I'm Happy Just To Dance With You
5. And I Love Her
6. Tell Me Why
7. Can't Buy Me Love
8. Any Time At All
9. I'll Cry Instead
10. Things We Said Today
11. When I Get Home
12. You Can't Do That
13. I'll Be Back

All compositions by John Lennon/Paul McCartney

John Lennon: vocals, guitar, harmonica, piano, percussion / George Harrison: vocals, guitar, percussion / Paul McCartney: vocals, bass guitar, guitar, piano, percussion / Ringo Starr: drums, percussion / George Martin: piano, producer

THE BEACH BOYS   ALL SUMMER LONG

I Get Around was the Beach Boys' breakthrough single in the UK, the first to enter the top ten, and it was also the group's first number one in the US. The album assembled around it, the sixth to be issued by the Beach Boys, was by far the strongest made by them to date. The Beatles had established themselves as the artists to set the standard for pop albums and *All Summer Long* finds the Beach Boys responding to the challenge and meeting the standard. Not that the album is without its flaws. *Carl's Big Chance* is a not particularly memorable instrumental, while *Our Favorite Recording Sessions* is a montage of studio silliness that in the digital age would have been saved for a hidden bonus item. It has no place on an album that is otherwise full of some particularly striking Brian Wilson songs. Although *I Get Around* is a stunning demonstration of the group's skilful vocal interplay, and *Don't Back Down* is the first surf song to successfully capture some of the power of a wave in its music, the real masterpiece is *Girls On The Beach*. This is a paean to the opposite sex, but delivered as an aching ballad, as if the singer kely to be

```
US release   July 1964   Capitol   (S)T 2110
UK release   June 1965   Capitol   (S)T 2110
```

1. I Get Around (Brian Wilson/Mike Love)
2. All Summer Long (Brian Wilson/Mike Love)
3. Hushabye (Doc Pomus/Mort Shuman)
4. Little Honda (Brian Wilson/Mike Love)
5. We'll Run Away (Brian Wilson/Gary Usher)
6. Carl's Big Chance (Brian Wilson/Carl Wilson)
7. Wendy (Brian Wilson/Mike Love)
8. Do You Remember? (Brian Wilson/Mike Love)
9. Girls On The Beach (Brian Wilson/Mike Love)
10. Drive-In (Brian Wilson/Mike Love)
11. Our Favorite Recording Sessions (Beach Boys)
12. Don't Back Down (Brian Wilson/Mike Love)

Mike Love: vocals / Carl Wilson: vocals, guitar / Brian Wilson: vocals, keyboards, tuned percussion, producer / Al Jardine: vocals, bass guitar, guitar / Dennis Wilson: vocals, drums, percussion / Hal Blaine: percussion / Glen Campbell: bass guitar / Ray Pohlman: bass guitar / Steve Douglas: tenor saxophone / Jay Migliori: baritone saxophone, piccolo / The Honeys (Diane Rovell, Marilyn Rovell, Ginger Blake): vocals

successful in that area. These songs do much to compensate for the fact that the album is extremely short. *Another Side Of Bob Dylan,* released the following month, has each of its sides lasting as long as the Beach Boys' entire album. As a songwriter, Brian Wilson clearly believed that two minutes will do. He liked to come quickly to the point and then quit, leaving the listener with no alternative than to play the song again, if they wanted more. In the UK, the album release was delayed by nearly a year, so that any momentum generated by the hit single was lost. The album did not enter the charts, although it sold well when it was reissued in 1973 as part of EMI's bargain Music for Pleasure series.

TOM PAXTON   RAMBLIN' BOY

Bob Dylan did not, of course, work in a vacuum and he was by no means the only contemporary folk singer to be performing in the US during the early sixties. Tom Paxton had previously recorded a limited edition live album, but *Ramblin' Boy* was his first release by an established record company. Much less acerbic than Dylan, Paxton's forays into social commentary were few and not the kind of songs to be taken up as anthems. *Daily News* and *What Did You Learn In School Today?* make valid points about the disconnect between American ideals and what was actually happening in society at the time, but they do so in a relatively light-hearted manner, with a strong sense of narrative, but not much poetry. That quality is reserved for the songs that were designed to touch the heart rather than the conscience. The title track, *The Last Thing On My Mind,* and *I Can't Help But Wonder Where I'm Bound* achieve their purpose and they swiftly entered the repertoire of folk singers performing in clubs on both sides of the Atlantic. Elsewhere, Tom Paxton followed a gently humorous approach, with songs aimed at children, as on *Goin' To The Zoo* on this album. Paxton has never achieved the influence and the innovation of Bob Dylan, but he has managed to maintain a career as lengthy. In 2019, at the age of eighty-one, he was still touring.

| US release | July 1964 | Elektra | EKS 7277 / EKL 277 |
| UK release | early 1965 | Elektra | EKS 7277 / EKL 277 |

1. A Job Of Work
2. A Rumblin' In The Land
3. When Morning Breaks
4. Daily News
5. What Did You Learn In School Today?
6. The Last Thing On My Mind
7. Harper
8. Fare Thee Well, Cisco
9. I Can't Help But Wonder Where I'm Bound
10. High Sheriff Of Hazard (Traditional)
11. My Lady's A Wild, Flying Dove
12. Standing On The Edge Of Town
13. Bound For The Mountains And The Sea
14. Goin' To The Zoo
15. Ramblin' Boy

All compositions by Tom Paxton except where stated

Tom Paxton: vocals, guitar / Barry Kornfeld: banjo, guitar, harmonica / Felix Pappalardi: guitarron / Paul Rothchild: producer

BOB DYLAN   ANOTHER SIDE OF

| US release | August 1964 | Columbia | CS 8993 / CL 2193 |
| UK release | August 1964 | CBS | (S)BPG 62429 |

1. All I Really Want To Do
2. Black Crow Blues
3. Spanish Harlem Incident
4. Chimes Of Freedom
5. I Shall Be Free No. 10
6. To Ramona
7. Motorpsycho Nitemare
8. My Back Pages
9. I Don't Believe You
10. Ballad In Plain D
11. It Ain't Me Babe

All compositions by Bob Dylan

Bob Dylan: vocals, guitar, harmonica, piano / Tom Wilson: producer

With *Another Side Of Bob Dylan*, the singer songwriter makes clear his refusal to be pigeon-holed. Defying the expectations of some of his fans was something he would be doing many times again as his career progressed. Musically, apart from the addition of a piano to one track, played with no greater expertise than his simple guitar, nothing has changed. The lyrics are a different matter, however. Bob Dylan the protest singer is gone, and in his place is Bob Dylan the singer of contemporary pop songs, albeit pop songs that do not really sound like those written by anyone else. His imagery is starting to become a little more obtuse too, not least in the adoption of titles like *I Don't Believe You* and *I Shall Be Free No.10*, where the connection with what is actually being sung seems tenuous. Where previously, Dylan had assembled his albums from the results of several recording sessions, this time all the songs are from a single day's work, delivered as first takes. Essentially, the appropriately titled *Another Side Of Bob Dylan* is the first indication that the world was dealing with a truly major artist – one who was intent on setting fashion, rather than following it. The ambition implicit in the music belies the apparent simplicity of what is in the groove.

THE SUPREMES   WHERE DID OUR LOVE GO

Berry Gordy founded the Motown company in 1959 and by the end of 1963 had turned it into the third highest seller of singles in the US. The Supremes, originally formed by Florence Ballard as a quartet called the Primettes, were signed to the label in 1961. *Where Did Our Love Go* was the group's first substantial hit, reaching number one in the R&B and National charts, and

| US release | August 1964 | Motown | MS/MT 621 |
Not released in UK

1. Where Did Our Love Go
2. Run Run Run
3. Baby Love
4. When The Lovelight Starts Shining Through His Eyes
5. Come See About Me
6. Long Gone Lover (Smokey Robinson)
7. I'm Giving You Your Freedom
8. A Breathtaking Guy (Smokey Robinson)
9. He Means The World To Me (Norman Whitfield)
10. Standing At The Crossroads Of Love
11. Your Kiss Of Fire (Berry Gordy/Harvey Fuqua)
12. Ask Any Girl

Tracks 1-5,7,10,12 composed by Brian & Eddie Holland/Lamont Dozier

Diana Ross: vocals / Florence Ballard: vocals / Mary Wilson: vocals / The Four Tops: vocals (2,4) / Brian Holland: vocals (2,4), producer (1-5,7,10,12) / Eddie Holland: vocals (2,4) / Lamont Dozier: vocals (2,4), producer (1-5,7,10,12) / The Love-Tones: vocals (10) / Smokey Robinson: producer (6,8) / Norman Whitfield: producer (9) / Robert Gordy: producer (11) / Robert White: guitar / Eddie Willis: guitar / Joe Messina: guitar / Joe Hunter: keyboards / Earl Van Dyke: keyboards / James Jamerson: bass guitar / Benny Benjamin: drums / Richard Allen: drums / Jack Ashford: percussion, tuned percussion / Eddie Brown: percussion / Jack Brokensha: tuned percussion / various horn players

getting to number three in the UK chart too. Not long previously, Berry Gordy had demoted Florence Ballard and Mary Wilson, who frequently sang lead, in favour of Diana Ross alone, who dominated the group from then on. She has a distinctive voice, though with less power and flexibility than the others, but she has enough charisma to compensate. Motown was now using the same team of musicians on all its sessions and favouring a strong dance beat that gave the company a sound of its own, so that there was a strong similarity between the records of all its artists. The Supremes lived up to their name, however, and remained the most successful Motown act through the Sixties. The *Where Did Our Love Go* album also included the next two hit singles, *Baby Love* and *Come See About Me*. The Stateside label was responsible for issuing Motown LPs in the UK and chose to release the group's previous album, *Meet The Supremes*, in place of this, in line with parent company EMI's policy of avoiding, in general, the placing of hit singles on albums. It was an unfortunate decision, as that album had been recorded two years previously, when the group was still a quartet, and it sounds even older than that, as the classic Motown sound is not yet in place. *Where Did Our Love Go*, the single and the album, are the records where that classic sound starts.

VARIOUS ARTISTS   R & B

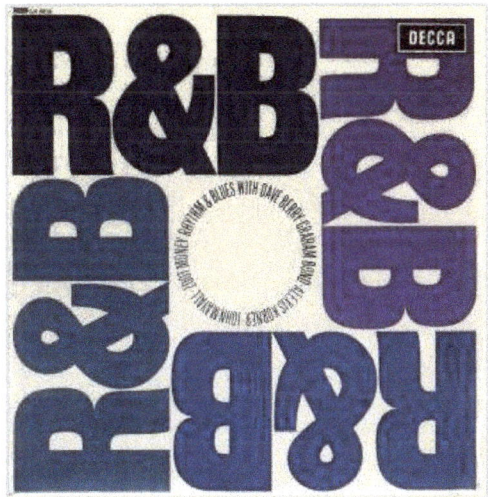

Decca produced what would have been a very useful showcase for the up-and-coming R&B bands impressing audiences at the clubs in the UK, if only people had known about it. Some of the tracks had been issued as singles, but by no means all of them, and none were hits. All of these groups made albums of their own subsequently, but it is significant that only those by John Mayall's Bluesbreakers and Dave Berry were for Decca. Alexis Korner had albums issued by several different companies, both before and after this time – two *were* released by Decca, but only on the company's bargain priced Ace of Clubs subsidiary. Dave Berry is something of an outsider in this company. Always much more of a rock 'n' roller than an enthusiast of the blues, he abandoned his backing band as soon as it began to struggle with the demands of the recording studio, and gained three top five hits in the UK with songs that were unapologetic pop. Berry apart, the sheer energy of these kes the album an exhilarating experience and it also provides a fascinating early opportunity for several musicians who went on to achieve much greater things. Information included with Alexis Korner reissues claims that the *R&B* album was not released until October, but John Mayall's *Looking Back* anthology gives August, which fits better with the album's catalogue number.

UK release   August 1964   Decca   LK 4616
Not released in US

1. Hi Heel Sneakers (Robert Higgenbotham)
2. Not Fade Away (Norman Petty/Buddy Holly)
3. Early In The Morning (Traditional)
4. Walking The Dog (Rufus Thomas)
5. Mr James (John Mayall)
6. Long Legged Baby (Graham Bond)
7. You Better Move On (Arthur Alexander)
8. Diddley Daddy (Bo Diddley / Harvey Fuqua)
9. Hoochie Coochie Man (Willie Dixon)
10. Get On The Right Track Baby (Joe Turner)
11. Little Girl (Graham Bond)
12. Crawling Up A Hill (John Mayall)
13. Strut Around (Graham Bond)
14. Night Time Is The Right Time (Nappy Brown/Ozzie Cadena/Lew Herman)

Tracks 1,6,9,11,13: The Graham Bond Organization – Graham Bond: vocals, organ / Dick Heckstall-Smith: tenor saxophone / Jack Bruce: bass guitar / Ginger Baker: drums / Vernon Lloyd: producer
Tracks 2,7: Dave Berry – Dave Berry: vocals / Big Jim Sullivan: guitar / Jimmy Page: guitar (7 only) / John Paul Jones: bass guitar / Bobby Graham: drums / Mike Smith: producer
Track 8: Dave Berry and the Cruisers – Dave Berry: vocals / Frank Miles: guitar / Roy Barber: guitar / John Fleet: bass guitar / Kenny Slade: drums
Tracks 3,14: Alexis Korner's Blues Incorporated– Alexis Korner: guitar / Ronnie Jones: vocals (14 only) / Graham Bond: alto saxophone / Dick Heckstall-Smith: tenor saxophone / Johnny Parker: piano / Jack Bruce: bass / Ginger Baker: drums / Roy Lister: producer
Tracks 4,10: Zoot Money's Big Roll Band – Zoot Money: vocals, organ / Andy Summers: guitar / Nick Newall: tenor saxophone / Clive Burrows: tenor saxophone / Paul Williams: bass guitar / Colin Allen: drums / Noel Walker: producer
Tracks 5,12: John Mayall's Bluesbreakers – John Mayall: vocals, organ piano,, harmonica / Bernie Watson: guitar / John McVie: bass guitar / Martin Hart: drums / Mike Vernon: producer

MANFRED MANN   THE FIVE FACES OF

5-4-3-2-1, a single issued at the start of the year, acted as a count down to the launch of the career of a successful hit-making group, named after the studious-looking keyboard player. The song was adopted too as the theme tune to a new music television show, *Ready Steady Go*, which presented live performances by contemporary stars and became the number one must-watch music programme in the UK. The fact that Paul Jones, lead singer and lyricist of the song, had got his ancient history wrong in a verse about the siege of Troy (deliberately, for the sake of the rhyming scheme – an important element in a song intended to add a touch of humour to its beat) gave the group considerable extra media exposure. The release of the group's first album followed closely after the third single hit, *Doo Wah Diddy Diddy*, had reached number one. Frustratingly for modern listeners, but in keeping with the policy at the time of EMI and other major

THE GOLDEN AGE OF ROCK Volume One 1963-1968

```
UK release    September 1964    HMV    CLP 1731
US release as THE MANFRED MANN ALBUM  September 1964
with three tracks replaced by the hit Doo Wah Diddy Diddy. Ascot
ALS 16015 / AM 13015 . The Ascot LP issued in Feb 1965 as
THE FIVE FACES OF MANFRED MANN is a different album.

1. Smokestack Lightning (Howlin' Wolf)
2. Don't Ask Me What I Say (Paul Jones)
3. Sack O' Woe (Cannonball Adderley)
4. What You Gonna Do? (Paul Jones/Manfred Mann)
5. Hoochie Coochie Man (Willie Dixon)
6. I'm Your Kingpin (Paul Jones/Mandred Mann)
7. Down The Road Apiece (Don Raye)

8. Got My Mojo Working (Preston Foster)
9. It's Gonna Work Out Fine (Rose Marie McCoy/Sylvia McKinney)
10. Mr Anello (Manfred Mann group)
11. Untie Me (Joe South)
12. Bring It To Jerome (Jerome Green)
13. Without You (Paul Jones)
14. You've Got To Take It (Paul Jones)

Paul Jones: vocals, harmonica, percussion / Manfred Mann: piano,
organ / Mike Vickers: guitar, flute, alto saxophone / Tom
McGuinness: bass guitar, guitar / Dave Richmond: bass guitar (13)
/ Mike Hugg: drums, vibes / John Burgess: producer
```

record companies, the album did not include any of the hit singles (although the US version happily included *Doo Wah Diddy Diddy*, which had become a number one hit in that country too). *The Five Faces Of Manfred Mann* revealed the group to be playing music that was something like a slightly more jazzy version of the Rolling Stones, albeit with piano replacing guitars as the dominant instrument. Rhythm and blues covers jostle against group originals in the same bluesy style. They found space to include a cover of a piece by Cannonball Adderley, *Sack O' Woe*, where the fact that Mike Vickers is no match as a soloist is camouflaged by underpinning the music with an R&B rhythm. The album sold well, reaching number three in the UK album charts.

JIMMY SMITH   THE CAT

```
US release    September 1964    Verve    V6/V 8587
UK release    September 1964    Verve    VLP 9079

1. Theme From Joy House (Lalo Schifrin)
2. The Cat (Lalo Schifrin)
3. Basin Street Blues (Spencer Williams)
4. Main Title From The Carpetbaggers (Elmer Bernstein)

5. Chicago Serenade (Eddie Harris)
6. St Louis Blues (W.C.Handy)
7. Delon's Blues (Jimmy Smith)
8. Blues In The Night (Johnny Mercer/Harold Arlen)

Jimmy Smith: organ / Lalo Schifrin: arranger, conductor / Kenny
Burrell: guitar / Bernie Glow, Ernie Royal, Jimmy Maxwell,
Marky Markowitz, Snooky Young, Thad Jones: trumpets / Billy
Byers, Jimmy Cleveland, Urbie Green: trombones / Tony Studd:
bass trombone / Bill Correa, Earl Chapin, Jim Buffington, Ray
Alonge: French horns / Don Butterfield: tuba / George Duvivier:
bass / Grady Tate: drums / Phil Kraus: percussion / Creed
Taylor: producer
```

Jimmy Smith began recording, for the Blue Note label, in 1956 and was enormously influential in boosting the appeal of the Hammond organ in jazz. Before Smith, organists in the music were extremely rare. Aware of his importance as an innovator, he happily allowed his name to be posted on his album sleeves as 'The Incredible' Jimmy Smith.

He tried various different line-ups to support his playing from album to album, and *The Cat* features a big band, directed by film composer Lalo Schifrin. Guitarist Kenny Burrell gets to play the theme on *Chicago Serenade*, but otherwise Jimmy Smith's Hammond is the only solo voice to be heard on the album. Smith made some thirty-six albums before this one, and they all favour the same kind of relaxed groove, but for some reason, *The Cat* was the one that caught the public's imagination. The album climbed to number twelve in the US album charts.

THE HONEYCOMBS

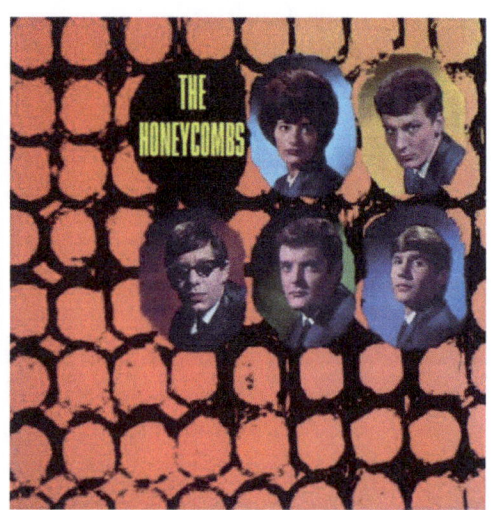

British producer Joe Meek had acquired a considerable reputation during the early sixties for his imaginative use of special effects and his unorthodox recording techniques. He achieved a huge international hit with his recording of *Telstar* by the Tornados. Producing *Have I The Right?* by the Honeycombs, he enhanced the drum beat by matching it to the

```
UK release    September 1964    Pye         NPL 18097
US release    September 1964    Interphon   INS-88001

1. Colour Slide (Ken Howard/Alan Blaikley)
2. Once You Know (Ken Howard/Alan Blaikley)
3. Without You It Is Night (Ken Howard/Alan Blaikley)
4. That's The Way (Ken Howard/Alan Blaikley)
5. I Want To Be Free (Jerry Leiber/Mike Stoller)
6. How The Mighty Have Fallen (Ken Howard/Alan Blaikley)
7. Have I The Right? (Ken Howard/Alan Blaikley)

8. Just A Face In The Crowd (Ken Howard/Alan Blaikley)
9. Nice While It Lasted (Joe Meek)
10. Me From You (Ken Howard/Alan Blaikley)
11. Leslie Anne (Martin Murray)
12. She's Too Way Out (Butch Davis/Joe Meek)
13. It Ain't Necessarily So (George & Ira Gershwin)
14. This Too Shall Pass Away (Ken Howard/Alan Blaikley)

Dennis D'Ell: vocals / Allan Ward: guitar / Martin Murray: guitar /
John Lantree: bass guitar / Honey Lantree: drums / Joe Meek:
producer
```

sound of stamping feet on a wooden staircase and speeded up the whole recording to give it extra bite. He was rewarded with another big hit, achieving number one in the UK, number five in the US, and a million sales overall. Much of the Honeycombs' enthusiastic pop material was the work of fledgling songwriting duo Ken Howard and Alan Blaikley – later to achieve even greater success with Dave Dee, Dozy, Beaky, Mick & Tich, although they struggled to find further hits for the Honeycombs. Ultimately, the group's biggest selling point appeared to be the fact that it had a female drummer, at a time when musical women were not expected to do anything other than sing.

THE KINKS   KINKS

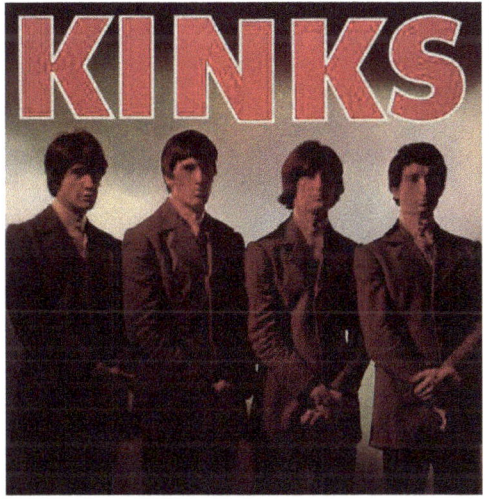

UK release   October 1964   Pye   N(S)PL 18096
US release   October 1964   Reprise   R(S) 6143
Three fewer tracks, retitled YOU REALLY GOT ME

1. Beautiful Delilah (Chuck Berry)
2. So Mystifying (Ray Davies)
3. Just Can't Go To Sleep (Ray Davies)
4. Long Tall Shorty (Don Covay/Herb Abramson)
5. I Took My Baby Home (Ray Davies)
6. I'm A Lover Not A Fighter (J.D.Miller)
7. You Really Got Me (Ray Davies)

8. Cadillac (Bo Diddley)
9. Bald Headed Woman (Shel Talmy)
10. Revenge (Larry Page/Ray Davies)
11. Too Much Monkey Business (Chuck Berry)
12. I've Been Driving On Bald Mountain (Shel Talmy)
13. Stop Your Sobbing (Ray Davies)
14. Got Love If You Want It (Slim Harpo)

Ray Davies: vocals, guitar, harmonica / Dave Davies: guitar, vocals / Peter Quaife: bass guitar, vocals / Mick Avory: drums, percussion / Arthur Greenslade: piano / Perry Ford: piano / Jon Lord: organ / Bobby Graham: drums / Rasa Didzpetris: vocals / Shel Talmy: producer

The Kinks reached number one in the UK charts in the summer, with *You Really Got Me*, a record which was also a hit in the US. The Kinks presented a stripped-down approach to British beat (not that their rivals were exactly complicated) in which driving guitar chords were the most important ingredient. The group seemed to be taking the Kingmen as their inspiration, as much as Chuck Berry, and indeed, they recorded a version of *Louie Louie* for inclusion on an EP release soon after the completion of the album. They cover Chuck Berry too, but very much in the manner that the Kingsmen would have adopted, translated from mature blues complaint to stroppy teen angst. Singer-guitarist Ray Davies wrote some of the Kinks' material, including the hit single, and he had the knack of finding memorable melody lines to distinguish songs based on simple rhythm and blues chord changes. The group seemed to have a less sympathetic management behind them than the Beatles or the Rolling Stones, however, so that they were forced to include considerably less inspired songs by their producer, Shel Talmy. Meanwhile, rumours persist that some of the guitar was played by session musician Jimmy Page, despite denials by all concerned.

SIMON & GARFUNKEL   WEDNESDAY MORNING, 3AM

US release   October 1964   Columbia   CS 9049 / CL 2249
UK release   November 1968   CBS   (S) 63370

1. You Can Tell The World (Bob Gibson/Bob Camp)
2. Last Night I Had The Strangest Dream (Ed McCurdy)
3. Bleecker Street (Paul Simon)
4. Sparrow (Paul Simon)
5. Benedictus (Orlande de Lassus)
6. The Sounds Of Silence (Paul Simon)

7. He Was My Brother (Paul Simon)
8. Peggy-O (Traditional)
9. Go Tell It On The Mountain)Traditional)
10. The Sun Is Burning (Ian Campbell)
11. The Times They Are A-Changin' (Bob Dylan)
12. Wednesday Morning, 3am (Paul Simon)

Paul Simon: vocals, guitar, banjo / Art Garfunkel: vocals / Barry Kornfeld: guitar / Bill Lee: bass guitat / Tom Wilson: producer

Paul Simon had achieved several minor pop hits in the US during the late fifties and early sixties, using a variety of different names, including 'Tom and Jerry' for a record made with his school friend, Art Garfunkel. In 1964, the duo auditioned for Columbia records and were signed for an album. They judged that the time was right for a folk recording, so applied their harmony singing (very much in the style of the Everly Brothers) to a set of appropriate material. This included the obligatory Bob Dylan song, alongside five songs written by Paul Simon himself. The album flopped, and was not released at all in the UK, but has acquired an importance retrospectively as the first significant record by an extremely popular and influential pair of artists.

GEORGIE FAME   FAME AT LAST

UK release   October 1964   Columbia   33SX 1638
US release   early 1965   Imperial   LP 12282 / LP 9282
as YEH YEH with two tracks replaced by both sides of the single

1. Get On The Right Track Baby (Titus Turner)
2. Let The Sunshine In (Billy Barberis/Bobby Weinstein/Teddy Randazzo)
3. The Monkey Time (Curtis Mayfield)
4. All About My Girl (Jimmy McGriff)
5. Point Of No Return (Gerry Goffin/Carole King)
6. Gimme That Wine (Jon Hendricks)
7. Pink Champagne (Joe Liggins)
8. Monkeying Around (William Bell)
9. Pride And Joy (Marvin Gaye/Norman Whitfield/William Stevenson)
10. Green Onions (Booket T and the MGs)
11. I Love The Life I Life (Willie Dixon)
12. I'm In The Mood For Love (Dorothy Fields/Jimmy McHugh)

Georgie Fame: vocals, organ / Peter Coe: tenor saxophone / Glenn Hughes: baritone saxophone / Eddie Thornton: trumpet / Tex Makins: bass guitar / Tommy Frost: drums / Speedy Acquaye: percussion / Earl Guest: director (2,3,8,9) / Ian Samwell: producer

Columbia must have had a considerable amount of faith in Georgie Fame, for although he had still not been responsible for any record release resembling a hit, he was allowed to make a second album. This time, the result, a collection of sophisticated studio songs played as though they were jazz, even if their origin was often somewhere else, justified the record company's confidence by entering the album charts and reaching number fifteen. It set the stage for a hit single, which followed in the New Year, as *Yeh Yeh*, retaining the jazz sound, went to number one in the UK and was a hit too in the US. Imperial, however, clearly thought that the jazz influence should be reduced if at all possible, and edited out Peter Coe's saxophone solo.

THE ROLLING STONES   12 x 5

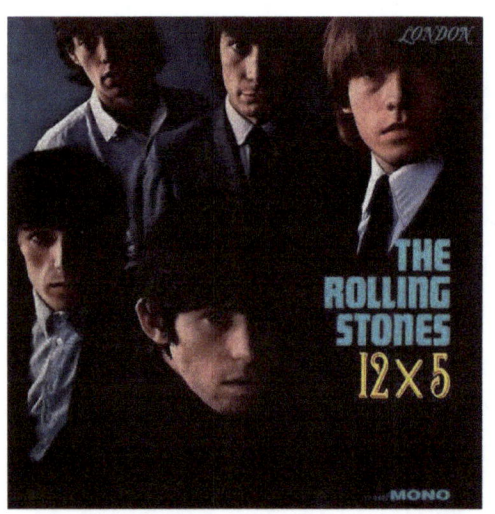

US release   October 1964   London   PS 402 / LL 3402
Not released in UK   1,2,3,7,11 issued on EP 5 x 5; 4,8,10,12 issued on LP THE ROLLING STONES No.2; 5,6 issued as a single; 9 issued on 1973 LP NO STONE UNTURNED

1. Around And Around (Chuck Berry)
2. Confessin' The Blues (Jay McShann/Walter Brown)
3. Empty Heart (Rolling Stones)
4. Time Is On My Side (Jerry Ragovoy)
5. Good Times Bad Times (Mick Jagger/Keith Richards)
6. It's All Over Now (Bobby & Shirley Womack)
7. 2120 South Michigan Avenue (Rolling Stones)
8. Under The Boardwalk (Arthur Resnick/Kenny Young)
9. Congratulations (Mick Jagger/Keith Richards)
10. Grown Up Wrong (Mick Jagger/Keith Richards)
11. If You Need Me (Robert Bateman/Wilson Pickett)
12. Susie Q (Dale Hawkins/Eleanor Broadwater/Stanley Lewis)

Mick Jagger: vocals, harmonica, percussion / Brian Jones: guitar, harmonica, percussion, vocals, organ (11) / Keith Richards: guitar, vocals / Bill Wyman: bass guitar, vocals, percussion / Charlie Watts: drums / Ian Stewart: keyboards / Andrew Loog Oldham: producer / Rolling Stones: producer

A five track EP, issued in the UK as *5 x 5*, and never intended to do much more than mark time, was expanded into a full album for the American market, with the same result. The album fulfils its task of keeping the group's momentum going, but it lacks the excitement, the sense of world-changing newness, that made the first album such a vital release. During the year, several other groups had emerged on to the world stage, delivering rhythm and blues covers just as effectively as the Stones. With the group's attempts at original songwriting remaining undistinguished, there is little here to give the Rolling Stones an edge over the competition. The tracks destined for the British EP had been recorded in Chicago, and on the album generally there is a slight shift in the direction of the Chicago urban blues that was the group's first love. Shortly after the release of *12 x 5*, the group issued a straightforward cover of a Howlin' Wolf song as a single, *Little Red Rooster*, complete with well-played slide guitar by Brian Jones. The record was more remarkable than anything on the album, with the exception of the group's transformation of soul singer Bobby Womack's *It's All Over Now* into a driving piece of blues-rock, but this had already been a hit single release.

ALEXIS KORNER'S BLUES INCORPORATED   AT THE CAVERN

This live recording was made a month before the studio recordings issued in June on the *Red Hot From Alex* album and with a slightly smaller band including only one saxophonist. The music is much less jazzy than on the studio session and Alexis Korner himself dominates the music far more, whether singing (which he does more often than the band's supposed vocalist, Herbie Goins) or delivering his gritty guitar playing, either as part of the rhythm or else stepping forward to play solos. For the most part, the band shuffles rather than rocks and the music has far less drive than that of the Rolling Stones or the Animals. Arguably, the period of his greatest influence was already over, with Korner's best band having left en masse to become the Graham Bond Organization, and his own version of the blues starting to sound over-polite and staid. But the audience at the Cavern is appreciative enough and the music is well recorded, which alone makes *At The Cavern* one of the more satisfactory live albums of the period.

```
UK release    October 1964    Oriole    PS 40058
Not released in US

1. Overdrive (Alexis Korner)
2. Whoa Babe (Alexis Korner)
3. Every Day I Have The Blues (Memphis Slim)
4. Hoochie Coochie Man (Willie Dixon)

5. Herbie's Tune (Alexis Korner)
6. Little Bitty Gal Blues (Joe Turner)
7. Well All Right, OK, You Win (Sid Wyche/Mayme Watts)
8. Kansas City (Jerry Leiber/Mike Stoller)

Alexis Korner: voca;s, guitar / Herbie Goins: vocals / Dave Castle: alto saxophone / Malcolm Saul: organ / Vernon Brown: bass / Mike Scott: drums
```

JOAN BAEZ   5

The many albums made by Joan Baez are all about the voice, blessed as she is with a pure natural soprano of great beauty. She made her first major performance at the 1959 Newport Folk Festival and was signed to the Vanguard record company as a result. Her first four albums all sold well enough to earn her gold records. *5* finds the singer moving significantly away from the traditional material that made her name, but without losing her audience. She even has the confidence to tackle a classical music piece, by Villa-Lobos. The arrangement, where her voice soars over a group of eight cellos, makes the track the only one to depart from her acoustic guitar accompaniment, but it manages to take its place seamlessly. Her cover of a Bob Dylan song makes it clear that her guitar playing is very much more skilful than his, although this is apparent on all the other tracks too. The album matched the sales of its predecessors and also spawned a hit single in both the US and the UK, her cover of a song by protest singer Phil Ochs, *There But For Fortune*.

```
US release    October 1964    Vanguard    VSD 79160 / VRS 9160
UK release    October 1964    Fontana     (S)TFL 6043

1. There But For Fortune (Phil Ochs)
2. Stewball (Ralph Rinzler/Bob Yellin/John Herald)
3. It Ain't Me Babe (Bob Dylan)
4. The Death Of Queen Jane (Traditional)
5. Bachianas Brasileiras No.5 – Aria (Heitor Villa-Lobos)
6. Go 'Way From My Window (John Jacob Niles)

7. I Still Miss Someone (Johnny Cash/Roy Cash Jr)
8. When You Hear Them Cuckoos Hollerin' (Traditional)
9. Birmingham Sunday (Richard Farina)
10. So We'll Go No More A-Roving (Richard Dyer-Bennet/Lord Byron)
11. O' Cangaceiro (The Bandit) (Alfredo Ricardo do Nascimento)
12. The Unquiet Grave (Traditional)

Joan Baez: vocals, guitar / David Soyer: cello (5)/ Maurice Abravanel: conductor of cello ensemble (5) / Gino Foreman: guitar (8) / Maynard Solomon: producer
```

THE ANIMALS

```
UK release    November 1964    Columbia    33SX 1669
US  release   October 1964     MGM    SE 4264    5 different tracks

1. Story Of Bo Diddley (Bo Diddley)
2. Bury My Body (Traditional)
3. Dimples (John Lee Hooker/James Bracken)
4. I've Been Around (Fats Domino)
5. I'm In Love Again (Fats Domino/Dave Bartholomew)
6. The Girl Can't Help It (Bobby Troup)

7. I'm Mad Again (John Lee Hooker)
8. She Said Yeah (Roddy Jackson/Sonny Bono)
9. Night Time Is The Right Time (Lew Herman)
10. Memphis (Chuck Berry)
11. Boom Boom (John Lee Hooker)
12. Around And Around (Chuck Berry)

Eric Burdon: vocals / Hilton Valentine: guitar / Alan Price: organ, piano / Chas Chandler: bass guitar / John Steel: drums / Mickie Most: producer
```

In June 1964, the Animals released their version of a traditional folk song, *House Of The Rising Sun*, that had appeared on the first album by Bob Dylan. The song was dramatically rearranged, so that it no longer sounds like a folk song. Organist Alan Price received the credit, which seems fitting, although various members have since maintained that the whole group was responsible. Introduced by a distinctive guitar arpeggio sequence, the song is delivered by a singer able to wind up the emotion from verse to verse to the point where his voice has become an anguished wailing, while the whole thing is underscored and carried along by organ playing that seems to be sounding through an open church door. The record was twice as long as most singles, yet seemed such an obvious hit, that it was no surprise when it went to number one in both the UK and the US. The American version of the Animals' first LP has the song as its first track, albeit in a shortened version. The UK issue does not and is a weaker collection of songs in consequence. The tough covers of rhythm and blues originals are well played and have more energy and conviction than anything else outside the Rolling Stones, but there is nothing there as distinguished and vital as *House Of The Riding Sun*. Alan Price, the organist, left the group a year later, to begin a successful solo career. Chas Chandler, the bass guitarist, moved into management some time after that, promoting the music of a left-handed guitarist he had discovered in America, by the name of Jimi Hendrix.

THE RONETTES   PRESENTING THE FABULOUS RONETTES

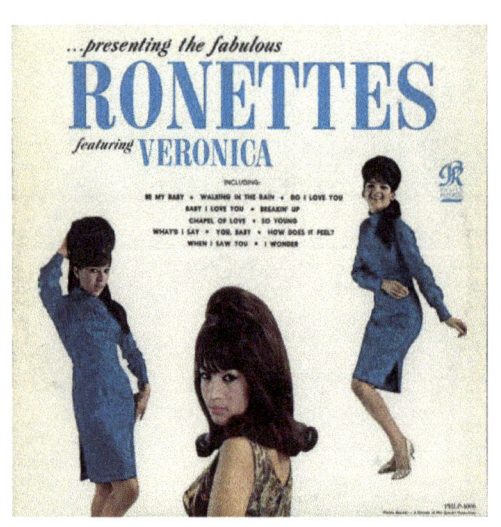

US release   November 1964   Philles   PHLP/ST   4006
UK release   November 1964   London   HA-U 8212

1. Walking In The Rain (Barry Mann/Cynthia Weil/Phil Spector)
2. Do I Love You? (Vini Poncia/Pete Andreoli/Phil Spector)
3. So Young (William Tyus)
4. (The Best Part Of) Breakin' Up (Poncia/Andreoli/Spector)
5. I Wonder (Jeff Barry/Ellie Greenwich/Phil Spector)
6. What'd I Say (Ray Charles)
7. Be My Baby (Jeff Barry/Ellie Greenwich/Phil Spector)
8. You, Baby (Barry Mann/Cynthia Weil/Phil Spector)
9. Baby, I Love You (Jeff Barry/Ellie Greenwich/Phil Spector)
10. How Does It Feel? (Vini Poncia/Pete Andreoli/Phil Spector)
11. When I Saw You (Phil Spector)
12. Chapel Of Love (Jeff Barry/Ellie Greenwich/Phil Spector)

Veronica Bennett: vocals / Nedra Talley: vocals / Estelle Bennett: vocals / The Blossoms – Darlene Love, Fanita James, Gracia Nitzsche: vocals (1,4,7,8,9,10,12) / Bobby Sheen: vocals (4,7,12) / Cher: vocals (1,4,7,8,9) / Ellie Greenwich: vocals (7) / Nino Tempo: vocals (7) / Sonny Bono: percussion, vocals (4,7) / Barney Kessel: guitar / Tom Tedesco: guitar / Carol Kaye: guitar / Bill Pitman: guitar / Vincent Poncia: guitar / Don Randi: piano / Al De Lory: piano / Leon Russell: piano / Harold Battiste: piano / Larry Knechtel: piano, bass guitar / Ray Pohlman: bass guitar / Jimmy Bond: bass guitar / Steve Douglas: saxophone / Jay Migliori: saxophone / Lou Blackburn: trombone / Roy Caton: trumpet / Hal Blaine: drums / Frank Capp: percussion / Julius Wechter: percussion / Jack Nitzsche: arranger / Phil Spector: producer

The sublime tones of Ronnie Bennett's voice, cushioned by the Ronettes and several other backing singers, together with the might of Phil Spector's wall-of-sound, was responsible for some of the most appealing examples of girl group music, of this time or since. The Ronettes achieved four unforgettable hits, all of which are included on *Presenting The Fabulous Ronettes*. The implication of the title is that this would be the first of many albums, but in fact the group never got to make another one. For Phil Spector, whose controlling attitude is emphasised by the addition of his name to those of established song-writing pairs in the album credits, the sound was always more important than the actual artists. The first tracks he made with the Ronettes were included on a Crystals album as being by that group, although Spector had always been inclined to use the Crystals name as a convenient cover-all device. There was a real group there, but the personnel kept changing, and several of the records, including the biggest hit, *He's A Rebel*, were actually recorded by different singers entirely. Phil Spector eventually married Ronnie Bennett and, by all accounts, treated her badly. It is interesting to note the presence of Cher on some of the tracks on the Ronettes album, taking part in her first recording sessions, although her voice cannot be distinguished inside the ensemble.

THE BEATLES   BEATLES FOR SALE

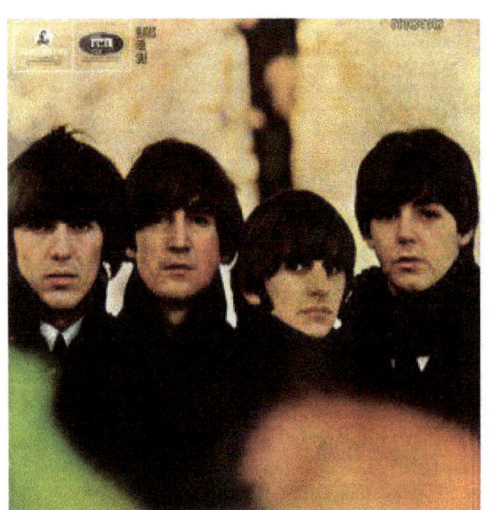

UK release   December 1964   Parlophone   PCS 3062 / PMC 1240
US release   Issued as two LPs, together with an assortment of tracks issued as singles or left over from other albums.   **BEATLES '65**   December 1964   Capitol (S)T 2228;   **BEATLES VI**   June 1965   Capitol   (S)T 2358

1. No Reply (John Lennon/Paul McCartney)
2. I'm A Loser (John Lennon/Paul McCartney)
3. Baby's In Black (John Lennon/Paul McCartney)
4. Rock And Roll Music (Chick Berry)
5. I'll Follow The Sun (John Lennon/Paul McCartney)
6. Mr Moonlight (Roy Lee Johnson)
7. Kansas City / Hey Hey Hey Hey (Jerry Leiber/Mike Stoller//Little Richard)
8. Eight Days A Week (John Lennon/Paul McCartney)
9. Words Of Love (Buddy Holly)
10. Honey Don't (Carl Perkins)
11. Every Little Thing (John Lennon/Paul McCartney)
12. I Don't Want To Spoil The Party (John Lennon/Paul McCartney)
13. What You're Doing (John Lennon/Paul McCartney)
14. Everybody's Trying To Be My Baby (Carl Perkins)

John Lennon: vocals, guitar, harmonica, percussion / George Harrison: guitar, vocals, percussion / Paul McCartney: vocals, bass guitar, guitar, piano, organ / Ringo Starr: drums, percussion, vocals / George Martin: producer, piano

For the Beatles' fourth UK album, they moved back to the formula of mixing their own songs with cover versions. *Mr Moonlight* was an obscure B-side by bluesman Piano Red and is an odd choice, given its less than classic status, and it had already been recorded by the Hollies (who arguably do a better job). The others are all rock 'n' roll songs – no Motown this time. The writer of the sleeve notes took great delight in listing such details as Ringo Starr playing a packing case in place of his drums on *Words Of Love* and George Harrison thumping an African drum on *Mr Moonlight*. Although it was commonplace for songs to come to an end by fading out, *Eight Days A Week* kicked off the album's second side by fading *in*. While the use of such instruments and effects hardly constituted an innovation of landmark proportions, it was significant that the Beatles were interested in introducing this kind of modest novelty at a time when the LP would have been commercially successful whatever it had sounded like. The effects are important because they show how the Beatles were beginning to search for new sounds in an effort to give each song a distinct character of its own.

THE YARDBIRDS   FIVE LIVE YARDBIRDS

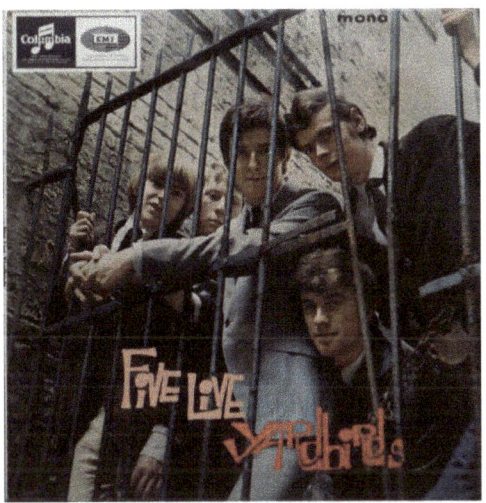

UK release   December 1964   Columbia   33SX 1677
Not released in US, but 4 tracks included on **HAVING A RAVE UP WITH THE YARDBIRDS**, issued by Epic in November 1965.

1. Too Much Monkey Business (Chuck Berry)
2. Got Love If You Want It (Slim Harpo)
3. Smokestack Lightnin' (Howlin' Wolf)
4. Good Morning Little Schoolgirl (Don Level/Bob Love)
5. Respectable (Isley Brothers) / Humpty Dumpty (Eric Morris)

6. Five Long Years (Eddie Boyd)
7. Pretty Girl (Bo Diddley)
8. Louise (John Lee Hooker)
9. I'm A Man (Bo Diddley)
10. Here 'Tis (Bo Diddley)

Keith Relf: vocals, harmonica, percussion / Eric Clapton: guitar, vocals / Chris Dreja: guitar / Paul Samwell-Smith: bass guitar, vocals / Jim McCarty: drums / Giorgio Gomelsky: producer

For the first album by London R&B group the Yardbirds, Columbia decided to repeat the formula it had used for Georgie Fame and made a live recording, at the Marquee Club in Soho. The acoustics of the tiny venue were less than ideal for creating a clear sound and although Keith Relf's voice and harmonica cut through well enough, everything else is distinctly murky. The group has a tendency to play everything at breakneck speed, but one slow blues, *Five Long Years*, makes it clear that the lead guitarist, Eric 'Slowhand' Clapton, is a particularly fluid player, even if his tone is the thin affair that was typical of the period. Supposedly, the Yardbirds would often stretch out some of their songs to as much as half an hour, but here they are all quite short. Relf solos often on harmonica, and Clapton does too, on guitar, but for no more than a couple of verses at a time. The guitarist, of course, would go on to acquire a legendary reputation, and whether deliberately or not, he does rather succeed in dominating the group photograph on the album cover.

1965

THE ROLLING STONES   No.2

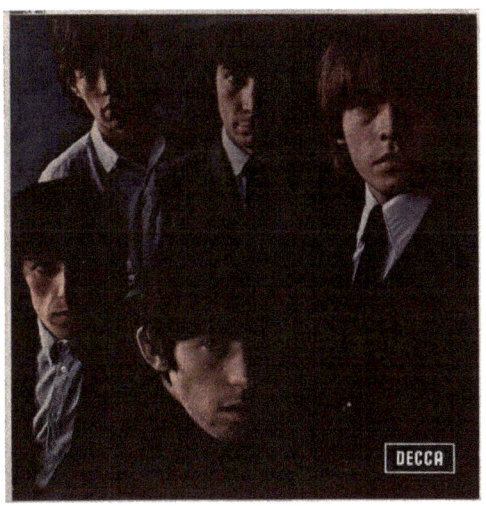

The Rolling Stones No.2 is a stronger, more cohesive collection than *12 x 5*, and it announces its authority with an energetic opening track, in which Mick Jagger takes on soul singer Solomon Burke and succeeds in forcing a draw. There are three Jagger/Richards compositions, which are memorable enough for the purpose, even if they would not have made Lennon and McCartney worry about the competition. It was already clear, however, that in common with the majority of their contemporaries, the Rolling Stones were channelling their best efforts into the production of sparkling singles. Although the album sold well, reaching the top chart position as its predecessor had done, it nevertheless proved that the Stones were following in the wake of the Beatles, rather than being creative rivals. The Beatles were delivering albums in which many of the tracks could have been released as singles. Thus far, the Rolling Stones were not managing to match this achievement. Perhaps aware that the album was not quite cutting it against the competition, manager Andrew Oldham decided to write a deliberately provocative essay in his sleeve notes, rather than rely on the music making its own impact. "Cast deep in your pockets for loot to buy this disc of groovies and fancy words. If you don't have bread, see that blind man, knock him on the head, steal his wallet and lo and behold you have the loot, if you put in the boot, good, another one sold!" Subsequent issues of the record presented a somewhat amended version of this text.

> UK release   January 1965   Decca   LK 4661
> 7 tracks included on US release THE ROLLING STONES NOW   February 1965
> London   PS 420 / LL 3420; 4 tracks had been included on US release 12 x 5
>
> 1. Everybody Needs Somebody To Love (Solomon Burke/Bert Berns/Jerry Wexler)
> 2. Down Home Girl (Jerry Leiber/Arthur Butler)
> 3. You Can't Catch Me (Chuck Berry)
> 4. Time Is On My Side (Jerry Ragovoy)
> 5. What A Shame (Mick Jagger/Keith Richards)
> 6. Grown Up Wrong (Mick Jagger/Keith Richards)
>
> 7. Down The Road Apiece (Don Raye)
> 8. Under The Boardwalk (Arthur Resnick/Kenny Young)
> 9. I Can't Be Satisfied (Muddy Waters)
> 10. Pain In My Heart (Allen Toussaint)
> 11. Off The Hook (Mick Jagger/Keith Richards)
> 12. Suzie-Q (Dale Hawkins/Stan Lewis/Eleanor Broadwater)
>
> Mick Jagger: vocals, harmonica, percussion / Brian Jones: guitar, percussion, vocals / Keith Richards: guitar, vocals / Bill Wyman: bass guitar, vocals / Charlie Watts: drums / Ian Stewart: piano (1,5,7), organ (4) / Jack Nitzsche: piano (2,10) / Andrew Loog Oldham: producer / Rolling Stones: producer

DAVY GRAHAM   FOLK, BLUES & BEYOND

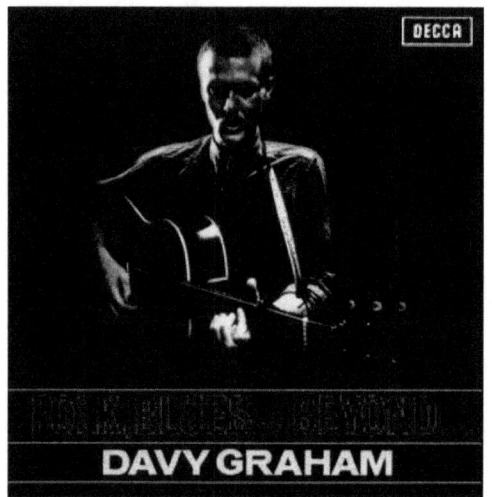

> UK release   January 1965   Decca   LK 4649
> Not released in US
>
> 1. Leavin' Blues (Leadbelly)
> 2. Cocaine (Rev Gary Davis)
> 3. Sally Free And Easy (Cyril Tawney)
> 4. Black Is The Colour Of My True Love's Hair (Traditional)
> 5. Rock Me Baby (Big Bill Broonzy)
> 6. Seven Gypsies (Traditional)
> 7. Ballad Of The Sad Young Man (Fran Landesman/Tommy Wolf)
> 8. Moanin' (Bobby Timmons/Jon Hendricks)
>
> 9. Skillet (Good 'N Greasy) (Traditional)
> 10. Ain't Nobody's Business What I Do (Porter Grainger/Everett Robbins)
> 11. Maajun (A Taste Of Tangier) (Davy Graham)
> 12. Can't Keep From Crying Sometimes (Blind Willie Johnson)
> 13. Don't Think Twice, It's All Right (Bob Dylan)
> 14. My Babe (Willie Dixon)
> 15. Goin' Down Slow Jimmy Oden)
> 16. Better Get Hit In Yo' Soul (Charles Mingus)
>
> Davy Graham: guitar, vocals / Tony Reeves: bass / Barry Morgan: drums / Ray Horricks: producer

Davy Graham was a virtuoso acoustic guitarist who served as a major inspiration for numerous players to come after him, although his own records were not commercially successful. His first recording was an EP made jointly with Alexis Korner in 1962, although the latter only played on one track out of the three. One of the others was *Angi*, composed by Graham, and which ended up becoming his most well-known piece. The technical challenge it presented encouraged several other guitarists to tackle it, with variable results. In 1963, Graham made an album, but it was released by Pye's bargain-priced Golden Guinea label, aimed at the easy-listening market, and it failed to attract much serious attention. *Folk, Blues & Beyond* did little better, despite a release by Decca, but it remains a convincing showcase for Davy Graham's remarkable abilities as a guitarist. These include his fondness for using alternative tunings, beyond the open chords favoured by blues slide guitar players, in which respect he was something of a pioneer. He sings on many of the tracks too, and his voice is unremarkable, although considerably more tuneful than Bob Dylan, one of whose songs Graham chooses to cover. Graham's interests, however, extended much more widely than just folk, as he incorporates blues and jazz (including a tune by Charles Mingus) and even a touch of world music into his style. The music includes a rhythm section, comprising two young British jazz performers. Tony Reeves would end up playing a significant part of his own (with John Mayall, Colosseum, and Greenslade) in the development of rock music. A little later in the year, Davy Graham issued an album made with folk singer Shirley Collins, although even here, he still managed to incorporate his other musical influences. In the long term, Graham's success was hampered by his belief, revealed in interview, that creativity generally was subject to a divinely inspired balance, whereby any positive action on his part would be offset by a negative somewhere else in the world. His recordings and performances became increasingly meagre.

HORACE SILVER   SONG FOR MY FATHER

Horace Silver played piano with the premier hard bop jazz unit of the fifties – Art Blakey's Jazz Messengers. *Song For My Father* is the most acclaimed album issued under his own name, even before the underlying riff of the title track was appropriated by Steely Dan some ten years later. The music has a bright, accessible sound, with memorable themes that wear their blues heritage proudly, even if they refuse to keep to the traditional form. Two different groups are at work here, one of them featuring the fluid playing of tenor saxophonist Joe

> US release   January 1965   Blue Note   BST 84185 / BLP 4185
> Not released in UK
>
> 1. Song For My Father (Horace Silver)
> 2. The Natives Are Restless Tonight (Horace Silver)
> 3. Calcutta Cutie (Horace Silver)
>
> 4. Que Pasa (Horace Silver)
> 5. The Kicker (Joe Henderson)
> 6. Lonely Woman (Horace Silver)
>
> Horace Silver: piano / Joe Henderson: tenor saxophone (1,2,4,5) / Junior Cook: tenor saxophone (3) / Carmell Jones: trumpet (1,2,4,5) / Blue Mitchell: trumpet (3) / Teddy Smith: bass (1,2,4,5) / Gene Taylor: bass (3,6) / Roger Humphries: drums (1,2,4,5) / Roy Brooks: drums (3,6) / Alfred Lion: producer

Henderson, who ultimately became a more significant jazz artist than his employer here. *Song For My Father* is not a ground-breaking album, but it does represent the dominant jazz style of its time played supremely well.

JOHN COLTRANE   A LOVE SUPREME

| US release | January 1965 | Impulse | AS-77/A-77 |
| UK release | January 1965 | HMV | CLP 1869 |

1. Part I – Acknowledgement
2. Part II – Resolution
3. Part III – Pursuance / Part IV – Psalm

All compositions by John Coltrane

John Coltrane: tenor saxophone / McCoy Tyner: piano / Jimmy Garrison: bass / Elvin Jones: drums / Bob Thiele: producer

A Love Supreme is widely acclaimed as the second most vital jazz album of all (after the Miles Davis record, *Kind Of Blue*, which also featured John Coltrane). It comprises a single work, divided into four movements, as though it was a jazz symphony. The inspiration behind the music is religious, the 'love' in the title referring to the love of God. Only the meditative final section, entitled *Psalm*, conforms with most people's ideas of what a religious work should sound like. For the rest, it is the jazz approach that John Coltrane had been working with for the previous six years or so, in which he delivers long improvisations based on a single chord. For an album that is usually counted as being part of the avant garde, *A Love Supreme* is very accessible. With no complicated sequence of chords to keep track of, the listener can concentrate on the sequence of notes, which manages to be extremely melodic in the soloing of all concerned. This is doubtless the reason for the album's continual popularity. Although it took a couple of years for its influence to take hold, as rock musicians started to warm to the idea of incorporating improvisation into their music, it was John Coltrane, and *A Love Supreme* in particular, that provided their basic template.

CILLA BLACK   CILLA

UK release   January 1965   Parlophone   PCS 3063 / PMC 1243
Not issued in US

1. Goin' Out Of My Head (Teddy Randazzo/Robert Weinstein)
2. Every Little Bit Hurts (Ed Cobb)
3. Baby It's You (Mack David/Barney Williams/Burt Bacharach)
4. Dancing In The Street (Ivy Jo Hunter/William Stevenson/Marvin Gaye)
5. Come To Me (George Martin/Bobby Willis)
6. Ol' Man River (Jerome Kern/Oscar Hammerstein III)
7. One Little Voice (Elio Isola/Hal Shaper/Mario Coppola)
8. I'm Not Alone Anymore (Clive Westlake/Kenny Lynch)
9. Whatcha Gonna Do 'Bout It (Doris Troy/Gregory Carroll)
10. Love Letters (Edward Heyman/Victor Young)
11. This Empty Place (Hal David/Burt Bacharach)
12. You'd Be So Nice To Come Home To (Cole Porter)

Cilla Black: vocals; Johnny Scott: bandleader (1-5,9,11) / Johnnie Spence: bandleader (6,12)/ George Martin: bandleader (7,8), producer / Sounds Incorporated (John Gilliard: guitar / Barrie Cameron: keyboards, baritone saxophone) / Griff West: tenor saxophone, clarinet / Alan Holmes: tenor and baritone saxophone, flute / Wes Hunter: bass guitar / Tony Newman: drums) (10) / other musicians not credited

Thanks to Sheridan Smith's wonderful portrayal of Cilla Black in the television series dramatising the early years of the singer's career, we now have a clear understanding of Cilla's years as a very successful chart performer. She worked as a solo singer at the Cavern and other Liverpool clubs, whenever she could persuade groups gigging there (including the Beatles) to act as her backing band. She was eventually taken on by Brian Epstein as part of his roster of Liverpool artists. By the time that Cilla issued her first album, she had already achieved four single hits in the UK, including two number ones. The album is a fine showcase for her talents. There is a nasal quality to her voice when she sings loudly, which is irritating for some, but her ability to give the songs she chooses a distinctive and emotional impact marks her out as one of the finest interpretive singers of her generation. The style is not Merseybeat – or any kind of beat music – but Cilla Black does succeed in presenting a totally contemporary set (the two standards from the Great American Songbook notwithstanding) of intelligent mid-sixties pop.

ALBERT AYLER SPIRITUAL UNITY

US release	January 1965	ESP-Disk	ESP-1002
UK release	late 1969	Fontana	SFJL 933

1. Ghosts: First Variation
2. The Wizard
3. Spirits
4. Ghosts: Second Variation

All compositions by Albert Ayler

Albert Ayler: tenor saxophone / Gary Peacock: bass / Sunny Murray: drums / Bernard Stollman: producer

Numerous recordings by Albert Ayler appeared during the early sixties, like bursts of shrapnel, which is appropriate, since that is what his music sounds like too. *Spiritual Unity* was the second release (after an obscure set of folk songs sung in Esperanto) for the experimental music label, ESP Disk. Ayler makes the music of other avant garde jazz performers, including both John Coltrane and Ornette Coleman, sound almost conservative. He plays his tenor saxophone as though it is a spray paint gun, or a flame thrower. His notes are smeared and gargled and spattered – very seldom indeed are they clear and precisely pitched. A few years later, Jimi Hendrix would play the electric guitar like this and make a big impact. Albert Ayler's impact was considerably less on music as a whole, although many of the critics who did hear the music were quick to describe it as worthless. For those who consider freely improvised music to be the ultimate emotional outpouring, however, a window on to the creative mind and heart of the improvising musician, *Spiritual Unity* can only truly be described as the ultimate soul music.

CHRIS BARBER GOOD MORNIN' BLUES

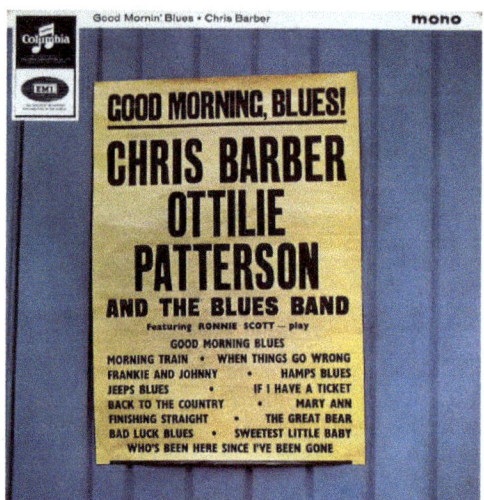

UK release	January 1965	Columbia	33SX 1657
Not released in US			

1. Good Mornin' Blues (Leadbelly)
2. Morning Train (Traditional/arranged Chris Barber)
3. Bad Luck Blues (Ottilie Patterson)
4. Mary-Ann (Ray Charles)
5. Who's Been Here Since I've Been Gone? (Bill Gaither/Kevin Williams)
6. Frankie And Johnny (Traditional/arranged Ottilie Patterson)
7. Finishing Straight (Chris Barber/Pat Halcox)
8. Hamp's Blues (Lionel Hampton)
9. If I Have A Ticket (Traditional/arranged Chris Barber)
10. The Great Bear (Chris Barber)
11. When Things Go Wrong (Tampa Red)
12. Sweetest Little Baby (Chris Barber)
13. Jeep's Blues (Duke Ellington/Johnny Hodges)
14. Back To The Country (Ottilie Patterson)

Chris Barber: trombone, vocals / Ottilie Patterson: vocals, piano / Pat Halcox: trumpet / Jimmy Deuchar: trumpet (2,8,13) / Ian Wheeler: harmonica, clarinet, alto saxophone / Ronnie Scott: tenor saxophone (2,8) / John Slaughter: guitar / Eddie Smith: banjo, guitar / Norrie Paramor: piano (10) / Peter Bardens: piano (10) / Dick Smith: double bass / Graham Burbidge: drums / No producer credited, but probably Norrie Paramor

Trombonist Chris Barber led a successful UK trad jazz band through the fifties and beyond. Always interested in the blues as well, he encouraged his banjo player, Lonnie Donegan, to switch to a guitar and deliver versions of songs by the likes of Leadbelly and Big Bill Broonzy during interludes in the band's live performances. One of these songs, *Rock Island Line*, with Barber himself playing double bass, became a substantial chart hit and launched an entire UK genre, known as skiffle. With this becoming a major ingredient in the development of British beat – not least because it inspired the teenage John Lennon to take up the guitar – it should not have been surprising that Chris Barber added an electric lead guitar to his line-up during 1964, following blues pioneer John Mayall's recommendation as to the guitarist (John Slaughter). Barber was, however, the only trad jazz band leader to make this move, and it was treated with suspicion. But *Good Mornin' Blues*, the first album to feature Slaughter's playing, is an unequivocal success, sounding rather like the music of the Rolling Stones reinterpreted by a robust jazz band. The presence of guest star Ronnie Scott serves as an endorsement for the project. Another guest, Peter Bardens, was hardly a star, but led a beat group by the name of the Cheynes, which made three singles at this time, one of them being produced by the Rolling Stones' bass player, Bill Wyman. Bardens later became a founding member of the progressive rock group Camel. *Good Mornin' Blues* was not a big seller and it yielded no hit singles, so that Barber's important place in the music of the era tends to be overlooked now. Not by John Mayall, however, who was delighted to include Chris Barber, alongside Eric Clapton and Mick Taylor, in the band assembled to celebrate Mayall's seventieth birthday in 2003.

ROGER MILLER   THE RETURN OF ROGER MILLER

```
US release      January 1965    Smash    SRS 67061 / MGS 27061
UK release      April 1965      Philips  BL 7669

1. Do-Wacka-Do
2. Atta Boy Girl
3. Reincarnation
4. That's The Way It's Always Been
5. As Long As There's A Shadow
6. Hard Headed Me
7. Ain't That Fine (Dorsey Burnette)

8. King Of The Road
9. You Can't Roller Skate In A Buffalo Herd
10. Our Hearts Will Play The Music
11. Love Is Not For Me
12. In The Summertime (You Don't Want My Love)
13. There I Go Dreamin'

All compositions by Roger Miller except track 7

Roger Miller: vocals, guitar / Buddy Killen: guitar / Bob Moore: bass /
Buddy Harman: drums / Jerry Kennedy: producer / unknown piano
```

For music fans in the UK, Roger Miller was a purveyor of novelty pop songs, like *You Can't Roller Skate In A Buffalo Herd*, *Do-Wacka-Do*, and later in the year, *England Swings* (like a pendulum do, apparently). For Americans, he was a country singer and songwriter, and a good one, albeit with an unusually whimsical approach. In both countries, the strikingly original *King Of The Road* was a big hit, entering the top ten in the US and reaching number one in the UK. The song is the highlight of Miller's second album and has a somewhat different sound to the rest of the songs on offer. It has more of a late-night jazz feel than anyone would usually associate with country. The others chug along in a cheerful manner, driven by a band with a sprightly strummed acoustic guitar to the fore, even when what Roger Miller is actually singing about is sometimes tinged with sadness. He maintained a successful career in music right up until his death in 1992, but never managed to create anything else as compelling as *King Of The Road*.

MICHAEL GARRICK QUINTET   OCTOBER WOMAN

```
UK release      January 1965    Argo    (Z)DA 33
Not released in US

1. Seven Pillars
2. Little Girl
3. Sweet And Sugary Candy
4. Blue Scene
5. Anthem

6. Return Of An Angel
7. Sketches Of Israel
8. October Woman
9. Echoes
10. Fairies Of Oneiros

All compositions by Michael Garrick

Michael Garrick: piano / Shake Keane: trumpet / Joe
Harriott: alto saxophone / Coleridge Goode: bass / Colin
Barnes: drums / probably Denis Preston: producer
```

Michael Garrick's musical interests ranged very widely. During the early sixties he was involved in a series of concerts in which various eminent contemporary poets read their work to the accompaniment of modern jazz played by his group. Shortly after he recorded *October Woman,* he also released a single on which he combined his jazz with church music, centred on organ playing and a choir. The album ignores all of this and focuses on jazz alone. It is his second album like this, but the first, *Moonscape,* issued a year earlier by the Michael Garrick Trio, was a privately produced item restricted, for the purposes of avoiding purchase tax, to just ninety-nine copies. *October Woman* does, however, cover a lot of ground stylistically, even if there is nothing here that would be of interest to British lovers of the trad jazz that had been a considerable commercial contender during the previous decade. Garrick is fortunate to be able to draw on the talents of Joe Harriott and Shake Keane for his front line, both of whom had made a number of records themselves and are very impressive players. Michael Garrick would later join the Ian Carr-Don Rendell Quintet, to continue the task of creating the finest contemporary jazz to be found in the UK.

THE SHANGRI-LAS   LEADER OF THE PACK

Producer George 'Shadow' Morton was hoping to achieve the reputation and sales success of Phil Spector. He used his girl group discovery, the Shangri-Las, initially comprising two pairs of teenage sisters, as the vehicle for his ambitions. Through the sixties, the group recorded a number of sparkling, memorable singles, with Morton at the helm. *Remember (Walking In The Sand)*, *Leader Of The Pack*, and *Give Him A Great Big Kiss* were the first three and the biggest hits. All are included on the Shangri-Las LP. Fewer instrumental resources are applied than on Spector productions, so there is no equivalent of the 'wall of sound', but instead, Shadow Morton adds significant and innovative sound effects to create a distinctive

```
US release    February 1965    Red Bird    RB 20-101
UK release    February 1965    Red Bird    RB 20-101 (different cover)

1. Give Him A Great Big Kiss (Shadow Morton)
2. Leader Of The Pack (Ellie Greenwich/Shadow Morton/Jeff Barry)
3. Bull Dog (Jerry Leiber/Mike Stoller)
4. It's Easier To Cry (J J Jackson/Joe DeAngelsi/Robert Steinberg)
5. What Is Love (Shadow Morton/Tony Michaels)
6. Remember (Walking In The Sand) (Shadowa Morton)
7. Twist And Shout (Phil Medley/Bert Berns)
8. Maybe (Richard Barrett)
9. So Much In Love (Billy Jackson/Roy Straigis)
10. Shout (Isley Brothers)
11. Goodnight My Love, Pleasant Dreams (George Motola/John Marascalco)
12. You Can't Sit Down (Cornell Muldow/Dee Clark)

Mary Weiss: vocals / Betty Weiss: vocals / Marge Ganser: vocals / Mary Ann
Ganser: vocals / Shadow Morton: producer / musicians uncredited
```

atmosphere – seagulls on the first record, a revving motorbike and breaking glass on the second. Alternatively, as on both the second and third records, he uses streetwise spoken word passages by the girls to make the songs stand out ("When I say I'm in love, you best believe I'm in love, l-u-v").

The Shangri-Las themselves rise to the challenge very well, with Mary Weiss's agonised lead vocals serving as an instantly recognisable focus. It is said that James Brown, alongside whom the girls were booked to appear, was surprised to discover that the singers were not black. The music is presented differently to that of the Ronettes or the Supremes, however. There is no over-riding dance beat and the singers are less concerned with conveying emotion than with telling a story as effectively as they can. The remainder of the LP, lacking the care lavished on the singles, is strictly make-weight, with the Shangri-Las moving more directly into Ronettes territory and failing to impress. A more recent greatest hits compilation would also include such later pieces of magnificence as *Out In The Streets, Give Us Your Blessings, I Can Never Go Home Anymore*, and, best of all, *Past, Present And Future* (on which the narrative, surprisingly but very effectively, is spoken over Beethoven's *Moonlight Sonata*). The Red Bird label (owned by veteran songwriters Jerry Leiber and Mike Stoller) collapsed in 1966 and the Shangri-Las disbanded two years later, although they have performed very sporadically since then. Mary Weiss made a well-received solo album as recently as 2007.

MILES DAVIS   MY FUNNY VALENTINE

```
US release    February 1965    Columbia    CS 9106 / CL 2306
UK release    April 1965       CBS         (S)BPG 62510

1. My Funny Valentine (Richard Rodgers/Lorenz Hart)
2. All Of You (Cole Porter)
3. Stella By Starlight (Ned Washington/Victor Young)
4. All Blues (Miles Davis)
5. I Thought About You (Jimmy Van Heusen/Johnny Mercer)

Miles Davis: trumpet / George Coleman: tenor saxophone /
Herbie Hancock: piano / Ron Carter: bass / Tony Williams:
drums / Teo Macero: producer
```

John Coltrane left Miles Davis in 1960, in order to start his own group, thereby bringing an end to the unit subsequently referred to as Miles Davis's first great quintet. It took the trumpeter some time to establish his second great quintet, but when the live recordings making up *My Funny Valentine* were made, the group was four fifths complete. Tenor saxophonist George Coleman was the one who did not stay the course – a fine player, but ultimately not one comfortable with the free-wheeling attitude that Miles Davis demanded. The album presents the slower pieces played at a concert in New York in February 1964 – the faster ones were retained for a second album, *Four And More*, issued a year later. The pieces chosen for improvised exploration are long and very much a showcase for Miles Davis himself, even though the other players are given some solo space. Miles was extremely familiar with the songs, which had been in his repertoire for a long time. He is well able, therefore, to take liberties with their harmonic structures and to turn them into modal pieces, in the manner of his ground-breaking *Kind Of Blue* album from 1959. His approach is to improvise on the actual melodies, to the point where the original tunes are seldom clearly stated at all, the listener being assumed to know already what these sound like. Most of them would not stay in the stage set for very much longer. Miles doubtless felt that the versions preserved in this album had succeeded in delivering the last word on them. *My Funny Valentine* is, therefore, very much a milestone recording (no pun intended), saying farewell to an era that was coming to an end and opening the way for new kinds of jazz improvisation made possible by the remarkable playing techniques, bravado, and empathy of the Herbie Hancock/Ron Carter/Tony Williams rhythm section. It is astonishing to realise that, at the time this album was made, Williams, already rated as one of the finest drummers playing anywhere, was only eighteen years old.

THE IMPRESSIONS PEOPLE GET READY

US release   February 1965   ABC-Paramount
                                ABC(S) 505
Not released in UK

1. Woman's Got Soul
2. Emotions
3. Sometimes I Wonder
4. We're In Love
5. Just Another Dance
6. Can't Work No Longer

7. People Get Ready
8. I've Found That I've Lost
9. Hard To Believe
10. See The Real Me
11. Get Up And Move
12. You Must Believe Me

All compositions by Curtis Mayfield

Curtis Mayfield: vocals, guitar / Fred Cash: vocals / Sam Gooden: vocals / Johnny Pate: arranger, producer

The Impressions' next album to the successful *Keep On Pushing* fared a little less well in the chart, but was still a hit. It provides plenty more evidence of Curtis Mayfield's soft soul mastery and includes what is perhaps his best known song of all, *People Get Ready*. Mayfield captures the flavour of the old spirituals and creates a song that itself became a significant civil rights anthem. Released as a single, it became a substantial chart hit and has been covered by several other artists since.

THE PRETTY THINGS

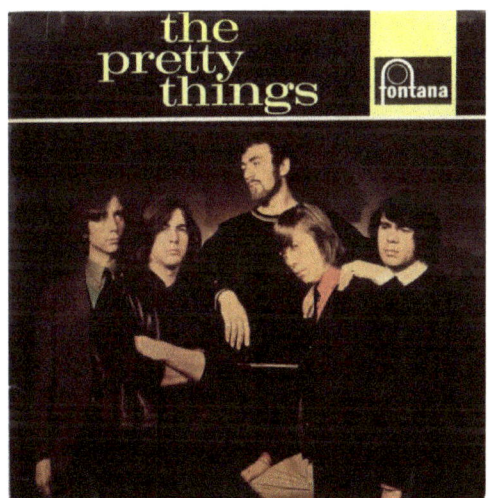

UK release   March 1965   Fontana   TL 5239
US release March 1965 several different tracks   Fontana SRF 67544

1. Road Runner (Bo Diddley)
2. Judgement Day (Bryan Morrison)
3. 13 Chester Street (Pretty Things)
4. Big City (Jimmy Duncan/Alan Klein)
5. Unknown Blues (Pretty Things)
6. Mama Keep Your Big Mouth Shut (Bo Diddley)

7. Honey I Need (D.Taylor/Lew Warburton/Peter Smith/Ian Stirling)
8. Oh Baby Doll (Chuck Berry)
9. She's Fine, She's Mine (Bo Diddley)
10. Don't Lie To Me (Tampa Red)
11. The Moon Is Rising (Jimmy Reed)
12. Pretty Thing (Willie Dixon)

Phil May: vocals / Dick Taylor: guitar / Brian Pendleton: guitar, vocals / John Stax: bass guitar, harmonica, vocals / Viv Prince: drums / Bobby Graham: producer

Listening to the first album by the Pretty Things blind, one would guess that it was a record by the Rolling Stones. The groups have the same influences – Bo Diddley, Jimmy Reed and the blues generally – except that the Pretty Things show no interest in the soul music that creeps into the Stones' repertoire. Nevertheless, singer Phil May sounds exactly like a slightly exaggerated version of Mick Jagger, while the guitarists adopt the same roughly interlocking riff-based style as favoured by Brian Jones and Keith Richards. Dick Taylor provides a more tangible link between the two bands – he was originally a member of the Rolling Stones, playing bass before deciding that he would rather concentrate on guitar and being replaced by Bill Wyman. *Honey I Need* was a modest chart hit in the UK. The American version of the LP also includes the group's other two UK hits, *Rosalyn* and *Don't Bring Me Down*, which make it a stronger album. Unlike the Rolling Stones, however, success in America eluded the Pretty Things.

THE KINKS KINDA KINKS

The Kinks' second album was the result of two sessions in December and January and a week in February. Shel Talmy and the record company liked the resulting rough edges, but the group would have preferred more time. Ray Davies did manage to ensure, however, that all but two of

UK release   March 1965   Pye   NPL 18112
US release   August 1965   Reprise   RS 6173   several different tracks, new cover

1. Look For Me Baby (Ray Davies)
2. Got My Feet On The Ground (Ray and Dave Davies)
3. Nothin' In The World Can Stop Me Worryin' 'Bout That Girl (Ray Davies)
4. Naggin' Woman (Jerry West/Jimmy Anderson)
5. Wonder Where My Baby Is Tonight (Ray Davies)
6. Tired Of Waiting For You (Ray Davies)

7. Dancing In The Street (Marvin Gaye/William Stevenson)
8. Don't Ever Change (Ray Davies)
9. Come On Now (Ray Davies)
10. So Long (Ray Davies)
11. You Shouldn't Be Sad (Ray Davies)
12. Something Better Beginning (Ray Davies)

Ray Davies: vocals, guitar, piano / Dave Davies: guitar, vocals / Peter Quaife: bass guitar, vocals / Mick Avory: drums / Bobby Graham: drums (6) / Rasa Davies: vocals (1,7,9,11) / Shel Talmy: producer

the songs were his own compositions. He rises to the challenge well, continuing his knack for creating distinctive songs out of the simplest of chord structures. The powerful and precise playing of the Quaife/Avory rhythm section is particularly effective in driving the hit single, *Everybody's Gonna Be Happy,* which was included on the American version of the LP, but it ensures that every track makes its mark. *Tired Of Waiting For You* was a well-deserved number one hit in the UK, and did well in the US too, although there it was left off the LP in favour of the following singles, *Everybody's Gonna Be Happy* and *Set Me Free. Tired Of Waiting For You* was included an an LP called *Kinks-Size*, alongside other tracks issued in the UK on singles and EPs. *Kinda Kinks* reached number three in the UK charts, the same position as had been achieved by its predecessor.

THE SONICS   HERE ARE THE SONICS

US release   March 1965   Etiquette   ET-LP(S)-024
Not released in UK

1. Witch (Gerry Roslie)
2. Do You Love Me (Berry Gordy)
3. Roll Over Beethoven (Chuck Berry)
4. Boss Hoss (Gerry Roslie)
5. Dirty Robber (John Greek/Kent Morrill)
6. Have Love Will Travel (Richard Berry)
7. Psycho (Gerry Roslie)
8. Money (Berry Gordy/Janie Bradford)
9. Walkin' The Dog (Rufus Thomas)
10. Nighttime Is The Right Time (Lew Herman/Nappy Brown/Ozzie Cadena)
11. Strychnine (Gerry Roslie)
12. Good Golly Miss Molly (John Marascalco/Robert Blackwell)

Gerry Roslie: vocals, piano / Larry Parypa: guitar, vocals / Rob Lind: tenor saxophone, vocals / Andy Parypa: bass guitar, vocals / Bob Bennett: drums / Buck Ornsby: producer / Kent Morrill: producer

The Sonics are a bar band, similar to the Kingmen, though with more aggression in their playing. Performing music that is superficially like that of the British beat groups, the Sonics actually stay much closer to the spirit and sound of fifties rock 'n' roll, particularly that of Little Richard. They are not interested in moving the music forward, but merely in delivering a rockin' beat as powerfully as they can manage. Doubtless aware of this, the producers settle for a primitive, muddy recording quality. Issued on a small local label, *Here Are The Sonics* made little impact at the time, although it has attracted the attention of more recent listeners, who hear a kinship with seventies punk.

THE BEACH BOYS   TODAY!

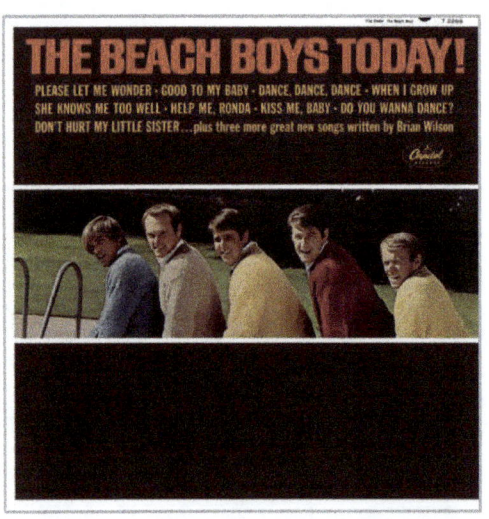

US release   March 1965   Capitol   (D)T 2269
UK release   April 1966   Capitol   (S)T 2269

1. Do You Wanna Dance? (Bobby Freeman)
2. Good To My Baby (Brian Wilson/Mike Love)
3. Don't Hurt My Little Sister (Brian Wilson/Mike Love)
4. When I Grow Up To Be A Man (Brian Wilson/Mike Love)
5. Help Me Ronda (Brian Wilson/Mike Love)
6. Dance Dance Dance (Brian Wilson/Carl Wilson/Mike Love)
7. Please Let Me Wonder (Brian Wilson/Mike Love)
8. I'm So Young (William Tyus)
9. Kiss Me Baby (Brian Wilson/Mike Love)
10. She Knows Me Too Well (Brian Wilson/Mike Love)
11. In The Back Of My Mind (Brian Wilson/Mike Love)
12. Bull Session With The Big Daddy (Beach Boys)

Mike Love: vocals / Brian Wilson: vocals, bass guitar, keyboards, producer / Carl Wilson: vocals, guitar, bass guitar / Al Jardine: vocals, guitar, bass guitar / Dennis Wilson: vocals, drums, percussion / Marilyn Wilson: vocals / Glen Campbell: guitar / Barney Kessel: guitar / Bill Pitman: guitar / Billy Strange: guitar, mandolin / Tommy Tedesco: guitar, autoharp, mandolin / John Gray: piano / Don Randi: piano, organ / Leon Russell: piano, organ / Carol Kaye: bass guitar / Larry Knechtel: bass guitar / Ray Pohlman: bass guitar / Hal Blaine: drums, percussion / Earl Palmer: drums, percussion / Ron Swallow: percussion / Russ Titelman: percussion / Julius Wechter: percussion, vibes / Jerry Williams: percussion, vibes / Carrol Lewis: harmonica / Billy Lee Riley: harmonica / Carl Fortina: accordion / Peter Christ: English horn / Steve Douglas: tenor saxophone / David Duke: French horn / Plas Johnson: tenor saxophone / Jack Nimitz: baritone saxophone / Jay Migliori: baritone saxophone / unknown strings

All Summer Long had suggested that the Beach Boys and their record company were finally grasping the concept of an album that was more than just a mechanism for extracting more revenue out of a hit single. *Today!* maintains that momentum, although once again the UK branch of Capitol waited an extraordinarily long time before issuing the album. Perhaps at least part of the problem was the group's frantic work rate, which had seen two other albums being squeezed into the company's release schedule during this period. Neither *Beach Boys Concert* nor *Beach Boys' Christmas Album* are exactly essential, adding little to the group's reputation, even if the former album proved that the Beach Boys could deliver an acceptable facsimile of their studio work in a live context. *Today!* is a little frustrating in its failure to explore its ideas as fully as it could have done. As before, the songs and the album itself are very short, despite which, one of the tracks (the last one) is a completely pointless recording of the Beach Boys enjoying a take-away meal. Brian Wilson employed a large number of session musicians to fill out the music, but they are largely hidden behind the group sound that still dominates. The album proves that Brian Wilson was continuing to develop his art, but more impressive work was to come.

BOB DYLAN   BRINGING IT ALL BACK HOME

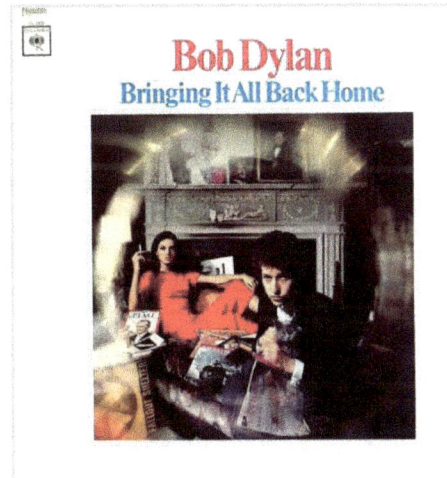

```
US release    March 1965    Columbia    CS 9128 / CL 2328
UK release    March 1965    CBS         (S)BPG 62515

1. Subterranean Homesick Blues
2. She Belongs To Me
3. Maggie's Farm
4. Love Minus Zero / No Limit
5. Outlaw Blues
6. On The Road Again
7. Bob Dylan's 115th Dream

8. Mr Tambourine Man
9. Gates Of Eden
10. It's Alright Ma (I'm Only Bleeding)
11. It's All Over Now, Baby Blue

All compositions by Bob Dylan

Bob Dylan: vocals, guitar, harmonica, piano (6) / Bruce Langhorne: guitar (1-8,11) / Al Gorgoni: guitar (3-7) / Kenny Rankin: guitar (3-7) / Paul Griffin: piano (4,5,7) / Frank Owens: electric piano (1,3,6) / Joseph Macho Jr: bass guitar (3-7) / Bill Lee: bass guitar (2-6) / John Sebastian or Steve Boone: bass guitar (1) / Bobby Gregg: drums (1-7) / Tom Wilson: producer
```

With his fifth LP, Bob Dylan moved across the divide separating folk music from rock 'n' roll and presented himself as the lead singer of a fully-fledged rock band, through the whole of side one. During the fifties, when Pete Seeger and others were exploring the folk music legacy of Woody Guthrie, followers of the genre were convinced that it was free from commercial considerations (despite paying money for their records) and was therefore inherently superior to rock 'n' roll.

Bob Dylan was perceived as belonging to this camp and the introduction of rock instrumentation on *Bringing It All Back Home* was, therefore, a considerable shock to many of his fans. As it happened, Dylan had already carried out the same experiment at the end of 1962, with the song *Mixed Up Confusion*, using an appropriate mixture of jazz and rock musicians, including guitarist Bruce Langhorne. Presented as the A-side of a single, the song flopped in the US and was not released at all in the UK. For less narrowly focused record buyers, *Bringing It All Back Home* sounded like Bob Dylan's most impressive album to date. It outsold all his previous albums, breaking into the US top ten for the first time and reaching number one in the UK charts. *Subterranean Homesick Blues* was Dylan's first top forty single hit in the US and entered the top ten in the UK. A ground-breaking video was made for the song – in an era when such things were hardly ever produced – although it was not shown until the release in 1967 of the film about Dylan's 1965 tour, *Don't Look Back,* which included the video. Bob Dylan was shown displaying his lyrics on a series of large hand-held flash cards, his appearance making it clear that he was far more concerned with being seen as part of the contemporary music vanguard than with conforming to anyone else's idea as to the music he should be performing and the image he should have. The flash card idea was borrowed, many years later, for a memorable scene in the film *Love Actually*.

JOHN MAYALL   PLAYS JOHN MAYALL

```
UK release        March 1965        Decca        LK 4680
Not released in US

1. Crawling Up A Hill (John Mayall)
2. I Wanna Teach You Everything (John Mayall)
3. When I'm Gone (John Mayall)
4. I Need Your Love (John Mayall)
5. The Hoot Owl (John Mayall)
6. R&B Time – Night Train (Jimmy Forrest/Oscar Washington/Lewis
                P. Simpkins); Lucille (Albert Collins/Little Richard)

7. Crocodile Walk (John Mayall)
8. What's The Matter With You (John Mayall)
9. Doreen (John Mayall)
10. Runaway (John Mayall)
11. Heartache (John Mayall)
12. Chicago Line (John Mayall)

John Mayall: vocals, harmonica, keyboards, guitar / Roger Dean: guitar / Nigel Stanger: tenor saxophone / John McVie: bass guitar / Hughie Flint: drums / Tony Clarke: producer
```

British blues pioneer Alexis Korner persuaded the like-minded John Mayall to move to London from his native Manchester, in order to build a following for his blues-based music. Signed to Decca, Mayall's new band, the Bluesbreakers, released a single, *Crawling Up A Hill*, which sold hardly at all, but was nevertheless allowed to make an album. (The song was rediscovered by Katie Melua, who recorded her own version for her debut album in 2003). Typically, the band's personnel changed in between the two records. *John Mayall Plays John Mayall* was recorded live in a club just a few yards away from Decca's own recording studio, with cables running out the club window to the desk. Alexis Korner wrote the lengthy sleeve notes for the album. The music, largely comprising songs written by Mayall himself, is more R&B than pure blues, and being dominated by Mayall's Hammond organ, it sounds like a rougher version of Georgie Fame's Blue Flames. Guitarist Roger Dean plays well, if unspectacularly, but was dumped just a few months later in favour of a more celebrated competitor. The saxophonist, Nigel Stanger, was not a regular member of the Bluesbreakers, but was drafted in for the recording in order to fill out the sound. He later turned up as a member of the Newcastle Big Band, an organisation chiefly remembered for being home to a bass player who later became rather famous under the name of 'Sting'. The Bluesbreakers rhythm section, out of many employed under John Mayall's volatile leadership, fared rather better in the long term. Hughie Flint had successful stints with the chart-topping McGuinness-Flint and with the Bonzo Dog Band, before joining the Blues Band, led by Paul Jones. John McVie is still an active performer, as a founding member of Fleetwood Mac. *Crocodile Walk* was re-recorded in the studio, for release as the band's second single, but it sold no better than its predecessor. The album sold poorly too and Decca terminated Mayall's record contract.

B.B. KING   LIVE AT THE REGAL

```
US release     March 1965     ABC-Paramount    ABC(S)-509
UK release     March 1965     HMV              CLP 1870

1. Every Day I Have The Blues (Memphis Slim)
2. Sweet Little Angel (BB King/Jules Taub)
3. It's My Own Fault (John Lee Hooker)
4. How Blue Can You Get (Jane Feathers)
5. Please Love Me (BB King/Jules Taub)

6. You Upset Me Baby (Joe Josea/Maxwell Davis)
7. Worry Worry (Davis Plumber/Jules Taub)
8. Woke Up This Mornin' (BB King)
9. You Done Lost Your Good Thing Now (Victoria Spivey/Reuben Floyd)
10. Help The Poor (Charlie Singleton)

B.B. King: guitar, vocals / Duke Jethro: piano / Bobby Forte: tenor saxophone / Johnny Board: tenor saxophone / Leo Lauchie: bass guitar / Sonny Freeman: drums / Johnny Pate: producer
```

Riley 'Blues Boy' King began recording the blues in 1949 and scored his first R&B number one three years later. He became known as a particularly expressive lead electric guitarist: never playing fast, never trying to impress with extreme technical virtuosity, but with the unerring ability to make each note count. *Live At The Regal* was recorded in Chicago in November 1964 and is the testament to what King was able to achieve on stage, night after night. His approach to the blues is far more sophisticated than that of the majority of his contemporaries, being close to jazz in its overall smooth professionalism. King always maintained that he was unable to sing and play the guitar at the same time, especially since he only ever played lead lines and never adopted any kind of rhythm guitar, chorded approach. The music therefore functions as a dialogue between voice and guitar, with the instrument continually providing a commentary and expansion on whatever is sung. The influence of *Live At The Regal* on other guitarists was instant and enormous, especially where the up and coming British blues players like Eric Clapton and Peter Green were concerned. The album was not a big chart success, yet it rapidly acquired the reputation of one of the key blues albums and it is one of the five hundred or so records from the entire twentieth century to have been preserved in the US Library of Congress as being of particular cultural or historical significance (alongside, from *Live At The Regal*'s own era, Bob Dylan's *Freewheelin'* and the Beatles' *Sgt Pepper* albums).

SPENCER DAVIS GROUP   THEIR FIRST LP

Although the group was named after him, Spencer Davis was neither the lead singer nor the main instrumentalist. Instead, both of these roles were taken by the young Steve Winwood, aged just seventeen at the time *Their First LP* was recorded. It is his voice, soulful beyond his years, that makes the Spencer Davis Group's brand of R&B immediately distinctive. Winwood is particularly impressive

```
UK release    March 1965    Fontana    TL 5242
Not released in US

1. My Babe (Bill Medley/Bobby Hatfield)
2. Dimples (John Lee Hooker)
3. Searchin' (Jerry Leiber/Mike Stoller)
4. Every Little Bit Hurts (Ed Cobb)
5. I'm Blue (Gong Gong Song) (Ike Turner)
6. Sittin' And Thinkin' (Spencer Davis Group)

7. I Can't Stand It (Smokey McAllister)
8. Here Right Now (Steve Winwood)
9. Jump Back (Rufus Thomas)
10. It's Gonna Work Out Fine (Michael Lee/Joe Seneca)
11. Midnight Train (Alvin Roy/Gerry Hicks)
12. It Hurts Me So (Steve Winwood)

Steve Winwood: vocals, guitar, piano, harmonica / Spencer Davis: guitar, vocals, harmonica / Muff Winwood: bass guitar, vocals / Pete York: drums / Kenny Salmon: organ (4,8) / Peter Asher: piano (5) / Millie Small: vocals (5) / Chris Blackwell: producer
```

on the ballad *Every Little Bit Hurts*. This was originally a US hit by Motown singer Brenda Holloway, but the Spencer Davis Group rendering emerges as a fine alternative version, not at all a pale cover. The song was issued as the group's second single – the first was *I Can't Stand It*, which is also included on the album – although single success eluded the Spencer Davis Group until the end of the year. It was a surprise, therefore, when *Their First LP* climbed into the album top ten in the UK, but this was an eminently deserved success. Producer Chris Blackwell had formed one of the first record companies in Jamaica. He brings no ska influence to the proceedings, but he does ensure that Millie Small, best known for her hit single of early 1964, *My Boy Lollipop*, is employed as a backing singer on one track.

THE RIGHTEOUS BROTHERS   YOU'VE LOST THAT LOVIN' FEELIN'

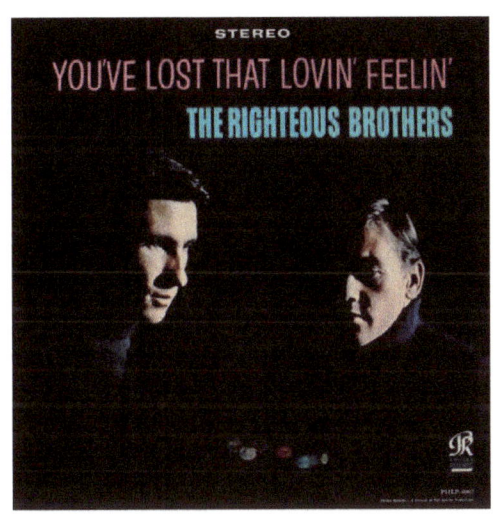

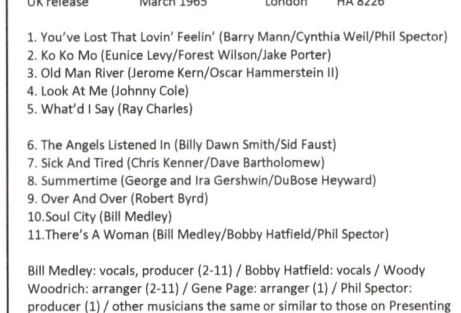

```
US release      March 1965    Philles    PHLP/ST 4007
UK release      March 1965    London     HA 8226

1.  You've Lost That Lovin' Feelin' (Barry Mann/Cynthia Weil/Phil Spector)
2.  Ko Ko Mo (Eunice Levy/Forest Wilson/Jake Porter)
3.  Old Man River (Jerome Kern/Oscar Hammerstein II)
4.  Look At Me (Johnny Cole)
5.  What'd I Say (Ray Charles)

6.  The Angels Listened In (Billy Dawn Smith/Sid Faust)
7.  Sick And Tired (Chris Kenner/Dave Bartholomew)
8.  Summertime (George and Ira Gershwin/DuBose Heyward)
9.  Over And Over (Robert Byrd)
10. Soul City (Bill Medley)
11. There's A Woman (Bill Medley/Bobby Hatfield/Phil Spector)

Bill Medley: vocals, producer (2-11) / Bobby Hatfield: vocals / Woody
Woodrich: arranger (2-11) / Gene Page: arranger (1) / Phil Spector:
producer (1) / other musicians the same or similar to those on Presenting
The Fabulous Ronettes
```

The single, *You've Lost That Lovin' Feelin'*, was a number one hit on both sides of the Atlantic during the beginning of 1965. Produced by Phil Spector, it was one of the finest achievements of his 'wall of sound' technique. Bill Medley and Bobby Hatfield, who were clearly not actually brothers, had powerful, soulful voices, with different ranges that enabled them to work well together. Medley was the singer with the lower, baritone voice. The duo's previous album had been titled *Some Blue-Eyed Soul*, a description that suited the singers well and quickly moved into common parlance for any white singer performing convincingly in the style. The Righteous Brothers had a few more, much smaller single hits, and they also made an extraordinary number of albums. There were twelve of these through the sixties, including four released in 1965 alone. Nothing on any of these recordings, however, succeeded in making the impact of the big hit single. *You've Lost That Lovin' Feelin'*, the song, is the one for which they will always be remembered, the one performance that really matters.

VARIOUS ARTISTS   A COLLECTION OF 16 TAMLA MOTOWN BIG HITS

Tamla Motown was launched as a label in its own right in the UK in March 1965 (before that Berry Gordy's releases appeared on London, Fontana, Oriole, or Stateside). The first album release was this various artists collection, which did an excellent job in promoting what the label had to offer. Despite the title, only the two songs by the Supremes and Mary Wells' *My Guy* were actually big hits

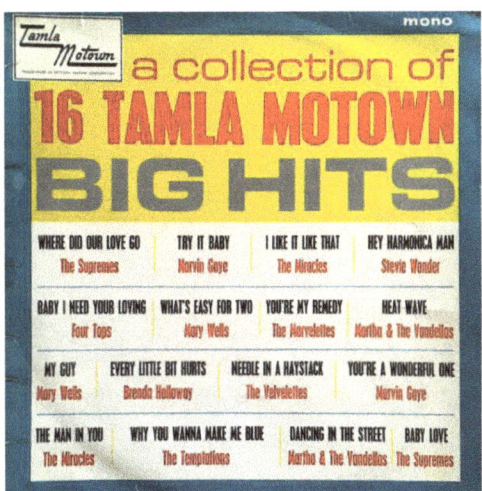

```
UK release      March 1965    Tamla Motown   TML 11001
Not released in US

1.  Where Did Our Love Go (Brian & Eddie Holland/Lamont Dozier)
2.  Try It Baby (Berry Gordy)
3.  I Like It Like That (Smokey Robinson/Marvin Tarplin)
4.  Hey Harmonica Man (Lou Josie/Marty Cooper)
5.  Baby I Need Your Loving (Holland/Dozier/Holland)
6.  What's Easy For Two Is So Hard For One (Smokey Robinson)
7.  You're My Remedy (Smokey Robinson)
8.  Heat Wave (Holland/Dozier/Holland)

9.  My Guy (Smokey Robinson)
10. The Man In You (Smokey Robinson)
11. Needle In A Haystack (Norman Whitfield/Mickey Stevenson)
12. Y ou're A Wonderful One (Holland/Dozier/Holland)
13. Every Little Bit Hurts (Ed Cobb)
14. Why You Wanna Make Me Blue (Eddie Holland/Norman Whitfield)
15. Dancing In The Street (Marvin Gaye/Mickey Stevenson)
16. Baby Love (Holland/Dozier/Holland)

The Supremes (Diana Ross/Mary Wilson/Florence Ballard) (1,16) / Marvin
Gaye (2,12) / The Miracles (Smokey Robinson/Ronnie White/Pete
Moore/Bobby Rogers/Claudette Robinson/ Marvin Tarplin) (3,10) / Stevie
Wonder (4) / The Four Tops (Levi Stubbs/Lawrence Payton/ Renaldo
Benson/Abdul Fakir) (5) / Mary Wells (6,9) / The Marvelettes (Wanda
Young/ Katherine Anderson/Georgeanna Tillman/Gladys Horton) (7) /
Martha & The Vandellas (Martha Reeves/Rosalind Ashford/Betty Kelley)
(8,15) / The Velvelettes (Bertha Barbee/Norma Barbee/Carolyn
Gill/Mildred Gill/Betty Kelley) (11) / Brenda Holloway (13) / The
Temptations (David Ruffin/Otis Williams/Melvin Franklin/Eddie
Kendricks/Paul Williams) (14)
```

in the UK, although several of the other songs have become very well-known regardless.

SOUNDTRACK   THE SOUND OF MUSIC

US release   March 1965   RCA Victor   LSOD/LOCD 2005
UK release   March 1965   RCA Victor   SB/RB 6616

1. Prelude and the Sound of Music
2. Overture and Preludium
3. Morning Hymn and Alleluia
4. How Do You Solve A Problem Like Maria?
5. I Have Confidence
6. Sixteen Going On Seventeen
7. My Favourite Things
8. Climb Every Mountain

9. The Lonely Goatherd
10. The Sound of Music
11. Do-Re-Mi
12. Something Good
13. Processional and Maria
14. Edelweiss
15. So Long, Farewell
16. Climb Every Mountain (Reprise)

All compositions by Oscar Hammerstein II / Richard Rodgers

Irwin Kostal: arranger, conductor / Julie Andrews, Dan Truhitte, Charmian Carr, Peggy Wood, Angela Cartwright, Nicholas Hammond, Kym Karath, Duane Chase, Heather Menzies, Debbie Turner, Christopher Plummer, Robert Tucker: vocals / Neely Plumb: producer

The soundtrack album to the film version of the Rodgers and Hammerstein musical, *The Sound Of Music*, was the second best-selling album of the sixties (behind the Beatles' *Sgt Pepper's Lonely Hearts Club Band*). In the US, it reached number one, remaining in the album chart for 238 weeks. In the UK, it also reached number one (twelve times, during 1965 to 1968, displaced by other records in between) and stayed in the chart for an astonishing 381 weeks. Any album that successful, that popular, can hardly have failed to exert an influence, even if its music is no different in conception from earlier musicals composed by Richard Rodgers and Oscar Hammerstein working together, beginning with *Oklahoma!* in 1943 (before the birth of rock 'n' roll.). Easy-listening singer Vince Hill achieved a number two hit in the UK in early 1967 with a version of *Edelweiss*, but only two covers of songs from the musical appear elsewhere within this book. John Coltrane realised that *My Favourite Things* could be re-invented as a vehicle for a lengthy modal jazz improvisation, presenting his first successful attempt at this on an album he released in March 1961 (titled after the song) as well as issuing further live versions in subsequent years. The Bonzo Dog Doo-Dah Band was even more sacrilegious than this in October 1967, using a savagely truncated interpretation of the *Sound Of Music* theme song as the butt of a piece of barbed humour (and still scrupulously giving the proper, original songwriting credit).

BARRY McGUIRE   EVE OF DESTRUCTION

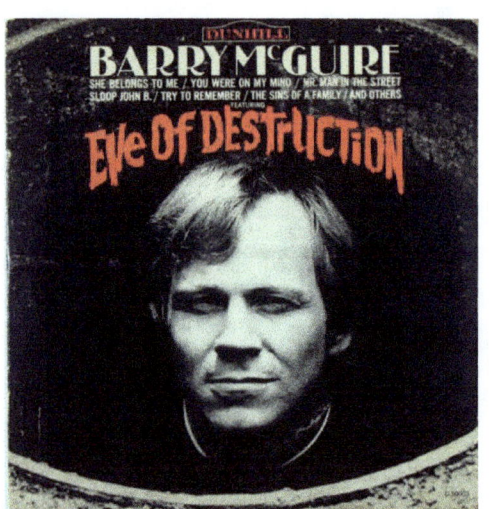

US release   March 1965   Dunhill   D(S)-50003
UK release   March 1965   RCA Victor   RD 7751

1. Eve Of Destruction (P.F. Sloan)
2. She Belongs To Me (Bob Dylan)
3. You Never Had It So Good (P.F. Sloan/Steve Barri)
4. Sloop John B (Traditional)
5. It's All Over Now, Baby Blue (Bob Dylan)
6. The Sins Of A Family (P.F. Sloan)

7. Try To Remember (Harvey Schmidt/Tom Jones)
8. Mr Man On The Street – Act One (P.F. Sloan)
9. You Were On My Mind (Sylvia Fricker)
10. Ain't No Way I'm Gonna Change My Mind (P.F. Sloan/Steve Barri)
11. What Exactly's The Matter With Me (P.F.Sloan)
12. Why Not Stop & Dig It While You Can (Barry McGuire)

Barry McGuire: vocals / P.F. Sloan: guitar, producer / Tommy Tedesco: guitar / Larry Knechtel: bass guitar / Hal Blaine: drums / Steve Barri: percussion, producer / Lou Adler: producer / Bones Howe: producer

Eve Of Destruction, owing everything to Bob Dylan, but delivered by a singer with a strikingly gruff voice, well able to enhance an already doom-laden message, was a substantial hit at the end of the summer in 1965. It was a number one in the US and reached number three in the UK, despite receiving a partial radio ban in both countries. Barry McGuire was previously a member of the folk group, the New Christy Minstrels, and was featured on their novelty hit, *Three Wheels On My Wagon*. *Eve Of Destruction*, the album, was his third solo record. P.F. Sloan, the man who wrote the title track and several of the other songs on the album, also performed as a solo folk artist, although he was much more successful in composing songs for other people. McGuire never achieved another big hit, but he managed to maintain a busy recording career through to the end of the century, much of it falling into the Christian music category.

BERT JANSCH

UK release April 1965 Transatlantic TRA 125
Not released in US

1. Strolling Down The Highway
2. Smokey River
3. Oh How Your Love Is Strong
4. I Have No Time
5. Finches
6. Rambling's Going To Be The Death Of Me
7. Veronica
8. Needle Of Death
9. Do You Hear Me Now?
10. Alice's Wonderland
11. Running, Running From Home
12. Courting Blues
13. Kasbah
14. Dreams Of Love
15. Angie (Davy Graham)

All compositions, apart from track 15, by Bert Jansch.

Bert Jansch: vocals, guitar / Bill Leader: producer

On his first album, the Scottish performer Bert Jansch was revealed as being a skilled acoustic guitarist, very much inspired by the work of Davy Graham. *Angie*, Graham's best known piece, is included (albeit with a slightly revised spelling of its title), as the only track not written by Jansch himself. Five other tracks are also instrumentals, designed to demonstrate what Jansch could do with his guitar. Although *Kasbah* toys with an Arab influence and *Alice's Wonderland* makes a nod towards Charles Mingus, Bert Jansch is much more focused than Graham on the world of folk music. Perhaps his prime significance, therefore, is that he represents the first British response to the American singer-songwriters and Bob Dylan in particular. The anti-war *Do You Hear Me Now?* and the poignant warning against hard drugs, *Needle Of Death*, are very much in the mould of early Bob Dylan protest songs. On the other hand, the charming *Courting Blues* displays a tenderness that would never have occurred to Bob Dylan at this time. To the extent that Davy Graham could be viewed as an isolated maverick, *Bert Jansch* marks the opening of a rich vein of contemporary British folk music, as important within that genre as the Beatles *Please Please Me* was in theirs.

THE ZOMBIES   BEGIN HERE

UK release April 1965 Decca LK 4679
US release Jan.1965 some different tracks Parrot PAS7 / PA6 1001

1. Road Runner (Bo Diddley)
2. Summertime (George & Ira Gershwin/DuBose Heyward)
3. I Can't Make Up My Mind (Chris White)
4. The Way I Feel Inside (Rod Argent)
5. Work 'n' Play (Ken Jones)
6. You Really Got A Hold On Me (Smokey Robinson)
7. She's Not There (Rod Argent)
8. Sticks And Stones (Henry Glover/Titus Turner)
9. Can't Nobody Love You (Phillip Mitchell)
10. Woman (Rod Argent)
11. I Don't Want To Know (Chris White)
12. I Remember When I Loved Her (Rod Argent)
13. What More Can I Do (Chris White)
14. I Got My Mojo Working (Muddy Waters)

Colin Blunstone: vocals, percussion, guitar / Paul Atkinson: guitar / Rod Argent: keyboards, vocals, harmonica / Chris White: bass guitar, vocals / Hugh Grundy: drums / Ken Jones: producer, piano (5), percussion (12)

Much was made, at the time of the group's first appearance, of the fact that most of the members of the Zombies had been educated at university, as if this would somehow make their music superior to that of their contemporaries. In truth, the group's first single from the previous July (and the only top twenty hit in the UK), *She's Not There*, was an extremely classy piece of music. Rod Argent's electric piano dominated the proceedings, including the delivery of a fluent solo, while singer Colin Blunstone was revealed as having a very distinctive voice, high, breathy, and full of emotion. The subsequent album, *Begin Here*, struggles to maintain the standard set by the single, a fine version of *Summertime* notwithstanding. This song had been the highlight of an EP issued in late 1964, and this had also included three impressive group compositions, including one, *It's Alright With Me*, that strikingly pulls off a smooth change in rhythm from beat to mid-tempo jazz and back again. Unfortunately, these were omitted from the album (two of them are included on the American version). *Begin Here* is an above-average debut, but, with the benefit of hindsight, it does help to make it understandable that the Zombies struggled to find continuing success after their hit. Again, the superior US version does include a worthy second single, *Tell Her No*, written by Rod Argent, which was a big hit in the US, but it was hardly a hit at all in the UK.

THE BEAU BRUMMELS   INTRODUCING

```
US release    April 1965    Autumn        (LP) 103
UK release    April 1965    Pye International    NPL 28062

1.  Laugh Laugh (Ron Elliott)
2.  Still In Love With You Baby (Ron Elliott)
3.  Just A Little (Ron Elliott/Robert Durand)
4.  Just Wait And See (Ron Elliott)
5.  Oh Lonesome Me (Don Gibson)
6.  Ain't That Loving You Baby (Deadric Malone)

7.  Stick Like Glue (Ron Elliott)
8.  They'll Make You Cry (Ron Elliott)
9.  That's, If You Want Me To (Ron Elliott)
10. I Want More Loving (Ron Elliott)
11. I Would Be Happy (Ron Elliott)
12. Not Too Long Ago (Ron Elliott)

Sal Valentino: vocals / Ron Elliott: guitar, vocals / Dec Mulligan: guitar, harmonica, vocals / Ron Meagher: bass guitar, vocals / John Petersen: drums / Sylvester Stewart: producer
```

The Beau Brummels, with a name intended to sound British, were the first notable American response to 'the British invasion' – the rush of British beat groups gaining chart hits in the US, following the first arrival of the Beatles. *Laugh Laugh* was a hit at the beginning of the year and could easily have been a Beatles song. Ron Elliott manages to recall the Lennon-McCartney songwriting style and the group's performance, incorporating an acoustic guitar into the beat group sound, is one that the Beatles themselves would have been proud of. Only Sal Valentino's idiosyncratic, quavery voice gives the game away. The rest of the group's debut album, with most of the songs also written by Ron Elliott, is a thoroughly worthwhile set, even if no other song can quite match the immediacy of *Laugh Laugh*. It is interesting to realise that, in contrast to all the British invasion albums, there is little R&B influence, although *Ain't That Loving You Baby* is a rip-off of a song by Jimmy Reed, with the blues stripped out and the the music transformed into harmony pop-rock. The other cover version is by a country singer, Don Gibson. Sylvester Stewart, the house producer for Autumn records, was no older than the band members, but already known as something of a musical marvel. He later formed a successful band of his own, using the stage name Sly Stone. *Introducing* did well in the US, but attracted little interest in the UK, where music fans probably felt that they already had enough beat groups of their own.

MARTHA AND THE VANDELLAS   DANCE PARTY

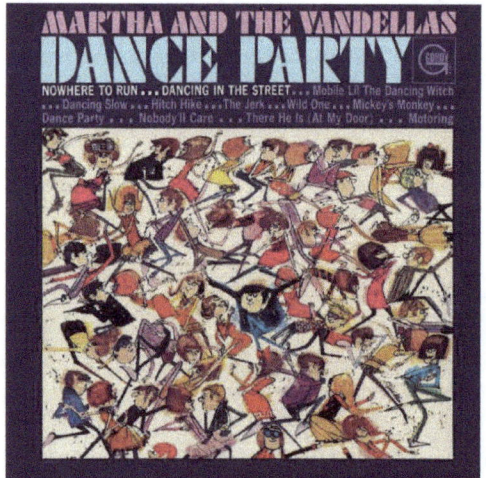

```
US release    April 1965    Gordy         GLP/S 915
UK release    April 1965    Tamla Motown TML 11013    different cover

1.  Dancing In The Street (Marvin Gaye/Mickey Stevenson)
2.  Dancing Slow (Stevenson/Ivy Jo Hunter/William Weatherspoon)
3.  Wild One (Stevenson/Hunter)
4.  Nowhere To Run (Brian & Eddie Holland/Lamont Dozier)
5.  Nobody'll Care (Stevenson/Hunter/Stevie Wonder)
6.  There He Is (At My Door) (Brian Holland/Freddie Gorman/Dozier)

7.  Mobile Lil The Dancing Witch (Stevenson/Hunter)
8.  Dance Party (Stevenson/Hunter)
9.  Motoring (Mickey Stevenson)
10. The Jerk (Stevenson/Hunter)
11. Mickey's Monkey (Holland/Dozier/Holland)
12. Hitch Hike (Clarence Paul/Marvin Gaye/Mickey Stevenson)

Martha Reeves: vocals / Rosalind Ashford: vocals / Betty Kelley: vocals / Annette Beard: vocals (6,12) / Mickey Stevenson: vocals, producer / Ivy Jo Hunter: vocals, producer / Earl Van Dyke: keyboards / Robert White: guitar / Eddie Willis: guitar / Joe Messina: guitar / James Jamerson: bass guitar / Benny Benjamin: drums / Richard Allen: drums / Jack Ashford: percussion / Eddie Brown: percussion / various horns and strings
```

Dancing In The Street is arguably the most iconic Motown track of all. It reached number two in the US charts, although it only just scraped into the top thirty in the UK when released in 1964 – it was reissued in 1969 and reached number four. Martha and the Vandellas achieved a number of smaller hits through the sixties, but were never as successful as the Supremes and were never seen as being as significant. But the Supremes never made a *Dancing In The Street*. The album built around the song also includes the songs issued as the next two singles, *Wild One* and *Nowhere To Run,* which are also memorable songs. So too, as it turns out, is the dubiously titled *Mobile Lil The Dancing Witch,* if only because it encourages Martha Reeves to deliver one of her funkiest performances.

ANDREW HILL   POINT OF DEPARTURE

With limited experience of playing in the top jazz groups during the fifties, pianist Andrew Hill was fortunate in gaining a recording contract with the prestigious Blue Note label in 1963. He made a number of critically acclaimed albums through the sixties, but without ever managing to become as well-known as the various musicians who played on his recordings. *Point Of Departure* features the playing of some of the most talented jazzmen of the period, with Eric Dolphy in particular

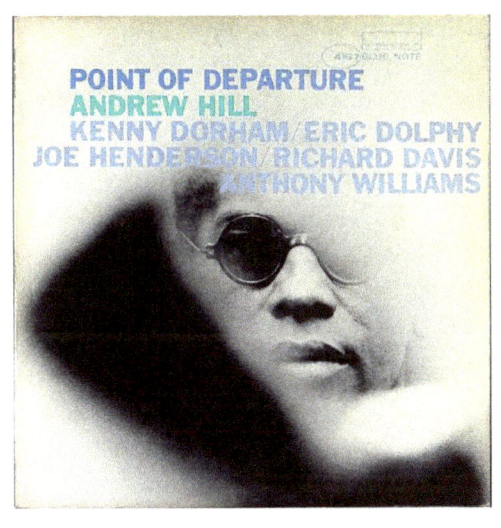

| US release | April 1965 | Blue Note | BST 84167 / BLP 4167 |

Not released in UK

1. Refuge
2. New Monastery
3. Spectrum
4. Flight 19
5. Dedication

All compositions by Andrew Hill

Andrew Hill: piano / Eric Dolphy: alto saxophone, bass clarinet, flute / Joe Henderson: tenor saxophone, flute / Kenny Dorham: trumpet / Richard Davis: bass / Tony Williams: drums / Alfred Lion: producer

feeling inspired enough to deliver some spectacular solos, eclipsing even those on his own *Out To Lunch* album, recorded just a month earlier. Andrew Hill himself is a fine pianist, sounding like a cross between Herbie Hancock and Thelonious Monk. His compositions too have the flavour of a similar hybrid. They do what they have to do in terms of providing a launch-pad for the various performers to demonstrate their skills, but fail to make the melodic impact that appeared to come naturally to both Hancock and Monk. In truth, Andrew Hill is outclassed by his own band and the fact that *Point Of Departure* emerges as a particularly fine example of mid-sixties jazz has everything to do with them, rather than him.

GEORGE JONES   THE RACE IS ON

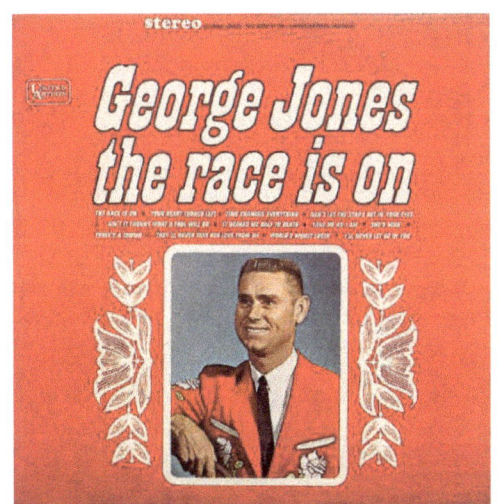

| US release | April 1965 | United Artists | UAS 6422 / UAL 3422 |

Not released in UK

1. The Race Is On (Don Rollins)
2. Don't Let The Stars Get In Your Eyes (Slim Willett)
3. I'll Never Let Go Of You (George Jones/George Riddle)
4. She's Mine (George Jones/Jack Ripley)
5. Three's A Crowd (Darrell Edwards/George Jones/Herbie Treece)
6. They'll Never Take Her Love From Me (Leon Payne)
7. Your Heart Turned Left (Harlan Howard)
8. Ain't It Funny What A Fool Will Do (Johnny Mathis/George Jones)
9. It Scares Me Half To Death (Audrey Allison/Joe Allison)
10. World's Worse Loser (Autry Inman)
11. Time Changes Everything (Tommy Duncan)
12. Take Me As I Am (Boudleaux Bryant)

George Jones: vocals, guitar / Don Adams: vocals, guitar / Jerry Starr: guitar / Charlie Justice: fiddle / Sonny Curtis: steel guitar / Donald Lyle: bass guitar, vocals / Glenn Davis: drums / unknown piano / Pappy Daily: producer

George Jones began recording in 1954. *The Race Is On* is something like his thirtieth album, mostly comprising songs already released during the previous few years, and titled after one of his biggest hits, from the autumn of 1964. During this time, George Jones very much epitomised the sound and the style of country music, with an emphasis on mournful lyrics set to slow or mid tempo ballads. Even when the rhythm gets a little faster and sounds cheerful, as it does on *The Race Is On* (a song using horse-racing metaphors throughout), the mood is still upset by the words. This is music that seems to have very little connection with the world of beat music, despite country in previous decades providing a major ingredient in the creation of rock 'n' roll, and despite it having a similar instrumentation.

HERB ALPERT'S TIJUANA BRASS   WHIPPED CREAM & OTHER DELIGHTS

| US release | April 1965 | A&M | SP 4110 / LP-110 |
| UK release | April 1966 | Pye International | N(S)PL 28058 |

1. A Taste Of Honey (Bobby Scott/Ric Marlow)
2. Green Peppers (Sol Lake)
3. Tangerine (Johnny Mercer/Victor Schertzinger)
4. Bittersweet Samba (Sol Lake)
5. Lemon Tree (Will Holt)
6. Whipped Cream (Allen Toussaint)
7. Love Potion No.9 (Jerry Leiber/Mike Stoller)
8. El Garbanzo (Sol Lake)
9. Ladyfingers (Toots Thielmans)
10. Butterball (Mike Henderson)
11. Peanuts (Luis Guerrero)
12. Lollipops And Roses (Tony Velona)

Herb Alpert: trumpet, producer / John Pisano: guitar / Bob Edmondson: trombone / Leon Russell: piano / Julius Wechter: marimba, vibraphone / Carol Kaye: bass guitar / Chuck Berghofer: bass / Hal Blaine: drums / Jerry Moss: producer

Easy-listening trumpeter Herb Alpert was one of the biggest selling artists of the sixties (and beyond – his most recent US chart album was in 1987), with fourteen hit albums in the US up to 1970, of which six reached number one. Five were top ten hits in the UK too. Their success was primarily responsible for propelling the record label started in 1962 by Herb Alpert and Jerry Moss (A&M Records) into the major league. The two most popular albums of all both came out in 1965. *Going Places,* released in October, includes the hit singles *Tijuana Taxi* and *Spanish Flea,* while *Whipped Cream* includes *A Taste Of Honey*. The earlier album also has a particularly iconic cover – arguably one of its major selling points – with an attractive woman apparently covered in a large quantity of the whipped cream mentioned (although closer inspection reveals that most of the white enveloping her is actually a blanket). Herb Alpert's style is nominally based on the traditional mariachi music of Mexico, but applied to more modern tunes that allow his smoothly melodic trumpet playing to dominate. The massed trumpets making up 'The Tijuana Brass' consisted of Alpert overdubbing himself several times, while the other instruments were handled by session musicians, including some well-known names more often associated with rockier material. The success of *Whipped Cream & Other Delights,* however, enabled him to form a full band for live performances.

MARIANNE FAITHFULL COME MY WAY / MARIANNE FAITHFULL

UK release   April 1965   Decca   LK 4688
Not released in US

1. Come My Way (Jon Mark)
2. Jaberwock (Lewis Carroll/Jon Mark)
3. Portland Town (Traditional)
4. House Of The Rising Sun (Traditional)
5. Spanish Is A Loving Tongue (Traditional)
6. Fare Thee Well (Traditional)
7. Lonesome Traveller (Lee Hays)
8. Down In The Salley Garden (Traditional)
9. Mary Ann (Traditional)
10. Full Fathom Five (William Shakespeare/Jon Mark)
11. Four Strong Winds (Traditional)
12. Black Girl (Traditional)
13. One I Had A Sweetheart (Traditional)
14. Bells Of Freedom (Traditional)

Marianne Faithfull: vocals / Jon Mark: guitar, producer / Big Jim Sullivan: guitar / uncredited bass and drums/percussion, possibly Danny Thompson and Terry Cox

UK release   April 1965   Decca   LK 4689
US release   April 1965   London PS 423 / LL 3423   Little Bird instead of Down Town

1. Come And Stay With Me (Jackie DeShannon)
2. If I Never Get To Love You (Burt Bacharach/Hal David)
3. Time Takes Time (Barry Fantoni/Marianne Faithfull)
4. He'll Come Back To Me (Claude Henri/Mike Leander/Robert Gall)
5. Down Town (Tony Hatch)
6. Plaisir D'Amour (Traditional)
7. Can't You Hear My Heartbeat (John Carter/Ken Lewis)
8. As Tears Go By (Mick Jagger/Keith Richards)
9. Paris Bells (Jon Birchell)
10. They Never Will Leave You (André Popp/Jean-Jacques Debout)
11. What Have They Done To The Rain (Malvina Reynolds)
12. In My Time Of Sorrow (Jackie DeShannon/Jimmy Page)
13. What Have I Done Wrong (Michael Farr)
14. I'm A Loser (John Lennon/Paul McCartney)

Marianne Faithfull: vocals / Jon Mark: guitar / Big Jim Sullivan: guitar / other musicians unknown / David Whittaker: arranger / Mike Leander: arranger / Andrew Oldham: producer (8) / Tony Calder: producer

Marianne Faithfull's fragile, tremulous singing voice made her music sound very attractive and her first single, *As Tears Go By,* written for her by Mick Jagger and Keith Richards of the Rolling Stones, was a chart hit in both the UK and the US. Her first album was a double, albeit issued as two separate discs (and one of them was not released in the US). *Come My Way* is almost entirely made up of traditional folk material, with guitarist Jon Mark providing most of the accompaniment, sometimes supported by a second guitar, bass, and percussion. The result is a welcome addition to the small body of British folk recordings at this time. The self-titled record is more folk-pop and includes the hit single. This much music definitely highlights Ms Faithfull's limitations as an interpretive singer, but it nevertheless announces the arrival of a significant new artist.

DONOVAN   WHAT'S BIN DID AND WHAT'S BIN HID

During the early weeks of 1965, a young Scottish folk singer by the name of Donovan Leitch was given a regular performance slot on the coolest of UK pop/rock television shows, *Ready Steady Go*. The singer's guitar was emblazoned with the slogan 'This Machine Kills', which few of the audience would have realised was an abbreviated version of a similar message on the guitar of American folk pioneer Woody Guthrie, 'This machine kills fascists'. Donovan's music was very much influenced by that of Woody Guthrie and, since Bob Dylan's early songs were too, it was easy to draw comparisons between Dylan and Donovan. *What's Bin Did And What's Bin Hid,*

Donovan's first album, does have much in common with the early albums of Bob Dylan, albeit with much less of the latter's authority and gravity. If he had made these recordings, he would not have considered them to be good enough. *Catch The Wind*, however, which became a hit single, stands up well against Dylan's own songs, although it is a much gentler, more romantic affair than anything in the American's repertoire.

```
UK release        May 1965      Pye       NPL 18117
US release as Catch The Wind   June 1965   Hickory   LPS/LPM 123

1. Josie (Donovan)
2. Catch The Wind (Donovan)
3. Remember The Alamo (Jane Bowers)
4. Cuttin' Out (Donovan)
5. Car Car (Woody Guthrie)
6. Keep On Truckin' (Traditional/arranged Donovan)

7. Goldwatch Blues (Mick Softley)
8. To Sing For You (Donovan)
9. You're Gonna Need Somebody On Your Bond (Trad./arr. Donovan)
10. Tangerine Puppet (Donovan)
11. Donna Donna (Aaron Zeitlin/Sholom Secunda/Arthur Kevess/Teddi Schwartz)
12. Ramblin' Boy (Donovan)

Donovan Leitch: vocals, guitar, harmonica / Brian Locking: bass guitar, bass / Skip Alan: drums / Gypsy Dave: kazoo / Terry Kennedy: producer / Peter Eden: producer / Geoff Stephens: producer
```

BAROCK & ROLL ENSEMBLE   EINE KLEINE BEATLEMUSIC EP

```
UK release     May 1965     HMV     7EG 8887
Not released in US

1. Allegro
2. Minuet And Trio
3. Finale

4. Star Of Eve Bossa Nova
5. My Old Man's A Dutchman – Twist
6. Tannhauser Lettered Rock

Side 1 compositions by John Lennon and Paul McCartney, arranged by Harry Wild and directed by Fritz Spiegl;
Side 2 compositions by Richard Wagner, arranged by Harry Wild and Fritz Spiegl, directed by Harry Wild
```

As confirmation of the impact that the Beatles were having outside the area of pop music alone, the classical musician and broadcaster, Fritz Spiegl, constructed a medley of Beatles songs, arranged as they might have sounded if Mozart had worked on the themes. Spiegl undoubtedly considered the results to be a joke at the Beatles' expense, but in fact the music sounds remarkably attractive. If nothing else, it proves that John Lennon and Paul McCartney had a real gift for melody. The second side of the EP works much less well. The reworking of themes composed by Richard Wagner into music that might have been produced by the Shadows mainly succeeds in demonstrating that Spiegl (and his probably imaginary colleague, Harry Wild) had no real understanding of how rock music worked.

DON RENDELL/IAN CARR QUINTET   SHADES OF BLUE

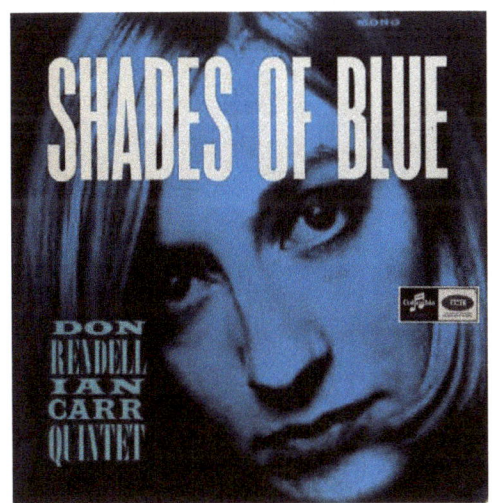

```
UK release     May 1965     Columbia    33SX 1733
Not released in US

1. Blue Mosque (Colin Purbrook)
2. Latin Blue (Don Rendell)
3. Just Blue (Don Rendell)
4. Sailin' (Mike Carr)

5. Garrison '64 (Don Rendell)
6. Blue Doom (Don Rendell/Ian Carr)
7. Shades Of Blue (Neil Ardley)
8. Big City Strut (Ian Carr)

Don Rendell: tenor and soprano saxophones / Ian Carr: trumpet, flugelhorn / Colin Purbrook: piano / Dave Green: bass / Trevor Tomkins: drums / Denis Preston: producer
```

The formation of the Don Rendell-Ian Carr Quintet marked a significant gear change up for British jazz in the world arena. With music displaying influences from Miles Davis and from Art Blakey's Jazz Messengers and with no trace at all of the British novelty-pop approach that trad had turned into, the Quintet made serious comparisons with the best contemporary American jazz possible. *Shades Of Blue*, featuring pieces inspired by the blues, cannot be realistically described as artistically superior to the music of John Coltrane or Charles Mingus or Miles Davis, or even as being on the same level, but it is at least worthy of being mentioned in the same breath. It is a modern jazz recording of considerable quality and an indication that British jazz musicians were now able to make a significant contribution to US-derived music, just as the beat musicians had already done. Although there is no hint of any rock influence in *Shades Of Blue*, it is worth noting that Don Rendell's previous album, from 1961, *Roarin'*, had featured some fine alto saxophone playing by Graham Bond, who made the decision to move away from pure jazz shortly afterwards.

THE NEW JAZZ ORCHESTRA   WESTERN REUNION LONDON 1965

The New Jazz Orchestra, a UK big band organised by Neil Ardley, attempted to emulate the sound and approach of the American bandleader and arranger Gil Evans, who was responsible for several innovative albums with Miles Davis and others during the late fifties and afterwards. Even though the NJO gigged very sporadically, it managed to serve as a vital

| UK release | May 1965 | Decca | LK 4690 |

Not released in US

1. Big P (Jimmy Heath)
2. Shades Of Blue (Neil Ardley)
3. So What (Miles Davis; arranged Les Carter/Paul Rutherford)
4. If You Could See Me Now (Tadd Dameron/Carl Sigman; arranged Lionel Grigson)
5. Tiny's Blues (Tiny Kahn/Al Cohn; arranged Dave Gelly)

6. Milestones (Miles Davis; arranged Les Carter)
7. Django (John Lewis; arranged Neil Ardley)
8. Maria (Leonard Bernstein/Stephen Sondheim; arr. Les Carter)
9. Western Reunion (Gerry Mulligan; arranged Neil Ardley)

Les Carter: flute, alto flute / Trevor Watts: alto saxophone, flute / Barbara Thompson: alto saxophone / Dave Gelly: tenor Saxophone / Tom Harris: tenor saxophone / Sebastian Freudenberg: baritone saxophone / Bob Leaper: trumpet / Mike Phillipson: trumpet / Tony Dudley: trumpet / Ian Carr: trumpet, flugelhorn / John Mumford: trombone / Paul Rutherford: trombone / Peter Harvey: bass trombone / Mick Palmer: French horn / Dick Hart: tuba / Mike Barrett: piano / Tony Reeves: bass / Jon Hiseman: drums / Neil Ardley: conductor / Ray Horricks: producer

training ground for young British musicians interested in modern jazz – leader Neil Ardley was just short of his twenty-eighth birthday at the time of the debut album's recording, while drummer Jon Hiseman and new recruit Barbara Thompson were only twenty. Much of the music on *Western Reunion* was recorded live at the Decca studios, in front of an invited audience, although the recording continued after the audience had left. Propelled by the dynamic Jon Hiseman/Tony Reeves rhythm section, the music features some fine solo playing and, just as with the Don Rendell/Ian Carr album issued the same month, provides a fine demonstration of the fact that British modern jazz had arrived. Much of the material derives from the work of American performers, but it is rearranged so thoroughly and imaginatively by members of the band, that it emerges rather as a set of new compositions.

HERBIE HANCOCK   MAIDEN VOYAGE

| US release | May 1965 | Blue Note | BST8 / BLP 4195 |

Not released in UK

1. Maiden Voyage
2. The Eye Of The Hurricane
3. Little One
4. Survival Of The Fittest
5. Dolphin Dance

All compositions by Herbie Hancock

Herbie Hancock: piano / Freddie Hubbard: trumpet / George Coleman: tenor saxophone / Ron Carter: bass / Tony Williams: drums / Alfred Lion: producer

Herbie Hancock recorded the fifth album issued in his name with the other members of the Miles Davis Quintet he was used to working with, bringing in Freddie Hubbard to replace Miles himself. Hancock intended this collection of pieces to be a musical portrait of the sea, and although it does not have the impressionistic quality of Claude Debussy's well-known composition with the same purpose, the music does indeed have a flowing quality. The melodic structures that Hancock sets up as the basis for improvisation are not based on the blues changes that dominate his soul jazz performances on the earlier albums. Instead the music follows the modal, empathic approach of Miles Davis's records. One track, *Little One*, is a slightly gentler reading of a piece that would be presented again, three months later, on Miles' *ESP* album. *Maiden Voyage* demonstrates how great, memorable music can be produced from the simplest of resources, always providing that skilled musicians who really listen to each other are involved. Nothing here is played faster than mid-tempo and yet the album manages to deliver a manifesto for a form of modern jazz that retains a powerful emphasis on melody. It emerges as determinedly cutting-edge as anything produced by its more avant garde contemporaries.

THE ANIMALS   ANIMAL TRACKS

During 1965, the Animals achieved a number of chart hits with impressive, memorable singles. The band's masterful reworking of Nina Simone's *Don't Let Me Be Misunderstood* and the angry complaint of *We've Gotta Get Out Of This Place* were particularly striking. The groups' second album is not at all in the same league as these, comprising a business-as-usual selection of enthusiastic but not very distinctive R&B covers. It is as though the group had already played its favourite songs on the first LP and is left with a less highly regarded selection to play now. Alan Price decided to leave what had

| UK release | May 1965 | Columbia | 33SX 1708 |

The US LP with the same title, issued in September 1965 on MGM an almost entirely different album, with only two tracks in common.

1. Mess Around (Ahmet Ertegun)
2. How You've Changed (Chuck Berry)
3. Hallelujah I Love Her So (Ray Charles)
4. I Believe To My Soul (Ray Charles)
5. Worried Life Blues (Major Merriweather)
6. Roberta (Huey Piano Smith)

7. I Ain't Got You (Billy Boy Arnold)
8. Bright Lights Big City (Jimmy Reed)
9. Let The Good Times Roll (Leonard Lee)
10. For Miss Caulker (Eric Burdon)
11. Roadrunner (Bo Diddley)

Eric Burdon: vocals / Hilton Valentine: guitar, vocals / Alan Price: keyboards, vocals / Chas Chandler: bass guitar, vocals / John Steel: drums / Mickie Most: producer

originally been his own group just as the album was coming out. His fear of flying was the official reason for this, but it seems more likely that he had simply become disenchanted with the lack of musical progress being displayed.

TOM JONES   ALONG CAME JONES

In 1999, Tom Jones managed to reinvent himself as an artist who should be considered as cool, with an album, *Reload*, where he collaborated with a number of more recent performers, who might have been expected to view the prospect somewhat warily. During the years before that, Tom Jones was not at all cool. His first hit single, *It's Not Unusual*, was a dynamic slice of blue-eyed soul, proving that the Jones voice, powerful, rich, and flexible, was an instrument to be taken seriously. It was cushioned, however, within the kind of pop big band arrangement that the Beatles had rendered largely irrelevant. The impression given was that Tom Jones would much rather have been wooing the socialites at Las Vegas than touring up and down the country in the name of rock 'n' roll. He seemed to be like a middle-aged crooner trapped in the body of a much younger man. He would have been impressive as the lead singer of a beat group, but that was not at all what he was interested in being. In 1969, when he had indeed been performing in Las Vegas, he sang on US television with Crosby, Stills, Nash and Young, with results that proved he could do it, but that still came over as weird. His debut album is the same. It sold well, reaching number eleven in the UK album chart, but it was bought by the people who were keeping Frank Sinatra and the *Sound Of Music* soundtrack in the list of best-sellers, not by those who had added *Beatles For Sale* or *The Rolling Stones No.2* to their growing collections. The inclusion of songs by the likes of Chuck Berry and Chuck Willis tries to make a connection with the world of rock 'n' roll, but these versions have the rock stripped out of them.

```
UK release    May 1965     Decca    LK 4693
US release    July 1965    Parrot   PA 6/7 1004    as    IT'S NOT UNUSUAL    with 4 fewer tracks

1. I've Got A Heart (Gordon Mills/Les Reed)
2. It Takes A Worried Man (Traditional)
3. Skye Boat Song (Traditional)
4. Once Upon A Time (Gordon Mills)
5. Memphis (Chuck Berry)
6. Whatcha Gonna Do (Chuck Willis)
7. I Need Your Loving (Don Gardner/Bobby Robinson/Clarence Lewis/James McDougall)
8. It's Not Unusual (Gordon Mills/Les Reed)

9. Autumn Leaves (Joseph Kosma/Johnny Mercer/Geoffrey Parsons/ Jacques Prévert)
10. The Rose – Version 2 (Gordon Mills)
11. If You Need Me (Wilson Pickett/Robert Bateman/Sonny Sanders)
12. Some Other Guy (Gordon Mills)
13. Endlessly (Brook Benton/Clyde Otis)
14. It's Just A Matter Of Time (B.Benton/C.Otis/Belford Hendricks)
15. Spanish Harlem (Jerry Leiber/Phil Spector)
16. When The World Was Beautiful (Paul Kaufman/Jerry Harris)

Tom Jones: vocals / Les Reed: musical director / Peter Sullivan: producer
```

THE ROCKIN' BERRIES   IN TOWN

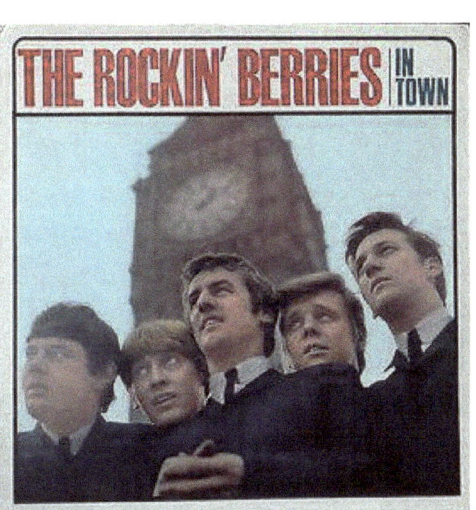

He's In Town is Carole King and Gerry Goffin's most moving song, especially when performed by the Rockin' Berries in a mournful, countryish soft rock style. (In the US, the Tokens achieved a minor hit with the song, but failed to deliver the required level of anguish.) The song was the Rockin' Berries' biggest hit in

```
UK release    May 1965    Piccadilly    NPL 38013
Not released in US

1. He's In Town (Gerry Goffin/Carole King)
2. Let's Try Again (John Carter/Ken Lewis)
3. Ich Liebe Dich (Doc Pomus/Phil Spector)
4. You Don't Know What You Do (Wendy King)
5. Brother Bill (The Last Clean Shirt) (Johnny Otis/Jerry Leiber/Mike Stoller)
6. Without Your Love (John Schroeder/Mike Hawker)
7. All Of Me (Gerald Marks/Seymour Simons)

8. Crazy Country Hop (Johnny Otis)
9. All I Want Is My Baby (Andrew Oldham/Keith Richards)
10. Lonely Avenue (Doc Pomus)
11. Shades Of Blue (Dave Mason/Jim Capaldi)
12. Follow Me (John Schroeder/Mike Hawker)
13. Ain't That Lovin' You Baby (Jimmy Reed)
14. Funny How Love Can Be (John Carter/Ken Lewis)

Clive Lea: vocals / Geoff Turton: vocals, guitar / Chuck Botfield: guitar / Roy Austin: bass guitar / Terry Bond: drums / Frank Barber: arranger (6,12) / John Schroeder: producer
```

the UK, but the group's reluctance to play songs to match its name prevented it from gaining long-term rock credibility. Instead it introduced a comedy element, working in a similar vein to the Barron Knights. The *In Town* album has a touch of this, with the group's version of the Jimmy Reed blues, *Ain't That Lovin' You Baby,* played for laughs. On the whole, however, the album presents a worthy set of guitar-based pop songs to accompany the hit, often sounding, with two strong lead singers, very much like the Everly Brothers. Curiously, *Ich Liebe Dich* is sung in German, which must have been the only time that a British group did this on its own album. *Funny How Love Can Be* suits Geoff Turton's voice particularly well and would have made a fine follow-up single to *He's In Town,* if the songwriters had not decided to record it themselves (as the Ivy League).

UNIT 4 + 2   #1 FEATURING CONCRETE AND CLAY

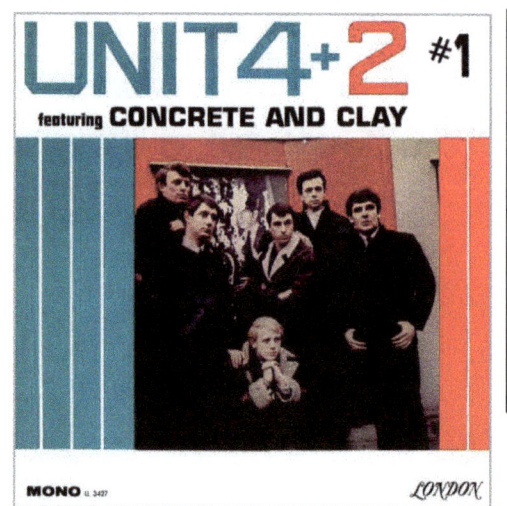

Propelled by attractive Spanish-sounding acoustic guitars and with an intensely memorable chorus, *Concrete And Clay* was a record that was bound to become a big hit. It reached number one in the UK and although it fared less well in the US, where it had to compete with a cover version, it was still a chart hit. Unit 4 + 2's intriguing name was a reference to the fact that the original four-piece band was helped out by two session musicians, Russ Ballard and Bob Henrit (members of Adam Faith's backing group, the Roulettes), both of whom eventually joined on a full-time basis. In the UK, Decca rush-released the group's first album, but in the US, London waited until the impressive second single, *You've Never Been In Love Like This Before,* became available, and included that on the album as well (together with its strong B side, *Tell Somebody You Know*). For this reason, the American first album is a superior collection to the British one. Brian Parker and Tommy Moeller were clearly talented songwriters, but they sadly never managed to take their group back into the charts again. Unit 4 + 2 eventually disbanded in 1970.

LESLEY GORE   GOLDEN HITS

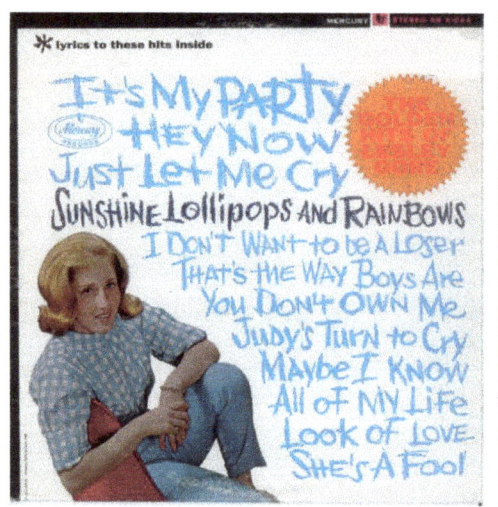

Lesley Gore was sixteen and still at school when she released her first single, *It's My Party,* in April 1963, and proceeded to sell over a million copies of it. The song was a number one hit in the US and reached the top ten in the UK too. She was a singer whose pop style was typical of those recording before the arrival of the Beatles and the Rolling Stones, sounding old-fashioned, with her double-tracked voice, next to them. But she went on to score several more hits in the US, through to 1967, even if none of them were as big as the first. Her music was produced by jazz bandleader Quincy Jones, making his first venture away from the music with which he was most comfortable. Perhaps surprisingly, he made no attempt to include any jazz influence on Lesley Gore's records. This was in spite of the fact that the man he employed to lead her band was Claus Ogerman, a man with a similar jazz background to Jones's own.

THEM   THE "ANGRY" YOUNG THEM

```
UK release      June 1965      Decca       LK 4700
US release      July 1965 as   THEM FEATURING HERE COMES THE NIGHT,
with several different tracks  Parrot  PAS 71005 / PA 61005

1. Mystic Eyes (Van Morrison)
2. If You And I Could Be As Two (Van Morrison)
3. Little Girl (Van Morrison)
4. Just A Little Bit (Rosco Gordon)
5. I Gave My Love A Diamond (Bert Berns)
6. Gloria (Van Morrison)
7. You Just Can't Win (Van Morrison)

8. Go On Home Baby (Bert Berns)
9. Don't Look Back (John Lee Hooker)
10. I Like It Like That (Van Morrison)
11. I'm Gonna Dress In Black (Tommy Scott/M. Howe)
12. Bright Lights Big City (Jimmy Reed)
13. My Little Baby (Bert Berns/Wes Farrell)
14. Route 66 (Bobby Troup)

Van Morrison: vocals, harmonica, tenor saxophone / Billy Harrison: guitar /
Peter Bardens: piano, organ / Alan Henderson: bass guitar / Pat McAuley:
drums (all tracks) / Bobby Graham: drums (6) / Arthur Greenslade: organ
(6) / Tommy Scott: producer (1-4,7,9-12,14) / Dick Rowe: producer (6) /
Bert Berns: producer (5,8,13)
```

Them was an R&B band with a slight difference; inspired by the Rolling Stones, but formed in Belfast by singer Van Morrison. The group scored UK chart hits with the singles *Baby Please Don't Go* and *Here Comes The Night,* which have justifiably acquired the status of classic sixties recordings, along with the B-side of the second single, *Gloria*. Only this last-named track is included on the UK first album, however. A product of the group's first recording session, it has an improvised feel, especially where Morrison's vocals are concerned, and an innovative twin drummer line-up. Van Morrison's love of singing spontaneously is apparent on all the songs credited to him, especially on the striking opening track, *Mystic Eyes*, which was extracted from a much longer studio jam. Even on the cover versions, Morrison makes the songs memorable with his wayward approach. Session guitarist Jimmy Page had been drafted in to help with *Baby Please Don't Go* (although its distinctive lead guitar line is the work of Them's own Billy Harrison). The group members prove throughout the album how such a move was unnecessary, providing fine support for their charismatic lead singer.

THE BYRDS   MR TAMBOURINE MAN

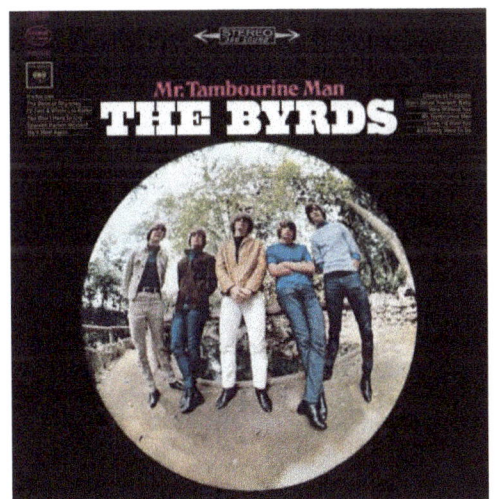

```
US release      June 1965      Columbia    CS 9172 / CL 2372
UK release      June 1965      CBS         (S)BPG 62571

1. Mr Tambourine Man (Bob Dylan)
2. I'll Feel A Whole Lot Better (Gene Clark)
3. Spanish Harlem Incident (Bob Dylan)
4. You Won't Have To Cry (Gene Clark/Jim McGuinn)
5. Here Without You (Gene Clark)
6. The Bells Of Rhymney (Pete Seeger/Idris Davies)

7. All I Really Want To Do (Bob Dylan)
8. I Knew I'd Want You (Gene Clark)
9. It's No Use (Gene Clark/Jim McGuinn)
10. Don't Doubt Yourself Babe (Jackie DeShannon)
11. Chimes Of Freedom (Bob Dylan)
12. We'll Meet Again (Hughie Charles/Ross Parker)

Gene Clark: vocals, guitar, percussion / David Crosby: vocals,
guitar / Jim McGuinn: vocals, guitar / Chris Hillman: bass guitar
/ Michael Clarke: drums / Jerry Cole: guitar (1,8) / Leon Russell:
piano (1,8) / Larry Knechtel: bass guitar (1,8) / Hal Blaine:
drums (1,8) / Terry Melcher: producer
```

In 1964, encouraged by the success of the Beatles, three established, albeit low-profile folk performers in the US, Gene Clark, David Crosby, and Jim McGuinn, decided to join forces. Adding a former bluegrass mandolin player as bassist and an enthusiastic, if inexperienced drummer, the quintet recorded an album as the Jet Set, with manager Jim Dickson as producer. Unfortunately, the results were not deemed good enough for release. (They appeared some years later as the album *Preflyte*, cashing in on the Byrds' later success.) Despite this, the group, now renamed as the Byrds, managed to secure a recording contract with Columbia and was entrusted to the services of producer Terry Melcher (the son of actress/singer Doris Day). Understandably, Melcher chose to employ session musicians to record a first single, retaining only McGuinn's distinctive twelve string guitar and the layered harmonies of the Byrds' three singers. *Mr Tambourine Man* went to number one on both sides of the Atlantic, giving its songwriter, Bob Dylan, his biggest single success thus far. For the album that followed, the Byrds themselves played everything, on a mixture of folk-derived material and songs written by group members, very much in the style of the Beatles. These songs had been included in the recordings made the year before, and the fact that they sound so much better is a testament to what can be achieved by a good producer. Although the Animals and the Searchers had previously recorded occasional rock interpretations of folk material, and Bob Dylan himself had started to favour rock instrumentation, the fact that the Byrds were doing this as the essential basis of their style encouraged critics to coin the term 'folk-rock' as a description of what the group was achieving. The music is important because it marks the bringing together of two divergent approaches to contemporary music – American folk and British beat. UK listeners should be aware that the surprise inclusion of *We'll Meet Again* at the end of the album has nothing to do with Vera Lynn, but is because the song was used within the Stanley Kubrick black comedy anti-nuclear film of 1964, *Dr Strangelove*.

THE ROLLING STONES   GOT LIVE IF YOU WANT IT! EP

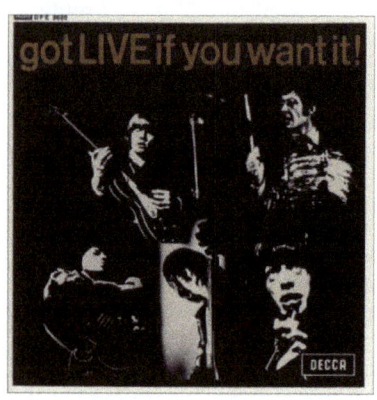

UK release   June 1965   Decca   DFE 8620
Not released in US

1. Everybody Needs Somebody To Love (Solomon Burke/Bert Russell/Jerry Wexler)
2. Pain In My Heart (Allen Toussaint [as Naomi Neville])
3. Route 66 (Bobby Troup)
4. I'm Moving On (Hank Snow)
5. I'm Alright (Rolling Stones)

Mick Jagger: vocals, harmonica, percussion / Brian Jones: guitar, vocals / Keith Richards: guitar, vocals / Bill Wyman: bass guitar, vocals / Charlie Watts: drums / Andrew Loog Oldham: producer

It was a sensible decision to release a live recording by the Rolling Stones on an EP, rather than turning it into a whole LP. The group plays well enough, and with enormous energy, but the recording quality is primitive, with Mick Jagger's vocals struggling to be heard above the noise of his band. To be fair, this is undoubtedly how the music sounded to the audience at the time, given the poor quality amplification systems available. As a concert memento for those who were there, or for those who wished they had been, the record serves a valuable purpose. The Solomon Burke song that opens the proceedings is just a single verse, used to introduce the following cover of an early Otis Redding song. Andrew Oldham gets the producer credit as usual, although no production was required for this recording. His business nous is in evidence, however, in his listing the audience cries of "We want the Stones!" as a separate track and giving it a 'Nanker-Phelge' songwritng credit, the fictitious partnership used to disguise songs actually written by the Stones themselves.

NINA SIMONE   I PUT A SPELL ON YOU

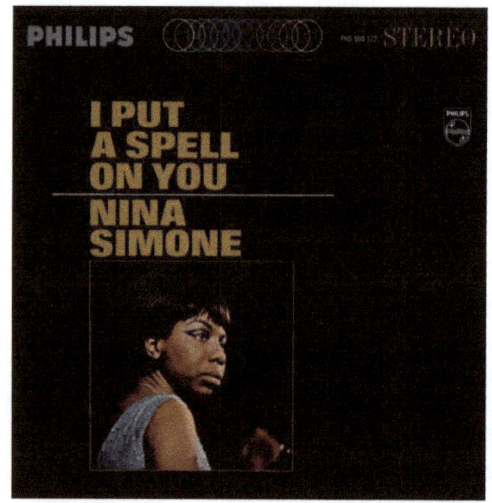

US release   June 1965   Philips   PHS 600-172 / PHM 200-172
UK release   June 1965   Philips   (S)BL 7671

1. I Put A Spell On You (Screamin' Jay Hawkins)
2. Tomorrow Is My Turn (Charles Aznavour/Marcel Stellman/Yves Stéphane)
3. Ne Me Quitte Pas (Jacques Brel)
4. Marriage Is For Old Folks (Leon Carr/Earl Shuman)
5. July Tree (Irma Jurist/Eve Merriam)
6. Gimme Some (Andy Stroud)
7. Feeling Good (Leslie Bricusse/Anthony Newley)
8. One September Day (Rudy Stevenson)
9. Blues On Purpose (Rudy Stevenson)
10. Beautiful Land (Leslie Bricusse/Anthony Newley)
11. You've Got To Learn (Charles Aznavour/Marcel Stellman)
12. Take Care Of Business (Andy Stroud)

Nina Simone: vocals, piano / Rudy Stevenson: guitar / Lisle Atkinson: bass / Bobby Hamilton: drums / Horace Ott: arranger / Hal Mooney: arranger, producer

Nina Simone is a jazz singer who sings soul, or a soul singer who sings jazz – it is hard to say which. She made her first recordings in the fifties and *I Put A Spell On You*, featuring lush arrangements for strings on most of the tracks and a night-club jazz sound on the rest, could easily have been made then. There is one really weak track, *Beautiful Land,* where Ms Simone adopts a child-like persona that does not work at all well. The album is saved, however, by three performances where she takes hold of songs already recorded by others and completely makes them her own. Jacques Brel's *Ne Me Quitte Pas* retains its poignancy, its sense of anguish, even when it is not translated into English. The title track transforms Screamin' Jay Hawkins' bizarre, drunken original into a statement of intent that unsettles and thrills in equal measure – later interpretations of this song by the likes of Manfred Mann, Alan Price, Arthur Brown, and Joe Cocker all used Nina Simone as their inspiration, rather than Hawkins. Best of all, *Feeling Good* sets its agenda as a candidate for the definitive Nina Simone performance. The song was not issued as a single, but has become one of the two or three recordings for which the singer is most fondly remembered. The album became one of Nina Simone's biggest commercial successes, by which we mean that it scraped into the US top hundred albums chart, although it made the top twenty in the UK.

THE YARDBIRDS — FOR YOUR LOVE

US release   June 1965   Epic   BN 26167 / LN 24167
Not released in UK

1. For Your Love (Graham Gouldman)
2. I'm Not Talking (Mose Allison)
3. Putty (In Your Hands) (Kay Rogers/John Patton)
4. I Ain't Got You (Calvin Carter)
5. Got To Hurry (Giorgio Gomelsky as Oscar Rasputin)
6. I Ain't Done Wrong (Keith Relf)

7. I Wish You Would (Billy Boy Arnold)
8. A Certain Girl (Allen Toussaint)
9. Sweet Music (Major Lance/Otis Cobb/Walter Bowie)
10. Good Morning Little Schoolgirl (H.G.Demarais)
11. My Girl Sloopy (Bert Berns/Wes Farrell)

Keith Relf: vocals, harmonica / Eric Clapton: guitar (1,3,4,5,7,8,9,10) / Jeff Beck:guitar (2,6,11) / Chris Dreja: guitar / Paul Samwell-Smith: bass guitar, vocals, producer / Jim McCarty: drums, vocals / Giorgio Gomelsky: producer (not 9), vocals (8) / Brian Auger: harpsichord (1) / Denny Pierce: bongos (1) / Ron Prentice: bass (1)/ Manfred Mann: producer (9)

For Your Love began a series of particularly imaginative and innovative singles made by the Yardbirds during 1965 and 1966. It was a big hit in the UK and the US in the spring of 1965. The song has an unusual harpsichord and bongos accompaniment (alongside a barely audible bowed bass and, eventually, Jim McCarty's drums), with the guitarists only joining in for a short, contrasting middle section, so that it is close to being a solo performance by singer Keith Relf. It was, nevertheless, very unexpected when lead guitarist Eric Clapton used this fact as an excuse for announcing his departure from the group. The B-side, *Got To Hurry*, was a blues instrumental highlighting Clapton's own playing, but this was clearly not enough to save the situation as far as the guitarist was concerned. The fact that the group's manager seized the composing credit for himself cannot have helped. Columbia in the UK was concerned enough to hold back from allowing the Yardbirds to record a studio album, but Epic in the US had no such qualms. It put together an LP, surrounding both sides of the hit single with a selection of earlier out-takes with Clapton and three tracks featuring the group's new lead guitarist, Jeff Beck. These three, issued on an EP in the UK, are the most dynamic and forward-looking pieces of music on the album and show that Clapton's replacement was at least as remarkable a player as Clapton himself. His lead lines on the two blues-based tracks, *I'm Not Talking* and *I Ain't Done Wrong*, sound like nobody else at this time. When Beck cheerfully carved away the top edge of his Fender Telecaster, to make the instrument more comfortable to play, he provided further demonstration of his willingness to ignore tradition. It is Jeff Beck who is pictured on the LP sleeve, in front of a keyboard that he did not play, and Eric Clapton is not mentioned anywhere, giving a rather false impression of the record's contents.

KENNY BURRELL — GUITAR FORMS

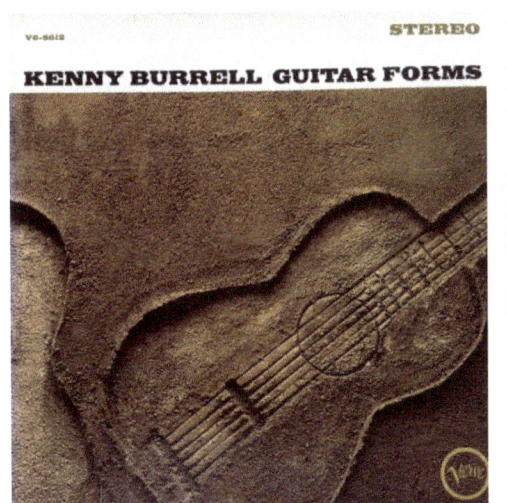

US release   June 1965   Verve   V(6)-8612
UK release   June 1965   Verve   VLP 9099

1. Downstairs (Elvin Jones)
2. Lotus Land (Cyril Scott)
3. Terrace Theme (Joe Benjamin)
4. Prelude #2 Excerpt (George Gershwin)

5. Moon And Sand (Alec Wilder)
6. Loie (Kenny Burrell)
7. Greensleeves (Traditional)
8. Last Night When We Were Young (E.Y.Harburg/Harold Arlen)
9. Breadwinner (Kenny Burrell)

Kenny Burrell: guitar / Creed Taylor: producer. Tracks 1,3,9: Roger Kellaway: piano / Joe Benjamin: bass / Grady Tate: drums / Willie Rodriguez: congas. Tracks 2,5,6,7,8: Gil Evans: arranger, conductor / Steve Lacy: soprano saxophone / Lee Konitz: alto saxophone / Bob Tricarico: tenor saxophone, bassoon, flute / Richie Kamuca: tenor saxophone, oboe / Ray Beckenstein: flute, bass clarinet / George Marge & Andy Fitzgerald: flute, English horn / Julius Watkins & Ray Alonge: French horn / Johnny Coles & Louis Mucci: trumpet / Jimmy Cleveland & Jimmy Knepper: trombone / John Barber: tuba / Ron Carter: bass / Charlie Persip & Elvin Jones: drums

Kenny Burrell is an acclaimed jazz guitarist who made his first recordings at the start of the fifties, and *Guitar Forms* is frequently favoured as his most remarkable LP. He performs on both the electric and the acoustic varieties of his instrument yet hardly alters his style of playing, whichever guitar it is. In truth, he would not fare particularly well in a cutting contest against Davy Graham and those seeking the display of obvious virtuosity to be found a few years later on records by John McLaughlin or Jimi Hendrix will not find it here. The central interest lies in the juxtaposition of Burrell's unspectacular style with the fascinating orchestrations of Gil Evans, which take up two thirds of the album's playing time. Originally employed by the Claude Thornhill orchestra in the forties, Evans found a modicum of fame when he became involved with Miles Davis's ground-breaking *Birth Of The Cool* band in 1948. Towards the end of the following decade and into the sixties, Evans and Davis recorded four albums together, of which *Sketches Of Spain*, the result of fusing classical music with jazz, attracted the most attention. The Gil Evans arrangements on *Guitar Forms* cannot match these, but they nevertheless provide further compelling evidence for Evans's consideration as one of the greatest organisers of multiple tones and timbres to be found in the whole of jazz.

THE RAMSEY LEWIS TRIO   THE IN CROWD

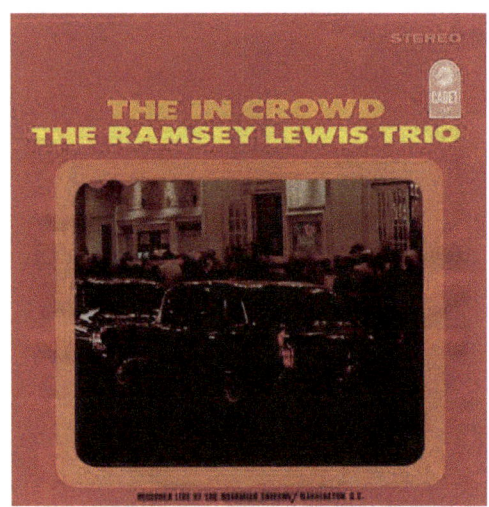

```
US release    June 1965    Cadet    LP(S)-757
UK release    June 1965    Chess    CRL 4511

1. The In Crowd (Billy Page)
2. Since I Fell For You (Buddy Johnson)
3. Tennessee Waltz (Pee Wee King/Redd Stewart)
4. You Been Talkin' 'Bout Me Baby (Gale Garnett/Ray Riviera/Walter Hirsch)
5. Love Theme From Spartacus (Alex North)
6. Felicidade (Antonio Carlos Jobim/Vinicius De Moraes)
7. Come Sunday (Duke Ellington)

Ramsey Lewis: piano / Eldee Young: bass, cello / Red Holt: drums / Esmond Edwards: producer
```

Pianist Ramsey Lewis had been making straightforward jazz records since the mid-fifties, when he hit upon the idea of playing a jazz version of a recent soul hit by Dobie Gray, *The In Crowd*. His improvisation, recorded live in a club in Washington D.C., is kept simple and heavy on the chords, so as to emphasise the strong rhythm being delivered by the bass and drums, and the result was a million-selling single in the US. The rest of the set captured on the album is less blatantly commercial, but the audience have been won over by the opening salvo and are in the mood to enjoy a good night. The group is very much a trio of equals, in which the contribution of each musician is vital. As a confirmation of this, a version of *Tennessee Waltz* is performed, where the theme statement and subsequent soloing is given to Eldee Young, demonstrating his fluency on a pizzicato cello. During the next year, the Ramsey Lewis Trio achieved two more million-selling singles, with *Hang On Sloopy* and *Wade In The Water*, played in the same soul-jazz style as *The In Crowd*.

THE BEACH BOYS   SUMMER DAYS (AND SUMMER NIGHTS!)

Summer Days (And Summer Nights!) shows signs of being a rushed job. Released just four months after *The Beach Boys Today!* it sounds very much like a continuation of that album, with less inspired songs. As before, a large number of session musicians are on hand to fill out the sound, but are given much too little to do. The revised version of *Help Me Rhonda* and *California Girls* were hit singles and are by far the best tracks on offer here. They are offset by a rather nondescript instrumental, *Summer Means New Love*, and a song that sounds like the demo of something that was not worth finishing, *I'm Bugged At My Ol' Man*. The unaccompanied harmony singing of the last track, *And Your Dream Comes True*, almost rescues the proceedings, but by then it feels like too little, too late.

```
US release    July 1965    Capitol    (D)T 2354
UK release    June 1966    Capitol    (S)T 2354

1. The Girl From New York City (Brian Wilson/Mike Love)
2. Amusement Parks USA (Brian Wilson/Mike Love)
3. Then I Kissed Her (Phil Spector/Ellie Greenwich/Jeff Barry)
4. Salt Lake City (Brian Wilson/Mike Love)
5. Girl Don't Tell Me (Brian Wilson)
6. Help Me Rhonda (Brian Wilson/Mike Love)

7. California Girls (Brian Wilson/Mike Love)
8. Let Him Run Wild (Brian Wilson/Mike Love)
9. You're So Good To Me (Brian Wilson/Mike Love)
10. Summer Means New Love (Brian Wilson)
11. I'm Bugged At My Ol' Man (Brian Wilson)
12. And Your Dream Comes True (Brian Wilson/Mike Love)

Mike Love: vocals / Carl Wilson: vocals, guitar / Al Jardine: vocals, guitar, bass / Brian Wilson: vocals, bass guitar, keyboards, producer / Dennis Wilson: vocals, drums / Bruce Johnston: vocals, keyboards / Glen Campbell: guitar / Jerry Cole: guitar / Bill Pitman: guitar / Howard Roberts: guitar / Tommy Tedesco: guitar / Billy Strange: guitar, ukulele, tambourine / Al De Lory: organ / Leon Russell: piano / Frank Capp: vibraphone / Steve Douglas: tenor saxophone / Plas Johnson: tenor saxophone / Jay Migliori: baritone saxophone / Jack Nimitz: bass saxophone / Roy Caton: trumpet / William Hinshaw: French horn / Billy Lee Riley: harmonica / Israel Baker, Arnold Belnick, James Getzoff, Bernard Kundell, Leonard Malarsky, Ralph Schaeffer, Sid Sharp, Tibor Zelig: violin / Harry Hyams: viola / Lyle Ritz: bass / Carol Kaye: bass guitar / Ray Pohlman: bass guitar / Hal Blaine: drums / Ron Swallow: percussion / Julius Wechter: percussion / Marilyn Wilson: vocals
```

THE MOODY BLUES   THE MAGNIFICENT MOODIES

The Moody Blues scored a number one hit in the UK at the beginning of the year (and it entered the top ten in the US) with an unusual soul ballad called *Go Now*, in waltz time and driven by a hard-hitting piano. It was closely modelled on a version recorded the previous year by Bessie Banks, although this was significantly slower and failed to chart. The album built around the hit is something of a disappointment. On the first side, the group's attempts to tackle other soul material fall rather flat. They are rash enough to cover two songs by James Brown, for which they lack the necessary rhythmic

```
UK release        July 1965      Decca     LK 4711
US release as   GO NOW - THE MOODY BLUES with some different
tracks   July 1965    London    PS 428 / LL 3428

1. I'll Go Crazy (James Brown)
2. Something You Got (Chris Kenner)
3. Go Now (Larry Banks/Milton Bennett)
4. Can't Nobody Love You (James Mitchell)
5. I Don't Mind (James Brown)
6. I've Got A Dream (Jeff Barry/Ellie Greenwich)
7. Let Me Go (Denny Laine/Mike Pinder)
8. Stop (Denny Laine/Mike Pinder)
9. Thank You Baby (Denny Laine/Mike Pinder)
10. It Ain't Necessarily So (George & Ira Gershwin/DuBose Heyward)
11. True Story (Denny Laine/Mike Pinder)
12. Bye Bye Bird (Willie Dixon/Sonny Boy Williamson)

Denny Laine: vocals, guitar, harmonica / Ray Thomas: harmonica,
flute, vocals, percussion / Mike Pinder: piano, organ, vocals / Clint
Warwick: bass guitar, vocals / Graeme Edge: drums, vocals / Elaine
Caswell: percussion / Denny Cordell: producer / Alex Wharton:
producer (3)
```

precision and do not have a singer with the excitement and emotional depth of Brown himself. The group's own compositions that dominate the album's second side are strictly forgettable. Contemporary listeners were unimpressed too, for the album did not sell very well. The group struggled to find a single to repeat the lightning strike of *Go Now* and the lack of success caused both Denny Laine and Clint Warwick to leave the band the following year, although the others resolved to keep trying.

LULU   SOMETHING TO SHOUT ABOUT

```
UK release        July 1965      Decca     LK 4719
Not released in US

1. You Touch Me Baby (Sammy Fain/Ed Silvers)
2. You'll Never Leave Her (Bert Russell/Mike Stoller)
3. I'll Come Running Over (Bert Berns/Ilene Stuart)
4. Not In This Whole World (Troy Davis/Joe Simmons)
5. She Will Break Your Heart (Jerry Butler/Clarence Carter/Curtis Mayfield)
6. Can I Get A Witness (Brian Holland/Lamont Dozier/Eddie Holland)
7. Tell Me Like It Is (Bob Brass/Al Kooper/Irwin Levine)
8. Shout (Isley Brothers)
9. Try To Understand (Lori Burton/Pam Sawyer)
10. Night Time Is The Right Time (Leroy Carr/Lew Herman)
11. Chocolate Ice (Mike Leander)
12. So In Love (Billy Jackson/George Williams/Roy Straigis)
13. Only One (Mike Leander)
14. Dream Lover (Clifford Grey/Victor Schertzinger)
15. He's Sure The Boy I Love (Barry Mann/Cynthia Weil)
16. Leave A Little Love (Robin Conrad/Les Reed)

Lulu: vocals / Ross Neilson: guitar / James Dewar: guitar / Jimmy Page:
guitar / Tommy Tierney: bass guitar / David Mullin: drums / Mike Leander:
arranger / Reg Guest: arranger / Peter Sullivan: producer
```

Lulu was only fifteen when she recorded a dynamic version of the Isley Brothers song, *Shout,* and took it into the UK charts. Her gritty, powerful voice is ideal for this kind of soul music, and ensured that she was able to maintain a lengthy career in music. Initially, however, she struggled to find a successful follow-up to *Shout,* with the result that her album was delayed for over a year. Sadly, the collection was not really worth waiting for. Producer Peter Sullivan opts for a set of old-fashioned orchestral arrangements rather than the beat group sound that would have been Lulu's natural environment. A beat group, the Luvvers, is indeed present on some of the material, but it is overwhelmed by the rest of the accompaniment. There are a few soul songs here, but the arrangements give them a pop ambience that is difficult for Lulu to overcome. When a version of the Bobby Darin hit, *Dream Lover,* is made to sound like a lacklustre re-run of *Shout,* then it becomes clear that Sullivan is short of ideas.

SOLOMON BURKE   THE BEST OF

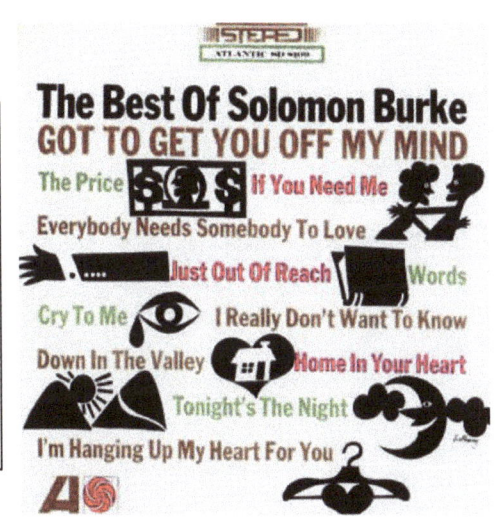

Everybody Needs Somebody To Love finds Solomon Burke as preacher, delivering a partly sung and partly spoken sermon over a soul music version of the basic *Louie Louie* riff. As much as any song of the period by Ray Charles or James Brown, it demonstrates exactly what is meant by soul music. It was a US hit in the summer of 1964, but not a big one. Sadly,

```
US release     July 1965     Atlantic   (SD) 8109
UK release     July 1965     Atlantic   588/587 016

1. Got To Get You Off My Mind (Delores Burke)
2. The Price (Solomon Burke Jr)
3. Down In The Valley (Bert Berns)
4. I'm Hanging Up My Heart For You (Don Covay/John Berry)
5. If You Need Me (Robert Bateman/Sonny Sanders/Wilson Pickett)
6. Just Out Of Reach (Virgil Stewart)
7. Cry To Me (Bert Russell)
8. Everybody Needs Somebody To Love (Bert Berns/Jerry Wexler)
9. Home In Your Heart (Otis Blackwell/Winfield Scott)
10. Tonight's The Night (Don Covay)
11. I Really Don't Want To Know (Don Robertson/Howard Barnes)
12. Words (Solomon Burke)

Solomon Burke: vocals / Bert Berns: producer / Jerry Wexler:
producer / musicians uncredited
```

this was very much the story of Solomon Burke's career. He enjoyed several chart hits during the early sixties, but only one of them reached anywhere near the top. This was not the classic *Everybody Needs Somebody To Love*, but the much less celebrated *Got To Get You Off My Mind,* written in 1965 as a tribute to Sam Cooke, who had just been murdered. It has a very close similarity to Cooke's own *I'll Come Running Back To You*. With the arrival of rather more dynamic soul singers like Wilson Pickett and Otis Redding, and with James Brown achieving primacy as the soul singer to follow, Solomon Burke found himself becoming increasingly sidelined. The emotional music on *The Best Of Solomon Burke* makes it clear how unfair this was to a man who was one of the great pioneers of the soul genre.

THE BEATLES   HELP!

UK release   August 1965   Parlophone   PCS 3071 / PMC 1255
US release   August 1965   Capitol   (S)MAS 2386
This mixes the UK side one tracks with instrumental music played by an orchestra led by Ken Thorne. The side two tracks are scattered over three US albums: **BEATLES VI, RUBBER SOUL** and **YESTERDAY AND TODAY.**

1. Help! (John Lennon/Paul McCartney)
2. The Night Before (John Lennon/Paul McCartney)
3. You've Got To Hide Your Love Away (Lennon/McCartney)
4. I Need You (George Harrison)
5. Another Girl (John Lennon/Paul McCartney)
6. You're Going To Lose That Girl (John Lennon/Paul McCartney)
7. Ticket To Ride (John Lennon/Paul McCartney)

8. Act Naturally (Johnny Russell/Voni Morrison)
9. It's Only Love (John Lennon/Paul McCartney)
10. You Like Me Too Much (George Harrison)
11. Tell Me What You See (John Lennon/Paul McCartney)
12. I've Just Seen A Face (John Lennon/Paul McCartney)
13. Yesterday (John Lennon/Paul McCartney)
14. Dizzy Miss Lizzy (Larry Williams)

John Lennon: vocals, guitar, piano, organ, percussion / George Harrison: vocals, guitar, percussion / Paul McCartney: vocals, bass guitar, guitar, piano / Ringo Starr: drums, percussion, vocals / John Scott: flutes (3) / uncredited string quartet (13) / George Martin: producer, piano

With the soundtrack to the Beatles' second film, expanded to album length by the addition of seven other new songs, the Beatles seemed to effortlessly trounce the competition. There are only two cover versions. One is the expected rock 'n' roll song (*Dizzy Miss Lizzy*), but the other is a piece of Buck Owens country, marking a new departure. George Harrison gets two songwriting credits and although he is not yet a match for Lennon/McCartney, he is nevertheless becoming a significant talent. The ten John Lennon-Paul McCartney songs making up the bulk of the album are all memorable and distinctive and any of them could have been chosen for release as a single. The group is starting to make a serious attempt to give each song a unique musical element for the album, in order to maximise their impact. Thus *You Like Me Too Much* is driven by three pianos, with Lennon, McCartney, and Martin all playing a keyboard part; *Another Girl* has Paul McCartney playing a striking wobbly-toned lead guitar. *Tell Me What You See* employs a touch of Latin American percussion, and *You've Got To Hide Your Love Away* employs a session musician to play a closing instrumental verse on a pair of flutes. Most remarkable of all, *Yesterday* has Paul McCartney singing and playing on his own, accompanied by a string quartet, the first time such a unit and sound had been employed on a popular music record. The American version of the album considerably reduced its musical impact by making it a strict film soundtrack, including orchestral music not played by the Beatles. The songs on side two of the British album were distributed across three other records, with the first album appearance of *Yesterday* being delayed until the *Yesterday And Today* LP of June 1966. Meanwhile, it made a strange choice for a US single in September 1965. The classical music establishment was starting to notice the Beatles at this point. Writing in the *Times* eighteen months earlier, the critic William Mann compared the songs of the Beatles with those of Schubert, but his was a lone appreciative voice. In the UK too, the writer given the task of reviewing popular records in the long-established *Gramophone* music magazine tore himself away from the easy-listening albums that were his usual fare just long enough to pen a few lines about *Help!* He did not think much of it. In this context, it is worth noting that a 1999 poll carried out by the BBC showed that a majority considered *Yesterday* to be the best song of the twentieth century.

BOB DYLAN   HIGHWAY 61 REVISITED

In July 1965, *Like A Rolling Stone* was issued as a single. It was an unprecedented six minutes long and it had a harder rock sound than anything already released by Bob Dylan, but it climbed into the top five in both the US and the UK, becoming the most successful single of Dylan's career. A solitary staccato snare drum hit and a bass drum kick usher in a striding, confident rock group sound, on a two chord vamp, anchored to a C in the bass, with a swirling organ adding distinction and a touch of fantasy. (It is the stuff of legend that this part was improvised by the young Al Kooper, muscling in on a session he was only supposed to be observing and on an instrument he had not previously played.) Even before Bob Dylan

```
US release      August 1965    Columbia    CS 9189 / CL 2389
UK release      August 1965    CBS         (S)BPG 62572

1. Like A Rolling Stone
2. Tombstone Blues
3. It Takes A Lot To Laugh, It Takes A Train To Cry
4. From A Buick 6
5. Ballad Of A Thin Man

6. Queen Jane Approximately
7. Highway 61 Revisited
8. Just Like Tom Thumb's Blues
9. Desolation Row

All songs composed by Bob Dylan

Bob Dylan: vocals, guitar, harmonica, piano / Mike Bloomfield: guitar / Charlie McCoy: guitar (9) / Al Kooper: organ / Paul Griffin: piano / Frank Owens: piano / Harvey Brooks: bass guitar / Joseph Macho Jr: bass guitar (1) / Russ Savakus: bass (9) / Bobby Gregg: drums / Bruce Langhorne: tambourine (1) / Bob Johnston: producer / Tom Wilson: producer (1)
```

starts singing, the listener feels that he is in the presence of something incendiary and new. Essentially, this is the first rock song – before this moment, even the Beatles, even the Rolling Stones were playing pop. When Dylan does start singing, the lyrics are finely judged and poetic, and they lead inexorably to an epic chorus, the kind that insists on audiences joining along: "How does it feel?!" Bob Dylan is sneering and he is ranting and he has never sounded so much in command, so magnificent. The song is chosen to open the proceedings on the *Highway 61 Revisited* album and, rather remarkably, the songs that follow keep the momentum and the sense of the new going through the rest of the album. Only *Desolation Row* presents a lighter sound, a return to all-acoustic playing to end the album. It achieves a distinction of its own, however, with its extraordinary length and its success in keeping the listener interested in the vivid imagery of the lyrics throughout the eleven minute marathon. The record is not perfect. *From A Buick 6* and the title track are the kind of blues filler that Dylan employed to pad out his earlier albums, although they are saved by the tumbling imagery of the lyrics and the energy. And Bobby Gregg's drumming is frequently ham-fisted to the point of becoming annoying. He appears to believe that the best way of making the music powerful is to simply hit everything as hard as possible, when a modicum of subtlety would actually be more effective. These are, however, minor complaints about an album that can claim to be the greatest set of music to have been released since the arrival of rock 'n' roll over a decade previously. Two more songs were recorded at the same sessions and issued as follow-up singles to *Like A Rolling Stone*. *Positively 4th Street* and *Can You Please Crawl Out Your Window* were not as successful, but are still remarkably compelling performances.

MILES DAVIS   E.S.P.

```
US release      August 1965    Columbia    CS 9150 / CL 2350
UK release      August 1965    CBS         (S)BPG 662577

1. E.S.P. (Miles Davis/Wayne Shorter)
2. Eighty-One (Miles Davis/Ron Carter)
3. Little One (Herbie Hancock/Miles Davis)
4. R.J. (Ron Carter)

5. Agitation (Miles Davis)
6. Iris (Wayne Shorter)
7. Mood (Ron Carter)

Miles Davis: trumpet / Wayne Shorter: tenor saxophone / Herbie Hancock: piano / Ron Carter: bass / Tony Williams: drums / Irving Townsend: producer
```

Wayne Shorter joined the Miles Davis group in September 1964, after several years playing with Art Blakey's Jazz Messengers, during which his reputation as one of the most impressive young saxophonists in jazz was established. Typically, Miles Davis took his newest recruit straight on to the concert stage, without any rehearsal. The first new music by the Quintet was recorded in three days, the following January, and released as the album *E.S.P.* The music is melodic and apparently based on shifting harmonies provided by the piano, except that it is very hard to work out exactly what these are. Only *Eighty-One*, which is clearly a blues, albeit one that is harmonised a little strangely, is at all easy to fathom. Meanwhile, Tony Williams' complex drumming underpins and drives everything along, using a variety of unpredictable rhythmic patterns. The album title is extremely appropriate, since the way the musicians are able to keep the music together despite the barest of actual structure suggests that they must have been in telepathic contact. Miles Davis later described the approach of his Quintet as being 'time, no changes'. He had little tolerance for the kind of avant garde jazz practised by the likes of Ornette Coleman or Albert Ayler and had previously sacked Sam Rivers as the saxophonist in his own group, for not being sufficiently melodic. In its own way, however, the music of *E.S.P.* is also a kind of jazz that is distinctly avant garde, but it does not immediately sound like it, which makes all the difference.

PAUL SIMON   THE PAUL SIMON SONGBOOK

UK release   August 1965   CBS   (S)BPG 62579
Not released in US

1. I Am A Rock
2. Leaves That Are Green
3. A Church Is Burning
4. April Come She Will
5. The Sound Of Silence
6. A Most Peculiar Man
7. He Was My Brother
8. Kathy's Song
9. The Side Of A Hill
10. A Simple Desultory Philippic
11. Flowers Never Bend With The Rainfall
12. Patterns

All compositions by Paul Simon (as Paul Kane on tracks 7 and 9)

Paul Simon: vocals, guitar / Reginald Warburton: producer / Stanley West: producer

During 1964 and 1965, Paul Simon lived in the UK, based for much of the time in Brentwood, Essex. He performed at Brentwood School for boys, at the invitation of future folk singer Nic Jones, then a pupil at the school and the organiser of the school folk club, and he began dating a girl from the Ursuline girls' school in the town, Kathy Chitty. She is pictured, along with Paul Simon himself, on the cover of a solo recording made by Simon in London, for the benefit of the fans who watched him perform at many folk clubs in London, Brentwood, and elsewhere. Most of the songs on *The Paul Simon Songbook* were subsequently re-recorded in a more elaborate manner with Art Garfunkel. Delivered here, simply by a man and his acoustic guitar, they are revealed as the work of a very accomplished songwriter. Paul Simon is working within the Bob Dylan tradition, but with a gentler approach and a much greater emphasis on attractive melody lines. The album was not a commercial success and Paul Simon himself became disenchanted with it, to the point where he blocked later attempts on the part of the record company to issue the record in the US. It remains, however, a delightful glimpse into the early creative world of one of the major talents of twentieth century songwriting. Kathy Chitty, celebrated in the lyrics of *Kathy's Song* and further mentioned in three more, chose to break off the relationship, rather than be forced to adopt a celebrity lifestyle. She was tracked down to her home in Wales by a journalist in 2014 and revealed, as a happily married grandmother, that she had no regrets.

SUN RA   THE HELIOCENTRIC WORLDS OF   VOLUME 1

US release   August 1965   ESP Disk 1014
UK release   1969   Fontana   STL 5514

1. Heliocentric
2. Outer Nothingness
3. Other Worlds
4. The Cosmos
5. Of Heavenly Things
6. Nebulae
7. Dancing In The Sun

All compositions by Sun Ra

Sun Ra: keyboards, percussion, producer / Danny Davis: flute, alto saxophone / Marshall Allen: piccolo, alto saxophone, percussion / John Gilmore: tenor saxophone, percussion / Pat Patrick: baritone saxophone, percussion / Robert Cummings: bass clarinet, percussion / Chris Capers: trumpet / Teddy Nance: trombone / Bernard Pettaway: bass trombone / Ronnie Boykins: bass / Jimhmi Johnson: percussion

From the mid-fifties until his death in 1993, the eccentric jazz bandleader Sun Ra, who claimed to have been born on Saturn, but was actually from Alabama (where he was known as Herman Blount), followed his own musical path with very little reference to what anyone else was doing. Enormously innovative – he was the first jazz musician to make extensive use of electric instruments, for example, and pioneered the wearing of elaborate stage costumes – Sun Ra released a huge number of albums, well over a hundred of them, mostly on his own El Saturn label. *The Heliocentric Worlds Of Sun Ra Vol.1* is one of his best known records (in so far as any of them are well known) because it was taken up by better organised record companies, although it is not particularly representative of the man's music overall. This is a ferociously avant garde affair, with the music ranging from solo electric keyboard tinkling, to dialogues for percussion and various wind instruments, like animal cries in the jungle, to dense work-outs for the entire band, engaging in collective improvisation at full tilt. Many of the musicians had played together for several years and they are able to interact with the same kind of musical telepathy as displayed by the more recently formed Miles Davis Quintet, although the sound they produce is rather different. Melody is not a major concern, but rather the effects produced by the juxtaposition of different timbres.

ARCHIE SHEPP   FIRE MUSIC

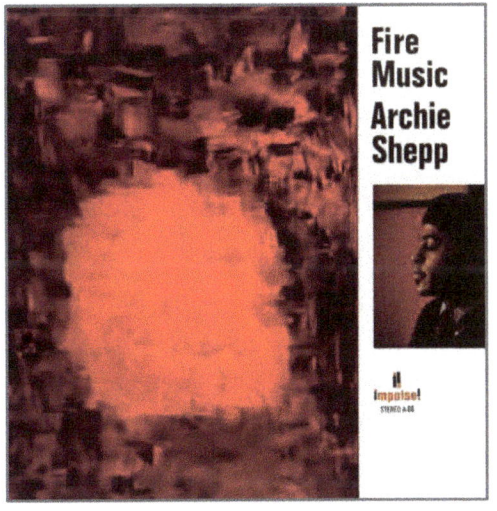

```
US release        August 1965      Impulse     A(S) 86
Not released in UK

1. Hambone (Archie Shepp)
2. Los Olvidados (Archie Shepp)

3. Malcolm, Malcolm, Semper Malcolm (Archie Shepp)
4. Prelude To A Kiss (Duke Ellington)
5. The Girl From Ipanema (Antonio Carlos Jobim/
                          Norman Gimbel/Vinicius De Moraes)

Archie Shepp: tenor saxophone, voice / Marion Brown:
alto saxophone / Ted Curson: trumpet / Joseph Orange:
trombone / Reggie Johnson: bass (1,2,4,5) / David Izenzon:
bass (3) / Joe Chambers: drums (1,2,4,5) / J.C.Moses:
drums (3) / Bob Thiele: producer
```

Archie Shepp is an avant garde tenor saxophonist, with both his own sound on his instrument and the approach of his band falling in between those of his contemporaries John Coltrane and Albert Ayler. *Fire Music* is the fourth album in which Shepp is involved, but the first to attract serious attention (if only due to the fascination of a scathing review in *Downbeat* magazine) and to establish the musician as a major player in his chosen genre. Much of the improvisation is collective, with Shepp's throaty-toned tenor saxophone rising out of the quirky, angular, written passages most often. The set includes two surprising standards, in which the familiar melodies can be easily distinguished, even if they are somewhat battered and distorted in the process. In dedicating one piece to black power activist Malcolm X, complete with a celebratory poem at the start, Archie Shepp had no hesitation in aligning himself with that movement. This was a logical extension of the significant black protest statements within jazz, as expressed some years earlier by such works as Billie Holiday's *Strange Fruit* and Max Roach's *Freedom Now Suite*.

DONOVAN   UNIVERSAL SOLDIER EP

```
UK release       August 1965      Pye      NEP 24219
Not released in US

1.  Universal Soldier (Buffy Sainte Marie)
2.  The Ballad Of A Crystal Man (Donovan)

3.  Do You Hear Me Now (Bert Jansch)
4.  The War Drags On (Mick Softley)

Donovan: vocals, guitar / Terry Kennedy: producer / Peter
Eden: producer / Geoff Stephens: producer
```

It would seem that Donovan, after being continually compared with Bob Dylan, decided to give further credence to the argument by recording a set of protest songs (ignoring the fact that Dylan himself was no longer doing this). The result is a powerful piece of vinyl, making a greater impact by embracing the concision of the EP format. The title track, which was a faithful cover of a song originally recorded by the Native American singer songwriter, Buffy Sainte Marie, became one of Donovan's most popular performances. His second album, *Fairytale*, was released the following October and included *The Ballad Of A Crystal Man*, but made less of an impression overall than the EP. The American version improved matters a little by also including *Universal Soldier*, which had been issued as a US single.

JAN AND DEAN   GOLDEN HITS VOLUME 2

```
US release       August 1965      Liberty    LST 7417/LRP 3417
UK release       August 1965      Liberty    LBY 1279

1.  Linda (Jack Lawrence)
2.  Surf City (Brian Wilson/Jan Berry)
3.  Honolulu Lulu (Jan Berry/Lou Adler/Roger Christian)
4.  Drag City (Brian Wilson/Jan Berry/Roger Christian)
5.  Dead Man's Curve (Brian Wilson/Jan Berry/Roger Christian/Artie Kornfeld)
6.  The New Girl In School (Brian Wilson/Jan Berry/Roger Christian/Bob Norman)

7.  The Little Old Lady From Pasadena (Don Altfeld/Roger Christian)
8.  The Anaheim, Azusa & Cucamonga Sewing Circle, Book Review & Timing
             Association (Don Altfeld/Jan Berry/Roger Christian)
9.  Ride The Wild Surf (Brian Wilson/Jan Berry/Roger Christian)
10. Sidewalk Surfin' (Brian Wilson/Roger Christian)
11. From All Over The World (P.F.Sloan/Steve Barri)
12. You Really Know How To Hurt A Guy (Jan Berry/Jill Gibson/Roger Christian)

Jan Berry: vocals, arranger, producer / Dean Torrence: vocals / similar musicians
as Beach Boys albums
```

Jan Berry and Dean Torrence achieved a certain amount of chart success in the US during the early sixties, but gained their biggest hits after they started to work with Brian Wilson. The songs have the same subject matter as those by the Beach Boys – surfing, cars, and generally being a teenager – and the music is close to being identical. All of the songs on *Golden Hits Volume 2* were US chart hits, some being listed in their own right even though they were the single B-sides, and *Surf City* reached number one. (*Volume 1* has the smaller hits from the pre-Brian Wilson days.) In a very real sense, Jan and Dean function as a Beach Boys tribute act, but the songs include many that are just as memorable as those by their heroes. The duo continued to perform music for many years after the hits stopped coming, even after Jan Berry was involved in a major car accident that left him brain damaged, but Berry and Torrence did not have the kind of creative minds that enabled Brian Wilson to move in a more ambitious direction.

THE ROLLING STONES   OUT OF OUR HEADS

```
UK release      September 1965    Decca    SKL/LK 4733
US release      July 1965         London   PS 429/LL 3429
Different cover and only six tracks in common with UK album. Four more
tracks appear on the US LP, December's Children, issued in December
1965. This has the same cover as the UK Out Of Our Heads

1. She Said Yeah (Sonny Bono/Roddy Jackson)
2. Mercy Mercy (Don Covay/Ronald Miller)
3. Hitch Hike (Clarence Paul/Marvin Gaye/William Stevenson)
4. That's How Strong My Love Is (Roosevelt Jamison)
5. Good Times (Sam Cooke)
6. Gotta Get Away (Mick Jagger/Keith Richard)

7. Talkin' 'Bout You (Chuck Berry)
8. Cry To Me (Bert Russell)
9. Oh Baby (We Got A Good Thing Going On) (Barbara Lynn Ozen)
10. Heart Of Stone (Mick Jagger/Keith Richard)
11. The Under Assistant West Coast Promotion Man (Rolling Stones)
12. I'm Free (Mick Jagger/Keith Richard)

Mick Jagger: vocals / Keith Richards: guitar, vocals / Brian Jones: guitar,
harmonica / Bill Wyman: bass guitar / Charlie Watts: drums / Ian Stewart:
piano, marimba (5) / Jack Nitzsche: organ (8) / Andrew Loog Oldham:
producer / Rolling Stones: producer
```

During 1965. the Rolling Stones became regular visitors to the top of the singles charts, with masterful songs written by the Jagger/Richards team – *The Last Time, Satisfaction,* and, shortly after the release of the third UK album, *Get Off My Cloud. Out Of Our Heads* is a much stronger collection of performances than its predecessor, but it is still dominated by the Stones' takes on a variety of R&B material. The group's songwriting energies would seem to have been largely exhausted by those vital singles. This was less apparent on the Rolling Stones' US albums, since those records include both sides of the singles, although in stretching the group's material over a larger number of albums, the American record company created further musical problems of its own. Andrew Oldham composed a sleeve essay, not as controversial as his words on the previous album, but still designed to make the release of the record seem of greater import than perhaps it really was. "The only message about this new ellpee is let's all live to enjoy it. And in the words of my local parson, if the bomb does go off, make sure you get higher than the bomb. It's the only way to go, and why not take this disc along – out of our heads."

OTIS REDDING   SINGS SOUL / OTIS BLUE

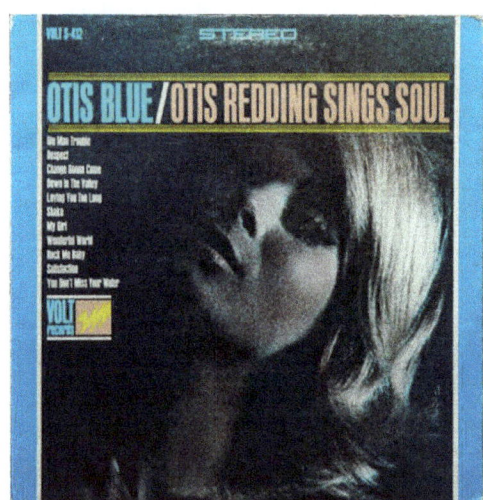

```
US release      September 1965    Volt       (S) 412
UK release      September 1965    Atlantic   SAL/ATL 5041

1. Ole Man Trouble (Otis Redding)
2. Respect (Otis Redding)
3. Change Gonna Come (Sam Cooke)
4. Down In The Valley (Solomon Burke)
5. I've Been Loving You Too Long (Jerry Butler/Otis Redding)

6. Shake (Sam Cooke)
7. My Girl (Ronald White/Smokey Robinson)
8. Wonderful World (Barbara Campbell)
9. Rock Me Baby (B.B.King/Joe Josea)
10. Satisfaction (Mick Jagger/Keith Richards)
11. You Don't Miss Your Water (William Bell)

Otis Redding: vocals / Steve Cropper: guitar / Booker T. Jones:
keyboards / Isaac Hayes: keyboards, producer / Gene Miller:
trumpet / Wayne Jackson: trumpet / Andrew Love: tenor
saxophone / Floyd Newman: baritone saxophone / Donald
Dunn: bass guitar / Al Jackson Jr: drums / Earl Sims: vocals / Jim
Stewart: producer / David Porter: producer
```

The Memphis recording studio was set up in 1960 and used by the recently established Stax record company to make soul records. The musicians responsible, under the name of the Mar-Keys, for a big instrumental hit in the US, *Last Night,* were employed to work on all the sessions. The rhythm section, without the brass instruments, achieved a big hit on its own as well, *Green Onions,* credited to Booker T and the MGs. Singer Otis Redding began recording for Stax (his records being issued on a new subsidiary label called Volt) in 1963 and the combination of his gruff, emotional vocals with the gritty rhythms and powerful brass seemed like a perfect match. *Otis Blue* was his third album and the most successful, reaching number one in the Billboard R&B LP chart and entering the National chart too. Three of its tracks became hit singles: *Respect, I've Been Loving You Too Long,* and *Shake.* The album also made a big impact in the UK, where it reached number six in the album chart, with two different tracks becoming hit singles, *My Girl* and *Satisfaction*. Redding's decision to record a version of the Rolling Stones song is remarkable for reversing the direction of the influence from American R&B to British beat. He very much succeeds in making the song his own and his mastery on the album generally had the effect of making him acclaimed as the finest male soul singer since the rise to fame of James Brown.

HERMAN'S HERMITS

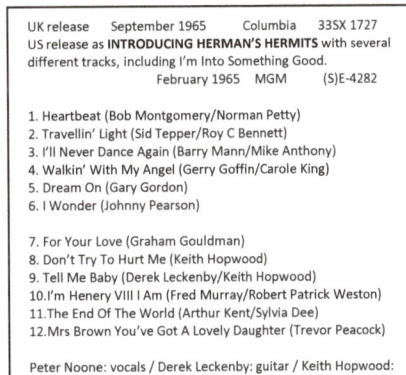

UK release   September 1965   Columbia   33SX 1727
US release as INTRODUCING HERMAN'S HERMITS with several different tracks, including I'm Into Something Good.
February 1965   MGM   (S)E-4282

1. Heartbeat (Bob Montgomery/Norman Petty)
2. Travellin' Light (Sid Tepper/Roy C Bennett)
3. I'll Never Dance Again (Barry Mann/Mike Anthony)
4. Walkin' With My Angel (Gerry Goffin/Carole King)
5. Dream On (Gary Gordon)
6. I Wonder (Johnny Pearson)

7. For Your Love (Graham Gouldman)
8. Don't Try To Hurt Me (Keith Hopwood)
9. Tell Me Baby (Derek Leckenby/Keith Hopwood)
10. I'm Henery VIII I Am (Fred Murray/Robert Patrick Weston)
11. The End Of The World (Arthur Kent/Sylvia Dee)
12. Mrs Brown You've Got A Lovely Daughter (Trevor Peacock)

Peter Noone: vocals / Derek Leckenby: guitar / Keith Hopwood: guitar / Karl Green: bass guitar / Barry Whitwam: drums / probably Nicky Hopkins: piano / Mickie Most: producer

Herman's Hermits, fronted by fifteen-year-old singer, Peter Noone, scored a number one UK hit in the autumn of 1964 with their first single, *I'm Into Something Good*, written by Carole King. The group favoured a light, pop version of British beat music, with little R&B influence at all. That first hit was a cover of a song recorded by a member of the Cookies, but the fact that one of the tracks on the debut album had been a pop hit for Cliff Richard and another was a mildly rocking update of a music hall song was far more significant. The group had several more UK hits during the next few years, though without ever reaching number one again. It did far better in the US, however, where the two novelty songs from the album, *I'm Henery VIII I Am* and *Mrs Brown You've Got A Lovely Daughter*, were both number one hits. For a little while, the group was considered as a serious rival to the Beatles, although its lack of songwriting expertise and its failure to progress beyond a comfortable soft rock formula eventually brought the success to an end.

FRANK SINATRA   SEPTEMBER OF MY YEARS

Frank Sinatra famously described rock 'n' roll as "the most brutal, ugly, desperate, vicious form of expression it has been my misfortune to hear". As late as 1967, he was reported as having smashed his car radio with his shoe when it kept playing a song he particularly disliked, *Light My Fire* by the Doors. Clearly, he was worried that his reign as the most successful singer in popular music was about to come to an end. In fact, he continued to sell very many records right up until his death in 1998. *September Of My Years* reached number five in the US album chart and the track *It Was A Very Good Year*

US release   September 1965   Reprise   (FS)1014
UK release   September 1965   Reprise   R9 1014

1. The September Of My Years (Jimmy Van Heusen / Sammy Cahn)
2. How Old Am I? (Gordon Jenkins)
3. Don't Wait Too Long (Sunny Skylar)
4. It Gets Lonely Early (Jimmy Van Heusen/Sammy Cahn)
5. This Is All I Ask (Gordon Jenkins)
6. Last Night When We Were Young (E.Y.Harburg/Harold Arlen)
7. The Man In The Looking Glass (Bart Howard)

8. It Was A Very Good Year (Ervin Drake)
9. When The Wind Was Green (Don Hunt)
10. Hello Young Lovers (Richard Rodgers/Oscar Hammerstein)
11. I See It Now (Alec Wilder/William Engvick)
12. Once Upon A Time (Charles Strouse/Lee Adams)
13. September Song (Kurt Weill/Maxwell Anderson)

Frank Sinatra: vocals / Gordon Jenkins: arranger, conductor / Sonny Burke: producer

was released as a single and was a hit too. The song was given two Grammy awards the following year. In the UK, both album and single did less well, but *It Was A Very Good Year* has acquired the status of one of Sinatra's most memorable and fondly regarded later performances regardless.

Robbie Williams obviously thought so, when he spliced a whole verse of Sinatra into his own interpretation of the song. When Frank Sinatra recorded the album, he was just about to celebrate his fiftieth birthday. The songs form a collective meditation on the ageing process and the fact that they must have seemed very personal pushes Sinatra into delivering some of his most heartfelt performances, demonstrating once again why he is considered to be such a sublime interpreter of song lyrics and melodies. As far as the purchasers of records by the Beatles and the Rolling

Stones were concerned, of course, this was indeed music for old people. Frank Sinatra at this time was not at all the epitome of cool that modern revisionists try to make him out to be. Removed from its context, however, *September Of My Years* remains a fine piece of work.

JAMES BROWN   PAPA'S GOT A BRAND NEW BAG

In February 1965, James Brown led his musicians in the recording of a song called *Papa's Got A Brand New Bag*. It is a crucial piece of music, because it marks the invention of the funk music style, that James Brown used as the basis for the rest of his career and became highly influential on a host of other musicians through the seventies and beyond. Although the band was a big one, it does not sound like it. The music has a spacious quality, with the instruments all contributing to the rhythm, rather than providing layers of texture. This is particularly apparent after the song proper is finished, but the band continues to play, with Brown cueing saxophonist Maceo Parker into a solo. The song is based on standard blues

```
US release     September 1965    King     (S) 938
UK release     September 1965    London   HA 8262    different cover

1. Papa's Got A Brand New Bag part 1 (James Brown)
2. Papa's Got A Brand New Bag part 2 (James Brown)
3. Mashed Potatoes USA (James Brown)
4. Cross Firing (James Brown)
5. Love Don't Love Nobody (Roy Brown)
6. I Stay In The Chapel Every Night (James Brown)

7. And I Do Just What I Want (James Brown)
8. This Old Heart (James Brown)
9. Baby, You're Right (James Brown/Joe Tex)
10. Have Mercy Baby (Billy Ward)
11. You Don't Have To Go (James Brown)
12. Doin' The Limbo (James Brown)
```

Personnel on tracks 1 & 2: James Brown: vocals, producer / Nat Jones: alto saxophone / Maceo Parker: tenor and baritone saxophones / St.Clair Pinckney: tenor saxophone / Eldee Williams: tenor saxophone / Al Clark: tenor saxophone / Joe Dupars: trumpet / Ron Tooley: trumpet / Levi Rasbury: trombone / Wilmer Milton: trombone / Jimmy Nolen: guitar / Nat Jones: organ / Sam Thomas: bass guitar / Melvin Parker: drums. Some of these musicians were overdubbed on to track 8.
Personnel on other tracks: James Brown: vocals, producer, organ (3,4), drums (12) / Johnny Terry: vocals (8) / Eugene Stalworth: vocals (8,11) / Bobby Bennett: vocals (8,11) / Bobby Byrd: vocals (6,11), organ (12) / James McGary: alto saxophone (8) / Alfred Corley: alto saxophone (5,7,9,11) / J.C.Davis: tenor saxophone (5,7,8,9,11) / St.Clair Pinckney: tenor saxophone (3,4,6,10,12) / Clifford MacMillan: tenor saxophone (3) / Al Clark: tenor & baritone saxophone (3,4,6,10,12) / Roscoe Patrick: trumpet (9,11,12) / Roosevelt Brown: trumpet (6) / Lewis Hamlin: trumpet (12) / Teddy Washington: trumpet (12) / Clarence Johnson: trombone (12) / Bobby Roach: guitar (8) / Les Buie: guitar (3-7,9-12) / Sonny Thompson: piano (8,9), producer (5,7,9) / Alvin Gonder: keyboards (6,11) / Bernard Odum: bass guitar (8) / Hubert Lee Parry: bass guitar (3-7,9-12) / Clayton Fillyua: drums (3) / Nat Kendrick: drums (4-12) / Hal Neely: producer (11)

chords, but for the extended coda, the chord changes are abandoned, as a groove based on just one chord is established. The rhythm is made up of four distinct ingredients, with none predominating. A light, jazz-inflected drum pattern is delivered by Melvin Parker (Maceo's brother), without any particular beat in the bar being emphasised. This is not the backbeat familiar to all rock 'n' roll players, where the second and fourth beats in each bar are stressed. Sam Thomas plays a dancing bass riff, placed in the middle of each bar, while the rhythm guitar strikes a staccato chord, using just two or three strings and placed well back in the mix, so that although Jimmy Nolen does indeed play on the second and fourth beats, he does not succeed in making this the major emphasis in the music. The brass section, playing tightly enough to sound like a single, albeit many-throated musician, compresses a triplet into a single pulse, adding its weight to the guitarist on the second beat of the bar. Although the one-chord structure Maceo Parker is working with for his solo is derived from the work of John Coltrane, Parker does not play like this, preferring to use short notes and brief phrases, so as not to divert attention from the groove. James Brown exhorts and directs the soloist and the other players throughout, to make it clear that what is happening musically is entirely under his command. The music was speeded up slightly for single release, spread over both sides. It became Brown's first US top ten entry, hit number one in the R&B charts, and gained a Grammy award for best rhythm and blues record of 1965. The song even scraped into the UK top thirty for the first time, inspiring the influential TV show, *Ready Steady Go*, to present a James Brown special the following March. Both sides of the single are placed at the beginning of the album titled after it and they succeed in making the album essential just on their own. Which is just as well, because rather than attempting to create further examples of the 'new bag', Brown fills the record with an assortment or lesser known vintage tracks, with recording dates varying between 1959 and 1962. The singer is incapable of producing a bad performance, but in the context of the major leap forward he had just achieved with the hit single, these songs seem irrelevant. James Brown was not at all unusual at this time in channelling most of his energies into the production of hit singles, but to allow an album to be released that is so blatantly made up of filler could have seriously undermined Brown's standing as a great artist.

MANFRED MANN   MANN MADE

UK release	October 1965	HMV	CSD 1628 / CLP 1911
US release	November 1965	Ascot	ALS/ALM 13024

1. Since I Don't Have You (Janet Vogel/Jimmy Beaumont/Joe Rock/John Taylor/Joseph Verscharen/Lennie Martin/Walter Lester)
2. You're For Me (Mike Vickers)
3. Look Away (Bert Russell/Norman Meade)
4. The Abominable Snowman (Mike Vickers)
5. Watch Your Step (Bobby Parker)
6. Stormy Monday Blues (T-Bone Walker)
7. I Really Do Believe (Paul Jones)

8. Hi Lili Hi Lo (Bronislaw Kaper/Helen Deitsch)
9. The Way You Do The Things You Do (Robert Rogers/Smokey Robinson)
10. Bare Hugg (Mike Hugg)
11. You Don't Know Me (Cindy Walker/Eddy Arnold)
12. L.S.D. (Tom McGuinness)
13. I'll Make It Up To You (Ben Raleigh/Norman Meade)

Paul Jones: vocals, harmonica / Manfred Mann: keyboards, vocals / Mike Vickers: guitar, saxophones, flute, vocals / Tom McGuinness: bass guitar, vocals / Mike Hugg: drums, vibes / John Burgess: producer

There is little sense of development from the first Manfred Mann LP to this one, and certainly no tracks as memorable as the singles, with which the group was gaining considerable chart success. The jazz influence is there as before, but overall the band is starting to move away from rhythm and blues towards a more straightforward pop approach. Mike Vickers emerges as the strongest musical voice, with his work on guitar, saxophones, and flute. He experiments with multiple overdubbing in places, turning himself into a one-man brass section. He must have felt himself to be restricted nevertheless, as soon after *Mann Made* was released, he left the band in order to set himself up as an independent arranger. It was a testament to his important role in the band that we was replaced by *three* new members. *Pretty Flamingo*, which was released the following April and included on the Canadian version of the LP, was released with the new line-up in place and, perhaps sadly for Mike Vickers, became Manfred Mann's biggest hit single to date. While wondering how the simple mid-tempo ballad chosen to open the album could possibly have needed seven songwriters for its construction (five of them being the members of the Skyliners vocal group which had scored a US hit with the song in 1958), modern listeners should be aware that the title of the Tom McGuinness song included on the second side refers to pounds, shillings, and pence and is not an unusually prescient tribute to a hallucinatory drug.

THE PAUL BUTTERFIELD BLUES BAND

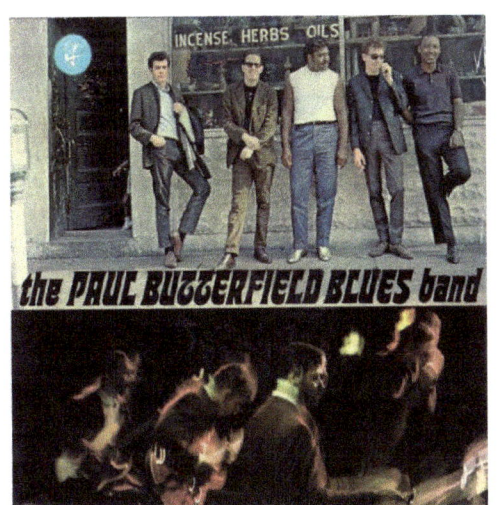

US release	October 1965	Elektra	EKS7294 / EKL 294
UK release	October 1965	Elektra	EKS7294 / EKL 294

1. Born In Chicago (Nick Gravenites)
2. Shake Your Money-Maker (Elmore James)
3. Blues With A Feeling (Little Walter Jacobs)
4. Thank You Mr Poobah (Bloomfield/Butterfield/Naftalin)
5. I Got My Mojo Working (Muddy Waters)
6. Mellow Down Easy (Willie Dixon)

7. Screamin' (Mike Bloomfield)
8. Our Love Is Drifting (Paul Butterfield/Elvin Bishop)
9. Mystery Train (Junior Parker/Sam Phillips)
10. Last Night (Little Walter Jacobs)
11. Look Over Yonders Wall (James Clark)

Paul Butterfield: vocals, harmonica / Mike Bloomfield: guitar / Elvin Bishop: guitar / Mark Naftalin: organ / Jerome Arnold: bass guitar / Sam Lay: drums, vocals (5) / Paul Rothchild: producer

It has been frequently maintained that, although people like Alexis Korner, John Mayall, Eric Clapton, and the Rolling Stones might perform using the blues style, their music could never really *be* the blues, because they were not African-American and were not part of the appropriate culture and experience. The argument became a little harder to sustain in the case of the American Paul Butterfield Blues Band. Hailing from Chicago, the home of the urban blues, Butterfield had fearlessly taken his harmonica into the city's blues clubs and learned to play the music first-hand, with the masters of the genre as his tutors. His playing skill very quickly overcame any problems arising from the fact that he had, in this context, the wrong skin colour. Forming his own blues band in 1963, Butterfield was able to persuade the bass player and drummer from Howlin' Wolf's band to join, by the simple expedient of offering them more money. By the time the group succeeded in recording an album they liked (on the third time of trying), guitarist Mike Bloomfield had already played on *Like A Rolling Stone* and other vital Bob Dylan recordings, and, together with Jerome Arnold and Sam Lay, had backed Dylan at the Newport folk festival in July. This was a performance that delighted many in the audience, but infuriated others, who could not abide the use of electric instruments in a folk concert. The music on the *Paul Butterfield Blues Band* album is exciting, mostly uptempo electric blues, in which Bloomfield and Butterfield deliver highly accomplished and frequently thrilling solos on every track. Bloomfield turns his amplifier up high and although his guitar does not achieve the thick overdriven sustain that Eric Clapton had started to use in his live performances with John Mayall's Bluesbreakers, it nevertheless cuts through the music with an authority unheard on any beat album released up to this time.

SONNY & CHER   LOOK AT US

US release   October 1965   Atco   (SD) 33-177
UK release   October 1965   Atlantic   SAL / ATL 5036

1. I Got You Babe (Sonny Bono)
2. Unchained Melody (Alex North/Hy Zaret)
3. Then He Kissed Me (Ellie Greenwich/Jeff Barry/Phil Spector)
4. Sing C'est La Vie (Brian Stone/Charles Greene/Sonny Bono)
5. It's Gonna Rain (Sonny Bono)
6. 500 Miles (Hedy West)

7. Just You (Sonny Bono)
8. The Letter (Dewey Terry/Don Sugarcane Harris)
9. Let It Be Me (Gilbert Becaud/Mann Curtis)
10. You Don't Love Me (Tommy Raye)
11. You've Really Got A Hold On Me (Smokey Robinson)
12. Why Don't They Let Us Fall In Love (Greenwich/Barry/Spector)

Sonny Bono: vocals, producer / Cher Bono: vocals / Barney Kessel: guitar / Don Peake: guitar / Howard Roberts: guitar / Monte Dunn: guitar / Steve Mann: guitar / Don Randi: piano / Harold Battiste: piano, arranger / Mike Rubini: harpsichord / Cliff Hils: bass guitar / Lyle Ritz: bass guitar / Earl Palmer: drums / Frank Capp: drums / Hal Blaine: drums / Gene Estes: percussion / Brian Stone: percussion / uncredited oboe on track 1

Sonny Bono and Cher Sarkisian were both involved in recording with Phil Spector and soon became a couple, despite an eleven year age-gap. They made a number of singles during 1964 as Caesar and Cleo, but without success. *I Got You Babe* did the trick, with an insanely catchy chorus featuring a prominent figure played on the oboe, a distinctly unusual instrument on any kind of popular music record. Credited to the duo's real names, the record reached number one in both the US and the UK, selling over a million copies in America alone. Both performers favoured the Bob Dylan approach to singing and Cher gained a solo hit with her version of Dylan's *All I Really Want To Do*. Sonny had a solo hit too, *Laugh At Me* elaborating on his persona as a misunderstood teen rebel, introduced on *I Got You Babe*. He was thirty years old. The album put together round the Sonny & Cher hit single is undistinguished, but managed to sell over seven million copies regardless. The couple divorced in 1975 and Cher eventually regained an even greater success as an international star than she had enjoyed during the sixties, having somehow acquired an impressive singing voice along the way. Sonny moved into politics, becoming a Republican member of the House of Representatives until his death in a skiing accident in 1998.

JOAN BAEZ   FAREWELL ANGELINA

US release   October 1965   Vanguard   VSD-79200/VRS-9200
UK release   October 1965   Fontana   (S)TFL 6058

1. Farewell Angelina (Bob Dylan)
2. Daddy, You Been On My Mind (Bob Dylan)
3. It's All Over Now, Baby Blue (Bob Dylan)
4. The Wild Mountain Thyme (Traditional)
5. Ranger's Command (Woody Guthrie)
6. Colours (Donovan)

7. A Satisfied Mind (Joe Hayes/Jack Rhodes)
8. The River In The Pines (Traditional)
9. Pauvre Ruteboeuf (Leo Ferré/Ruteboeuf)
10. Sagt Mir wo die Blumen Sind (Where Have All The Flowers Gone) (Pete Seeger)
11. A Hard Rain's A-Gonna Fall (Bob Dylan)

Joan Baez: vocals, guitar / Bruce Langhorne: guitar (2,3,6,7,11) / Ralph Rinzler: mandolin (7) / Richard Romoff: bass (4,10) / Russ Savakus: bass / Maynard Solomon: producer

Joan Baez makes a very tentative move towards folk rock, adding Bruce Langhorne's gentle electric guitar on several tracks, although there are no drums and the occasional bass players use the acoustic instrument. The traditional material with which she made her name is very much in the minority now and she includes four songs by Bob Dylan, placing three of them together to make a particularly strong opening for the album as a whole. The album sold as well as its predecessor, *Joan Baez 5*, achieving high placings in the album charts in both the US and the UK.

THE KINKS   THE KINK KONTROVERSY

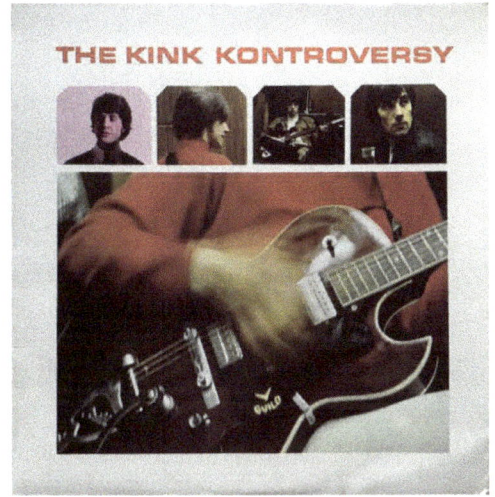

```
UK release      November 1965    Pye        N(S)PL 18131
US release      November 1965    Reprise    R(S)-6197

1.  Milk Cow Blues (Sleepy John Estes or Kokomo Arnold)
2.  Ring The Bells (Ray Davies)
3.  Gotta Get The First Plane Home (Ray Davies)
4.  When I See That Girl Of Mine (Ray Davies)
5.  I Am Free (Dave Davies)
6.  Till The End Of The Day (Ray Davies)

7.  The World Keeps Going Round (Ray Davies)
8.  I'm On An Island (Ray Davies)
9.  Where Have All The Good Times Gone (Ray Davies)
10. It's Too Late (Ray Davies)
11. What's In Store For Me (Ray Davies)
12. You Can't Win (Ray Davies)

Ray Davies: vocals, guitar, harmonica / Dave Davies: vocals,
guitar / Peter Quaife: bass guitar, vocals / Mick Avory: drums
(1,2,9), percussion / Clem Cattini: drums (3-8,10-12) / Nicky
Hopkins: piano / Rasa Davies: vocals (6,9) / Shel Talmy:
producer, guitar (10)
```

The roughness is becoming a characteristic sound of the Kinks' music. Even when switching to acoustic guitars, as the Davies brothers do on a few of the tracks on this third group album, the music still has an abrasiveness and a toughness quite different to the smoother approach that the Beatles brought to the same instrumentation. Inevitably, the track released as a single, *Till The End Of The Day*, is the most distinctive, but *Where Have All The Good Times Gone*, its anthemic B-side, *I'm On An Island*, with its hints of calypso, and *The World Keeps Going Round*, with a spacious harmony at the end of its chorus that would be described as 'psychedelic' a year or so later, are almost as good. Overall, *The Kink Kontroversy* is not really a classic album, but still provides enough worthwhile music to make it clear that the Kinks have enough talent to keep them moving forward.

THE LOVIN' SPOONFUL   DO YOU BELIEVE IN MAGIC

```
US release    November 1965    Kama Sutra    KLP(S) 8050
UK release    November 1965    Pye           NPL 28069

1.  Do You Believe In Magic (John Sebastian)
2.  Blues In The Bottle (Traditional)
3.  Sportin' Life (Traditional)
4.  My Gal (Traditional)
5.  You Baby (Barry Mann/Cynthia Weil/Phil Spector)
6.  Fishin' Blues (Traditional)

7.  Did You Ever Have To Make Up Your Mind (John Sebastian)
8.  Wild About My Lovin' (Traditional)
9.  Other Side Of This Life (Fred Neil)
10. Younger Girl (John Sebastian)
11. On The Road Again (John Sebastian)
12. Night Owl Blues (John Sebastian)

John Sebastian: vocals, guitar, autoharp, harmonica / Zalman
Yanovsky: guitar, vocals / Steve Boone: bass guitar, vocals /
Joe Butler: drums, vocals / Erik Jacobsen: producer
```

Like the Byrds, the Lovin' Spoonful had its roots in folk music, and the group has a lighter sound than the other American bands attempting to counter the flow of British beat. This is especially noticeable in the various blues performances included on the group's first album, which owe far more to the traditional Southern jug bands than to the modern Chicago urban blues inspiring many of the British groups. The songs are all credited as 'traditional', avoiding the need to worry about contentious songwriting claims on songs going back several decades, despite versions by the likes of Brownie McGhee, Henry Thomas, and Lightnin' Hopkins being readily available. Most interesting, however, are John Sebastian's own compositions. The first three included on the album are highly memorable songs, two of which became big American hits when issued as singles, while the third, *Younger Girl*, was covered by the Critters and taken into the charts by them. In the UK, the songs received extensive airplay on the pirate stations Radio London and Radio Caroline, but still managed to avoid going anywhere near the charts.

THE YARDBIRDS   HAVING A RAVE UP

The chaotic state of the Yardbirds' recording catalogue, which has been a feature of the group's discography for half a century, is epitomised by this LP release. The first side comprises songs made with lead guitarist Jeff Beck, including the group's most recent singles. The opening track was recycled as the B-side to the next single, the ground-breaking *Shapes Of Things* (with which the group invented the high-powered psychedelic genre later known as freakbeat), although that crucial song was recorded too late to be included on the album. The second side presents an assortment of live recordings already issued as part of the *Five Live Yardbirds* LP, with Eric Clapton on lead guitar. The LP sleeve-notes entirely fail to make clear what is going on, ironically enough referring to the old tracks with a guitarist no longer in the band as 'the sound of the

THE GOLDEN AGE OF ROCK Volume One 1963-1968

```
US release      November 1965    Epic    BN 26177 / LN 24177
Not issued in UK

1. You're A Better Man Than I (Mike Hugg)
2. Evil Hearted You (Graham Gouldman)
3. I'm A Man (Bo Diddley)
4. Still I'm Sad (Jim McCarty/Paul Samwell-Smith)
5. Heart Full Of Soul (Graham Gouldman)
6. The Train Kept A-Rollin' (Tiny Bradshaw/Lois Mann/Howard Kay)

7. Smokestack Lightning (Howlin' Wolf)
8. Respectable (Isley Brothers)
9. I'm A Man (Bo Diddley)
10. Here 'Tis (Bo Diddley)

Keith Relf: vocals, harmonica / Jeff Beck: guitar (1-6) / Eric Clapton:
guitar (7-10) / Chris Dreja: guitar / Paul Samwell-Smith: bass guitar,
vocals / Jim McCarty: drums, vocals / Ron Prentice: bass guitar (5) /
Giorgio Gomelsky: vocals (4), producer
```

future'. As it happens, the music on side one is outstanding, with inventive songwriting being uplifted by Jeff Beck's extraordinary guitar playing, utilising a biting tone and a sustain that nobody else (apart from Eric Clapton in his work subsequent to what is included on the album) was managing to achieve.

THE TEMPTATIONS   TEMPTIN'

```
US release      November 1965    Gordy    G/S 914
UK release      November 1965    Tamla Motown    (S)TML 11023

1. Since I Lost My Baby (Smokey Robinson/Pete Moore)
2. The Girl's Alright With Me (Norman Whitfield/Eddie Holland/Eddie Kendricks)
3. Just Another Lonely Night (Ivy Jo Hunter/Mickey Stevenson)
4. My Baby (Smokey Robinson/Pete Moore/Bobby Rogers)
5. You've Got To Earn It (Smokey Robinson/Cornelius Grant)
6. Everybody Needs Love (Norman Whitfield/Eddie Holland)

7. Girl (Why You Wanna Make Me Blue) (Whitfield/Holland)
8. Don't Look Back (Smokey Robinson/Ronnie White)
9. I Gotta Know Now (Norman Whitfield/Eddie Holland)
10. Born To Love You (Ivory Jo Hunter / Mickey Stevenson)
11. I'll Be In Trouble (Smokey Robinson)
12. You're The One I Need (Smokey Robinson)

David Ruffin: vocals / Eddie Kendricks: vocals / Paul Williams: vocals / Melvin
Franklin: vocals / Otis Williams: vocals / Jimmy Ruffin: vocals (10) / The Andantes
– Jackie Hicks, Marlene Barrow, Louvain Demps: vocals / musicians as on
following Miracles album / Smokey Robinson: producer
```

The Temptations were originally brought together in the late fifties as the Primes, alongside a female group called the Primettes, who eventually became the Supremes. The group did not achieve its first hit until 1964, with the Smokey Robinson produced *The Way You Do The Things You Do,* but after that it was seldom out of the charts until the mid-seventies. *Temptin'* was the group's third album, and a hit in its own right, as well as including four single hits, *I'll Be In Trouble, Girl (Why You Wanna Make Me Blue), Since I Lost My Baby,* and *My Baby*. The other two big hits from this period, *My Girl* and *It's Growing,* are to be found on the previous album, *The Temptations Sing Smokey,* issued in March. More than the other Motown artists, the Temptations were very much an outlet for the songwriters and producers who worked with them. They deliver the songs with considerable artistry, but without seeming to put a particularly distinctive stamp on them. This was due to the fact that, in contrast to the other vocal groups signed to Berry Gordy's Motown labels, the Temptations used different members as the lead singer on different songs. Eventually, the fact that all of them were strong singers would enable producer Norman Whitfield to work with the group on some particularly memorable music, but that remained in the future in 1965.

SMOKEY ROBINSON AND THE MIRACLES   GOING TO A GO-GO

```
US release      November 1965    Tamla    T(S)-267
UK release      November 1965    Tamla Motown    (S)TML 11024

1. The Tracks Of My Tears (Robinson/Marvin Tarplin/Warren Moore)
2. Going To A Go-Go (Robinson/Tarplin/Moore/Bobby Rogers)
3. Ooo Baby Baby (Smokey Robinson/Warren Moore)
4. My Girl Has Gone (Robinson/Tarplin/Moore/Rogers)
5. In Case You Need Love (Smokey Robinson)
6. Choosey Beggar (Smokey Robinson/Warren Moore)

7. Since You Won My Heart (Smokey Robinson/Mickey Stevenson)
8. From Head To Toe (Smokey Robinson/Bobby Rogers)
9. All That's Good (Smokey Robinson/Warren Moore)
10. My Baby Changes Like The Weather (Frank Wilson/Hal Davis)
11. Let Me Have Some (Smokey Robinson/Bobby Rogers)
12. A Fork In The Road (Robinson/Ronnie White/Moore)

Smokey Robinson: vocals, producer / Ronnie White: vocals / Bobby
Rogers: vocals / Warren Moore: vocals / Claudette Robinson: vocals /
Marvin Tarplin: guitar / Earl Van Dyke: keyboards / James Jamerson:
bass guitar / Benny Benjamin: drums / Jack Ashford: percussion /
Eddie Brown: percussion / others / members of the Detroit
Symphony Orchestra, directed by Gordon Staples / Frank Wilson:
producer / Mickey Stevenson: producer
```

It was Smokey Robinson who advised Berry Gordy to start the Tamla label and who gave the record company its first million selling hit, *Shop Around,* issued by Robinson's group, the Miracles, in 1960. *Going To A Go-Go* was the group's ninth album, the first to elevate Robinson's name to equal billing with that of the group,

66

and the first to achieve conspicuous chart success. Four of its tracks were released as singles and did well in both the R&B and National charts in the US, while *The Tracks Of My Tears* became a top ten hit in the UK too, although, for some reason, it took four years for this to happen. The group's music is quintessential Motown, with smooth harmonies supporting Smokey's immediately distinctive voice, which is apparently able to hit the highest notes without entering a falsetto register. A large number of musicians, usually including string players, are employed to flesh out the sound. Smokey favours a higher proportion of ballads than his label-mates, but whatever the tempo, the powerful lines of Motown's star bass player, James Jamerson, provide a crucial underpinning. Curiously, Smokey's wife, Claudette, can easily be heard singing on the Miracles' songs, but she was seldom photographed with the group or performed live.

JIMMY SMITH   ORGAN GRINDER SWING

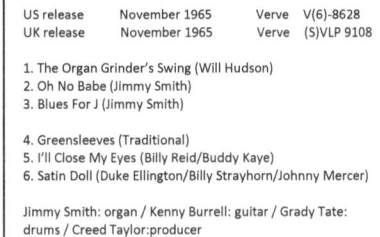

US release   November 1965   Verve   V(6)-8628
UK release   November 1965   Verve   (S)VLP 9108

1. The Organ Grinder's Swing (Will Hudson)
2. Oh No Babe (Jimmy Smith)
3. Blues For J (Jimmy Smith)
4. Greensleeves (Traditional)
5. I'll Close My Eyes (Billy Reid/Buddy Kaye)
6. Satin Doll (Duke Ellington/Billy Strayhorn/Johnny Mercer)

Jimmy Smith: organ / Kenny Burrell: guitar / Grady Tate: drums / Creed Taylor: producer

Jimmy Smith was a prolific artist and in the year following the release of his best-selling album, *The Cat*, he recorded three more albums before this one. *Who's Afraid Of Virginia Woolf*, recorded with a big band under the direction of Oliver Nelson and Claus Ogerman, was another big seller. For *Organ Grinder Swing*, he returns to the trio format with which he had made his name. There is no bass player, because Smith fills the lower register with the pedals of his Hammond organ. Kenny Burrell is a fine second soloist, and within a trio he is able to make his presence felt even more than on his own *Guitar Forms* album, where his playing is swathed within orchestral arrangements. He rises to the challenge by employing a rather more biting tone than before. Jimmy Smith himself is able to shine too, easily making the listener aware that he is in the company of a master musician. Hammond organ aficionados like Georgie Fame and Graham Bond, and future stars Keith Emerson, Jon Lord, and Brian Auger would have been listening very closely. *Organ Grinder Swing* became a top twenty album in the US, selling almost as many copies as *The Cat*.

MICHAEL GARRICK SEXTET   PROMISES

UK release   November 1965   Argo   (Z)DA 36
Not released in US

1. Promises
2. Parting Is Such
3. I've Got Rhythm (George and Ira Gershwin)
4. A Thing Of Beauty
5. Merlin The Wizard
6. Second Coming
7. Requiem
8. Leprechaun Leap
9. Portrait Of A Young Lady
10. Song By The Sea

All compositions apart from track 3 by Michael Garrick

Michael Garrick: piano, electric piano (10) / Ian Carr: trumpet, flugelhorn / Joe Harriott: alto saxophone / Tony Coe: tenor saxophone, clarinet / Coleridge Goode: bass (1,2,5-9) / Dave Green: bass (3,4,10) / Colin Barnes: drums / Harley Usill: producer

For Michael Garrick's second album for Argo, trumpeter Ian Carr was brought in to replace Shake Keane, who was playing elsewhere. Three tracks, those where Dave Green plays bass, are by a trio, but the rest feature a sextet, with three horns in the front line. They are, however, employed for the sake of their tonal variety, not for making the music sound particularly powerful. Much of Garrick's writing consists of bright, happy melodies with the blues tonality stripped out, so that the music has a somewhat different character to most other jazz, even while sounding as though it belongs to the same modern jazz genre. The soloists, including Michael Garrick himself (switching to the electric version of his instrument for just one track) meet the challenge presented very well indeed, helping to create music that provides a distinctly British slant on an American form.

THE McCOYS   HANG ON SLOOPY

US release   November 1965   Bang   BLP(S)-212
UK release   November 1965   Immediate   IMLP 001

1. Meet The McCoys
2. Hang On Sloopy (Wes Farrell/Bert Russell)
3. Fever (Eddie Cooley/John Davenport)
4. Sorrow (Bob Feldman/Jerry Goldstein/Richard Gottehrer)
5. If You Tell A Lie (Feldman/Goldstein/Gottehrer)
6. I Don't Mind (James Brown)
7. Stubborn Kind Of Fellow (Marvin Gaye/Mickey Stevenson/George Gordy)
8. I Can't Help Fallin' In Love (George Weiss/Hugo Peretti/Luigi Creatore)
9. All I Really Want To Do (Bob Dylan)
10. Papa's Got A Brand New Bag (James Brown)
11. I Can't Explain It (Feldman/Goldstein/Gottehrer)
12. High Heel Sneakers (Robert Higginbotham)
13. Stormy Monday Blues (T-Bone Walker)

Richard Zehringer: vocals, guitar / Ronnie Brandon: organ, vocals / Randy Hobbs: bass guitar, vocals / Randy Zehringer: drums, vocals / Bassett Hand: brass arrangements / Bob Feldman, Jerry Goldstein, Richard Gottehrer: producers

The McCoys recorded an updated version of the Kingsmen's *Louie Louie*, called *Hang On Sloopy*, with a new melody and new words over the same chords, and were rewarded with a number one million seller in the US. In the UK too, the single reached the top five. The album produced around the hit single starts off with guitarist Richard Zehringer (later to change his name to the more user-friendly Rick Derringer) literally introducing the members of the band, who each play for a few seconds. This gives the impression that the listener is about to experience the work of a decent bar band, an impression that is confirmed by the efficient pop covers that follow. The version of *Fever*, however, is rather good, turning the Peggy Lee classic into an effective piece of beat music. It was issued as a second single and did well in the US charts, though without matching the sales of *Hang On Sloopy*. On several tracks, including both singles, Richard Zehringer shows himself to be a pretty good guitarist, with the ability to create fine, original solos. *Sorrow*, a song written by the album's production team, was itself treated to a cover version and taken into the UK charts six months later by the Merseys. The first single and album by the McCoys were the first releases in the UK on the new Immediate record label, formed by the manager of the Rolling Stones, Andrew Loog Oldham.

THE SORROWS   TAKE A HEART

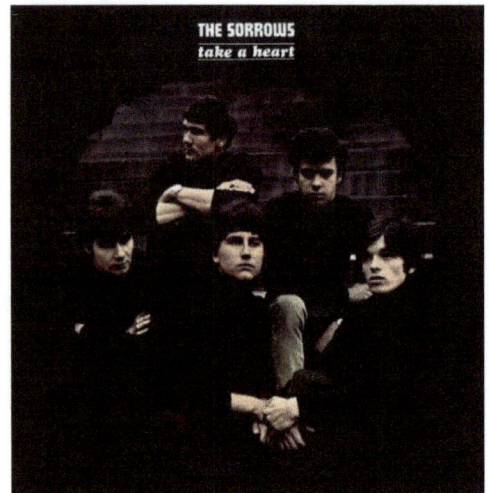

UK release   November 1965   Piccadilly   N(S)PL 38023
Not issued in US

1. Baby (Clive Westlake/Mort Shuman)
2. No No No (Don Fardon/Pip Whitcher)
3. Take A Heart (Miki Dallon)
4. She's Got The Action (Miki Dallon)
5. How Love Used To Be (Michael Redfern/Richard O'Sullivan)
6. Teenage Letter (Renald Richard)
7. I Don't Wanna Be Free (Don Fardon/Pip Whitcher)
8. Don't Sing No Sad Songs For Me (Al Stillman/Joey Brooks)
9. Cara-Lin (Bob Feldman/Jerry Goldstein/Richard Gottehrer)
10. We Should Get Along Fine (Don Fardon/Pip Whitcher)
11. Come With Me (Zakss/Formula 5)
12. Let Me In (Miki Dallon)

Don Maughn (Don Fardon): vocals / Pip Whitcher: guitar / Wez Price: guitar / Philip Packham: bass guitar / Bruce Finley: drums / John Schroeder: producer

The failure of the Sorrows to achieve great stardom is a considerable mystery, given that the group's brand of rhythm and blues is harder and more powerful than either the Rolling Stones or the Pretty Things, and does not rely on cover versions of American originals. The brooding roller-coaster that is *Take A Heart* is one of the most impressive singles of its time, yet could manage no higher than number twenty-one in the UK chart. The group's storming album has no weak tracks, with the possible exception of *We Should Get Along Fine*, which is the only song to descend into relatively mundane harmony pop. The song was written by members of the group, whose lack of expertise in this direction might have been at least part of the problem. The Sorrows did not make another album and lead singer Don Fardon left the following year. Ironically, he scored a number three hit in 1970 with *Indian Reservation*, a song that, stripped of its brass section, would have suited the Sorrows very well.

THE PRETTY THINGS   GET THE PICTURE?

With drummer Viv Prince becoming increasingly unreliable, the Pretty Things were forced to find alternatives for much of the group's second album. Regardless, *Get The Picture?* is a remarkably hip record, with the R&B underpinning largely abandoned in favour of a more generalised kind of driving beat music without blues chord changes. Dick Taylor's lead guitar dominates the proceedings, complete with a newly-acquired fuzz box in places and a touch of feedback at the

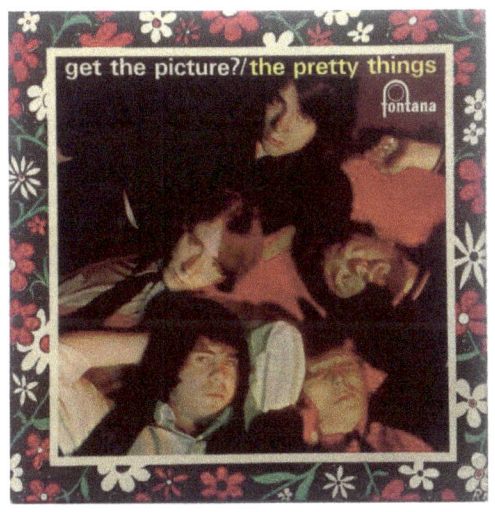

```
UK release      December 1965     Fontana    TL 5280
Not released in US

1. You Don't Believe Me (Phil May/Wandra Merrell/Bobby Graham/Jimmy Page)
2. Buzz The Jerk (Dick Taylor/Phil May)
3. Get The Picture? (Dick Taylor/Phil May)
4. Can't Stand The Pain (Dick Taylor/Phil May/Bobby Graham)
5. Rainin' In My Heart (James Moore/Jerry West)
6. We'll Play House (Dick Taylor/Phil May/Fred Gandy/John Alder)

7. You'll Never Do It Baby (Brian Smith/Terry Fox)
8. I Had A Dream (Jimmy Witherspoon)
9. I Want Your Love (Jack Tarr/Johnnie Dee)
10. London Town (Dick Taylor)
11. Cry To Me (Bert Russell)
12. Gonna Find Me A Substitute (Ike Turner)

Phil May: vocals / Dick Taylor: guitar / Brian Pendleton: guitar, vocals / John Stax: bass guitar, vocals / Viv Prince: drums / Bobby Graham: drums, producer / John Alder (Twink): drums / Jimmy Page: guitar / uncredited piano (4,8) possibly Arthur Greenslade / Glyn Johns: producer
```

beginning of *We'll Play House*. The result is an altogether stronger collection of music than to be found on the albums delivered by Taylor's former group, the Rolling Stones, although it was much less successful commercially. *Get The Picture?* did not appear in the UK album charts, and it was not even released in the US. It did not help that the Pretty Things were much less accomplished when it came to producing singles. *Cry To Me* had been chosen from this album and it is one of the least distinguished tracks here – it was no match for the Stones' *Satisfaction*, released at about the same time.

THE BEATLES   RUBBER SOUL

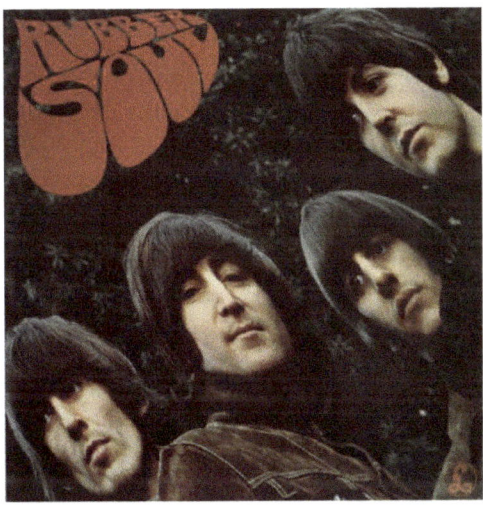

```
UK release   December 1965   Parlophone   PCS 3075 / PMC 1267
US release   December 1965   Capitol   (S)T 2442   4 tracks held back for YESTERDAY & TODAY LP   June 1966; replaced by 2 tracks not included on the US version of HELP!

1. Drive My Car (John Lennon/Paul McCartney)
2. Norwegian Wood (John Lennon/Paul McCartney)
3. You Won't See Me (John Lennon/Paul McCartney)
4. Nowhere Man (John Lennon/Paul McCartney)
5. Think For Yourself (George Harrison)
6. The Word (John Lennon/Paul McCartney)
7. Michelle (John Lennon/Paul McCartney)

8. What Goes On (John Lennon/Paul McCartney/Ringo Starr)
9. Girl (John Lennon/Paul McCartney)
10. I'm Looking Through You (John Lennon/Paul McCartney)
11. In My Life (John Lennon/Paul McCartney)
12. Wait (John Lennon/Paul McCartney)
13. If I Needed Someone (George Harrison)
14. Run For Your Life (John Lennon/Paul McCartney)

John Lennon: vocals, guitar, organ (5), percussion / George Harrison: vocals, guitar, sitar (2), percussion / Paul McCartney: vocals, bass guitar, piano (1,3,6), percussion / Ringo Starr: drums, vocals, organ (10) / Mal Evans: organ (3) / George Martin: producer, harmonium (6), piano (11)
```

Less than three years after releasing their first album, inventing British beat but displaying their influences clearly, the Beatles produced the sublime state-of-the-art pop-rock album that is *Rubber Soul*, with every track composed by the group. Even more remarkably, the album appeared just four months after the previously released *Help!* It conveys the impression of being a coherent song suite, in which every element has been carefully considered in terms of the impact and balance it brings to the whole work (an approach that was sadly undermined by Capitol's usual procedure in the US, where the album was truncated and bowdlerised with no regard to the Beatles' own wishes). As before, each song is given a distinctive, unique musical element, with George Harrison's innovative use of the sitar on *Norwegian Wood*, Paul McCartney's fuzz pedal-effected bass on *Think For Yourself*, and George Martin's baroque piano solo on *In My Life* being the most striking. The strength of the songwriting here encouraged other artists to record their own versions of many of the songs, since the Beatles clearly had no intention of issuing any of them as singles themselves. Both the Truth and the St Louis Union scored with *Girl*, the Hollies achieved a hit with *If I Needed Someone*, and the Overlanders took *Michelle* to number one. Judy Collins recorded *In My Life* as the title track of an album, Nancy Sinatra included *Run For Your Life* on hers, and even old-timer Frankie Vaughan had a go with a version of *Wait*, although this was a step too far for his particular audience and the record sold hardly at all. The punning title of the album might have been intended to imply that these were songs with a high emotional, or even personal content, and this was certainly born out by the thought-provoking themes of songs like *Nowhere Man* and *In My Life*, although in marked contrast to what most of the group's contemporaries were still producing, there is no obvious connection with the work of people like James Brown or Otis Redding.

THE WHO   MY GENERATION

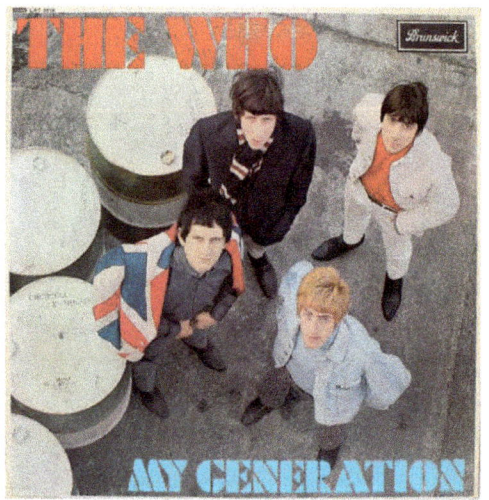

```
UK release    December 1965    Brunswick  LAT 8616
US release    April 1966    Decca  DL4664  different cover and one
                                           different track

1. Out In The Street (Pete Townshend)
2. I Don't Mind (James Brown)
3. The Good's Gone (Pete Townshend)
4. La-La-La-Lies (Pete Townshend)
5. Much To Much (Pete Townshend)
6. My Generation (Pete Townshend)

7. The Kids Are Alright (Pete Townshend)
8. Please Please Please (James Brown/Johnny Terry)
9. It's Not True (Pete Townshend)
10. I'm A Man (Bo Diddley)
11. A Legal Matter (Pete Townshend)
12. The Ox (Townshend/John Entwistle/Keith Moon/Nicky Hopkins)

Roger Daltrey: vocals, harmonica / Pete Townshend: guitar, vocals /
John Entwistle: bass guitar, vocals / Keith Moon: drums / Nicky
Hopkins: piano / Shel Talmy: producer
```

The Who began playing in London during 1964, frequently incorporating some equipment destruction as part of the act. Keith Moon would knock over his drum kit and Pete Townshend would thrust his guitar neck through the speaker of a spare amplifier, or even break the guitar itself. While playing, he developed his characteristic windmill right-arm action and used the squeal of guitar feedback as a deliberate ingredient in his sound. The feedback was included in the group's groundbreaking second single, *Anyway Anyhow Anywhere*, issued in May 1965 and just scraping into the top ten. The group's management encouraged the members to identify with the mod fashion movement and make their choice of clothing an essential part of their image. The Union Jack jacket draped across John Entwistle's shoulders on the album picture derives from this. It was the mod taste for soul music that encouraged the Who to include two rather ill-advised James Brown covers on the album, for which Roger Daltrey at this stage simply did not possess sufficient vocal expertise to avoid sounding foolish. Overall, however, *My Generation* is a triumph. Pete Townshend wrote most of the songs in a style that owes much to Ray Davies of the Kinks, but with enough of his own to make the songs distinctive. The producer, Shel Talmy, of course, carried out the same duties on the records made by the Kinks. The title track was issued as a single and just missed the number one spot in the charts. As an anthem for the teenagers the Who purported to represent, the song, *My Generation*, was perfect, propelled by Keith Moon's tumultuous drumming, with Roger Daltrey stuttering his lines in imitation of a youngster charged with pep pills, and John Entwistle capping the proceedings with a fluent bass guitar solo.

THE BYRDS   TURN! TURN! TURN!

```
US release    December 1965    Columbia  CS 9254 / CL 2454
UK release    December 1965    CBS       (S)BPG 62652

1. Turn! Turn! Turn! (Pete Seeger)
2. It Won't Be Wrong (Jim McGuinn/Harvey Gerst)
3. Set You Free This Time (Gene Clark)
4. Lay Down Your Weary Tune (Bob Dylan)
5. He Was A Friend Of Mine (Traditional, arranged Jim McGuinn)

6. The World Turns All Around Her (Gene Clark)
7. Satisfied Mind (Jack Rhodes/Red Hayes)
8. If You're Gone (Gene Clark)
9. The Times They Are A-Changin' (Bob Dylan)
10. Wait And See (Jim McGuinn/David Crosby)
11. Oh! Susannah (Traditional, arranged Jim McGuinn)

Gene Clark: vocals, percussion, harmonica / Jim McGuinn: guitar,
vocals / David Crosby: guitar, vocals / Chris Hillman: bass guitar,
vocals / Mike Clark: drums / Terry Melcher: producer, organ (5)
```

The second album by the Byrds continues in much the same vein as the first. During the six months since that initial album, Jim McGuinn had clearly been practising hard on his twelve string guitar, so that rather than simply strumming it, he is able to play a picked accompaniment with lead lines on nearly every track. The exception is the group's respectful recasting of the traditional song *He Was A Friend Of Mine* as a lament for President John Kennedy. Although *Turn! Turn! Turn!* was a second number one single for the group (in the US, not in the UK), there is no track on the second album as instantly memorable as *Mr Tambourine Man*. Overall, however, it is a strong collection of songs, making it clear that the Byrds were perfectly capable of building a music career on their folk-rock innovation.

BERT JANSCH   IT DON'T BOTHER ME

UK release   December 1965   Transatlantic   TRA 132
Not released in US

1. Oh My Babe (Bert Jansch)
2. Ring-A-Ding Bird (Bert Jansch)
3. Tinker's Blues (Bert Jansch)
4. Anti Apartheid (Bert Jansch)
5. The Wheel (Bert Jansch)
6. A Man I'd Rather Be (Bert Jansch)
7. My Lover (Bert Jansch)
8. It Don't Bother Me (Bert Jansch)
9. Harvest Your Thoughts Of Love (Bert Jansch)
10. Lucky Thirteen (John Renbourn)
11. As The Day Grows Longer Now (Bert Jansch)
12. So Long (Alex Campbell)
13. Want My Daddy Now (Bert Jansch)
14. 900 Miles (Traditional, arranged Bert Jansch)

Bert Jansch: vocals, guitar, banjo (14) / Roy Harper: vocals (6), guitar (7) / John Renbourn: guitar (7,10) / Nathan Joseph: producer / Bill Leader: producer

The second album by Bert Jansch provides further evidence of his remarkable guitar expertise. The songwriting is perhaps not as strong as previously, however. *Harvest Your Thoughts Of Love* is lovely, but many of the songs are not at all memorable and his tackling of a major socio-political theme with *Anti Apartheid* fails entirely to hit as hard as it needs to, for all that its heart is in the right place. But the collaborations with other contemporary folk artists are very encouraging, particularly when Jansch's guitar crosses strings with those of John Renbourn, delivering music with just enough strangeness to make it extremely interesting.

STAN TRACEY QUARTET   JAZZ SUITE – UNDER MILK WOOD

UK release   December 1965   Columbia   SCX 3589 / 33SX 1774
Not released in US

1. Cockle Row
2. Starless And Bible Black
3. I Lost My Step In Nantucket
4. No Good Boyo
5. Panpals
6. Llareggub
7. Under Milk Wood
8. A.M. Mayhem

All compositions by Stan Tracey

Stan Tracey: piano / Bobby Wellins: tenor saxophone / Jeff Clyne: bass / Jack Dougan: drums / Denis Preston: producer

Born in 1926, Stan Tracey was of the same generation as the conservative trad and swing players that dominated jazz in the UK in the fifties and beyond. He made his first recording in 1952 with the trumpeter Kenny Baker and, like Baker, he spent some time playing with Ted Heath's popular big band. His own first album dated from 1958 and through the sixties he worked as the house pianist at Ronnie Scott's jazz club, providing backing for the visiting American jazz stars. His masterpiece, the *Jazz Suite Inspired by Dylan Thomas's Under Milk Wood*, looks forward, away from the safe sounds and styles of the British jazz in his background, although he struggled to be taken seriously by fans of the new breed of jazz players coming to the fore during the sixties. There is, to be fair, little trace of the avant garde in Tracey's music, which sounds very like something Thelonious Monk might have produced with his saxophonist Charlie Rouse, if for some reason he was feeling less inclined to hammer the keyboard than usual. *Under Milk Wood* was one of a large number of albums that Stan Tracey recorded, right up to his death in 2013, but clearly he had a strong affection for this one. He re-recorded the music in 1976, and again in 2001, though inevitably without quite managing to surpass the freshness of the original.

JACKSON C. FRANK

UK release   December 1965   Columbia   33SX 1788
Not released in US

1. Blues Run The Game
2. Don't Look Back
3. Kimbie (Traditional)
4. Yellow Walls
5. Here Come The Blues
6. Milk And Honey
7. My Name Is Carnival
8. Dialogue (I Want To Be Alone)
9. Just Like Anything
10. You Never Wanted Me

All compositions by Jackson C. Frank except track 3

Jackson C. Frank: vocals, guitar / Al Stewart: guitar (4) / Paul Simon: producer

American singer songwriter Jackson C. Frank recorded his only album in London, where it was produced by Paul Simon. Frank sounds like a confident performer, but was apparently so shy during the recording that he played and sang behind a screen, to prevent him from being seen by the other people in the studio. He has one particularly memorable song, simple but effective, and placed as the opening track on the album. *Blues Run The Game* was subsequently covered by Paul Simon himself, by Bert Jansch, and by several other artists. The gentle *Milk And Honey* is strikingly reminiscent of Nick Drake, whose own version of the song eventually appeared as an out-take. Sadly, Frank was prevented by mental problems from doing much to build his career beyond this initial album.

THE WAILERS   THE WAILING WAILERS

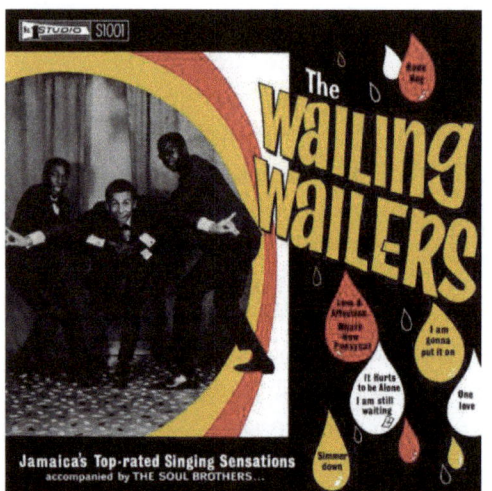

The first album involving future superstar Bob Marley was a compilation of Jamaican singles made during 1964 and 1965. The earliest of these was *Simmer Down,* a number one hit in February 1964. The Wailers at this time was a vocal group, the singers dressed in smart suits and with short hair, and using the Studio One resident band, the Soul Brothers, to provide the instrumental support. The music is firmly within the ska style that dominated Jamaican music at the time, propelled by a strident afterbeat, giving a characteristic bouncy, sprung quality. The standard procedure at Studio One was for the Soul Brothers to lay down a variety of instrumental backing tracks, after which singers like the Wailers would come in and fit their own melodies and lyrics over the top. Coxsone Dodd, the owner and operator of Studio One, felt totally justified, therefore, in adding his name to the songwriting credits for most of the Wailers' songs. This is how they are presented on modern reissues, although the label information on the first pressings attaches only Bob Marley's name to most of them, (including songs not written by him) or else no name at all. In 1965, of course, most record buyers in the UK or the US would have had no access to the *Wailing Wailer*s LP and would not even have been aware of its existence. For modern listeners, the chance to discover the musical roots of one of the most important twentieth century musicians is invaluable.

Not released in UK or US
Jamaican release   December 1965   Studio One   S1001

1. Ten Commandments Of Love (Marshall Paul)
2. Rude Boy (Bob Marley)
3. It Hurts To Be Alone (Junior Braithwaite/Coxsone Dodd)
4. Love And Affection (Bob Marley/Bunny Livingston/Coxsone Dodd)
5. I'm Still Waiting (Bob Marley/Coxsone Dodd)
6. Simmer Down (Bob Marley/Coxsone Dodd)
7. Put It On (Bob Marley/Coxsone Dodd)
8. I Need You (Bob Marley)
9. Lonesome Feeling (Bob Marley/Bunny Livingston/Peter Tosh)
10. What's New Pussycat? (Burt Bacharach/Hal David)
11. One Love (Bob Marley/Bunny Livingston/Coxsone Dodd)
12. When The Well Runs Dry (William Bell)

Bob Marley: vocals / Bunny Livingston: vocals / Peter Tosh: vocals / Junior Braithwaite: vocals / Berverley Kelso: vocals / Cherry Smith: vocals / Coxsone Dodd: producer / The Soul Brothers – Ernest Ranglin: guitar / Wallin Cameron: guitar / Harry Haughton: guitar / Jackie Mittoo: piano, organ / Roland Alphonso: tenor saxophone / Dennis Campbell: tenor saxophone /Johnny Moore: trumpet / Bobby Ellis: trumpet / Bryan Atkinson: bass guitar / LLoyd Brevett: bass / Bunny Williams: drums / Joe Isaacs: drums

THE GRAHAM BOND ORGANIZATION   THERE'S A BOND BETWEEN US

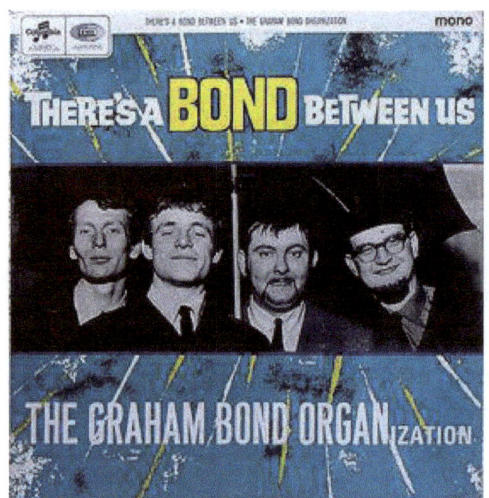

UK release   December 1965   Columbia   33SX 1750
Not released in US

1. Who's Afraid Of Virginia Woolf? (Don Kirkpatrick/Kevin Knox)
2. Hear Me Calling Your Name (Jack Bruce)
3. The Night Time Is The Right Time (Lew Herman)
4. Walkin' In The Park (Graham Bond)
5. Last Night (The Markeys)
6. Baby Can IT Be True? (Graham Bond)
7. What'd I Say (Ray Charles)
8. Dick's Instrumental (Dick Heckstall-Smith)
9. Don't Let Go (Jesse Stone)
10. Keep A-Drivin' (Chuck Willis)
11. Have You Ever Loved A Woman? (Graham Bond)
12. Camels And Elephants (Ginger Baker)

Graham Bond: vocals, organ, mellotron, alto saxophone / Dick Heckstall-Smith: tenor and baritone saxophones / Jack Bruce: bass guitar, harmonica, vocals / Ginger Baker: drums / Robert Stigwood: producer

This is the second album released by the Graham Bond Organization: *The Sound Of 65,* a rather more determinedly commercial collection, was released in March. The musicians had all previously been members of Alexis Korner's Blues Incorporated, and had played in various jazz groups before that. With the opening track on the album, a tune associated with the jazz organist Jimmy Smith, it is very hard to decide whether the Graham Bond Organization is playing jazz or rock. The jazz sensibility permeates through the rest of the album, even if most of the tracks are more obviously rhythm and blues. Graham Bond, performing on both the Hammond organ and the alto saxophone, and tenor saxophonist Dick Heckstall-Smith are fine soloists and prove that they are, with instrumental breaks on nearly every track. *Camels And Elephants* presents an extended drum solo, only the second one of these to be played on a rock album (the first being the responsibility of Ginger Baker as well, on the earlier Graham Bond Organization LP). Bond also pioneers a new keyboard instrument on two tracks, the mellotron, although he has not spent much time exploring its full potential. Neither of the Organization albums sold at all well. By the time *There's A Bond Between Us* was released, Jack Bruce was playing with Manfred Mann, having been fired from the Organization in August. Ginger Baker would not stay much longer, although Bond and Heckstall-Smith soldiered on until the end of 1967, with a new drummer, Jon Hiseman.

MARTIN CARTHY

UK release December 1965 Fontana (S)TL 5269
Not released in US

1. High Germany
2. The Trees They Do Grow High
3. Sovay
4. Ye Mariners All
5. The Queen Of Hearts
6. Broomfield Hill
7. Springhill Mine Disaster (Ewan MacColl/Peggy Seeger)
8. Scarborough Fair
9. Lovely Joan
10. The Barley And The Rye
11. The Wind That Shakes The Barley
12. The Two Magicians
13. The Handsome Cabin Boy
14. And A-Begging I Will Go

Martin Carthy: vocals, guitar / Dave Swarbrick: violin, mandolin

Martin Carthy had previously issued an album as a member of the Three City Four, playing contemporary folk songs, many of them written by group member Leon Rosselson. For his first solo LP, however, Carthy presents a selection of traditional folk material, with the fiddle player from the Ian Campbell Folk Group providing support on some of the songs. Carthy is a skilled guitarist, albeit not in the league of Bert Jansch or Davy Graham, but his playing is very much subservient to the song. Three of the tracks are delivered by his unaccompanied voice and a fourth has Dave Swarbrick's sprightly violin playing, but no guitar. Although a number of artists had been recording traditional folk material since the beginning of the fifties, Martin Carthy was responsible for a surge of interest in the music. The guitar part he invents to decorate the lyrics of *Scarborough Fair* was borrowed a little later by Paul Simon for his own reworking of the song and, much to Carthy's annoyance, his role in the creation of the hit song was not acknowledged.

THE WATERSONS   FROST AND FIRE

UK release December 1965 Topic 12T136
US release February 1967 Elektra EKS 7/EKL 321
different cover

1. Here We Come A-Wassailing
2. The Derby Ram
3. Jolly Old Hawk
4. Pace-Egging Song
5. Seven Virgins Or The Leaves Of Life
6. The Holly Bears A Berry
7. Hal-An-Tow
8. Earlsdon Sword Dance Song
9. John Barleycorn
10. Harvest Song: We Gets Up In The Morn
11. Souling Song
12. Christmas Is Now Drawing Near At Hand
13. Herod And The Cock
14. Wassail Song

All songs Traditional

Norma Waterson: vocals / Mike Waterson: vocals / Lal Waterson: vocals / John Harrison: vocals / Bill Leader: producer

The Watersons are a family singing group from Yorkshire, performing traditional material unaccompanied. *Frost And Fire,* a collection of seasonal songs, including several for Christmas, was the group's first album. Each singer has one song that they deliver on their own, but the rest are four-part harmony performances. Although there are two male singers and two female singers, the result sounds little like the music of the Mamas and the Papas, partly because the Watersons' Yorkshire accents are clear, but equally because the group is not particularly concerned with sounding smooth or sweet. Hugely influential within British folk music, members of the Waterson family, which include Martin Carthy, who married Norma Waterson, and their daughter Eliza Carthy, have recorded and performed, to much acclaim, right up to the present day.

DOWNLINERS SECT THE COUNTRY SECT

UK release   December 1965   Columbia   33SX 1745
Not released in US

1. If I Could Just Go Back (Tommy Collins)
2. Rocks In My Bed (Traditional)
3. Ballad Of The Hounds (Johnny Fitzmorris/Jack Rhodes)
4. Little Play Soldiers (Marty Cooper)
5. Hard Travellin' (Keith Grant/Don Craine/Mike Collier)
6. Wait For The Light To Shine (Fred Rose)

7. I Got Mine (Tommy Collins)
8. Waiting In Heaven (Keith Grant/Don Craine/Mike Collier)
9. Above And Beyond (Harlan Howard)
10. Bad Storm Coming (Keith Grant/Don Craine/Mike Collier)
11. Midnight Special (Traditional)
12. Wolverton Mountain (Claude King/Merle Kilgore)

Don Craine: vocals, guitar / Terry Gibson: guitar / Keith Grant: bass guitar, vocals / Johnny Sutton: drums / Michael Sutton: washboard / Pip Harvey: vocals (3) / John Paul Jones: piano (2,8) / Mike Collier: producer

Downliners Sect started as a British R&B band, sounding very much like the Rolling Stones and the Pretty Things, but without the charisma, the star quality of either of those bands. Lead singer Don Craine always wore a deerstalker hat, which was supposedly an ironic gesture, but in totally failing to become a popular fashion item, it succeeded only in making Craine look foolish.

The Downliners Sect first album, released the previous year, was the familiar blend of Chuck Berry, Bo Diddley, and Muddy Waters, with a few group compositions in the same style thrown in to make up the numbers. This follow-up was a bold departure in that it switched the music's focus to American country music, even if this was largely performed as though it was simply another kind of R&B. Ironically, therefore, the music recalls Hank Williams rather than Nashville, although to judge from its choice of songs to cover, it is doubtful whether the Sect was aware of who the country pioneer was. The group incorporates the strange addition of a washboard, borrowed not from country, but from skiffle, the British interpretation of folk-blues invented by Lonnie Donegan in the fifties. The two major features distinguishing proper contemporary county music, the powerfully melodic singing and the intricate guitar playing, are absent from *The Country Sect*, which ends up as an uncomfortable hybrid, not so much landing a strike before its time as simply missing the target altogether. Sales of the album were minimal, although Columbia kept faith with the group long enough to release just one more album, which did not persevere with the country experiment.

ALBERT AYLER SPIRITS REJOICE

US release   c.December 1965   ESP-Disk   ESP 1020
Not released in UK

1. Spirits Rejoice
2. Holy Family

3. D.C.
4. Angels
5. Prophet

All compositions by Albert Ayler

Albert Ayler: tenor saxophone / Charles Tyler: alto saxophone / Donald Ayler: trumpet / Gaey Peacock: bass / Henry Grimes: bass / Sunny Murray: drums / Call Cobbs: harpsichord (4) / David Hancock: producer

Spirits Rejoice is a recording by a slightly larger group than the one led by Albert Ayler on the earlier *Spiritual Unity*. It was carried out in a New York concert hall for the sake of the ambience, although there was no audience present. Even more than previously, the martial-style themes that Ayler uses as the basis for the group improvisation (*Spirits Rejoice* itself quotes from the French National Anthem) give the music a considerable gravity and presence, within which his own impassioned tenor saxophone playing is able to soar. *Angels* provides a surprising diversion in which Albert Ayler, as the only soloist, is supported by a frantic electric harpsichord part, although the impact of this is reduced by being recorded very softly. Throughout the album, Ayler proves once more that he has a very individual approach to avant garde playing and that he is a very important jazz innovator.

ROLAND KIRK RIP, RIG & PANIC

Roland Kirk has to be the most idiosyncratic and single-minded musician working in jazz. He makes a virtue out of being able to play two or three wind instruments simultaneously (including saxophone and flute, which ought to be impossible, given their different blowing actions). He incorporates the technique of circular breathing, whereby a saxophonist takes in air through his nose while blowing out through the instrument, enabling long, seamless phrases to be played with no apparent breath taken. And he uses unusual instruments that appear to be unique to him – the manzello is a modified

tenor saxophone with an upturned bell and no U-curve, while the stritch is a straight alto saxophone. When playing the saxophone conventionally, it becomes apparent that Kirk's primary influence is John Coltrane, although the pieces on *Rip, Rig & Panic* are based on chord changes and are very accessible. He does, of course, have Coltrane's drummer, Elvin Jones, supporting him here. The passages where more than one saxophone can be heard at a time could have been achieved by overdubbing, but the music gains an extra dimension with the knowledge that Kirk is actually playing live. He introduces a little unexpected electronic noise on *Slippery, Hippery, Flippery*, weaving it through the sound of sirens and percussion, while he solos on saxophone over the top. Roland Kirk's influence turned out to be greatest on rock musicians. Saxophonists like Dick Heckstall-Smith and Blodwyn Pig's Jack Lancaster adopted the technique of playing two instruments together, while Ian Anderson borrowed Kirk's breathy, vocalised flute playing style in its entirety.

RICHARD & MIMI FARINA   REFLECTIONS IN A CRYSTAL WIND

Joan Baez's little sister Mimi married folk singer Richard Farina when she was just seventeen and the couple proceeded to make two albums, of which *Reflections In A Crystal Wind* is the second. The duo perform their songs in close harmony, with the voices evenly balanced so that neither of them is singing a clearly defined lead line. The result is very attractive, although at the expense of making the songs melodically distinctive. Mimi's guitar and Richard's dulcimer integrate as easily as the voices and provide the primary instrumental support, although other musicians are frequently added. Lead guitarist Bruce Langhorne is able to demonstrate his prowess much more effectively than he does on his recordings with Bob Dylan. Four tracks employ a complete rock group line-up, although in a much more polished manner than Bob Dylan chose to follow on his ground-breaking *Highway 61 Revisited* album, so that the music causes much less upset to the delicate sensibilities of contemporary folk music fans. Another four tracks are entirely instrumental, allowing the interplay between guitar and dulcimer to be more clearly appreciated. The Farinas never made another album because just over four months after the release of *Reflections In A Crystal Wind*, Richard was killed while riding as a pillion passenger on a friend's motorbike. The suggestion that he was on the point of providing serious artistic competition for Bob Dylan is not backed up by the existing recordings, but the album remains a worthy addition to the American folk catalogue.

MAURICE JARRE   DOCTOR ZHIVAGO ORIGINAL SOUNDTRACK

French composer Maurice Jarre wrote the scores for several David Lean films beginning with *Lawrence Of Arabia* in 1961/2. His music for *Doctor Zhivago* is suitably epic and evocative and includes the sounds of appropriate Russian balalaikas, as well as some Japanese instruments, mixed in with the conventional orchestra. One of the most memorable musical sequences is *Lara's Theme*, which later became recast as the song, *Somewhere My Love*, and became a big easy-listening hit in the US for the

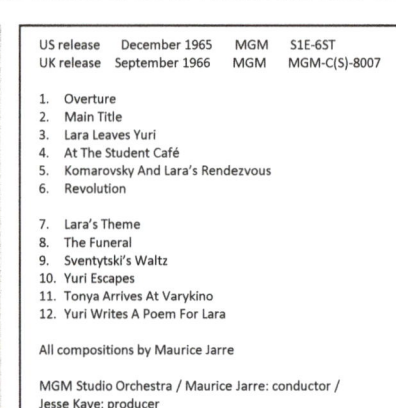

US release	December 1965	MGM	S1E-6ST
UK release	September 1966	MGM	MGM-C(S)-8007

1. Overture
2. Main Title
3. Lara Leaves Yuri
4. At The Student Café
5. Komarovsky And Lara's Rendezvous
6. Revolution

7. Lara's Theme
8. The Funeral
9. Sventytski's Waltz
10. Yuri Escapes
11. Tonya Arrives At Varykino
12. Yuri Writes A Poem For Lara

All compositions by Maurice Jarre

MGM Studio Orchestra / Maurice Jarre: conductor / Jesse Kaye: producer

Ray Conniff Singers. David Lean liked the melody so much that he edited it into the music in several other places, despite Jarre's fears that the soundtrack would be spoilt. It received a best soundtrack Oscar regardless. The film was hugely successful and, as a result, the soundtrack album was too. In the UK, it reached number three and stayed in the chart for two years.

1966

SONNY BOY WILLIAMSON & THE YARDBIRDS

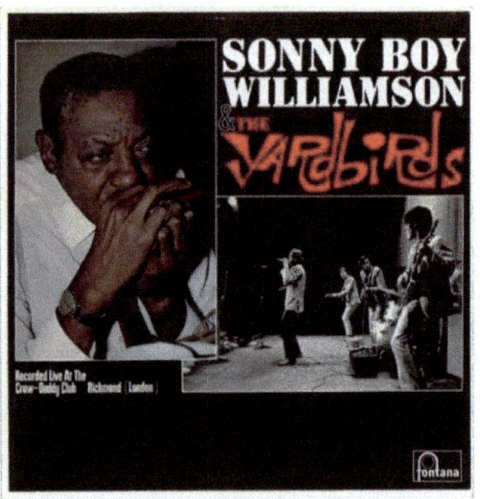

UK release	January 1966	Fontana	TL 5277
US release	February 1966	Mercury	SR 61071 / MG 21071

1. Bye Bye Bird (Willie Dixon/Sonny Boy Williamson)
2. Mister Downchild
3. 23 Hours Too Long
4. Out On The Water Coast
5. Baby Don't Worry

6. Pontiac Blues
7. Take It Easy Baby
8. I Don't Care No More
9. Do The Weston

All compositions apart from track 1 by Sonny Boy Williamson

Sonny Boy Williamson: vocals, harmonica / Keith Relf: not much / Eric Clapton: guitar / Chris Dreja: guitar / Paul Samwell-Smith: bass guitar / Jim McCarty: drums / Horst Lippmann: producer / Giorgio Gomelsky: producer

Sonny Boy Williamson II (real name Rice Miller), the premier Chicago blues harmonica player (although Little Walter would have argued the point), toured Europe several times during the early sixties. *Sonny Boy Williamson & The Yardbirds* is a recording made in December 1963 at a London club, when the Yardbirds were hired to provide the accompaniment, without Williamson having much say in the matter. The suggestion, however, that he remarked "those British boys want to play the blues real bad, and they do" is not backed up by any evidence. In truth, the Yardbirds do what they have to do, enabling Sonny Boy to impress. Eric Clapton gets to play several solos too and he rises to the occasion very well, despite a tendency to show off his skill by playing too many notes. As a learning experience, this encounter with one of the blues greats must have been of great value for the Yardbirds and it provides much to enjoy for the rest of us too. It is Fontana that comes out of this least well. After sitting on the tapes for two years, the record company packaged the music in a cover showing the wrong line-up of the Yardbirds, with Jeff Beck, who does not play on the album, in a prominent position.

THE KNICKERBOCKERS   LIES

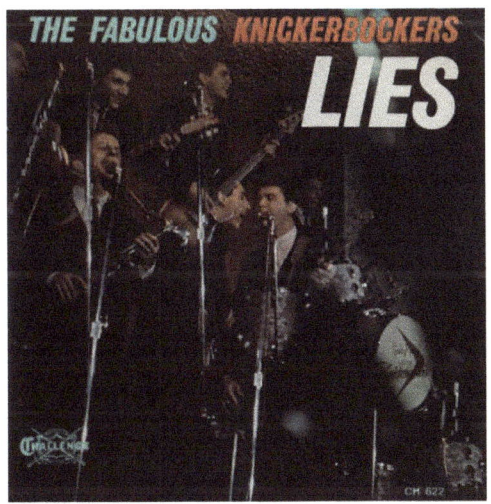

US release   January 1966   Challenge   CH(S)-622
UK release   January 1966   London   HAH 8294

1. Lies (Beau Charles/Buddy Randell)
2. I Can Do It Better (James Seals/Dash Crofts)
3. Can't You See I'm Tryin' (Glen Campbell/Jerry Fuller)
4. Please Don't Fight It (Jerry Fuller)
5. Just One Girl (Beau Charles)

6. I Believe In Her (James Seals/John Trombatore)
7. Wishful Thinking (Wynn Stewart)
8. You'll Never Walk Alone (Richard Rodgers/Oscar Hammerstein)
9. Your Kind Of Lovin' (Annette Tucker/Jill Jones)
10. Harlem Nocturne (Dick Rogers/Earle Hagen)

Beau Charles: vocals, guitar / Buddy Randell: saxophone, vocals / John Charles: bass guitar, vocals / Jimmy Walker: drums, vocals / Jerry Fuller: producer

The Knickerbockers were a busy bar band with a reputation for being able to provide very fine impersonations of the various hit artists of the day. Two earlier albums are full of well-played sound-alike cover versions. With the original song *Lies*, the group did such a good job of reproducing the sound and the style of the Beatles, that many people would have assumed that it was the Beatles, when hearing the song played on the radio. It reached number 20 in the National charts, but was not a hit in the UK, despite being played often on the pirate radio stations. Some of the tracks on the album are almost as good, although the group is no more capable of turning the turgid *You'll Never Walk Alone* into a classic rock performance than was Gerry and the Pacemakers. Sadly, the Knickerbockers were saddled with a rather inept record company and the hits rapidly dried up, despite the group recording some highly memorable singles through the remainder of the sixties. No more albums were made, but a compilation issued in 2006 by Sundazed Records, *Rockin' With The Knickerbockers*, proves that the group is one of the great lost talents of the Golden Age.

THE SPENCER DAVIS GROUP   THE SECOND ALBUM

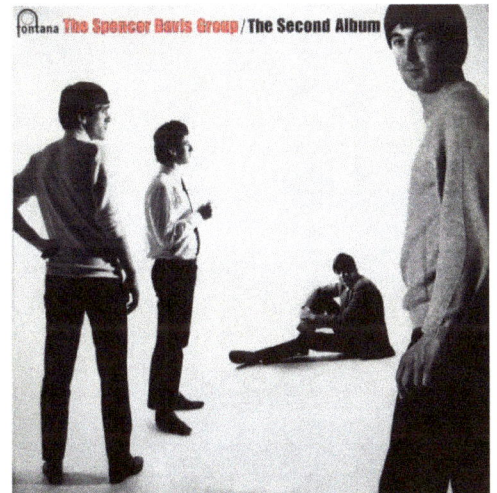

UK release   January 1966   Fontana   TL 5295
Not released in US

1. Look Away (Bert Russell/Norman Meade)
2. Keep On Running (Jackie Edwards)
3. This Hammer (Spencer Davis Group)
4. Georgia On My Mind (Hoagy Carmichael/Stuart Gorrell)
5. Please Do Something (Don Covay)
6. Let Me Down Easy (James McDougal/Wrecia Holloway)

7. Strong Love (Deadric Malone/Eddie Silvers/Mary Brown)
8. I Washed My Hands In Muddy Water (Joe Babcock)
9. Since I Met You Baby (Ivory Joe Hunter)
10. You Must Believe Me (Curtis Mayfield)
11. Hey Darling (Spencer Davis/Steve Winwood)
12. Watch Your Step (Bobby Parker)

Spencer Davis: guitar, vocals / Steve Winwood: vocals, piano, guitar, harmonica / Muff Winwood: bass guitar / Peter York: drums / Chris Blackwell: producer

The Spencer Davis Group had become an altogether stronger proposition at the time of the release of *The Second Album*, having just achieved a number one hit with *Keep On Running*. Because it has a singer with a superlative soul voice, the group draws on soul music for its material, rather than the more rocking R&B styles, and acquires in the process a rather different sound to that of the majority of its competitors. The single is by far the most impressive track, however. It is sourced from Jamaican songwriter Jackie Edwards, but turned into a driving piece of sixties rock, framed by a distinctive bass guitar riff and slashing fuzz guitar chords to clinch the deal. The guitar sound was still new enough that at least one reviewer believed that he was listening to the playing of a raucous saxophonist with a split reed. The album repeated the success of its predecessor by climbing to near the top of the album charts.

JOHN RENBOURN

The influence of Davy Graham continues, with the release of an album by a third British virtuoso acoustic guitarist, John Renbourn, who had already impressed with guest appearances on records by Bert Jansch. Renbourn is much more interested in the blues and the songs marked as 'traditional' on his album (including two that are properly attributed to Blind Boy Fuller and the Rev Gary Davis) are not the English folk songs to be found on Martin Carthy's record, but are borrowed from the blues and spirituals of black American culture. He plays slide guitar on three tracks and on the two pieces where Bert Jansch joins in, Renbourn essentially plays blues lead guitar over Jansch's rhythm. In purely technical terms, he out-plays the original American blues guitarists that are his inspiration, but he arguably brings much less emotion to his playing. As producer, Nathan Joseph does John Renbourn few favours – everything is clear enough, but the ambience affecting the overall quality of sound varies considerably from track to track. It should be noted that this is actually the second album to feature John Renbourn. The previous month, an album jointly credited to Renbourn and American expatriate folk singer Dorris Henderson, *There You Go!*, was issued by Columbia records. Sadly, the record company did such a bad job of promoting the album, that hardly anyone was aware of its existence.

```
UK release      January 1966      Transatlantic    TRA 135
Not released in US

1. Judy (John Renbourn)
2. Beth's Blues (Blind Boy Fuller/John Renbourn)
3. Song (John Donne/John Renbourn)
4. Down On The Barge (John Renbourn)
5. John Henry (Traditional)
6. Plainsong (John Renbourn)
7. Louisiana Blues (Muddy Waters)
8. Blue Bones (Bert Jansch/John Renbourn)

9. Train Tune (John Renbourn)
10. Candy Man (Rev Gary Davis)
11. The Wildest Pig In Captivity (John Renbourn)
12. National Seven (John Renbourn)
13. Motherless Children (Traditional)
14. Winter Is Gone (Traditional)
15. Noah And Rabbit (Bert Jansch/John Renbourn)

John Renbourn: guitar, vocals / Bert Jansch: guitar (8,15) /
Nathan Joseph: producer
```

SIMON & GARFUNKEL   SOUNDS OF SILENCE

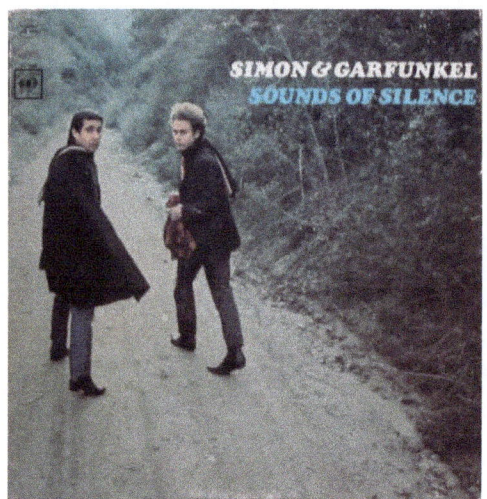

```
US release      January 1966    Columbia    CS 9269 / CL 2469
UK release      April 1966      CBS (S)BPG 62690    Homeward Bound added

1. The Sounds Of Silence
2. Leaves That Are Green
3. Blessed
4. Kathy's Song
5. Somewhere They Can't Find Me
6. Angie (Davy Graham)

7. Richard Cory
8. A Most Peculiar Man
9. April Come She Will
10. We've Got A Groovey Thing Goin'
11. I Am A Rock

All compositions by Paul Simon except track 6

Paul Simon: vocals, guitar / Art Garfunkel: vocals / Fred Carter Jr: guitar /
Glen Campbell: guitar / Joe South: guitar / Al Gorgoni: guitar (1) / Vinnie
Bell: guitar (1) / Larry Knechtel: keyboards / Joe Osborn: bass guitar /
Joe Mack: bass guitar (1) / Hal Blaine: drums / Bobby Gregg: drums (1) /
Bob Johnston: producer / Tom Wilson: producer (1)
```

In June, producer Tom Wilson turned the recording of *The Sound Of Silence* included on Simon and Garfunkel's first album into a band performance, by overdubbing extra parts using some of the musicians who had played on recent records made by Bob Dylan. The result was issued as a single without the duo being consulted, but any objections they might have had were forgotten when the record reached number one in the US charts. Paul Simon, who had been working as a solo artist in the UK, returned to the US and reunited with Art Garfunkel. The album that followed was recorded in the same folk-rock style as the single, applied for the most part to songs that Paul Simon had originally recorded on his own in the UK. It was a substantial hit in its own right, without reaching the top ten in the album charts, although in the UK, the album remained in the chart for two years.

THEM   AGAIN

```
UK release      January 1966      Decca       LK 4751
US release      April 1966        Parrot      PAS7 / PA6 1008    6 tracks omitted

1. Could You, Would You (Van Morrison)
2. Something You Got (Chris Kenner)
3. Call My Name (Tommy Scott)
4. Turn On Your Love Light (Deadric Malone/Joseph Wade Scott)
5. I Put A Spell On You (Screamin' Jay Hawkins)
6. I Can Only Give You Everything (Phil Coulter/Tommy Scott)
7. My Lonely Sad Eyes (Van Morrison)
8. I Got A Woman (Ray Charles/Renald Richard)

9. Out Of Sight (James Brown/Ted Wright)
10. It's All Over Now, Baby Blue (Bob Dylan)
11. Bad Or Good (Van Morrison)
12. How Long Baby (Tommy Scott)
13. Hello Josephine (Dave Bartholomew/Fats Domino)
14. Don't You Know (Tommy Scott)
15. Hey Girl (Van Morrison)
16. Bring 'em On In (Van Morrison)

Van Morrison: vocals, saxophone / Jim Armstrong: guitar / Ray Elliot:
keyboards, saxophone, flute/ Alan Henderson: bass guitar / John
Wilson: drums / Tommy Scott: producer
```

The key track on a collection of worthy but not particularly memorable R&B is a Van Morrison song called *Hey Girl*. The music moves slowly back and forth between two chords, while a lazy flute part provides decoration, and Morrison delivers his vocal lines, sounding very much as though he is improvising both the melody and the lyrics. It is, in short, the template for the music that the singer spent the rest of his career exploring. Elsewhere, Van Morrison turns out a fine version of *I Put A Spell On You* and has a strong enough voice to do justice to a James Brown song. The band does its best with four indifferent songs thrust on to them by the producer, but overall it is not too surprising that the album failed to enter the charts. Later in the year, Van Morrison left the band, at the end of an American tour.

THE ARANBEE POP SYMPHONY ORCHESTRA   TODAY'S POP SYMPHONY

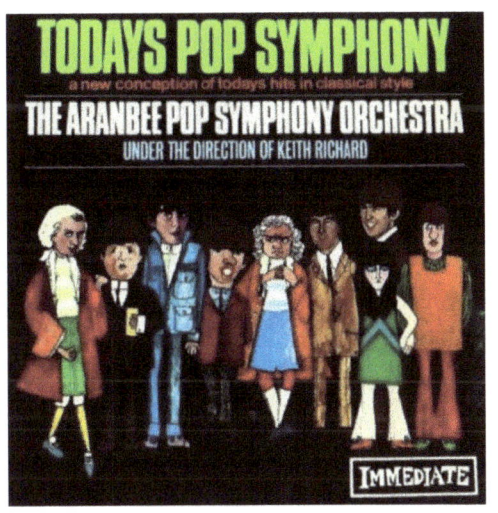

UK release   February 1966   Immediate   IMSP 003 / IMLP 003
Not released in US

1. There's A Place (John Lennon/Paul McCartney)
2. Rag Doll (Bob Crewe/Bob Gaudio)
3. I Got You Babe (Sonny Bono)
4. We Can Work It Out (John Lennon/Paul McCartney)
5. Play With Fire (Mick Jagger/Keith Richards/Bill Wyman/Brian Jones)
6. Mother's Little Helper (Mick Jagger/Keith Richards)
7. In The Midnight Hour (Steve Cropper/Wilson Pickett)
8. Take It Or Leave It (Mick Jagger/Keith Richards)
9. Sittin' On A Fence (Mick Jagger/Keith Richards)
10. I Don't Want To Go On Without You (Bert Berns/Jerry Wexler)

The Andrew Loog Oldham Orchestra / Keith Richards: producer

The Rolling Stones' manager, Andrew Loog Oldham, started his own record label in late 1965 and released the first album and single by the American group, the McCoys. For a second album, Oldham was able to get the rights to an old Sam Cooke record for reissue, but after that he was struggling to find music he could release. As a stopgap, he decided to make a fifth album of instrumental versions of well-known rock and pop songs, played by a non-musician's idea of what a chamber orchestra on the cusp of the medieval and baroque eras should sound like. It was not an obvious decision, given that Oldham's previous four orchestral albums had not exactly been big sellers. This time he renamed his Andrew Oldham Orchestra in order to distance himself a little from the project, using a rather cute pun instead. Keith Richards was credited as supervising the record, but it is doubtful whether he had very much to do with it. Previously, the arrangements had been the work of either John Paul Jones or David Whittaker, so it is likely that one of these was involved this time as well. It is difficult to argue that these slightly bizarre recastings of songs by the Rolling Stones, the Beatles, and others represent any kind of recognition of the music's intrinsic worth, but the results are undoubtedly great fun. It is interesting to note that two of the songs destined for the Rolling Stones' *Aftermath* album are included, in advance of the release of the Stones' own versions.

JOHN COLTRANE   ASCENSION

US release   February 1966   Impulse   A(S)-95
UK release   February 1966   HMV   CSD/CLP 3543

1. Ascension Part One
2. Ascension Part Two

Composed by John Coltrane

John Coltrane: tenor saxophone / Pharoah Sanders: tenor saxophone / Archie Shepp: tenor saxophone / Marion Brown: alto saxophone / John Tchicai: alto saxophone / Freddie Hubbard: trumpet / Dewey Johnson: trumpet / McCoy Tyner: piano / Art Davis: bass / Jimmy Garrison: bass / Elvin Jones: drums / Bob Thiele: producer

In 1961, Ornette Coleman issued an album called *Free Jazz*, in which the saxophonist led a double quartet in the performance of a work that was entirely improvised. *Ascension* finds John Coltrane leading an eleven piece band doing the same thing. There is a kinship between the opening of *Ascension* and the opening of the earlier *A Love Supreme*, although the meditative mood very quickly changes into something much more frantic. Eventually, the horns drop out to allow John Coltrane space to deliver a turbulent solo, after which ensemble passages alternate with individual solos by the various musicians. For the most part, Coltrane himself, having set the music into motion, makes quite a small contribution to the album. The band played the music twice in the studio – the versions are similar in overall conception and sound, but different in detail. The soloists perform in almost the same order; Elvin Jones does not solo at all on the second version (which is over two minutes longer despite this), although this hardly matters since he is effectively delivering a solo throughout. After the initial release of the album, John Coltrane decided that he liked the other take better and subsequent issues used this in place of the one used at first. The music was enormously influential, but it is not for those who place a premium on melody, on music that is easy on the ear.

THE SUPREMES   I HEAR A SYMPHONY

```
US release     February 1966     Motown      M(S) 643
UK release     February 1966     Tamla Motown (S)TML 11028

1. Stranger In Paradise (George Forrest/Robert Wright)
2. Yesterday (John Lennon/Paul McCartney)
3. I Hear A Symphony (Brian & Eddie Holland/Lamont Dozier)
4. Unchained Melody (Alex North/Hy Zaret)
5. With A Song In My Heart (Lorenz Hart/Richard Rodgers)
6. Without A Song (Billy Rose/Edward Eliscu/Vincent Youmans)
7. My World Is Empty Without You (Holland/Dozier/Holland)
8. A Lover's Concerto (Denny Randell/Sandy Linzer)
9. Any Girl In Love (Holland/Dozier/Holland)
10. Wonderful Wonderful (Ben Raleigh/Sherman Edwards)
11. Everything Is Good About You (Holland/Dozier/Holland)
12. He's All I Got (Holland/Dozier/Holland/James Dean)

Diana Ross: vocals / Florence Ballard: vocals / Mary Wilson: vocals /
The Andantes (as on Temptations LP above): vocals (6,9) / The Funk
Brothers (as on Temptations & Miracles LPs above) / Brian Holland &
Lamont Dozier: producer / Norman Whitfield: producer
```

The eighth album issued by the Supremes was also one of the biggest selling. It contained two of the group's hit singles, *My World Is Empty Without You* and the title track. Many of the remaining songs are taken from the classic pop song-book, including one very recent addition, the Beatles' *Yesterday*, The syrupy arrangements used for these do not fit well against the customary Motown sound of the singles and the other tracks written by the Holland-Dozier-Holland team, and Diana Ross's voice does not have the emotional depth to make her versions of the songs satisfying. The other two singers are given far too little to do and are swamped beneath the overbearing sound of the orchestra. What emerges is a very misguided attempt to make the Supremes sound 'sophisticated'. It does not work.

THE MAMAS AND THE PAPAS   IF YOU CAN BELIEVE YOUR EYES AND EARS

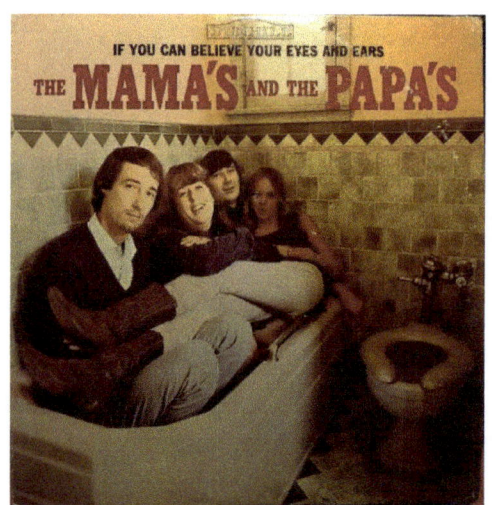

```
US release     February 1966     Dunhill      D(S)-50006
UK release     February 1966     RCA Victor   RD 7803

1. Monday Monday (John Phillips)
2. Straight Shooter (John Phillips)
3. Got A Feelin' (John Phillips/Denny Doherty)
4. I Call Your Name (John Lennon/Paul McCartney)
5. Do You Wanna Dance (Bobby Freeman)
6. Go Where You Wanna Go (John Phillips)
7. California Dreamin' (John Phillips/Michelle Phillips)
8. Spanish Harlem (Jerry Leiber/Phil Spector)
9. Somebody Groovy (John Phillips)
10. Hey Girl (John Phillips/Michelle Phillips)
11. You Baby (P F Sloan/Steve Barri)
12. In Crowd (Billy Page)

Michelle Phillips: vocals / Cass Elliot: vocals / John Phillips:
vocals, guitar / Denny Doherty: vocals / P F Sloan: guitar,
vocals / Larry Knechtel: keyboards / Peter Pilafian: electric
violin / Bud Shank: flute (7) / Joe Osborn: bass guitar / Hal
Blaine: drums / Lou Adler: producer
```

The members of the Mamas and the Papas had backgrounds in folk music groups, but came together in an attempt to make harmony pop music cool. *California Dreamin'* and *Monday Monday* have the stamp of classic song recordings and were substantial hits – both being awarded gold discs in the US, for one million dollars worth of retail sales. The first album is a sparkling collection with no weak tracks, showing off the group's immaculate four-part harmony singing, and announcing the arrival of a major new act. Some critics have described the album as a celebration of Californian alternative culture, on no more evidence than that one track, *Go Where You Wanna Go*, has the female singers refusing to commit themselves to a monogamous relationship. It seems more reasonable to view the album as being a celebration of being young. Its cover, however, was considered controversial in many parts of the US, where people apparently did not like to admit that they sometimes had to use a toilet. Alternative covers were printed in which the toilet shown was covered up. The album reached number one in the album charts regardless, although it was much less successful in the UK, despite the toilet not really being an issue there.

SUN RA   THE MAGIC CITY

Sun Ra's Arkestra functioned like an exclusive club for musicians who stayed absolutely loyal over the course of numerous albums and did not record elsewhere. *The Magic City* presents collective free improvisation as startling and as innovative as similarly conceived records by Ornette Coleman and John Coltrane, but with much less impact on the jazz world as a whole. Issued as always on Sun Ra's own label, sales of the album were minimal. The album was reissued in 1973 on the Impulse label, which would have generated a few more sales, though still not many. Although *The Shadow World* presents its improvisation carried out over a busy drum rhythm, the rest of the music does not have a regular pulse at all, with a generally sparse sound in which the instruments use space as part of their emphasis on timbre and texture. This marks the music as being rather different from the Coleman and Coltrane records. On the album's title track, Sun Ra improvises simultaneously on piano and an electric keyboard called a clavioline – presumably he is playing the piano with his left hand and the clavioline with his right, in a manner that would become ubiquitous for keyboard players in the seventies, but was highly unusual in September 1965, when the recording was made.

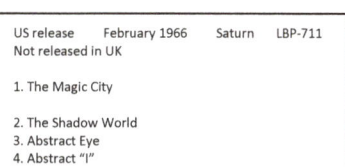

US release   February 1966   Saturn   LBP-711
Not released in UK

1. The Magic City
2. The Shadow World
3. Abstract Eye
4. Abstract "I"

All compositions by Sun Ra

Sun Ra: keyboards, percussion / Danny Davis: alto saxophone, flute / Harry Spencer: alto saxophone (1) / Marshall Allen: alto saxophone, flute, piccolo, oboe / Pat Patrick: baritone saxophone, flute, percussion / John Gilmore: tenor saxophone / Robert Cummings: bass clarinet / Walter Miller: trumpet (1) / Chris Capers: trumpet (2-4) / Ali Hassan: trombone (1) / Bernard Pettaway: trombone (2-4) / Teddy Nance: trombone (2-4) / Ronnie Boykins: bass / Roger Blank: percussion (1) / Jimhmi Johnson: percussion (2-4) / Alton Abraham: producer

SANDIE SHAW   THE GOLDEN HITS OF

UK release   February 1966   Pye Golden Guinea   GGL 0360
Not released in US

1. (There's) Always Something There To Remind Me (Burt Bacharach / Hal David)
2. Long Live Love
3. Don't You Know
4. I've Heard About Him
5. I'd Be Far Better Off Without You
6. I'll Stop At Nothing

7. How Can You Tell
8. You Can't Blame Him
9. Don't You Count On It
10. Message Understood
11. If Ever You Need Me
12. Girl Don't Come

All compositions except track 1 by Chris Andrews

Sandie Shaw: vocals / Ken Woodman: arranger, producer / Chris Andrews: producer

Sandie Shaw was one of the most successful female singers in Britain during the sixties, scoring eight top ten hits, three of them reaching number one. The songs on this compilation include five of these hits, dating from 1964 and 1965. Chris s is responsible for composing nearly all of the material. He has the knack of writing catchy melodies with memorable hook lines, so that Sandie Shaw does not have to do very much to make the songs sound good, but she proves on the touching *I'd Be Far Better Off Without You* (a B-side originally) that she is perfectly capable of using her voice as a powerful emotional instrument if she needs to.

LOVE

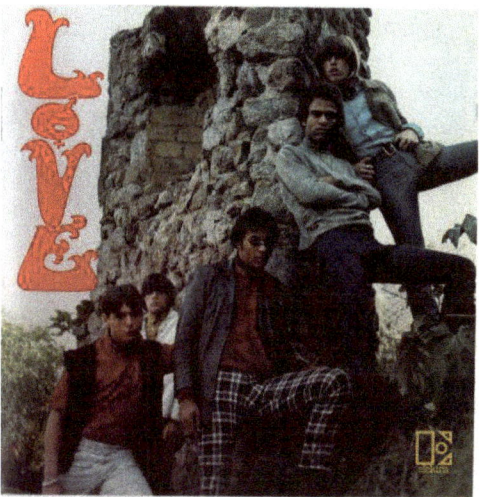

US release   March 1966   Elektra   EKS-74001 / EKL-4001
UK release   June 1966   Elektra   EKS-74001 / EKL-4001

1. My Little Red Book (Burt Bacharach/Hal David)
2. Can't Explain (Arthur Lee/John Echols/John Fleckenstein)
3. A Message To Pretty (Arthur Lee)
4. My Flash On You (Arthur Lee)
5. Softly To Me (Bryan Maclean)
6. No Matter What You Do (Arthur Lee)
7. Emotions (Arthur Lee/John Echols)

8. You I'll Be Following (Arthur Lee)
9. Gazing (Arthur Lee)
10. Hey Joe (Dino Valenti)
11. Signed D.C. (Arthur Lee)
12. Colored Balls Falling (Arthur Lee)
13. Mushroom Clouds (Lee/Bryan Maclean/John Echols/Ken Forssi)
14. And More (Arthur Lee/Bryan Maclean)

Arthur Lee: vocals, percussion, harmonica / Bryan Maclean: vocals, guitar / John Echols: guitar / Ken Forssi: bass guitar / Snoopy Pfisterer: drums / Jac Holzman: producer / Mark Abramson: producer

Love was the first rock group signed to the Elektra label, previously known for the variety of its folk music releases. Arthur Lee, the leader of the the group, had produced a single for a singer called Rosa Lee Brooks, *My Diary,* which would have remained completely obscure had it not happened to include some of the earliest recorded work of guitarist Jimi Hendrix. The music on the first LP by Love is very much in the style that later came to be called 'garage rock' or 'punk', before the latter term was hijacked by a different musical movement in the seventies. It is music played by a set of musicians, impressed by British beat and the Beatles, and certainly in Love's case, even more impressed by the Byrds, but slightly younger and lacking the experience of playing within the American folk music scene. Several of the tracks sound like unused demos for Byrds recordings, while songs like *My Flash On You* and *My Little Red*

Book do have very much in common with the punk music of ten years later, full of energy and enthusiasm, but not much finesse. But the slightly odd structure of *Softly To Me* is much more interesting, revealing a group that could achieve much more in the future.

VARIOUS ARTISTS   CHICAGO THE BLUES TODAY! VOLUMES 1-3

Realising that there was a growing interest amongst young white musicians and fans in both the US and the UK in the blues, Vanguard Records sent producer Sam Charters to Chicago to record some of the blues bands playing in the clubs there. The big names – B.B. King, Muddy Waters, Howlin' Wolf, Little Walter, Sonny Boy Williamson, Elmore James, Jimmy Reed – were already contracted to other record companies, so to some extent the bands included on the three LP

US release	March 1966	Vanguard	VSD7/VRS 9216/9217/9218
UK release	March 1966	Fontana	TFL 6068/6069/6070

The Junior Wells Chicago Blues Band: (Vol 1)
Junior Wells: harmonica, vocals / Buddy Guy: guitar / Jack Myers: bass / Fred Below: drums

1. Help Me (Sonny Boy Williamson/Ralph Bass)
2. It Hurts Me Too (When Things Go Wrong) (Melvin London)
3. Messin' With The Kid (Melvin London)
4. Vietcong Blues (Junior Wells)
5. All Night Long (Junior Wells)

J.B. Hutto and his Hawks: (Vol 1)
J.B. Hutto: guitar, vocals / Herman Hassell: bass guitar / Frank Kirkland: drums

6. Going Ahead (J.B. Hutto)
7. Please Help (J.B. Hutto)
8. Too Much Alcohol (J.B. Hutto)
9. Married Woman Blues (J.B. Hutto)
10. That's The Truth (J.B. Hutto)

Otis Spann's South Side Piano: (Vol 1)
Otis Spann: piano, vocals / S.P. Leary: drums

11. Marie (Otis Spann)
12. Burning Fire (Otis Spann)
13. S.P. Blues (Otis Spann)
14. Sometimes I Wonder (Otis Spann)
15. Spann's Stomp (Otis Spann)

The Jimmy Cotton Blues Quartet: (Vol 2)
Jimmy Cotton: harmonica, vocals / James Madison: guitar / Otis Spann: piano / S.P. Leary: drums

1. Cotton Crop Blues (Jimmy Cotton)
2. The Blues Keep Falling (Jimmy Cotton)
3. Love Me Or Leave Me (Jimmy Cotton)
4. Rocket 88 (Jackie Brenston)
5. West Helena Blues (Jimmy Cotton)

The Otis Rush Blues Band: (Vol 2)
Otis Rush: guitar, vocals / Robert 'Sax' Crowder: alto sax / Luther Tucker: guitar / Ernest Gatewood (as Roger Jones): bass / Jesse Green (as Willie Lion): drums

6. Everything's Going To Turn Out Alright (Rose Marie McCoy/Sylvia McKinney)
7. It's A Mean Old World (T-Bone Walker/Marl Young)
8. I Can't Quit You Baby (Willie Dixon)
9. Rock (Otis Rush)
10. It's My Own Fault B.B. King/Jules Taub/Muddy Waters)

Homesick James and his Dusters: (Vol 2)
Homesick James Williamson: guitar, vocals / Willie Dixon: bass / Frank Kirkland: drums

11. Dust My Broom (Robert Johnson)
12. Somebody Been Talkin' (James Williamson)
13. Set A Date (Memphis Minnie)
14. So Mean To Me (James Williamson)

Johnny Young's South Side Blues Band (Vol 3)
Johnny Young: guitar, mandolin, vocals / Walter Horton: harmonica / Hayes Ware: bass guitar / Elga Edmonds: drums

1. One More Time (Johnny Young)
2. Kid Man Blues (Johnny Young)
3. My Black Mare (Arthur Crudup)
4. Stealin' Back (Johnny Young)
5. I Got Mine In Time (Johnny Young)
6. Tighten Up On It (Johnny Young)

The Johnny Shines Blues Band: (Vol 3)
Johnny Shines: guitar, vocals / Walter Horton: harmonica / Floyd Jones: bass guitar / Frank Kirkland: drums

7. Dynaflow Blues (Johnny Shines)
8. Black Spider Blues (Johnny Shines)
9. Layin' Down My Shoes And Clothes (Johnny Shines)
10. If I Get Lucky (Johnny Shines)
12. Mr. Boweevil (Johnny Shines)
13. Hey, Hey (Johnny Shines)

Big Walter Horton's Blues Harp Band with Memphis Charlie: (Vol 3)
Walter Horton: harmonica / Charlie Musselwhite: harmonica / Johnny Shines: guitar / Floyd Jones: bass guitar / Frank Kirkland: drums

11. Rockin' My Bridge (Johnny Shines)

All produced by Sam Charters

set, *Chicago The Blues Today* are the second division. But nobody would guess this from the way that they sound. All the musicians are determined to make the most of the opportunity presented to them and play with a passion that is obvious. Modern critics who suggest that the music on these albums would have been revelatory at the time forget the fact that the big names mentioned had been releasing singles and albums since the fifties and had achieved considerable sales success with them. Individual enthusiasts like John Mayall, Eric Clapton, and Paul Butterfield had already made a considerable effort in promoting other significant blues names, so that musicians like Otis Spann and Otis Rush, with several recordings for small labels behind them, were not completely obscure. Nevertheless, the LP set serves very well as a demonstration of how the blues should be played, always bearing in mind that these musicians prefer to be working within the tradition and are not at all interested in breaking any new ground. The impression given that the music was thriving as a vital part of contemporary black American culture is somewhat undermined too by the uncomfortable truth that none of these musicians is particularly young. Guitarist Buddy Guy, for all that he was yet to make the impact he managed later on, was thirty when these records were released, and he is the youngest performer here (apart from the twenty-two year old Charlie Musselwhite, who is white, paying his dues, and lucky to be included). Homesick James Williamson and Johnny Shines were both in their fifties. In 1966, the R&B charts, primarily listing the music being bought by young people, were full of soul music, not the blues.

THE LOVIN' SPOONFUL   DAYDREAM

US release   March 1966   Kama Sutra   KLP(S)-8051
UK release   March 1966   Pye   NPL 28078

1. Daydream (John Sebastian)
2. There She Is (John Sebastian)
3. It's Not Time Now (John Sebastian/Zalman Yanovsky)
4. Warm Baby (John Sebastian)
5. Day Blues (John Sebastian/Joe Butler)
6. Let The Boy Rock And Roll (John Sebastian/Joe Butler)
7. Jug Band Music (John Sebastian)
8. Didn't Want To Have To Do It (John Sebastian)
9. You Didn't Have To Be So Nice (John Sebastian/Steve Boone)
10. Bald Headed Lena (Edward Sneed/Willie Perryman)
11. Butchie's Tune (John Sebastian)
12. Big Noise From Speonk (Lovin' Spoonful)

John Sebastian: vocals, guitar, autoharp, harmonica / Zalman Yanovsky: guitar, vocals / Steve Boone: bass guitar, vocals, piano / Joe Butler: drums, vocals / Erik Jacobsen: producer

There is a considerable leap in inspiration and performance between the first and second albums by the Lovin' Spoonful, the key factor being the rapid development of John Sebastian into a world-class songwriter. *Daydream* is a classic pop-rock album of the period, comparable to the Beatles *Help!* in the variety and confidence of its material. Sebastian has not forgotten his love of the blues, even if he no longer particularly wants to play it. *Day Blues* has the sound and the tonality, but not the blues structure; *Jug Band Music* is a song praising the genre, but it is not an example of it. John Sebastian cannot resist paraphrasing John Lee Hooker at the start of *Let The Boy Rock and Roll*, but the song itself is not a rewrite of *Boogie Chillun*. Both the title track and *You Didn't Have To Be So Nice* were issued as singles, with the former reaching number two in both the US and the UK. The second song was treated to a faithful copy by the Boston Crabs in the UK, which divided the loyalties of radio listeners and resulted in neither version becoming a hit, although it did well in the US. The album proved to be the Lovin' Spoonful's most successful, becoming a top ten album on both sides of the Atlantic – the group's only album success in the UK.

THE BLUES PROJECT   LIVE AT THE CAFE AU GO GO

The first album by the Blues Project is made up of live recordings in a New York club, but it is not a single complete gig. The music consists mostly of fast, exciting interpretations of blues songs, with a couple of surprising folk-rock performances for contrast. The members of the band are fine musicians, with lead guitarist Danny Kalb being particularly outstanding. Al Kooper, of course, was already well-known for his contributions to some key Bob Dylan recordings and he was a late addition to the band, after first playing with the others as a session musician. Lead singer Tommy Flanders left the band during the club engagement, but he is hardly missed since the others can sing just as well, although realistically, none of them is a Mick Jagger or a Van Morrison. The music is different – harder – than that of the Lovin' Spoonful,

US release   March 1966   Verve Folkways   FV(S)-9024
Not released in UK

1. Goin' Down Louisiana (Muddy Waters)
2. You Go, I'll Go With You (Willie Dixon)
3. Catch The Wind (Donovan)
4. I Want To Be Your Driver (Chuck Berry)
5. Alberta (Traditional)
6. The Way My Baby Walks (Andy Kulberg)
7. Violets Of Dawn (Eric Andersen)
8. Back Door Man (Willie Dixon/Howlin' Wolf)
9. Jelly Jelly Blues (Billy Eckstine/Earl Hines)
10. Spoonful (Willie Dixon)
11. Who Do You Love? (Bo Diddley)

Tommy Flanders: vocals (7,8,10,11) / Steve Katz: guitar, harmonica, vocals / Danny Kalb: guitar, vocals / Al Kooper: organ, vocals / Andy Kulberg: bass guitar / Roy Blumenfeld: drums / Jerry Schoenbaum: producer

although the Blues Project does not have a great songwriter, but both bands provide ample evidence that the US was now producing home-grown performers to easily counter the British invasion. Despite this, the Blues Project sadly achieved little in the way of chart success.

THE FUGS

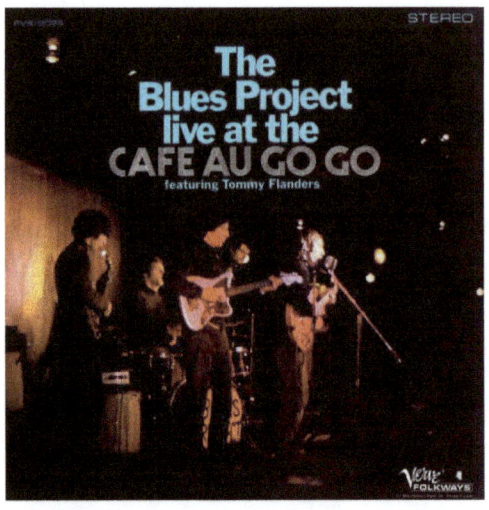

To describe the music of the Fugs as being like that of the Mothers of Invention, only without the humour or a musical genius in the driving seat, is accurate, but not entirely helpful at this point, given that in March 1966, Frank Zappa's group had yet to issue any records. Lurking behind the irreverent vocals of performance poets Ed Sanders and Tuli Kupferberg is the playing of a surprisingly skilled group of rock musicians, made to sound less competent than they are by an emphasis on shock value for its own sake and a rather poor recording quality. The Fugs present themselves as the voice of the Underground and they are clearly dissatisfied with the society they find themselves in, although they are more like stroppy adolescents than angry revolutionaries. Musically, by far the most interesting track is the last one, *Virgin Forest*, which is an eleven minute sound collage in which several short recordings are jammed together, more or less at random. The Fugs made an album during the previous year, but this is the one that attracted some attention, just managing to creep into the top hundred list of albums in the US.

US release   March 1966   ESP   1028
Not issued in UK

1. Frenzy (Ed Sanders)
2. I Want To Know (Charles Olson/Ed Sanders)
3. Skin Flowers (Pete Kearney/Ed Sanders)
4. Group Grope (Ed Sanders)
5. Coming Down (Ed Sanders)
6. Dirty Old Man (Ed Sanders/Lionel Goldbart)
7. Kill For Peace (Tuli Kupferberg)
8. Morning Morning (Tuli Kupferberg)
9. Doin' All Right (Richard Alderson/Ted Berrigan/Lee Crabtree)
10. Virgin Forest (Richard Alderson/Lee Crabtree/Ed Sanders)

Ed Sanders: vocals, producer / Tuli Kupferberg: vocals, percussion / Pete Kearney: guitar / Vinny Leary: guitar / Lee Crabtree: keyboards, bells / John Anderson: bass guitar, vocals / Ken Weaver: drums, percussion, vocals / Betsy Klein: vocals / Richard Alderson: producer

NANCY SINATRA   BOOTS

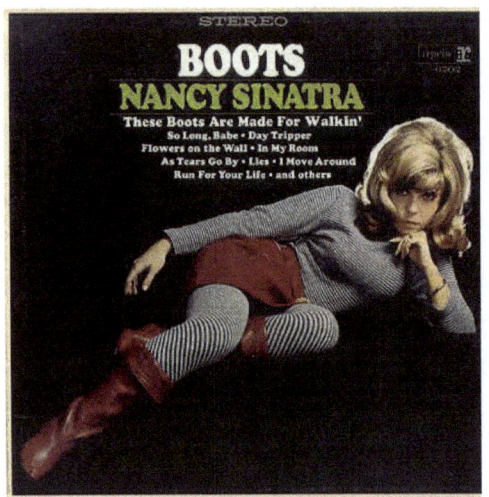

US release   March 1966   Reprise   R(S)-6202
UK release   March 1966   Reprise   R 6202

1. As Tears Go By (Mick Jagger/Keith Richards/Andrew Oldham)
2. Day Tripper (John Lennon/Paul McCartney)
3. I Move Around (Lee Hazlewood)
4. It Ain't Me Babe (Bob Dylan)
5. These Boots Are Made For Walkin' (Lee Hazlewood)
6. In My Room (Lee Pockriss/Paul Vance)
7. Lies (Beau Charles/Buddy Randall)
8. So Long Babe (Lee Hazlewood)
9. Flowers On The Wall (Lewis De Witt)
10. If He'd Love Me (Mirriam Eddy)
11. Run For Your Life (John Lennon/Paul McCartney)

Nancy Sinatra: vocals / Billy Strange: arranger / Lee Hazlewood: producer

Frank Sinatra's daughter hit the music world hard with the release of a striking country-pop single, *These Boots Are Made For Walkin'*, framed by a distinctive descending bass line. It reached number one in both the US and the UK. The album including the hit single is spoilt by Billy Strange's unimaginative arrangements. He uses that same bass line on two other songs and generally gives the music a clichéd, old-fashioned sound – the kind of thing heard in period films trying to convey the spirit of the sixties without having a proper understanding of how the music actually worked. The worst offender is *Lies,* where the Knickerbockers' sparkling original, whose whole point was that it sounded like the Beatles, is turned into an embarrassing piece of kitsch. Nancy Sinatra proves on the opening *As Tears Go By* that she has a very good voice, but too often the songs are pitched too low for her to put any real emotion into her singing, simply because the novelty effect of making her sound like a bored socialite worked well on the hit single. The album definitely has its moments, and the actual choice of song material is good, but it was not until the next year, when Nancy Sinatra was asked to perform a James Bond theme song (*You Only Live Twice*), that the singer was able to show what she could really do.

THE YOUNG RASCALS

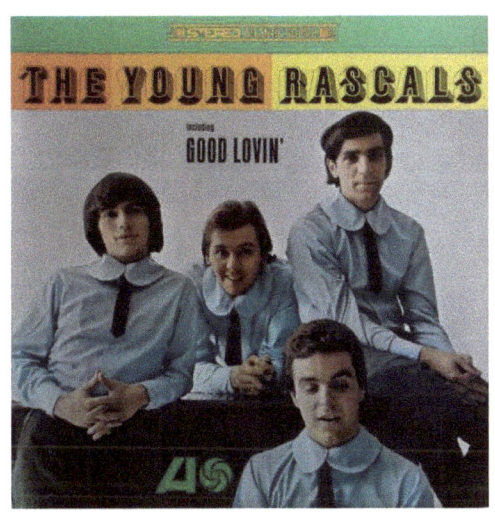

```
US release    March 1966    Atlantic  (SD) 8123
UK release    March 1966    Atlantic  588/587 012

1. Slow Down (Larry Williams)
2. Baby Let's Wait (Laurie Burton/Pam Sawyer)
3. Just A Little (Robert Durand/Ronald Elliott)
4. I Believe (Al Stillman/Ervin Drake/Irvin Graham/Jimmy Shirl)
5. Do You Feel It (Felix Cavaliere/Gene Cornish)

6. Good Lovin' (Arthur Resnick/Rudy Clark)
7. Like A Rolling Stone (Bob Dylan)
8. Mustang Sally (Bonny Rice)
9. I Ain't Gonna Eat Out My Heart Anymore (Burton/Sawyer)
10. In The Midnight Hour (Steve Cropper/Wilson Pickett)

Felix Cavaliere: vocals, organ / Gene Cornish: vocals, guitar /
Eddie Brigati: vocals,  percussion / Dino Danelli: drums / Arif
Mardin: producer / Tom Dowd: producer
```

Somewhat belatedly, an American group responded to the British beat invasion, not by directly copying the sound of the groups, but by exploring the same R&B and soul influences and creating its own response to those. The Young Rascals scored a US number one hit with their energetic second single, *Good Lovin'*, which sets out the characteristics of the group's sound – slightly lighter and with a little more rhythmic sophistication than the average British beat group, soulful vocals, and an organ moved forward in the mix to play on equal terms with the guitar. Curiously, the group decided to include a version of Bob Dylan's *Like A Rolling Stone* on the album, despite being unable to add anything worthwhile to the sound of the original. It is impossible to ignore the awkwardness of the costumes that someone decided would be a good look for a group calling itself the Young Rascals, but fortunately the music is for the most part strong enough to compensate.

WAYLON JENNINGS   FOLK – COUNTRY

```
US release    March 1966    RCA Victor    LSP/LPM 3523
Not released in UK

1. Another Bridge To Burn (Harlan Howard)
2. Stop The World (And Let Me Off) (Carl Belew/WS Stevenson)
3. Cindy Of New Orleans (Waylon Jennings)
4. Look Into My Teardrops (Don Bowman/Harlan Howard)
5. Down Came The World (Bozo Darnell/Waylon Jennings)
6. I Don't Mind (Harlan Howard/Richard Johnson)

7. Just For You (Don Bowman/Jackson King/Jerry Williams)
8. Now Everybody Knows (Don Bowman)
9. That's The Chance I'll Have To Take (Jackson King)
10. What Makes A Man Wander (Harlan Howard)
11. I'm A Man Of Constant Sorrow (Waylon Jennings)
12. What's Left Of Me (Harlan Howard)

Waylon Jennings: vocals, guitar / The Waylons – Jerry Gropp: guitar
(1-5,7,8,10-12) / Paul Foster: guitar (2,3,5,11,12), bass guitar (1,5,8) /
Richie Albright: drums (1,2,3,5,8,11,12) // Jerry Reed: guitar (3,4,9,10) /
Fred Carter Jr: guitar (2,5,11) / Pete Wade: guitar (1,8) / Floyd Cramer:
piano (2,4,5,11) / Hargus Robbins: piano (1,8) / Ray Stevens: piano
(3,9,10,12) , vibraphone (4) / Bob Moore: bass guitar (3,9,12) / Henry
Strzelecki: bass guitar (5,11) / Buddy Harman: drums (9,10) / Kenny
Buttrey: drums (4) / / Anita Carter: vocals / Dorothy Ann Dillard: vocals /
Louis Nunley: vocals / William Wright: vocals / Chet Atkins: producer
```

Waylon Jennings played bass guitar with Buddy Holly on the star's ill-fated last tour and released a number of country singles after that without much success. He managed to sign a record deal with RCA, however, after being recommended by singer Bobby Bare, and released *Folk – Country* as his first album for the label. The title is misleading, since there is little discernible trace of folk music in any of the songs. His rewrite of a traditional song associated with Bob Dylan, *I'm A Man Of Constant Sorrow*, takes a few words from the original, but nothing else. The album is standard commercial country music, such as could be heard on many other records during this period. It was moderately successful in terms of sales, certainly enough to keep RCA interested, but it bears little relation to the 'outlaw' country music pioneered by Jennings a few years later.

THE SEEDS

The Seeds take the music of R&B groups like Them and the Rolling Stones and reduce it to its simplest elements: a beat, a snarl, and just one or two chords, repeated over and over until fatigue declares the song to be finished. In the case of the fast-moving *Pushin' Too Hard*, released as a single, the result works extremely well, but most of the other songs are just variations on the same theme, with different words and played at different speeds. *Pushin' Too Hard* scraped into the US top forty on its second time of release and defined a 'sixties punk rock' genre. It inspired numerous other bands playing in more or less the same style, because the music was easy to put together and perform. In the UK, however, where bands like the Yardbirds and John Mayall's Bluesbreakers were already demonstrating the merits of instrumental expertise, the music made very much less impact.

```
US release      April 1966    GNP Crescendo   GNP(S) 2023
Not released in UK

1. Can't Seem To Make You Mine (Sky Saxon)
2. No Escape (Sky Saxon/Jan Savage/Jimmy Lawrence)
3. Lose Your Mind (Sky Saxon)
4. Evil Hoodoo (Sky Saxon/Daryl Hooper)
5. Girl I Want You (Sky Saxon)
6. Pushin' Too Hard (Sky Saxon)

7. Try To Understand (Sky Saxon)
8. Nobody Spoil My Fun (Sky Saxon)
9. It's A Hard Life (Sky Saxon)
10. You Can't Be Trusted (Sky Saxon)
11. Excuse Excuse (Marcus Tybalt)
12. Fallin' In Love (Sky Saxon)

Sky Saxon (aka Marcus Tybalt): vocals, bass guitar, harmonica, producer / Jan Savage: guitar, vocals / Daryl Hooper: piano, organ, vocals / Rick Andridge: drums / Harvey Sharpe: bass guitar
```

THE ANIMALS   THE MOST OF

```
UK release      April 1966       Columbia    SX 6035
US release      February 1966    11 track similar compilation, THE BEST OF
                                                  THE ANIMALS    MGM   SE 4324

1. We Gotta Get Out Of This Place (Barry Mann/Cynthia Weil)
2. Don't Let Me Be Misunderstood (Bennie Benjamin/Sol Marcus/
                                                      Gloria Caldwell)
3. Boom Boom (John Lee Hooker)
4. Baby Let Me Take You Home (Bob Russell/Wes Farrell)
5. Bright Lights Big City (Jimmy Reed)
6. I'm Crying (Alan Price/Eric Burdon)
7. The House Of The Rising Sun (Traditional)

8. It's My Life (Roger Atkins/Carl D'Errico)
9. Mess Around (Ahmet Ertegun)
10. Dimples (John Lee Hooker)
11. Bring It On Home To Me (Sam Cooke)
12. Gonna Send You Back To Walker (Johnnie Matthews/Jake Hammonds)
13. I'm Mad Again (John Lee Hooker)
14. Talkin' 'Bout You (Ray Charles)

Eric Burdon: vocals / Hilton Valentine: guitar, vocals; Alan Price: organ, piano, vocals (except 1 & 8) / Dave Rowberry: organ, vocals (1,8) / Chas Chandler: bass guitar, vocals / John Steel: drums / Mickie Most: producer
```

The Most of the Animals is the group's greatest hits compilation, named in honour of the producer, Mickie Most. It includes all the Animals' single A-sides up to the end of 1965, alongside a few selected album tracks, and it is by far the best album issued by the group. It easily makes clear why the Animals should be considered one of the essential acts of the time. It is not very surprising that the record became the group's highest charting album up to that point. The fact that the songs are not presented in chronological order is mildly irritating, except that it makes the overall impact of the music greater by ensuring a better balance of moods and tempos. An album issued in 1971 on EMI's Music for Pleasure label is also called *The Most Of The Animals,* but has an almost entirely different set of tracks.

JOE HARRIOTT - JOHN MAYER DOUBLE QUINTET   INDO-JAZZ SUITE

```
UK release      April 1966       Columbia    S(C)X 6025
US release      April 1966       Atlantic    (SD) 1465

1. Overture (John Mayer)
2. Contrasts (John Mayer)

3. Raga Megha (John Mayer)
4. Raga Gaud-Saranga (John Mayer)

Joe Harriott: alto saxophone / Kenny Wheeler: trumpet / Pat Smythe: piano / Coleridge Goode: bass / Alan Ganley: drums / John Mayer: violin, harpsichord / Chris Taylor: flute / Diwan Motihar: sitar / Chandrahas Paigankar: tambura / Keshav Sathe: tabla / Denis Preston: producer
```

Jamaican-British saxophonist Joe Harriott released five albums under his own name during the early sixties, three of them being adventurous free jazz sessions in a similar vein to those of the American pioneer, Ornette Coleman. John Mayer was an Indian violinist who performed for several years with the Royal Philharmonic Orchestra and composed works that combined Indian and Western classical music forms. His suggestion of forging a different fusion, between Indian music and jazz was initially ignored by producer Denis Preston, but it became possible when Ahmet Ertegun, the proprietor of Atlantic records in the US, came out in favour of the idea. The album *Indo-Jazz Suite* was the first result – with John Mayer being shown holding a sitar on the cover in order to emphasise what was being achieved, although the instrument was actually played by another member of the band. A full integration between the two styles of music is seldom to be heard, as for the most part the Indian and the jazz musicians take turns. Coleridge Goode's bass playing does manage to provide a unifying link, however, as he continues to provide an underlying counterpoint, regardless of who is playing over the top. The modal approach of Indian music had become recently adopted as part of the vocabulary of modern jazz soloists, and Joe Harriott and John Mayer have no difficulty in showing how this can make the two styles of music easily compatible. Their innovative album can only be considered as a very successful experiment, even if its sales were unfortunately very low.

SAM & DAVE   HOLD ON, I'M COMIN'

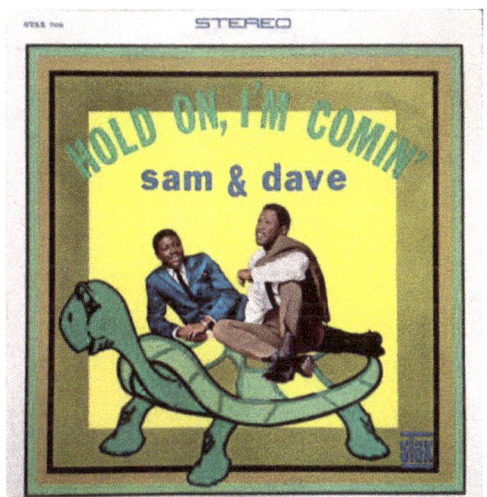

```
US release    April 1966    Stax        (SD)708
UK release    April 1966    Atlantic    589/587 045

1. Hold On, I'm Comin' (Isaac Hayes/David Porter)
2. If You Got The Loving (Steve Cropper/Isaac Hayes/David Porter)
3. I Take What I Want (Mabon Hodges?Isaac Hayes/David Porter)
4. Ease Me (Isaac Hayes/David Porter)
5. I Got Everything I Need (Steve Cropper/Eddie Floyd/Alvertis Isbell)
6. Don't Make It So Hard On Me (Eddie Floyd/Willia Dean Parker)

7. It's A Wonder (Isaac Hayes/David Porter)
8. Don't Help Me Out (Isaac Hayes/David Porter)
9. Just Me (Randall Catron/Mary Frierson/Willia Dean Parker)
10. You Got It Made (Isaac Hayes/David Porter)
11. You Don't Know Like I Know (Isaac Hayes/David Porter)
12. Blame Me (Don't Blame My Heart) (Steve Cropper/Alvertis Isbell)

Sam Moore: vocals / Dave Prater: vocals / Steve Cropper: guitar /
Booker T Jones: keyboards / Isaac Hayes: organ / Donald Dunn: bass
guitar / Al Jackson: drums / Wayne Jackson: trumpet, trombone / Packy
Axton: tenor saxophone / Don Nix: baritone saxophone / Jim
Stewart: producer
```

Performing as a duo, Sam Moore and Dave Prater were able to bring the exciting call and response patterns of gospel music directly into soul. The title track of this album was a big US hit, qualifying for a gold disc, while the previous Stax singles, *You Don't Know Like I Know* and *I Take What I Want*, also did well. All three records received extensive radio play in the UK too, but remarkably they all avoided becoming actual chart hits. Nevertheless, Sam & Dave became acknowledged as the third crucial ingredient in the Stax sound, alongside Otis Redding and Wilson Pickett, in the UK as in the US. Only the later hit, *Soul Man*, is missing from this otherwise ideal primer for the essential sixties soul music of Sam and Dave.

THE ROLLING STONES   AFTERMATH

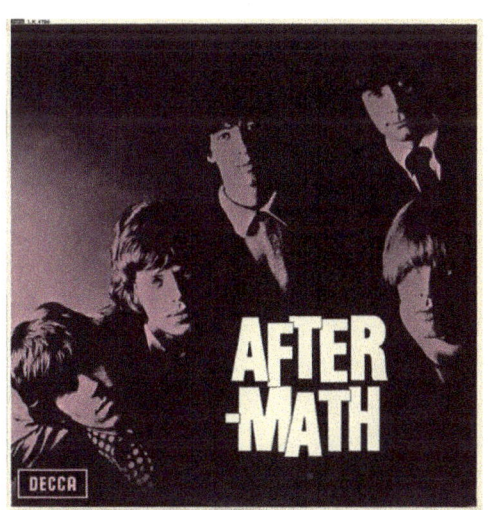

```
UK release   April 1966   Decca    SKL/LK 4786
US release   June 1966    London   PS 476/LL 3476
different cover, 4 tracks omitted, Paint It Black added

1. Mother's Little Helper
2. Stupid Girl
3. Lady Jane
4. Under My Thumb
5. Doncha Bother Me
6. Goin' Home

7. Flight 505
8. High And Dry
9. Out Of Time
10. It's Not Easy
11. I Am Waiting
12. Take It Or Leave It
13. Think
14. What To Do

All compositions by Mick Jagger and Keith Richards

Mick Jagger: vocals, percussion, harmonica / Brian
Jones: guitar, dulcimer, harmonica, marimba, koto /
Keith Richards: guitar, bass guitar, vocals / Bill Wyman:
bass guitar, bells, organ (on Paint It Black) / Charlie
Watts: drums, percussion / Ian Stewart: piano, organ /
Jack Nitzsche: piano, organ, harpsichord, percussion /
Andrew Loog Oldham, Rolling Stones: producer
```

Aftermath is the Rolling Stones' artistic breakthrough on album. All the songs are written by Mick Jagger and Keith Richards and, for the first time, they and the rest of the group have put as much effort into making all the music sound memorable and distinctive as they had been doing for some time with the singles. Many of the songs sever the group's connection with R&B, most notably the gentle, acoustic *Lady Jane*, underpinned by the sound of a dulcimer, and the cheeky *Mother's Little Helper*, referencing medically prescribed barbiturates while propelled by a suitably spaced-out riff delivered in unison by a Japanese koto and a guitar made to sound like a sitar (the real thing is played on the single *Paint It Black*, included on the US version of the album). Many of the songs are arranged as imaginatively as these, with Keith Richards often attaching the fuzz pedal he used on the single, *Satisfaction*, to both guitar and bass guitar, while Brian Jones experiments with a number of instruments not often employed in a rock context. The music is made to sound very varied from track to track as a result, although the Stones have not quite grasped the Beatles' principle of reserving each new sound for just one song. The album reaches a climax with *Goin' Home*, placed strategically at the end of side one on the UK version (at the end of side two in the US). This breaks entirely new ground by presenting the result of a studio jam, stretching a song that might otherwise not be particularly notable into an eleven-minute marathon, that most definitely is, even if the jamming is essentially a rhythmic exercise, without obvious instrumental solos.

THE SMALL FACES   SMALL FACES

UK release   May 1966   Decca   LK 4790
Not released in US

1. Shake (Sam Cooke)
2. Come On Children (Jones/Lane/Marriott/Winston)
3. You'd Better Believe It (Kenny Lynch/Jerry Ragavoy)
4. It's Too Late (Jones/Lane/Marriott/Winston)
5. One Night Stand (Lane/Marriott)
6. Whatcha Gonna Do About It (Ian Samwell/Lane/Marriott)

7. Sorry She's Mine (Kenny Lynch)
8. Own Up Time (Jones/Lane/Marriott/McLagan)
9. You Need Loving (Lane/Marriott)
10. Don't Stop What You're Doing (Jones/Lane/Marriott/Winston)
11. E Too D (Lane/Marriott)
12. Sha-La-La-La-Lee (Kenny Lynch/Mort Shuman)

Steve Marriott: vocals, guitar / Ronnie Lane: bass guitar, vocals / Jimmy Winston: keyboards, guitar, vocals (2,4,6,10,11) / Ian McLagan: keyboards, vocals (1,3,5,7, 8,9,12) / Kenney Jones: drums / Kenny Lynch: vocals, producer (3,7,12) / Ian Samwell: producer / Don Arden: producer

Although the Who had made the decision to appeal to the mod audience, the Small Faces were already a part of it. In Steve Marriott, the group had a singer with a particularly compelling and soulful voice. The first single, *Whatcha Gonna Do About It*, borrowed its underlying riff from soul singer Solomon Burke and was a modest hit. The song also employed the kind of extreme approach to the guitar favoured by the Who, in this case delivering a whining solo achieved by rubbing the guitar neck against a microphone stand. The second single, *I Got Mine,* entirely failed to capitalise on the initial success and a disillusioned Jimmy Winston decided to leave the group. Ian McLagan was swiftly recruited as a replacement and a third single, *Sha-La-La-La-Lee,* proceeded to climb to number three. It is McLagan who is included in the group portrait used on the LP sleeve. The album starts off with a convincing cover of a Sam Cooke song, but after that the group prefers to use material written in soul style by black British songwriter Kenny Lynch, or else by the Small Faces themselves. *You Need Loving* is a very thinly disguised version of a song by Muddy Waters, but it failed to attract the attention that Led Zeppelin received in appropriating the same song some three years later. It is the sound of the group that dominates the album, however, rather than the actual songs. Steve Marriott's powerful singing is ably supported by group playing that is harder and more fiery than any of its contemporaries, even the Who. The combination produces a particularly exciting record.

GEORGIE FAME   SWEET THINGS

UK release   May 1966   Columbia   SX 6043
US release as **GET AWAY,** different cover and two different tracks   July 1966   Imperial   LP-12331 / LP-9331

1. Sweet Thing (Mickey Stevenson)
2. See Saw (Don Covay)
3. Ride Your Pony (Allen Toussaint as Naomi Neville)
4. Funny How Time Slips Away (Willie Nelson)
5. Sitting In The Park (Billy Stewart)
6. Dr Kitch (Chris Blackwell/Lord Kitchener)

7. My Girl (Smokey Robinson/Ronald White)
8. Music Talk (Clarence Paul/Stevie Wonder/Ted Hull)
9. The In Crowd (Billy Page)
10. The World Is Round (Rufus Thomas)
11. The Whole World's Shaking (Sam Cooke)
12. Last Night (The Markeys)

Georgie Fame: vocals, organ / Colin Green: guitar / Peter Coe: alto and tenor saxophones / Glen Hughes: tenor and baritone saxophones, flute / Edward Thornton: trumpet / Cliff Barton: bass guitar / John (Mitch) Mitchell: drums / Speedy Acquaye: percussion/ Denny Cordell: producer

Georgie Fame continued to refine his jazz-slanted approach to soul singing and playing with his second studio album and was rewarded with a top ten chart placing. *Get Away* was released as a single a little afterwards, in time to be included on the American version of the album, and it reached number one in the UK. The more relaxed *Sitting In The Park* was chosen as a single towards the end of the year and also did well, although it failed to enter the top ten. The new Cliff Barton/Mitch Mitchell rhythm section delivers a considerable punch, making the music sound more dynamic than previously. It anticipates by three years the jazz-rock of bands like Colosseum and Chicago, except that little opportunity is provided for instrumental soloing, other than Georgie Fame's own Hammond organ playing.

THE STANDELLS   DIRTY WATER

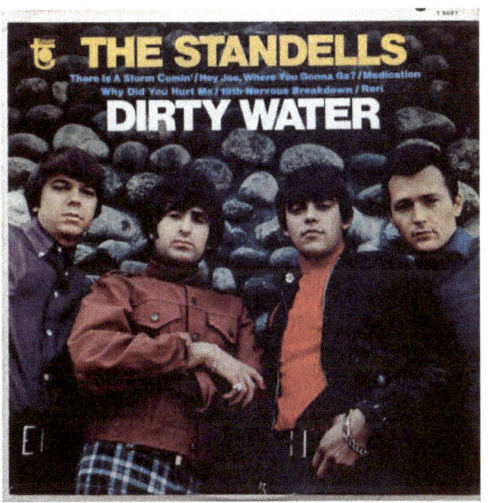

```
US release      May 1966    Tower   (S)T 5027
Not released in UK

1. Medication (Ben DiTosti/Minette Allton)
2. Little Sally Tease (Jim Valley)
3. There Is A Storm Comin' (Ed Cobb)
4. 19th Nervous Breakdown (Mick Jagger/Keith Richard)
5. Dirty Water (Ed Cobb)

6. Pride And Devotion (Larry Tamblyn)
7. Sometimes Good Guys Don't Wear White (Ed Cobb)
8. Hey Joe, Where You Gonna Go? (Billy Roberts)
9. Why Did You Hurt Me (Dick Dodd/Tony Valentino)
10. Rari (Ed Cobb)

Tony Valentino: guitar, harmonica / Larry Tamblyn: keyboards, vocals /
Gary Lane: bass guitar / Dick Dodd: vocals, drums / Ed Cobb: producer
```

Of the many American punk, garage bands to emerge in the wake of the Seeds, the Standells were the most convincing. The title track of the album was released as a single and became a big US hit. The group is clearly taking Them and the Rolling Stones as its primary influences, even if it is apparently unaware of the R&B that underlies the music of its mentors. The Standells even throw in a cover of a recent Stones' single, although this entirely lacks the authority of the original and seems like a pointless exercise in hero-worship. There is also the inevitable nod in the direction of the Byrds, most obviously on *Pride And Devotion*, composed by the group's keyboard player. The most interesting track is the one that opens the album, with an oscillating guitar underscoring lyrics that are blatantly concerned with mind-altering substances. The song suggests a fertile path to be explored, although it was not one that the Standells chose to follow themselves.

THE MONKS   BLACK MONK TIME

```
German release    May 1966    Polydor   249 900
Not released in the UK or US

1. Monk Time
2. Shut Up
3. Boys Are Boys And Girls Are Choice
4. Higgle-dy Piggle-dy
5. I Hate You
6. Oh, How To Do Now

7. Complication
8. We Do Wie Du
9. Drunken Maria
10. Love Came Tumblin' Down
11. Blast Off!
12. That's My Girl

All compositions by the Monks

Gary Burger: vocals, guitar / Dave Day: banjo, vocals /
Larry Clark: organ, vocals / Eddie Shaw: bass guitar,
vocals / Roger Johnston: drums, vocals / Jimmy Bowen:
producer
```

The one album made by the Monks, issued only in Germany and failing to sell many copies even there, would have remained completely obscure were it not for its rediscovery in more recent years by critics determined to prove its seminal influence on the punk rock of the late seventies. The Monks were a group of former American soldiers who liked to perform while wearing the habits suggested by their chosen name and with the tops of their heads shaved in a crude imitation of monks' tonsures. The music is similarly demented. It is as though five accomplished musicians have decided to form a rock band without having any idea as to what rock is supposed to sound like. The rhythms are mostly played in a strident two four time, resembling those of a barn-dance or a bierkeller. The lead singer, Gary Burger, declaims his words histrionically over the top, without trying to deliver anything much in the way of a melody. During the first track, *Monk Time*, he mentions that the group does not think much of the American involvement in Vietnam, but the rest of the album is steadfastly non-political. His guitar interjections, which include a small number of unexpectedly phrased solos, are frequently distorted with a fuzz box and even a little feedback in a couple of places. Larry Clark's organ plays in much the same way. But the most distinctive element in the group's sound is the cheerfully tuneless clattering of Dave Day's strummed banjo. This idiosyncratic music is fascinating to listen to, and has a superficial resemblance in places to the far more rocking Pere Ubu a decade later, but it is diametrically opposed to the punk aesthetic, where musicians with limited skills do the best that they can regardless. The Monks play like this on purpose.

THE BEACH BOYS   PET SOUNDS

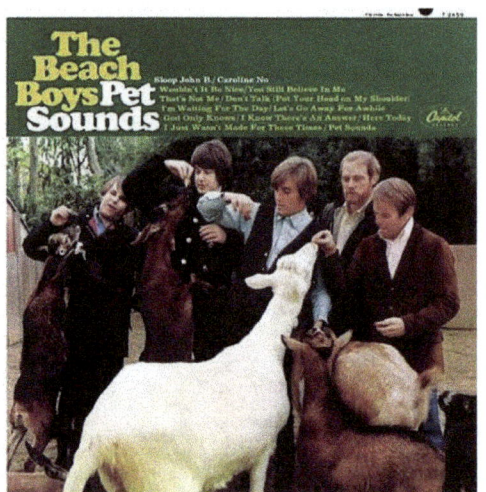

| US release | May 1966 | Capitol | (D)T 2458 |
| UK release | June 1966 | Capitol | (S)T 2458 |

1. Wouldn't It Be Nice (Brian Wilson/Tony Asher/Mike Love)
2. You Still Believe In Me (Brian Wilson/Tony Asher)
3. That's Not Me (Brian Wilson/Tony Asher)
4. Don't Talk (Put Your Head On My Shoulder) (Wilson/Asher)
5. I'm Waiting For The Day (Brian Wilson/Tony Asher)
6. Let's Go Away For A While (Brian Wilson)
7. Sloop John B (Traditional)

8. God Only Knows (Brian Wilson/Tony Asher)
9. I Know There's An Answer (Wilson/Terry Sachen/Mike Love)
10. Here Today (Brian Wilson/Tony Asher)
11. I Just Wasn't Made For These Times (Brian Wilson/Tony Asher)
12. Pet Sounds (Brian Wilson)
13. Caroline, No (Brian Wilson/Tony Asher)

Mike Love: vocals / Brian Wilson: vocals, piano (2,12), organ (3,9), bass guitar (3), producer / Al Jardine: vocals / Carl Wilson: vocals, guitar (3,8) / Bruce Johnston: vocals / Dennis Wilson: vocals, drums (3) / Tony Asher: piano (2) / Steve Korthof: percussion (3) / Terry Melcher: percussion (3,8) / Glen Campbell: guitar, banjo / Al Casey: guitar / Jerry Cole: guitar / Mike Deasy: guitar / Barney Kessell: guitar / Bill Pitman: guitar / Billy Strange: guitar / Tommy Tedesco: guitar / Al De Lory: keyboards / Larry Knechtel: keyboards / Mike Melvoin: harpsichord / Don Randi: piano / Paul Tanner: theremin (tannerin) / Carl Fortina: accordion / Frank Marocco: accordion / Tommy Morgan: bass harmonica / Carol Kaye: bass guitar / Ray Pohlman: bass guitar / Lyle Ritz: bass, ukulele / Hal Blaine: drums, percussion / Frank Capp: percussion, tuned percussion / Gary Coleman: percussion / Ritchie Frost: drums, percussion / Jim Gordon: drums, percussion / Nick Martinis: drums / Jerry Williams: percussion / Julius Wechter: percussion, vibraphone / Roy Caton: trumpet / Gail Martin: bass trombone / Ernie Tack: bass trombone / Alan Robinson: French horn / Steve Douglas: alto and tenor saxophone, clarinet, flute, piano, percussion / Jay Migliori: baritone and bass saxophone, clarinet, bass clarinet, flute / Jack Nimitz: baritone and bass saxophone / Bill Green: alto saxophone, clarinet, flute, percussion / Jim Horn: alto and baritone saxophone, clarinet, flute / Plas Johnson: tenor saxophone, clarinet, flute, piccolo, percussion / Bobby Klein: clarinet / Paul Horn: flute / Jules Jacob: flute / Leonard Hartman: clarinet, bass clarinet, English horn / The Sid Sharp Strings

Brian Wilson finally manages to create the music that he must have been hearing inside his head all along. He does this by largely abandoning the Beach Boys' own instrumental playing and using them purely as a vocal group. Despite this, Wilson cannot ignore his love of instrumentals, resulting in a track, *Pet Sounds* itself, where he is the only group member present, and another, *Let's Go Away For A While*, on which no member of the Beach Boys performs at all. The playing of an orchestra of session musicians, however, employed to do much more than merely add colour, makes the music throughout the album sound gorgeous. Fortunately, Brian Wilson has supplied a collection of his strongest songs to date, songs that would have sounded impressive even without the elaborate arrangements they receive. There are several very imaginative touches to help to make the music stand out. These include the use of a theremin in *I Just Wasn't Made For These Times*, plucked piano strings in *You Still Believe In Me*, and sampled train noise and dog barking at the end of *Caroline, No*. Legend has it that Brian Wilson saw himself as being in competition with the Beatles and that he intended *Pet Sounds* to be an album to surpass *Rubber Soul*. Arguably, this is exactly what it does. Curiously, *Caroline, No* was issued as a Brian Wilson solo single (with an instrumental B-side, *Summer Means New Love*, taken from the *Summer Days (And Summer Nights!)* album), but it was overwhelmed by the release, just two weeks later, of *Sloop John B*, properly credited to the Beach Boys.

FRANK SINATRA   STRANGERS IN THE NIGHT

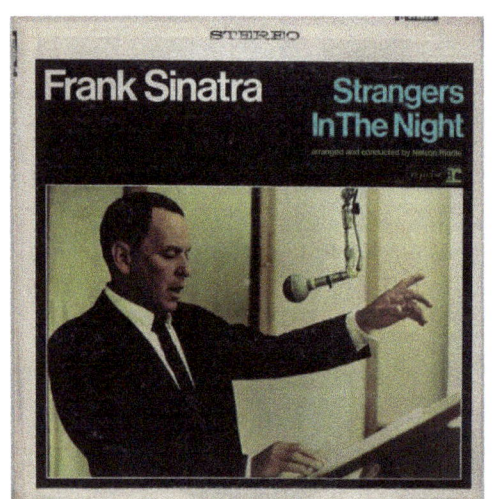

| US release | May 1966 | Reprise | F(S) 1017 |
| UK release | May 1966 | Reprise | R(9) 1017 |

1. Strangers In The Night (Bert Kaempfert/Charles Singleton/Eddie Snyder)
2. Summer Wind (Henry Mayer/Johnny Mercer)
3. All Or Nothing At All (Arthur Altman/Jack Lawrence)
4. Call Me (Tony Hatch)
5. You're Driving Me Crazy (Walter Donaldson)

6. On A Clear Day (Al Lerner/Burton Lane)
7. My Baby Just Cares For Me (Gus Kahn/Walter Donaldson)
8. Downtown (Tony Hatch)
9. Yes Sir, That's My Baby (Gus Kahn/Walter Donaldson)
10. The Most Beautiful Girl In The World (Richard Rogers/Lorenz Hart)

Frank Sinatra: vocals / Ernie Freeman: arranger (1) / Nelson Riddle: arranger (2-10) / Jimmy Bowen: producer (1) / Sonny Burke: producer (2-10) / Musicians on track 1 include Glen Campbell: guitar / Hal Blaine: drums

Frank Sinatra made three albums in 1966 and this middle one, *Strangers In The Night*, was very much business as usual, with no significant musical differences from Sinatra's other albums in the fifties and sixties. By including two songs associated with Petula Clark and written by Tony Hatch, Sinatra probably imagined that he was being modern, but they fit comfortably into his usual style. Petula Clark returned the favour by including the song, *Strangers In The Night*, on an album of her own later the same year. For some reason, the Frank Sinatra album became the most successful of his entire career and its title track reached number one in both the US and the UK when released as a single. Frank Sinatra made it clear that he hated the song, possibly because the arrangement opts for a light orchestral pop sound, including a few musicians more used to working with the Beach Boys, rather than the jazz-influenced big band with which he was familiar. The record buying public, however, clearly did not agree with him.

JOHN HANDY   RECORDED LIVE AT THE MONTEREY JAZZ FESTIVAL

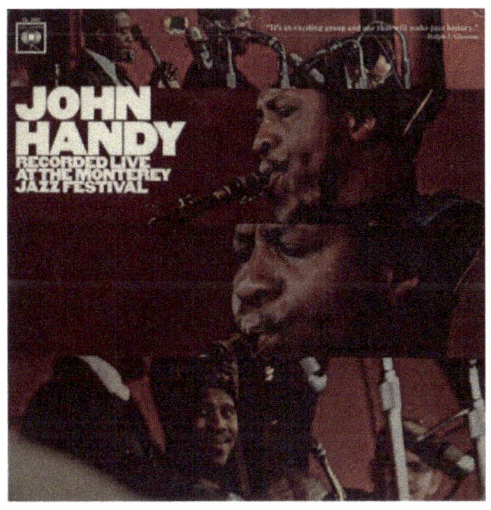

| US release | May 1966 | Columbia | CS 9262 / CL 2462 |
| UK release | May 1966 | CBS | (S)BPG 62678 |

1. Spanish Lady (John Handy)
2. If Only We Knew (John Handy)

John Handy: alto saxophone / Michael White: violin / Jerry Hahn: guitar / Don Thompson: bass / Terry Clarke: drums / John Hammond: producer

The acceptable face of avant garde jazz: these are long modal improvisations in the manner of John Coltrane, but with playing that stays on the right side of the safety barrier, keeping everything nicely melodic and avoiding anything harsh or upsetting. John Handy had previously been a member of Charles Mingus' band, but at this performance, recorded live at the 1965 Monterey Jazz Festival, he is presenting a band of his own for the first time. The line-up is the familiar jazz quintet, except that instead of a trumpet alongside the leader's alto saxophone, a violin plays, and instead of a piano, an electric guitar is heading up the rhythm section. This level of innovation is commendable, especially when it is clear that all concerned are fine players. They must have gone down very well at Monterey, but ultimately, the lack of an edge makes the music sound just a little bland. *Spanish Lady* tears along at a considerable speed, but still sounds as though the musicians' feet are hovering just above the brake pedals. Critic Ralph Gleason declaims on the front cover of the album, "It's an exciting group and one that will make jazz history", but really it's not particularly and it didn't.

VARIOUS ARTISTS   WHAT'S SHAKIN'

| US release | June 1966 | Elektra | EKS 74002/EKL 4002 |
| UK release | June 1966 | Elektra | EKS 74002/EKL 4002 |

Reissued early 1968 with a different cover as **GOOD TIME MUSIC** Elektra EUK(S) 260

1. Good Time Music (John Sebastian)
2. Almost Grown (Chuck Berry)
3. Spoonful (Willie Dixon)
4. Off The Wall (Walter Jacobs)
5. I Can't Keep From Crying Sometimes (Blind Willie Johnson)
6. I Want To Know (Paul Jones as Sheila McLeod)
7. Crossroads (Robert Johnson)
8. Lovin' Cup (Paul Butterfield)
9. Good Morning Little Schoolgirl (Bob Love/Don Level)
10. Steppin' Out (Memphis Slim)
11. I'm In Love Again (Dave Bartholomew/Fats Domino)
12. Don't Bank On It Baby (John Sebastian)
13. Searchin' (Jerry Leiber/Mike Stoller)
14. One More Mile (James Cotton)

Tracks 1,2,12,13: The Lovin' Spoonful – John Sebastian: vocals, guitar / Zalman Yanovsky: guitar / Steve Boone: bass guitar / Joe Butler: drums. Tracks 3,4,8,9,14: The Paul Butterfield Blues Band – Paul Butterfield: vocals, harmonica / Elvin Bishop: guitar / Mike Bloomfield: guitar / Jerome Arnold: bass guitar / Sam Lay: drums. Tracks 5: Al Kooper: vocals, piano / Bruce Langhorne: guitar / Harvey Brooks: bass guitar / Bobby Gregg: drums. Tracks 6,7,10: Eric Clapton and the Powerhouse – Eric Clapton: guitar / Steve Winwood: vocals / Paul Jones: harmonica / Ben Palmer: piano / Jack Bruce: bass guitar / Pete York: drums. Track 11: Tom Rush: vocals, guitar / band as on track 5. Producers – Paul Rothchild / Mark Abramson / Joe Boyd

The Lovin' Spoonful is given pride of place on the front cover of the album issued by Elektra as the second release in its new 4000 series (set up to acknowledge the company's launch in the UK). In fact, the group only plays on four tracks on what is actually a compilation album, conveniently gathering together some significant recordings not otherwise destined for LP. The Lovin' Spoonful tracks are the first to have been recorded by the group, when it was still very much a rhythm and blues band, without the folk influences that were adopted soon afterwards. The five tracks by the Paul Butterfield Blues Band are similarly the first to have been recorded by them, in advance of keyboard player Mark Naftalin joining. These are songs that were intended as part of a first album by the band, but were replaced by later recordings. Despite being deemed to be not good enough, the songs sound like a perfectly fine representation of the Butterfield Band's strengths. The Eric Clapton tracks were recorded by a band specially assembled by new producer Joe Boyd, following the musicians' high placings in the annual *New Musical Express* readers' poll. The Powerhouse did not survive beyond the recording session, although two of the songs became part of Clapton's subsequent repertoire with different groups. *Steppin' Out* and *Crossroads* achieved greater stature than can be claimed by the rather basic versions presented here. The remaining tracks, by Al Kooper and Tom Rush, are left-overs from a Bob Dylan recording session, snatched out of the down-time. Rush was a folk singer with an album of his own already issued by Elektra.

MANFRED MANN   INSTRUMENTAL ASYLUM EP

UK release   June 1966   HMV   7EG 8949
Not released in US

1. Still I'm Sad (Paul Samwell-Smith)
2. My Generation (Pete Townshend)
3. Satisfaction (Mick Jagger/Keith Richards)
4. I Got You Babe (Sonny Bono)

Manfred Mann: keyboards / Tom McGuinness: guitar / Henry Lowther: trumpet / Lyn Dobson: tenor saxophone, flute / Jack Bruce: bass guitar / Mike Hugg: drums, vibraphone / John Burgess: producer

Manfred Mann seemed very keen on using the EP to promote itself. The group reserved some of its strongest material for a succession of releases in the format. *Instrumental Asylum* is something different and marks, together with the previous EP, *Machines,* and the *Pretty Flamingo* single, the recorded legacy of an influential transitional line-up. With Mike Vickers having departed, and Paul Jones about to follow suit, Tom McGuinness moved to guitar, leaving room for Jack Bruce to fill the bass slot. As a former member of Alexis Korner's Blues Incorporated and of the Graham Bond Organization, as well as, briefly, John Mayall's Bluesbreakers, where he performed alongside guitarist Eric Clapton, Bruce had already acquired the reputation as a particularly gifted player. The other new members of Manfred Mann – trumpeter Henry Lowther and saxophonist Lyn Dobson – had similar jazz backgrounds to Bruce. *Instrumental Asylum* comprises four well-known contemporary beat songs, reworked as though they were jazz instrumentals. The results work surprisingly well, making the EP a significant milestone on the road to jazz-rock. The tracks were included on a Manfred Mann LP issued in the UK in 1967, *Soul Of Mann,* a largely instrumental compilation of the group's more jazz-slanted material, but their main impact was made here.

WAYNE SHORTER   SPEAK NO EVIL

US release   June 1966   Blue Note   BST 84194/BLP 4194
Not released in UK

1. Witch Hunt
2. Fee-Fi-Fo-Fum
3. Dance Cadaverous
4. Speak No Evil
5. Infant Eyes
6. Wild Flower

All compositions by Wayne Shorter

Wayne Shorter: tenor saxophone / Freddie Hubbard: trumpet / Herbie Hancock: piano / Ron Carter: bass / Elvin Jones: drums / Alfred Lion: producer

While playing as a member of the Miles Davis Quintet, Wayne Shorter still found time to record a number of albums of his own for the Blue Note label. Inevitably, the music sounds remarkably like that on the Miles Davis albums, especially since Shorter tended to employ other members of the Quintet whenever he could. Herbie Hancock's piano playing is the key where *Speak No Evil* is concerned, thanks to his ability to supply continually shifting harmonies even when the root notes of the chords do not change. Curiously, the one weak link in the band assembled here is drummer Elvin Jones, who reins in the tumultuous rhythms he favours when playing with John Coltrane, but without managing to discover a talent to surprise in the manner of Tony Williams. He sounds efficient, but ordinary – a remarkable position for one of the great drummers of his time to be in. Wayne Shorter himself plays superbly, so that *Speak No Evil* cannot avoid being revealed as an impressive album regardless, even if it is one that breaks no new ground.

THE BEATLES   YESTERDAY AND TODAY

US release   June 1966   Capitol   (S)T 2553
Not released in UK

1. Drive My Car (John Lennon/Paul McCartney)
2. I'm Only Sleeping (John Lennon/Paul McCartney)
3. Nowhere Man (John Lennon/Paul McCartney)
4. Dr Robert (John Lennon/Paul McCartney)
5. Yesterday (John Lennon/Paul McCartney)
6. Act Naturally (John Russell/Voni Morrison)
7. And Your Bird Can Sing (John Lennon/Paul McCartney)
8. If I Needed Someone (George Harrison)
9. We Can Work It Out (John Lennon/Paul McCartney)
10. What Goes On? (John Lennon/Paul McCartney/Ringo Starr)
11. Day Tripper (John Lennon/Paul McCartney)

John Lennon: vocals, guitar, harmonium / George Harrison: guitar, vocals, percussion / Paul McCartney: vocals, bass guitar, guitar, piano / Ringo Starr: drums, vocals / George Martin: producer, harmonium

Yesterday And Today was originally issued with the extraordinary sleeve shown, where the white-coated Beatles are festooned with decapitated dolls and pieces of raw meat. This was appropriately dubbed the 'butcher sleeve'. Ignoring the fact that, as British citizens, the Beatles were not directly concerned with American foreign policy and were not, in any case, accustomed to making political statements, several commentators decided that the album cover was intended as a criticism of the war in Vietnam. It is more logical, however, to assume that the criticism was aimed at Capitol itself, for 'butchering' the Beatles' albums and completely ignoring the group's own wishes with regard to album

coherence and sequencing. The contents of *Yesterday And Today* are a case in point: a random assortment of tracks originally included on the UK *Help!* and *Rubber Soul* albums, two tracks issued as a single, and three tracks stolen from the album *Revolver*, which had not yet been released, with mixes that would be changed. The cover was hastily withdrawn and changed to something much more bland as soon as Capitol realised what it had done, but the album's contents remained as they were. Musically, the album cannot help sounding good, because the songs are good, but in terms of its contribution towards revealing the Beatles' musical development, it remains a travesty. Original copies of the album in this sleeve have, of course, become serious collectors' items, with prices rising steadily over time. In 2016, a mint copy of the LP was sold at auction for $125,000.

THE INCREDIBLE STRING BAND

```
UK release    June 1966    Elektra    EUK 254
US release    April 1967   Elektra    EKS 7322/EKL 322    different cover

1. Maybe Someday (Mike Heron)
2. October Song (Robin Williamson)
3. When The Music Starts To Play (Mike Heron)
4. Schaeffer's Jig (Traditional)
5. Womankind (Robin Williamson)
6. The Tree (Mike Heron)
7. Whistle Tune (Traditional)
8. Dandelion Blues (Robin Williamson)

9. How Happy I Am (Mike Heron)
10. Empty Pocket Blues (Clive Palmer)
11. Smoke Shovelling Song (Robin Williamson)
12. Can't Keep Me Here (Mike Heron)
13. Good As Gone Robin Williamson)
14. Footsteps Of The Heron (Mike Heron)
15. Niggertown (Traditional)
16. Everything's Fine Right Now (Mike Heron)

Mike Heron: vocals, guitar / Robin Williamson: vocals, guitar, violin, mandolin, whistle / Clive Palmer: vocals, guitar, banjo, kazoo / Joe Boyd: producer
```

The Scottish folk trio, the Incredible String Band, was not so much a band on its first album, as a co-operative. Several of the tracks are performed by just one person, others by a duo, with only three tracks (*How Happy I Am*, *Empty Pocket Blues*, and *Everything's Fine Right Now*) being the work of all three musicians singing and playing together. Clive Palmer only plays on five of the sixteen tracks, one of them being a solo banjo performance with, for modern listeners, an unfortunately insensitive title. On the cover of the album, the three are shown holding a variety of exotic stringed instruments, as apparent justification for the band name. At gigs too, the Incredibles would surround themselves with a similar assortment. Sadly, none are played on the album and for the most part the singers accompany themselves with acoustic guitars. The melody lines and the wayward manner of their delivery are delightfully eccentric, however. Mike Heron was a late addition to the group, but he is a natural fit, since his song-writing and singing styles are very similar to those of Robin Williamson.

MIKE TAYLOR QUARTET   PENDULUM

Any album that opens with a drum solo is announcing its intention to be a little different. The music on the first side of *Pendulum* comprises improvisations on three jazz standards in which the familiar tunes are deconstructed and turned into new pieces that border on the avant garde. The second side presents three surprising original compositions based on the use of twisting improvised themes laid over subtle riffs. Soprano saxophonist Dave Tomlin plays well enough, although he would never be likely to give John Coltrane any sleepless nights. But the rhythm section,

```
UK release    June 1966    Columbia    SX 6042
Not released in US

1. But Not For Me (George Gershwin)
2. Exactly Like You (Jimmy McHugh/Dorothy Fields)
3. A Night In Tunisia (Dizzy Gillespie/Frank Paparelli)

4. Pendulum (Mike Taylor)
5. To Segovia (Mike Taylor)
6. Leeway (Mike Taylor)

Mike Taylor: piano / Dave Tomlin: soprano saxophone / Tony Reeves: bass / Jon Hiseman: drums / Denis Preston: producer
```

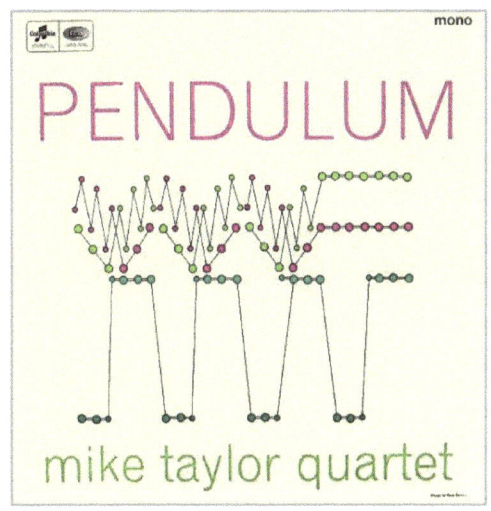

borrowed from the New Jazz Orchestra, is outstanding and so too is the playing of the group's leader, pianist Mike Taylor. He is not an extrovert performer, but sounds like no other pianist in jazz. The album very successfully sets out the credentials of a major new voice in British jazz, although disappointingly its sales were minimal.

SPONTANEOUS MUSIC ENSEMBLE   CHALLENGE

UK release   c.June 1966   Eyemark   EMPL 1002
Not released in US

1. E.D.'s Message (Trevor Watts)
2. 2 B Ornette (Paul Rutherford)
3. Club 66 (Trevor Watts)
4. Day Of Reckoning (Trevor Watts)

5. Travelling Together (John Stevens)
6. Little Red Head (John Stevens)
7. After Listening (Paul Rutherford)
8. End To A Beginning (John Stevens)

Trevor Watts: alto and soprano saxophones / Kenny Wheeler: flugelhorn / Paul Rutherford: trombone / Bruce Cale: bass (2-7) / Jeff Clyne: bass (1,8) / John Stevens: drums / Eddie Kramer: producer

This is the first recording by a group of British improvising musicians, under the nominal leadership of drummer John Stevens and saxophonist Trevor Watts. It was to become very influential within the related worlds of avant garde jazz and free improvisation, essentially bringing together the music of Ornette Coleman and Sun Ra on the one hand with the music of AMM and Il Gruppo (Nuova Consonanza) on the other, although *Challenge* predates the first albums by both of those last-named units. Alto saxophonist Joe Harriott was the first British jazz player to explore the new vocabulary pioneered by Ornette Coleman, with the albums, *Free Form* and *Abstract*, recorded right at the start of the sixties. *Challenge* continues this work, proving how well these British musicians have absorbed the approach of the American avant garde. It is an outstanding album, in which the members of the Spontaneous Music Ensemble are able to improvise simultaneously, with little more than brief predetermined melodic phrases to launch the proceedings, but with close attention at all times to each other's playing. The result is that the music is given an organic cohesiveness even while the musicians are improvising freely. It is not surprising that music so removed from the British mainstream in any genre should have needed the daring of a tiny independent record company for its release. Within a catalogue that also included steam train recordings, a singing drag act, and a paean to oral sex, Eyemark doubtless considered the Spontaneous Music Ensemble to be a tribute to British eccentricity, but as it turned out, the music succeeds in entirely transcending this lowly idea.

THE MOTHERS OF INVENTION   FREAK OUT!

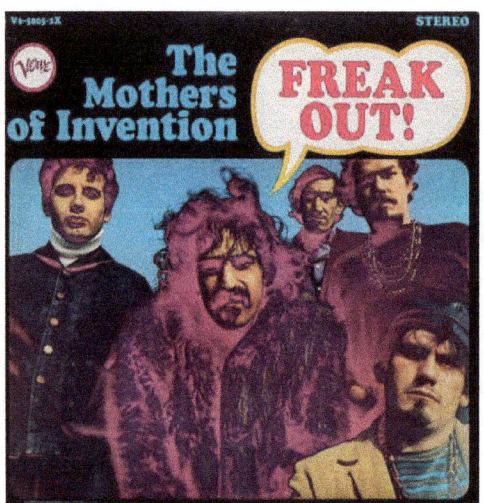

US release   June 1966   Verve   V(6)-5005-2   double LP
UK release March 1967   Verve (S)VLP 9154   single LP with 3 tracks missing

1. Hungry Freaks, Daddy
2. I Ain't Got No Heart
3. Who Are The Brain Police?
4. Go Cry On Somebody Else's Shoulder (Frank Zappa/Ray Collins)
5. Motherly Love
6. How Could I Be Such A Fool

7. Wowie Zowie
8. You Didn't Try To Call Me
9. Any Way The Wind Blows
10. I'm Not Satisfied
11. You're Probably Wondering Why I'm Here

12. Trouble Every Day
13. ..Help, I'm A Rock (Okay To Tap Dance - In Memoriam, Edgar Varese - It Can't Happen Here)

14. The Return Of The Son Of Monster Magnet (Ritual Dance Of The Child Killers - Nullis Pretii [No Commercial Potential)

All compositions by Frank Zappa except track 4

Frank Zappa: guitar, vocals, arranger / Ray Collins: vocals, harmonica, percussion / Elliot Ingber: guitar / Roy Estrada: bass guitar, guitarron, vocals / Jimmy Carl Black: drums, vocals / Jeannie Vassoir (Suzy Creamcheese): voice / Neil Le Vang: guitar / Carol Kaye: guitar / Eugene Di Novi: piano / John Rotella: clarinet, saxophone / Arthur Maebe: French horn, tuba / Gene Estes: percussion / Kurt Reher, Raymond Kelley, Paul Bergstrom, Emmet Sargeant, Joseph Saxon, Edwin Beach: cellos / George Price: French horn /John Johnson: tuba / Virgil Evans: trumpet / David Wells: trumpet, trombone / Kenneth Watson: percussion / Plas Johnson: tenor saxophone / Roy Caton: trumpet / Benjamin Barrett: violin / Tom Wilson: producer

The music of Frank Zappa was introduced to music followers in the UK by the inclusion of *It Can't Happen Here* as a new single release on the TV programme, *Juke Box Jury*. Presenter David Jacobs assured the panel whose task it was to assess the hit potential of the records that this one, in contrast to how it sounded, was intended to be entirely serious, with no deliberately humorous component whatsoever. Frank Zappa was no stranger to being misunderstood – no stranger either to being dismissed as unsaleable, as the title chosen for the last track on the *Freak Out!* album wryly recognises. Humour runs right through the music of the Mothers of Invention, but so does serious music making. Frank Zappa demonstrates how these qualities are not at all incompatible. There is more invention and variety here than could be found even on the recent Beatles albums, but tied to an irreverent approach and a love of the avant garde that was not at all guaranteed to win supporters. Most startling are the two long tracks making up most of the second record in the double set issued in the US (and still included on the slightly truncated UK version). These are elaborate sound collages, mostly held together by an underlying rhythm, but ranging widely through assorted styles borrowing equally from rhythm and blues and pop, electronic, jazz, and the avant garde. Unsurprisingly, *Freak Out!* was not a big seller, although it did well enough to keep the record company interested, and it established a cult following for the Mothers of Invention, particularly in Europe.

BOB DYLAN   BLONDE ON BLONDE

Less than two months before the release of his double album masterpiece, *Blonde On Blonde*, Bob Dylan had played at a concert in Manchester. Some of the audience did not appreciate the high-volume rock music they were hearing, from an artist they still wanted to be a folk singer: one person called out, loudly enough to be picked up by a microphone, "Judas!". Dylan responded with an incendiary performance of his greatest song, *Like A Rolling Stone*, as the perfect rebuttal and justification for the nature of his art. *Blonde On Blonde* provides further evidence of Dylan's vital importance to the status of rock music in the mid-sixties.

```
US release      July 1966    Columbia    C2S 841 / C2L 41
UK release      July 1966    CBS         (S)DDP 66012

1. Rainy Day Women #12 & 35
2. Pledging My Time
3. Visions Of Johanna
4. One Of Us Must Know

5. I Want You
6. Stuck Inside Of Mobile With The Memphis Blues Again
7. Leopard-Skin Pill-Box Hat
8. Just Like A Woman

9. Most Likely You Go Your Way And I'll Go Mine
10. Temporary Like Achilles
11. Absolutely Sweet Marie
12. 4th Time Around
13. Obviously 5 Believers

14. Sad Eyed Lady Of The Lowlands

All compositions by Bob Dylan

Bob Dylan: vocals, guitar, harmonica / Al Kooper: guitar, organ / Jerry Kennedy: guitar / Robbie Robertson: guitar / Wayne Moss: guitar, vocals / Hargus Robbins: piano / Bill Aikins: keyboards / Henry Strzelecki: bass / Joe South: bass guitar, vocals / Charlie McCoy: harmonica, trumpet / Kenny Buttrey: drums / Wayne Butler: trombone / Paul Griffin: piano / Rick Danko: bass guitar / Bobby Gregg: drums / Bob Johnston: producer
```

Recording was carried out in New York and in Nashville, with the majority of it being in the southern studio. Al Kooper, who had been the key to the success of the recording of *Like A Rolling Stone*, and Robbie Robertson, the lead guitarist in Dylan's live band, were employed in both venues. Bob Dylan's method of recording was not one that was familiar to the seasoned session musicians, used to working with well-rehearsed country singers. He wrote his songs in the studio, expecting the musicians to wait for each one to be completed, before recording the result quickly. The resulting freshness is important to the success of these songs. On an album made up entirely of highlights, *Visions Of Johanna* and *One Of Us Must Know* stand out as perfect demonstrations of how Bob Dylan's personal form of rock music works, with inspiring lyrics delivered by a voice less concerned with pitch than with meaning, and a band on fire, seemingly incapable of sounding a note out of place. The melody of *4th Time Around* makes a cheeky nod towards the Beatles' *Norwegian Wood*, with Dylan secure in the knowledge that the Beatles had absorbed much influence from him. *Sad Eyed Lady Of The Lowlands* presents a song as long as the earlier marathon, *Desolation Row*, and equally able to sustain interest over numerous verses. It is placed on its own on the album's fourth side, to make sure that it is noticed, even if the album side that results is only a little over eleven minutes – long for a song, but not for a side. *Blonde On Blonde* sold two million copies in the US and achieved platinum status too in the UK (with a smaller qualifying number of 300,000 sales), but did not manage to reach the top of either chart. It remains one of the crucial albums of the Golden Age, the end-point of a trilogy of immeasurably influential records made by Bob Dylan. Wikipedia gives a release date in June, other authorities suggest May, which would make *Blonde On Blonde* the first double album of new rock music. A well-researched article by Jake Brown on the gloriousnoise.com website proves that these dates must be incorrect, not least because overdubs were still being recorded in mid-June. The double album accolade, therefore, belongs with the Mothers of Invention.

THE BYRDS   FIFTH DIMENSION

Eight Miles High, issued as a single in March, introduced a startling new sound. The Byrds took the modal improvisation of John Coltrane, translated it from saxophone to lead twelve-string guitar, and changed the setting from jazz to surging folk-rock, complete with the group's sublime close-harmony vocals, but retaining a single-chord structure. The innovation works incredibly well, ushering in a style eventually christened psychedelic rock. The implication was that this was music

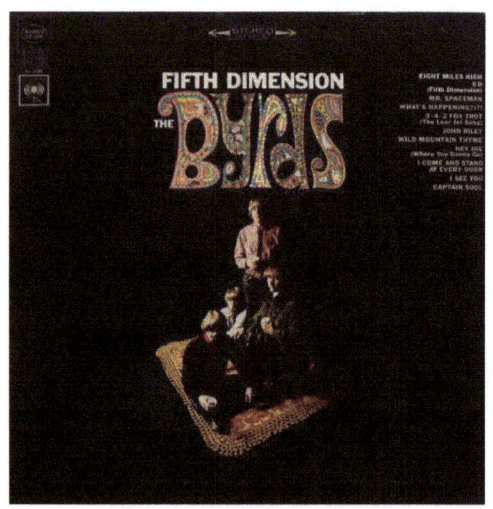

```
US release    July 1966    Columbia   CS 9349 / CL 2549
UK release    July 1966    CBS        (S)BPG 62783

1.  5 D (Fifth Dimension) (Jim McGuinn)
2.  Wild Mountain Thyme (Traditional)
3.  Mr Spaceman (Jim McGuinn)
4.  I See You (David Crosby/Jim McGuinn)
5.  What's Happening?!?! (David Crosby)
6.  I Come And Stand At Every Door (Nazim Hikmet)
7.  Eight Miles High (David Crosby/Gene Clark/Jim
                                          McGuinn)
8.  Hey Joe (Billy Roberts)
9.  Captain Soul (Chris Hillman/David Crosby/Mike
                                  Clarke/Jim McGuinn)
10. John Riley (Traditional)
11. 2-4-2 Fox Trot (The Lear Jet Song) (Jim McGuinn)

Gene Clark: vocals (7), harmonica (9) / Jim McGuinn:
guitar, vocals / David Crosby: guitar, vocals / Chris
Hillman: bass guitar, vocals / Michael Clarke: drums /
Allen Stanton: strings arranger (2,10), producer /
Van Dyke Parks: organ (1)
```

inspired by mind-altering drugs, although it is equally possible in this case that the Byrds simply had fertile musical imaginations. The song is one of the major creations of its era regardless. Unfortunately, the Byrds did not feel able to make an entire album in the new style. Some of the tracks on *Fifth Dimension* are the tried and trusted folk-rock of the previous two albums, while three are just not very good. *Mr Spaceman* is trite, *Hey Joe* is performed with much less authority than some of the other versions of the song issued during the year, and *Captain Soul* is a not particularly interesting rhythm and blues instrumental. It is left to four tracks with elements of the *Eight Miles High* approach (*5 D*, *I See You*, *What's Happening?!?!*, and possibly *I Come And Stand At Every Door* – to which the single B-side *Why* should have been added) to provide the core components of the great album that was not made.

THE LEAVES   HEY JOE

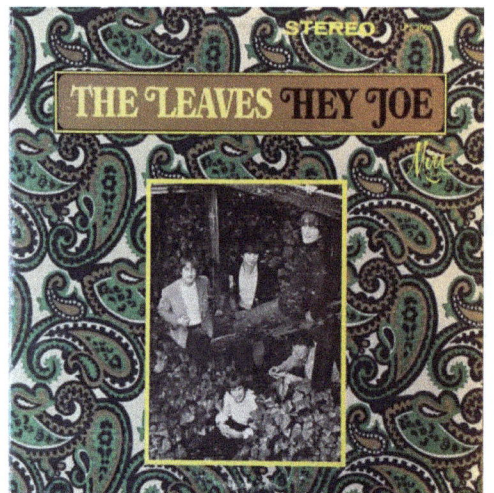

```
US release    July 1966    Surrey/Mira   LP(S) 3005
Not released in UK

1.  Dr Stone (Jim Pons/John Beck)
2.  Just A Memory (Bob Arlin)
3.  Get Out Of My Life Woman (Allen Toussaint)
4.  Girl From The East (Bobby Jameson)
5.  He Was A Friend Of Mine Traditional)
6.  Hey Joe (Billy Roberts)
7.  Words (Tommy Boyce/Bobby Hart)
8.  Back On The Avenue (The Leaves)
9.  War Of Distortion (Bob Arlin)
10. Tobacco Road (John Loudermilk)
11. Goodbye My Love (John McNally/Mike Pender)
12. Too Many People (Bill Rinehart/Jim Pons)

John Beck: vocals, percussion, harmonica / Bobby Arlin:
guitar / Bill Rinehart: sitar (12) / Robert Lee Reiner: guitar /
Jim Pons: bass guitar, vocals / Tom Ray: drums / Norm
Ratner: producer
```

Hey Joe, a song expressing sympathy for a wife-murderer, was a very popular choice for recording during 1966. Often the song was attributed to Jet Powers, a name used by singer Dino Valenti, best known as a member of Quicksilver Messenger Service, but it was actually copyrighted by folk singer Billy Roberts. Until Jimi Hendrix decided to weigh in with a powerful version near the end of the year, the most musically exciting interpretation of the song (and certainly one that trounces the recording made by the Byrds) was the one issued by Californian group, the Leaves. It became a substantial chart hit in the US in May, after two earlier recordings of the song by the Leaves had failed to make any impression. Ironically, the album made by the group around the hit single sounds very influenced by the Byrds and includes one song previously recorded by them, *He Was A Friend Of Mine,* although the Leaves remove the references to John Kennedy. To be fair, however, if the album had been made by the Byrds, it would have been disappointing. The Leaves barely survived the sixties – bass player Jim Pons subsequently became a member of the Turtles and Frank Zappa's Mothers of Invention.

THE YARDBIRDS   YARDBIRDS

The Yardbirds' studio album with Jeff Beck was recorded very quickly, without the care and imagination lavished on the singles, and it shows. The astonishing guitar-driven extravaganzas of the two single sides released near the beginning of the year, *Shapes Of Things* and *You're A Better Man Than I,* had demonstrated what the group was capable of when Jeff Beck was allowed to unleash the full power of his imagination as a soloist. The album starts well, with the driving *Lost Woman* and the single, *Over Under Sideways Down,* consciously dragging Bill Haley's rock 'n' roll into the approaching psychedelic age, but after that the album largely runs out of steam. The songs try hard to exhibit the same kind of forward-looking innovation as the singles, but without the necessary time being given to properly developing the ideas, the results sound half-hearted. Jeff Beck was brought in after the initial recording sessions in order to overdub his lead guitar contributions and he frequently struggles to make an impact within songs not properly designed to highlight his playing. A further

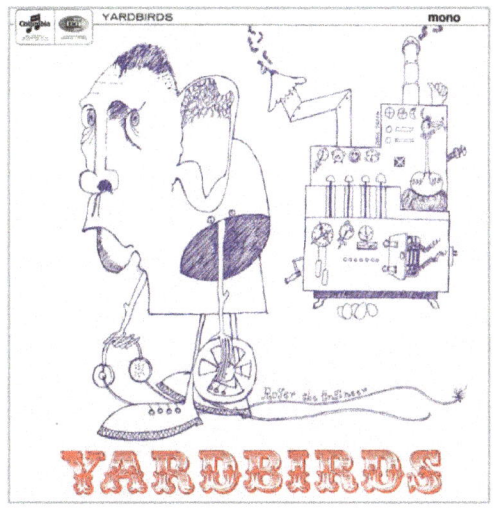

UK release	July 1966 Columbia S(C)S 6063
US release	July 1966 Epic BN26210 / LN24210
as **OVER UNDER SIDEWAYS DOWN** with 2 tracks missing	

1. Lost Woman
2. Over Under Sideways Down
3. The Nazz Are Blue
4. I Can't Make Your Way
5. Rack My Mind
6. Farewell

7. Hot House Of Omagararshid
8. Jeff's Boogie
9. He's Always There
10. Turn Into Earth
11. What Do You Want
12. Ever Since The World Began

All compositions by the Yardbirds

Keith Relf: vocals, harmonica / Jeff Beck: guitar, bass guitar (2), vocals (3) / Chris Dreja: guitar, piano, vocals / Paul Samwell-Smith: bass guitar, vocals, producer / Jim McCarty: drums, vocals / Simon Napier-Bell: producer

consequence of this manner of recording is that the mono and stereo versions of the album, with overdubs recorded as part of the separate mixing procedures, sound considerably different to each other. The album is frequently referred to as 'Roger the Engineer' after the caption applied by Chris Dreja to his cover drawing, but the wording elsewhere on the sleeve and on the record labels makes it clear that this is not intended to be the album's title.

JOHN MAYALL WITH ERIC CLAPTON   BLUES BREAKERS

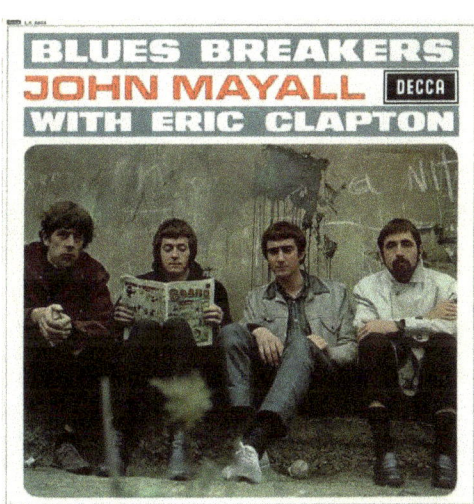

UK release	July 1966 Decca LK 4804
Stereo edition	SKL 4804 released in 1969
US release	July 1966 London PS 492 / LL 3492

1. All Your Love (Otis Rush/Willie Dixon)
2. Hideaway (Freddie King/Sonny Thompson)
3. Little Girl (John Mayall)
4. Another Man (Traditional)
5. Double Crossing Time (Eric Clapton/John Mayall)
6. What'd I Say (Ray Charles)

7. Key To Love (John Mayall)
8. Parchman Farm (Mose Allison)
9. Have You Heard (John Mayall)
10. Ramblin' On My Mind (Robert Johnson)
11. Steppin' Out (LC Frazier)
12. It Ain't Right (Walter Jacobs)

John Mayall: vocals, harmonica, organ, piano / Eric Clapton: guitar, vocals (10) / John McVie: bass guitar / Hughie Flint: drums / Alan Skidmore: tenor saxophone (7,9,11) / Johnny Almond: baritone saxophone (5,7,9,11) / Dennis Healey: trumpet (7,9,11) / Mike Vernon: producer

When former Yardbird, Eric Clapton, joined forces with John Mayall in April 1965, they both began to dig deeply into the blues that they loved. The music on the *Blues Breakers* album is based on the Chicago amplified blues performed by the likes of Otis Rush and Freddie King, rather than the older styles favoured by Alexis Korner and the Rolling Stones. *All Your Love*, the first track on the album, is an Otis Rush song played almost note-for-note the same as Rush's own 1958 version. The difference is in the sound of Eric Clapton's guitar. He had discovered that the high output of the pick-ups on a vintage Gibson Les Paul created a rich, sustained tone, just on the edge of feeding back, when connected to a powerful valve amplifier, with the volume controls turned to maximum. The British manufacturer, Jim Marshall, had just produced an updated version of the Fender Bassman amplifier, designed to cope with the less cutting notes of a bass guitar. With a power of 45 watts, high for the time, it was ideal for Clapton's purposes. Fortunately, producer Mike Vernon was prepared to allow the group to play in the studio at the high volume of a stage performance. As a result, the sound of Eric Clapton's guitar throughout the album is revelatory. It allows the listener to ignore the fact that John Mayall's singing voice is sometimes uncertainly pitched and that the group's version of the blues is, for the most part, not quite as authentic as the musicians would have liked it to be. Decca clearly had faith in the music, as the company had happily re-signed Mayall and his band to the label. It was rewarded with a hit album, reaching number six in the UK charts and qualifying for a gold disc. Meanwhile, the mercurial Eric Clapton had already left the band in order to try something else.

ARCHIE SHEPP   LIVE IN SAN FRANCISCO

These live recordings are taken from a club gig in February and represent slightly less than half of the complete set. *The Lady Sings The Blues* and *In A Sentimental Mood* are the kind of rough-hewn versions of jazz standards that Archie Shepp played on his *Fire Music* album. The Ellington tune is prefaced by a tumultuous solo by Shepp, playing on his own and demonstrating his remarkable virtuosity on the tenor saxophone. *Keep Your Heart Right* acts as a kind of calling card for the band. It demonstrates the effectiveness of its collective improvisation approach in the space of less than two minutes. The lengthy *Wherever June Bugs Go* would seem to provide a more extended version of this, except that the musicians this time take turns to solo, in the conventional jazz manner. *Sylvia* provides a fascinating diversion in which, with Roswell Rudd

US release	July 1966	Impulse	A(S)-9118
UK release	July 1966	HMV	CSD/CLP 3600

1. Keep Your Heart Right (Roswell Rudd)
2. The Lady Sings The Blues (Herbie Nichols)
3. Sylvia (Oley Speaks)
4. The Wedding (Archie Shepp)
5. Wherever June Bugs Go (Archie Shepp)
6. In A Sentimental Mood (Duke Ellington/Irving Mills/Manny Kurtz)

Archie Shepp: tenor saxophone, piano (3), voice (4) / Roswell Rudd: trombone / Donald Garrett: bass / Lewis Worrell: bass / Beaver Harris: drums / Bob Thiele: producer

silent, Archie Shepp takes to the piano. He proves himself to be a convincing player, with an original style that blends the ornamental flourishes of an Art Tatum with the more haphazard tonality of a Thelonious Monk. *The Wedding* is different again, as Shepp intones a bleakly evocative poem against the arco playing of the two bassists. The natural climax of the original set, a reading of a Shepp composition, *Three For A Quarter, One For A Dime,* lasting for over half an hour, was kept back for a second LP, released three years later. In its absence, *Live In San Francisco* becomes an album whose primary purpose is to demonstrate the variety of which Archie Shepp was capable, something that it manages to do extremely well.

DON RENDELL / IAN CARR 5TET   DUSK FIRE

UK release	July 1966	Columbia	SX 6064

Not release in US

1. Ruth (Don Rendell)
2. Tan Samfu (Don Rendell)
3. Jubal (Don Rendell)
4. Spooks (Don Rendell/Ian Carr)
5. Prayer (Michael Garrick)
6. Hot Rod (Ian Carr/Michael Garrick)
7. Dusk Fire (Michael Garrick)

Ian Carr: trumpet, flugelhorn / Don Rendell: tenor and soprano saxophones, flute, clarinet / Michael Garrick: piano / Dave Green: bass / Trevor Tomkins: drums / Denis Preston: producer

The second album by Britain's premier modern jazz group turns up the quality even higher, with the help of new pianist and composer, Michael Garrick. *Ruth,* the opening track, is a reflective showcase for flute and sets the mood for the cerebral music that follows. Only *Hot Rod* presents anything in the way of a driving rhythm and even then there is a sense of the power being deliberately reined in. The track is clearly inspired by the Miles Davis piece, *Milestones,* which introduced the idea of modal improvisation in 1958, but *Hot Rod* seems to lack the vitality of its source, despite being played rather faster. But the focus throughout the album is on the finely judged, melodic playing of the two main soloists, who prove themselves to be well up to the challenge. The quintet made three more albums after this one in much the same style, including a live recording, but it is *Dusk Fire* that demonstrates the strengths of these musicians particularly well.

TIM HARDIN   1

US release	July 1966	Verve	FT(S) 3004
UK release	July 1966	Verve	(S)VLP 5018

1. Don't Make Promises
2. Green Rocky Road
3. Smugglin' Man
4. How Long
5. While You're On Your Way
6. It'll Never Happen Again
7. Reason To Believe
8. Never Too Far
9. Part Of The Wind
10. Ain't Gonna Do Without
11. Misty Roses
12. How Can We Hang On To A Dream

All compositions by Tim Hardin

Tim Hardin: vocals, guitar, piano / John Sebastian: harmonica / Gary Burton: vibraphone / Phil Krauss: vibraphone / Bob Bushnell: bass guitar / Walter Yost: bass / Buddy Saltzman: drums / Earl Palmer: drums / Artie Butler: string arrangements / Erik Jacobsen: producer

Like Bob Dylan on his early albums, Tim Hardin falls back on the blues when song inspiration fails to arrive, but he lacks Dylan's skills as a wordsmith to lift the results above the routine. The singer-songwriter's debut album suffers a little as a result, which is a pity, because it also includes some very memorable songs indeed, most notably the first and last on each side. Hardin prefers to write songs tinged with sadness, for which the naturally mournful, fragile quality of his voice makes it an ideal instrument. Both *Reason To Believe* and *How Can We Hang On To A Dream* were covered by other singers after their first appearance here, but even Rod Stewart could not manage to better the pathos of Tim Hardin's originals. Many of the musicians employed to perform on the album are jazz players and they give the songs a rhythmic subtlety not found on the records by Bob Dylan and the Byrds. It would be overstating the case somewhat to describe the music as folk-jazz, but certainly it is not folk-rock.

BUCK OWENS   CARNEGIE HALL CONCERT

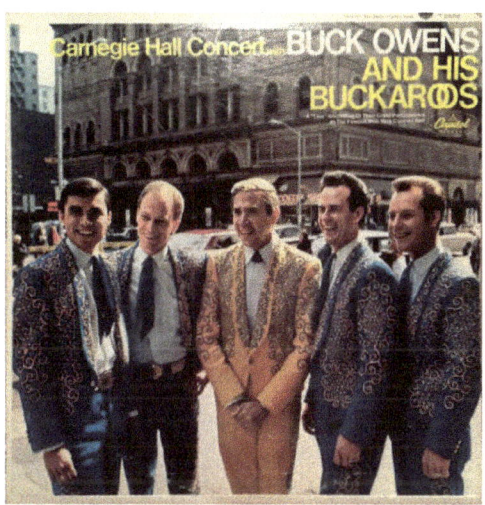

```
US release    July 1966    Capitol (S)T 2556
UK release    July 1966    Capitol (S)T 2556

1. Act Naturally (Johnny Russell/Voni Morrison)
2. Together Again (Buck Owens)
3. Love's Gonna Live Here (Buck Owens)
4. Medley: In The Palm Of Your Hand (Owens), Cryin' Time (Owens), Don't
           Let Her Know (Owens), Only You (Owens)
5. Medley: I Don't Care (Owens), My Heart Skips A Beat (Owens), Gonna
           Have Love (Buck Owens/Red Simpson)
6. Waitin' In Your Welfare Line (Buck Owens/Nat Stuckey/Don Rich)

7. Buckaroo (Bob Morris)
8. The Streets Of Laredo (Traditional)
9. I've Got A Tiger By The Tail (Harlan Howard/Buck Owens)
10.Medley: Under Your Spell Again (Buck Owens/Dusty Rhodes),
           Above And Beyond (Harlan Howard), Excuse Me (Howard/
           Owens), Foolin' Around (Howard/Owens), Hello Trouble (Eddie
           McDuff/Orville Chouch), Truck Drivin' Man (Terry Fell)

Buck Owens: vocals, guitar / Don Rich: guitar, vocals / Tom Brumley:
pedal steel guitar / Doyle Holly: bass guitar, vocals / Willie Cantu: drums /
Ken Nelson: producer
```

Buck Owens was one of country music's most successful artists during the sixties and the sound of his band, with pedal steel guitar to the fore, defines how country in this period was supposed to sound. Even so, it is said that Owens was reluctant to become one of the few country artists to perform at New York's Carnegie Hall, believing that his following would not extend so far north. In the event, the concert was a sell-out and the audience was enthusiastic in its appreciation of Owens and his group, the Buckaroos. The recording makes clear the difference between country and beat music, because even with a similar instrumentation – electric guitars and drums – the rhythms are different. And there is no escaping the emotional effect of the keening pedal steel guitar, one instrument that never is found in beat music at this time. The Buckaroos are consummate professionals, with a clarity and a tightness that beat groups would have envied, but they do not rock, because they do not intend to. The CD reissue of the concert recording includes much between-song banter by the group, which clearly knew how to win over an audience. There is also a lengthy section during which Owens and company play humorous tributes to some of their contemporaries. These include the Beatles, with a rendering of *Twist And Shout* that ends up sounding much more like the Tex-Mex hit, *La Bamba*. Owens was doubtless aware of, and grateful for the star group having covered one of his hit songs, *Act Naturally*. It is not surprising that this is what Owens chose to open his set, emphasising how well the Beatles had captured the style with their own version.

THE BEATLES   REVOLVER

```
UK release    August 1966    Parlophone    PCS/PMC 7009
US release    August 1966    Capitol (S)T 2576    tracks 3,9,11 omitted

1. Taxman
2. Eleanor Rigby
3. I'm Only Sleeping
4. Love You To
5. Here, There And Everywhere
6. Yellow Submarine
7. She Said She Said

8. Good Day Sunshine
9. And Your Bird Can Sing
10.For No One
11.Doctor Robert
12.I Want To Tell You
13.Got To Get You Into My Life
14.Tomorrow Never Knows

All compositions by John Lennon/Paul McCartney except 1,4,12 by
George Harrison

John Lennon: vocals, guitar, keyboards, percussion, sound effects /
George Harrison: vocals, guitar, bass guitar, sitar, tamboura, percussion,
sound effects / Paul McCartney: vocals, bass guitar, guitar, keyboards,
percussion, sound effects / Ringo Starr: drums, percussion, vocals /
George Martin: producer, piano (8,14), organ (13) / Anil Bhagwat: tablas
(4) / Alan Civil: French horn (10) / Mal Evans: bass drum, vocals (6) / Neil
Aspinall: vocals (6) / Brian Jones: vocals (6) / Pattie Boyd: vocals (6) /
Marianne Faithfull: vocals (6) / Alf Bicknell: vocals (6) / Tony Gilbert,
Sidney Sax, John Sharpe,Jurgen Hess: violins (2) / Stephen Shingles,John
Underwood: violas (2) / Derek Simpson,Norman Jones: cello (2) / Eddie
Thornton,Ian Hamer, Les Condon: trumpets (13) / Peter Coe, Alan
Branscombe: tenor saxophones (13)
```

For the music on *Revolver*, the Beatles started to use the resources of the recording studio as creative tools in their own right, rather than simply as a means for capturing the sound of song performances. They were not the first artists to do this, as earlier recordings by the likes of Les Paul and Joe Meek can testify, but the Beatles applied a level of imagination and innovation that was remarkable. Two songs stand out in particular. *Yellow Submarine* (issued as a single with *Eleanor Rigby*, at the same time as the album) presents a panoply of sound and spoken word effects in order to turn what might otherwise be regarded as a children's song into something altogether grander. This includes the playing of the brass band introduced in the words of the song, although opinions are divided as to whether the musicians were hired for the recording or are the result of a pioneering exercise in sampling an old record. *Tomorrow Never Knows* is entirely artifice, from treating John Lennon's voice by feeding the sound through the rotating speaker cabinet of a Hammond organ and reversing the fragments of the lead guitar playing, to underscoring the whole affair with a melange of mellotron sounds and prearranged electronic tape loops. The reversed guitar turns up on *I'm Only Sleeping* as well, a song that is also distinguished by a beautifully recorded yawn at an appropriate moment in the mix. The Beatles' customary insistence on giving each song at least one unique element for the record is brought to perfection on this album and they do not hesitate to employ session musicians in places to help with the procedure. A string octet is added to *Eleanor Rigby* and a Stax-style brass section to *Got To Get You Into My Life*; a tabla player enhances *Love You To,* while classical French horn specialist Alan Civil delivers a delightful solo to *For No One* (and copes admirably with the fact that the music he was required to perform with was not at proper concert pitch). Significantly, however, the standard of the song writing throughout *Revolver* is such as to prevent any of these effects and additions sounding like buttresses for poor quality compositions. The songs come first, by virtue of their interesting melody lines, harmonies, and lyrics – everything else is a bonus. Through it all, the Beatles manage to sound more as modern ears expect a rock group to sound, with guitar playing that is more insistent than before, and the Paul McCartney/Ringo Starr rhythm section as tight and as powerful as it has ever been. Many critics argue that *Revolver* is the number one rock album of all – certainly it is the number one rock music highlight of a year filled with many inspirational albums.

WILSON PICKETT   THE EXCITING

| US release | August 1966 | Atlantic | (SD) 8129 |
| UK release | August 1966 | Atlantic | 588/587 029 |

1. Land Of 1000 Dances (Chris Kenner)
2. Something You Got (Chris Kenner)
3. 634-5789 (Eddie Floyd/Steve Cropper)
4. Barefootin' (Robert Parker)
5. Mercy Mercy Mercy (Don Covay/Ronald Miller)
6. You're So Fine (Lance Finney/Robert West/Willie Schofield)
7. In The Midnight Hour (Steve Cropper/Wilson Pickett)
8. Ninety-Nine And A Half (Won't Do) (Floyd/Cropper/Pickett)
9. Danger Zone (Steve Cropper/Wilson Pickett)
10. I'm Drifting (Darrell Banks/David Porter/Wilson Pickett)
11. It's All Over (Steve Cropper/Wilson Pickett)
12. She's So Good To Me (Bobby Womack)

Wilson Pickett: vocals / Steve Cropper: guitar, producer / Jimmy Johnson: guitar / Chips Moman: guitar / Joe Hall: keyboards / Isaac Hayes: keyboards / Spooner Oldham: keyboards / Wayne Jackson: trumpet / Gene Miller: trumpet / Charles Axton: tenor saxophone / Andrew Love: tenor saxophone / Charles Chalmers: tenor saxophone / Floyd Newman: baritone saxophone / Donald Dunn: bass guitar / Tommy Cogbill: bass guitar / Al Jackson: drums / Roger Hawkins: drums / Jerry Wexler: producer / Jim Stewart: producer / Rick Hall: producer / Tom Dowd: producer

Beginning his professional career in 1955, as a member of a gospel group, the Violinaires, Wilson Pickett made the easy transition to R&B as lead singer with the Falcons, before seeking success as a solo artist. The breakthrough came with *In The Midnight Hour,* written by Pickett in collaboration with the session guitarist at the Stax studio, Steve Cropper. The single did well in the charts in both the US and the UK, eventually qualifying for a gold disc for a million sales. It set the standard for Wilson Pickett's brand of soul music, like a slightly more muscular version of Otis Redding, with a strident brass section vying with the vocals for attention and driven by strong rhythm playing. Some of the songs on *The Exciting Wilson Pickett* were recorded at Stax in Memphis, others at the Fame studios in Muscle Shoals, Alabama, but the sound does not change even with different musicians involved. Three more tracks became substantial single hits – *Ninety-Nine And A Half (Won't Do), 634-5789,* and *Land Of 1000 Dances* – while the album itself became a hit in the US album charts. It established Wilson Pickett as one of the major soul stars of the sixties, with only James Brown and Otis Redding attracting more acclaim as far as male singers were concerned.

THE SUPREMES   A' GO-GO

The ninth studio album released by the Supremes includes one of the trio's biggest singles, *You Can't Hurry Love,* and was itself a considerable hit, reaching number one in the US album chart and selling an estimated three and a half million copies worldwide. Curiously the album mainly comprises Supremes' versions of other people's hits. If the intention was to display the singers' superiority over their rivals, then it is something of a failure, because in every case the familiar original versions remain definitive. But the Supremes do acquit themselves well and the album is a strong one.

LARRY YOUNG   UNITY

US release   August 1966   Blue Note   BST8/BLP 4221
Not released in UK

1. Zoltan (Woody Shaw)
2. Monk's Dream (Thelonious Monk)
3. If (Joe Henderson)
4. The Moontrane (Woody Shaw)
5. Softly As A Morning Sunrise (Oscar Hammerstein/
   Sigmund Romberg)
6. Beyond All Limits (Woody Shaw)

Larry Young: organ / Woody Shaw: trumpet / Joe Henderson: tenor saxophone / Elvin Jones: drums / Alfred Lion: producer

US release   August 1966   Motown   M(S) 649
UK release   August 1966   Tamla Motown   (S)TML 11039

1. Love Is Like An Itching In My Heart
2. This Old Heart Of Mine
3. You Can't Hurry Love
4. Shake Me Wake Me (When It's Over)
5. Baby I Need Your Loving
6. These Boots Are Made For Walking (Lee Hazlewood)
7. I Can't Help Myself
8. Get Ready (Smokey Robinson)
9. Put Yourself In My Place (H-D-H/John Thornton)
10. Money (Berry Gordy/Janie Bradford)
11. Come And Get These Memories
12. Hang On Sloopy (Bert Russell/Wes Farrell)

All compositions by Brian Holland/Lamont Dozier/Eddie Holland except where stated

Diana Ross: vocals / Mary Wilson: vocals / Florence Ballard: vocals / The Andantes: vocals (11) / similar musicians to those on I Hear A Symphony / Brian Holland and Lamont Dozier: producers (1,3,5,7,9,11) / Hal Davis and Frank Wilson: producers (2,4,6,8,10,12)

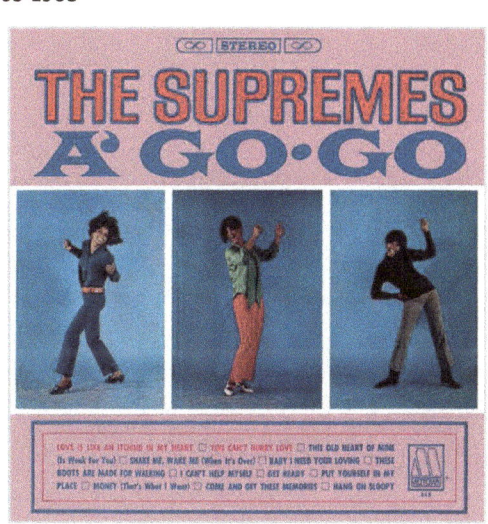

Jazz organist Larry Young made a number of albums under his own name during the sixties, but *Unity* is the one that has become the most highly regarded. Following the success of Jimmy Smith, the Blue Note record company issued albums by several different organists. Larry Young is as accomplished as any of them and he is also the only one to lean towards the music that John Coltrane was producing at the time. In this respect, Young is greatly aided by the presence of Coltrane's drummer, Elvin Jones, who delivers his usual assortment of expertly played polyrhythms. *Unity* is not a startlingly innovative record, and it did not sell particularly well, but it is a fine example of the Blue Note sound. It is also an interesting glimpse into the formative part of the career of a player who would make a much bigger impact on jazz just a few years later.

THE BUTTERFIELD BLUES BAND   EAST-WEST

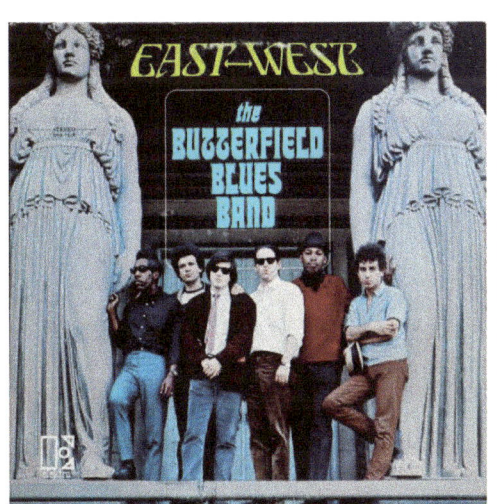

US release   August 1966   Elektra   EKS7/EKL 315
UK release   August 1966   Elektra   EKS7/EKL 315

1. Walkin' Blues (Robert Johnson)
2. Get Out Of My Life Woman (Allen Toussaint)
3. I Got A Mind To Give Up Living (B B King)
4. All These Blues (Junior Parker)
5. Work Song (Nat Adderley)
6. Mary Mary (Mike Nesmith)
7. Two Trains Running (Muddy Waters)
8. Never Say No (Percy Mayfield)
9. East-West (Mike Bloomfield/Nick Gravenites)

Paul Butterfield: vocals, harmonica / Mike Bloomfield: guitar / Elvin Bishop: guitar, vocals / Mark Naftalin: keyboards / Jerome Arnold: bass guitar / Billy Davenport: drums / Paul Rothchild: producer / Mark Abramson: producer / Barry Friedman: producer (6)

The second album by Paul Butterfield's band departs considerably from the straightforward Chicago blues policy of the debut. Elektra was extremely lax in giving proper songwriting credits, disguising the fact that the band was drawing on R&B performers like Percy Mayfield and Allen Toussaint as much as the obvious blues names, with one track being the work of Mike Nesmith, shortly to gain fame as a member of the Monkees. The album is dominated, however, by two long instrumental tracks, placed at the end of each side. *Work Song* has a theme statement followed by a succession of improvised solos; *East-West* is entirely improvised, using a one chord, modal structure rather than the blues. The result is to give the piece a flavour of Indian music, hence the title chosen for it. Essentially, this music would be jazz if the rhythms were different, and it has the effect of making a positive statement with regard to the technical playing abilities of the most accomplished musicians choosing to work in rock. This studio recording of *East-West* is over eleven minutes long, but in live performance, the group would often create versions much longer than this. Mike Bloomfield is particularly impressive and he is given by far the most solo space to emphasise his fluency and his imagination. He employs a gritty tone but without much sustain, sounding loud but without pushing his amplifier into overdrive, so that his playing sounds quite different to that of Eric Clapton, the UK guitarist who is Bloomfield's closest equivalent.

JEFFERSON AIRPLANE   TAKES OFF

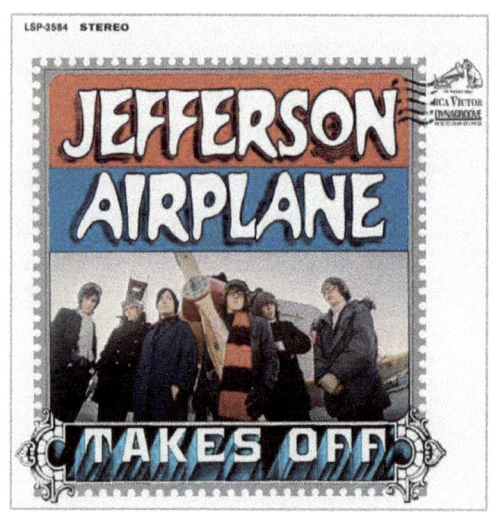

US release   August 1966   RCA Victor   LSP/LPM 3584
UK release   1971   RCA Victor   SF 8195

1. Blues From An Airplane (Skip Spence/Marty Balin)
2. Let Me In (Marty Balin/Paul Kantner)
3. Bringing Me Down (Marty Balin/Paul Kantner)
4. Its No Secret (Marty Balin)
5. Tobacco Road (John D Loudermilk)
6. Come Up The Years (Marty Balin/Paul Kantner)
7. Run Around (Marty Balin/Paul Kantner)
8. Let's Get Together (Chet Powers)
9. Don't Slip Away (Skip Spence/Marty Balin)
10. Chauffeur Blues (Lester Melrose)
11. And I Like It (Jorma Kaukonen/Marty Balin)

Marty Balin: vocals, guitar / Signe Toly Anderson: vocals, percussion / Paul Kantner: guitar, vocals / Jorma Kaukonen: guitar / Jack Casady: bass guitar / Skip Spence: drums / Tommy Oliver: producer / Matthew Katz: producer

During the latter part of 1965 and through 1966, a number of groups performing at the Avalon Ballroom, the Fillmore, the Matrix, and other venues in San Francisco turned the city into a focus for a new rock music movement, just as had been the case with Liverpool some four years earlier. The first of the groups to gain a recording contract was Jefferson Airplane. The essence of the San Francisco sound lay in finding ways to explore the approach presented by the Byrds with their song *Eight Miles High*, combining layered vocals and a vaguely folk-song sensibility with bouts of improvisation. On stage, the results often sounded revolutionary, but this quality does not really come through on the Jefferson Airplane *Takes Off* album. Certainly the group had to make compromises to satisfy the record company – indeed the very first pressings were withdrawn so that some of the vocal lines could be redone with less controversial lyrics, at RCA's insistence. Explicit sexual and possible drug references were not yet acceptable. Overall, the album does sound very like a Byrds record, albeit with one of the voices being female and another (Marty Balin) adopting a much more soulful style than McGuinn or Crosby ever employed. Paul Kantner often plays solos on a twelve string guitar, but with less imagination than Jim McGuinn. Jorma Kaukonen is a much more remarkable soloist, but is given comparatively little to do. Bass player Jack Casady, however, is in fine form throughout, using a slightly distorted tone to drive the music along even more than the drumming. *Takes Off* is a worthy debut, but the Airplane was to make much better records later on.

DON CHERRY   COMPLETE COMMUNION

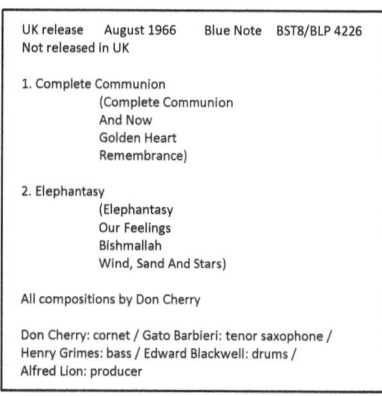

UK release   August 1966   Blue Note   BST8/BLP 4226
Not released in UK

1. Complete Communion
   (Complete Communion
   And Now
   Golden Heart
   Remembrance)

2. Elephantasy
   (Elephantasy
   Our Feelings
   Bishmallah
   Wind, Sand And Stars)

All compositions by Don Cherry

Don Cherry: cornet / Gato Barbieri: tenor saxophone / Henry Grimes: bass / Edward Blackwell: drums / Alfred Lion: producer

Don Cherry played trumpet with Ornette Coleman during the late fifties and very early sixties; *Complete Communion* is his debut for Blue Note as the leader of his own band. The music is very similar to Coleman's, although as the long pieces move from section to section, it becomes apparent that this is not happening purely organically, that the music depends on a certain amount of prearranged composition. Gato Barbieri would soon become a significant name in his own right: though a fluent player on this album, he has yet to discover the distinctive screaming tone that would make his playing immediately recognisable. *Complete Communion* can be regarded as formative for both Barbieri and Don Cherry himself, but is a fine example of mid-sixties jazz avant garde all the same.

ORNETTE COLEMAN AT THE GOLDEN CIRCLE STOCKHOLM VOLUMES ONE & TWO

US release   August 1966   Blue Note   BST8/BLP 4224/4225
Not released in UK

1. Faces And Places
2. European Echoes
3. Dee Dee
4. Dawn
5. Snowflakes And Sunshine
6. Morning Song
7. The Riddle
8. Antiques

All compositions by Ornette Coleman

Ornette Coleman: alto saxophone, trumpet, violin / David Izenzon: bass / Charles Moffett: drums / Francis Wolff: producer

It was Ornette Coleman who introduced the concept of avant garde jazz. Initially he released a series of albums in the late fifties that appeared to present a version of the prevailing hard bop style played by musicians who were not particularly concerned with hitting the true notes, and then he recorded the groundbreaking *Free Jazz* album of 1961, in which two quartets improvise simultaneously without any agreed theme or chord structure, though with a considerable rhythmic drive producing exhilarating results. Five years on, Ornette Coleman is working with a trio, which makes the music sound much more spacious, though it is still very much freely improvised. These live recordings make it clear that Coleman has found a rhythm section able to match his own virtuosity as a player and able to easily respond to the changes in mood that guide how the improvisations proceed. He has also extended his range by adding both trumpet and violin on *Snowflakes And Sunshine*. He plays neither of them in a conventional manner and may not have the authority on these instruments that he undoubtedly does on alto saxophone, but this matters not at all – they sound totally effective in this context. Given that Jack Bruce, the bass player with Cream, maintained that his own group's approach to improvisation was very much influenced by Ornette Coleman's trio (in an interview given in 2000), it makes sense to listen to the *Golden Circle* recordings with that in mind.

DONOVAN   SUNSHINE SUPERMAN

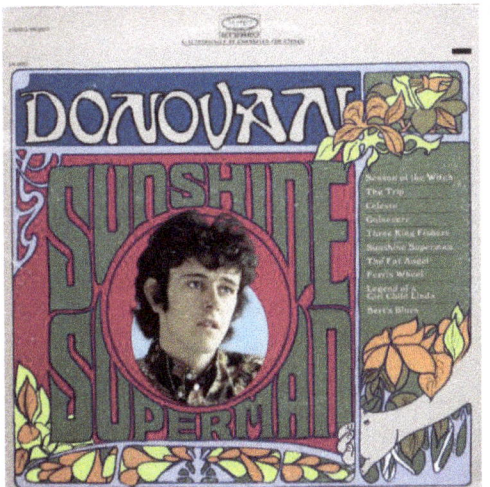

US release   August 1966   Epic   LN 24217 / BN 26217
Not released in UK in this form

1. Sunshine Superman
2. Legend Of A Girl Child Linda
3. Three King Fishers
4. Ferris Wheel
5. Bert's Blues
6. Season Of The Witch
7. The Trip
8. Guinevere
9. The Fat Angel
10. Celeste

All compositions by Donovan Leitch

Donovan: vocals, guitar, organ (10) / Mickie Most: producer / Bobby Ray: bass guitar / Eddie Hoh: drums / Shawn Phillips: sitar / Cyrus Faryar: electric violin / Candy John Carr: percussion (tracks 3,4,7,8,9.10) / Jimmy Page: guitar / Eric Ford: guitar / John Cameron: keyboards, arranger / Spike Healey: bass / John Paul Jones: bass guitar / Bobby Orr: drums / Tony Carr: percussion (tracks 1,2,5,6)

Donovan released a single in July 1966 in the US that was notably different from his previous material. Just as Bob Dylan had already done, the UK folk singer added extra instrumentation in order to move away from an obvious folk music sound. Even with the adventurous session guitarist Jimmy Page involved, however, the result was much lighter than Dylan's, mainly because Donovan was becoming interested in jazz and was trying to employ some of the flavour of that. The single, *Sunshine Superman*, reached number one in the US chart. An album built around it proved to be wide-ranging and inventive. With some of the material recorded in the US and some in the UK, different sets of session musicians were employed, increasing the variety of sound heard on the album. String arrangements were in place for some of the music, while an unusual combination of sitar with electric violin featured on other tracks. A climax is reached with the last song, *Celeste*, where the sitar and violin mesh with sustained organ notes played by Donovan himself to create an emotion-filled sound striking enough to fool some later critics into believing that a mellotron was being played. Unfortunately, Donovan's new manager, Allen Klein, had decided to sign a US contract with Epic, ignoring the agreement already in place between Pye and Warner Brothers. The result was that Donovan's remarkable album did not get released in the UK and the singer's bold adoption of some of the Beatles' production methods to his folk-based music – ensuring that each track had a unique element of its own – went unrecognised. The *Sunshine Superman* single was eventually given a UK release in December (and reached number two in the chart) but no album appeared until the following June.

THE KINKS   WELL RESPECTED KINKS

UK release   September 1966   Marble Arch   MAL(S) 612
Not released in US   **GREATEST HITS**   released in US in August 1966, Reprise R(S) 6217 has four different tracks.

1. A Well Respected Man
2. Where Have All The Good Times Gone
3. Till The End Of The Day
4. Set Me Free
5. Tired Of Waiting For You
6. All Day And All Of The Night
7. I Gotta Move
8. Don't You Fret
9. Wait Till The Summer Comes Along (Dave Davies)
10. You Really Got Me

All compositions by Ray Davies except where stated

Ray Davies: vocals, guitar / Dave Davies: guitar, vocals / Peter Quaife: bass guitar / Mick Avory: drums / Shel Talmy: producer

Well Respected Kinks was issued on Pye's cheap reissue label and served as a Greatest Hits compilation. It emphasised the strength of the Kinks' run of hit singles and became the group's most successful album, helped by the fact that its selling price was only a third of the normal price for an album. In the US, Reprise issued a proper *Greatest Hits* with an even stronger selection of tracks, including *Dedicated Follower Of Fashion* and *Everybody's Gonna Be Happy*, which are missing from the UK collection. Either album is a tribute to Ray Davies' astonishing ability to create memorable and distinctive beat songs without often using more than three chords.

MANFRED MANN   MANN MADE HITS

K release   September 1966   HMV   CLP 3559
Not released in US. **GREATEST HITS**, United Artists UAS6 / UAL3 551, has just five tracks in common

1. Pretty Flamingo (Mark Barkan)
2. The One In The Middle (Paul Jones)
3. Oh No, Not My Baby (Gerry Goffin/Carole King)
4. John Hardy (Group)
5. Spirit Feel (Jon Hendricks/Milt Jackson)
6. Come Tomorrow (Bob Elgin/Dolores Phillips/Frank Augustus)
7. Do Wah Diddy Diddy (Ellie Greenwich/Jeff Barry)
8. There's No Living Without Your Loving (Jerry Harris/Paul Kaufman)
9. With God On Our Side (Bob Dylan)
10. Groovin' (Ben E King/James Bethea)
11. I'm Your Kingpin (Manfred Mann/Paul Jones)
12. Sha La La (Robert Mosely/Robert Napoleon Taylor)
13. 5,4,3,2,1 (Paul Jones/Mike Hugg/Manfred Mann)
14. If You Gotta Go, Go Now (Bob Dylan)

Manfred Mann: keyboards / Paul Jones: vocals, harmonica / Mike Vickers: guitar, alto saxophone, flute, orchestra arranger (not 1) / Tom McGuinness: bass guitar, guitar / Mike Hugg: drums / Jack Bruce: bass guitar (1) / The Three Bells: Carol, Sue & Jean Bell: vocals (8) / John Burgess: producer

The release of Manfred Mann's Greatest Hits album coincided with the end of the original group line-up and the impending move to a new record company. It is a strong collection, although it makes clear that the group did not worry too much about staying true to its jazz and blues roots when selecting material for singles. Without much in-house songwriting ability at this stage, the group was happy to take songs from various of the pop writers of the day, songs having an emphasis on catchy melodies and sing-along choruses. Of course, everything is very well played and, to be fair, the group does find room to accommodate two Bob Dylan songs. But the music fails to convince that it is essential, its impact on the development of mid-sixties music seeming to be much smaller than that of the Kinks, for example.

IKE & TINA TURNER   RIVER DEEP – MOUNTAIN HIGH

By 1966, Ike and Tina Tuner were veteran performers. Ike formed his Kings of Rhythm in the late forties and was responsible for one of the founding records of rock 'n' roll, *Rocket 88,* credited to the band's Jackie Brenston. Anna Mae Bullock began singing with the band in the late fifties and Ike gave her the 'Tina Turner' stage name even before they became married. The 1961 album, *The Soul Of Ike & Tina Turner,* was one of the first records to use the name 'soul' to

| UK release | September 1966 | London | SHU / HAU 8298 |
| US release | 1969 | A&M | SP-4178 one track change |

1. River Deep – Mountain High (Phil Spector/Ellie Greenwich/Jeff Barry)
2. I Idolize You (Ike Turner)
3. A Love Like Yours (Edward Holland/Lamont Dozier/Brian Holland)
4. A Fool In Love (Ike Turner)
5. Make 'Em Wait (Ike Turner)
6. Hold On Baby (Ellie Greenwixh/Jeff Barry)
7. Save The Last Dance For Me (Doc Pomus/Mort Shuman)
8. Oh Baby (Kent Harris)
9. Every Day I Have To Cry (Arthur Alexander)
10. Such A Fool For You (Ike Turner)
11. It's Gonna Work Out Fine (Michael Lee/Joe Seneca)
12. You're So Fine (Lance Finney/Robert West/Willie Schofield)

Tina Turner: vocals / Ike Turner: piano, vocals, producer (2,4,5,8,10,11,12) / Barney Kessel, Don Peake, John Ewing: guitar / Robert Gerstlauer: guitar, baritone saxophone / Harold Battiste: piano / Larry Knechtel: piano / Michael Rubini: piano / Jimmy Bond: bass / Carol Kaye, Ray Pohlman, Lyle Ritz: bass guitar / Jim Gordon, Earl Palmer: drums / Frank Capp, Gene Estes: percussion / Roy Caton, Oliver Mitchell: trumpet / John Ewing, Lew McCreary: trombone / Plas Johnson: tenor saxophone / Jim Horn: tenor and baritone saxophone / Jim Migliori: tenor saxophone / Claudia Lennear: vocals / Bonnie Bramlett: vocals / Jack Nitzsche: arranger / Gene Page: arranger / Perry Botkin Jr: arranger / Phil Spector: producer (1,3,6,7

describe its music. Producer Phil Spector hired the Turners for a single, the title track of *River Deep – Mountain High*, that turned out to be the most perfect realisation of his trademark wall-of-sound style, although he supposedly paid Ike Turner to stay at home while the recording was done. Unfortunately, Spector had succeeded in alienating much of the music industry in the US and the record did not become a hit. It was different in the UK, however, and the single reached number three in the chart. The album release was cancelled in the US, but went ahead in the UK. It is a fine showcase for Tina Turner's singing and she has no difficulty in convincing the listener that she is one of the great soul singers, whether she is encased within Phil Spector's sound or when she is fronting an altogether funkier R&B band, as she does on the tracks produced by Ike Turner. In the light of what we now know about the Turners' relationship, however, *It's Gonna Work Out Fine*, with its spoken interjections from Ike Turner, cannot help sounding a little spooky.

FLATT & SCRUGGS   GREATEST HITS

| US release | September 1966 | Columbia | CS 9370 / CL 2570 |
Not released in UK

1. The Ballad Of Jed Clampett (Paul Henning)
2. Flint Hill Special (Earl Scruggs)
3. Jimmy Brown, The Newsboy (A.P. Carter)
4. I Still Miss Someone (Johnny Cash/Roy Cash)
5. Petticoat Junction (Curt Massey/Paul Henning)
6. Fire ball (Burkett Graves/Earl Scruggs/Lester Flatt)
7. Earl's Breakdown (Earl Scruggs)
8. You Are My Flower (A.P.Carter)
9. Pearl Pearl Pearl (Paul Henning)
10. The Good Things (Out-Weigh The Bad) (Burkett Graves/Jake Lambert)
11. My Saro Jane (Lester Flatt/Earl Scruggs)

Lester Flatt: guitar, vocals / Earl Scruggs: guitar, banjo, vocals / The Foggy Mountain Boys: fiddles, guitars, basses

Virtuoso bluegrass players Lester Flatt and Earl Scruggs were members of Bill Monroe's Blue Grass Boys in the forties, pioneering and developing their distinctive form of acoustic, roots country music. The pair began working with their own band, the Foggy Mountain Boys, in 1948 and were very successful with numerous hit singles through the fifties and presented their own WSM radio show. WSM is a specialist country music station, based in Nashville, and home of the Grand Ole Opry concerts that define and oversee the history of the music. Even greater success followed in 1962, when the pair recorded *The Ballad Of Jed Clampett*, which was used as the theme song for the long-running American TV show, *The Beverly Hillbillies*. The following year, Flatt and Scruggs gave the first of two concerts at New York's prestigious Carnegie Hall. The *Greatest Hits* compilation presents the duo's hits from the first part of the sixties, when they were still very much concerned with performing bluegrass as it always had been, with all-acoustic instruments. Later, Earl Scruggs became interested in tackling a more modern approach, which eventually led to the breakup of the Foggy Mountain Boys.

JOHN COLTRANE   MEDITATIONS

Although this album follows the religiously inspired *A Love Supreme*, it becomes clear from the first few bars that John Coltrane's idea of a meditation is not a calm affair. *The Father And The Son And The Holy Ghost* features some of the saxophonist's most tumultuous playing to date and the rest of the band respond in the same manner. There are two drummers, each playing a multitude of intense polyrhythms, yet somehow managing to mesh together as though a single eight-limbed player is responsible. There is a second saxophonist too, often playing at the same time as Coltrane. Pharoah

```
US release    September 1966   Impulse  A(S)-9110
UK release    September 1966   HMV      CSD/CLP 3575

1. The Father And The Son And The Holy Ghost
2. Compassion

3. Love
4. Consequences
5. Serenity

All compositions by John Coltrane

John Coltrane: tenor saxophone, percussion / Pharoah
Sanders: tenor saxophone, percussion / McCoy Tyner:
piano / Jimmy Garrison: bass / Elvin Jones: drums /
Rashied Ali: drums / Bob Thiele: producer
```

Sanders is an equally fluent improviser, but with a distinctive tone of his own, relying on a harsher timbre, with the frequent use of screaming overtones and split notes. Although the music is identified with the names of individual tracks, it is actually a continuous performance. *Compassion* is where McCoy Tyner solos and the saxophonists are silent (although they add to the percussion maelstrom with bells and tambourines). *Love* is Jimmy Garrison's feature initially, before the rest of the band (without Sanders) return in a slightly more reflective mood than before. Pharoah Sanders joins in as the piece becomes *Consequences* and is soon soloing in place of Coltrane, relishing the chance to display his full range of effects, as the drummers turn up the fury. Coltrane adds some notes of his own briefly, before both saxophonists, followed by the rest of the band, once again leave the proceedings for McCoy Tyner. As a conclusion to the work, John Coltrane delivers a solo that might indeed be considered serene if the rhythm section was not still concerned with keeping the fire burning.

CECIL TAYLOR   UNIT STRUCTURES

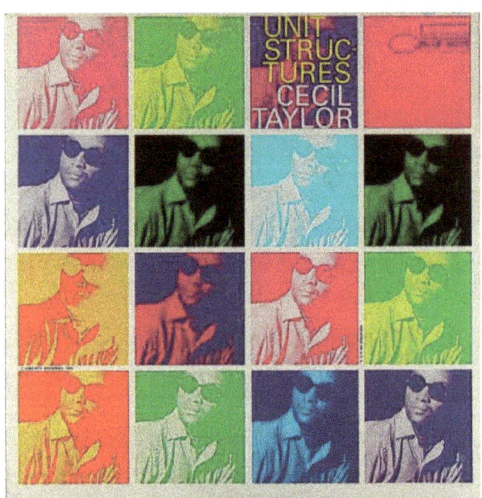

```
US release   September 1966   Blue Note   BST8/BLP 4237
Not released in UK

1. Steps
2. Enter Evening (Soft Line Structure)

3. Unit Structure / As Of A Now / Section
4. Tales (8 Whisps)

All compositions by Cecil Taylor

Cecil Taylor: piano, percussion / Eddie Gale: trumpet / Jimmy
Lyons: alto saxophone / Ken McIntyre: alto saxophone, oboe,
bass clarinet / Henry Grimes: bass / Alan Silva: bass / Andrew
Cyrille: drums / Alfred Lion: producer.
```

Cecil Taylor's approach to avant garde jazz is as much intellectual as emotional. In contrast to the free-ranging outpouring of John Coltrane, Taylor applies carefully worked out construction methods. In the case of the music on *Unit Structures*, the first of two similar Taylor albums issued by Blue Note in 1966, a series of particular events is set in advance for the musicians to work through in order, taking as long as they like on each one, but not deviating from the plan. The sound of the music is extremely turbulent, chaotic even, except that the band does clearly know what it is doing and the musicians move together as they play. Cecil Taylor's own playing is virtuosic and not immediately reminiscent of any other pianist, unless it is one of the classical performers interpreting the work of Olivier Messiaen or Pierre Boulez. His fingers race around the keyboard, striking quickly and percussively, incorporating huge leaps and complex note clusters. It is the kind of playing that inspires listeners who have not thought the matter through to suggest that they know three-year-olds who can play in the same way, but, in reality, they do not! Meanwhile, the saxophonists, and particularly Taylor's regular collaborator, Jimmy Lyons, provide some kind of link to the music of Charlie Parker, making it clear that this difficult music does belong within the long jazz tradition.

BERT JANSCH (AND JOHN RENBOURN)   JACK ORION / BERT AND JOHN

These two albums by Bert Jansch (and John Renbourn) were issued at the same time and with consecutive catalogue numbers, so that effectively they function as a double LP. The first record is primarily devoted to traditional folk material, including one, *Jack Orion* itself, that is of marathon proportions, while the second LP has two cover versions but is otherwise mainly made up of pieces composed by Jansch and Renbourn together. Bert Jansch has abandoned any intention of being considered a singer songwriter, however, with *Soho* being his only offering in that direction. Instead, the focus is very much on the guitar playing. The joint compositions are all instrumentals and many of the tracks on the first LP are too. If there is little development in the performance of either guitarist in comparison with their previous

recordings, that is only because they were both already consummate performers. The fact that they were beginning to be noticed outside the world of folk music was very much emphasised when, two years later, Jimmy Page borrowed Bert Jansch's arrangement of the traditional *Black Water Side* for a piece he tried to pass off as his own, under the title *Black Mountain Side*.

JOHN RENBOURN — ANOTHER MONDAY

```
UK release   October 1966   Transatlantic   TRA 149
Not released in US

1. Another Monday (John Renbourn)
2. Ladye Nothing's Toye Puffe (John Renbourn)
3. I Know My Babe (Traditional)
4. Waltz (John Renbourn)
5. Lost Lover Blues (Traditional)
6. One For William (John Renbourn)

7. Buffalo (John Renbourn)
8. Sugar Babe (Traditional)
9. Debbie Anne (John Renbourn)
10. Can't Keep From Crying (Traditional)
11. Day At The Seaside (John Renbourn)
12. Nobody's Fault But Mine (Traditional)

John Renbourn: guitar, vocals / Jacqui McShee: vocals
(5,10,12) / Jennifer de Montforte-Jones: oboe / Bill
Leader: producer
```

```
UK release   September 1966   Transatlantic   TRA 143/144
US release   1968/1971   Vanguard VSD 6544 / VSD 6506
(different covers; 1 extra track and 2
extra tracks respectively; 2nd LP retitled Stepping Stones)

1. The Waggoner's Lad (Traditional)
2. The First Time Ever I Saw Your Face (Ewan MacColl)
3. Jack Orion (Traditional)

4. The Gardener (Traditional)
5. Nottamun Town (Traditional)
6. Henry Martin (Traditional)
7. Black Water Side (Traditional)
8. Pretty Polly (Traditional)

9. East Wind (Bert Jansch/John Renbourn)
10. Piano Tune (John Renbourn)
11. Goodbye Pork Pie Hat (Charles Mingus)
12. Soho (Bert Jansch)
13. Tic-Tocative (Bert Jansch/John Renbourn)
14. Orlando (Bert Jansch/John Renbourn)

15. Red's Favourite (Bert Jansch/John Renbourn)
16. No Exit (Bert Jansch/John Renbourn)
17. Along The Way (Bert Jansch/John Renbourn)
18. The Time Has Come (Ann Briggs)
19. Stepping Stones (Bert Jansch/John Renbourn)
20. After The Dance (Bert Jansch/John Renbourn)

Bert Jansch: guitar, vocals, banjo (1) / John Renbourn: guitar
(1,3.6.8,9-20) / Bill Leader: producer
```

Bert Jansch does not play on the second solo album by John Renbourn and, left on his own, it becomes even more clear what a remarkable guitarist Renbourn is. He has a tendency to play his music – primarily comprising blues tunes – very fast, simply because he can. This becomes particularly noticeable on the piece he calls *Waltz*, which may be in three-four time, but charges along like an express train. Good luck to anyone attempting to dance a waltz to this! Two tracks, *Ladye Nothing's Toye Puffe* and *One For William,* break new ground by adopting a distinctly medieval flavour. The second piece adds an oboe to the mix, which is extremely effective. Three songs present Renbourn's singing discovery, a young lady by the name of Jacqui McShee, who duets quite delightfully with Renbourn. Overall, *Another Monday*, despite its air of unprepossessing simplicity, is something of a gem.

GRUPPO DI IMPROVVISAZIONE — NUOVA CONSONANZA

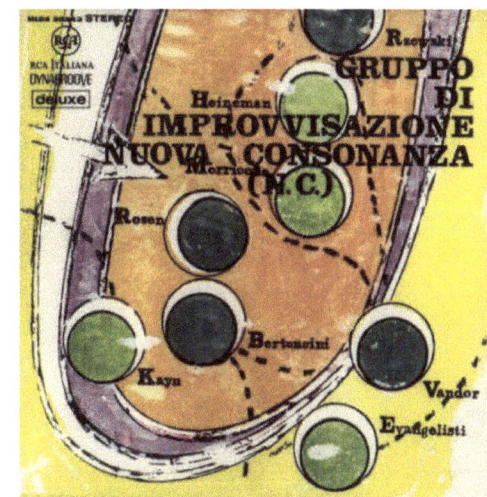

In English, the group responsible for this album is called New Harmony and it is described, perfectly accurately, as an improvisation group. The members are all classically trained composers, indeed one of them, Ennio Morricone, was becoming very well-known after directing his energies towards the creation of film soundtrack music. The music on the album is entirely improvised, but without any melodic or rhythmic content at all. This is not jazz, although it does bear comparison with some of the music produced by Sun Ra. The emphasis is on timbre and texture, delivered quietly to focus the listener's attention, and with every performer trying to find sounds that his instruments would not usually be expected to

Italian release   c.October 1966   RCA   MLDS 20243
US release   October 1967   RCA Victor   LSP/LPM 3846 as **THE PRIVATE SEA OF DREAMS** by Il Gruppo, different cover, some tracks retitled as indicated, order of tracks changed.
Not released in UK

1. Improvvisazione Per Otto (Sunrise)
2. Trio Di Fiati (Conversations)
3. String Quartet (Springs Quartet)
4. Improvvisazione Per Cinque (Waves)

5. Quartetto (Side One Band Four)
6. Trio Per Violoncello, Tromba E Lastra Di Cristallo (Perfect Union)
7. RKBA 1675/1
8. Cantata (Lip Service)

All compositions by Gruppo Di Improvvisazione Nuova Consonanza

Mario Bertoncini: percussion, prepared piano, mouth percussion / Franco Evangelisti: piano, celeste, percussion, mouth percussion / John Heineman: trombone, prepared piano, cello / Roland Kayn: organ, prepared piano, vibraphone, marimba, mouth percussion / Ennio Morricone: trumpet, mouth percussion / Jerry Rosen: clarinet / Frederic Rzewski: piano, percussion, mouth percussion / Ivan Vandor: tenor saxophone / Pasquale Santomartino: producer

deliver. The opening track, the only one on which all eight musicians play, is spacious and light, allowing every sound to be clearly heard. Each musician spends more time in silence than in playing anything, which remains the approach through the rest of the album. The closing track, with the performers' mouths becoming the instruments (aided by a little echo), could be said to be anticipating the rise of beatboxing in the eighties, except that, as always, Nuova Consonanza is interested purely in the sounds it can make and does not attempt to organise them into anything so obvious as a beat. Music so uncompromising was never likely to reach a mass market and, initially, the record was only issued in Italy, the country where this composers' collective was based. But a year later, with the development of psychedelia, RCA in America clearly felt that the album might appeal to the fans of that and re-released it with an appropriate new cover design and title. Sales were not impressive, although it is hard to believe that the likes of Pink Floyd and Organisation (the precursor of Kraftwerk) were not aware of music that relates so closely to some of what they were trying to achieve.

THE SEEDS   A WEB OF SOUND

US release   October 1966   GNP Crescendo   GNP(S) 2033
UK release   October 1966   Vocalion   VA-N 8062

1. The Farmer (Sky Saxon)
2. Pictures And Designs (Daryl Hooper/Sky Saxon)
3. Tripmaker (Daryl Hooper/Marcus Tybalt)
4. I Tell Myself (Marcus Tybalt)
5. A Faded Picture (Daryl Hooper/Sky Saxon)
6. Rollin' Machine (Sky Saxon)

7. Just Let Go (Daryl Hooper/Jan Savage/Sky Saxon)
8. Up In Her Room (Sky Saxon)

Sky Saxon (aka Marcus Tybalt): vocals, bass guitar, producer / Jan Savage: guitar, vocals / Cooker: slide guitar / Daryl Hooper: keyboards, vocals / Rick Andridge: drums / Harvey Sharpe: bass guitar

The second album by the Seeds is an altogether more adventurous affair than the group's debut. Jan Savage attaches a fuzzbox to his guitar and plays lead lines through every song, as counterpoint to Sky Saxon's vocals. Nobody plays any chords explicitly, not even Daryl ooper, whose primary role on keyboards is to deliver quirky solos. He revels in choosing notes that are not those the listener would expect, making his playing very memorable. Overall, the music is constructed out of tightly interlocking parts played by the entire band, in which the simple phrases added by the group's new member, slide guitarist Cooker, are an essential ingredient. The approach enables the long track on side two, *Up In Her Room*, to proceed through its fourteen minutes or so without becoming at all tiresome, despite the song being nothing more than a rhythmic jam in an unchanging A major. It would be overstating the case to describe *A Web Of Sound* as a masterpiece, but it certainly presents the most durable music to be created by any of the 'punk' groups of the time.

SIMON AND GARFUNKEL
PARSLEY, SAGE, ROSEMARY AND THYME

Many of the songs are still amongst the most fondly remembered that Paul Simon has ever written. Martin Carthy was annoyed at Simon taking his guitar arrangement for the traditional *Scarborough Fair*, and claiming the writing credit on the song for himself, but in truth the duo transforms the original, taking it to a place far removed from Carthy's more prosaic rendering. Simon interpolates lines of his own (*Canticle*) in between the lines of the original song, giving it a call and response structure, and he adds a delicate harpsichord part to the mix, alongside his and Art Garfunkel's most sublime vocal harmonies. The closing track places an ethereal version of the Christmas carol, *Silent Night,* over a contrasting reconstruction of a radio news broadcast, full of violence and mayhem. The album reached number four in the US album chart and eventually achieved triple platinum status. In the UK, the album did not enter the chart until nearly two years later, following an increased interest in Simon and Garfunkel, kindled by the use of their music in the very successful film, *The Graduate*. Glorying in their position of Columbia star artists, Simon and Garfunkel took their time recording this album, and it shows.

Paul Simon: vocals, guitar / Art Garfunkel: vocals, piano (12) / Joe South: guitar / Larry Knechtel: keyboards / John Mezzar: harpsichord (1) / Joe Osborn: bass guitar / Eugene Wright: bass (6) / Carol Kaye: bass guitar (1,4) / Hal Blaine: drums / Joe Morello: drums (6) / Charlie O'Donnell: narration / Bob Johnston: producer

| US release | October 1966 | Columbia | CS9/CL2 363 |
| UK release | October 1966 | CBS | (S)BPG 62860 |

1. Scarborough Fair / Canticle (Traditional/Paul Simon/Art Garfunkel)
2. Patterns (Paul Simon)
3. Cloudy (Paul Simon/Bruce Woodley)
4. Homeward Bound (Paul Simon) (not included on UK album)
5. The Big Bright Green Pleasure Machine (Paul Simon)
6. The 59th Street Bridge Song (Feelin' Groovy) (Paul Simon)
7. The Dangling Conversation (Paul Simon)
8. Flowers Never Bend With The Rainfall (Paul Simon)
9. A Simple Desultory Philippic (Paul Simon)
10. For Emily, Whenever I May Find Her (Paul Simon)
11. A Poem On The Underground Wall (Paul Simon)
12. 7 O'Clock News / Silent Night (Josef Mohr/Franz Gruber/Paul Simon)

TIM BUCKLEY

| US release | October 1966 | Elektra | EKS7/EKL 4004 |
| UK release | October 1966 | Elektra | EKS7/EKL 4004 |

1. I Can't See You (Tim Buckley/Larry Beckett)
2. Wings (Tim Buckley)
3. Song Of The Magician (Tim Buckley/Larry Beckett)
4. Strange Street Affair Under Blue (Tim Buckley/Larry Beckett)
5. Valentine Melody (Tim Buckley/Larry Beckett)
6. Aren't You The Girl (Tim Buckley)
7. Song Slowly Song (Tim Buckley/Larry Beckett)
8. It Happens Every Time (Tim Buckley)
9. Song For Jainie (Tim Buckley)
10. Grief In My Soul (Tim Buckley/Larry Beckett)
11. She Is (Tim Buckley/Larry Beckett)
12. Understand Your Man (Tim Buckley)

Tim Buckley: vocals, guitar / Lee Underwood: guitar / Van Dyke Parks: keyboards / Jim Fielder: bass guitar / Billy Mundi: drums / Jack Nitzsche: strings arranger / Paul Rothchild: producer / Jac Holzman: producer

The first album by Tim Buckley is a confident set of folk rock performances by someone who is clearly a considerable talent. The songs are not exactly catchy, but they are made to sound effective, beautiful even, by the sensitive playing of the accompanying musicians – particularly the delicate lead guitar of Lee Underwood running through most of the songs and the inventive string parts added to some of them. It is Tim Buckley's voice that is the most crucial element, however – a high, clear tenor like no other singer of the time. The album was not a huge commercial success, but promised much interesting music to come.

GEORGIE FAME   SOUND VENTURE

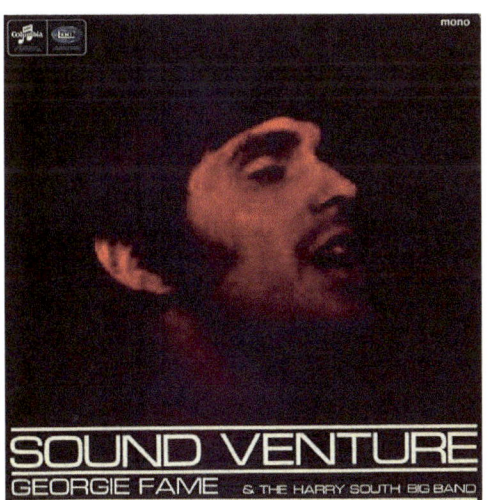

For his third studio album, Georgie Fame moved entirely into the role of jazz singer, fronting a big band made up of some of the best British jazz musicians of the time and abandoning his own Hammond organ playing. In terms of his own career, Fame undoubtedly saw this as a positive venture (to paraphrase the title of the album), giving himself an increased artistic credibility within the wider world of music

| UK release | October 1966 | Columbia | SX 6076 |
| Not released in US | | | |

1. Many Happy Returns (Norman Hurricane Smith)
2. Down For The Count (Jon Hendricks/Dave Lambert/Freddie Green)
3. It's For Love The Petals Fall (Jack Ashford)
4. And I Am Missing You (Georgie Fame)
5. Funny How Time Slips Away (Willie Nelson)
6. Lil' Pony (Jon Hendricks, Neal Hefti)
7. Lovey Dovey (King Curtis/Ahmet Ertegun)
8. Lil' Darlin' (Jon Hendricks/Neal Hefti)
9. Three Blind Mice (Jon Hendricks)
10. Dawn Yawn (Georgie Fame)
11. Feed Me (Jon Hendricks)
12. Papa's Got A Brand New Bag (James Brown

Georgie Fame: vocals / Colin Green: guitar / Stan Tracey: piano / Gordon Beck: piano / Kenny Wheeler: trumpet / Jimmy Deuchar: trumpet / Bert Courtley: trumpet / Tony Fisher: trumpet / Ian Hamer: trumpet / Greg Bowen: trumpet / Les Condon: trumpet / Chris Smith: trombone / Gib Wallace: trombone / Johnny Marshall: trombone / Keith Christie: trombone / Ken Goldie: trombone / Alan Branscombe: alto saxophone / Ray Warleigh: alto saxophone / Roy Willox: alto saxophone / Tubby Hayes: tenor saxophone / Ronnie Scott: tenor saxophone / Dick Morrissey: tenor saxophone / Tony Coe: tenor saxophone, flute / Harry Klein: baritone saxophone / Jackie Sharpe: baritone saxophone / Phil Bates: bass / Bill Eyden: drums / Phil Seamen: drums / Harry South: arranger, conductor / Denny Cordell: producer / Tony Palmer: producer

by adopting the sophisticated sound and style already established by the likes of Tony Bennett, Mel Tormé, Jon Hendricks, and Frank Sinatra. To be fair, Georgie Fame does a good job in entering the musical territory of these older performers. But only an enthusiastic cover version of a James Brown song, *Papa's Got A Brand New Bag*, gives a hint of what could have been achieved in the way of creating a convincing sixties jazz-soul fusion. *Sound Venture* is undoubtedly a good album, with fine performances throughout, but it was something of an irrelevance to the exciting developments taking place elsewhere in popular music. During 1967, Georgie Fame performed with an innovative jazz-rock small band, including saxophonist Lyn Dobson, drummer Jon Hiseman, and guitarist John McLaughlin, alongside his own keyboard work, but sadly nothing was recorded for an album. Instead, Fame chose to further pursue his direction on record as a jazz/cabaret singer, finding himself increasingly marginalised within a rock music scene that was finding more adventurous paths to follow. His last big hit, at the end of 1967, was a novelty song, *The Ballad Of Bonnie And Clyde*, which would have fitted well within the trad jazz/pop approach of an earlier performer like Kenny Ball – an odd choice to pick as an influence.

THE MONKEES

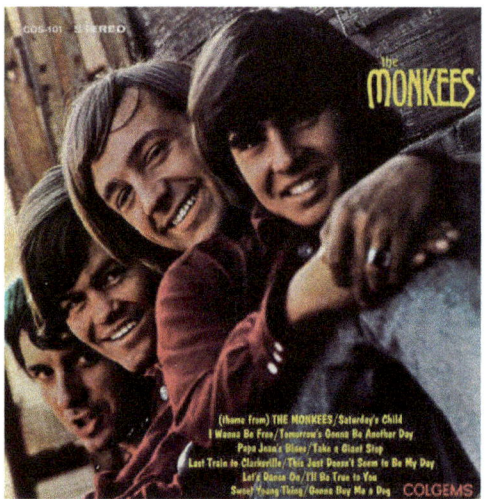

| US release | October 1966 | Colgems | COS/COM 101 |
| UK release | October 1966 | RCA Victor | RD 7844 |

1. Theme From The Monkees (Tommy Boyce/Bobby Hart)
2. Saturday's Child (David Gates)
3. I Wanna Be Free (Tommy Boyce/Bobby Hart)
4. Tomorrow's Gonna Be Another Day (Tommy Boyce/Steve Venet)
5. Papa Gene's Blues (Mike Nesmith)
6. Take A Giant Step (Gerry Goffin/Carole King)
7. Last Train To Clarksville (Tommy Boyce/Bobby Hart)
8. This Just Doesn't Seem To Be My Day (Tommy Boyce/Bobby Hart)
9. Let's Dance On (Tommy Boyce/Bobby Hart)
10. I'll Be True To You (Yes I Will) (Gerry Goffin/Russ Titleman)
11. Sweet Young Thing (Gerry Goffin/Carole King/Mike Nesmith)
12. Gonna Buy Me A Dog (Tommy Boyce/Bobby Hart)

Davy Jones: vocals / Micky Dolenz: vocals / Peter Tork: vocals, guitar (5), bass guitar (11) / Mike Nesmith: vocals, producer (5,11) / Ron Hicklin: vocals / Wayne Erwin: guitar, vocals / Gerry McGee: guitar / Louie Shelton: guitar / James Burton: guitar, bass guitar / Glen Campbell: guitar, bass guitar / Al Casey: guitar, bass guitar / James Helms: guitar / Don Peake: guitar / Michael Deasy: guitar / Michael Rubini: harpsichord / Larry Knechtel: piano / Keith Allison: harmonica / Larry Taylor: bass guitar / William Pitman: bass guitar / Bob West: bass guitar / Billy Lewis: drums / Hal Blaine: drums / Frank De Vito: drums / Jim Gordon: drums, percussion / Gene Estes: percussion / Gary Coleman: percussion / David Walters: percussion / Bob Cooper: oboe / Bonnie Douglas: violin / Paul Shane: violin / Jimmy Bryant: violin / Myra Kestenbaum: viola / Fred Seykora: cello / Joseph Ditullio: cello / Leon Russell: arranger (6) / Tommy Boyce: producer, vocals, guitar / Bobby Hart: producer, vocals, organ, glockenspiel / Jack Keller: producer, piano

The Monkees consisted of four actors, hired to play the parts of the members of a group for a television series that began showing in the US in September 1966. Heavily influenced by the Beatles' films, *A Hard Day's Night* and *Help!*, the TV show was a sitcom, presenting the light-hearted antics of four young men, sharing accommodation and playing music together. Each episode had the Monkees pretending to play at least one song as a group, and the album, *The Monkees,* was intended as a soundtrack for the series, with the first title being the theme song playing during the opening credits of each programme. The back cover artwork introduced the group members in their TV series personae, complete with instrument credits. In fact, virtually everything on the album was played by session musicians. Davy Jones and Micky Dolenz had substantial roles as lead singers, but the musical contributions of the other two were little more than cameos, although Mike Nesmith was allowed to include and produce two of his own songs. The element of confusion introduced, that this was an album by an actual group, was one that suited both the programme producers and the record company, who proceeded to muddy the waters further by sending the Monkees out on tour, in the real world. Fortunately, both Peter Tork and Mike Nesmith were accomplished guitarists, although Micky Dolenz, cast as the group's drummer, had never played his instrument before. The album comprises a highly professional and attractive set of songs, deliberately reminiscent of the Beatles, though without any of that group's innovation. With the regular advertisement provided by the television programmes, it had no difficulty in reaching the top of the charts in both the US and the UK.

THE KINKS   FACE TO FACE

| UK release | October 1966 | Pye | N(S)PL 18149 |
| US release | December 1966 | Reprise | R(S) 6228 |

1. Party Line (Ray and Dave Davies)
2. Rosy Won't You Please Come Home
3. Dandy
4. Too Much On My Mind
5. Session Man
6. Rainy Day In June
7. House In The Country
8. Holiday In Waikiki
9. Most Exclusive Residence For Sale
10. Fancy
11. Little Miss Queen Of Darkness
12. You're Looking Fine
13. Sunny Afternoon
14. I'll Remember

All compositions by Ray Davies except track 1

Ray Davies: vocals, guitar / Dave Davies: guitar, vocals / Pete Quaife: bass guitar, vocals / Mick Avory: drums / Nicky Hopkins: keyboards / John Dalton: bass guitar (11) / Rasa Davies: vocals / Shel Talmy: producer

The fourth album by the Kinks has a notably psychedelic cover, with brightly coloured butterflies emerging from the top of a man's head, but the music is rather less strikingly arranged than this might suggest. The Kinks are not interested in adding the extra instrumental timbres to be found on the recent Beatles album, *Revolver*. It is a very strong collection, however, because Ray Davies' songwriting has reached a new high level, finding further ways to present the insightful social observation of the recent singles, *Well Respected Man* and *Dedicated Follower of Fashion*, within songs that are melodically distinctive. *Sunny Afternoon* had been an obvious choice for a memorable single, and was a well-deserved number one in the

UK, but many of the other songs on the album are almost as good as this. There is still a roughness to the Kinks' playing, albeit softened on many tracks by the addition of Nicky Hopkins on a variety of keyboard instruments, but it is sounding like a deliberate effect now, rather than any kind of indication of a lack of skill or rehearsal. *Face To Face* represents a considerable leap in quality from the previous Kinks albums, marking the group as one to be particularly worth following, even if the LP was a little less successful in the charts than its predecessors.

MANFRED MANN   AS IS

```
UK release    October 1966    Fontana    (S)TL 5377
US release    October 1966    Philips    PDS 260

1.  Trouble And Tea (Mike D'Abo)
2.  A Now And Then Thing (Tom McGuinness)
3.  Each Other's Company (Mike Hugg)
4.  Box Office Draw (Mike D'Abo)
5.  Dealer Dealer (Manfred Mann/Mike Hugg/Peter Thomas)
6.  Morning After The Party (Mike Hugg)
7.  Another Kind Of Music (Manfred Mann/Mike Hugg)
8.  As Long As I Have Lovin' (Mike D'Abo)
9.  Autumn Leaves (Johnny Mercer/Joseph Kosma)
10. Superstitious Guy (Mike Hugg)
11. You're My Girl (Manfred Mann/Mike Hugg/Peter Thomas)
12. Just Like A Woman (Bob Dylan)

Manfred Mann: organ, mellotron, piano, harpsichord / Mike D'Abo:
vocals, piano (8) / Tom McGuinness: guitar, mandolin / Klaus
Voormann: bass guitar, recorder, flute, guitar (7) / Mike Hugg: drums,
vibraphone / Dave Richmond: bass (9) / Shel Talmy: producer
```

As Is presents another new line-up for Manfred Mann, with Mike D'Abo replacing Paul Jones as lead singer and Klaus Voormann, a long-standing friend of the Beatles and designer of the cover for their *Revolver* album, drafted in to play bass. One track, an efficient cover of the standard, *Autumn Leaves,* with Dave Richmond, a member of the group before it became famous, recalled to play double bass, proves that the group has not entirely abandoned its interest in jazz. This might otherwise be assumed from the rest of the album, which is made up of not particularly ambitious pop. The group members have discovered an interest in writing their own material, but this is not remarkable, even if it displays the right influences (Ray Davies mainly). Manfred Mann himself has acquired a mellotron – still a considerable novelty, despite it being nearly a year since the instrument's first recorded appearance in the hands of Graham Bond. He uses it throughout much of the album, although it remains an effect, rather than a fully integrated aspect of the overall sound. By far the most notable track on the album is the group's interpretation of a song by Bob Dylan, *Just Like A Woman,* where the mellotron does not sound. Released as a single, the song was the first of several top ten UK hits by this revamped edition of Manfred Mann, confirming the group's standing as a creator of memorable singles rather than entirely convincing albums.

THE 13th FLOOR ELEVATORS

```
US release    October 1966    International Artists    IA-LP-1
Not released in UK

1.  You're Gonna Miss Me (Roky Erickson)
2.  Roller Coaster (Roky Erickson/Tommy Hall)
3.  Splash 1 (Now I'm Home) (Clementine Hall/Roky Erickson)
4.  Reverberation (Roky Erickson/Stacy Sutherland/Tommy Hall)
5.  Don't Fall Down (Roky Erickson/Tommy Hall)
6.  Fire Engine (Roky Erickson/Stacy Sutherland/Tommy Hall)
7.  Thru The Rhythm (Stacy Sutherland/Tommy Hall)
8.  You Don't Know (John St.Powell)
9.  Kingdom Of Heaven (John St.Powell)
10. Monkey Island (John St.Powell)
11. Tried To Hide (Stacy Sutherland/Tommy Hall)

Roky Erickson: vocals, guitar, harmonica / Stacy Sutherland:
guitar / Ronnie Leatherman: bass guitar / Benny Thurman: bass
guitar (1,11) / John Walton: drums / Tommy Hall: jug, vocals /
Lelan Rogers: producer / Gordon Bynum: producer (1,11)
```

The back cover of the first album by the 13th Floor Elevators states 'The Psychedelic Sounds Of: The 13th Floor Elevators', but as a description of the album's contents, rather than its title. The wording appears on neither the front cover nor on the record labels. The group actually plays the garage, punk rock made familiar by the Seeds, the Standells, and many others, though with the customary keyboard player replaced by what sounds like a demented chicken clucking in the background. This is achieved by group member Tommy Hall chortling into a large aluminium jug and amplifying the noise with a microphone – a rather different approach to the jug playing employed by blues bands in the twenties, where the device was used to create burping bass tones. Whether this is enough to characterise the group's music as 'psychedelic' is doubtful, although fans of the group in recent years clearly believe that it is. Certainly the chosen cover design seems to be appropriate and was ultimately rather more influential than the music. The album, released on an independent Texan record label, was not particularly successful, although *You're Gonna Miss Me* was a small hit in the US singles chart.

THE DEEP   PSYCHEDELIC MOODS

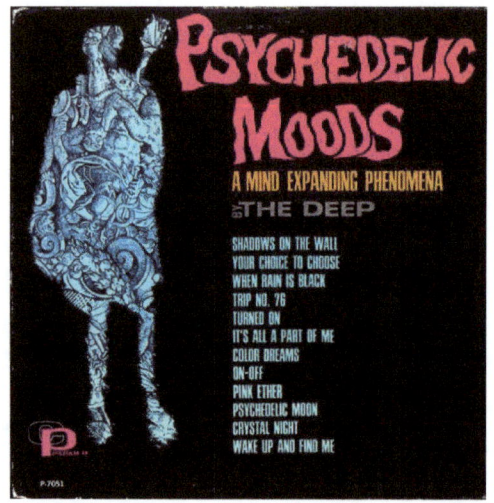

US release   October 1966   Parkway   (S)P-7051
Not released in UK

1. Color Dreams (Rusty Evans)
2. Pink Ether (David Blackhurst/Rusty Evans)
3. When Rain Is Black (Caroline Blue/Rusty Evans)
4. It's All A Part Of Me (Rusty Evans)
5. Turned On (David Blackhurst/Rusty Evans)
6. Psychedelic Moon (David Blackhurst/Rusty Evans)
7. Shadows On The Wall (Rusty Evans)
8. Crystal Nite (David Blackhurst/Mark Barkan)
9. Trip #76 (Lenny Pogan/Mark Barkan/Rusty Evans)
10. Wake Up And Find Me (Rusty Evans)
11. Your Choice To Choose (Arthur Geller/Rusty Evans)
12. On Off – Off On (Rusty Evans)

Rusty Evans: vocals, guitar, producer / David Bromberg: guitar, bass guitar, vocals / Mark Barkan: producer / David Blackhurst: / Arthur Geller: / Lenny Pogan: / Caroline Blue: vocals

The word 'psychedelic' refers to drugs that produce mind-altering, hallucinogenic effects when taken. Psychedelic music is therefore music that seeks to recreate some of these effects in the mind of the listener by means of unusual and unexpected sounds and timbres. The people making this music may or may not be acting under the influence of drugs themselves. Songwriter Rusty Evans and producer Mark Barkan (the composer of the Manfred Mann hit, *Pretty Flamingo* and several hit songs for Lesley Gore) conceived the idea of a rock music album with psychedelic qualities and released the result as being by a group they called the Deep. Many of the songs are based on the familiar punk rock style of the time, with a couple of more pastoral efforts for contrast. The songs are much less interesting than they need to be, because clearly Evans is not much of a composer and neither he nor Barkan have sufficient imagination to make the project work. They considered that the best idea for an extra ingredient was to include the sounds of a couple making love, on *When Rain Is Black*. A template for what they wanted to achieve was already available for them, in the form of the Beatles track *Tomorrow Never Knows*, included on the *Revolver* album, but Evans and Barkan were apparently satisfied with a much lower level of creativity. The album was not a commercial success, although Columbia records gave the duo the chance to make a follow-up during the next year, which was released as *Psychedelic Psoul* and credited to the Freak Scene.

GARY LEWIS AND THE PLAYBOYS   GOLDEN GREATS

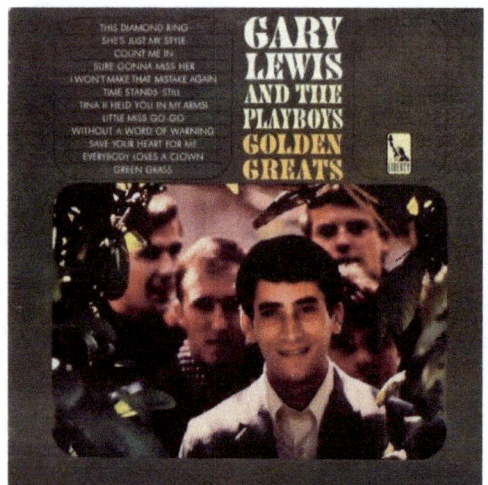

US release   October 1966   Liberty   LST/LRP 7468
Not released in UK

1. This Diamond Ring (Al Kooper/Bob Brass/Irwin Levine)
2. Count Me In (Glen Hardin)
3. She's Just My Style (Gary Lewis/Leon Russell/Snuff Garrett/Al Capps)
4. Tina (I Held You In My Arms) (Gary Lewis/Sonny Curtis/Leon Russell/Snuff Garrett)
5. Without A Word Of Warning (Snuff Garrett/Leon Russell/Gary Lewis)
6. Sure Gonna Miss Her (Leon Russell)
7. Everybody Loves A Clown (Snuff Garrett/Leon Russell/Gary Lewis)
8. I Won't Make That Mistake Again (Leon Russell/Snuff Garrett/Gary Lewis)
9. Save Your Heart Just For Me (Gary Geld/Peter Udell)
10. Little Miss Go-Go (Snuff Garrett/Leon Russell/Brown)
11. Time Stands Still (Leon Russell/Snuff Garrett/Gary Lewis)
12. Green Grass (Roger Greenaway/Roger Cook)

Gary Lewis: drums, vocals / Dave Walker: guitar, vocals (1) / Tommy Tripplehorn: guitar, vocals / Dave Castell: guitar / Al Ramsay: bass guitar (1) / Carl Radle: bass guitar / John R West: keyboards / Jimmy Karstein: drums / Leon Russell: keyboards, arranger / Tommy Allsup: guitar / Mike Deasy: guitar / Joe Osborn: bass guitar / Hal Blaine: drums / Ron Hicklin: vocals / Snuff Garrett: producer

Gary Lewis and the Playboys performed undemanding pop with a beat, sounding very like Herman's Hermits. Lewis is the son of comedian and actor Jerry Lewis and was persuaded by producer Snuff Garrett to capitalise on his name by taking the role of lead singer, even though his voice was weak and had to be supported by session singer Ron Hicklin. The group gained several big hits in the US. *This Diamond Ring* went to number one and sold a million copies, while the following six singles (tracks 2, 9, 7, 3, 6, and 12) were all top ten hits. The run came to an end when Gary Lewis was drafted into the US army. After his discharge, the momentum was dissipated and the group only had one more hit, its version of Bryan Hyland's *Sealed With A Kiss* stalling at number nineteen. Gary Lewis and the Playboys were largely ignored in the UK and had no hits at all.

ELVIS PRESLEY   SPINOUT

The cover of the soundtrack album for Elvis Presley's twenty-second film shows the singer making a half-hearted attempt to update his image, but the music remains stuck in the early sixties style where rock 'n' roll was becoming subverted and smoothed into just another branch of showbiz. A fuzz-toned electric guitar tries hard to bring the music into

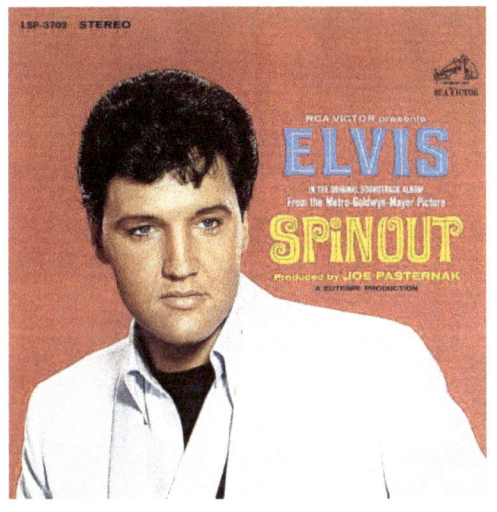

| US release | October 1966 | RCA Victor | LSP / LPM-3702 |
| UK release | October 1966 | RCA Victor | SF/ RD 7820 |

1. Stop, Look And Listen (Joy Byers)
2. Adam And Evil (Fred Wise/Randy Starr)
3. All That I Am (Sid Tepper/Roy C.Bennett)
4. Never Say Yes (Doc Pomus/Mort Shuman)
5. Am I Ready (Sid Tepper/Roy C.Bennett)
6. Beach Shack (Bill Giant/Bernie Baum/Florence Kaye)
7. Spinout (Ben Weisman/Dolores Fuller/Sid Wayne)
8. Smorgasbord (Sid Tepper/Roy C.Bennett)
9. I'll Be Back (Ben Weisman/Sid Wayne)
10. Tomorrow Is A Long Time (Bob Dylan)
11. Down In The Alley (Jesse Stone)
12. I'll Remember You (Kui Lee)

Elvis Presley: vocals / The Jordanaires (Hoyt Hawkins, Neal Matthews Jr, Gordon Stoker, Ray Walker): vocals / Scotty Moore: guitar / Tommy Tedesco: guitar / Tiny Timbrell: guitar / Boots Randolph: tenor saxophone / Floyd Cramer: piano / Charlie Hodge: piano (6) / Bob Moore: double bass / D.J. Fontana: drums / Buddy Harman: drums / George Stoll: producer

1966 on *I'll Be Back*, but it is fighting a losing battle against the corny cabaret band arrangements surrounding it on the album. With Elvis LPs like this being churned out twice a year, only his most loyal fans continued to be interested and if the records always managed to make an appearance in the US chart, it was a rare event if any managed to get near the top. *Spinout* peaked at number eighteen and it was a similar story in the UK, where the album (retitled *California Holiday*) reached number seventeen. On this occasion, however, the album is redeemed by one outstanding performance, an interpretation of a Bob Dylan song, one of three bonus tracks not included in the film, but added to the album to make it long enough for release. *Tomorrow Is A Long Time* was recorded during the session that produced the gospel songs later released as the album, *How Great Thou Art*. Elvis loved this kind of material, and devoted much more care and effort into the recordings than he bothered to do with the insipid songs chosen for his films. He sings the Dylan song as though this too is a gospel classic and in the process manages to give it a depth and a stature to completely transcend any of the composer's own recordings. (It originally appeared as a 1962 publisher's demo, included as part of what are known as the 'Witmark demos'.) For once, too, Elvis is presented with a gentle country-rock arrangement that suits his singing very well. He proves that, given half a chance, he is worthy of all the hype aimed in his direction. It is such a shame that Elvis was generally not given the opportunity to interpret material that he actually cared about.

DUSTY SPRINGFIELD   GOLDEN HITS

| UK release | October 1966 | Philips | (S)BL 7737 |
| US release | October 1966 | Philips | PHS-600-220 |

1. I Only Want To Be With You (Ivor Raymonde/Mike Hawker)
2. I Just Don't Know What To Do With Myself (Burt Bacharach/Hal David)
3. In The Middle Of Nowhere (Beatrice Verdi/Buddy Kaye)
4. Losing You (Clive Westlake/Tom Springfield)
5. All Cried Out (Buddy Kaye/Philip Springer)
6. Some Of Your Lovin' (Gerry Goffin/Carole King)
7. Wishin' And Hopin' (Burt Bacharach/Hal David)
8. My Colouring Book (John Kander/Fred Ebb)
9. Little By Little (Beatrice Verdi/Buddy Kaye/Eddie Gin)
10. You Don't Have To Say You Love Me (Pino Donaggio/Simon Napier-Bell/ Vicki Wickham/Vito Pallavicini)
11. Goin' Back (Gerry Fohhin/Carole King)
12. All I See Is You (Ben Weisman/Clive Westlake)

Dusty Springfield: vocals / Ivor Raymonde: arranger / Peter Knight: arranger (11) / Wally Stott: arranger (12) / Johnny Franz: producer

By late 1966, Dusty Springfield had become a big star, with eight top ten hits in the UK, including a number one (*You Don't Have To Say You Love Me*), and three top twenty hits in the US. All the songs on *Golden Hits* have orchestral arrangements with no trace of anything that could be described as rock, but such is the appeal and resonance of Dusty's voice, that the songs are made completely memorable. The collection proves Dusty Springfield to be the most convincing singer of her generation in the UK and it was the most successful of her career, reaching number two in the album chart.

PAT KILROY   LIGHT OF DAY

Pat Kilroy was one of many American folk performers given the chance to record for the Elektra label, although in many cases, (and certainly that of Kilroy, who died of cancer just a year later), one album was all they got. The sleeve notes of *Light Of Day* mention a plethora of world music influences, but the evidence of the music itself is that Kilroy's ambition very much outstrips his actual ability. He has nothing to match Davy Graham's *Maajun* or Bert Jansch's *Kasbah,* folk recordings displaying world music flavours over a year earlier. The gentle flute and percussion that is used to decorate most of his songs provides a hippy ambience that is very slightly ahead of its time, but the music is continually undermined by Kilroy's annoying vocal mannerisms. Some of the singing is improvised, but again his talent is not really great enough to make the approach work. Wikipedia claims that *Light Of Day* is a psychedelic prototype (a claim that provides the reason for the album to be included here), but clearly the author of the entry has not heard the album. At a considerable stretch, it can be viewed as a precursor of *Astral Weeks*, recorded two years later, but Van Morrison is so much more adept and inspired, that the comparison does not really do Pat Kilroy any positive favours.

```
US release    October 1966    Elektra    EKS-7311 / EKL-311
UK release    October 1966    Elektra    EKL-311

1.  The Magic Carpet
2.  Roberta's Blues
3.  Cancereal
4.  A Day At The Beach
5.  The Pipes Of Pan
6.  Mississippi Blues

7.  Vibrations
8.  Light Of Day
9.  The Fortune Teller
10. Canned Heat
11. The River
12. Star Dance

All compositions by Pat Kilroy

Pat Kilroy: vocals, guitar, bass guitar, glockenspiel, percussion /
Bob Amacker: tablas / Susan Gaubard: flute, glockenspiel /
Stefan Grossman: guitar / Marc Silber: guitar, bass guitar / Eric
Katz: harmonica / Jim Welch: congas / Peter K. Siegel: producer
```

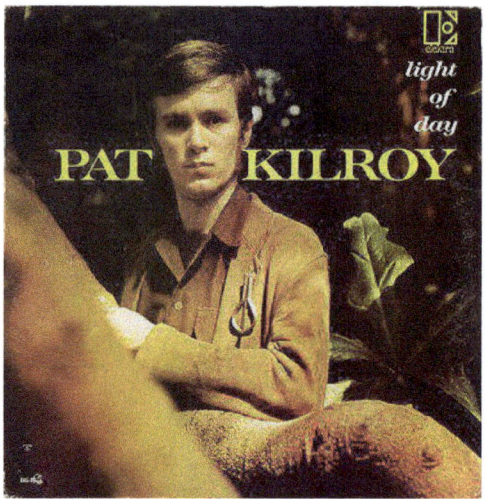

BLUES MAGOOS   PSYCHEDELIC LOLLIPOP

```
US release    November 1966    Mercury    SR6 / MG2 1096
UK release    November 1966    Fontana    (S)TL 5402

1.  (We Ain't Got) Nothin' Yet (Mike Esposito/Ron Gilbert/Ralph Scala)
2.  Love Seems Doomed (Mike Esposito/Ron Gilbert/Ralph Scala)
3.  Tobacco Road (John D Loudermilk)
4.  Queen Of My Nights (David Blue)
5.  I'll Go Crazy (James Brown)

6.  Gotta Get Away (Ritchie Adams/Alan Gordon)
7.  Sometimes I Think About (Mike Esposito/Ron Gilbert/Ralph Scala)
8.  One By One (Ron Gilbert/Emil Theilhelm)
9.  Worried Life Blues (Big Maceo Merriweather)
10. She's Coming Home (Roger Atkins/Helen Miller)

Mike Esposito: guitar / Emil Theilhelm: guitar, vocals / Ralph Scala:
keyboards, vocals / Ron Gilbert: bass guitar, vocals / Geoff Daking:
drums / Art Polhemus: producer / Bob Wyld: producer
```

More garage punk rock in the manner of the Seeds and the Standells, this time with a particularly ethereal organ sound and a finely-honed sense of song structure and dynamics. There are more smouldering ballads than usually tolerated within this genre and one track (*Love Seems Doomed*) even appears to be anticipating a fragment of King Crimson. With the organ playing as justification, Blues Magoos adopt an album title that attempts to seize the happening word of the time, 'psychedelic', as its own. The music does not have any of the musical sound effects of the Deep, however, even if the songs are more distinctive. *(We Ain't Got) Nothin' Yet* was a substantial US hit and the album did well too, but the group struggled to find a satisfactory follow-up, despite two attempts, and had broken up before the end of the decade.

THE WHO   READY STEADY WHO EP

```
UK release    November 1966    Reaction    592001
Not released in US

1. Disguises (Pete Townshend)
2. Circles (Pete Townshend)

3. Batman (Neil Hefti)
4. Bucket T (Dean Torrence/Don Altfield/Roger Christian)
5. Barbara Ann (Fred Fassert)

Roger Daltrey: vocals / Pete Townshend: guitar, vocals /
John Entwistle: bass guitar, French horn, vocals / Keith
Moon: drums, vocals / Kit Lambert: producer
```

During October, the Who were given the accolade of a dedicated edition of the UK television show, *Ready Steady Go*. This EP was released as a memento of the occasion, with studio recordings of some of the songs played by the group on the programme. The cover versions comprising side two are essentially whimsical in nature and include a rare example of a Keith Moon lead vocal on the Jan and Dean song, *Bucket T*. The Pete Townshend songs on side one, however, are two of his strongest compositions to date, effortlessly matching the originality of the group's two big hit singles earlier in the year, *Substitute* and *I'm A Boy*. On the opening *Disguises*, John Entwistle demonstrates his surprising fluency on the French horn, as Keith Moon delivers a drum part dominated by cascading, reverberating cymbals. With the group's second album being released only a month later, *Ready Steady Who* served as a very effective appetiser for this, reminding listeners that the Who had already managed to achieve the status of more established stars like the Kinks and the Rolling Stones.

THE ROLLING STONES   BIG HITS (HIGH TIDE AND GREEN GRASS)

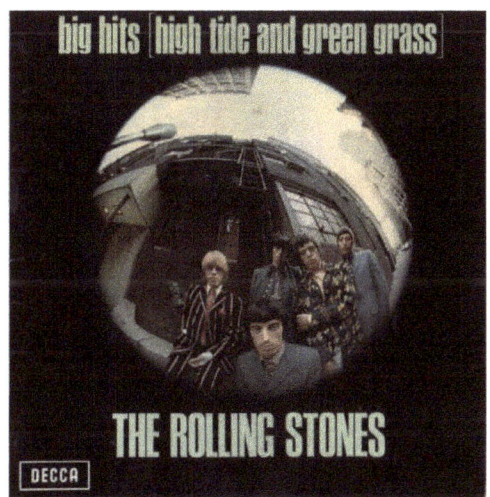

UK release   November 1966   Decca   TXS / TXL 101
US release   March 1966   London NP(S) 1   different tracks and cover

1. Have You See Your Mother, Baby, Standing In The Shadow?
2. Paint It Black
3. It's All Over Now (Bobby and Shirley Womack)
4. The Last Time
5. Heart Of Stone
6. Not Fade Away (Charles Hardin/Norman Petty)
7. Come On (Chuck Berry)

8. (I Can't Get No) Satisfaction
9. Get Off My Cloud
10. As Tears Go By (Mick Jagger/Keith Richards/Andrew Oldham)
11. 19th Nervous Breakdown
12. Lady Jane
13. Time Is On My Side (Norman Meade/Jimmy Norman)
14. Little Red Rooster (Willie Dixon)

All compositions by Mick Jagger and Keith Richards unless otherwise stated.

Mick Jagger: vocals, harmonica, percussion / Keith Richards: guitar, vocals / Brian Jones: guitar, sitar, dulcimer, electric piano, harmonica, vocals / Bill Wyman: bass guitar, organ, vocals / Charlie Watts: drums / Ian Stewart: piano / Jack Nitzsche: piano, percussion / Phil Spector: percussion / Andrew Loog Oldham: producer / Rolling Stones: producer

The first greatest hits compilation issued by the Rolling Stones includes all the single A sides released up to that point, apart from *I Wanna Be Your Man*, together with a further four tracks issued as singles in the US. The omission of the second single, which had been written by John Lennon and Paul McCartney, was presumably done to maintain the fiction that the Beatles and the Rolling Stones were adversaries. A similar selection was released in the US eight months earlier, but with four of the hits missing. The songs are arranged so as to make maximum impact, rather than chronologically, but the album succeeds in making clear the strength of the second most influential set of hit singles of the sixties. The Rolling Stones had channelled most of their creative energies into the singles, all but the earliest of them being composed by the group's own team of Mick Jagger and Keith Richards. Each one is a a small masterpiece, where the vibrant songwriting and performance are enhanced further by the considerable imagination applied to the arrangements. The fuzz guitar on *Satisfaction*, the bottleneck playing on *Little Red Rooster*, the sitar on *Paint It Black*, and the drone underscore of *Have You Seen Your Mother, Baby, Standing In The Shadow* are four examples where a fresh musical element provides the finishing touch to a song that is already distinctive. The album was hugely successful, of course, and in the US it remained in the album charts for just under two years.

THE BEACH BOYS   BEST OF

UK release   November 1966   Capitol   (S)T 20856
A greatly inferior version of the album, with only 4 tracks in common, was released in the US in July 1966.   Capitol (D)T 2545

1. Surfin' Safari (Brian Wilson/Mike Love)
2. Surfin' USA (Brian Wilson/Chuck Berry)
3. Little Deuce Coupe (Brian Wilson/Roger Christian)
4. Fun, Fun, Fun (Brian Wilson/Mike Love)
5. I Get Around (Brian Wilson)
6. All Summer Long (Brian Wilson)
7. In My Room (Brian Wilson/Gary Usher)

8. Do You Wanna Dance? (Bobby Freeman)
9. Help Me, Rhonda (Brian Wilson)
10. California Girls (Brian Wilson)
11. Barbara Ann (Fred Fassert)
12. You're So Good To Me (Brian Wilson)
13. Sloop John B (Traditional)
14. God Only Knows (Brian Wilson/Tony Asher)

Mike Love: vocals / Brian Wilson: vocals, bass guitar, keyboards, producer / Carl Wilson: vocals, guitar / Al Jardine: vocals, guitar / Dennis Wilson: vocals, drums / Bruce Johnston: vocals, keyboards / various session musicians

Presented in chronological order, the tracks on the UK version of *The Best Of The Beach Boys* provide a perfect manifesto for the development of Brian Wilson into one of the greatest songwriters of his generation. These are the songs that were the highlights of the albums where they first appeared and although only a few of them (*I Get Around* and the last four on the album, with *You're So Good To Me* being a B-side) were actually top ten hits in the UK, by late 1966 the Beach Boys had reached a position of popularity and influence where all these singles were fondly remembered as if they had been big hits. The album matched the achievement of *Pet Sounds* in reaching number two in the album chart, ultimately remaining in the chart for nearly three years. The US version of the album was a huge hit in that country, but it has a largely different selection of tracks, concentrating on the early part of the group's career and missing out all the songs that UK listeners at least would consider to be truly the best of the Beach Boys.

THE ARTWOODS   ART GALLERY

UK release   November 1966   Decca   LK 4830
Not released in US

1. Can You Hear Me (Allen Toussaint)
2. Down In The Valley (Bert Berns/Solomon Burke)
3. Things Get Better (Eddie Floyd/Steve Cropper/Wayne Jackson)
4. Walk On The Wild Side (Elmer Bernstein/Mack David)
5. I Keep Forgettin' (Jerry Leiber/Mike Stoller)
6. Keep Lookin' (Delores, Mark, & Solomon Burke)
7. One More Heartache (Smokey Robinson & the Miracles)
8. Work, Work, Work (Naomi Neville)
9. Be My Lady (Booker T & the MGs)
10. If You Gotta Make A Fool Of Somebody (Rudy Clarke)
11. Stop And Think It Over (Nat Jones)
12. Don't Cry No More (Deadric Malone)

Art Wood: vocals / Derek Griffiths: guitar / Jon Lord: organ / Malcolm Poole: bass guitar / Keef Hartley: drums / Mike Vernon: producer

The Artwoods made an impressive single, *I Take What I Want*, that nearly became a hit. But by the time the group got to make an LP, the R&B cover versions in which they specialised were beginning to sound distinctly passé. The album, which would have been greatly improved if it had included the single (or the jazz-inspired tunes included on an earlier EP called *Jazz in Jeans*), was not a success and Decca dropped the group soon afterwards. The Artwoods' significance, however, lies in the fact that the group served as a training arena for two musicians making important contributions to rock a little later on. Drummer Keef Hartley (who had previously been Ringo Starr's replacement in the Liverpool group, Rory Storm and the Hurricanes) joined John Mayall's Bluesbreakers and subsequently formed his own band, while organist Jon Lord became a founder member of Deep Purple. Singer Art Wood sadly had to content himself with whatever reflected glory came his way from the success of his brother Ron, who ended up as guitarist with the Faces and the Rolling Stones.

CHRIS FARLOWE   THE ART OF

UK release   November 1966   Immediate   IMSP/IMLP 006
Not released in US

1. What Becomes Of The Broken Hearted (James Dean/Paul Riser/William Weatherspoon)
2. We're Doing Fine (Horace Ott)
3. Life Is But Nothing (Andrew Rose/David Skinner)
4. Paint It Black (Mick Jagger/Keith Richards)
5. Cuttin' In (Johnny Guitar Watson)
6. Open The Door To Your Heart (Darrell Banks)
7. Out Of Time (Mick Jagger/Keith Richards)
8. North South East West (Albert Lee/Chris Farlowe)
9. You're So Good For Me (Andrew Oldham/Andrew Rose/David Skinner/William Bell)
10. It Was Easier To Hurt Her (Bert Russell/Jerry Ragovoy)
11. I'm Free (Mick Jagger/Keith Richards)
12. I've Been Loving You Too Long (Jerry Butler/Otis Redding)
13. Reach Out I'll Be There (Brian & Eddie Holland/Lamont Dozier)
14. Ride On Baby (Mick Jagger/Keith Richards)

Chris Farlowe: vocals / Albert Lee: guitar, vocals / Dave Greenslade: keyboards / Bruce Waddell: bass guitar / Ian Hague: drums / Dave Quincy: tenor saxophone / Gerry Temple: vocals, percussion / Mick Jagger: vocals, producer / Jimmy Page: guitar (4) / Andy White: drums (7) / Art Greenslade: strings arranger, conductor / Andrew Loog Oldham: producer

The Art of Chris Farlowe was the third album to be released during the year by the British blue-eyed soul singer, but the only one to include a big hit single – *Out Of Time,* which reached number one in July. Farlowe was a superb singer, able to deliver impressive versions of the soul (and Rolling Stones) songs he chose to cover, but his uncool appearance – short hair and a tight suit, like a bank clerk – worked against him being taken seriously as a star in 1966. Apart from his voice, however, Chris Farlowe did have an extra asset in his backing band, the Thunderbirds. Guitarist Albert Lee, saxophonist Dave Quincy, keyboard player Dave Greenslade, and drummer Carl Palmer, who joined the band three months after the release of *The Art of Chris Farlowe*, all proceeded to have substantial music careers with a number of well-known groups, which provides an indication of their quality.

THE LOVIN' SPOONFUL   HUMS OF

In September, the Lovin' Spoonful released an album of soundtrack music recorded for a Woody Allen film, *What's Up, Tiger Lily?*, but neither the group nor its followers considered the collection of hastily thrown-together, largely instrumental music to be the proper third album. *Hums Of The Lovin' Spoonful* is therefore the official third album by the group. It reveals the Lovin' Spoonful as retreating from the rock group concept, thereby avoiding any further comparisons with the Beatles, and presenting instead music that is much lighter and more folk-based than previously. Although when the group does decide to turn in a fully-fledged rock track, as it does on the concluding *Summer In The City*, it succeeds in creating the most memorable song in its entire catalogue. Released as a single, this became the group's only number one in the US. *Coconut Grove* reworked an instrumental from the soundtrack album into a full song, while *Nashville Cats* attempted to create a song that would appeal to the country market. This it largely failed to do,

| US release | November 1966 | Kama Sutra | KLP(S) 8054 |
| UK release | November 1966 | Kama Sutra | KLP 401 |

1. Lovin' You (John Sebastian)
2. Bes' Friends (John Sebastian)
3. Voodoo In My Basement (John Sebastian)
4. Darlin' Companion (John Sebastian)
5. Henry Thomas (John Sebastian)
6. Full Measure (John Sebastian/Steve Boone)
7. Rain On The Roof (John Sebastian)
8. Coconut Grove (John Sebastian/Zalman Yanovsky)
9. Nashville Cats (John Sebastian)
10. 4 Eyes (John Sebastian)
11. Summer In The City (John Sebastian/Mark Sebastian/Steve Boone)

John Sebastian: vocals, guitar, autoharp, keyboards, pedal steel guitar, Irish harp, occarina / Zalman Yanovsky: guitar, vocals, banjo, whistle / Steve Boone: bass guitar, bass, keyboards, percussion / Joe Butler: drums, vocals / Henry Dilitz: clarinet (2) / Larry Hankin: jew's harp (5) / Artie Schroeck: electric piano (11) / Erik Jacobsen: producer

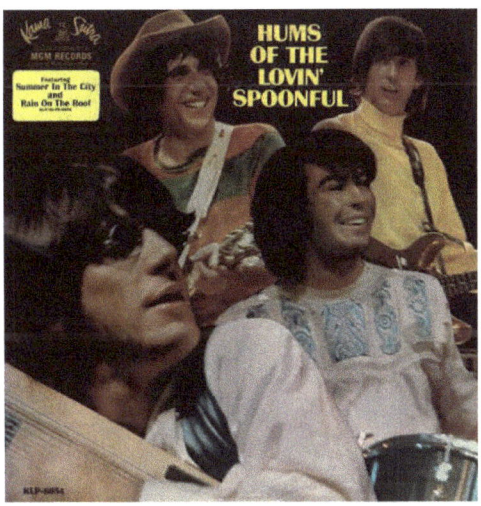

despite a cover version being recorded by Flatt and Scruggs, although the song was a substantial pop hit.

LOVE   DA CAPO

| US release | November 1966 | Elektra | EKS7/EKL 4005 |
| UK release | November 1966 | Elektra | EKS7/EKL 4005 |

1. Stephanie Knows Who (Arthur Lee)
2. Orange Skies (Bryan Maclean)
3. ¡ Que Vida ! (Arthur Lee)
4. 7 And 7 Is (Arthur Lee)
5. The Castle (Arthur Lee)
6. She Comes In Colors (Arthur Lee)
7. Revelation (Arthur Lee/Bryan Maclean/Johnny Echols/Ken Forssi)

Arthur Lee: vocals, guitar, harmonica, percussion / Bryan Maclean: vocals, guitar / Johnny Echols: guitar / Ken Forssi: bass guitar / Snoopy Pfistrer: keyboards, drums (4) / Tjay Cantrelli: saxophone, flute, percussion / Michael Stuart-Ware: drums / Paul Rothchild: producer

The second album by Love marks an enormous increase in quality and ambition from the first, despite maintaining a link by using artwork taken from the same photo session. The music no longer has much in common with sixties punk rock, even if one track, *7 And 7 Is*, does deliver an extraordinary energy. Elsewhere, harpsichords and flutes make a frequent appearance within the group sound, turning the music into a prime early example of a style dubbed 'baroque pop'. Side one of the album has six short songs, all different, all memorable, and all displaying a remarkable freshness and originality. This is perhaps the strongest album side to have been released outside of a Beatles record at this date. Side two is something else – a song lasting nineteen minutes and based on a group jam in the manner of the Rolling Stones track, *Goin' Home* (on the *Aftermath* album), but with more overt soloing from the various members of the group. The track had been a feature of Love's live set for some time and Arthur Lee maintained that the Rolling Stones had copied the idea from him, even though their song was released first. Regardless, *Da Capo* remains a hugely impressive achievement, although its sales in both the US and the UK were modest.

THE BLUES PROJECT   PROJECTIONS

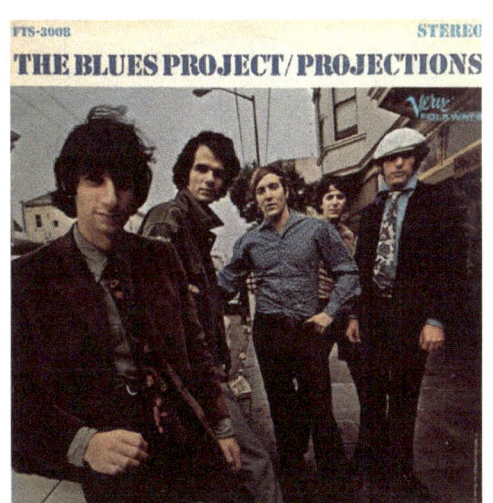

For the Blues Project's studio album, the group moves away from any attempt to deliver authentic interpretations of the blues and instead uses the material as a source from which to create a thoroughly contemporary form of blues- rock. *Two Trains Running* is the crucial work here, where the group slows the music down to a

| US release | November 1966 | Verve Folkways | FT(S)-3008 |
| UK release | summer 1967 | Verve Forecast | (S)VLP 6004 |

1. I Can't Keep From Crying (Blind Willie Johnson)
2. Steve's Song (Steve Katz)
3. You Can't Catch Me (Chuck Berry)
4. Two Trains Running (Muddy Waters)
5. Wake Me, Shake Me (Traditional)
6. Cheryl's Going Home (Bob Lind)
7. Flute Thing (Al Kooper)
8. Caress Me Baby (Jimmy Reed)
9. Fly Away (Al Kooper)

Al Kooper: keyboards, vocals / Danny Kalb: guitar, vocals / Steve Katz: guitar, vocals, harmonica, bass guitar (7) / Andy Kulberg: bass guitar, flute / Roy Blumenfeld: drums / Tom Wilson: producer / Billy James: producer (7,9) / Jeff Chase: producer (7,9)

crawl and delivers a long modal improvisation, highlighting the instrumental skills of all concerned. Elsewhere, the Blues Project abandons the blues altogether, as on the cover of a song by folk singer-songwriter Bob Lind and the pastoral/baroque approach of guitarist Steve Katz's own *Steve's Song*. Another showcase for the musicians' soloing abilities, with Andy Kulberg demonstrating a considerable skill on the flute, is provided by *Flute Thing*, which is revealed as being an early example of jazz-rock. *Projections* is a confident and influential body of work, but sadly it was not a big commercial success.

JUDY COLLINS   IN MY LIFE

| US release | November 1966 | Elektra | EKS7/EKL 320 |
| UK release | November 1966 | Elektra | EKS7/EKL 320 |

1. Tom Thumb's Blues (Bob Dylan)
2. Hard Lovin' Loser (Richard Farina)
3. Pirate Jenny (Bertolt Brecht/Kurt Weill/Marc Blitzstein)
4. Suzanne (Leonard Cohen)
5. La Colombe (Alasdair Clayre/Jacques Brel)
6. Marat / Sade (Richard Peaslee)
7. I Think It's Going To Rain Today (Randy Newman)
8. Sunny Goodge Street (Donovan)
9. Liverpool Lullaby (Stan Kelly)
10. Dress Rehearsal Rag (Leonard Cohen)
11. In My Life (John Lennon/Paul McCartney)

Judy Collins: vocals, guitar / Joshua Rifkin: keyboards, arrangements / Mark Abramson: producer

Folksinger Judy Collins emerged at about the same time as Bob Dylan and Joan Baez, with a voice almost as pure as that of Ms Baez herself. Her first album, *A Maid Of Constant Sorrow*, was issued in 1961 and contained a song by Ewan MacColl, but was otherwise made up entirely of traditional material. *In My Life* was her sixth album and marked a considerable departure. There are no traditional folk songs at all. Although Judy Collins plays her acoustic guitar on a couple of songs, the bulk of the accompaniment on these and all the other songs consists of imaginatively constructed orchestral and chamber music arrangements. Some of the performances are very theatrical in nature, and most present the work of significant contemporary singer-songwriters, including Bob Dylan, Randy Newman, and Leonard Cohen. The latter two of these had yet to make any albums themselves. Most controversially as far as the folk world was concerned, the title track is a beautiful version of a song by John Lennon and Paul McCartney, presented as being songwriters on a par with Dylan and Cohen. The album sold slowly, but by 1970 had achieved a fully justified gold record status.

THE SEARCHERS   SMASH HITS

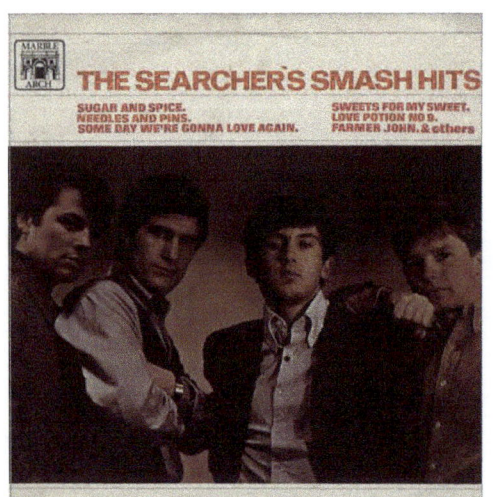

UK release   December 1966   Marble Arch   MAL(S) 640
Not released in US

1. Needles And Pins (Jack Nitzsche/Sonny Bono)
2. Farmer John (Terry/Harris)
3. Sugar And Spice (Tony Hatch as Fred Nightingale)
4. What Have They Done To The Rain (Malvina Reynolds)
5. Take Me For What I'm Worth (P.F.Sloan)
6. Love Potion No.9 (Jerry Leiber/Mike Stoller)
7. Till I Met You (Mike Pender/John McNally/Frank Allen/Chris Curtis)
8. He's Got No Love (Chris Curtis/Mike Pender)
9. Someday We're Gonna Love Again (Sharon McMahan)
10. Sweets For My Sweet (Doc Pomus/Mort Shuman)

Mike Pender: vocals, guitar / John McNally: guitar, vocals / Tony Jackson: vocals, bass guitar (1,2,3,10) / Frank Allen: bass guitar, vocals (4-9) / Chris Curtis: drums, vocals / Tony Hatch: producer

The Searchers played a kind of folk rock before there was such a term and scored ten top twenty hits in the UK (including three number ones) between 1963 and 1966. Pye delayed issuing a compilation of the group's hits until a year after its last chart entry and then effectively sabotaged the effort by putting it out on the company's bargain price label, so that it was not taken seriously as a proper album release. The company also made the record extremely short by only including ten tracks and it omitted several of the biggest hits, cynically keeping therm back for a second volume a year later, by which time interest in the group had plummeted. The Searchers deserved better. Although they lacked song-writing ability and were less than convincing as album artists, they certainly had the knack of picking the right songs to cover for single release and they had a sound that was very distinctive at the time.

CHICO HAMILTON   THE DEALER

Drummer Chico Hamilton began leading his own bands in the mid-fifties and *The Dealer* is something like his twenty-ninth album. Along the way, he employed several musicians whose later careers found them deliberately courting popularity in a manner not expected of jazz musicians, including guitarist Gabor Szabo and tenor saxophonist Charles Lloyd. Hamilton himself incorporated modest avant garde elements into his band's music and the style of many of his albums suggests that

```
US release      December 1966       Impulse   A(S)-9130
Not released in UK

1. The Dealer (Chico Hamilton/Jimmy Cheatham)
2. For Mods Only (Archie Shepp)
3. A Trip (Chico Hamilton/Jimmy Cheatham)
4. Baby You Know (Chico Hamilton/Jimmy Cheatham)

5. Larry Of Arabia (Larry Coryell)
6. Thoughts (Chico Hamilton)
7. Jim - Jeannie (Chico Hamilton)

Arnie Lawrence: alto saxophone / Larry Coryell: guitar /
Richard Davis: bass / Chico Hamilton: drums, voice (6) / Ernie
Hayes: organ (4,5) / Archie Shepp: piano (2) / Bob Thiele:
producer
```

he would have loved to be creating cutting edge jazz in the manner of Miles Davis, but did not quite have the imagination (or the players) to bring it off. Many of his pieces have a Latin-jazz approach, inspired by the collaborations between Stan Getz and people like Joao Gilberto and Antonio Carlos Jobim. On the title track of *The Dealer*, Hamilton sets up a rhythmic pattern forceful enough to lend credence to any argument proposing that the fusion jazz of the seventies has its origin here. Unfortunately, Hamilton's policy, on this track and most of the others too, is to keep the pattern going throughout the piece, without any deviation. The relationship between soloists and rhythm is not an interactive one. Hamilton provides a percussive background for the other players to solo against, but makes no reaction to anything they play and fails to provide any particular stimulus for them to respond to. Ultimately, the real focus of interest for the album is provided by guitarist Larry Coryell, making his recording debut and impressing his new employer sufficiently to gain a credit on the front cover. Coryell adopts a more biting tone than other jazz guitarists, approaching the sound of Mike Bloomfield on his recordings with the Butterfield Blues Band, and his solo on the title track includes some atonality created by sliding his fingers on the fretboard, an effect only made possible by the amplification of his guitar.

CREAM   FRESH CREAM

```
UK release     December 1966    Reaction    593/594 001
US release     January 1967     Atco        (SD) 33-206
                       Spoonful replaced by I Feel Free

1. N.S.U. (Jack Bruce)
2. Sleepy Time Time (Jack Bruce/Janet Godfrey)
3. Dreaming (Jack Bruce)
4. Sweet Wine (Ginger Baker/Janet Godfrey)
5. Spoonful (Willie Dixon)

6. Cat's Squirrel (Isaiah Ross)
7. Four Until Late (Robert Johnson)
8. Rollin' And Tumblin' (Muddy Waters)
9. I'm So Glad (Skip James)
10. Toad (Ginger Baker)

Eric Clapton: guitar, vocals / Jack Bruce: vocals, bass guitar,
harmonica / Ginger Baker: drums / Robert Stigwood:
producer
```

In July 1966, Ginger Baker asked Eric Clapton to join a new group: Clapton said that he would, if Jack Bruce became the bass player. Baker and Bruce had a history of feuding while playing in the Graham Bond Organization, but agreed to work together again in Cream. Eric Clapton had already developed his huge, sustaining guitar tone while playing with John Mayall. As a member of Cream, he did little more than refine his approach and bring it to a wider audience. There is nothing on *Fresh Cream* that he could not have played earlier, although his solos on tracks like *N.S.U.* and *I'm So Glad* do emphasise that his style was essentially melodic even when at its most tonally extreme. These solos derive a considerable strength from the fact that they contain what are themselves memorable tunes. Although the music on *Fresh Cream* takes the blues as its starting point and includes several cover versions, all three musicians succeed in imposing their own signatures on it, so that the album emerges with less of a purist feel than that of the John Mayall *Blues Breakers* LP. Realistically, despite a couple of lighter tracks, this is the first hard rock album.

THE BEATLES   A COLLECTION OF BEATLES OLDIES

With no new Beatles album ready to be released for the Christmas market, Parlophone assembled a Greatest Hits compilation. *Michelle* and *Yesterday* were not issued as singles in the UK, while the rock 'n' roll cover, *Bad Boy*, clearly included as an inducement for fans to buy the album even if they already had everything, had not previously been issued in the UK at all. The rest of the tracks are not just hits, but number one hits. The album provides a perfect soundtrack for the Beatlemania phenomenon as well as emphasising the sureness of touch displayed by John Lennon and Paul McCartney as songwriters. The album sold less well than all the other Beatles albums, stalling at number seven in the chart, but this was presumably because the group's fans did already have all the singles.

```
UK release    December 1966    Parlophone    PCS / PMC 7016
Not released in US

1. She Loves You
2. From Me To You
3. We Can Work It Out
4. Help!
5. Michelle
6. Yesterday
7. I Feel Fine
8. Yellow Submarine

9. Can't Buy Me Love
10. Bad Boy (Larry Williams)
11. Day Tripper
12. A Hard Day's Night
13. Ticket To Ride
14. Paperback Writer
15. Eleanor Rigby
16. I Want To Hold Your Hand

All compositions apart from track 10 by John Lennon and Paul McCartney.   John Lennon: vocals, guitar, keyboards / Paul McCartney: vocals, bass guitar / George Harrison: guitar, vocals / Ringo Starr: drums, vocals / George Martin: producer
```

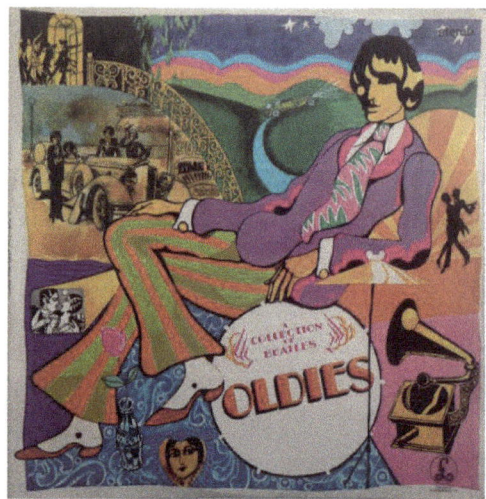

THE ROLLING STONES   GOT LIVE IF YOU WANT IT!

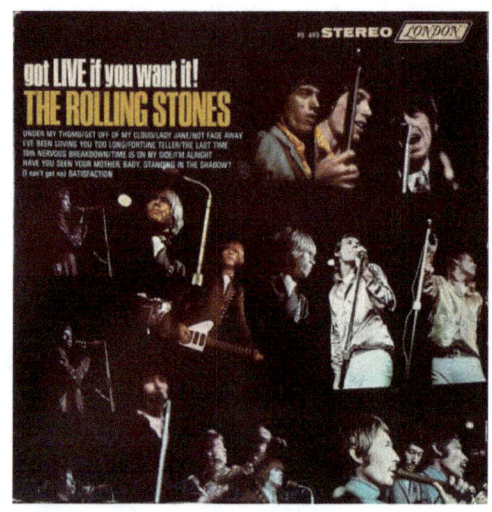

```
US release    December 1966    London    PS / LL3 493
UK release    December 1966    Decca     SKL / LK 4838
Issued for export only, retitled HAVE YOU SEEN YOUR MOTHER LIVE!

1. Under My Thumb
2. Get Off My Cloud
3. Lady Jane
4. Not Fade Away (Norman Petty/Charles Hardin)
5. I've Been Loving You Too Long (Otis Redding/Jerry Butler)
6. Fortune Teller (Naomi Neville)

7. The Last Time
8. 19th Nervous Breakdown
9. Time Is On My Side (Norman Meade)
10. I'm Alright (Bo Diddley)
11. Have You Seen Your Mother, Baby, Standing In The Shadow?
12. (I Can't Get No) Satisfaction

Mick Jagger: vocals, percussion / Keith Richards: guitar, vocals / Brian Jones: guitar, dulcimer, vocals, harmonica / Bill Wyman: bass guitar / Charlie Watts: drums / Ian Stewart: organ (5) / Andrew Loog Oldham: producer
```

The Rolling Stones had not wanted this album of live performances to be issued, but the US record company went ahead with it anyway. In the UK, Decca cancelled the full release, but made it available for export to Europe. It is easy to understand the group's reluctance, since the recordings reveal the Stones to be somewhat rough and ready live performers, although the primitive sound quality does not help. Despite the back cover claiming that this is a single concert from London's Albert Hall, the tracks actually derive from several different concerts during 1965 and 1966 at several different venues, none of which are the Albert Hall. Two tracks, *I've Been Loving You Too Long* and *Fortune Teller*, are not even live, but are made to sound as though they are with the addition of overdubbed audience noise. The clear sound is a bit of a give-away, however. The LP has no tracks in common with the earlier EP that used the same title – the performances of *I'm Alright* are different (with this one correctly crediting Bo Diddley as the composer).

THE HOLLIES   FOR CERTAIN BECAUSE

```
UK release    December 1966         Parlophone    PCS / PMC 7011
US release    as STOP! STOP! STOP!  December 1966 Imperial LP 12/9 339

1. What's Wrong With The Way I Live
2. Pay You Back With Interest
3. Tell Me To My Face
4. Clown
5. Suspicious Look In Your Eyes
6. It's You

7. High Classed
8. Peculiar Situation
9. What Went Wrong
10. Crusader
11. Don't Even Think About Changing
12. Stop! Stop! Stop!

All compositions by Allan Clarke/Tony Hicks/Graham Nash

Allan Clarke: vocals, harmonica / Graham Nash: guitar, vocals / Tony Hicks: guitar, banjo, vocals / Bernie Calvert: bass guitar, piano / Eric Haydock: bass guitar (11) / Bobby Elliott: drums / Mike Vickers: orchestral arrangements (7,9,10) / Ron Richards: producer
```

After a couple of lacklustre albums, the Hollies finally discovered the confidence to fill a whole record with their own songs. The three song-writing Hollies are an efficient rather than inspired composing team. Only the single, *Stop! Stop! Stop!*, adding a banjo to the mix, but without recalling country music, makes an immediate strong impact. *For Certain Because* has many of the characteristics of a Beatles album, even if it is one that the more successful group would have rejected as not being quite good enough. To be fair, by the usual standards, the album is impressive – musically varied and expertly performed. It did reasonably well in the UK charts, reaching number twelve (with the single having been a number two hit).

THE WHO   A QUICK ONE

UK release   December 1966   Reaction   593 002
US release   as **HAPPY JACK**, with the title track replacing Heatwave   May 1967   Decca   DL(7) 4892

1. Run Run Run (Pete Townshend)
2. Boris The Spider (John Entwistle)
3. I Need You (Keith Moon)
4. Whiskey Man (John Entwistle)
5. Heatwave (Brian and Eddie Holland/Lamont Dozier)
6. Cobwebs And Strange (Keith Moon)

7. Don't Look Away (Pete Townshend)
8. See My Way (Roger Daltrey)
9. So Sad About Us (Pete Townshend)
10. A Quick One, While He's Away (Pete Townshend)

Roger Daltrey: vocals, trombone (6) / Pete Townshend: guitar, vocals, tin whistle (6) / John Entwistle: bass guitar, vocals, French horn, trumpet (6) / Keith Moon: drums, vocals / Kit Lambert: producer

Apart from a rather unnecessary cover of a song by Martha and the Vandellas, the Who move away from R&B on their second album. Manager Kit Lambert had negotiated a publishing advance for all the group's members, so that the writing credits on the album are more evenly spread than on Who records before or since. Pete Townshend still has the greatest share, however, and one of his four songs is over nine minutes long. This is the title track, which is constructed as a medley of six, not particularly serious, short songs, linked together in a kind of mini-opera. Further evidence that the Who was determined to be musically surprising is provided by the madcap instrumental, *Cobwebs And Strange*, with the group members making cameo performances on instruments they could barely play, and the curious conflation of children's song and Hammer horror provided by *Boris The Spider*. Letting humour interlace with rock music made the Who unlikely bedfellows with Frank Zappa but also emphasised the originality of a group that was becoming increasingly influential.

SONNY ROLLINS   EAST BROADWAY RUN DOWN

US release   December 1966   Impulse   A(S)-9121
UK release   January 1967   HMV   CSD / CLP 3610

1. East Broadway Run Down (Sonny Rollins)
2. Blessing In Disguise (Sonny Rollins)
3. We Kiss In A Shadows (Richard Rodgers/Oscar Hammerstein II)

Sonny Rollins: tenor saxophone / Freddie Hubbard: trumpet (1) / Jimmy Garrison: bass / Elvin Jones: drums / Bob Thiele: producer

Sonny Rollins was the most highly regarded tenor saxophonist of the fifties and early sixties, building on the bop inventions and achievements of alto player Charlie Parker, translated on to the larger horn. For the album *East Broadway Run Down*, Rollins explores for the first time some of the ideas of avant garde jazz, employing John Coltrane's rhythm section for the purpose. The result is an accessible kind of avant garde, with Rollins' love of melody still very much controlling the way he builds his improvisations. He must have been aware that what he was producing was a compromise and he proceeded to retire from active music making for six years, perhaps hoping that the jazz cutting edge would move on and he would not have to tackle further a style that did not really suit his natural approach. Nevertheless, *East Broadway Run Down* is an impressive and durable album, which would have been a fine swansong to an illustrious career, if that is what it had turned out to be.

JOHN COLTRANE   LIVE AT THE VILLAGE VANGUARD AGAIN

John Coltrane played at New York's Village Vanguard in 1961, with the results being issued on the LPs *Impressions* and *Live At The Village Vanguard*. Five years later, he played at the club again, with the resulting album comprising improvisations on just two pieces. *Naima* was included in the earlier set too; *My Favourite Things* entered Coltrane's live repertoire shortly afterwards, so this music is very familiar to the saxophonist in 1966. But the group is mostly new, bringing interpretations of the music that are inevitably a little different. Alice Coltrane (John's wife) and Rashied Ali have performance styles not

US release	December 1966	Impulse	A(S)-9124
UK release	December 1966	HMV	CSD / CLP 3599

1. Naima (John Coltrane)
2. Introduction To My Favorite Things (Jimmy Garrison)
3. My Favorite Things (Richard Rodgers/Oscar Hammerstein II)

John Coltrane: tenor and soprano saxophones, flute, bass clarinet / Pharoah Sanders: tenor saxophone, flute / Alice Coltrane: piano / Jimmy Garrison: bass / Rashied Ali: drums / Emanuel Rahim: percussion / Bob Thiele: producer

unlike those of the men they replace, except that both are slightly more diffident, providing a rich underlay for the saxophonists without particularly propelling them forwards. Jimmy Garrison gets to play a solo feature (*Introduction To My Favorite Things*), which is just as well, since he tends to disappear when the whole group is playing. Surprisingly, it is Pharoah Sanders who has the largest amount of solo space, and it is his tortured, tonally extreme sound that is primarily responsible for giving the music its character. In comparison, John Coltrane seems to be coasting and certainly never attempts to lock horns with Sanders to deliver any twin improvisation. He plays a little flute and a little bass clarinet in behind Sanders during the long version of *My Favorite Things*, but seems to be doing no more than adding textural decoration to the proceedings. *Live At The Village Vanguard Again* shows how Coltrane was well able to keep up with the musicians who were starting to run with the discoveries that he himself had made, but in truth more spectacular live recordings from this last part of John Coltrane's career have emerged more recently.

VARIOUS ARISTS   THE REAL BAHAMAS

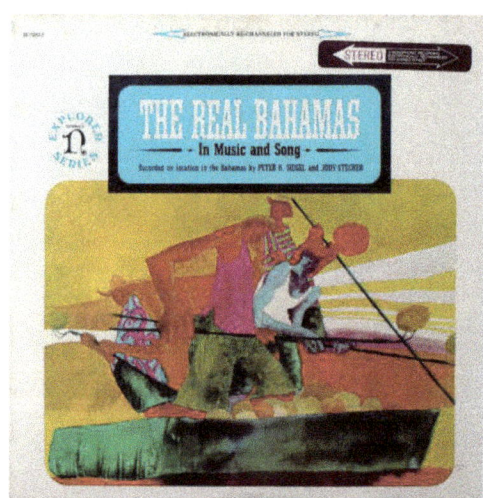

The fact that the origins of the blues and gospel date from before the start of recording technology has encouraged numerous musicologists to search for contemporary performers whose music seems to have a direct link with the music lost to history. During the thirties and forties, several recordings were made by John and Alan Lomax at prisons in the Southern USA. They believed that the music performed by long-stay prisoners was likely to be relatively free of contemporary influences and might, therefore, give some clues as to how the roots of the blues might have sounded. The recordings made by Jody Stecher and Peter K Siegel in rural communities in the Bahamas in 1965 are of a similar nature. The music on *The Real Bahamas* sounds a hundred years old and it can be assumed that these songs do go back at least that far. Performed for the most part by unaccompanied amateur singers, the spiritual and fishing songs sound strange and often dissonant, but always compelling. The natural response might be to use the word 'primitive' to describe the music, except that it would not be at all easy to reproduce using singers not brought up within the Bahamian culture. It is difficult to assess the impact that this album might have made on the wider rock music audience, but certainly the fact that the Grateful Dead later performed a respectful version of one of its songs, *I Bid You Goodnight*, is enough to prove that the influence was there.

US release	December 1966	Nonesuch	H-(7)2013
UK release	1969	Polydor	236 581

1. We Will Understand It Better By And By
2. Sheep Know When Thy Shepherd Calling
3. I Told You People Judgement Coming
4. Don't Take Everybody To Be Your Friend
5. Sailboat Malarkey
6. Up In The Heaven Shouting
7. Won't That Be A Happy Time
8. Out On The Rolling Sea

9. I Am So Glad
10. Come For Your Dinner
11. God Locked The Lion's Jaw
12. Great Dream From Heaven
13. My Lord Help Me To Pray
14. Numberless As The Sands On The Seashore
15. I Ain't Got Long
16. I Bid You Goodnight

The Pinder Family (Edith, Geneva, Raymond): vocals (1,12,16) / Joseph Spence: vocals, guitar (1,4,7,12,16) / Frederick McQueen: vocals (2,5,8,10,11) / Rev. W. G. McPhee: vocals (2,14) / Sam Green and group: vocals (3,15) / Bruce Green: vocals (6,9,13) / Tweedie Gibson: vocals (6,9,13) / Clifton Green: vocals (6,9,13) / Louise Spence: vocals (7) / Shelton Swain: vocals (8,11,14) / George McKenzie: vocals (8,14) / Stanley Thompson: vocals (11) / Stanley Swain: vocals (14) / Ronald Swain: vocals (14) / Jody Stecher: producer / Peter K.Siegel: producer

FRED NEIL

Folk singer-songwriter Fred Neil attracted attention with one song from his previous album in 1965. *Other Side To This Life* was covered by Jefferson Airplane, who became personal friends, by the Lovin' Spoonful, the Animals, and many other artists. His self-titled album has a song making even more impact. *Everybody's Talkin'* was included in the hit film *Midnight Cowboy*, though not Neil's own version, and in 1969, his album was re-released with that song's name as its new title. It is Fred Neil's voice that is his most distinctive feature, much lower than any of his contemporaries, yet capable of carrying a considerable amount of emotion. Sadly, none of this was enough to make him a star and he virtually gave up performing after 1970, although it has been reported that there are three unreleased albums made by him during the seventies.

```
US release      December 1966    Capitol    (S)T 2665
Not released in UK

1. The Dolphins
2. I've Got A Secret (Didn't We Shake Sugaree) (Elizabeth Cotten)
3. That's The Bag I'm In
4. Badi-Da
5. Faretheewell (Fred's Tune)

6. Everybody's Talkin'
7. Everything Happens
8. Sweet Cocaine
9. Green Rocky Road
10. Cynicrustpetefredjohn Raga

All compositions by Fred Neil apart from track 2

Fred Neil: vocals, guitar / John T. Forsha: guitar / Peter Childs: guitar / Cyrus Faryar: guitar, bouzouki / Al Wilson: harmonica / James E. Bond: bass / Billy Mundi: drums / Rusty Faryar: percussion / Nick Venet: producer
```

BUFFALO SPRINGFIELD

Folk-rock in the manner of the Byrds, but with a slightly harder edge, the first album by Buffalo Springfield introduces the work of two singer songwriters destined to make a major impact on the development of rock music, Stephen Stills and Neil Young. It would appear, however, that Neil Young did not yet have total confidence in his somewhat unique singing voice and he only sings two of his songs as lead vocalist. These early songs by both men are good enough, although there is little here that is particularly outstanding and both men would soon start to produce better material. In fact, after the album was completed, Stephen Stills wrote *For What It's Worth,* a powerful political song with a distinctive chorus and a simple two note pattern of electric guitar harmonics to give the song extra impact. This became a top ten hit in the US, with the result that the Atco record company pressed a new version of the album to include the hit single as the opening track. Unfortunately, rather than simply adding the song, Atco decided to remove one to make way for it. The track they chose, *Baby Don't Scold Me,* was doubtless considered to be too like the Beatles, but it was also one of the most attractive songs on the album.

```
US release      December 1966    Atco    (SD)33-/ 200
Reissued      March 1967      same number    For What It's Worth added, Baby Don't Scold Me dropped
UK release    March 1967      Atlantic   587070

1. Go And Say Goodbye (Stephen Stills)
2. Sit Down, I Think I Love You (Stephen Stills)
3. Leave (Stephen Stills)
4. Nowadays Clancy Can't Even Sing (Neil Young)
5. Hot Dusty Roads (Stephen Stills)
6. Everybody's Wrong (Stephen Stills)

7. Flying On The Ground Is Wrong (Neil Young)
8. Burned (Neil Young)
9. Do I Have To Come Right Out And Say It (Neil Young)
10. Baby Don't Scold Me (Stephen Stills)
11. Out Of My Mind (Neil Young)
12. Pay The Price (Stephen Stills)

Stephen Stills: vocals, guitar, keyboards / Neil Young: vocals, guitar, harmonica, piano / Richie Furay: vocals, guitar / Bruce Palmer: bass guitar / Dewey Martin: drums, vocals / Charles Greene: producer / Brian Stone: producer
```

ROSCOE MITCHELL SEXTET   SOUND

```
US and UK release    c.December 1966    Delmark    DS/DL-408

1. Ornette
2. The Little Suite
3. Sound

All compositions by Roscoe Mitchell

Roscoe Mitchell: alto saxophone, clarinet, flute, recorder, percussion / Lester Bowie: trumpet, flugelhorn, harmonica, percussion / Maurice McIntyre: tenor saxophone, percussion / Lester Lashley: trombone, cello, percussion / Malachi Favors: bass, percussion / Alvin Fielder: drums, percussion / Robert G Koester: producer
```

Sound is the first album by the group that became the Art Ensemble of Chicago, the premier free improvisation jazz group working through the seventies. The album sounds loose in the extreme, but the musicians spent several days rehearsing the material, honing the structure to make it sound spontaneous. Even so, the long title track is the result of editing and combining two different takes. For the most part, the group is not much interested in working with rhythm for more than a few moments at a time, and the various pieces of percussion that all the musicians play in addition to their main instruments are employed to add texture and timbre to the proceedings. For the same reason, a significant role is played by recorder and harmonica, instruments not often used much in jazz. This is the equivalent approach adopted by Sun Ra on many of his recordings, but Roscoe Mitchell and company are well able to put their own distinctive mark on it.

OLIVIER MESSIAEN   ET EXSPECTO RESURRECTIONEM MORTUORUM / COULEURS DE LA CITÉ CÉLESTE

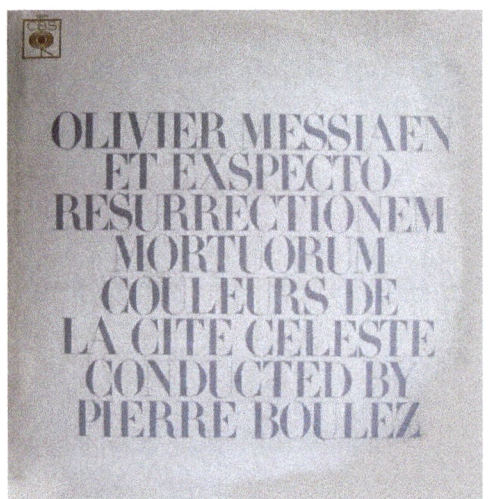

| UK release | December 1966 | CBS | (S)BRG 72471 |
| US release | 1969 | Columbia Masterworks | MS 7356 |

1. Et Expecto Resurrectionem Mortuorum Parts 1-4
2. Et Expecto Resurrectionem Mortuorum Part 5
3. Couleurs De La Cité Céleste

All compositions by Olivier Messiaen

Orchestre Du Domaine Musical / Groupe Instrumental A Percussion De Strasbourg / Pierre Boulez: conductor / Yvonne Loriod: piano

French composer Olivier Messiaen developed a highly individual style, beginning in the nineteen thirties, and depending on three major elements: the use of birdsong, carefully notated and reproduced by orchestral instruments, the use of elaborate percussion structures, influenced by the gamelan music of Indonesia; and the use of complicated harmonies, in which elaborate chords are built out of an unusually large number of notes. All of these elements are apparent in the two works included on this LP, originally composed in 1964 and 1963 respectively. Both employ the resources of an orchestra without a string section and with a large number of percussionists playing a variety of different instruments. *Et Exspecto Resurrectionem Mortuorum* is a particularly striking piece, built on a succession of slow, ominous chords and climaxing with a rush of sound generated by the beating of a tam-tam (a type of very large gong). Messiaen was gifted with a form of synaesthesia, in which he interpreted different notes and timbres as colours (hence the title of the second piece), although he did not expect that listeners would appreciate this themselves. While undoubtedly avant garde compared to the classical music of the nineteenth century, the music of Messiaen is far more approachable than what was being produced by some of his contemporaries. His influence is enormous, not least because as a professor at the Paris Conservatoire, he taught many of the people who themselves became well-known and respected composers.

1967

THE DOORS

The front cover of the first album by the Doors makes it clear that the focus of the group was intended to be its charismatic lead singer, Jim Morrison. Musically, the Doors build on the garage punk of the Seeds and their kin, except that they reverse the usual positions of guitar and keyboards by making Ray Manzarek's organ playing the dominant feature. The group's signature song, *Light My Fire,* derives

| US release | January 1967 | Elektra | EKS7 / EKL 4007 |
| UK release | January 1967 | Elektra | EKS7 / EKL 4007 |

1. Break On Through (To The Other Side) n
2. Soul Kitchen
3. The Crystal Ship
4. Twentieth Century Fox
5. Alabama Song (Whisky Bar) (Bertolt Brecht/Kurt Weill)
6. Light My Fire
7. Back Door Man (Howlin' Wolf/Willie Dixon)
8. I Looked At You
9. End Of The Night
10. Take It As It Comes
11. The End

All compositions by the Doors, except where stated

Jim Morrison: vocals / Ray Manzarek: keyboards, zither (5), vocals (5) / Robbie Krieger: guitar, bass guitar (2,7), vocals (5) / John Densmore: drums, vocals (5) / Larry Knechtel: bass guitar (4,6,8,10) / Paul Rothchild: vocals (5), producer

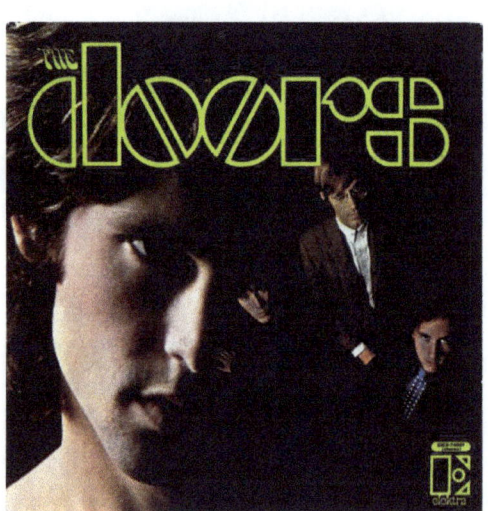

much of its impact from the distinctive organ riff that frames the song. Although both organ and guitar deliver substantial solos, the organ goes first and is far more confident, while it is Manzarek's left-hand bass figure that keeps the whole thing going. Creating a cover version of an old theatre song by Kurt Weill and Bertolt Brecht is a surprising departure, while the jam session responsible for *The End* attracted immediate attention not so much for its length, as for the sexual bravado of Morrison's performance. The Doors were hugely successful very quickly in the US – an edited version of *Light My Fire* was a number one hit, while the album reached number two and eventually sold four million copies. They were much less acclaimed in the UK, where neither the single nor the album were hits (and no subsequent album or single managed to break into the top ten). American punk had been largely ignored, with the version supplied by the Doors seeming to be only a little more interesting. The UK, after all, had the Stones and the Who; the Kinks, the Animals, and the Small Faces.

THE ROLLING STONES   BETWEEN THE BUTTONS

UK release   January 1967   Decca   LK/SKL 4852
US release   February 1967   London PS 499 / LL 3499   2 different tracks

1. Yesterday's Papers
2. My Obsession
3. Back Street Girl
4. Connection
5. She Smiled Sweetly
6. Cool, Calm & Collected
7. All Sold Out
8. Please Go Home
9. Who's Been Sleeping Here?
10. Complicated
11. Miss Amanda Jones
12. Something Happened To Me Yesterday

All compositions by Mick Jagger / Keith Richards

Mick Jagger: vocals, percussion, harmonica / Brian Jones: guitar, keyboards, vibraphone, marimba, recorder, kazoo, harmonica, trumpet, trombone, vocals / Keith Richards: guitar, bass guitar, bass, keyboards, vocals / Bill Wyman: bass guitar, bass, vocals / Charlie Watts: drums / Ian Stewart: keyboards / Jack Nitzsche: keyboards / Nick de Caro: accordion / Andrew Loog Oldham: producer / Rolling Stones: producer

Between The Buttons is a kind of hard pop album, with thoughtful, imaginative playing in the service of a set of Jagger-Richards compositions, of which only a couple deliver the kind of straight-ahead rock rhythms in which the Stones had previously specialised. Guitars, bass, and keyboards are used in a variety of interesting ways, but with the exception of the raucous Bo Diddley-inspired *Please Go Home*, they tend to be applied sparingly, giving the album a slightly sparse quality overall. The fact that the fuzz box is frequently attached to both guitar and bass guitar does not change this essential character. Although Brian Jones contributes marimba to *Yesterday's Papers* and, surprisingly, trumpet and trombone to *Something Happened To Me Yesterday,* his love of unusual timbres is bypassed for the most part. No longer much interested in guitar, he makes minor contributions on recorder and kazoo and does not play at all on four of the tracks. The music does contrive to be very varied through the album, but is ultimately hampered by the fact that the songs are not in themselves particularly memorable. The American version of the album includes both sides of the single issued at the same time, *Let's Spend The Night Together* and *Ruby Tuesday,* and becomes a much stronger proposition as a result.

VARIOUS ARTISTS   RAW BLUES

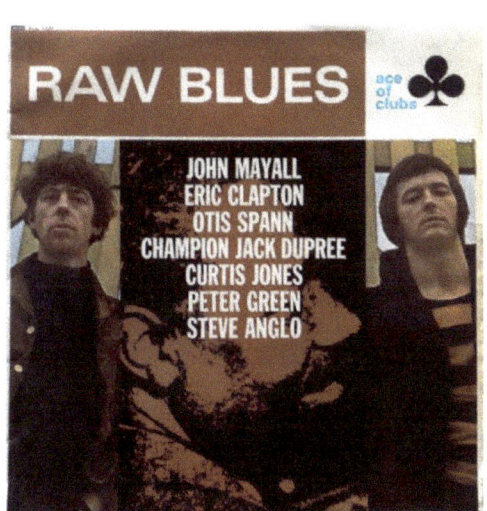

UK release   January 1967   Decca Ace of Clubs   SCL/ACL 1220
US release   January 1967   London   PS 543

1. Pretty Girls Everywhere (Eugene Church/Thomas Williams)
2. Burn Out Your Blind Eyes (John Mayall)
3. Calcutta Blues (Traditional)
4. Long Night (John Mayall/Steve Winwood)
5. Country Boy (Muddy Waters)
6. You Got Good Business (Curtis Jones)
7. Lonely Years (John Mayall)
8. Evil Woman Blues (Peter Green)
9. My Home In The Desert (Traditional)
10. Milkman Strut (John Mayall)
11. 24 Hours (Eddie Boyd)
12. Roll Me Over (Curtis Jones)
13. Bernard Jenkins (Eric Clapton)
14. You're Gonna Need My Help (Muddy Waters)

John Mayall: vocals, harmonica, piano, guitar (2,3,4,7,8,10,11,13) / Eric Clapton: guitar (1,3,7,13) / Otis Spann: vocal, piano (1,5,9,14) / Muddy Waters: guitar (1,5,9,14) / Ransom Knowling: bass (1,5,9,14) / Little Willie Smith: drums (1,5,9,14) / Champion Jack Dupree: vocals, piano (3,11) / Tony McPhee: guitar (3,11) / Malcolm Poole: bass guitar (3,11) / Keef Hartley: drums (3,11) / Steve Winwood: organ (4) / John McVie: bass guitar (4) / Aynsley Dunbar: drums (4) / Curtis Jones: vocals, piano (6,12) / Peter Green: vocals, guitar (8) / Mike Vernon: producer

Perhaps with the intention of proving that some of the best British blues musicians were now capable of holding their own in the company of the American inventors of the form, Decca issued this compilation of tracks recorded by Britons and Americans performing together. The argument is won on the very first track, where Eric Clapton contributes a remarkable example of his fluent, melodic lead guitar playing to a group led by blues pianist Otis Spann and including the great Muddy Waters (disguised for contractual reasons under the name of 'Brother'). Clapton succeeds in turning what might have been a fairly routine affair into something almost magical, entirely justifying his prominent position on the right side of the album front cover. The man pictured on the left, of course, is John Mayall, who takes his place as one of the blues greats with his playing on fully half of the album's tracks. On *Evil Woman Blues*, he introduces his new guitarist with the Bluesbreakers, and Peter Green demonstrates immediately, with a typically atmospheric piece of playing, alongside some fine singing, that he is a worthy successor to Eric Clapton. The ebullient Champion Jack Dupree easily dominates the tracks on which he performs, although the rhythm section from the Artwoods supports him well. The two are joined by a new name, guitarist Tony McPhee, who is given no opportunity to shine on this occasion (he is in the shadow of Eric Clapton on one of the two tracks), although he would become a significant performer later on. Only veteran pianist Curtis Jones keeps his distance from the Brits. Two anonymous and quiet guitarists do their best to make an impression, but in reality the music is a one-man show.

VARIOUS ARTISTS   LIVING LEGENDS

US release   January 1967   Verve Folkways   FT(S) 3010
Not released in UK

1. Son House – Levee Camp Moan (Son House)
2. Bukka White – Black Bottom (Bukka White)
3. Bukka White – Aberdeen, Mississippi Blues (Bukka White)
4. Big Joe Williams – Whiskey-Headed Woman (Big Joe Williams)
5. Skip James – Devil Got My Woman (Skip James)
6. Skip James – I'm So Glad (Skip James)
7. Big Joe Williams – So Soon (Big Joe Williams)
8. Big Joe Williams – Somebody Evil (Big Joe Williams)
9. Bukka White – Thunderbird Blues (Bukka White)
10. Bukka White – Poor Boy (Bukka White)

Jerry Schoenbaum: producer

Living Legends is an accurately titled souvenir of a series of concerts recorded at the Café Au-Go-Go in New York's Greenwich Village in November 1966. The four veteran country blues performers are men in their sixties who had made their first recordings over thirty years previously, before the late Robert Johnson had made the recordings that defined the sound and structure of the blues. Although this emphasises the fact that the country blues, played on acoustic guitars, is no longer an ongoing creative genre, at least as far as the black American community is concerned, there is no gainsaying the playing abilities and emotional resonance that these musicians bring to their performances. Compared to the work of revivalists like John Fahey and John Renbourn, the guitars sound heavy-handed and lacking in finesse, but that is a deliberate effect, designed for making the music sound loud and forceful. *Living Legends* provides a vital glimpse into the musical world that gave birth to rock music and is a hugely valuable historical document.

THE MONKEES   MORE OF THE MONKEES

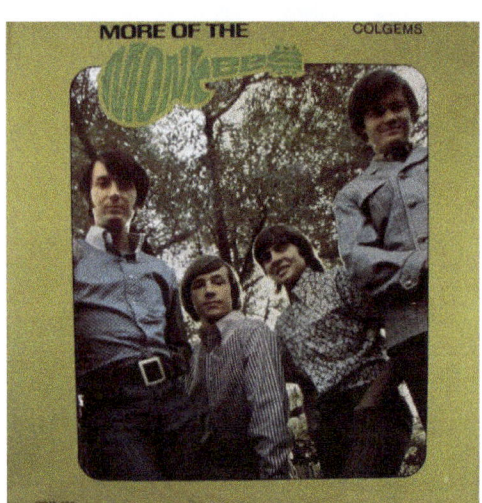

US release   January 1967   Colgems   COS/COM-102
UK release   January 1967   RCA Victor   SF/RD 7868

1. She (Tommy Boyce/Bobby Hart)
2. When Love Comes Knockin' (Carole Bayer/Neil Sedaka)
3. Mary Mary (Mike Nesmith)
4. Hold On Girl (Ben Raleigh/Billy Carr/Jack Keller)
5. Your Auntie Grizelda (Diane Hilderbrand/Jack Keller)
6. (I'm Not Your) Steppin' Stone (Tommy Boyce/Bobby Hart)
7. Look Out (Here Comes Tomorrow) (Neil Diamond)
8. The Kind Of Girl I Could Love (Mike Nesmith/Roger Atkins)
9. The Day We Fall In Love (Denny Randell/Sandy Linzer)
10. Sometime In The Morning (Gerry Goffin/Carole King)
11. Laugh (Mitch Margo/Phil Margo/Hank Medress/Jay Siegel)
12. I'm A Believer (Neil Diamond)

Davy Jones: vocals / Micky Dolenz: vocals / Peter Tork: vocals, guitar / Mike Nesmith: vocals, pedal steel guitar, producer (3,8) / Ron Hicklin: vocals / WayneErwin: guitar, vocals / Gerry McGee: guitar / Louie Shelton: guitar / Al Gafa: guitar / Willard Suyker: guitar / Donald Thomas: guitar / James Burton: guitar / Glen Campbell: guitar / Al Casey: guitar / Michael Deasy: guitar / Neil Diamond: guitar / Al Gorgoni: guitar / Sal DiTroia: guitar / Neil Sedaka: piano / Michael Cohen: piano / Larry Knechtel: piano / George Butcher: piano / Maurgan Cheff: organ / Michel Rubini: organ / Stan Free: organ / Don Randi: harpsichord / Larry Taylor: bass guitar / Russell Savakus: bass guitar / Bob West: bass guitar / Carol Kaye: bass guitar, guitar / Ray Pohlman: bass guitar / Billy Lewis: drums / Herbert Lovell: drums / Hal Blaine: drums / Buddy Salzman: drums / Norm Jefferies: percussion / Gary Coleman: percussion / Jim Gordon: percussion / Henry Lewy: percussion / Kauren Seguer: percussion / Frank Capp: percussion / Julius Wechter: percussion / George Deveny: percussion / Louis Haber: violin / Irving Spice: violin / Lousi Stone: violin / David Sackson: viola / Murray Sandry: viola / Seymour Barab: cello / Arthur Butler: conductor / Don Peake: arranger / Jeff Barry: producer (4,5,7,9,10,11,12) / Tommy Boyce: producer (1,6) / Bobby Hart: producer (1,6), organ / Neil Sedaka: producer (2) / Carole Bayer: producer (2) / Gerry Goffin: producer (10) / Carole King: producer (10)

A second Monkees album follows just three months after the first, in order to take maximum advantage of a TV show whose popularity is likely to be short-lived. This one includes the group's biggest hit, *I'm A Believer,* which quickly reached number one in both the US and the UK and eventually sold over ten million copies worldwide. The rest of the album is much weaker than the first and was probably something of a rushed job. There is one really dreadful track – *The Day We Fall In Love,* with a mawkish spoken word recitation by Davy Jones in place of a proper vocal – but perhaps the purposeful

THE YOUNG RASCALS   COLLECTIONS

```
US release      January 1967    Atlantic   (SD) 8134
UK release      January 1967    Atlantic   587060

1. What Is The Reason (Eddie Brigati/Felix Cavaliere)
2. Since I Fell For You (Buddy Johnson)
3. (I've Been) Lonely Too Long (Felix Cavaliere)
4. No Love To Give (Gene Cornish)
5. Mickey's Monkey (Brian & Eddie Holland/Lamont Dozier);
        Turn On Your Love Light (Deadric Malone/Joseph Scott)
6. Come On Up (Felix Cavaliere)
7. Too Many Fish In The Sea (Eddie Holland/Norman Whitfield)
8. More (Riz Ortolani/Nino Oliviero/Norman Newell/Marcello Ciorciolini)
9. Nineteen Fifty-Six (Gene Cornish)
10. Love Is A Beautiful Thing (Felix Cavaliere/Eddie Brigati)
11. Land Of A Thousand Dances (Chris Kenner)

Felix Cavaliere: organ, piano, vocals / Eddie Brigati: vocals, percussion /
Gene Cornish: guitar, bass guitar, vocals / Dino Danelli: drums / Produced
by the group
```

The second album by the Young Rascals continues the group's love of soul music, but this time the musicians write half the material themselves. Eddie Brigati, Felix Cavaliere, and Gene Cornish are efficient rather than inspired songwriters. None of their songs is especially noteworthy, but this did not stop two of them (tracks 3 and 10) from doing well in the US charts, and indeed the album itself was a substantial hit, eventually achieving a gold record award. Just one track, *No Love To Give,* marks a bold departure in terms of its arrangement, replacing the rock instruments with a chamber string orchestra. The result is striking, if only because it sounds distinctly out of place on the album, but it does indicate a group which might, after all, be open to extending its range.

THE YOUNGBLOODS

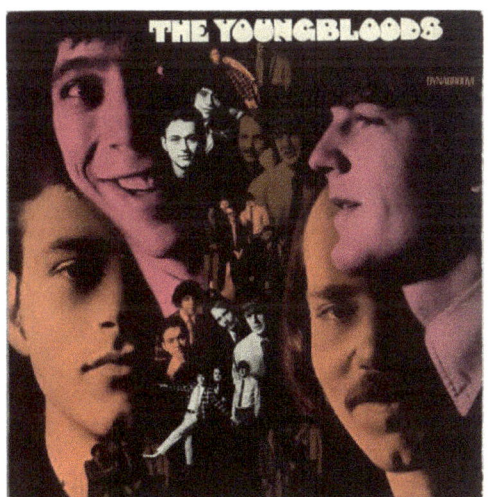

```
US release      January 1967    RCA Victor   LSP/LPM 3724
Not released in UK

1. Grizzly Bear (Jerry Corbitt)
2. All Over The World (La-La) (Jerry Corbitt)
3. Statesboro Blues (Blind Willie McTell)
4. Get Together (Chet Powers)
5. One Note Man (Paul Arnaldi)
6. The Other Side Of This Life (Fred Neil)
7. Tears Are Falling (Jesse Colin Young)
8. Four In The Morning (George Remailly)
9. Foolin' Around (The Waltz) (Jesse Colin Young)
10. Ain't That Lovin' You Baby (Jimmy Reed)
11. C C Rider (Mississippi John Hurt)

Jerry Corbitt: vocals, guitar, harmonica / Jesse Colin Young: vocals,
guitar, bass guitar / Lowell Levinger: guitar, piano, vocals, percussion /
Joe Bauer: drums / George Ricci: cello (9) / Felix Pappalardi: producer
```

The Youngbloods were an American folk rock group sounding quite similar to the Lovin' Spoonful, on that group's first recordings. They have the same mix of contemporary folk songs and the blues. Despite being led by two singer songwriters, however, the debut album makes it clear that neither of them is in the same league as John Sebastian. The Youngbloods' big US hit was a song written by neither of them, the hippy anthem *Get Together*. This had already been recorded by several other artists, but the Youngbloods version was used in advertising two years later by the National Conference for Christians and Jews and it became a hit on the back of that. Both Jerry Corbitt and Jesse Colin Young maintained sporadically interesting careers as solo artists for several years, but they were considerably upstaged by their producer, making his debut on the first Youngbloods album. Felix Pappalardi produced many records by Cream and went on to become the bass player for the successful hard rock band, Mountain.

JACQUES BREL   67

Jacques Brel was a Belgian singer, performing in the grand French *chanson* tradition, but writing his own material. First recording in 1953, he found international acclaim during the sixties and his songs were recorded by several other artists, usually with the lyrics translated and adapted into English. His best known song, *Ne Me Quitte Pas (If You Go Away)* first appeared in 1959 and was subsequently interpreted by a huge number of other singers, including Dusty Springfield, Scott Walker, and Frank Sinatra, and, more recently, Marc Almond, Cindy Lauper, and Madonna. *67* is Brel's eleventh album and

French release	January 1967	Barclay	80334S
UK release	April 1967	Fontana	TL 5429
US release	December 1967	Vanguard	VSD7/VRL 9265

as LE FORMIDABLE JACQUES BREL, different cover

1. Mon Enfance (Jacques Brel)
2. Le Cheval (Jacques Brel/Gérard Jouannest)
3. Mon Père Disait (Jacques Brel)
4. La La La (Jacques Brel)
5. Les Coeurs Tendres (Jacques Brel)

6. Fils De… (Jacques Brel/Gérard Jouannest)
7. Les Bonbons 67 (Jacques Brel)
8. La Chanson Des Vieux Amants (Jacques Brel/Gérard Jouannest)
9. À Jeun (Jacques Brel/Gérard Jouannest)
10. Le Gaz (Jacques Brel/Gérard Jouannest)

Jacques Brel: vocals / François Rauber: piano, arranger, conductor / other musicians and producer not credited

a particularly fine example of his art. The emotional, dramatic nature of the music makes a strong impression even if the listener does not know what Brel is singing about. In fact, he does not so much sing the songs as declaim them, act them out. It is as though each song is part of a stage show. The illusion is completed by the varied, cinematic arrangements provided by François Rauber. Scott Walker covered *Fils De…* (as *Sons Of…*) and Judy Collins covered *La Chanson Des Vieux Amants*: both of them used great singing voices to extract as much emotion from the songs as possible, something that Jacques Brel achieves with a voice that is much less beautiful, but still absolutely capable of drawing the listener into his world. The music on *67*, like all of Brel's music, is enormously attractive and it is easy to understand why he is held in such high regard.

JOHN COLTRANE   KULU SE MAMA

| US release | January 1967 | Impulse | A(S)-9106 |
| UK release | January 1967 | HMV | CSD/CLP 3617 |

1. Kulu Sé Mama (Juno Sé Mama) (Juno Lewis)

2. Vigil (John Coltrane)
3. Welcome (John Coltrane)

John Coltrane: tenor and soprano saxophones, producer / Pharoah Sanders: tenor saxophone (1) / Donald Garrett: bass, bass clarinet (1) / Juno Lewis: vocals, percussion (1) / McCoy Tyner: piano (1,3) / Jimmy Garrison: bass (1,3) / Frank Butler: drums (1) / Elvin Jones: drums (2,3) / Bob Thiele: producer

The music on *Kulu Sé Mama* was recorded in June and October 1965, so it pre-dates the music on the already released *Meditations* and *Live At The Village Vanguard Again* albums. The title track is a unique experiment in John Coltrane's catalogue, with a distinct African influence, dominated by various percussion instruments played by Juno Lewis, together with his chanting in a Creole language. Coltrane and Sanders improvise simultaneously over the dense rhythmic carpet laid down by the rest of the band, then McCoy Tyner takes over with a striking performance that is full of trills and riffs and note clusters, in keeping with the character of the piece. Donald Garrett delivers a creaking bass clarinet solo as a duet with Juno Lewis's singing, and the piece comes to an end. The overall result sounds a little chaotic in places, but exhilarating. *Vigil* on the second side of the album is an intense duet for tenor saxophone and drums, with no other instruments playing, then *Welcome* revisits the classic John Coltrane quartet format for a piece that is almost rhapsodic in comparison with what went before. The variety of these three long tracks emphasises the fertility of John Coltrane's last three years, already made clear by the other albums released during this period. *Kulu Sé Mama* was the last record to be released in his lifetime: on July 17 he succumbed to liver cancer at the age of just forty.

PAUL McCARTNEY   THE FAMILY WAY

| UK release | January 1967 | Decca | SKL/LK 4847 |
| US release | June 1967 | London | M 76007/MS 82007 |

No individual track titles

George Martin: orchestrations, producer

John Lennon published two volumes of his humorous writing in 1964 and 1965, but the first solo music project by a member of the Beatles was this recording of the soundtrack for the Roy Boulting film, *The Family Way,* starring Hayley Mills and Hywel Bennett. Paul McCartney's contribution was rather less than it appears, since he composed just two short piano pieces, which were then given several different arrangements by George Martin. Although the album does not list any titles, we know that the two pieces were *A Theme From The Family Way* and *Love In The Open Air*, because they were issued as the two sides of two different editions of a single, credited to the Tudor Minstrels and to the George Martin Orchestra. Paul McCartney's melodic gift is much in evidence, but the music otherwise has no stylistic connection with the work of the Beatles, which is undoubtedly the reason that many fans of the group are not even aware of this soundtrack album.

B. B. KING   BLUES IS KING

Blues Is King is a live recording, made in a Chicago club towards the end of 1966. It has much more of a laid-back jazz sound than the earlier *Live At The Regal*, which is probably the reason that it is less acclaimed. But B.B.King plays more guitar this time, so that it functions rather better as a showcase for his expressive playing, despite the lack of uptempo rhythms. He shows no interest in the latest developments taken up by other guitarists: he uses no effects nor even much sustain, and yet he manages to deliver a tone that sounds rich and sweet, purely as a result of the way he places his fingers on the fretboard. He proves that the title of the album is indeed entirely appropriate.

JOHN FAHEY   THE TRANSFIGURATION OF BLIND JOE DEATH

The first album by American acoustic guitarist John Fahey, *Blind Joe Death*, was issued in 1959, with only a hundred copies being pressed. Fahey assumed that the established record companies would not be interested in instrumental guitar music, so released the album himself. *The Transfiguration Of Blind Joe Death* was Fahey's fourth album and was also originally issued as a limited edition, with just fifty copies being pressed in 1965. The guitarist tried again in 1967 and this time, with better distribution, the album attracted considerable ongoing attention and became frequently reissued on different labels. John Fahey's love of the blues as his primary inspiration makes comparisons with the work of John Renbourn very easy, although Fahey favours a rather more earthy approach over technical precision. He is accompanied by a banjo player on two of the tracks, although Mayne Smith is careful not to steal the limelight and keeps his playing simple. John Fahey's dog starts barking near the start of *Poor Boy*, but the guitarist decided to keep this on the record, to emphasise the primitive, 'authentic' nature of the recording. This was carried out using a home tape recorder, rather than the resources of a professional studio. The genre known as 'American primitive guitar' derives from John Fahey, though with reference to the fact that the guitarists are self-taught, rather than any implied criticism of the standard of playing or recording.

AMM   AMMMUSIC

UK release   c.January 1967   Elektra   EUK(S7) 256
Not released in US

1. Later During A Flaming Riviera Sunset
2. After Rapidly Circling The Plaza

Cornelius Cardew: piano, cello, radio / Lou Gare: tenor saxophone, violin / Eddie Prévost: drums, percussion / Keith Rowe: guitar, radio / Lawrence Sheaff: cello, accordion, clarinet, radio / Harry Davis: producer / Jac Holzman: producer

AMM (the members have never revealed what this stands for) started life in 1965 as an extreme free jazz trio, Lou Gare, Keith Rowe, and Eddie Prévost having all previously worked in more conventional jazz bands. Later arrival Cornelius Cardew, however, had a background in avant garde classical music and had worked with Karlheinz Stockhausen as well as composing several works of his own. The music on the group's first album is neither jazz nor classical, but is certainly avant garde and free. Relying on spontaneous interactions between the musicians, in which neither melody nor rhythm is allowed to feature at all, the music has much in common with that produced by the Italian Nuova Consonanza, with the addition of feedback deriving from Keith Rowe's electric guitar, and a random element generated by the use of transistor radios allowed to contribute whatever happens to be broadcasting for a few seconds at a time. AMM was adopted for a while by Pink Floyd's management, who must have imagined that a group capable of being viewed as even more psychedelic than the Floyd's most far-out moments might just become a commercial success. Of course, despite the LP being issued on that coolest of sixties labels, Elektra, it did not happen, although the core trio continued with a similar musical philosophy (separately for the most part) through to recent times (Lou Gare died in 2017).

LUCIANO BERIO   CIRCLES/SEQUENZA I, III, V

German release   c.January 1967   Wergo   WER 60021
UK release   1970   Heliodor   2549 020
Not released in US

1. Circles (composed in 1960)
2. Sequenza I (composed in 1958)
3. Sequenza III (composed in 1966)
4. Sequenza V (composed in 1966)

All compositions by Luciano Berio / lyrics on track 1 by E.E.Cummings

Cathy Berberian: vocals (1,3) / Francis Pierre: harp (1) / Jean-Claude Casadesus: percussion (1) / Jean-Pierre Drouet: percussion (1) / Aurèle Nicolet: flute (2) / Vinko Globokar: trombone (4)

Luciano Berio was an Italian composer (he died in 2003), who gained a first public performance of one of his works in 1947, when he was twenty-two. He gradually achieved recognition as one of the foremost avant-garde composers during the sixties, with the series of works for solo instruments that he called *Sequenze* being a key to his success. Each work explored the limits of what the chosen instrument could do, and required considerable virtuosity on the part of the musician concerned. *Sequenza I* and *V*, for flute and trombone respectively, sound like pieces of free improvisation, except that everything is written down. *Sequenza III* for soprano voice is performed by Berio's ex-wife, Cathy Berberian, who clearly remained on friendly terms with her former husband. Making the human voice deliver extreme sounds, not all of them pitched, runs the risk of being received as a series of comic effects, but the skill of both Berio and Berberian ensures that this does not happen here. The extraordinary performance opens the door for the other experimental singers that followed, including Meredith Monk and Yoko Ono, Mark Greenway (of the grindcore band Napalm Death) and Robert Plant, even if not all of these vocalists would have been aware of their predecessor. *Circles* is a more extended showcase for Cathy Berberian's voice, although on this occasion she is not expected to deliver the more surprising vocal effects. She is, however, supported and underscored by a mass of percussion instruments, both tuned and not, among them a harp, which is played as though it too is a member of the percussion family, a kind of plucked marimba.

THE FREE SPIRITS   OUT OF SIGHT AND SOUND

```
US release    c.January 1967    ABC    ABC(-S) 593
Not released in UK

1. Don't Look Now (But Your Head Is Turned Around) (Larry Coryell)
2. I'm Gonna Be Free (Larry Coryell)
3. LBOD (Bob Moses/Larry Coryell)
4. Sunday Telephone (Chip Baker/Larry Coryell)
5. Blue Water Mother (Chip Baker/Larry Coryell)
6. Girl Of The Mountain (Chip Baker/Larry Coryell)

7. Cosmic Daddy Dancer (Chip Baker/Larry Coryell)
8. Bad News Cat (Larry Coryell)
9. Storm (Chip Baker/Larry Coryell)
10. Early Mornin' Fear (Larry Coryell/Nick Hyams)
11. Angels Can't Be True (Larry Coryell)
12. Tattoo Man (Chip Baker/Larry Coryell)

Jim Pepper: tenor saxophone, flute / Larry Coryell: guitar, sitar /
Chip Baker: guitar / Chris Hills: bass guitar, vocals / Bob Moses:
drums / Bob Thiele: producer
```

In the UK during the early sixties, there were very limited opportunities for jazz musicians to play the music they loved and get paid for doing it. As a result, a number of rock bands, such as Alexis Korner's Blues Incorporated, the Graham Bond Organization, and Manfred Mann, included musicians whose primary passion was jazz and who were very influential on the way that these bands developed. In the US, where jazz had a much bigger following, its musicians were not generally very interested in having anything to do with music they viewed as being beneath their abilities. Which is why the Free Spirits, an American band made up of jazz musicians attempting to play rock, is so unusual. Unfortunately, they do not seem to have a very good grasp of how rock music works. The free-wheeling drumming of Bob Moses and the tendency of saxophonist Jim Pepper to introduce an avant garde element would have been great in the right context, but the ersatz Bob Dylan songs written quickly by the two guitarists, with frequently embarrassing lyrics, are not it. Larry Coryell had already proved his abilities as a guitarist during the few months he played with Chico Hamilton, but here he prefers to let Jim Pepper deliver the majority of the short solos. It is apparent that the members of the Free Spirits had never listened to what the Butterfield Blues Band and the Blues Project were achieving in the US with regard to incorporating jazz improvisation into rock music. They appeared to believe that bringing their jazz backgrounds to a rock album was enough, but the reality is that the album proves it is not and that the musicians are simply not at all as innovative as they think they are.

ROY HARPER   SOPHISTICATED BEGGAR

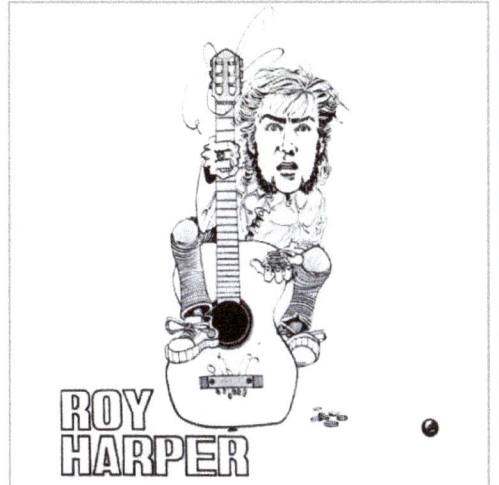

```
UK release    c.January 1967    Strike    JHL 105
Not released in US

1. China Girl
2. Goldfish
3. Sophisticated Beggar
4. My Friend
5. Big Fat Silver Aeroplane
6. Blackpool
7. Legend

8. Girlie
9. October 12th
10. Black Clouds
11. Mr Stationmaster
12. Forever
13. Committed

All compositions by Roy Harper

Roy Harper: vocals, guitar / Lon Goddard: guitar (2,9) /
Ritchie Blackmore: guitar (1,13) / unknown organ (11)
/ unknown bass guitar and drums (11,13) / Pierre Tubbs
(as Peter Richards): producer
```

The first album by Roy Harper presents idiosyncratic songwriting allied with skilful acoustic guitar playing in the manner of Bert Jansch. Harper's singing voice is an expressive instrument, with a tendency to incorporate vague pitching and a melismatic approach reminiscent of the singers in the Incredible String Band. *Sophisticated Beggar* is a low-budget affair, recorded in the producer's garage and released by a small, independent record company that would not, as it turned out, survive the year. Although most tracks feature Roy Harper performing on his own, session players are added on a few of the tracks, with a full band appearing on *Mr Stationmaster* and *Committed*. The last track is introduced by an extended burst of electric guitar feedback, probably the work of Ritchie Blackmore, later to play with Deep Purple, although he is not credited. The guitarist also delivers some effective reverse playing on the opening *China Girl*. The album announces the arrival of a significant new talent and has been reissued on several occasions, sometimes using the title *The Return Of The Sophisticated Beggar*, although Roy Harper has been able to resist the temptation of making new recordings of these songs.

DON CHERRY   SYMPHONY FOR IMPROVISERS

```
US release    c.January 1967    Blue Note    BST8/BLP 4247
Not released in UK

1. Symphony For Improvisers:
   Symphony for Improvisers/Nu Creative Love/What's Not Serious/
   Infant Happiness

2. Manhattan Cry:
   Manhattan Cry/Lunatic/Sparkle Plenty/Om Nu

All compositions by Don Cherry

Don Cherry: cornet / Gato Barbieri: tenor saxophone / Pharoah
Sanders: tenor saxophone, piccolo / Karl Berger: vibraphone, piano /
Henry Grimes: bass / Jean François Jenny-Clark: bass / Ed Blackwell:
drums / Alfred Lion: producer
```

Don Cherry's second album for Blue Note continues the approach begun on *Complete Communion* to even greater effect. The focus of the music moves quickly from soloist to soloist, so that while every musician has a generous amount of playing time in the spotlight, it is divided into several quite short segments. Although the music on each side of the album is subdivided with several titles, the performances are continuous. The *Manhattan Cry* suite starts slowly and is remarkably lyrical for an avant garde piece, even when Gato Barbieri unleashes his newly characteristic wailing tone on tenor saxophone, although the tempo tempo moves back up again when the part called *Lunatic* begins. Overall, the album provides a valuable lesson in how effective free improvisation can be when given a little pre-planned guidance and delivered by performers as skilled as these.

JOHNNY RIVERS   REWIND

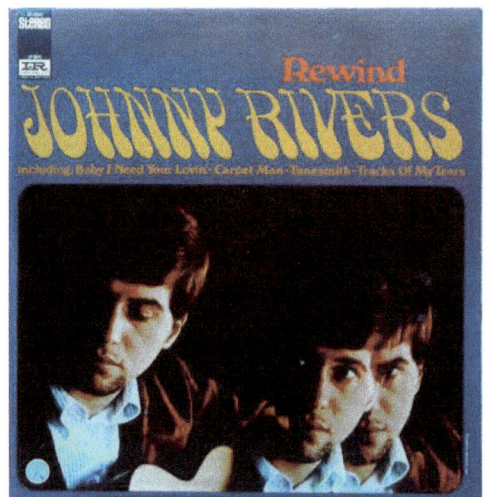

```
US release    January 1967    Imperial    LP-12/LP-9 341
UK release    January 1967    Liberty     LBS/LBL 83040

1. The Tracks Of My Tears (Smokey Robinson/Marvin Tarplin/Warren Moore)
2. Carpet Man (Jimmy Webb)
3. Tunesmith (Jimmy Webb)
4. Sidewalk Song / 27th Street (Jimmy Webb)
5. It'll Never Happen Again (Tim Hardin)
6. Do What You Gotta Do (Jimmy Webb)
7. Baby I Need Your Lovin' (Brian Holland/Lamont Dozier/Eddie Holland)
8. For Emily, Wherever I May Find Her (Paul Simon)
9. Rosecrans Boulevard (Jimmy Webb)
10. The Eleventh Song (Jimmy Webb)
11. Sweet Smiling Children (Jimmy Webb)

Johnny Rivers: vocals, guitar / Mike Dacy: guitar / Larry Knechtel: piano / Joe
Osborne: bass guitar / Hal Blaine: drums / Jimmy Webb: arranger / Marty
Paich: arranger (1,4,7,10) / Lou Adler: producer
```

Johnny Rivers scored several US hits from 1964 with cheerful covers of rock 'n' roll and R&B material, presenting himself as a home-grown answer to the British beat invasion. *Rewind* is his eighth album for Imperial and it finds Rivers winding down for a softer, more easy-listening approach, with lush string arrangements. Most of the songs, however, are by Jimmy Webb, who is making his first significant commercial breakthrough here. It is the originality of his songwriting that prevents the album from sliding into easy-listening territory and Rivers proves that he has a voice of sufficient flexibility to do justice to the songs. *Rewind* was a top twenty album in the US, becoming one of his best-selling albums, although it meant little to music fans in the UK.

EDDIE FLOYD   KNOCK ON WOOD

Eddie Floyd was fairly prolific as a songwriter for Stax records, but as a singer he lagged behind Otis Redding and Wilson Pickett in terms of sales success and impact. His song, *Knock On Wood*, however, is one of the best known soul tracks of the sixties. It has been covered by numerous other artists and was taken back into the charts by Amii Stewart in 1979. Floyd's original reached a respectable number 28 in the US chart and just scraped into the top twenty in the UK, but it was a big club success and exerted an influence out of proportion to its record sales. Eddie Floyd was able to maintain a lengthy career on the back of this early success, with his most recent album being released in 2013.

THE BYRDS YOUNGER THAN YESTERDAY

```
US release    January 1967    Stax    (SD) 714
UK release    April 1967      Stax    589006

1. Knock On Wood (Eddie Floyd/Steve Cropper)
2. Something You Got (Chris Kenner/Fats Domino)
3. But It's Alright (J J Jackson/Pierre Tubbs)
4. I Stand Accused (Billy Butler/Jerry Butler)
5. If You Gotta Make A Fool Of Somebody (Rudy Clark)
6. I Don't Want To Cry (Chuck Jackson/Luther Dixon)
7. Raise Your Hand (Alvertis Isbell/Eddie Floyd/Steve Cropper)
8. Got To Make A Comeback (Eddie Floyd/Joe Shamwell)
9. 634-5789 (Eddie Floyd/Steve Cropper)
10. I've Just Been Feeling Bad (Eddie Floyd/Steve Cropper)
11. High-Heel Sneakers (Robert Higginbotham)
12. Warm And Tender Love (Bobby Robinson)

Eddie Floyd: vocals / Steve Cropper: guitar / Booker T Jones: keyboards / Isaac Hayes: keyboards / Donald Dunn: bass guitar / Al Jackson: drums / Wayne Jackson: trumpet / Andrew Love: tenor saxophone / Floyd Newman: baritone saxophone / Jim Stewart: producer
```

```
US release    February 1967    Columbia    CS 9442/CL 2642
UK release    February 1967    CBS         (S)BPG 62988

1. So You Want To Be A Rock 'n' Roll Star (Hillman/McGuinn)
2. Have You Seen Her Face (Chris Hillman)
3. C.T.A. - 102 (Jim McGuinn/Robert Hippard)
4. Renaissance Fair (David Crosby/Jim McGuinn)
5. Time Between (Chris Hillman)
6. Everybody's Been Burned (David Crosby)
7. Thoughts And Words (Chris Hillman)
8. Mind Gardens (David Crosby)
9. My Back Pages (Bob Dylan)
10. The Girl With No Name (Chris Hillman)
11. Why (David Crosby/Jim McGuinn)

Jim McGuinn: vocals, guitar / David Crosby: vocals, guitar / Chris Hillman: vocals, bass guitar / Michael Clarke: drums / Hugh Masekela: trumpet (1) / Cecil Barnard (Hotep Idris Galeta): piano (2) / Vern Gosdin: guitar (5) / Clarence White: guitar (5,10) / Daniel Ray: percussion / Gary Usher: producer
```

Even without Gene Clark, the group's original lead singer, *Younger Than Yesterday* is the Byrds' most confident album to date, albeit one in which the Beatles influence is displayed most clearly. The tracks written by Chris Hillman, most notably, sound very much as though they have been left over from the recording of the album *Rubber Soul*. *Have You Seen Her Face* is arguably one of the most memorable Beatles songs not actually having anything to do with them. Only the final track on the album, *Why*, makes any attempt to continue with the modal experimentation of the earlier *Eight Miles High*, and an adventure of a different kind on *Mind Gardens*, with a melody that sounds improvised and the accompaniment drenched in backwards guitar effects, is something of a failure. The inclusion of an African-inspired bass line to underscore the trumpet cries of guest artist Hugh Masekela on the opening *So You Want To Be A Rock 'n' Roll Star* more than makes up for this, however, as does the preview of the summer of love provided by the ecstatic harmonies of *Renaissance Fair*, along with one of the most striking Bob Dylan covers yet, *My Back Pages*.

GENE CLARK WITH THE GOSDIN BROTHERS

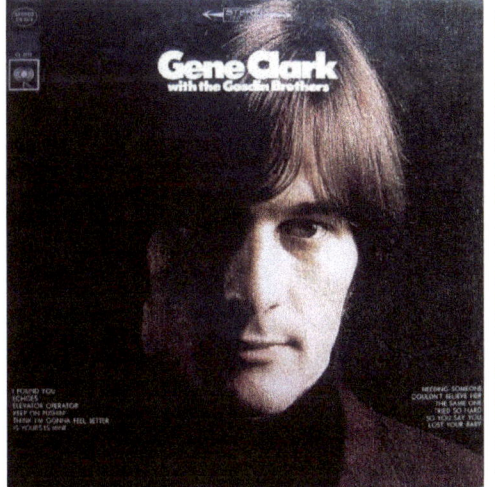

```
US release    February 1967    Columbia    CS 9418/CL 2618
UK release    February 1967    CBS         (S)BPG 62934

1. Echoes
2. Think I'm Gonna Feel Better
3. Tried So Hard
4. Is Yours Is Mine
5. Keep On Pushin' (Gene Clark/Bill Rinehart)
6. I Found You
7. So You Say You Lost Your Baby
8. Elevator Operator (Gene Clark/Bill Rinehart)
9. The Same One
10. Couldn't Believe Her
11. Needing Someone

All compositions by Gee Clark unless stated

Gene Clark: vocals, guitar, harmonica / Vern Gosdin: vocals / Rex Gosdin: vocals / Bill Rinehart: guitar / Glen Campbell: guitar / Jerry Cole: guitar / Clarence White: guitar (3,9,11) / Doug Dillard: banjo (5) / Leon Russell: keyboards, arrangements (1,7) / Chris Hillman: bass guitar / Mike Clarke: drums / Larry Marks: producer (1,2,5,6,8,10) / Gary Usher: producer (3,4,7,9,11)
```

Gene Clark, the original lead singer with the Byrds, left the group in early 1966, following the recording of the single *Eight Miles High*. Although he had been partially responsible for that song, he felt increasingly sidelined as a songwriter and by the elevation of Jim McGuinn to handle most of the lead vocals. *Gene Clark with the Gosdin Brothers* is his first solo album, even if he does give a joint credit to the duo providing harmony vocals. Not surprisingly, the music is quite similar to that of the Byrds, albeit with the addition of a chamber orchestra to the first track on each side. The album is a strong collection of folk rock material, with the Byrds' rhythm section lending its support, but unfortunately there is no single track as distinctive as *So You Want To Be A Rock 'n' Roll Star*, or *Have You Seen Her Face*, or *Renaissance Fair*, on the album by the Byrds that was released at the same time. As a result, Gene Clark's album did not sell very well, although it did make clear that he was far from spent as a creative force.

JOHN MAYALL   A HARD ROAD

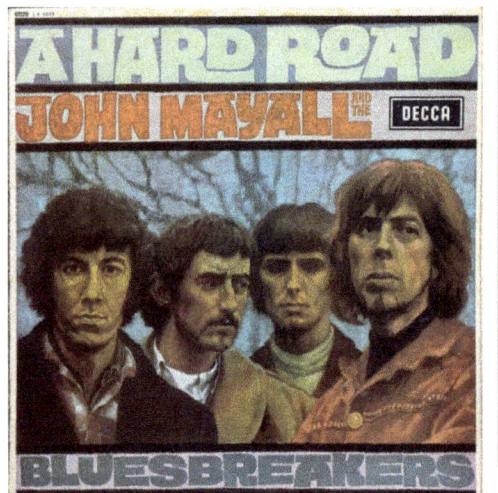

| UK release | February 1967 | Decca | LK/SKL 4853 |
| US release | February 1967 | London | PS / LL3 502 |

1. A Hard Road (John Mayall)
2. It's Over (John Mayall)
3. You Don't Love Me (Willie Cobbs)
4. The Stumble (Freddie King/Sonny Thompson)
5. Another Kinda Love (John Mayall)
6. Hit The Highway (John Mayall)
7. Leaping Christine (John Mayall)
8. Dust My Blues (Elmore James)
9. There's Always Work (John Mayall)
10. The Same Way (Peter Green)
11. The Supernatural (Peter Green)
12. Top Of The Hill (John Mayall)
13. Someday After A While (You'll Be Sorry) (Freddie King)
14. Living Alone (John Mayall)

John Mayall: vocals, harmonica, keyboards, guitar / Peter Green: guitar, vocals / John McVie: bass guitar / Aynsley Dunbar: drums / saxophones on tracks 5,7,13: Ray Warleigh: alto, Alan Skidmore: tenor, Johnny Almond: baritone / Mike Vernon: producer

Eric Clapton left the Bluesbreakers in order to form Cream and John Mayall was fortunate to find a replacement guitarist who was very much in the same league. Peter Green plays well throughout the *Hard Road* album and is primarily responsible for the standout track, an instrumental called *The Supernatural*. Green is able to produce tuned feedback, whereby his guitar holds smoothly sustained notes that sound for as long as a verse. At a time when there was no pedal available to create the effect, the result is a remarkable demonstration of Peter Green's skill, as well as being extremely atmospheric. The rest of the album is made up of more routine blues performances and is a worthy follow-up to the Eric Clapton *Blues Breakers* album, although it lacks the sense of excitement, of a band knowing that it is about to make a breakthrough, that permeates the older record. During the short time that Peter Green was a member of the band, John Mayall's Bluesbreakers also made a number of interesting singles, with performances that are generally more distinguished than those on the album, *The Supernatural* apart, but none were considered worth preserving on LP at the time. Sadly, none of these sold enough copies to trouble the charts at all, although the album followed its predecessor into the top ten.

JEFFERSON AIRPLANE   SURREALISTIC PILLOW

| US release | February 1967 | RCA Victor | LSP/LPM 3766 |
| UK release | February 1967 | several different tracks | RCA SF/RD 7889 |

1. She Has Funny Cars (Jorma Kaukonen/Marty Balin)
2. Somebody To Love (Darby Slick)
3. My Best Friend (Skip Spence)
4. Today (Marty Balin/Paul Kantner)
5. Comin' Back To Me (Marty Balin)
6. 3/5 Of A Mile In 10 Seconds (Marty Balin)
7. D.C.B.A.-25 (Paul Kantner)
8. How Do You Feel (Tom Mastin)
9. Embryonic Journey (Jorma Kaukonen)
10. White Rabbit (Grace Slick)
11. Plastic Fantastic Lover (Marty Balin)

Marty Balin: vocals, guitar / Grace Slick: vocals, keyboards, recorder / Paul Kantner: vocals, guitar / Jorma Kaukonen: guitar, vocals / Jack Casady: bass guitar / Spencer Dryden: drums / Jerry Garcia: arranger, possibly guitar / Rick Jarrard: producer

The UK version of Jefferson Airplane's definitive album is a hybrid, combining songs from both of the band's US albums (with different line-ups) and managing in the process to omit two particularly powerful and significant tracks, *White Rabbit* and *Plastic Fantastic Lover*. This is as much of a travesty as the similar mangling of UK Beatles albums in the US, because the original US version of *Surrealistic Pillow* is a landmark release, marking the first flowering on record of the San Francisco sound that provided a key ingredient in the psychedelic music of 1967. Not that the songs have any of the special effects that characterise much of the other music described as being 'psychedelic'. The influence of folk-rock and the Byrds is obvious, but the Airplane manages to build on this, giving its sound a freshness and a confidence that makes it seem newly invented. The classy playing by all concerned helps enormously, especially in the case of the inventive bass lines constructed by Jack Casady and the fluent and imaginative lead guitar playing of Jorma Kaukonen. He also gets to perform a solo feature, *Embryonic Journey*, played on a spaciously recorded acoustic guitar in a manner that is worthy of a John Fahey. *Somebody To Love* and *White Rabbit* became big US singles, the unusual non-repeating melody structure of the latter, its *Bolero* rhythm, and surreal lyrics relating to *Alice in Wonderland*, making the song stand out and giving it the stature of a psychedelic cornerstone to set alongside the Byrds' *Eight Miles High*. Grace Slick had brought both songs from her previous band, the Great Society, but it took the playing of Jefferson Airplane to make them sound special, providing an exquisite support for Grace's extraordinary voice.

MILES DAVIS   MILES SMILES

```
US release      February 1967    Columbia  CS9401 / CL2601
UK release      February 1967    CBS       (S)BPG 62933

1. Orbits (Wayne Shorter)
2. Circle (Miles Davis)
3. Footprints (Wayne Shorter)

4. Dolores (Wayne Shorter)
5. Freedom Jazz Dance (Eddie Harris)
6. Ginger Bread Boy (Jimmy Heath)

Miles Davis: trumpet / Wayne Shorter: tenor saxophone / Herbie
Hancock: piano / Ron Carter: bass / Tony Williams: drums / Teo
Macero: producer
```

An eighteen-month gap separates *Miles Smiles* from the previous studio album, *E.S.P.*, the longest break in Miles Davis's recording career since the early fifties, and until his forced retirement due to illness in 1976. The album begins a period of extraordinarily busy creativity and inspiration for Miles, that lasted for some eight years and was documented by twenty-one original Columbia LPs, both studio and live, of which twelve were doubles. Miles's manner of working on the first album of the series is well-described in the sleevenotes for a 2016 CD set of out-takes from the sessions. Having decided to tackle a version of a recent tune by Eddie Harris, *Freedom Jazz Dance*, Miles started by asking Ron Carter to demonstrate what he would play for the crucial underlying bass part. Carter had performed on the original record too, but Miles wanted something fresh. "No, that's too common, c'mon," he responded to what Carter was now trying. Miles expected his musicians to do what he did himself, avoid the common and always play beyond what he already knew he could play. It is an approach that informs all the music on *Miles Smiles*. As with *E.S.P.*, the group is stretching the original themes beyond breaking point, delivering improvisation that is free, but melodic and rhythmically based. One track, *Footprints*, is a little different in that it is constructed around a repetitive bass riff – albeit one that Ron Carter does frequently subvert – an approach that would be used again very frequently in subsequent years. The album is the first studio record by Miles Davis to be produced by Teo Macero, who immediately takes a role beyond that of merely recording complete takes as they are played. He edits the master-tape whenever he feels that the result will be a stronger finished product, trimming what are often much longer performances and even combining parts of different takes, in a manner that was distinctly revolutionary for jazz, if not for other kinds of music.

ORNETTE COLEMAN   CHAPPAQUA SUITE

```
UK release      c.February 1967    CBS    66203
French release  late 1966          CBS    66203
Not released in US

1. Part I
2. Part II
3. Part III
4. Part IV

Composed by Ornette Coleman

Ornette Coleman: alto saxophone / David Izenzon:
bass / Charles Moffett: drums / Pharoah Sanders:
tenor saxophone / Joseph Tekula: orchestral
arranger / Henri Renaud: producer
```

The music on the double LP *Chappaqua Suite* was commissioned in 1965 by American film director Conrad Rooks for an avant garde, psychedelic film. In the event, the music was not used and Rooks employed an alternative soundtrack from Indian sitar player Ravi Shankar. The album sleeve-notes quote Rooks as feeling that Ornette Coleman's music would have overwhelmed his film because it was "too beautiful", although one suspects that this was his way of politely admitting that he did not like the music very much. Essentially, Coleman delivers four twenty-minute, themeless solos, supported by his rhythm section, while a twelve-piece wind orchestra plays occasional discordant stabs behind him. It is a tribute to the saxophonist's skill and power as an improviser that the result works extremely well. The music is not exactly beautiful, but it would certainly have distracted the viewer from Rooks' rather meandering visuals. Pharoah Sanders functions as part of the orchestra and only gets to play a very brief solo towards the end of *Part IV*, but then it is not his show.

.

LAURA NYRO   MORE THAN A NEW DISCOVERY

US release   February 1967   Verve Folkways   FT(S) 3020
UK release   1969   as FIRST SONGS   Verve Forecast SVLP 6022 (also reissued 1969 in US with that title)

1. Goodbye Joe
2. Billy's Blues
3. And When I Die
4. Stoney End
5. Lazy Susan
6. Hands Off The Man (Flim Flam Man)
7. Wedding Bell Blues
8. Buy And Sell
9. He's A Runner
10. Blowin' Away
11. I Never Meant To Hurt You
12. California Shoeshine Boys

All compositions by Laura Nyro

Laura Nyro: vocals / Jay Berliner: guitar / Stan Free: piano / Buddy Lucas: harmonica / Lou Mauro: bass / Bill Lavorgna: drums / James Sedlar: French horn, flugelhorn / Herb Bernstein: arranger, conductor / Milton Okun: producer

Composing her songs on the piano and influenced by girl-group soul music rather than folk, Laura Nyro sounds rather different from the other singer songwriters of her generation. Her powerful singing voice, matched to busy arrangements and a strong beat, makes her album an obvious release for Motown, rather than Verve Folkways. The artists who had hits with songs taken from the album were Fifth Dimension and Barbra Streisand. They are hardly folk or rock performers either, although Blood Sweat And Tears later recorded *And When I Die,* having previously invited Lauro Nyro to be the lead singer. She was managed as his first client by David Geffen, the future proprietor of Asylum and Geffen Records, and rapidly became wealthy under his skilful entrepreneurship, although her own record sales, including those of this impressive debut album, remained modest.

THE LEFT BANKE   WALK AWAY RENEE / PRETTY BALLERINA

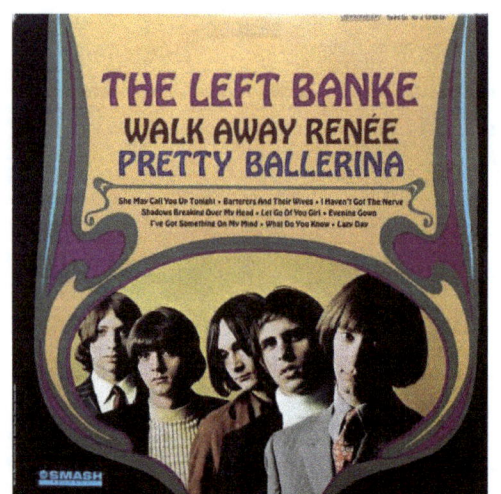

US release   February 1967   Smash   SRS-67088 / MGS-27088
UK release   February 1967   Phillips   SBL 7773

1. Pretty Ballerina (Michael Brown)
2. She May Call You Up Tonight (Michael Brown/Steve Martin)
3. Barterers And Their Wives (Michael Brown/Tom Feher)
4. I've Got Something On My Mind (George Cameron/Brown/Martin)
5. Let Go Of You Girl (George Cameron/Michael Brown/Steve Martin)
6. Evening Gown (Michael Brown/Tom Feher)
7. Walk Away Renee (Michael Brown/Bob Calilli/Tony Sansone)
8. What Do You Know (Michael Brown/Tom Feher)
9. Shadows Breaking Over My Head (Michael Brown/Steve Martin)
10. I Haven't Got The Nerve (George Cameron/Steve Martin)
11. Lazy Day (Michael Brown/Steve Martin)

Steve Martin: vocals / Michael Brown: keyboards, vocals / Rick Brand: guitar / Tom Finn: bass guitar, vocals / George Cameron: drums, vocals / John Abbott: arranger / Harry Lookofsky: producer, arranger, violin / Jackie Kelso: flute

The clumsily titled album by the Left Banke (after the group's two US hits) is the defining example of the music style known as baroque pop. On the face of it, the group has the standard beat group line-up, but in practice the sounds of keyboards (piano and harpsichord) dominate, together with a chamber string ensemble and delicate, harmony vocals. It is the style of the Beatles songs *Yesterday* and *Eleanor Rigby* turned into a complete group aesthetic. The guitar is so underplayed as to be hardly audible at all — when it finally makes an appearance on the one piece of country-rock to be included, *What Do You Know,* the result is something of a shock (though not as great as the one provided by the last track on the album, *Lazy Day,* where the guitarist plugs in a fuzzbox and the group switches into punk rock mode). Most of the songwriting is the responsibility of keyboard player Michael Brown (the son of the group's producer), who has the knack of creating melodies that are distinctive and rather beautiful. He must have been pleased when the Four Tops gained a big hit with a cover version of *Walk Away Renee,* although in the long term his career was disappointing (he died in 2015).

CHARLES LLOYD   FOREST FLOWER

US release   February 1967   Atlantic   (SD) 1473
Not released in UK

1. Forest Flower – Sunrise (Charles Lloyd)
2. Forest Flower – Sunset (Charles Lloyd)
3. Sorcery (Keith Jarrett)
4. Song Of Her (Cecil McBee)
5. East Of The Sun (Brooks Bowman)

Charles Lloyd: tenor saxophone, flute / Keith Jarrett: piano / Cecil McBee: bass / Jack DeJohnette: drums / George Avakian: producer

Forest Flower was recorded live at the 1966 Monterey Jazz Festival by the first permanent group formed by saxophonist Charles Lloyd, formerly a member of groups led by Chico Hamilton and by Cannonball Adderley. As was proved by the subsequent careers of at least two of them, the musicians in Charles Lloyd's Quartet were highly skilled. They play a kind of jazz that is modern and has considerable depth, but is also easy to listen to, with only a very peripheral touch of the avant garde. The rhythms are clear and danceable, the themes and the solos are melodic. Lloyd had realised that, in the context of a rock music world that was becoming increasingly driven by players with abilities not too far removed from those of jazz musicians, there was a good chance that his kind of jazz could find a much bigger audience than the music was accustomed to. *Forest Flower* achieved respectable sales, even if did not actually enter the charts, but it also opened the way for Charles Lloyd and his group to play at prestigious rock venues such as the Fillmore in San Francisco.

CANNONBALL ADDERLEY   MERCY, MERCY, MERCY!

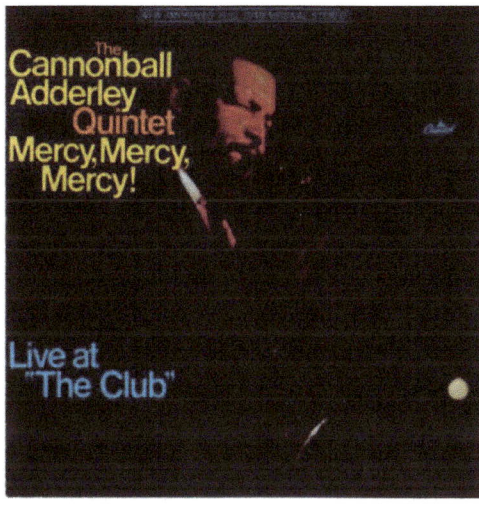

US release   February 1967   Capitol   (S)T 2663
UK release   February 1967   Capitol   (S)T 2663

1. Fun (Nat Adderley)
2. Games (Nat Adderley)
3. Mercy, Mercy, Mercy (Josef Zawinul)
4. Sticks (Cannonball Adderley)
5. Hippodelphia (Josef Zawinul)
6. Sack O' Woe (Cannonball Adderley)

Cannonball Adderley: alto saxophone / Nat Adderley: cornet / Josef Zawinul: piano / Victor Gaskin: bass / Roy McCurdy: drums / David Axelrod: producer

Julian 'Cannonball' Adderley was the *other* saxophonist in the sextet led by Miles Davis, with John Coltrane, at the end of the fifties. He played on the landmark recording, *Kind Of Blue*. His own groups during this time and afterwards played a slightly more rootsy version of the prevailing hard bop style – derived from the playing of Charlie Parker – frequently referred to as 'soul jazz'. The soul is much in evidence on the title track of this album, written by the Austrian keyboard player, Josef Zawinul, who played with the group through the sixties. To emphasise this, Zawinul plays an electric piano, immediately conjuring up the presence of the great soul pioneer, Ray Charles. Released as a single, *Mercy Mercy Mercy* became a rare jazz hit, reaching number eleven in the US chart. The other tracks on the album are less striking, and Zawinul sticks to the conventional non-electric version of his instrument, but the music succeeds in making it clear why Adderley should be considered as one of the major jazz soloists. The audience at 'The Club' are very appreciative, but they are not actually in Chicago, where the real venue was situated, but are in the Capitol main recording studio in Hollywood. Producer David Axelrod skilfully reproduces the ambience of a live club recording, but it is an illusion.

THE MAMAS & THE PAPAS   DELIVER

US release   February 1967   Dunhill   D(S)50014
UK release   February 1967   RCA Victor   SF / RD 7880

1. Dedicated To The One I Love (Ralph Bass/Lowman Pauling)
2. My Girl (Smokey Robinson/Ronald White)
3. Creeque Alley (John & Michelle Phillips)
4. Sing For Your Supper (Lorenz Hart/Richard Rodgers)
5. Twist And Shout (Phil Medley/Bert Russell)
6. Free Advice (John & Michelle Phillips)
7. Look Through My Window (John Phillips)
8. Boys And Girls Together (John Phillips)
9. String Man (John & Michelle Phillips)
10. Frustration (John Phillips)
11. Did You Ever Want To Cry (John Phillips)
12. John's Music Box (John Phillips)

John Phillips: vocals, guitar / Michelle Phillips: vocals / Cass Elliot: vocals / Denny Doherty: vocals / Eric Hord: guitar / P.F. Sloan: guitar / Larry Knechtel: keyboards / Jim Horn: flute, tenor saxophone / Joe Osborn: bass guitar / Hal Blaine: drums / Gary Coleman: Percussion / Lou Adler: producer

The third album by the Mamas and the Papas continued the group's run of success in the album charts in both the US and the UK, but it is a fairly lacklustre affair (as indeed was its predecessor). It is likely that John and Michelle Phillips' ongoing marriage problems were affecting their creativity – most of the songs written by them both or by John alone are not very distinguished. Two of them, on an album by a group famed for its harmony singing, are instrumentals, with the closing *John's Music Box* being exactly what it says, a short piece played by a clockwork music box. The three songs issued as singles are terrific, however, and succeed in saving the album. *Dedicated To The One I Love* is an inspired cover of a song by the fifties doo-wop group, the Five Royales, while *Creeque Alley* is a light-hearted history lesson about the early years of the group. *Look Through My Window* is something of a masterpiece, full of twisting chord changes and the quartet's most sublime harmonies, and topped with a particularly moving arrangement for strings. The song shows what can happen when effort and inspiration are combined in equal measure, making it all the more sad that the same qualities are seldom apparent on the rest of the album.

RICHIE HAVENS   MIXED BAG

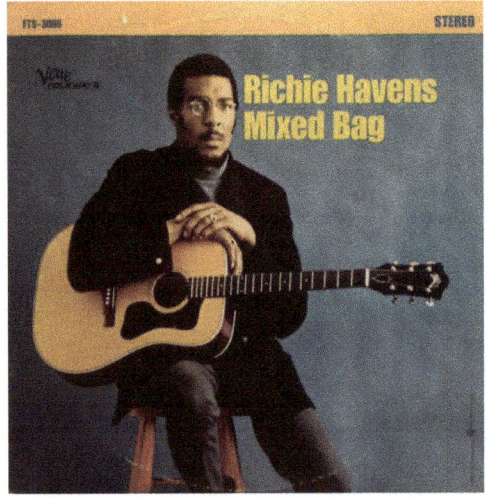

```
US release     February 1967    Verve   VT(S)-3006
UK release     February 1967    Verve   (S)VLP 6008

1. High Flyin' Bird (Billy Edd Wheeler)
2. I Can't Make It Anymore (Gordon Lightfoot)
3. Morning Morning (Tuli Kupferberg)
4. Adam (Richie Havens)
5. Follow (Jerry Merrick)

6. Three Day Eternity (Richie Havens)
7. Sandy (Jean Pierre Cousineau)
8. Handsome Johnny (Lou Gossett/Richie Havens)
9. San Francisco Bay Blues (Jesse Fuller)
10. Just Like A Woman (Bob Dylan)
11. Eleanor Rigby (John Lennon/Paul McCartney)

Richie Havens: vocals, guitar / Howard Collins: guitar / Paul Williams: guitar (5) / Paul Harris: keyboards / Harvey Brooks: bass guitar / Bill LaVorgna: drums / Joe Price: percussion (4) / Bruce Langhorne: arranger (02) / Felix Pappalardi: arranger (3) / John Court: producer
```

A black American with a guitar, Richie Havens chooses to defy expectations and rather than playing the blues or some kind of soul music, instead delivers his own take on folk. The opening *High Flyin' Bird* defines the characteristic Havens sound – a furiously strummed acoustic guitar tuned to an open chord, over jazzy rhythms from the session band, then the Havens voice, a smoky, grainy instrument capable of considerable emotional impact. He would have been a great blues singer if he had made that choice. Many of the songs that follow are slower, but continue to be dominated by the acoustic guitar and that magnificent voice. It took an appearance at Woodstock, two years later, to turn Richie Havens into a major star, but *Mixed Bag* sold well enough to attract attention and was a small US hit in both the pop and jazz album charts.

DOLLY PARTON   HELLO, I'M DOLLY

```
US release     February 1967    Monument   SLP/MLP 18085
Not released in UK

1. Dumb Blonde (Curly Putman)
2. Your Ole Handy Man (Dolly Parton)
3. I Don't Wanna Throw Rice (Dolly Parton/Bill Owens)
4. Put It Off Until Tomorrow (Dolly Parton/Bill Owens)
5. I Wasted My Tears (Dolly Parton/Bill Owens)
6. Something Fishy (Dolly Parton)

7. Fuel To The Flame (Dolly Parton/Bill Owens)
8. The Giving And The Taking (Dolly Parton/Bill Owens)
9. I'm In No Condition (Dolly Parton)
10. The Company You Keep (Dolly Parton/Bill Owens)
11. I've Lived My Life (Lola Jean Dillon)
12. The Little Things (Dolly Parton/Bill Owens)

Dolly Parton: vocals / Fred Foster: producer / other musicians uncredited
```

The first album by Dolly Parton introduces the voice and the songs of a country singer songwriter who would become one of the biggest stars of the music, to some extent transcending her chosen genre. *Hello, I'm Dolly* breaks no new ground, keeping closely to the conventions of country, and hoping that Dolly's attractive, little-girl voice will be enough to win through. The opening *Dumb Blonde* serves as her calling card, insisting that she is not a dumb blonde at all, although, ironically, this is one of the few songs on the album that she did not write. Released as a single, the song was her first country hit and it was followed into the chart by another track from the album, *Something Fishy*. Three other tracks had already been successful for other artists; *Hello I'm Dolly* stalled just short of the country album chart top ten.

LORETTA LYNN   DON'T COME HOME A DRINKIN'

Loretta Lynn made her first recordings in 1960 and achieved a number of country hits during the following years. She achieved something of a commercial breakthrough with the single, *Don't Come Home A Drinkin'*, which was her first country number one, and the associated album, which not only reached number one in the country albums chart, but became the first album by a female country singer to be awarded a gold disc. Most of the songs had previously been recorded by other people, but Loretta Lynn's strong, expressive voice ensures that she makes them entirely her own. The title track, with the crucial phrase "with lovin' on your mind" added to the title in parentheses, was co-written by Ms Lynn herself and one of her sisters, and tackles a realistic issue, but one sufficiently risqué to get the record banned by many of the specialist country music radio stations.

```
US release        February 1967     Decca  DL (7)4842
Not released in UK

1. Don't Come Home A Drinkin' (Loretta Lynn/Peggy Sue Wells)
2. I Really Don't Want To Know (Howard Barnes/Don Robertson)
3. Tomorrow Never Comes (Johnny Bond/Ernest Tubb)
4. There Goes My Everything (Dallas Frazier)
5. The Shoe Goes On The Other Foot Tonight (Billy Mize)
6. Saint To A Sinner (Betty Sue Perry)

7. The Devil Gets His Dues (Darrell Statler)
8. I Can't Keep Away From You (Darrell Statler)
9. I'm Living In Two Worlds (Jan Crutchfield)
10. Get Whatcha Got And Go (Loretta Lynn/Ron & Leona Williams)
11. Making Plans (Voni Morrison/Johnny Russell)
12. I Got Caught (Loretta Lynn)

Loretta Lynn: vocals / Fred Carter: guitar / Ray Edenton: guitar / Grady Martin: guitar / Johnny Russell: guitar / Hal Rugg: pedal steel guitar / David Briggs: piano / Floyd Cramer: piano / Harold Bradley: bass guitar / Junior Huskey: bass / Joe Zinkan: bass / Buddy Harman: drums / The Jordanaires (Hoyt Hawkins, Neal Matthews, Gordon Stoker, Ray Walker): vocals / Owen Bradley: producer
```

JOE HARRIOTT - JOHN MAYER DOUBLE QUINTET   INDO-JAZZ FUSIONS

```
UK release   c. February 1967   Columbia   S(C)X 6122
US release   c. February 1967   Atlantic   (SD) 1482   different cover

1. Partitia (John Mayer)

2. Multani (John Mayer)
3. Gana (John Mayer)
4. Acka Raga (John Mayer)
5. Subject (John Mayer/Joe Harriott)

Joe Harriott: alto saxophone / Shake Keane: trumpet, flugelhorn / John Mayer: violin, harpsichord / Diwan Motihar: sitar / Chris Taylor: flute / Pat Smythe: piano / Chandrahas Paigankar: tambura / Coleridge Good: bass / Alan Ganley: drums / Keshav Sathe: tablas / Denis Preston: producer
```

The follow-up to the previous year's *Indo-Jazz Suite* achieves a much greater integration of the jazz and Indian elements than its predecessor, as is suggested by the album's title. No longer do the separate quintets take turns to play, instead the ten musicians play together throughout, with the crucial rhythm section being a true fusion of the two musical worlds. The music is fairly thoroughly composed, but with enough space to allow the musicians to contribute short solo passages. The overall effect is rather different from the theme plus variations structure of pure jazz recordings. It is the skill of John Mayer in redirecting improvising musicians in the service of music requiring considerable discipline that ultimately makes more impact than his use of Indian instruments alongside the jazz. Joe Harriott continues to make his claim as a world-class improviser, although his total personal playing time is quite short.

VARIOUS COMPOSERS   THE NEW MUSIC

```
US release   c. February 1967   RCA Victrola   VIC(S) 1239
UK release   1968               RCA Victrola   VICS 1239   different cover

1. Karlheinz Stockhausen – Kontra-Punkte
2. Krzysztof Penderecki – Threnody For The Victims Of Hiroshima

3. Earle Brown – Available Forms I
4. Henri Pousseur – Rimes Pour Differentes Sources Sonores

Bruno Maderna: conductor / Rome Symphony Orchestra / Frederick Rzewski: piano
```

It is symptomatic of the slow rate at which the classical music world moves, that a compilation of works dating from 1953, 1960, 1961, and 1958 could be described as representing 'the new music' when issued on record several years later, although, to be fair, all but the Stockhausen piece were making their first recorded appearance. As a showcase for the state of classical music composition just past the middle of the twentieth century, however, *The New Music* serves very well. With the featured composers hailing from Germany, Poland, the USA, and Belgium, the record also manages to make a point about the international nature of the music. The Stockhausen piece, which pre-dates his pioneering electronic works from later in the fifties, sets the tone for the album as a whole. An assortment of ten instruments deliver a succession of musical fragments, just two or three sounding together at any one moment, like a forest of birds at dawn. There is no obvious key, little melodic development, and yet the result is surprisingly attractive. The Earle Brown piece is similar, although it is busier, with some sustained tones which are absent from the Stockhausen, and it employs a slightly larger ensemble including brass instruments and percussion, which tend to propel the music in a more strident direction. The Pousseur piece uses larger resources still and incorporates some electronic sounds within the mix, which manage to blend remarkably well with the acoustic instruments, functioning as a particularly exotic part of the percussion section. These pieces are fascinating, but the true masterpiece is the work by Penderecki. *Threnody For The Victims Of Hiroshima* is scored for a large orchestra of strings, which are made to shriek, and cry, and chatter discordantly, pushed to the tonal extremes of which the instruments are capable. Because there are many instruments playing together, they achieve the powerful impact of rock guitars, without the electricity. The music succeeds in conveying both the anguish and the horror of a war involving nuclear weapons in a highly evocative manner. As a companion piece to Bob Dylan songs like *Masters Of War* and *A Hard Rain's A-Gonna Fall*, it is perfect.

BOB DYLAN   GREATEST HITS

US release   March 1967   Columbia KCS 9463 / KCL 2663
UK release   January 1967 CBS (S)BPG 92847   different cover and tracks

1. Rainy Day Women #12 & 35
2. Blowin' In The Wind
3. The Times They Are A-Changin'
4. It Ain't Me Babe
5. Like A Rolling Stone

6. Mr Tambourine Man
7. Subterranean Homesick Blues
8. I Want You
9. Positively 4th Street
10. Just Like A Woman

Bob Dylan: vocals, guitar, harmonica / Other musicians as on original albums

With rumours that Bob Dylan was suffering the results of a bad motorbike accident and with no new studio album forthcoming, Columbia decided that this would be a good time to issue a *Greatest Hits* compilation. Dylan was far more an album artist than a purveyor of hit singles, but the anthology does very well in providing a snap manifesto for the singer songwriter's greatness and chooses the right tracks. It is a better album than the UK equivalent that the company issued two months earlier. The UK version has two more tracks, but places them in chronological order, so that the whole of the first side comprises Dylan's earlier acoustic material, which struggles to avoid sounding dull in this populist context. It also fails to include the majestic *Positively 4th Street*, extracted from the *Highway 61 Revisited* sessions as a worthy follow-up to the great *Like A Rolling Stone,* and not otherwise available on an album at this time. *Bob Dylan's Greatest Hits* became, by a large margin, his best selling album in the US.

THE SMOKE   …IT'S SMOKE TIME

Germany release   March 1967   Metronome   MLP 15279
Not released in UK or US

1. My Friend Jack
2. Waterfall
3. You Can't Catch Me
4. High In A Room
5. Wake Up Cherylina
6. Don't Lead Me On (Jerry Reno/Terry Brown)

7. We Can Take It
8. If The Weather's Sunny
9. I Wanna Make It With You
10. It's Getting Closer
11. It's Just Your Way Of Lovin'
12. I Would If I Could But I Can't

All compositions apart from track 6 by the Smoke

Mick Rowley: vocals, guitar / Mal Luker: guitar / Zeke Lund: bass guitar / Geoff Gill: drums / Monty Babson: producer

My Friend Jack is a magnificent piece of high energy freakbeat, dominated by a squalling, juddering guitar, with the amplifier's reverb setting turned up high. It failed to reach the number one spot in the UK chart that it deserved, after it became victim of a BBC ban for its drug references, and it did not even manage to make the top forty. In Germany, however, the single climbed to number two and it was in that country, therefore, that the Smoke, a group from Yorkshire, released its only album. Nothing on *…It's Smoke Time* is as remarkable as *My Friend Jack,* despite the frequent efforts of guitarist Mal Luker to wrench the group's music away from being the lightweight pop that the singer would so much like it to be. The Smoke struggled on for several more years, but were never given the opportunity to make another album and never again produced anything like *My Friend Jack*.

THE GRATEFUL DEAD   GRATEFUL DEAD

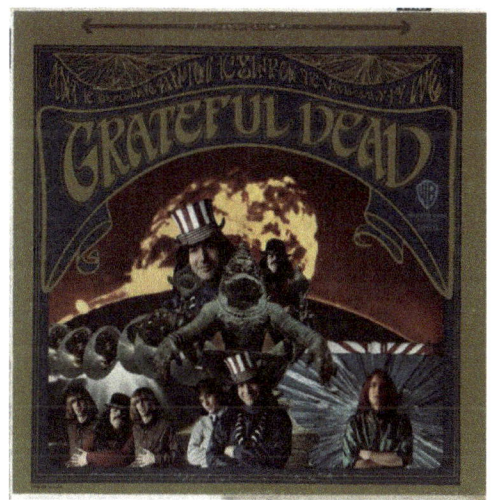

```
US release        March 1967    Warner Bros   W(S) 1689
UK release        March 1967    Warner Bros   W 1689

1. The Golden Road (To Unlimited Devotion) (Grateful Dead)
2. Beat It On Down The Line (Jesse Fuller)
3. Good Morning Little School Girl (Sonny Boy Williamson)
4. Cold Rain And Snow (Obray Ramsey)
5. Sitting On Top Of The World (Lonnie Chatmon/Walter Vinson)
6. Cream Puff War (Jerry Garcia)

7. Morning Dew (Bonnie Dobson/Tim Rose)
8. New New Minglewood Blues (Noah Lewis)
9. Viola Lee Blues (Noah Lewis)

Bob Weir: guitar, vocals / Jerry Garcia: guitar, vocals / Rod 'Pigpen' McKernan: organ, harmonica, vocals / Phil Lesh: bass guitar, vocals / Bill Kreutzmann: drums / David Hassinger: producer
```

The Grateful Dead had already acquired the reputation as a particularly fine live act, having been gigging in the San Francisco Bay area for two years before releasing a first album. *Grateful Dead* does not really succeed in making clear why the band was so acclaimed. The music emerges as a set of not very inspired folk/blues covers by a band in desperate need of a decent lead singer. Psychedelic it is not. But the extended, ten-minute *Viola Lee Blues* does allow the group to demonstrate its ability to improvise at length, with the interplay between the members pushing lead guitarist Jerry Garcia into delivering fluid, intricate lines, marking him as a considerable talent.

ARETHA FRANKLIN   I NEVER LOVED A MAN THE WAY I LOVE YOU

```
US release        March 1967    Atlantic    (SD) 8139
UK release        July 1967     Atlantic    587066

1. Respect (Otis Redding)
2. Drown In My Own Tears (Henry Glover)
3. I Never Loved A Man (The Way I Love You) (Ronnie Shannon)
4. Soul Serenade (King Curtis/Luther Dixon)
5. Don't Let Me Lose This Dream (Aretha Franklin/Ted White)
6. Baby Baby Baby (Aretha Franklin/Carolyn Franklin)

7. Dr Feelgood (Aretha Franklin/Ted White)
8. Good Times (Sam Cooke)
9. Do Right Woman, Do Right Man (Dan Penn/Chips Moman)
10. Save Me (Aretha Franklin/Carolyn Franklin/King Curtis)
11. A Change Is Gonna Come (Sam Cooke)

Aretha Franklin: vocals, piano / Jimmy Johnson: guitar / Chips Moman: guitar / Spooner Oldham: keyboards / Melvin Lastie: trumpet / Charles Chalmers: tenor saxophone / King Curtis: tenor saxophone / Willie Bridges: baritone saxophone / Tommy Cogbill: bass guitar / Gene Chrisman: drums / Roger Hawkins: drums / Carolyn Franklin: vocals / Erma Franklin: vocals / Cissy Houston: vocals / Rick Hall: producer
```

The Reverend Cecil L. Franklin's daughter made a gospel album in 1956, when she was fourteen. She was signed to Columbia in 1960, which issued nine albums by her, without a tremendous amount of success. Switching to Atlantic at the end of 1966, she was encouraged to explore her musical roots once again, instead of trying to be the pop-jazz singer, in the manner of Dinah Washington, that Columbia wanted her to be. One song was enough. The title track of this album uses a stirring electric piano figure and crisp drum beat to propel Aretha Franklin into delivering a performance that defines soul music. Released as a single, *I Never Loved A Man (The Way I Love You)* became a US top ten hit and announced, a little ironically, the arrival of a brand new star. Her singing on the rest of the album is no less inspirational, not least on her version of the Otis Redding song, *Respect*, which manages to completely make the song her own – as Redding himself was happy to acknowledge when speaking to the crowd at the Monterey festival. Released as a second single, Aretha's version of *Respect* became a number one hit in the US and was a top ten hit in the UK too. Eleven years after her recording debut, Aretha Franklin had finally made it.

JAMES CARR   YOU GOT MY MIND MESSED UP

You Got My Mind Messed Up is very like an Otis Redding album, and deserves to be as celebrated as *Otis Blue*. There is even a highly effective guitarist, adding crucial phrases to most of the tracks, and he may well be Steve Cropper. James Carr has a richer, smoother voice than that of Otis Redding, like dark chocolate to Redding's honeycomb, and he rolls the lyrics round his larynx rather than declaiming them in the manner of a preacher, as Otis Redding is inclined to do. Signed to the tiny independent Goldwax label, however, rather than the mighty Atlantic, James Carr does not appear to have access to the best songwriters (and his own *That's What I Want To Know* is a thinly disguised rewrite of the Four Tops' *I Can't Help Myself*, without the hook line). But he does have the knack of making the songs sound good regardless and he succeeds in revealing *The Dark End Of The Street* as something of a soul classic.

```
US release      March 1967      Goldwax      3001
UK release      March 1967      Stateside    SL 10205

1.  Pouring Water ON A Drowning Man (Danny McCormick/Drew Baker)
2.  Love Attack (Quinton Claunch)
3.  Coming Back To Me Baby (George Jackson)
4.  I Don't Want To Be Hurt Anymore (Dan Greer)
5.  That's What I Want To Know (James Carr/Roosevelt Jamison)
6.  These Ain't Raindrops (Quinton Claunch)

7.  The Dark End Of The Street (Chips Moman/Dan Penn)
8.  I'm Going For Myself (Edgar Campbell/Ernest Johnson)
9.  Lovable Girl (Obie McClinton)
10. Forgetting You (Obie McClinton)
11. She's Better Than You (Obie McClinton)
12. You've Got My Mind Messed Up (Obie McClinton)

James Carr: vocals / musicians uncredited / Quinton Claunch: producer / Rudolph Russell: producer
```

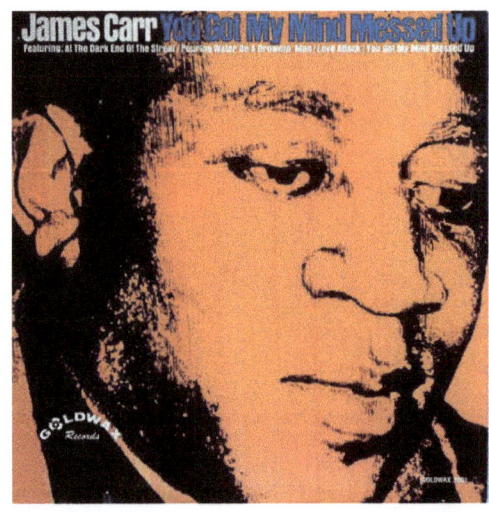

PATSY CLINE   GREATEST HITS

```
US release      March 1967      Decca    DL (7)4854
UK release      1988 (on CD)    MCA      DMCL 1875

1.  Walkin' After Midnight (Don Hecht/Alan Block)
2.  Sweet Dreams (Of You) (Don Gibson)
3.  Crazy (Willie Nelson)
4.  I Fall To Pieces (Hank Cochran/Harlan Howard)
5.  So Wrong (Carl Perkins)
6.  Strange (Fred Burch/Mel Tillis)

7.  Back In Baby's Arms (Bob Montgomery)
8.  She's Got You (Hank Cochran)
9.  Faded Love (Bob Wills/John Wills)
10. Why Can't He Be You (Hank Cochran)
11. You're Stronger Than Me (Hank Cochran/Jimmy Key)
12. Leavin' On Your Mind (Wayne Walker/Webb Pierce)

Patsy Cline: vocals / Ray Edenton: guitar / Hank Garland: guitar / Randy Hughes: guitar / Grady Martin: guitar / Walter Haynes: pedal steel guitar / Rita Faye Wilson: autoharp / Floyd Cramer: piano, organ / Hargus Robbins: piano / Bill Pursell: organ, vibraphone / Harold Bradley: bass guitar / Joe Jenkins: bass / Bob Moore: bass / Millie Kirkham: vocals / The Jordanaires (Hoyt Hawkins, Neal Matthews Jr, Gordon Stoker, Ray Walker): vocals / Owen Bradley: producer
```

Patsy Cline died in a plane crash in March 1963 at the age of thirty: the songs included on her *Greatest Hits* compilation were recorded between November 1960 and February 1963. She continued to have numerous single and album hits, however, right through until the twenty-first century. Even in the UK, where country music has always been a minority taste, a reissue of *Crazy* managed to enter the top twenty in 1990. *Greatest Hits* was released in 1967, but it remained in the US country album chart continuously until 2001, eventually selling ten million copies – without ever entering the main US album chart. It is all about her voice. Patsy Cline has one of the most mellifluous, most moving voices of any singer in any genre. It would hardly have mattered what songs she chose to perform, although as it happens, songs like *Walkin' After Midnight*, *Crazy*, and *She's Got You* are highly memorable in their own right.

THE VELVET UNDERGROUND & NICO

```
US release      March 1967       Verve    V(6)-5008
UK release      November 1967    Verve    (S)VLP 9184

1.  Sunday Morning (Lou Reed)
2.  I'm Waiting For The Man (Lou Reed)
3.  Femme Fatale (Lou Reed)
4.  Venus In Furs (Lou Reed)
5.  Run Run Run (Lou Reed)
6.  All Tomorrow's Parties (Lou Reed)

7.  Heroin (Lou Reed)
8.  There She Goes Again (Lou Reed)
9.  I'll Be Your Mirror (Lou Reed)
10. The Black Angel's Death Song (John Cale/Lou Reed)
11. European Son (Velvet Underground)

Lou Reed: vocals, guitar / Nico: vocals / John Cale: viola, piano, celeste, bass guitar / Sterling Morrison: guitar, bass guitar / Maureen Tucker: drums / Tom Wilson: producer / Andy Warhol: producer
```

The involvement of artist Andy Warhol in the first album by the Velvet Underground was what attracted attention initially. He provided financial support and was responsible for the cover design (a more conventional group photograph, together with the name and the album title, appears on the back). On the first American issues, the banana skin could be peeled off, revealing a pink-coloured fruit underneath, presumably intended to be phallic. Warhol is also credited as producer, although he largely managed to fulfil the role without entering the studio. It was Tom Wilson who carried out the actual work. It was Warhol, however, who insisted that the Velvet Underground should add his discovery, former model Nico, to the line-up. Welshman John

Cale, the group's viola and bass guitar player, had studied and worked with composer LaMonte Young and had acquired a love of the avant garde – and the use of drones in particular. Applying the drone technique to songs like *All Tomorrow's Parties, The Black Angel's Death Song, Heroin,* and *Venus In Furs* gives them a sound that is utterly unique as far as rock music at this time is concerned. A crucial element in this is also the major role taken by John Cale's viola, which provides a distinctly unusual lead voice. There is a roughness to the playing on the album that makes it seem linked to the artless punk rock styles of the sixties and the seventies, except that the subsequent musical careers of both Lou Reed and John Cale have made it clear that they are musicians of considerable skill and intelligence. If some of the playing sounds slapdash, that is because it is intended as a deliberate effect. *The Velvet Undergound & Nico* presents its music as a piece of pop art, to be set alongside Andy Warhol's similar efforts to turn the mundane into Art in his portraits of Marilyn Monroe in changing colours and of cans of soup.

THE PEANUT BUTTER CONSPRACY   IS SPREADING

US release   March 1967   Columbia   CS 9454 / CL 2654
Not released in UK

1. It's A Happening Thing (Al Brackett)
2. Then Came Love (John Merrill)
3. Twice Is Life (John Merrill)
4. Second Hand Man (Daniel Dalton)
5. You Can't Be Found (Al Brackett)
6. Why Did I Get So High (Al Brackett)
7. Dark On You Now (John Merrill)
8. The Market Place (Lance Fent)
9. You Should Know (John Merrill)
10. The Most Up Till Now (Al Brackett)
11. You Took Too Much (John Merrill)

Sandi Robison: vocals, percussion / Lance Fent: guitar / John Merrill: guitar, vocals / Al Brackett: bass guitar, vocals / Jim Voight: drums / Glen Campbell: guitar / James Burton: guitar / Gary Usher: producer

The Los Angeles group, the Peanut Butter Conspiracy, combine the vocal harmonies and pop sensibility of the Mamas and the Papas with the instrumental dexterity of Jefferson Airplane (whose drummer, Spencer Dryden, had previously been a member). The combination should have proved to be irresistible, especially when applied to bright, happy songs with powerful, memorable melodies. Unfortunately, *It's A Happening Thing,* released as a single, barely scraped into the US top hundred, while the album did no better. This is completely mysterious, since *The Peanut Butter Conspiracy Is Spreading* is a hugely attractive album, a great album even.

DONOVAN   MELLOW YELLOW

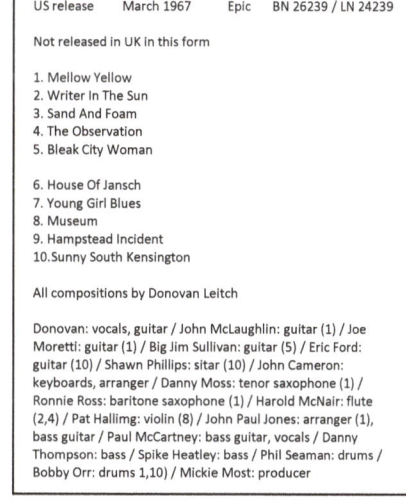

US release   March 1967   Epic   BN 26239 / LN 24239

Not released in UK in this form

1. Mellow Yellow
2. Writer In The Sun
3. Sand And Foam
4. The Observation
5. Bleak City Woman
6. House Of Jansch
7. Young Girl Blues
8. Museum
9. Hampstead Incident
10. Sunny South Kensington

All compositions by Donovan Leitch

Donovan: vocals, guitar / John McLaughlin: guitar (1) / Joe Moretti: guitar (1) / Big Jim Sullivan: guitar (5) / Eric Ford: guitar (10) / Shawn Phillips: sitar (10) / John Cameron: keyboards, arranger / Danny Moss: tenor saxophone (1) / Ronnie Ross: baritone saxophone (1) / Harold McNair: flute (2,4) / Pat Halling: violin (8) / John Paul Jones: arranger (1), bass guitar / Paul McCartney: bass guitar, vocals / Danny Thompson: bass / Spike Heatley: bass / Phil Seaman: drums / Bobby Orr: drums 1,10) / Mickie Most: producer

Mellow Yellow continues the eclectic approach adopted by Donovan on his previous album, *Sunshine Superman.* It provides a second set of memorable songs with interesting arrangements. The title track, complete with what sounds like an inebriated (or stoned) brass band, had previously been issued as a single and reached number two in the US. It fared a little less well in the UK, but still made the top ten. Curiously, the most lastingly effective songs are perhaps the two where Donovan uses only his own voice and acoustic guitar, *Sand And Foam* and *Young Girl Blues.* Overall, however, the album provides much ammunition for the argument that Donovan was now creating the most worthwhile pop albums outside the Beatles. (It is perhaps more than mere rumour that an uncredited Paul McCartney gave his blessing to the album by playing bass and/or singing on a couple of the tracks). The ongoing record company dispute prevented the album from being released in the UK, although it was recorded in London.

THE LOVIN' SPOONFUL   THE BEST OF

| US release | March 1967 | Kama Sutra | KLP(S) 8056 |
| UK release | March 1967 | Kama Sutra | KLP 403 |

1. Do You Believe In Magic (John Sebastian)
2. Did You Ever Have To Make Up Your Mind? (John Sebastian)
3. Butchie's Tune (Steve Boone)
4. Jug Band Music (John Sebastian)
5. Night Owl Blues (The Lovin' Spoonful)
6. You Didn't Have To Be So Nice (John Sebastian/Steve Boone)
7. Daydream (John Sebastian)
8. Blues In The Bottle (Traditional)
9. Didn't Want To Have To Do It (John Sebastian)
10. Wild About My Lovin' (Traditional)
11. Younger Girl (John Sebastian)
12. Summer In The City (John & Mark Sebastian/Steve Boone)

John Sebastian: vocals, guitar, autoharp, harmonica / Zalman Yanovsky: guitar, vocals / Steve Boone: bass guitar, vocals / Joe Butler: drums, vocals / Artie Schroek: electric piano (12) / Erik Jacobsen: producer

For all those who had not succumbed to the delights of the Lovin' Spoonful's original albums, Kama Sutra released a convenient sampler of the best tracks, including those issued as singles. The collection has no difficulty in demonstrating what a special group the Lovin' Spoonful was, and how inspirational a songwriter John Sebastian could be. The album became the group's best selling LP record, reaching number three in the US chart, although it achieved its greatest success in the UK when issued a couple of years later on Pye's bargain priced Marble Arch label.

CAT STEVENS   MATTHEW & SON

| UK release | March 1967 | Deram | SML/DML 1004 |
| US release | March 1967 | Deram | 16/18 005 some different tracks |

1. Matthew And Son
2. I Love My Dog
3. Here Comes My Baby
4. Bring Another Bottle Baby
5. Portobello Road (Cat Stevens/Kim Fowley)
6. I've Found A Love
7. I See A Road
8. Baby Get Your Head Screwed On
9. Granny
10. When I Speak To The Flowers
11. The Tramp
12. Come On And Dance
13. Hummingbird
14. Lady

All compositions by Cat Stevens apart from track 5

Cat Stevens: vocals, guitar, keyboards / John Paul Jones: bass guitar / Nicky Hopkins: keyboards / Alan Tew: arranger / Mike Hurst: arranger, producer

At the start of his career, Cat Stevens was much more of a mainstream pop artist than he became later on. His first album, building on the big hit single that is the title track, suggests that there is a talented folk rock artist trying to be heard (which his later albums proved to be the case). But the music is swathed in lush orchestral arrangements and soft rhythms which give the music more of an easy-listening flavour. The title track is the exception as it happens. The song *Matthew And Son* is fully orchestrated too, but it is driven by a strong bass line (played by future Led Zeppelin member John Paul Jones) that gives the distinctive melody far more of a rock character. The album confirms its young singer songwriter as a significant talent, although one that has yet to discover a convincing performance style. The producer, Mike Hurst, had previously been a member of the Springfields (alongside singer Dusty Springfield), a group that had followed a similar policy of making undemanding pop out of folk music.

ARCHIE SHEPP   MAMA TOO TIGHT

| US release | March 1967 | Impulse | A(S) 9134 |
| UK release | March 1967 | Impulse | SIPL/MIPL 508 |

1. A Portrait Of Robert Thompson (As A Young Man) (Archie Shepp) including: Prelude To A Kiss (Duke Ellington/Irving Gordon/Irving Mills); The Break Strain - King Cotton (Traditional); Dem Basses (Traditional)
2. Mama Too Tight (Archie Shepp)
3. Theme For Ernie (Fred Lacey)
4. Basheer (Archie Shepp)

Archie Shepp: tenor saxophone / Perry Robinson: clarinet / Tommy Turrentine: trumpet / Grachan Moncur III: trombone / Roswell Rudd: trombone / Howard Johnson: tuba / Charlie Haden: bass / Beaver Harris: drums / Bob Thiele: producer

The first side of the *Mama Too Tight* album presents a ferocious collective improvisation that storms along for over sixteen minutes, with just a brief and typically wayward Duke Ellington interlude to provide a little respite. Then, unexpectedly, the music dissolves and is taken over by a slightly manic marching band. The surprises continue on side two, when the title track demonstrates what happens when an avant garde jazz band decides to tackle some James Brown-style funk. *Theme For Ernie* is a ballad, albeit one whose smeared playing prevents any suggestion of sentimentality. Then, to conclude a fascinating album, *Basheer* takes the music to the theatre, moving rapidly from section to section as though accompanying an unseen drama, somewhat in the manner of a cartoon soundtrack. Archie Shepp's own tenor saxophone playing dominates the music throughout the album, proving once again what a remarkable improviser he is.

THE PRETTY THINGS   EMOTIONS

UK release   April 1967   Fontana   (S)TL 5425
Not released in US

1. Death Of A Socialite (Phil May/Dick Taylor/Ian Stirling)
2. Children (Phil May/Dick Taylor/Wally Waller)
3. The Sun (Phil May/Wally Waller)
4. There Will Never Be Another Day (Phil May/Dick Taylor/Wally Waller)
5. House Of Ten (Phil May/Dick Taylor/Wally Waller)
6. Out In The Night (Dick Taylor/Ian Stirling)
7. One Long Glance (Phil May/Dick Taylor/Wally Waller)
8. Growing In My Mind (Phil May/Dick Taylor)
9. Photographer (Phil May/Dick Taylor/Wally Waller)
10. Bright Lights Of The City (Phil May/Wally Waller)
11. Tripping (Phil May/Dick Taylor)
12. My Time (Phil May/Dick Taylor/Wally Waller)

Phil May: vocals / Dick Taylor: guitar / Brian Pendleton: guitar / Jon Povey: keyboards, vocals / Wally Waller: bass guitar, guitar, vocals / John Stax: bass guitar / Skip Alan: drums / Reg Tilsley: conductor / Johnnie Gray: saxophones / Keith Christie: trombone / Johnny Edwards: valve trombone / G. Wallace: bass trombone / Albert Hall: trumpet / Bert Ezzard: trumpet / Greg Bowen: trumpet / John Shinebourne: cello / Lionel Ross: cello / R. Kok: cello / William de Mont: cello / Marie Goossens: harp / J. Collier: bass / Steve Rowland: producer

Brian Pendleton and John Stax left the Pretty Things during the early recording sessions for the *Emotions* album and were replaced by Jon Povey and Wally Waller. These two were previously members of Bern Elliott and the Fenmen, best known for their late 1963 hit, an energetic cover of the Motown song, *Money,* to rival the one recorded by the Beatles. At this point, the Pretty Things were looking forward to signing a new contract with EMI, so had little enthusiasm for making a last album for Fontana. This rather shows in a set of songs that give every impression of having been composed quickly and have had to be made interesting by orchestral and brass arrangements, added without reference to the group members themselves. *Emotions* is not a bad album, but it largely fails to deliver on the promise of the previous *Get The Picture?*

THE BUCKINGHAMS   TIME & CHARGES

US release   April 1967   Columbia   CS 9469 / CL 2669
Not released in UK

1. Don't You Care (Gary Biesbier/James Holvay)
2. Pitied Be The Dragon Hunter (James Guercio/Larry Fitzgerald)
3. And Our Love (James Guercio)
4. Why Don't You Love Me (Gary Biesbier/James Holvay)
5. You Are Gone (James Guercio)
6. I'll Be Back (John Lennon/Paul McCartney)
7. Mercy Mercy Mercy (Joe Zawinul/L. Williams/J. Watson))
8. Remember (James Guercio)
9. The Married Life (James Guercio)
10. Foreign Policy (James Guercio)

Dennis Tufano: vocals / Carl Giammorese: guitar, vocals / Marty Grebb: keyboards, vocals / Nick Fortuna: bass guitar, vocals / John Poulas: drums, vocals / Dennis Budimir: guitar / Lincoln Mayorga: piano / John Johnson: tenor saxophone, flute / Bud Childers: trumpet / Bill Peterson: trumpet / James Henderson: trombone / Lew McCreary: trombone / Richard Leith: trombone / Carol Kaye: bass guitar / John Guerin: drums / James William Guercio: producer

The Buckinghams achieved a number one US hit in February 1967 with *Kind Of A Drag*, released on an independent Chicago label. Columbia bought the group's contract and handed the Buckinghams over to producer James Guercio for the album, *Time And Charges*. Noting that *Kind Of A Drag* had used brass instruments added to the beat group sound, Guercio decided to employ a full brass section on most of the tracks, in the manner used on records by Otis Redding and Wilson Pickett, creating the genre later referred to as 'brass rock' in the process. He used more elaborate orchestral arrangements on a few of the songs and it seems very likely that the group members themselves did nothing but sing, with their instruments being played by session musicians. With James Guercio being responsible for much of the songwriting too, *Time & Charges* is as much his album as one by the Buckinghams. One track is a definite failure. *Mercy, Mercy, Mercy*, already taken into the charts as a jazz instrumental by Cannonball Adderley, is given trite teen romance lyrics which only succeed in robbing the music of its spirituality. Regardless, the song still managed to become a US hit when issued as a single. James Guercio provides a major compensation, however, with the last track on the album, *Foreign Policy*. This song wraps a powerful political message within a shifting musical palette, incorporating dissonant orchestral passages, sampled speech, and sounds created in the studio by reversing the tape. The hugely impressive result can be regarded as being psychedelic, but is more properly considered as a piece of proto-progressive rock, two years before its time.

THE ELECTRIC PRUNES

US release   April 1967   Reprise   R(S) 6248
UK release   April 1967   Reprise   RLP 6248

1. I Had Too Much To Dream (Last Night) (Annette Tucker/Nancy Mantz)
2. Bangles (John Walsh)
3. Onie (Annette Tucker/Nancy Mantz)
4. Are You Lovin' Me More (Annette Tucker/Nancy Mantz)
5. Train For Tomorrow (Electric Prunes)
6. Sold To The Highest Bidder (Annette Tucker/Nancy Mantz)
7. Get Me To The World On Time (Annette Tucker/Jill Jones)
8. About A Quarter To Nine (Al Dubin/Harry Warren)
9. The King Is In The Counting House (Annette Tucker/Nancy Mantz)
10. Luvin' (Mark Tulin/James Lowe)
11. Try Me On For Size (Annette Tucker/Jill Jones)
12. Tunerville Trolley (Annette Tucker/Nancy Mantz)

James Lowe: vocals, guitar, autoharp, percussion / Ken Williams: guitar / James Spagnola (Weasel): guitar, vocals / Mark Tulin: bass guitar, keyboards / Preston Ritter: drums / Perry Botkin Jr: arranger / Dave Hassinger: producer

I Had Too Much To Dream, complete with guitars that shudder, and buzz, and play backwards, is an outstanding piece of freakbeat to set alongside the Smoke's *My Friend Jack*. Released as a single towards the end of 1966, it reached to just outside the top ten in the US. The sounds of distorted, effects-laden guitars are to be heard on most of the subsequent album made by the Electric Prunes. These establish themselves as the group's signature, so that when a couple of tracks are delivered without them, they seem like a pointless aberration. The album cannot match the impact of the hit single and only *Get Me To The World On Time*, released as a second single, is really in the same league, but the songs are varied and do manage to sustain the listener's interest all the way through. Essentially, this is the album that the Standells should have made in order to move on from the innovative sound of their song, *Medication*. It has been suggested that the Electric Prunes were not entirely happy about having to play songs written by external songwriters, but in truth the two songs written by themselves are much weaker than the others.

THE FREE DESIGN   KITES ARE FUN

US release   April 1967   Project 3 Total Sound   PR 5019 M/SD
Not released in UK

1. Kites Are Fun (Chris Dedrick)
2. Make The Madness Stop (Chris Dedrick/Sandy Zynczak/Sandy Dedrick)
3. When Love Is Young (Sandy Zynczak/Sandy Dedrick)
4. The Proper Ornaments (Chris Dedrick)
5. My Brother Woody (Chris Dedrick)
6. 59th Street Bridge Song (Feelin' Groovy) (Paul Simon)
7. Don't Turn Away (Chris Dedrick)
8. Umbrellas (Bruce Dedrick)
9. Michelle (John Lennon/Paul McCartney)
10. Never Tell The World (Sandy Zynczak)
11. A Man And A Woman (Francis Lai/Jerry Keller/Pierre Barouh)
12. Stay Another Season (Chris Dedrick)

Chris Dedrick: vocals, guitar, trumpet, recorder / Sandy Dedrick: vocals, keyboards / Bruce Dedrick: vocals, guitar, trombone / Jay Berliner: guitar / Ralph Casale: guitar / Tony Mottola: guitar / Paul Griffin: organ / Dick Hyman: organ / Stan Freeman: harpsichord / Bob Rosengarden: vibraphone / George Ricci: cello / Marvin Stamm: trumpet / Ted Weiss: trumpet / Joe Wilder: trumpet / Rusty Dedrick: trumpet / Bernie Glow: trumpet / Buddy Morrow: trombone / Ray Alonge: French horn / Tony Miranda: French horn / Phil Bodner: flute / Ray Beckenstein: flute / Romeo Penque: flute / Stanley Webb: flute / Russ Savakus: bass guitar / Bill Lavorgna: drums / Enoch Light: producer

The music of the Free Design is like the Mamas and the Papas given much more of an easy listening emphasis, with gorgeous harmony vocals layered over light, jazzy rhythms. It epitomises a sound and style later referred to as 'sunshine pop'. Chris Dedrick, his brother Bruce, and sister Sandy were signed to Enoch Light's Project 3 label and made six albums, of which *Kites Are Fun* was the first. The title track is a particularly appealing piece of froth, providing sufficient reason on its own for the group to be celebrated. Enoch Light, the leader of several dance bands recording through the thirties, had moved into record production with the aim of creating very high quality recordings. The sound of *Kites Are Fun* is beautifully clear, adding to the appeal of the music. Unfortunately, none of the Free Design's records were at all successful at the time, although a revival of interest in the trio's music at the turn of the century led to it being able to carry out some new recording and play several concerts. Independently of this, Chris Dedrick also achieved considerable success as a film and television soundtrack composer in Canada.

THE TURTLES   HAPPY TOGETHER

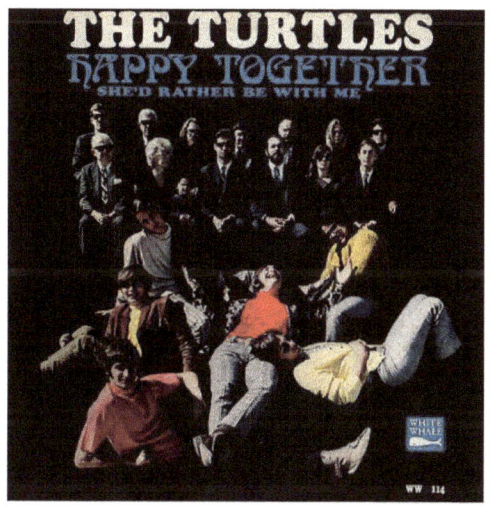

| US release | April 1967 | White Whale | WW(S7) 114 |
| UK release | July 1967 | London | HAU 8330 |

1. Makin' My Mind Up (Jack Dalton/Gary Montgomery)
2. Guide For The Married Man (John Williams/Leslie Bricusse)
3. Think I'll Run Away (Howard Kaylan/Mark Volman)
4. The Walking Song (Howard Kaylan/Al Nichol)
5. Me About You (Garry Bonner/Alan Gordon)
6. Happy Together (Garry Bonner/Alan Gordon)
7. She'd Rather Be With Me (Garry Bonner/Alan Gordon)
8. Too Young To Be One (Eric Eisner)
9. Person Without A Care (Al Nichol)
10. Like The Seasons (Warren Zevon)
11. Rugs Of Woods And Flowers (Howard Kaylan/Al Nichol)

Howard Kaylan: vocals / Mark Volman: vocals / Al Nichol: guitar, vocals / Jim Tucker: guitar / Jim Pons: bass guitar, vocals / John Barbata: drums / Bones Howe: producer (1,10) / Joe Wissert: producer

The Turtles scored a US top ten hit in the summer of 1965 with a cover of Bob Dylan's *It Ain't Me Babe*. Despite its use of harmony vocals and a folk-rock sound, the performance was not particularly reminiscent of the Byrds. The group made a bigger impact a couple of years later, with two compelling hit singles, *Happy Together* and *She'd Rather Be With Me*, the first of which was a US number one, and both songs became hits in the UK as well. The album featuring the singles is a strong set of songs, with the group's harmony vocals and beat group sound being enhanced by modest orchestral arrangements. The group featured an extra member, Mark Volman, who functioned as something of a clown on stage, like a more tubby Eric Morecombe. On record, the humour is restricted to the tongue-in-cheek *Rugs Of Woods And Flowers*, Volman being content to be a mere backing singer elsewhere. The hit songs apart, the Turtles' ultimate significance lay in providing a drummer for Crosby Stills Nash & Young and Jefferson Starship, a producer for the Monkees (Chip Douglas, who had already left the Turtles when the *Happy Together* album was recorded), and a bass player and a pair of singers with comedy leanings for Frank Zappa's Mothers of Invention.

TIM HARDIN   2

| US release | April 1967 | Verve | FT(S) 3022 |
| UK release | April 1967 | Verve | (S)VLP 6002 |

1. If I Were A Carpenter
2. Red Balloon
3. Black Sheep Boy
4. Lady Came From Baltimore
5. Baby Close Its Eyes
6. You Upset The Grace Of Living When You Lie
7. Speak Like A Child
8. See Where You Are And Get Out
9. It's Hard To Believe In Love For Long
10. Tribute To Hank Williams

All compositions by Tim Hardin

Tim Hardin: vocals, guitar, keyboards / David Cohen: guitar / Don Peake: arranger / other musicians unknown / Charles Koppelman: producer / Don Rubin: producer

The second Verve album made by Tim Hardin builds on the good reputation of the first and includes his best-known song. *If I Were A Carpenter* was recorded by several other artists over the years and was a chart hit in both the US and UK for Bobby Darin and for the Four Tops. The song is given an extra resonance, however, when delivered in Tim Hardin's fragile, mournful voice. It is that voice that sets the mood for the whole album, and on several of the songs it sounds as though Hardin is simply allowing his sadness to create the music on its own, improvising the melody and the words as the outcome of a stream of consciousness. It is left to the supporting musicians, including a string orchestra on many of the tracks, to give shape to the whole affair. Curiously, when Hardin decides to increase the tempo, which he does on tracks 8 and 9, he manages to sound exactly like John Sebastian singing with the Lovin' Spoonful.

JOHN FAHEY   GUITAR VOL.4 (THE GREAT SAN BERNARDINO BIRTHDAY PARTY & OTHER EXCURSIONS)

John Fahey's fifth album is labelled 'Volume 4' because he had decided, for reasons known only to him, that the earlier *The Transfiguration Of Blind Joe Death* should become Volume 5 when reissued. *The Great San Bernardino Birthday Party And Other Excursions* contains material recorded over a few years, going back to 1962, but Fahey brought the music together for release soon after a compilation on his own Takoma label, featuring his own playing alongside other blues-based acoustic guitarists, *Contemporary Guitar Spring '67*. The title track is a nineteen-minute extravaganza, although it is made up of several shorter pieces, recorded separately and joined together. The real experimentation begins with the second track on the album, where two extended passages are inserted with the tape reversed and the guitar therefore sounding backwards.

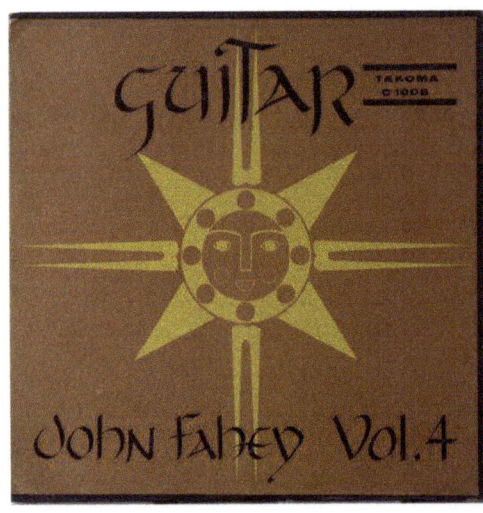

```
US release      April 1967      Takoma      C1008
Not released in UK

1. The Great San Bernardino Birthday Party (John Fahey)
2. Knott's Berry Farm Molly (John Fahey)

3. Will The Circle Be Unbroken (Traditional)
4. Guitar Excursions Into The Unknown (John Fahey)
5. 900 Miles (Traditional)
6. Sail Away Ladies (Traditional)
7. Oh Come, Oh Come Emanuel (Traditional)

John Fahey: guitar, producer / R. Anthony Lee (Flea): organ (3) /
Nancy McLean: flute (5) / Alan Wilson: veena (6) / Ed Denson:
producer
```

There are three duets with other instruments, one of them being a stringed Indian cousin of the sitar, played here by the slide guitarist with Canned Heat, Alan Wilson. There is the appropriately titled *Guitar Excursions Into The Unknown*, where John Fahey is using a prepared instrument, partially detuned and with some of the strings damped. And the album concludes with *Oh Come, Oh Come Emanuel*, played hesitantly, as though following the instruction given by Miles Davis to John McLaughlin, two years later for the recording of *In A Silent Way*, that he should play "as though (he) didn't know how to play".

GRAHAM COLLIER SEPTET   DEEP DARK BLUE CENTRE

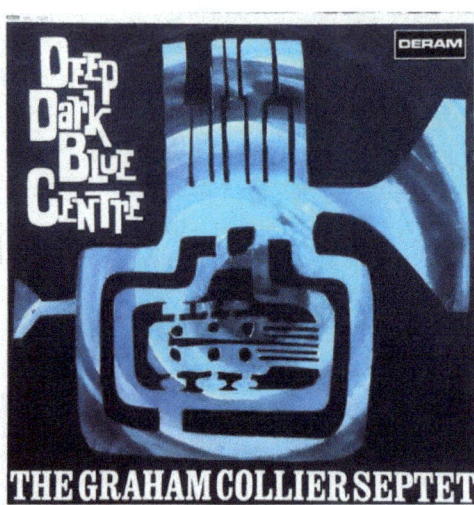

```
UK release      April 1967      Deram      SML/DML 1005
Not released in US

1. Blue Walls (Charlie Mariano)
2. El Miklos (Graham Collier)
3. Hirayoshi Suite (Graham Collier)
4. Crumblin Cookie (Graham Collier)

5. Conversations (Graham Collier)
6. Deep Dark Blue Centre (Graham Collier)

Graham Collier: bass / Kenny Wheeler: trumpet, flugelhorn
(2,5,6) / Harry Beckett: trumpet, flugelhorn (1,3,4) / Mike Gibbs:
trombone / Dave Aaron: alto saxophone, flute / Karl Jenkins:
baritone saxophone, oboe / Philip Lee: guitar / John Marshall:
drums / John and Malcolm Jackson: producer
```

The band led by Graham Collier provides yet further evidence of the ability of the new breed of British jazzmen to compete with the Americans on equal terms. Despite using a somewhat different set of instruments, the music on *Deep Dark Blue Centre* operates within the same territory as recent albums by Miles Davis and Herbie Hancock, and does so extremely successfully. There are echoes too, in the clever writing of Collier himself, of the big band composer Gil Evans, despite the septet being a much smaller ensemble than the American ever worked with. Apart from Graham Collier himself, the album provides a first outing for a number of players destined to make a significant contribution in subsequent years – Kenny Wheeler, Karl Jenkins, and John Marshall – all of whom prove that they have the necessary skills already in place. In compositional terms, the lengthy title track is the masterpiece here, providing plenty of solo space for flute, trumpet, baritone saxophone, and guitar over a continually changing musical backcloth.

PHAROAH SANDERS   TAUHID

```
US release      April 1967      Impulse      A(S)-9138
Not released in UK

1. Upper Egypt And Lower Egypt

2. Japan
3. Aum / Venus / Capricorn Rising

All compositions by Pharoah Sanders

Pharoah Sanders: tenor and alto saxophones, piccolo, voice / Sonny
Sharrock: guitar / Dave Burrell: piano / Henry Grimes: bass / Roger
Blank: drums / Nat Bettis: percussion / Bob Thiele: producer
```

The first album led by John Coltrane's protégé, two years earlier, was an unsatisfactory affair, in which the musicians accompanying Pharoah Sanders did not really understand what he was trying to achieve. *Tauhid*, the second album, is a different matter altogether. Inevitably, much of it sounds like an album that John Coltrane himself could have made, although the presence of guitarist Sonny Sharrock, already sounding startling in a jazz context, provides an element not found in the master's own recordings. Sanders waits over five minutes before joining the proceedings on side one, and then he does so on piccolo, not his accustomed tenor saxophone. Eventually, the musicians settle on a distinctly funky groove, which persuades Sanders to deliver the passionate tenor solo we have been waiting for. The first track on side two seems to be less concerned with Japan than with a Hare Krishna procession, and Sanders chants but does not play anything. The following medley, however, allows him full reign. To begin with, he is playing alto saxophone in place of his usual tenor, but sounds little different on the smaller horn. When he does switch, he moves into spiritual mode, favouring long, anthemic tones of great emotional power. With only three tracks, albeit long ones, *Tauhid* seems like a sampler for a distinguished group that has much more music waiting to be played.

THE DEVIANTS   PTOOFF!

UK release   April 1967   Underground Impresarios   IMP1
US release   late 1968   Sire   SES 97001

1. Opening (The Deviants)
2. I'm Coming Home (Mick Farren/Russell Hunter/Sid Bishop)
3. Child Of The Sky (Cord Rees/John Hammond/Mick Farren)
4. Charlie (Mick Farren/Sid Bishop)
5. Nothing Man (J Henry Moore/Mick Farren)
6. Garbage (Mick Farren/Russell Hunter/Sid Bishop)
7. Bun (Cord Rees)
8. Deviation Street (Mick Farren)

Mick Farren: vocals, keyboards / Sid Bishop: guitar, sitar / Cord Rees: bass guitar, guitar / Russell Hunter: drums, vocals / Duncan Sanderson: vocals / Stephen Sparks: vocals / Jennifer Ashworth: vocals / J Henry Moore: electronics (5) / Jonathon Weber: producer

Mick Farren's gang of social and musical anarchists produced their first album themselves, without the involvement of any record company, advertising it in the pages of the underground newspaper, *International Times*, whose logo appears on the top right corner of the record sleeve. The collection of semi-improvised rock jams, delivered with enthusiasm but not much expertise, has much in common with the music and attitude of the Fugs, if the American group had been notably influenced by the Rolling Stones. Essentially this is a British punk record, made a decade before the Sex Pistols, albeit with much less aggression and much less energy, even if Sid Bishop is reasonably adept at pushing his guitar into fuzz-toned overdrive. Decca picked up the album two years later and reissued it, but by then the Deviants' brand of stoned mayhem was already sounding very dated.

THE WEST COAST POP ART EXPERIMENTAL BAND   PART ONE

The band with the unwieldy name was the result of the more succinctly titled Laughing Wind accepting a sponsorship deal from the wealthy entrepreneur Bob Markley, in exchange for him being allowed to mastermind its career as a member. *Part One* was the first album over which he had full control – the earlier *Volume One*, dominated by cover versions, was largely completed before Markley became involved. It is a very varied affair, with the WCPAE band seeming to be determined to prove that it can emulate any other that it chooses. The Electric Prunes, the Mothers of Invention, the Left Banke, and the Byrds are conjured up convincingly, although the overall result is that the WCPAE band is left without much of a

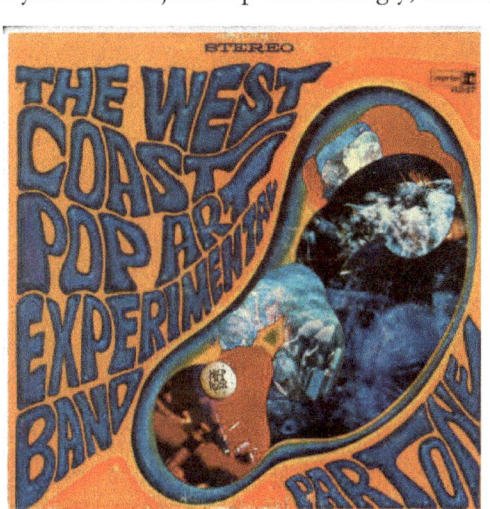

US release   May 1967   Reprise   R(S) 6247
Not released in UK

1. Shifting Sands (Baker Knight)
2. I Won't Hurt You (Michael Lloyd/Bob Markley/Danny Harris)
3. 1906 (Bob Markley/Ron Morgan)
4. Help, I'm A Rock (Frank Zappa)
5. Will You Walk With Me (Morning Dew) (Bonnie Dobson/Danny Harris)
6. Transparent Day (Bob Markley/Danny Harris)
7. Leiyla (Bob Markley/Danny Harris)
8. Here's Where You Belong (P.F. Sloan)
9. If You Want This Love (Baker Knight)
10. 'Scuse Me, Miss Rose (Bob Johnston)
11. High Coin (Van Dyke Parks)

Bob Markley: voice, producer / Michael Lloyd: vocals, guitar / Danny Harris: vocals, guitar / Ron Morgan: guitar / Shaun Harris: vocals, bass guitar / John Ware: drums

sound that it can call its own. *Part One* is an interesting album, very much a product of its time, but not one that stays with the listener for very long. *Transparent Day* would have been a good choice for a single, making a strong pop record out of a basic Byrds template, but Bob Markley opted for the much less radio-friendly *1906* and *Help I'm A Rock*. The second of these attempts to make a Frank Zappa song sound more outrageous than the original, but misses the avant garde sensibility that Zappa brought to the Mothers of Invention.

COSMIC SOUNDS   THE ZODIAC

```
US release      May 1967    Elektra    EKS7/EKL 4009
UK release      May 1967    Elektra    EKS7/EKL 4009

1. Aries – The Fire-Fighter
2. Taurus – The Voluptuary
3. Gemini – The Cool Eye
4. Cancer – The Moon Child
5. Leo – The Lord Of Lights
6. Virgo – The Perpetual Perfectionist
7. Libra – The Flower Child
8. Scorpio – The Passionate Hero
9. Sagittarius – The Versatile Daredevil
10. Capricorn – The Uncapricious Climber
11. Aquarius – The Lover Of Life
12. Pisces – The Peace Piper

Poems by Jacques Wilson; music by Mort Garson

Cyrus Faryar: voice / Paul Beaver: synthesizer / Mike Melvoin:
keyboards / Bud Shank: flute / Carol Kaye: bass guitar / Hal
Blaine: drums / Emil Richards: percussion / unknown guitar,
sitar / Mort Garson: arranger / Alex Hassilev: producer
```

Percussionist Emil Richards, working with Paul Beaver, recorded the first album to feature the Moog synthesizer, a month or two before their involvement with Cosmic Sounds. The fact that Richards chose to keep *Stones* within easy-listening territory, however, prevented it from making a significant impact. *The Zodiac* did rather better than this by retaining obvious links with the world of rock music, even if the first track is the only one that is delivered with prominent electric guitars and a strong beat. Cosmic Sounds is not a real group – the music was put together in the studio by composer Mort Garson, at the instigation of Elektra boss, Jac Holzman. The music comprises exotic soundscapes with the Moog synthesizer taking centre stage, over which singer Cyrus Faryar narrates a set of evocative poems based on the signs of the Zodiac. The album fits in very well with the growing psychedelic mood of the time, as Jac Holzman would have realised.

THE EASYBEATS   GOOD FRIDAY

The Easybeats released three albums in Australia during 1965 to 1966 and another four after moving to the UK, of which *Good Friday* was the first. A big-name band in Australia, the Easybeats in the UK are famous for one song, *Friday On My Mind*. Issued as a single in October 1966, the song entered the top ten in the UK, although somehow it failed to reach number one. It is a classic piece of guitar pop, with a highly catchy melody and chorus and energetic singing and playing.

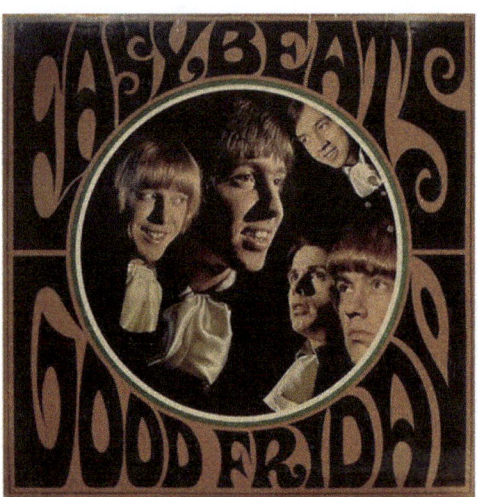

```
UK release      May 1967    United Artists    (S)ULP 1167
US release      May 1967    United Artists    UAS 6588 / UAL 3588 as
                                              FRIDAY ON MY MIND, different cover

1. River Deep Mountain High (Phil Spector/Ellie Greenwich/Jeff Barry)
2. Do You Have A Soul (Harry Vanda/George Young)
3. Saturday Night (Harry Vanda/George Young)
4. You Me, We Love (Harry Vanda/George Young)
5. Pretty Girl (Harry Vanda/George Young)
6. Friday On My Mind (Harry Vanda/George Young)
7. Happy Is The Man (Harry Vanda/George Young)
8. Hound Dog (Jerry Leiber/Mike Stoller)
9. Who'll Be The One (Harry Vanda/George Young)
10. Made My Bed Gonna Lie In It (George Young)
11. Remember Sam (Harry Vanda/George Young)
12. See Line Woman (Traditional)

Stevie Wright: vocals / Harry Vanda: guitar / George Young: guitar /
Dick Diamonde: bass guitar / Snowy Fleet: drums / Shel Talmy:
producer
```

Unfortunately, nothing else on the album has anything near the quality of the hit and the group makes the mistake of including a cover of a particularly iconic song as the first track on the album, yet do not play it at all well. The Easybeats struggled through to the end of 1969 before deciding to stop trying. The team of Harry Vanda and George Young did have considerable success later on, however, most notably as producers for the band featuring Young's brothers, AC/DC.

MIKE TAYLOR   TRIO

Mike Taylor's second album was recorded with Jack Bruce playing bass on many of the tracks, less than a week before he began rehearsing with Cream. Drummer Jon Hiseman was still playing with the Graham Bond Organization, although that band would disintegrate a couple of months later. The album follows a similar format to that of the earlier *Pendulum*, balancing reworked standards against quirky originals, but this time there is no saxophonist. The trio format allows the listener to focus more directly on the piano playing, and quickly realise what an imaginative and original player Mike Taylor is. The rhythm section, whichever bass player is

```
UK release      May 1967    Columbia    S(C)X 6137
Not released in US

1. All The Things You Are (Oscar Hammerstein/Jerome Kern)
2. Just A Blues (Mike Taylor)
3. While My Lady Sleeps (Gus Kahn/Bronislaw Kaper)
4. The End Of A Love Affair (Edward Redding)
5. Two Autumns (Mike Taylor)
6. Guru (Mike Taylor)
7. Stella By Starlight (Victor Young)
8. Abena (Mike Taylor)

Mike Taylor: piano / Jack Bruce: bass / Ron Rubin: bass / Jon
Hiseman: drums / Denis Preston: producer
```

involved (and sometimes it is both of them), is clearly inspired by what is going on in front of it, with Jon Hiseman in particular delivering some of his most forceful and complex playing to date. Typically, *Just A Blues* is nothing of the kind, with no blues chord changes being played, just an unstoppable energy, while the closing *Abena* is almost gentle, but not quite. Subsequently, Taylor wrote unusual rock songs for Cream (*Passing The Time, Those Were The Days, Pressed Rat And Warthog*) and for Colosseum (*Jumping Off The Sun*), but he lived a chaotic, drug-fuelled lifestyle and was found drowned less than two years after the release of this album, at the age of just thirty.

THE JIMI HENDRIX EXPERIENCE
ARE YOU EXPERIENCED

UK release   May 1967   Track 612 001   1973   Track 613 001 (stereo)
US release   August 1967   Reprise R(S) 6261   different cover and tracks

1. Foxy Lady
2. Manic Depression
3. Red House
4. Can You See Me
5. Love Or Confusion
6. I Don't Live Today
7. May This Be Love
8. Fire
9. 3rd Stone From The Sun
10. Remember
11. Are You Experienced?

All compositions by Jimi Hendrix

Jimi Hendrix: guitar, vocals / Noel Redding: bass guitar, vocals / Mitch Mitchell: drums, vocals / Chas Chandler: producer

In December 1966, a single release by a new band, the Jimi Hendrix Experience, was performed on the TV show, *Ready Steady Go*, the most influential and significant pop music programme in the UK. With his wild hair and extravagant clothing, the focus of the band, Jimi Hendrix himself, seemed exotic enough to have beamed down from outer space that same evening. The fact that his skin was brown seemed to be just another part of what made him spectacular. He sang a dark, violent song, *Hey Joe*, in a smoky, blues voice, and played an exhilarating guitar part throughout, using an upside-down Fender Stratocaster that he raised to his mouth in order to play a solo with his teeth. Some viewers may have been aware of versions of the song already recorded by other artists, but Jimi Hendrix managed to make those seem irrelevant. The single entered the charts the next week and climbed quickly into the top ten. Jimi Hendrix had spent his formative years as a musician playing backing guitar to second division soul acts in the US, like Lonnie Youngblood, Curtis Knight, Little Richard (whose time had passed), and the Isley Brothers (whose time, a couple of early hits notwithstanding, had yet to come). Seldom was he given much chance to flex his imagination in these circumstances, for no singer struggling to maintain a paying career was likely to want to risk being upstaged by one of his supporting musicians. He was discovered playing in a club by the bass player with the Animals, Chas Chandler, who recognised the guitarist's talent and persuaded him to move to the UK, correctly assessing that he would be able to make a big impact within the British music scene. Chandler made the decision to leave the Animals and commit himself to working full-time as the manager for his protégé. Jimi Hendrix's group was completed by two British musicians. Noel Redding, the guitarist with the Loving Kind, veterans of three unsuccessful singles, was persuaded to switch to bass guitar, while the drummer, Mitch Mitchell, was snatched from Georgie Fame's band. Two more singles quickly followed *Hey Joe*, different again, but still highlighting some extraordinary guitar playing. The first album by the Jimi Hendrix Experience, including the singles on its US version, but eleven new tracks in the UK, was a startling compendium of guitar possibilities. There was a noticeable blues undercurrent and, indeed, one track, *Red House*, was a straightforward twelve-bar, but Jimi Hendrix was taking the music in directions that no previous performer had considered. It was clear that Hendrix's understanding of his instrument was so complete as to enable him to make it do almost anything he wanted. He presented a style in which the electronic potential of the guitar was devastatingly realised, so that in a very real sense, it could be said that Hendrix's instrument was not so much the guitar itself as the electronics that fed it. Much of the music would have been impossible to play on an acoustic guitar. This was particularly apparent on the largely instrumental *3rd Stone From The Sun*, a science-fiction extravaganza essentially designed to demonstrate the range of sounds that Hendrix was capable of creating. Right at the start of the album, a burst of tuned feedback introduces the song, *Foxy Lady,* although the cascade of notes that opens side two, on *May This Be Love,* is generated by the familiar technique of Hendrix manipulating a metal slide on the guitar's fretboard, even if the effect is enhanced by a little studio-generated echo. The guitarist and producer Chas Chandler incorporated the full range of studio techniques now available, including echo, but also multiple overdubbing, varying the recording speed, and reversing the tape. Remarkably, this was done without attempting to produce the music in stereo, since mono recording was still the standard mode for rock and pop music at this time. The stereo editions that appeared in the US and Europe were artificially enhanced, causing degradation of the sound quality. It was not until 1973 that a true stereo mix appeared. This did not matter at all – *Are You Experienced* retained its impact as the most revolutionary debut album since the Beatles' *Please Please Me*.

THE MONKEES   HEADQUARTERS

US release   May 1967   Colgems   COS/COM-103
UK release   May 1967   RCA Victor   SF/RD 7886

1. You Told Me (Mike Nesmith)
2. I'll Spend My Life With You (Tommy Boyce/Bobby Hart)
3. Forget That Girl (Douglas Hatlelid)
4. Band 6 (The Monkees)
5. You Just May Be The One (Mike Nesmith)
6. Shades Of Gray (Barry Mann/Cynthia Weil)
7. I Can't Get Her Off My Mind (Tommy Boyce/Bobby Hart)

8. For Pete's Sake (Joey Richards/Peter Tork)
9. Mr Webster (Tommy Boyce/Bobby Hart)
10. Sunny Girlfriend (Mike Nesmith)
11. Zilch (The Monkees)
12. No Time (Hank Cicalo)
13. Early Morning Blues And Greens (Diane Hilderbrand/Jack Keller)
14. Randy Scouse Git (Micky Dolenz)

Davy Jones: vocals, percussion / Mike Nesmith: vocals, guitar, pedal steel guitar, organ / Peter Tork: vocals, guitar, bass guitar, banjo, keyboards / Micky Dolenz: vocals, drums, guitar / Chip Douglas: bass guitar, vocals / Jerry Yester: bass guitar / John London: bass guitar / Fred Seykora: cello / Vince DaRosa: French horn / Chip Douglas (as Douglas Hatlelid): producer

The third album to be released by the Monkees in eight months finds the four young men attempting to seize the status of a real group, playing most of the instruments and contributing half of the songs (if the brief rehearsal, *Band 6,* and the collection of speech loops, *Zilch,* can really be counted as songs). The result is a less immediately appealing album than its predecessors, but a worthy collection of performances nonetheless. Chuck Berry would have been justified in claiming royalties for *No Time,* credited to the album's recording engineer, although actually largely the work of Micky Dolenz and Mike Nesmith, while the introduction to *Sunny Girlfriend* is lifted directly from the Rolling Stones. Chip Douglas plays a bass line on *You Told Me* that is slightly reminiscent of the one played by Paul McCartney on the Beatles' *Taxman,* although it is simplified enough to avoid direct comparisons, especially within a song context that is quite different. But *For Pete's Sake* is a highly attractive original and strong enough to be adopted as the closing music in the Monkees' TV series. And the highly inventive *Randy Scouse Git* is sufficiently striking for it to be selected as a single release in the UK, even if RCA baulked at Micky Dolenz's use of language, causing the song to be renamed as *Alternate Title.*

PAUL REVERE & THE RAIDERS   GREATEST HITS

US release   May 1967   Columbia   KCS 9462 / KCL 2662
Not released in UK

1. Louie Louie (Richard Berry)
2. Louie Go Home (Mark Lindsay/Paul Revere)
3. Steppin' Out (Mark Lindsay/Paul Revere)
4. Just Like Me (Richard Dey/Roger Hart)
5. Melody For An Unknown Girl (Mark Lindsay/Paul Revere)
6. Kicks (Barry Mann/Cynthia Weil)

7. Hungry (Barry Mann/Cynthia Weil)
8. The Great Airplane Strike (Mark Lindsay/Paul Revere/Terry Melcher)
9. Good Thing (Mark Lindsay/Terry Melcher)
10. Ups And Downs (Mark Lindsay/Terry Melcher)
11. Legend of Paul Revere (Mark Lindsay/Terry Melcher)

Paul Revere: keyboards / Mark Lindsay: vocals, saxophone / Drake Levin: guitar / Jim Valley: guitar / Mike Holliday: bass guitar / Phil Volk: bass guitar / Mike Smith: drums / Bruce Johnston: producer / Terry Melcher: producer

Paul Revere and the Raiders recorded a version of *Louie Louie* at the same time as the Kingsmen, but lost the race for chart success. The group achieved its first US chart hit with *Just Like Me* in late 1965 and proceeded to score four more US hits through the following year: *Kicks, Hungry, The Great Airplane Strike,* and *Good Thing.* The songs are driving and melodic and it is easy to understand why they were successful, but the group is taking the British beat sound as its inspiration rather than the punk or folk rock or psychedelia of its

American rivals. With a singer who copies Van Morrison very closely and a band that reminds the listener in turn of the Kinks or the Animals or the Rolling Stones, Paul Revere and the Raiders have a convincing sound even if they are not at all original. The group was beset with personnel changes, with only singer Mark Lindsay and Paul Revere himself remaining for every track on *Greatest Hits*.

COUNTRY JOE & THE FISH   ELECTRIC MUSIC FOR THE MIND AND BODY

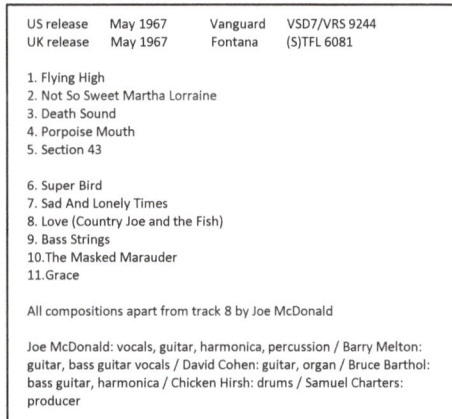

US release   May 1967   Vanguard   VSD7/VRS 9244
UK release   May 1967   Fontana   (S)TFL 6081

1. Flying High
2. Not So Sweet Martha Lorraine
3. Death Sound
4. Porpoise Mouth
5. Section 43

6. Super Bird
7. Sad And Lonely Times
8. Love (Country Joe and the Fish)
9. Bass Strings
10. The Masked Marauder
11. Grace

All compositions apart from track 8 by Joe McDonald

Joe McDonald: vocals, guitar, harmonica, percussion / Barry Melton: guitar, bass guitar vocals / David Cohen: guitar, organ / Bruce Barthol: bass guitar, harmonica / Chicken Hirsh: drums / Samuel Charters: producer

Joe McDonald and Barry Melton began performing together as a folk/protest duo in 1965, adopting the stage names 'Country Joe' and 'The Fish'. McDonald and his audiences would have totally understood the antipathy felt by the country music community towards the young hippy generation (made explicit in 1969 in the lyrics of the Merle Haggard song, *Okie From Muskogee*) and the irony involved in his choice of name. Expanded to a full rock group, Country Joe and the Fish became one of the major performers of the new psychedelic music to be heard at the Avalon Ballroom and the Fillmore in San Francisco. The group's first album provides as strong a set of songs as those on Jefferson Airplane's *Surrealistic Pillow*. Barry Melton's stinging guitar lines and David Cohen's ethereal organ playing act as a focus for music that presents a fully worked-out sound, for which 'Electric Music for the Mind and Body' is a very appropriate description. There is a lightness, a spaciousness to the group's music, as though the musicians are taking the time to savour the sounds they can hear themselves making, rather than doing anything so coarse as rocking out. Joe McDonald delivers his lyrics with his tongue apparently stuck in his cheek throughout, even when tackling themes of politics and death. According to rumour, the members of the group recorded the whole album while high, although their parts are integrated too well for this really to be true. Nevertheless, the album does epitomise the hippy ethos of the period, the summer of love, particularly well.

THE LITTER   DISTORTIONS

US release   May 1967   Warick   9445-671
Not released in UK

1. Action Woman (Warren Kendrick)
2. Whatcha Gonna Do About It? (Brian Potter/Ian Samwell)
3. Codine (Buffy Sainte Marie)
4. Somebody Help Me (Jackie Edwards)
5. Substitute (Pete Townshend)

6. I'm So Glad (Skip James)
7. A Legal Matter (Pete Townshend)
8. Rack My Mind (The Yardbirds)
9. Soul Searchin' (Warren Kendrick)
10. I'm A Man (Doc Pomus/Mort Shuman)

Dennis Waite: vocals, keyboards, harmonica / Tom Caplan: guitar, vocals / Dan Rinaldi: guitar, vocals / Bill Strandlof: guitar (1,7,9) / James Kane III: bass guitar, organ, vocals / Tom Murray: drums / Warren Kendrick: producer

The heavily fuzzed guitars and a decent drummer cannot hide the fact that if the Litter had not been sponsored by local Minneapolis producer Warren Kendrick for his own record label, it would have been unlikely to have made an album. The collection of mostly cover material is very much the kind of music to be played by a fledgling bar band learning its craft. At the time, *Distortions* made little impact, although the group did get to make two more albums, the last of which, *Emerge,* was on a major label (Probe). Only the rhythm section of Rinaldi, Kane, and Murray survived from the first album line-up. In truth, contemporary interest in the Litter lies in the group's appeal to the collectors' market, where records that sold poorly and are now very hard to find, but which have electric guitars distorted enough to qualify as 'psychedelic', are in great demand.

THE MOTHERS OF INVENTION   ABSOLUTELY FREE

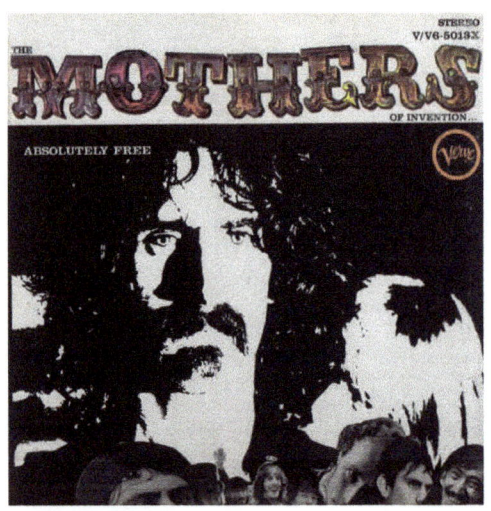

| US release | May 1967 | Verve | V(6)-5013 |
| UK release | May 1967 | Verve | (S)VLP 9174 |

1. Plastic People
2. The Duke Of Prunes/Amnesia Vivace/The Duke Regains His Chops
3. Call Any Vegetable/Invocation And Ritual Dance Of The Young Pumpkin/Soft-Sell Conclusion
4. America Drinks
5. Status Back Baby
6. Uncle Bernie's Farm
7. Son Of Suzy Creamcheese
8. Brown Shoes Don't Make It
9. America Drinks & Goes Home

All compositions by Frank Zappa

Frank Zappa: guitar, vocals, conductor, producer / Ray Collins: vocals, percussion, harmonica / Jim Fielder: guitar, piano / Don Preston: keyboards / Bunk Gardner: woodwind instruments / Roy Estrada: bass guitar, vocals / Jimmy Carl Black: drums, vocals / Billy Mundi: drums, percussion / John Balkin: bass (3,4) / Suzy Creamcheese (Lisa Cohen): voice (8) / Jim Getzoff: violin (8) / Marshall Sosson: violin (8) / Alvin Dinkin: viola (8) / Armand Kaproff: cello (8) / Don Ellis: trumpet (8) / John Rotella: bass clarinet (8) / Herb Cohen: cash register (9) / Terry Gilliam: voice (9) / Tom Wilson: producer

The second album by Frank Zappa's Mothers Of Invention (with several new members in place) continues to highlight the leader's love of the absurd, featuring songs devoted, among other topics, to positive relationships with vegetables and to the possibility of creating a love song in which the expected vocabulary is replaced by references to prunes, cheese, and go-carts. At the same time, Zappa achieves a significant step-up in the complexity of his music writing, combined with a virtuoso approach to studio production to enable him to make the ideas work. Although Tom Wilson received a producer credit, Frank Zappa was in reality the man carrying out the necessary work and he is revealed as a master tape-editor, able to combine fragments recorded at different sessions into a seamless whole. He weaves phrases from classical composers Igor Stravinsky and Gustav Holst into his own music and incorporates passages of solo improvisation (most notably on the lengthy central section of *Call Any Vegetable*), for which saxophonist/flautist Bunk Gardner and Frank Zappa himself, in his role as lead guitarist, prove themselves to be skilled players. There are innovations here that anticipate their later deployment within the progressive and jazz rock genres, although Zappa had little interest in trying to become an influence on other bands, preferring to simply follow his own muse in the creation of music that reveals an original and distinctive composer's voice. *Absolutely Free* is presented as rock music, but it is rock music that ranges particularly widely, displaying an imagination and an expertise that only the Beatles were capable of matching.

THE 5th DIMENSION   UP, UP AND AWAY

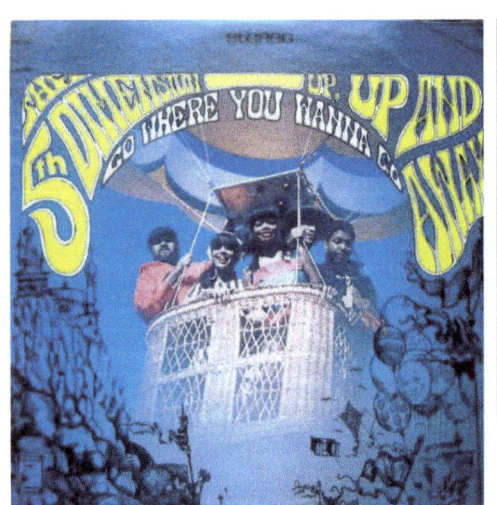

| US release | May 1967 | Soul City | SCS-92000/SCM-91000 |
| UK release | May 1967 | Liberty | LBS/LBL 83038 |

1. Up, Up And Away (Jimmy Webb)
2. Another Day, Another Heartache (P.F. Sloan/Steve Barri)
3. Which Way To Nowhere (Jimmy Webb)
4. California My Way (Willie Hutch)
5. Misty Roses (Tim Hardin)
6. Go Where You Wanna Go (John Phillips)
7. Never Gonna Be The Same (Jimmy Webb)
8. Pattern People (Jimmy Webb)
9. Rosencrans Boulevard (Jimmy Webb)
10. Learn How To Fly (Willie Hutch)
11. Poor Side Of Town (Johnny Rivers/Lou Adler)

Billy Davis, Florence LaRue, Lamonte McLemore, Marilyn McCoo, Ron Townson: vocals / Tommy Tedesco: guitar / Al Casey: guitar / Larry Knechtel: keyboards / Jimmy Webb: keyboards, arranger / Joe Osborn: bass guitar / Hal Blaine: drums / Marty Paich: arranger (1,2,5,6) / Johnny Rivers: producer / Marc Gordon: producer

Signed to Johnny Rivers' Soul City label, the frothy harmony vocals of the 5th Dimension lacked any obvious gospel influence and sound more like the music of an easy-listening than a soul group. *Go Where You Wanna Go*, a close copy of the original by the Mamas and Papas, but with a funkier bass line, and the joyous *Up, Up And Away* were nevertheless substantial chart hits in the US, with the second song winning no fewer than five Grammy awards. The song served as the breakthrough for both the 5th Dimension themselves and songwriter Jimmy Webb. The group's first album included the two hits and achieved gold record status itself, although sales in the UK were poor.

THE BEATLES — SGT PEPPER'S LONELY HEARTS CLUB BAND

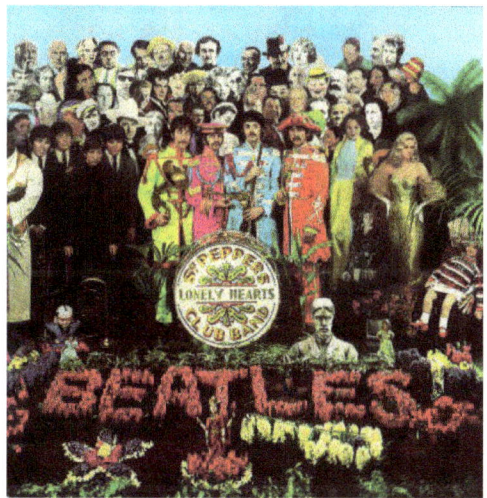

The Beatles' most famous album was foreshadowed by the release in February of an extraordinary double A-side single, coupling *Penny Lane* with *Strawberry Fields Forever*. This was the first record to have appeared since the Beatles' announcement, the previous August, that they were giving up playing live and would be concentrating entirely on producing new music in the studio. *Strawberry Fields Forever* most obviously provides a defining example of the way that the Beatles were now using the recording studio itself as a tool in the creation and development of new works. The group used the recording and playback process to suggest new ideas and approaches, gradually feeling the way forwards to the finished version. The first take of *Strawberry Fields Forever* is very different from the familiar performance of the song. All the details of the arrangement, including the basic parts played by the Beatles themselves, and even the song's final structure, were worked out in the studio during the course of successive recordings, with each change and addition being made as a direct response to the sound of the previous recorded take. This method of recording is much more complex than the simple transfer of performance to tape that was the norm for all kinds of music before this time. For this reason, the *Sgt Pepper's Lonely Hearts Club Band* album was a comparatively long time in the making – certainly by the standards of the time, where the usual procedure had always been to bash out a rock album in a matter of days – and the benefit derived is apparent in the tremendous attention to detail within every song. Here is the final development of the Beatles' instinctive ability to create maximum effect with minimum resources, such as the comb and paper sound which occurs early in *Lovely Rita* and retains its novelty unspoilt by being omitted from later repeats of that part of the tune. Where on *Help!* and its successors each song was given a distinct musical colour by the addition of one particular instrumental sound, here this technique is expanded to create for every song a complete palette of musical colours. There is, for example, the combination of Lowrey organ and helium-altered singing on *Lucy In The Sky With Diamonds*, forming the perfect accompaniment to the world of childish fantasy conjured up by the words of the song. (John Lennon, not wanting to incur any further wrath from an establishment set on making examples of big rock stars, insisted that the lyrics of the song had nothing to do with drugs, although it is impossible to imagine that he was not aware of the fortuitously initialled title of the painting by his son that was his first inspiration. In a song as complex as this, with its shifting key centres, we do not have to be satisfied that it is only about one thing.) Then there is the culmination of George Harrison's dalliance with the sitar in his employment of only Indian musicians to play the music of *Within You, Without You*; and there is the extraordinary tension and release generated by the string crescendos in *A Day In The Life*. Much has since been made of the presumption that the album is intended to be listened to as a continuous work, this being made all the easier by the fact that the ending of one song often blends into the beginning of the next. However, apart from the obvious link between the first two songs and the reprise of the title track towards the end of the second side, there is little thematic continuity. It cannot realistically be described as a 'concept album' – Mr Kite is at a different show to Billy Shears! The record is better viewed as a musical collage, where sound follows sound in a kind of aural feast. Mark Lewisohn, in his meticulously researched *The Complete Beatles Recording Sessions*, quotes Jerry Boys, who was a tape operator at Abbey Road studios at the time the Beatles were recording *Sgt Pepper*. "If you listen to the album now, there are noises which are still impossible to make, even with today's computerised 48-track equipment and all the microchips imaginable. It's a very very clever record. In terms of creative use of recording it has been one of *the* major steps forward." The cleverness included placing a fragment of melody, sung by several voices together, on the run-out groove at the end of side two, even though many sixties listeners, with record players that automatically parked the tone arm as soon as the side came to an end, never got to hear it. Happily, the Beatles

---

UK release June 1967 Parlophone PCS/PMC 7027
US release June 1967 Capitol (S)MAS 2653

1. Sgt Pepper's Lonely Hearts Club Band
2. With A Little Help From My Friends
3. Lucy In The Sky With Diamonds
4. Getting Better
5. Fixing A Hole
6. She's Leaving Home
7. Being For The Benefit Of Mr Kite
8. Within You Without You (George Harrison)
9. When I'm Sixty-Four
10. Lovely Rita
11. Good Morning Good Morning
12. Sgt Pepper's Lonely Hearts Club Band (Reprise)
13. A Day In The Life

All compositions except track 8 by John Lennon/Paul McCartney

John Lennon: vocals, guitar, keyboards, harmonica, percussion, effects / George Harrison: vocals, guitar, sitar, tambura, harmonica, percussion / Paul McCartney: vocals, bass guitar, guitar, keyboards, percussion, effects / Ringo Starr: drums, percussion, vocals, harmonica, piano / George Martin: producer, keyboards, effects / Neil Aspinall: harmonica, tambura / Geoff Emerick: effects / Mal Evans: harmonica, effects, piano / members of Sounds Incorporated (Alan Holmes/Griff West/Barrie Cameron): saxophones (11) / Neill Sanders, James W Buck, John Burden, Tony Randall: French horns (1) / Mike Leander: arranger (6) / Robert Burns, Henry MacKenzie, Frank Reidy: clarinets (9) / orchestra (13) / strings (6,8) / Indian musicians (8)

were able to insist that Capitol released the album in the US without changing the contents, so that, for the first time, the two versions of the album are the same. (Or almost – the voices in the run-out groove, and the high frequency dog whistle that introduced them, were omitted from the American release.) The packaging for the album was intended to emphasise that we should indeed consider the music inside to be special, creating a sense of delicious anticipation even before the record was played. The collection of celebrity (and non-celebrity) faces assembled by artist Peter Blake is striking enough, but the cover was made gatefold so that a large colour photograph of the Beatles dressed as Sgt Pepper's Lonely Hearts Club Band could be included; a cardboard sheet of cut-outs was inserted in the pocket where there was no record; the vinyl was given a uniquely patterned inner sleeve with red flames on a white background; and for the first time, the words of all the songs were printed on the back of the cover, making it clear that they were worthy of study.

It is difficult for modern listeners to appreciate the huge impact that *Sgt Pepper* had, when first heard by fans and other musicians alike. It seemed to have pushed rock music on to a new pinnacle of artistic endeavour that other performers would find difficult to replicate (although that did not stop many of them from making the attempt). Jimi Hendrix demonstrated his personal appreciation of the album by learning the title song and delivering his own version of it at a gig just two days after the album was released. There has been, to be sure, a notable critical retreat in the UK in recent years from granting *Sgt Pepper's Lonely Hearts Club Band* the accolade of best album or even best Beatles album, but it is not too difficult to work out why this rethink has taken place. Certainly, the music itself has not changed. The arrival of punk ten years later, however, brought with it a revised, narrower definition of what was to be counted as rock music. Another thirty to forty years on, within a musical climate that is still inclined to take the release of *Anarchy In The UK* by the Sex Pistols as its ground zero, *Sgt Pepper* simply does not conform with the contemporary audience's idea of what rock music is supposed to sound like. Some of the tracks do not even have guitars on them! For the rest of us, that is precisely what makes the music so great – it ignores musical boundaries, refusing to be placed in any predefined genre other than that of 'Beatle music'. The album spent a remarkable twenty-seven weeks at the top of the UK chart, fifteen weeks in the US, and is, by a considerable margin, the best-selling album of the sixties.

THE SMALL FACES   FROM THE BEGINNING

Earlier in the year, the Small Faces left Decca, which responded by issuing a compilation of the group's hits with an assortment of previously unreleased tracks. The album would not have been issued if the Small Faces had continued to work with Decca, but it manages to keep the group's reputation intact, if only because the singles (and in particular the magnificent slice of blue-eyed soul that is the group's number one hit, *All Or Nothing*) are so impressive. *Yesterday, Today And Tomorrow* and *That Man* find the group moving in a more adventurous direction, in keeping with the mood of the time, but a rather poor recording quality considerably diminishes the impact of the songs. The album only scraped into the bottom of the top twenty, but it is likely that the group's fans realised that the proper second album was only just around the corner.

```
UK release      June 1967    Decca    LK 4879
Not released in US

1. Runaway (Del Shannon/Max Crook)
2. My Mind's Eye (Ronnie Lane/Steve Marriott)
3. Yesterday, Today And Tomorrow (Ronnie Lane/Steve Marriott)
4. That Man (Ronnie Lane/Steve Marriott)
5. My Way Of Giving (Ronnie Lane/Steve Marriott)
6. Hey Girl (Ronnie Lane/Steve Marriott)
7. Tell Me Have You Ever Seen Me (Steve Marriott)

8. Come Back And Take This Hurt Off Me (Ronald Miller)
9. All Or Nothing (Ronnie Lane/Steve Marriott)
10. Baby Don't Do It (Brian & Eddie Holland/Lamont Dozier)
11. Plum Nellie (Ronnie Lane/Steve Marriott)
12. Sha La La La Lee (Kenny Lynch/Mort Shuman)
13. You Really Got A Hold On Me (Smokey Robinson)
14. Whatcha Gonna Do About It (Brian Potter/Ian Samwell)

Steve Marriott: vocals, guitar, producer / Ian McLagan: keyboards, vocals / Ronnie Lane: bass guitar, vocals, producer / Kenney Jones: drums / Jimmy Winston: keyboards (14), guitar, vocals (10) / Ian Samwell: producer / Kenny Lynch: producer / Don Arden: producer
```

MOBY GRAPE

Moby Grape, with music driven by three interlocking electric guitars, presented a high energy version of the San Francisco sound. The group played songs that if they had been made ten or fifteen years later would have been described as 'power pop', albeit tinged with a little country, and with a couple of slower performances for contrast. The group's first album is that rare thing, a record with no weak tracks. In recognition of this, Columbia decided to issue no fewer than five singles,

| US release | June 1967 | Columbia | CS 9498 / CL 2698 |
| UK release | June 1967 | CBS | (S)BPG 63090 |

1. Hey Grandma (Don Stevenson/Jerry Miller)
2. Mr Blues (Bob Mosley)
3. Fall On You (Peter Lewis)
4. 8:05 (Don Stevenson/Jerry Miller)
5. Come In The Morning (Bob Mosley)
6. Omaha (Skip Spence)
7. Naked If I Want To (Jerry Miller)
8. Someday (Skip Spence/Don Stevenson/Jerry Miller)
9. Ain't No Use (Don Stevenson/Jerry Miller)
10. Sitting BY The Window (Peter Lewis)
11. Changes (Don Stevenson/Jerry Miller)
12. Lazy Me (Bob Mosley)
13. Indifference (Skip Spence)

Peter Lewis: guitar, vocals / Jerry Miller: guitar, vocals / Skip Spence: guitar, vocals / Bob Mosley: bass guitar, vocals / Don Stevenson: drums, vocals / David Rubinson: producer

simultaneously with the album, comprising ten of the tracks. Unfortunately, the radio stations in America and the record-buying public decided that this was a matter of distinct overkill and reacted with the indifference that was, ironically enough, the title of one of the tracks. Neither the singles nor the album sold very well. The exhilarating *Omaha,* with 'classic hit single' written all over it, nevertheless only reached number eighty-eight in the Billboard chart, although this was better than any of its companion singles. The album struggled to number twenty-four and hardly sold at all in the UK.

THE HOLLIES   EVOLUTION

| UK release | June 1967 | Parlophone | PCS/PMC 7022 |
| US release | June 1967 | Epic | LN24/BN26 315 |

three tracks omitted, Carrie Anne added

1. Then The Heartaches Begin
2. Stop Right There
3. Water On The Brain
4. Lullaby To Tim
5. Have You Ever Loved Somebody?
6. You Need Love
7. Rain On The Window
8. Heading For A Fall
9. Ye Olde Toffee Shoppe
10. When Your Light Turned On
11. Leave Me
12. The Games We Play

All compositions by Allan Clarke/Tony Hicks/Graham Nash

Allan Clarke: vocals, harmonica / Graham Nash: vocals, guitar / Tony Hicks: guitar, vocals / Bernie Calvert: bass guitar, harpsichord (9) / Bobby Elliott: drums (4,5,10) / Elton John: organ (11) / Dougie Wright: drums / Mitch Mitchell: drums / Clem Cattini: drums / additional instruments directed by Mike Vickers / Ron Richards: producer

The Hollies recorded their *Evolution* LP at EMI's Abbey Road studios at the same time as the Beatles were working on *Sgt Pepper,* and there are hints in places that the Hollies were aware of what was taking place next door. They try hard to vary the instrumental sounds from track to track and apart from a guitar solo on *When Your Light Turned On,* all the breaks are played by session musicians on brass instruments, or fifes, or bass harmonica, or gypsy violin. The sliding vocals that punctuate *Water On The Brain* provide a touch of psychedelia to go with the cover and Graham Nash's voice on *Lullaby To Tim* is treated to give it a peculiar warbling quality. The songs are distinctive enough to stand these additions without being overwhelmed and overall the Hollies are managing to rise to the challenges set by the Beatles recordings during the previous year, even if *Evolution* cannot hope to compete with *Sgt Pepper.*

DAVID BOWIE

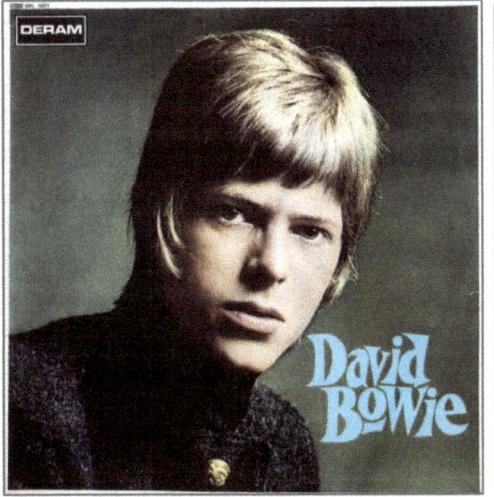

| UK release | June 1967 | Deram | SML/DML 1007 |
| US release | August 1967 | Deram | DES 1800300 /DE 16003 |

tracks 6 and 13 omitted

1. Uncle Arthur
2. Sell Me A Coat
3. Rubber Band
4. Love You Till Tuesday
5. There Is A Happy Land
6. We Are Hungry Men
7. When I Live My Dream
8. Little Bombardier
9. Silly Boy Blue
10. Come And Buy My Toys
11. Join The Gang
12. She's Got Medals
13. Maid Of Bond Street
14. Please Mr Gravedigger

All compositions by David Bowie

David Bowie: vocals, arranger / Big Jim Sullivan: guitar, sitar / Derek Boyes: organ / Dek Fearnley: bass guitar, arranger / John Eager: drums / Mike Vernon: producer

David Bowie issued eight singles between 1964 and 1967, many of them as the singer with different rhythm and blues groups. None was successful. The music on his first solo album is not rhythm and blues. The songs are given sparse orchestral arrangements, allowing Bowie's voice to dominate, as he presents what seems like a cabaret performance. It is as though these are extracts from a stage musical production, albeit one whose plot remains impossibly diverse and obscure. The closest comparison is with the work of Jacques Brel, except that these songs do not have the emotional impact of the Belgian singer songwriter's work. The album is nevertheless an extraordinarily bold venture for someone who has yet to find an audience, but it is not at all a recipe for any kind of commercial success. The record made no impact at the time of its release, but has to be included here because of what we know about David Bowie's subsequent career.

CATHY BERBERIAN   BEATLES ARIAS

```
UK release      June 1967     Polydor    583 702
US release      c.June 1967   Fontana    SRF 67564
                                         as REVOLUTION

1. Ticket To Ride
2. I Want To Hold Your Hand
3. Michelle
4. Eleanor Rigby
5. Yellow Submarine
6. Here There And Everywhere

7. Help!
8. You've Got To Hide Your Love Away
9. Yesterday
10. Can't Buy Me Love
11. Girl
12. A Hard Day's Night

All compositions by John Lennon/Paul McCartney

Cathy Berberian: vocals / Guy Boyer: harpsichord, organ,
arranger / string quartet / wind quintet
```

The late Cathy Berberian was a soprano singer who specialised in the avant-garde, so her decision to record an album of Beatles songs and release it as her first recital seemed like an unexpected side-project. The songs are given pseudo-baroque chamber arrangements, with *Eleanor Rigby*, which used strings when recorded by the Beatles, keeping close to the original (although *Yesterday* uses a different string part to the one conceived by George Martin). Cathy Berberian sings the melodies note-perfect, taking the trouble to enunciate the words very clearly indeed. One suspects that she is well aware of the comic aspect of what she is doing, something that is taken up by Gerald Scarfe in the design he has created for the album cover. In its own way, *Beatles Arias* is as much an avant-garde exercise for Cathy Berberian as her performances of works by her former husband, Luciano Berio (which also have their comic moments). Certainly it emphasises the impact that the Beatles were making on the wider world of the Arts.

CAPTAIN BEEFHEART & HIS MAGIC BAND   SAFE AS MILK

```
UK release      June 1967     Pye        NPL 281110
US release      June 1967     Buddah     BDS 5001 / BDM 1001

1. Sure 'Nuff 'N Yes I Do (Don Van Vliet/Herb Bermann)
2. Zig Zag Wanderer (Don Van Vliet/Herb Bermann)
3. Call On Me (Don Van Vliet)
4. Dropout Boogie (Don Van Vliet/Herb Bermann)
5. I'm Glad (Don Van Vliet)
6. Electricity (Don Van Vliet/Herb Bermann)

7. Yellow Brick Road (Don Van Vliet/Herb Bermann)
8. Abba Zaba (Don Van Vliet)
9. Plastic Factory (Don Van Vliet/Herb Bermann/Jerry Handley)
10. Where There's Woman (Don Van Vliet/Herb Bermann)
11. Grown So Ugly (Robert Pete Williams)
12. Autumn's Child (Don Van Vliet/Herb Bermann)

Don Van Vliet (Captain Beefheart): vocals, harmonica, marimba,
shenai / Alex St Clair Snouffer: guitar, bass guitar, percussion,
vocals / Ry Cooder: guitar, bass guitar, percussion / Jerry Handley:
bass guitar, vocals / John French: drums, vocals / Samuel Hoffman:
theremin (6,12) / Russ Titelman: guitar (12) / Milt Holland:
percussion (2,4,8) / Taj Mahal: percussion (7) / Richard Perry:
harpsichord (3), producer / Bob Krasnow: producer
```

Captain Beefheart and his Magic Band started as a more or less straightforward rhythm and blues band, for which the Captain's gruff singing voice, reminiscent of Howlin' Wolf, was a considerable asset. They issued two singles for A&M in 1966, but by the time of the first album, made for a different company, were already starting to move away from obvious interpretations of the blues. The band delights in subverting the listeners' expectations, as when *Yellow Brick Road* 'explains' the theremin with a distinct touch of humour, when *I'm Glad* brings in a surprising doo-wop throw-back, or when the impetus of *Dropout Boogie* is deliberately sabotaged by somewhat bizarre piano-led inserts. Overall, however, one suspects that the tendencies of Don Van Vliet (Captain Beefheart himself) to introduce more extreme elements are kept in check by the presence of guitarist Ry Cooder, already a fine musician, but one with a greater respect for tradition. The track *Electricity* provides the clearest indication of what was to come later, with its stop-start rhythms, its runaway theremin, and a lead vocal delivered in two voices so distinct as to give the impression that different singers are involved. *Safe As Milk* serves well as an easy introduction to the music of a band and an artist that would soon become very much more challenging.

KALEIDOSCOPE   SIDE TRIPS

US release   June 1967   Epic   BN 26304/LN24304
Not released in UK

1. Egyptian Gardens (Solomon Feldthouse)
2. If The Night (Chris Darrow)
3. Hesitation Blues (Charlie Poole)
4. Please (Mark Feedman/Solomon Feldthouse)
5. Keep Your Mind Open (Chris Darrow)

6. Pulsating Dream (Chris Darrow/David Lindley/Solomon Feldthouse)
7. Oh Death (Doc Boggs)
8. Come On In (Traditional)
9. Why Try (David Lindley)
10. Minnie The Moocher (Cab Calloway/Clarence Gaskill/Irving Mills)

Solomon Feldthouse: vocals, saz, bouzouki, dobro, vina, oud, doumbek, dulcimer, violin, guitar / David Lindley: guitar, mandolin, banjo, violin / Fenrus Epp: violin, viola, bass guitar, piano, organ, harmonica / Chris Darrow: vocals, bass guitar, mandolin, guitar / John Vidican: drums, timpani / Barry Friedman: producer

The American group Kaleidoscope, whose lead singer Solomon Feldthouse had spent six years living in Turkey, introduced a pronounced Middle Eastern flavour to rock music. *Egyptian Gardens*, the opening track of the group's first album, *Side Trips*, is as startling a world music fusion as was the Beatles' *Within You Without You,* issued the same month. The other tracks are less explicit in their cross-culture aspirations than this but most of them still succeed in introducing a remarkably exotic flavour. The members of the band perform on a large variety of stringed instruments, some of them making their first appearance on a rock album. In this way, Kaleidoscope functions as an American version of Britain's Incredible String Band. Even in 1967, the year of *Sgt Pepper's Lonely Hearts Club Band* and *Are You Experienced,* Kaleidoscope struggled to find an audience for its daring, innovative music, although the album sold well enough for the group to be able to make several more, building on the fine achievement of the debut.

THE RED CRAYOLA   THE PARABLE OF ARABLE LAND

The songs on the first album by the Red Crayola are layered between a series of noise celebrations, all titled *Free Form Freak-Out,* although they are different recordings. These are the work of a fifty-piece ensemble given the name 'The Familiar Ugly', friends of the band who were handed instruments if they wanted them and instructed to simply make

US release   June 1967   International Artists   IA-LP 2
Not released in UK

1. Free Form Freak-Out
2. Hurricane Fighter Plane
3. Free Form Freak-Out
4. Transparent Radiation
5. Free Form Freak-Out
6. War Sucks
7. Free Form Freak-Out

8. Free Form Freak-Out
9. Pink Stainless Tail
10. Free Form Freak-Out
11. Parable Of Arable Land
12. Free Form Freak-Out
13. Former Reflections Enduring Doubt

All compositions by the Red Crayola

Mayo Thompson: guitar, vocals / Steve Cunningham: bass guitar / Rick Barthelme: drums / The Familiar Ugly: assorted instruments and percussion / Roky Erickson: organ (2), harmonica (4) / Lelan Rogers: producer

whatever sounds they wanted to make, without attempting a melody or any coherence. The result is an American equivalent of the music created by AMM and Gruppo Di Improvvisazione Nuova Consonanza, albeit created by people who are not professional musicians and therefore lacking much in the way of subtlety. Many listeners would argue, of course, that noise is noise, but the kind produced by the Familiar Ugly has a relentless density not much favoured by the Europeans. The Red Crayola's own songs incorporate a noise element as well, so that there is no great contrast in effect between the album's alternating layers, apart from the presence or absence of vocals. The only precedent for rock music that deliberately tries to sound ugly, with all the instruments distorted to a greater or lesser extent, lies in the long tracks included on the Mothers of Invention album, *Freak Out!,* an album that *The Parable Of Arable Land* comes close to in terms of sheer impact, even if the Red Crayola proved to be much less influential than Frank Zappa.

ADRIAN HENRI & ROGER McGOUGH   THE INCREDIBLE NEW LIVERPOOL SCENE

The rhythms and the rhymes of poetry have long been an inspiration for composers of all kinds of music, who have explored ways of combining the two art forms. A particularly tight bond between poetry and music was achieved when the music started to be rock. This was the underlying basis for much of Bob Dylan's output, as was explicitly recognised when

the songwriter was awarded the Nobel Prize for Literature in 2016. In the UK, two poetry anthologies were published in early 1967, featuring the work of Liverpool poets Roger McGough, Adrian Henri, and Brian Patten. The fact that they were from the home of the Beatles was undoubtedly a factor in their gaining a publishing deal. *The Mersey Sound*, published by Penguin Books as number ten in its series of *Penguin Modern Poets*, achieved a rapid success that must have surprised all concerned, eventually selling around half a million copies. *The Liverpool Scene*, edited by Edward Lucie-Smith, sold much less well, but provided a title and a cover design for the LP, in which Henri and McGough were accompanied by the acoustic guitar playing of Andy Roberts. It was Henri who made most effort to work closely with the guitar playing, with the result that some of his performances have the character of songs, in which the lines just happen to be spoken. Aware of a certain lineage in this respect (from Christopher Bouchillon in 1926, through Woody Guthrie and Lonnie Donegan, to Bob Dylan himself), Henri presented one of the tracks as a talking blues – *Adrian Henri's Talking After Christmas Blues*. The album is the first stage in what turned out to be a fascinating series of poetry-and-music fusion works for both of these major poets.

```
UK release      c.June 1967    CBS    BPG 63045
US release      c.June 1967    Epic   LN 24336   different cover

1. Knees Down Mother Brown
2. I Say I Say I Say
3. For You, Everything's Gonna Be All Right
4. My Johnny Joined The Army/Let's Do It While We're Waiting/Poem
                                        For National LSD Week
5. Let Me Die A Young Man's Death
6. The New 'Our Times'
7. Adrian Henri's Talking After Christmas Blues
8. Don't Worry, Everything's Going To Be All Right
9. Classroom Blues

10. Tonight At Noon
11. Love Is
12. In The Midnight Hour
13. The Day Before Yesterday
14. Mother, There's A Strange Man Waiting At The Door
15. Mother, The Wardrobe Is Full Of Infantrymen
16. At Lunchtime, A Story Of Love
17. Mrs Albion, You've Got A Lovely Daughter
18. Car Crash Blues
19. Adrian Henri's Last Will And Testament

Poems on tracks 1-5, 13-16 by Roger McGough / Poems on tracks
6-12,17-19 by Adrian Henri / All music composed by Andy Roberts

Roger McGough: voice / Adrian Henri: voice / Andy Roberts: guitar /
Hal Shaper: producer
```

THE SMALL FACES   SMALL FACES

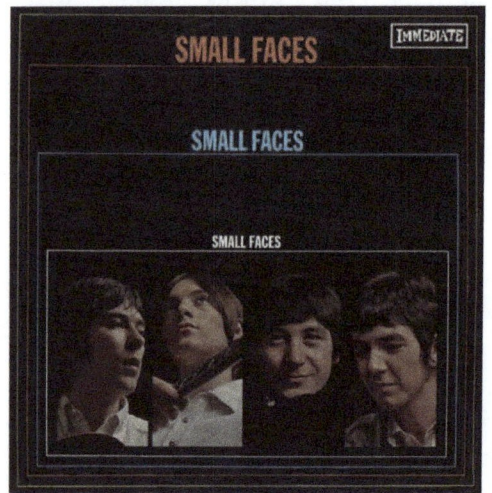

```
UK release      June 1967        Immediate    IMSP/IMLP 008
US release      December 1967    Immediate    Z12 52 002
different cover and title, THERE ARE BUT FOUR SMALL FACES, some
track differences

1. (Tell Me) Have You Ever Seen Me
2. Something I Want To Tell You
3. Feeling Lonely
4. Happy Boys Happy
5. Things Are Going To Get Better
6. My Way Of Giving
7. Green Circles (Steve Marriott/Ronnie Lane/Michael O'Sullivan)

8. Become Like You
9. Get Yourself Together
10. All Our Yesterdays
11. Talk To You
12. Show Me The Way
13. Up The Wooden Hills To Bedfordshire (Ian McLagan)
14. Eddie's Dreaming (Steve Marriott/Ronnie Lane/Ian McLagan)

All compositions by Steve Marriott and Ronnie Lane except where stated

Steve Marriott: vocals, guitar, piano, producer / Ian McLagan:
keyboards, bass guitar, guitar, vocals / Ronnie Lane: bass guitar, vocals,
producer / Kenney Jones: drums / uncredted brass and flute on track 14
```

Just three weeks after the Decca release, *From The Beginning*, came the Small Faces' proper second album, issued on Andrew Oldham's Immediate label and, confusingly, given the same title as the group's first LP. All of the songs are written by the group's members and they make a solid, if unspectacular collection, with the R&B largely abandoned in favour of a more generalised pop-rock approach. The singles issued during the year – *Here Come The Nice, Tin Soldier,* and, especially, *Itchycoo Park* (complete with its innovative use of the phasing effect) – are very much more distinguished than anything on the album and the American version includes all three of them, making it a much stronger record. Overall, *Small Faces* keeps the group's momentum going, but its failure to break into the top ten in the UK album chart was not altogether surprising, at a time when the music bar had been raised by the competition to a level that the Small Faces were struggling to reach.

THE ROLLING STONES   FLOWERS

Flowers is a compilation album released in the US, comprising a ragbag assortment of singles, out-takes, and tracks left off the American versions of recent British LPs. A UK edition of the record was prepared, but used for export only and not given a full commercial release. It is tempting to imagine that *Flowers* was intended as a Rolling Stones response to

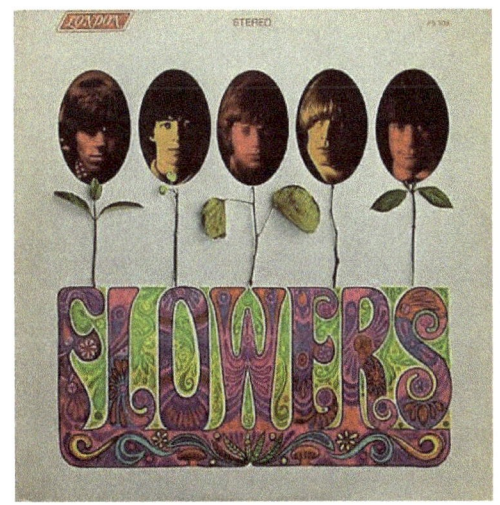

| US release | June 1967 | London | PS 509 / LL 3509 |
| UK release | June 1967 | Decca | SKL/LK 4888 export only |

1. Ruby Tuesday
2. Have You Seen Your Mother, Baby, Standing In The Shadow?
3. Let's Spend The Night Together
4. Lady Jane
5. Out Of Time
6. My Girl (Ronnie White/Smokey Robinson)
7. Back Street Girl
8. Please Go Home
9. Mother's Little Helper
10. Take It Or Leave It
11. Ride On, Baby
12. Sittin' On A Fence

All compositions by Mick Jagger/Keith Richards except track 6

Mick Jagger: vocals, percussion / Keith Richards: guitar, vocals, bass (1), bass guitar (3) / Brian Jones: guitar, keyboards, bass guitar, koto (10,11), dulcimer (4), recorder (1) / Bill Wyman: bass guitar, organ, percussion, vocals, bass (1) / Charlie Watts: drums / Andrew Loog Oldham: producer

Sgt Pepper, before the group had managed to record a new album to do the job properly, but realistically, the release came too quickly after the Beatles album for it to have been really designed in this way. The song selection works surprisingly well as a coherent album, if only because the Mick Jagger/Keith Richards songwriting team was producing some very strong material at this time. With a cover design that slips comfortably into the 'summer of love' idea, and a wide variety of pop and rock styles on offer, the album makes the Rolling Stones seem to have judged the music public's expectations exactly right for what is presented as a new record release. *Flowers* climbed to number three in the US album chart and earned itself a gold disc award.

DONOVAN   SUNSHINE SUPERMAN

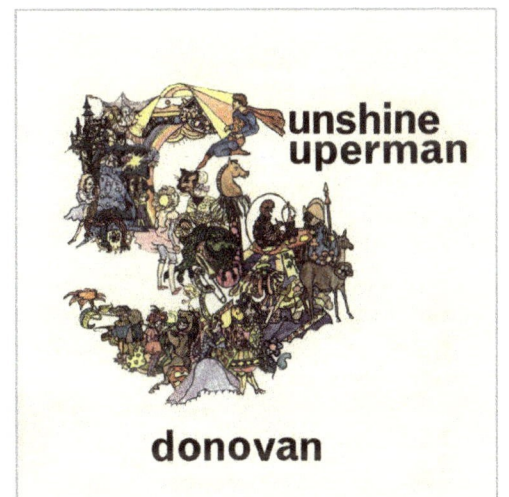

| UK release | June 1967 | Pye | NPL 18181 |

Not released in US

1. Sunshine Superman
2. Legend Of A Girl Child Linda
3. The Observation
4. Guinevere
5. Celeste
6. Writer In The Sun
7. Season Of The Witch
8. Hampstead Incident
9. Sand And Foam
10. Young Girl Blues
11. Three Kingfishers
12. Bert's Blues

All compositions by Donovan Leitch

Donovan: vocals, guitar / other musicians as on the US editions of Sunshine Superman and Mellow Yellow.

With the record company dispute regarding rights to Donovan's music resolved, Pye was finally able to release the singer's recent music in the UK. The album titled *Sunshine Superman* takes the best tracks on the US *Sunshine Superman* and *Mellow Yellow* albums, combining them on a single LP. Released just a few weeks after *Sgt Pepper*, the impression is given that Donovan is deliberately producing a folk equivalent of it, whereas in reality, of course, the music originates from the previous August and March, some time before the appearance of the Beatles album. But the approach is the same, with Donovan creating songs in a wide variety of styles, using instrumentation carefully tailored to each song to make them distinctive and different. The song selection means that two excellent albums are turned into one that is a masterpiece. The album fared rather less well commercially than might have been expected – a collection of remarkable songs by an artist who was a frequent visitor to the singles charts somehow failing to get into the top twenty albums – but it remains one of the most essential recordings of the period. Curiously, although stereo mixes of the the songs were available, Pye chose to issue a mono version only.

THE STONE PONEYS   EVERGREEN VOL.2

The Stone Poneys, a folk rock trio from Los Angeles, made three albums during 1967 and early 1968, of which *Evergreen*, the middle release, achieved the greatest success. *Different Drum*, composed by Mike Nesmith before he joined the Monkees, was a top twenty hit in the US, but with singer Linda Ronstadt attracting the most attention (Bobby Kimmel and Kenny Edwards did not play on the track), it had the effect of hastening the end of the group. Linda Ronstadt's voice, of course, is a wondrous thing, smooth and seductive, and making it fairly inevitable that she would become a big star. The gentle arrangements used on the album, many of them with added strings that turn the music into baroque pop, leave her as the major focus for the music, as the album cover recognises. For the third record, she was elevated to being the primary named artist and, after that, she was gone, launching her highly successful solo career.

JAKE HOLMES   THE ABOVE GROUND SOUND OF

```
US release    June 1967    Tower (S)T 5079
Not released in UK

1. Lonely
2. Did You Know
3. She Belongs To Me
4. Too Long
5. Genuine Imitation Life
6. Dazed And Confused
7. Penny's
8. Hard To Keep My Mind On You
9. Wish I Was Anywhere Else
10. Signs Of Age

All compositions by Jake Holmes

Jake Holmes: vocals, guitar / Tim Irwin: guitar / Rick Randle: bass guitar / Maximillian Productions: producer
```

```
US release    June 1967    (S)T 2763
Not released in UK

1. December Dream (John Braheny)
2. Song About The Rain (Steve Gillette)
3. Autumn Afternoon (Kenny Edwards/Bobby Kimmel)
4. I've Got To Know (Pam Polland)
5. Evergreen Part One (Kenny Edwards/Bobby Kimmel)
6. Evergreen Part Two (Kenny Edwards/Bobby Kimmel)
7. Different Drum (Mike Nesmith)
8. Driftin' (Kenny Edwards/Bobby Kimmel)
9. One For One (Al Silverman/Austin DeLone)
10. Back On The Street Again (Steve Gillette)
11. Toys In Time (Kenny Edwards/Bobby Kimmel)
12. New Hard Times (Mayne Smith/Bobby Kimmel)

Linda Ronstadt: vocals / Bobby Kimmel: guitar, vocals / Kenny Edwards: guitar, sitar / Dennis Budimir: guitar / Peter Childs: guitar / Steve Gillette: guitar, vocals / Bernie Leadon: guitar (7) / Don Randi: harpsichord / Joe Osborn: bass guitar / Jimmy Bond: bass. arranger / Jim Gordon: drums / Sidney Sharp, Harry Hyams, Jesse Ehrlich, Leonard Malersky, Norman Botnick, Robert Sushel, Stanley Plummer, William Kurasch: strings / Nick Venet: producer
```

Jake Holmes is an inventive singer songwriter, performing with a skilful, jazz-inspired lead guitarist and a bass player, but no drums. His rather bland singing voice means that the songs make less impression than they deserve to, but the album is nevertheless very interesting for modern listeners because it includes a song with the title *Dazed and Confused*. The Yardbirds added this to their live set after Holmes had performed as a support act for them, and when the group metamorphosed into Led Zeppelin, the song was included on the new group's first album, with a Jimmy Page writing credit. He had indeed changed some of the words and given the music a makeover, but the result was a new arrangement of a song that very definitely belonged to Jake Holmes. Many years later, the matter was settled out of court for an undisclosed sum. Holmes now gets his writing credit on the *Led Zeppelin* album, but Jimmy Page's name continues to appear there as well. Page, of course, was involved in a similar radical rearrangement of an original song when Joe Cocker released his own version of *With A Little Help From My Friends*, but Page was unable to pull off the trick he had managed with Jake Holmes with the rather more powerful John Lennon and Paul McCartney.

DUKE ELLINGTON   FAR EAST SUITE

```
US release    June 1967    RCA    LSP/LPM-3782
UK release    June 1967    RCA    SF/RD-7894

1. Tourist Point Of View
2. Bluebird Of Delhi (Mynah)
3. Isfahan
4. Depk
5. Mount Harissa
6. Blue Pepper (Far East Of The Blues)
7. Agra
8. Amad
9. Ad Lib On Nippon

All compositions by Duke Ellington/Billy Strayhorn (track 9 Duke Ellington alone)

Duke Ellington: piano / Mercer Ellington: trumpet, flugelhorn / Herbie Jones: trumpet, flugelhorn / Cat Anderson: trumpet / Cootie Williams: trumpet / Lawrence Brown: trombone / Buster Cooper: trombone / Chuck Connors: trombone / Johnny Hodges: alto saxophone / Russell Procope: alto saxophone, clarinet / Jimmy Hamilton: tenor saxophone, clarinet / Paul Gonsalves: tenor saxophone / Harry Carney: baritone saxophone / John Lamb: bass / Rufus Jones: drums / Brad McKuen: producer
```

Jazz pianist and composer, Edward 'Duke' Ellington, formed his first professional band, the Duke's Serenaders, in 1917, the year that the earliest jazz records were released, and made his own first recordings in 1924. During the thirties, the big band swing music in which he specialised became very popular and the Duke Ellington Orchestra became a considerable star attraction. At the same time, in the manner of the Beatles some thirty years later, Ellington became adept at stretching the form. He created a number of elaborate musical works, incorporating improvisation and enabling his musicians to display their expertise, both within the ensemble and as individual players, to the point where he established the reputation of being the finest and most vital composer working in jazz. He is the only jazz musician judged worthy to be included in Alex Ross' academic history of what he would call the 'serious music' of the twentieth century, *The Rest Is Noise*.

Remarkably, after jazz became replaced by rock 'n' roll as the dominant popular music genre, Ellington was able to keep working with a big band, despite financial difficulties that famously, as reported by Frank Zappa, led to him having to endure the humiliation of begging for a ten dollar advance from George Wein, organiser of an American jazz package tour in 1969 and also the man who ran the Newport Jazz Festival. His musicians were nevertheless extremely loyal and many of the performers on the *Far East Suite* album had been with him for thirty years or more. Baritone saxophonist Harry Carney, alto saxophonist Johnny Hodges, and trumpeter Cootie Williams all first played with the Duke Ellington Orchestra in the late twenties. During 1963, the Orchestra undertook a world tour, and the pieces included in the *Far East Suite* were largely composed during this, by Ellington in collaboration with his frequent writing partner, Billy Strayhorn. The Asian influence is subtle, but definitely present in some of the melody lines, although the rich voicings and harmonies are those that characterise all of Ellington's work. The soloists – typically just a couple on each track – emerge from the ensemble to deliver some sparkling playing, though always in keeping with the flavour set by the composed parts. None of the music is particularly fast, but all the tracks dovetail together very well, resulting in one of Duke Ellington's most impressive sets. Although he does not play here, it is interesting to note that drummer Sam Woodyard, included in the Orchestra when it played in the UK in early 1966, was an early user of a double bass drum set-up. He inspired Ginger Baker and Keith Moon to copy the idea after seeing him perform in Birmingham, on the only occasion during the Who/Graham Bond Organization tour in the same period when the drummers had a night off. It should be no surprise that two particularly influential rock musicians at this time should have been interested in attending a live concert by one of the greatest jazz bands of all, exploring influences that they in turn could bring to their own music.

BOOKER T & THE MG's   HIP HUG-HER

US release   June 1967   Stax   (S) 717
UK release   June 1967   Atco   228004   as GET READY different cover

1. Hip Hug-Her
2. Soul Sanction
3. Get Ready (Smokey Robinson)
4. More (Marcello Ciorciolini/Nino Oliviero/Norman Newell/Riz Ortolani)
5. Double Or Nothing
6. Carnaby St.
7. Slim Jenkins' Place
8. Pigmy (Billy Larkin/Henry Swarn/Mel Brown)
9. Groovin' (Eddie Brigati/Felix Cavaliere)
10. Booker's Notion
11. Sunny (Bobby Hebb)

All compositions by Booker T & The MG's except where stated

Booker T Jones: organ, piano / Steve Cropper: guitar, piano (9), percussion (10) / Donald Dunn: bass guitar / Al Jackson: drums / Jim Stewart: producer

The compelling instrumental R&B played by Booker T & the MG's hardly changed at all from its beginnings with the 1962 hit single and accompanying album, *Green Onions*. *Hip Hug-Her* was the group's fifth album and the one that returned it to the charts, with both the album itself and its two hit singles, the title track and *Groovin'*, doing well. By this time, the quartet had played as backing group for many Stax artists as well as performing on its own and could doubtless play this kind of undemanding material in its sleep. It is a sound that works, however, as Booker T & the MG's deliver their strong melodies with short solos that let the rhythm take most of the strain.

THE BEACH BOYS   BEST OF VOLUME 2

Brian Wilson was busy making an album to be called *Smile*, intended as a major artistic statement and his personal masterwork, but he was having trouble finishing it. Capitol took the opportunity to release a second volume of Beach Boys hits, ignoring any

UK release   July 1967   Capitol   (S)T20956
A US album with the same title, but a very different, inferior track selection, was released in July 1967   Capitol   (D)T 2706

1. Surfer Girl (Brian Wilson)
2. Don't Worry Baby (Brian Wilson/Roger Christian)
3. Wendy (Brian Wilson/Mike Love)
4. When I Grow Up (To Be A Man) (Brian Wilson/Mike Love)
5. Good To My Baby (Brian Wilson/Mike Love)
6. Dance, Dance, Dance (Brian and Carl Wilson, Mike Love)
7. Then I Kissed Her (Phil Spector/Ellie Greenwich/Chuck Barry)
8. The Girl From New York City (Brian Wilson/Mike Love)
9. Girl Don't Tell Me (Brian Wilson)
10. The Little Girl I Once Knew (Brian Wilson)
11. Mountain Of Love (Harold Dorman)
12. Here Today (Brian Wilson/Tony Asher)
13. Wouldn't It Be Nice (Brian Wilson/Tony Asher/Mike Love)
14. Good Vibrations (Brian Wilson/Mike Love)

Mike Love: vocals / Brian Wilson: vocals, bass guitar, keyboards, producer / Carl Wilson: vocals, guitar / Al Jardine: vocals, guitar / Dennis Wilson: vocals, drums / Bruce Johnston: vocals, keyboards / various session musicians

problems caused by the fact that the best of them had already been issued on Volume One. The track selections chosen for the UK and the US are almost entirely different, with the UK version being very much more to the point. It emerges as a fine collection despite the problems mentioned, especially as it includes one very recent hit, the sublime *Good Vibrations* – one song not included on the US edition of the album.

THE TROGGS   BEST OF

UK release   July 1967   Page One   FOR 001
Not released in US

1. Night Of The Long Grass (Reg Presley)
2. Gonna Make You (Colin Frechter/Larry Page)
3. Anyway That You Want Me (Chip Taylor)
4. 66-5-4-3-2-1 (Reg Presley)
5. I Want You (Colin Frechter/Larry Page)
6. With A Girl Like You (Reg Presley)
7. I Can't Control Myself (Reg Presley)
8. Girl In Black (Colin Frechter/Larry Page)
9. Give It To Me (Reg Presley)
10. You're Lying (Colin Frechter/Larry Page)
11. From Home (Reg Presley)
12. Wild Thing (Chip Taylor)

Reg Presley: vocals, ocarina (12) / Chris Britton: guitar, vocals / Pete Staples: bass guitar, vocals / Ronnie Bond: drums / Larry Page: producer

The Troggs issued *Wild Thing*, a classic slice of rock minimalism, complete with an unusual ocarina solo, as their second single, in the summer of 1966, and watched it climb to the top of the charts (number two in the UK, number one in the US). A British music journalist, expecting the Troggs to be not much more than a one-hit wonder, promised to treat the group to a meal at a top London restaurant if they were still selling records at the end of the following year. The group was able to collect on the promise, but only just – the uncharacteristically mellow *Love Is All Around* was the last substantial hit, towards the end of 1967. The Troggs' simple music is prototype heavy rock for the most part, sounding forceful but without making demands on the listener's close attention. Of the many groups credited with anticipating seventies punk, the claim of the Troggs is as good as any.

JOHN MAYALL'S BLUESBREAKERS   CRUSADE

UK release   July 1967   Decca   SKL/LK 4890
US release   July 1967   London   PS/LL3 529

1. Oh Pretty Woman (A C Williams/Albert King)
2. Stand Back Baby (John Mayall)
3. My Time After Awhile (Bob Geddins/Buddy Guy)
4. Snowy Wood (John Mayall/Mick Taylor)
5. Man Of Stone (Eddie Kirkland)
6. Tears In My Eyes (John Mayall)
7. Driving Sideways (Freddie King)
8. The Death Of J B Lenoir (John Mayall)
9. I Can't Quit You Baby (Otis Rush/Willie Dixon)
10. Streamline (John Mayall)
11. Me And My Woman (Gene Barge/Little Joe Blue)
12. Checking Up On My Baby (Sonny Boy Williamson)

John Mayall: vocals, keyboards, guitar, harmonica / Mick Taylor: guitar / Chris Mercer: tenor saxophone / Rip Kant: baritone saxophone / John McVie: bass guitar / Keef Hartley: drums / Mike Vernon: producer

Another album by John Mayall, this time with an almost entirely new band line-up. Despite assuring fans in the sleeve notes to the previous record, *A Hard Road*, that he had no intention of making brass instruments a permanent feature of the Bluesbreakers, that is exactly what Mayall does on *Crusade*. The guitarist is now eighteen-year-old Mick Taylor, originally discovered at a gig when, as a member of the audience, he volunteered to stand in for an absent Eric Clapton. He is not entirely a match for either Eric Clapton or Peter Green on *Crusade*, although he certainly acquits himself well. The title of the album ties in with Mayall's sleeve notes, in which he laments the acclaim given to pop musicians who do not play with much skill, and offers the blues as a music form whose exponents are much more gifted. He lists the key in which each song is played, in order to emphasise that they are all different and include some that are relatively difficult for inexperienced musicians to play. The band delivers convincing covers of some blues originals as well as some songs written by Mayall himself and overall the album shows how John Mayall, with the support of an accomplished band, is developing into a blues interpreter of considerable authority.

CANNED HEAT

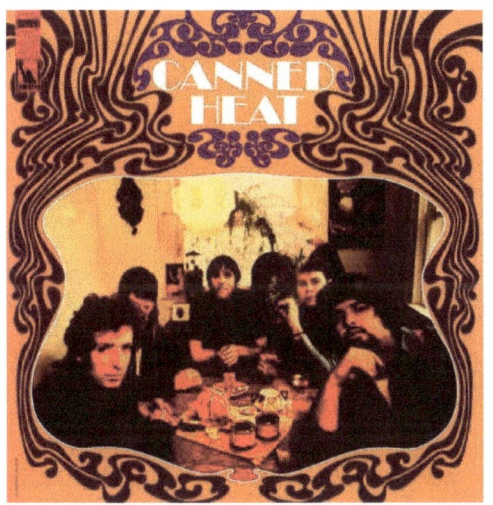

| US release | July 1967 | Liberty | LST 7526/LRP 3526 |
| UK release | July 1967 | Liberty | LBS/LBL 83059 |

1. Rollin' And Tumblin' (Muddy Waters)
2. Bullfrog Blues (Canned Heat)
3. Evil Is Going On (Willie Dixon)
4. Goin' Down Slow (James Oden)
5. Catfish Blues (Robert Petway)
6. Dust My Broom (Elmore James/Robert Johnson)
7. Help Me (Ralph Bass/Sonny Boy Williamson/Willie Dixon)
8. Big Road Blues (Canned Heat)
9. The Story Of My Life (Eddie Guitar Slim Jones)
10. The Road Song (Canned Heat)
11. Rich Woman (Dorothy La Bostrie/McKinley J Millet)

Bob Hite: vocals / Al Wilson: vocals, guitar, harmonica / Henry Vestine: guitar / Larry Taylor: bass guitar / Frank Cook: drums / Ray Johnson: piano / Cal Carter: producer

Bob Hite and Henry Vestine were enthusiasts of the blues and had amassed a huge collection of original 78 rpm recordings. Vestine was friends with guitarist John Fahey and the pair were primarily responsible for veteran bluesman Skip James recording several LPs through the sixties. Playing the blues themselves, Hite, Vestine, and the other members of Canned Heat, adopt a reverential approach to the material, making little attempt to use the songs they are copying as the basis for any kind of personal virtuosity or innovation. The result is a likeable, but not especially exciting record. *Catfish Blues* is the exception, with the band stretching out and allowing Henry Vestine to deliver a longer improvisation over a sprightly rhythm driven by a single chord. Elsewhere, Vestine turns up the distortion on his guitar on *The Story Of My Life* and *The Road Song*, giving him a more original sound.

OTIS REDDING   LIVE IN EUROPE

| US release | July 1967 | Volt | (S) 416 |
| UK release | July 1967 | Stax | 589 016 |

1. Respect (Otis Redding)
2. Can't Turn You Loose (Otis Redding/Steve Cropper/Smokey Robinson)
3. I've Been Loving You Too Long (Jerry Butler/Otis Redding)
4. My Girl (Ronald White/Smokey Robinson)
5. Shake (Sam Cooke)
6. Satisfaction (Mick Jagger/Keith Richards)
7. Fa-Fa-Fa-Fa (Sad Song) (Otis Redding/Steve Cropper)
8. These Arms Of Mine (Otis Redding)
9. Day Tripper (John Lennon/Paul McCartney)
10. Try A Little Tenderness (Harry Woods/Jimmy Campbell/Reg Connelly)

Otis Redding: vocals / Steve Cropper: guitar / Wayne Jackson: trumpet / Andrew Love: tenor saxophone / Joe Arnold: tenor saxophone / Booker T Jones: organ / Donald 'Duck' Dunn: bass guitar / Al Jackson: drums / Tom Dowd: producer

Otis Redding released three more albums after the ground-breaking *Otis Blue* (one of which, *King And Queen*, was a collection of duets with Carla Thomas), but it was his live performances that cemented his reputation. *Live In Europe* was recorded in March at the Olympia Theatre in Paris, where he was supported by the Mar-Keys, the band heard on the singer's studio albums. *Live In Europe* serves well as a greatest hits collection, with Otis Redding pulling no surprises in his choice of set-list. The sheer energy he applies to the performances, however, with a band that sounds to be perfectly rehearsed, means that these live versions are superior to the original studio recordings, good though these are. For much of the time, Otis Redding does not so much deliver melody as sermonise, but with so much passion that the songs make their impact regardless of the fact that the tunes are more implied than sung. It is clear that the Parisian audience was being given a considerable treat – and a masterclass in the art and dynamics of soul singing.

THE YARDBIRDS   LITTLE GAMES

Soon after the release of the Yardbirds' previous, self-titled album, Paul Samwell-Smith left the group to move into production and session guitarist Jimmy Page was persuaded to join as the new bass guitarist. It was agreed that Chris Dreja would switch to bass as soon as he had learned to play it effectively and for a short time Jimmy Page and Jeff Beck were featured as twin lead guitarists. This was the line-up that recorded the dramatic single, *Happenings Ten Years Time Ago* and the powerful *Stroll On*, included in the Michelangelo Antonioni film, *Blow Up*. When the time came to record the album *Little Games*, however, Jeff Beck had moved on to become a solo artist and Jimmy Page was the only guitarist. The album has its inspired moments, but on the whole it is less than it could have been. Page's guitar playing is a marvel throughout, but it is continually held back by songwriting that is rather weak. Producer Mickie Most's indifference to songs not

THE GOLDEN AGE OF ROCK Volume One 1963-1968

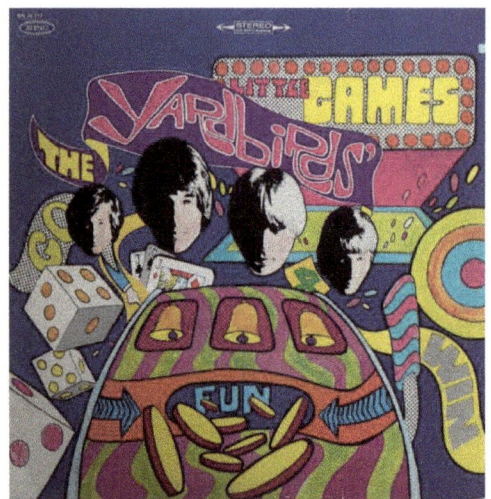

```
US release     July 1967     Epic   BN 26313 / LN 24313
Not released in UK

1.  Little Games (Harold Spiro/Phil Wainman)
2.  Smile On Me (Yardbirds)
3.  White Summer (Jimmy Page)
4.  Tinker, Tailor, Soldier, Sailor (Jim McCarty/Jimmy Page)
5.  Glimpses (Yardbirds)
6.  Drinking Muddy Water (Yardbirds)
7.  No Excess Baggage (Carl D'Errico/Roger Atkins)
8.  Stealing, Stealing (Yardbirds)
9.  Only The Black Rose (Keith Relf)
10. Little Soldier Boy (Jim McCarty/Jimmy Page/Keith Relf)

Keith Relf: vocals, harmonica, percussion / Jimmy Page: guitar / Chris Dreja: bass guitar, vocals / Jim McCarty: drums, vocals / Bobby Gregg: drums (1) / Dougie Wright: drums (1) / John Paul Jones: bass guitar (1,7), cello arrangement (1) / Chris Karan: tablas (3) / Ian Stewart: piano (2,6,8) / unknown oboe (3) / Mickie Most: producer
```

destined to become hit singles does not help. The interesting *White Summer* is an early version of the piece that became *Black Mountain Side*, even if its reliance on an oboe solo sounds odd in this context, while the blues, *Smile On Me*, also has some of the character of a Led Zeppelin prototype. Later in the year, the Yardbirds introduced a song called *Dazed And Confused* into their stage set (adapted from the original version by singer songwriter Jake Holmes) and recorded a single B-side, *Think About It*, that would have been a perfect fit on the first Led Zeppelin album. Meanwhile, with the *Little Games* single failing to gain the chart success of its predecessors, with the commercial failure of an album not even given a release in the UK, and with three further lacklustre pop singles thoroughly deserving to be ignored, the Yardbirds were heading for a sad demise.

SOUNDTRACK   BLOW-UP

```
US release     July 1967     MGM    (S)E-4447 ST
UK release     July 1967     MGM    C(S)-8039

1.  Main Title
2.  Verushka (Part I)
3.  Verushka (Part II)
4.  The Naked Camera
5.  Bring Down The Birds
6.  Jane's Theme
7.  Stroll On (The Yardbirds)
8.  The Thief
9.  The Kiss
10. Curiosity
11. Thomas Studies Photos
12. The Bed
13. End Title

All compositions except track 7 by Herbie Hancock

Herbie Hancock: piano, melodica / Freddie Hubbard: trumpet / Joe Newman: trumpet / Phil Woods: alto saxophone / Joe Henderson: tenor saxophone / Jimmy Smith or Paul Griffin: organ / Jim Hall: guitar / Ron Carter: bass / Jack DeJohnette: drums / Pete Spargo: producer / Track 7: Keith Relf: vocals, harmonica / Jeff Beck: guitar / Jimmy Page: guitar / Chris Dreja: bass guitar / Jim McCarty: drums
```

Producer Michelangelo Antonioni included a short performance by the Yardbirds in his film, *Blow-Up*, miming to their updated version of the rock 'n' roll song, *Train Kept A-Rollin'*, written by Tiny Bradshaw, but made famous by the Johnny Burnette Trio. The performance features both Jeff Beck and Jimmy Page playing lead guitars, blending together and creating an extraordinarily powerful sound. In the film, Beck is playing a cheap semi-acoustic guitar, not used on the recording, because he refused to destroy the expensive Gibson Les Paul that Antonioni wanted him to use – indeed the Yardbirds were not in the habit of destroying any of their equipment in the real world outside the film. The rest of the music is very different, being a set of jazz performances written by Herbie Hancock and played by a band assembled for the purpose. Having said that, it is nevertheless the case that the Ron Carter/Jack DeJohnette rhythm section plays with much more of a rock beat on some of the material than these musicians were accustomed to, and the other performers, most notably including guitarist Jim Hall, rise to the challenge of delivering some pioneering jazz-rock. Sadly, the constraints of the film medium mean that the band does not really stretch out in the way that the music style demands, and most of the tracks fade out early, so that the impact of what is being achieved is considerably reduced. Herbie Hancock himself plays very infrequently, clearly accepting that a band already including both guitar and Hammond organ leaves little space for his piano, although it is when he does perform that the music sounds most like the work of the band providing his main employment, the Miles Davis Quintet.

BERT JANSCH   NICOLA

The opening track of Bert Jansch's fifth album sounds very familiar and gives no indication that the rest of the music is going to sound rather different. Many of the songs are orchestrated with a rhythm section and on two of them Bert Jansch plays an electric guitar, although he still uses his accustomed fingerstyle technique. On *Woe Is Love My Dear*, the bass player

THE GOLDEN AGE OF ROCK Volume One 1963-1968

| UK release | July 1967 | Transatlantic | TRA 157 |

Not released in US

1. Go Your Way My Love (Bert Jansch/Anne Briggs)
2. Woe Is Love My Dear (Bert Jansch)
3. Nicola (Bert Jansch)
4. Come Back Baby (Walter Davis)
5. A Little Sweet Sunshine (Bert Jansch)
6. Love Is Teasing (Traditional)
7. Rabbit Run (Bert Jansch)
8. Life Depends On Love (Bert Jansch)
9. Weeping Willow Blues (Traditional)
10. Box Of Love (Bert Jansch)
11. Wish My Baby Was Here (Bert Jansch)
12. If The World Isn't There (Bert Jansch)

Bert Jansch: vocals, guitar / David Palmer: arranger / Nathan Joseph: producer

is clearly Danny Thompson, while he is joined by a drummer who is presumably Terry Cox on the title track. This pair, working with Alexis Korner at the time, would shortly begin playing with Bert Jansch on a permanent basis. Where Jansch plays solo, he has clearly learned from his friend John Renbourn and is performing blues material. Arguably, a couple of the orchestrated tracks (*Life Depends On Love* and *Wish My Baby Was Here*) try a little too hard to be commercial, although neither was released as a single. Overall, however, *Nicola* is the work of a musician determined to move forward.

THE BEE GEES   BEE GEES 1st

| UK release | July 1967 | Polydor | 582012/583012 |
| US release | August 1967 | Atco | (SD) 33-223 |

1. Turn Of The Century
2. Holiday
3. Red Chair, Fade Away
4. One Minute Woman
5. In My Own Time
6. Every Christian Lion Hearted Man Will Show You
7. Craise Finton Kirk Royal Academy Of Arts
8. New York Mining Disaster 1941
9. Cucumber Castle
10. To Love Somebody
11. I Close My Eyes
12. I Can't See Nobody
13. Please Read Me
14. Close Another Door

All compositions by Barry and Robin Gibb; tracks 6,11,14 also by Maurice Gibb

Barry Gibb: vocals, guitar / Robin Gibb: vocals, organ / Maurice Gibb: vocals, guitar, bass guitar, keyboards / Vince Melouney: guitar / Colin Petersen: drums / Phil Dennys: arrangements (3,4,8,11) / Bill Shepherd: arrangements (1,9.10,12,14) / Ossie Byrne: producer

The group led by three Gibb brothers made two albums in Australia before moving to the UK in order to establish an international music career. The Bee Gees scored a number twelve hit in the UK with *New York Mining Disaster 1941* and Polydor clearly thought that this was sufficient justification for an album. It did indeed sell well, even though *To Love Somebody*, released as a second single (and subsequently earning its place as one of the Bee Gees' most highly regarded early songs), was not a hit. The music on *Bee Gees 1st* is mildly psychedelic, melodic harmony pop, very much in the style of the Beatles, but delivered with rather less energy. It is clear that the Gibbs are talented songwriters, capable of creating songs made to last, even if they are not especially innovative or original. But *Bee Gees 1st* is undoubtedly a fine album, one that would be much more highly regarded if it had been released at any other time than the summer of 1967, when the competition was particularly intense.

THE YOUNG RASCALS   GROOVIN'

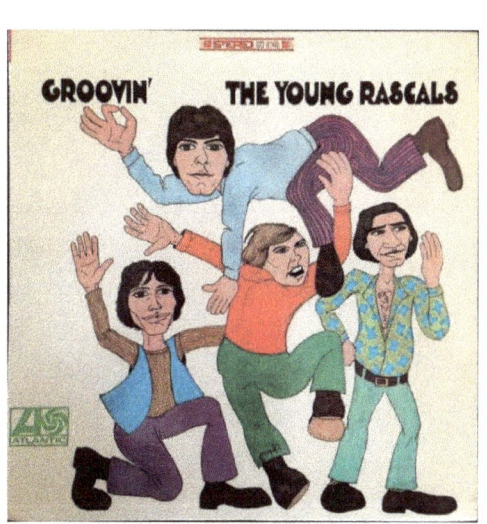

Groovin', with its lazy drum-less rhythm and its accompanying birdsong, is the perfect summer anthem and a well-deserved chart hit in both the US (where it reached number one) and the UK. The songs on the rest of the album demonstrate that the song's success was not a fluke. They are proof that Eddie Brigati and Felix Cavaliere have

| US release | July 1967 | Atlantic | (SD) 8148 |
| UK release | July 1967 | Atlantic | 588074/587074 |

1. A Girl Like You (Eddie Brigati/Felix Cavaliere)
2. Find Somebody (Eddie Brigati/Felix Cavaliere)
3. I'm So Happy Now (Gene Cornish)
4. Sueno (Eddie Brigati/Felix Cavaliere)
5. How Can I Be Sure (Eddie Brigati/Felix Cavaliere)
6. Groovin' (Eddie Brigati/Felix Cavaliere)
7. If You Knew (Eddie Brigati/Felix Cavaliere)
8. I Don't Love You Anymore (Gene Cornish)
9. You Better Run (Eddie Brigati/Felix Cavaliere)
10. A Place In The Sun (Brian Wells/Ronald Miller)
11. It's Love (Eddie Brigati/Felix Cavaliere)

Felix Cavaliere: vocals, keyboards / Eddie Brigati: vocals, percussion / Gene Cornish: vocals, guitar, bass guitar, harmonica / Dino Danelli: drums / David Brigati: vocals / Hubert Laws: flute / Chuck Rainey: bass guitar / Arif Mardin: orchestral arranger / The Young Rascals: producer

developed into a world-class songwriting team. *A Girl Like You* and *How Can I Be Sure* were also big single hits in the US, but several other songs on the album could have done the job just as well. The flute and backwards percussion effects on *It's Love* indicate a willingness to be inventive with regard to arrangements, although for the most part the group is content to let the excellence of the songwriting win through, which it does. *Groovin'* is not a spectacular album, but it is one that demands repeat plays and very much deserves the gold disc award that it achieved for sales in the US. Although the group does not have the cachet of its San Francisco rivals and has a much more mainstream pop approach, *Groovin'* confirms the Young Rascals as one of the more interesting American groups of the period.

THE SERPENT POWER

US release   July 1967   Vanguard
VSD-7/VRS 9252
Not released in UK

1. Don't You Listen To Her
2. Gently, Gently
3. Open House
4. Flying Away
5. Nobody Blues
6. Up And Down

7. Sky Baby
8. Forget
9. Dope Again
10. Endless Tunnel

All compositions by David Meltzer

Tina Meltzer: vocals / David Meltzer: guitar, harmonica, vocals / Denny Ellis: guitar / John Payne: organ / David Stenson: bass guitar / Clark Coolidge: drums / Jean-Paul Pickens: banjo (10) / Samuel Charters: producer

San Francisco in 1967 was a rock music nexus in the way that Liverpool had been five years earlier. If Jefferson Airplane was the Beatles, then the Serpent Power was, perhaps, the rather less successful Lee Curtis and the All Stars, except that with LP sales in the ascendant, the group got to make one, even without any hit singles to its name. David Meltzer was, however, a successful poet, with five published collections. The music on the album is very much what one would expect from a group used to playing at venues like the Avalon Ballroom, and includes the obligatory marathon track, *Endless Tunnel,* allowing Melzer to display his skills as a lead guitarist, favouring a lightly amplified tone with no distortion. He shares the spotlight with an electric banjo player, brought in just for this track, who provides an unusual sound within music of this kind. The Serpent Power did not survive the commercial failure of its album, although the Melzers maintained a sporadic recording career as a duo and David Melzer published many more books, both poetry and prose.

THE BEAU BRUMMELS   TRIANGLE

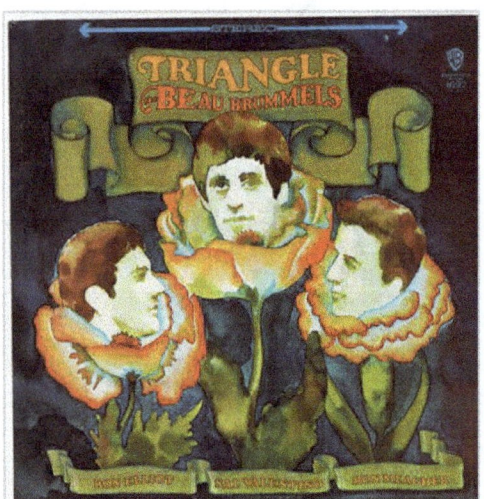

US release   July 1967   Warner Bros   W(S) 1692
Not released in UK

1. Are You Happy? (Robert Durand/Ron Elliott)
2. Only Dreaming Now (Ron Elliott/Sal Valentino)
3. Painter Of Women (Robert Durand/Ron Elliott)
4. The Keeper Of Time (Robert Durand/Ron Elliott)
5. It Won't Get Better (Ron Elliott/Sal Valentino)
6. Nine Pound Hammer (Merle Travis)

7. Magic Hollow (Ron Elliott/Sal Valentino)
8. And I've Seen Her (Robert Durand/Ron Elliott)
9. Triangle (Ron Elliott/Sal Valentino)
10. The Wolf Of Velvet Fortune (Ron Elliott/Sal Valentino)
11. Old Kentucky Home (Randy Newman)

Sal Valentino: vocals / Ron Elliott: guitar / Ron Meagher: bass guitar / Van Dyke Parks: harpsichord (7) / James Burton: guitar / Donnie Lanier: guitar / Gene Garf: accordion / Dick Hyde: trombone / David Duke: French horn / George Hyde: French horn / Gale Robinson: French horn / Lou Klass: violin / Shari Zippert: violin / Jesse Ehrlich: cello / Raymond Kelley: cello / Carol Kaye: bass guitar / Jim Gordon: drums / The Blossoms (Fanita James, Jean King, Darlene Love): vocals / Lenny Waronker: producer

Reduced to a trio, the Beau Brummels called on the support of a number of session musicians and their own increased songwriting expertise and produced by far the finest album of their career. Although Ron Elliott's folk/country guitar dominates the arrangements, it is surrounded by light orchestral instrumentation that turns every song into a fully worked-out piece of chamber music of frequently great beauty. The sleeve notes provide a narrative to link the songs together, but the music works perfectly well without this. Sal Valentino's voice continues to sound like that of no other singer and its wayward pitching prevents the use of any harmony singing, although its sits well next to the brass instruments, strings, and, as a particularly effective touch, accordion, that provide an alternative. *Triangle* celebrates the art of the song and there are no solos played by guitar or anything else. The album has much in common with the rather more celebrated *Forever Changes,* issued by Love four months later, and equally deserves to be described as a masterpiece.

THE INCREDIBLE STRING BAND   THE 5000 SPIRITS OR THE LAYERS OF THE ONION

```
UK release    July 1967    Elektra    EUKS 7/EUK 257
US release    July 1967    Elektra    EKS7/EKL 4010

1. Chinese White (Mike Heron)
2. No Sleep Blues (Robin Williamson)
3. Painting Box (Mike Heron)
4. The Mad Hatter's Song (Robin Williamson)
5. Little Cloud (Mike Heron)
6. The Eyes Of Fate (Robin Williamson)

7. Blues For The Muse (Robin Williamson)
8. The Hedgehog's Song (Mike Heron)
9. First Girl I Loved (Robin Williamson)
10. You Know What You Could Be (Mike Heron)
11. My Name Is Death (Robin Williamson)
12. Gently Tender (Mike Heron)
13. Way Back In The 1960s (Robin Williamson)

Mike Heron: vocals, guitar / Robin Williamson: vocals,
guitar, bowed gimbri, flute, percussion, oud, mandolin /
Danny Thompson: bass / Licorice McKechnie: vocals,
percussion / Soma: sitar, tambura / John Hopkins: piano /
Joe Boyd: producer
```

With the departure of Clive Palmer, the remaining two Incredibles function as a coherent unit, with the occasional help of a small number of guest musicians. Mike Heron sticks to his acoustic guitar, but Robin Williamson begins to experiment with the wider range of stringed instruments implied by the duo's name. They write the songs separately, but they have compatible styles, although the more whimsical material is all Mike Heron's. They produce one classic song each, Williamson's *First Girl I Loved* (later memorably covered by Judy Collins as *First Boy I Loved*) and Heron's *The Hedgehog's Song*, but there are no weak songs anywhere on the album. With album artwork produced by the design team, the Fool (who also decorated the guitars played by Cream and the Beatles and later did the same for the Beatles' Apple shop), the Incredible String Band was deliberately aligning itself with the other music presented in the 'summer of love' and the Beatles' *Sgt Pepper* in particular. The variety and strength of the songs ensures that this is not at all a vain hope. The mystically titled *The 5000 Spirits Or The Layers Of The Onion* is very much the folk music world's rootsy answer to the Beatles album, setting new benchmarks for other performers to match.

CHARLES LLOYD   LOVE-IN

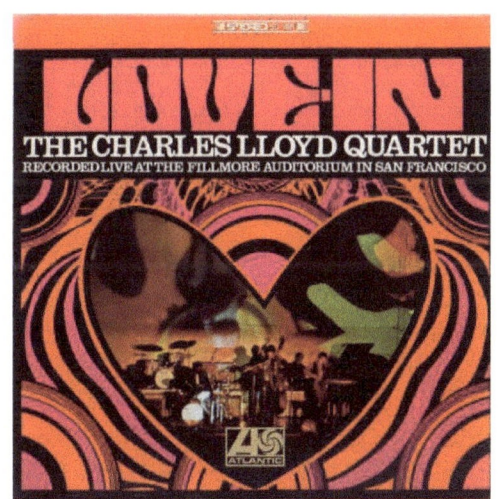

```
US release    July 1967    Atlantic    (SD) 1481
UK release    July 1967    Atlantic    588/587 077

1. Tribal Dance (Charles Lloyd)
2. Temple Bells (Charles Lloyd)
3. Is It Really The Same? (Keith Jarrett)
4. Here There And Everywhere (John Lennon/Paul McCartney)

5. Love-In (Charles Lloyd)
6. Sunday Morning (Keith Jarrett)
7. Memphis Dues Again / Island Blues (Charles Lloyd)

Charles Lloyd: tenor saxophone, flute / Keith Jarrett: piano /
Ron McClure: bass / Jack DeJohnette: drums / George Avakian:
producer
```

Love-In is a live recording made at the Fillmore in San Francisco the previous January. Charles Lloyd brings jazz to the hippies and succeeds in attracting their attention, although he is careful not to present anything too extreme. The opening *Tribal Dance* sounds like an out-take from John Coltrane's *A Love Supreme*, rejected because both the tenor saxophone and the piano were performing way below par. Keith Jarrett makes up for this elsewhere on the album, most notably on his buoyant soul-jazz feature, *Sunday Morning*, and on the thoughtful solo he plays during the Beatles interpretation, *Here There And Everywhere*. He strums the piano strings directly on *Temple Bells*, which sounds like a fresh approach in this context, even if the technique was a very familiar one elsewhere. Charles Lloyd himself, however, sounds throughout as though he is intimidated by the occasion, playing with a lack of passion despite the best efforts of his rhythm section, especially on the tracks where he switches to flute. Curiously, when the rest of the concert was issued on a second album, *Journey Within*, at the end of the year, it was revealed as consisting of a much stronger set of performances, by Lloyd and by the rest of his group too, so that the audience at the Fillmore would have been left feeling well satisfied at the end of the night. Charles Lloyd deserves full credit for trying to enlarge the audience for jazz improvisation, but the full revolution would only be achieved when musicians with rather more daring and imagination were involved.

STAN GETZ   SWEET RAIN

| US release | July 1967 | Verve | V(6)-8693 |
| UK release | July 1967 | Verve | S)VLP 9178 |

1. Litha (Chick Corea)
2. O Grande Amor (Antonio Carlos Jobim/Vinicius de Moraes)
3. Sweet Rain (Mike Gibbs)
4. Con Alma (Dizzy Gillespie)
5. Windows (Chick Corea)

Stan Getz: tenor saxophone / Chick Corea: piano / Ron Carter: bass / Grady Tate: drums / Creed Taylor: producer

Now this is what masterful, virtuoso tenor saxophone playing sounds like! As someone who had been a professional player since the forties, Stan Getz did not have youth on his side and was not particularly trendy, but the tumbling, fluid notes that burst out of the early lines of the album's first track, *Litha*, contain more passion than the whole of Charles Lloyd's *Love-In* record. Getz still favours the Latin-American rhythms that suit his mellow tone so well, but he manages to vary the tempos from track to track (or even within one track) so that any chance of the music descending to the level of easy-listening is dispelled. Future star Chick Corea is in fine form within the rhythm section and gets to play a few solos, but without any real chance of stealing even a little of the glory from his employer – although he tries very hard to do just that on his own composition, *Windows*. The fact that the occasional reed squeak from Stan Getz is allowed to remain in the finished takes tells us that these are genuinely spontaneous performances; the fact that the saxophone is so compelling throughout the album is a tribute to the skills of a truly inspired melodic improviser.

MORTON SUBOTNICK   SILVER APPLES OF THE MOON

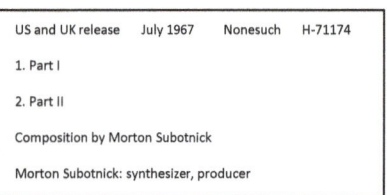

| US and UK release | July 1967 | Nonesuch | H-71174 |

1. Part I
2. Part II

Composition by Morton Subotnick

Morton Subotnick: synthesizer, producer

Silver Apples Of The Moon is an extended work composed and performed using the newly developed Buchla synthesizer. The instrument uses an innovative array of touch and pressure sensitive surfaces for its control, rather than the more user-friendly keyboard favoured by the rival Moog synthesizer, but this enabled Morton Subotnick to incorporate slurs and notes of indeterminate pitch that would be much more difficult to create on an instrument whose keys are linked to specific frequencies. There is also an element of unpredictability involved, forcing the composer to respond to patterns of sound generated by the instrument, whose character and detail he did not know in advance would be produced. Essentially, therefore, Subotnick is creating his music in the same intuitive way as the Beatles created pieces like *Strawberry Fields Forever* and *A Day In The Life*. Because the instrument is monophonic – it can only produce one note at a time and cannot play chords – Subotnick recorded three or four separate parts and overlaid them, although the result still employs a considerable amount of space, with most of the notes consisting of staccato stabs rather than sustained tones. It has some of the character of an improvised avant garde solo (or trio), except that it also has a distinct science-fiction ambience, as though human beings are not involved at all. It does, however, succeed in building a considerable rhythmic momentum during the second part. Within the context of the rock music scene of the time, *Silver Apples Of The Moon* provides the ultimate psychedelic trip. Nonesuch Records, which had commissioned Subotnick to create the work, proudly stated on the record sleeve that this was "the first time an original, full-scale composition had been created expressly for the record medium", although this was a rather dubious claim, given that rock and jazz musicians had been making albums in this way for some time. Arguably, *Sgt Pepper's Lonely Hearts Club Band* and Charles Mingus's *The Black Saint And The Sinner Lady*, to name two obvious examples, were also works to fit the Nonesuch description. The statement also served to minimise the true innovation of the album, that it was the first to present music played entirely on a commercially available synthesizer, rather than created by means of the tape manipulation that had been employed on earlier electronic works.

THE TEMPTATIONS   WITH A LOT O' SOUL

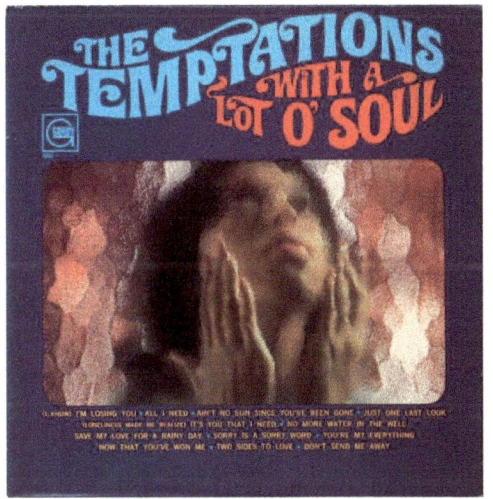

```
US release    July 1967    Gordy          GS/GM 922
UK release    July 1967    Tamla Motown   (S)TML 11057

1.  (I Know) I'm Losing You (Cornelius Grant/Eddie Holland/Norman Whitfield)
2.  Ain't No Sun Since You've Been Gone (Cornelius Grant/Norman Whitfield/Sylvia Moy)
3.  All I Need (Eddie Holland/Frank Wilson/R.Dean Taylor)
4.  (Loneliness Made Me Realise) It's You That I Need (Eddie Holland/Norman Whitfield)
5.  No More Water In The Well (Robert Rogers/Warren Moore/Smokey Robinson)
6.  Save My Love For A Rainy Day (Norman Whitfield/Roger Penzabene)

7.  Just One Last Look (Brian Holland/Lamont Dozier/Eddie Holland)
8.  Sorry Is A Sorry Word (Eddie Holland/Ivy Jo Hunter)
9.  You're My Everything (Cornelius Grant/Norman Whitfield/Roger Penzabene)
10. Now That You've Won Me (Smokey Robinson)
11. Two Sides To Love (Norman Whitfield/Sylvia Moy)
12. Don't Send Me Away (Eddie Kendricks/Smokey Robinson)

David Ruffin, Eddie Kendricks, Paul Williams, Melvin Franklin, Otis Williams: vocals / The
Funk Brothers / Smokey Robinson (5,10,12), Frank Wilson (3), Brian Holland and Lamont
Dozier (7), Ivy Jo Hunter (8), Norman Whitfield (rest): producer
```

As with many other record companies, the Motown albums of the sixties comprise a hit song or two and a lot of filler (which may or may not also have a lot of soul). This one by the Temptations is good, however, easily justifying its name, and it also happens to be the group's best selling album to date, in both the US and the UK. The big hit single is *(I Know) I'm Losing You,* driven by a memorable guitar figure and a robust David Ruffin vocal, which almost turns the song into a solo performance. But three other tracks also did well as singles (tracks 3, 4, and 9) even if they are less immediate in their appeal. Although Ruffin leads most of the singles, different singers are given some of the other album tracks and help to make the music sound varied. As always, bass player James Jamerson is a marvel throughout. Several producers are used, although they all keep to the expected Motown sound. *No More Water In The Well* is noticeably more funky than the rest, however, with its typically busy arrangement muted and mixed, unusually, well behind the rhythm section. Given that Norman Whitfield would eventually move the Temptations more conclusively in this direction, it is surprising to discover that the producer on the track is actually Smokey Robinson.

PINK FLOYD   A PIPER AT THE GATES OF DAWN

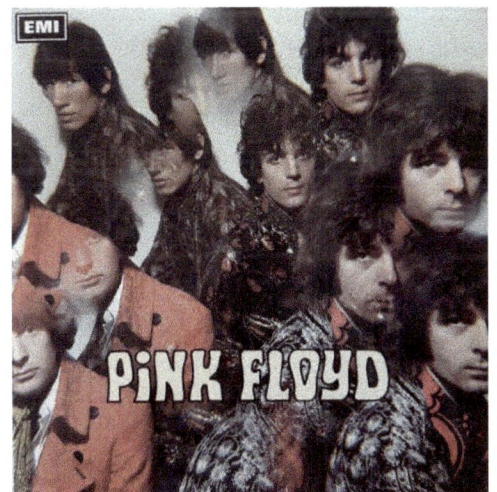

```
UK release    August 1967     Columbia   S(C)X 6157
US release    October 1967    Tower      (S)T 5093    some different tracks

1.  Astronomy Domine (Syd Barrett)
2.  Lucifer Sam (Syd Barrett)
3.  Matilda Mother (Syd Barrett)
4.  Flaming (Syd Barrett)
5.  Pow R Toc H (Pink Floyd)
6.  Take Up Thy Stethoscope And Walk (Roger Waters)

7.  Interstellar Overdrive (Pink Floyd)
8.  The Gnome (Dyd Barrett)
9.  Chapter 24 (Syd Barrett)
10. The Scarecrow (Syd Barrett)
11. Bike (Syd Barrett)

Syd Barrett: vocals, guitar / Richard Wright: keyboards, vibraphone, cello, violin,
vocals / Roger Waters: bass guitar, vocals / Nick Mason: drums, percussion /
Norman Smith: producer
```

Pink Floyd began as a rhythm and blues band, choosing to combine the names of two very obscure bluesmen for its own. Perhaps taking this more seriously than he should have, and noticing the "Waters" credit on one of the tracks, the reviewer in Melody Maker blithely assumed that *Take Up Thy Stethoscope And Walk* was a Muddy Waters cover. In fact, the music on *A Piper At The Gates Of Dawn* displays no discernible blues influence at all. During live performances, Pink Floyd would deliver lengthy freeform improvisations, albeit maintaining the rhythm for the most part, in which a psychedelic ambience, enhanced by a colourful liquid light show, took precedence over obvious melody. Most of the songs on the album include elements of this approach, while the instrumental, *Interstellar Overdrive,* is based entirely on it, using a descending guitar riff as the springboard for some lengthy musical free association. As the main songwriter, Syd Barrett produces lyrics and song structures that are decidedly odd, requiring only Richard Wright's ethereal organ tones and his battery of special effects to turn them into psychedelic extravaganzas. Barrett's own playing is surprisingly restrained, mainly keeping to a rhythm guitar role and not using any of the distortion becoming such a notable feature in other cutting edge groups, although he does like to employ some atonal slide guitar work from time to time. Overall, the sound of *A Piper At The Gates Of Dawn* is very much that of a group determined to follow its own path with as little reference to the work of other groups as it can manage, yet succeeding in remaining sufficiently accessible to be able to enter the top ten album chart in the UK, even if it did rather less well in the US.

BIG BROTHER AND THE HOLDING COMPANY

US release	August 1967	Mainstream	(S/)6099
UK release	c March 1968	Fontana	(S)TL 5457

1. Bye Bye Baby (Powell St John)
2. Easy Rider (James Gurley)
3. Intruder (Janis Joplin)
4. Light Is Faster Than Sound (Peter Albin)
5. Call On Me (Sam Andrew)

6. Women Is Losers (Janis Joplin)
7. Blindman (Big Brother and the Holding Company)
8. Down On Me (Traditional)
9. Caterpillar (Peter Albin)
10. All Is Loneliness (Moondog)

Janis Joplin: vocals / Sam Andrew: guitar, vocals / James Gurley: guitar, vocals / Peter Albin: bass guitar / Dave Getz: drums / Bob Shad: producer

This is the first album to feature singer Janis Joplin, then the lead vocalist with the San Francisco group, Big Brother and the Holding Company. She was not the first woman to employ the raw tones associated with the most effective rock singing – Wanda Jackson, Brenda Lee, and Lulu all made successful records before she did (and so, for that matter, did the likes of Etta James and Sugar Pie DeSanto, soul singers with the same kind of sound). But Janis Joplin's voice has an extra edge and she performs within a pure rock setting provided by electric guitars and a forceful rhythm, to push home her credentials. Despite this, the music on *Big Brother and the Holding Company* makes much less impact than it should have done. The problem lies with the band. The guitarists in particular, who had probably not heard what Eric Clapton and Jimi Hendrix were able to do, sound weak and unexciting. Janis Joplin almost makes up for this with her authority on tracks like *Down On Me* and *Women Is Losers*, but overall the album must have been something of a disappointment to those who had just witnessed the group's impressive performance at the Monterey Pop Festival in June.

VANILLA FUDGE

US release	August 1967	Atco	(SD) 33-224
UK release	October 1967	Atlantic	588/587 086

1. Ticket To Ride (John Lennon/Paul McCartney)
2. People Get Ready (Curtis Mayfield)
3. She's Not There (Rod Argent)
4. Bang Bang (Sonny Bono)

5. Illusions Of My Childhood Part One (Vanilla Fudge)
6. You Keep Me Hanging On (Brian Holland/Lamont Dozier/Eddie Holland)
7. Illusions Of My Childhood Part Two (Vanilla Fudge)
8. Take Me For A Little While (Trade Martin)
9. Illusions Of My Childhood Part Three (Vanilla Fudge)
10. Eleanor Rigby (John Lennon/Paul McCartney)

Mark Stein: vocals, keyboards / Vince Martell: guitar, vocals / Tim Bogert: bass guitar, vocals / Carmine Appice: drums, vocals / Shadow Morton: producer

The members of Vanilla Fudge came up with the idea of taking a well-known song, *You Keep Me Hanging On* (a hit for the Supremes in late 1966), and turning it into an extended work of considerable grandeur by slowing the music down and recasting it within a dramatic rock arrangement driven by portentous organ playing. Released as a single, *You Keep Me Hanging On* became a big hit in both the US and the UK. The group's self-titled first album presents six more songs treated in the same way, with the addition of three brief instrumental interludes whose primary function is to give the group some songwriting royalties. The full version of the single is included, its music now lasting more than twice as long. The album proves the value of the group's approach, being revealed as a thoroughly worthwhile and original project. It repeated the sales success of the single.

THE ELECTRIC PRUNES   UNDERGROUND

The second album by the Electric Prunes has a much greater proportion of group originals than before and includes two tracks, *The Great Banana Hoax* and *Long Day's Flight*, that are almost the equal of the hit songs included on the first album. The sounds of distorted and effects-laden electric guitars dominate the music as before. These include the newly developed wah-wah pedal, although it is used with such subtlety (on *I Happen To Love You*) that it makes far less impact than the device did on the single B-side issued two months previously by Cream, *Tales Of Brave Ulysses*. *Underground* is a strong addition to the small catalogue of determinedly psychedelic albums, but in a musical world that now included the outstandingly imaginative and skilful work of Jimi Hendrix, a guitarist with whom Ken Williams could not hope to compete, the group's dependence on guitar effects was never likely to be a recipe for success in the longer term.

```
US release    August 1967    Reprise    R(S) 6262
Not released in UK

1. The Great Banana Hoax (Mark Tulin/James Lowe)
2. Children Of Rain (Goodie Williams/Ken Williams)
3. Wind-Up Toys (Mark Tulin/James Lowe)
4. Antique Doll (Annette Tucker/Nancy Mantz)
5. It's Not Fair (Mark Tulin/James Lowe)
6. I Happen To Love You (Gerry Goffin/Carole King)

7. Dr Do-Good (Annette Tucker/Nancy Mantz)
8. I (Annette Tucker/Nancy Mantz)
9. Hideaway (Mark Tulin/James Lowe)
10. Big City (Johnny Walsh/Dan Walsh)
11. Capt Glory (James Lowe)
12. Long Day's Flight (Michael Weakley/Don Yorty)

James Lowe: vocals, autoharp, harmonica / Ken Williams: guitar / James Spagnola: guitar (not 1,12), vocals / Mike Gannon: guitar (1,12) / Mark Tulin: bass guitar, keyboards / Michael Weakley: drums (2,4,8,11,12) / Preston Ritter: drums (1,3,5,6,7,9,10) / Dave Hassinger: producer
```

THE CREATION   WE ARE PAINTERMEN

Eddie Phillips was an imaginative guitarist who decided to try using a violin bow on his instrument, in order to produce some unusual timbres. He plays like this on both *Making Time* and *Painterman*, which were minor hits in the UK during 1966. *Making Time* is something of a freakbeat classic. Signed to producer Shel Talmy's own Planet label, Phillips' group, the Creation, suffered a considerable setback when the label folded. The group was apparently unable to gain the interest of another record company in the UK, so that its album ended up being released in Germany, where the group had been more successful. The album has its strengths, being very reminiscent of the Who, though without songwriting as distinguished as that of Pete Townshend. Phillips and singer Kenny Pickett try rather too hard to create catchy pop melodies, often forgetting to add sufficient rock earthiness or depth. It is not too surprising that *Painterman* was later turned into a more substantial hit by the pop vocal group Boney M. Meanwhile, Pickett achieved what he wanted, even if this was at the cost of any attempt to be still considered cool, when a song he had co-written, *Grandad*, was taken to the top of the UK charts by Clive Dunn and a gaggle of schoolchildren.

```
German release    August 1967    Hit-Ton Schallplatten    HTSLP 340037
Not issued in UK or US

1. Cool Jerk (Donald Storball)
2. Making Time (Eddie Phillips/Kenny Pickett)
3. Through My Eyes (Bob Garner/Eddie Phillips)
4. Like A Rolling Stone (Bob Dylan)
5. Can I Join Your Band (Eddie Phillips)
6. Tom Tom (Bob Garner/Eddie Phillips)

7. Try And Stop Me (Eddie Phillips/Kenny Pickett)
8. If I Stay Too Long (Bob Garner/Eddie Phillips)
9. Biff Bang Pow (Eddie Phillips/Kenny Pickett)
10. Nightmares (Eddie Phillips/Kenny Pickett)
11. Hey Joe (Billy Roberts)
12. Painterman (Eddie Phillips/Kenny Pickett)

Kenny Pickett: vocals / Eddie Phillips: guitar, vocals / Bob Garner: bass guitar, vocals / Jack Jones: drums, vocals / Shel Talmy: producer
```

SIMON DUPREE & THE BIG SOUND   WITHOUT RESERVATIONS

```
UK release    August 1967    Parlophone    PMC/PCS 7029
US release    August 1967    Tower         (S)T-5097

1. Medley: 60 Minutes Of Your Love/A Lot Of Love (Isaac Hayes/David Porter)
2. Love (Jackie Edwards)
3. Get Off My Bach (Eve King/Ray Shulman)
4. There's A Little Picture Playhouse (Eric Hine)
5. Day Time, Night Time (Mike Hugg)

6. I See The Light (John Durrill/Mike Rabon/Norman Ezell)
7. What Is Soul (Ben E King/Bob Gallo)
8. Teacher Teacher (Derek, Phil, Ray Shulman)
9. Amen (Sam Cooke)
10. Who Cares (Eve King/Ray Shulman)
11. Reservations (Albert Hammond)

Derek Shulman: vocals / Phil Shulman: vocals, alto and tenor saxophone, trumpet / Ray Shulman: guitar, violin, trumpet, vocals / Eric Hine: keyboards / Peter O'Flaherty: bass guitar / Tony Ransley: drums / Dave Paramor: producer
```

Simon Dupree and the Big Sound, led by three brothers, performed as a British soul band and their album proves that they played the music well, with a considerable energy. *I See The Light*, *Reservations*, and *Day Time Night Time* were issued as singles and deserved to be hits, although sadly they were not. In November, the band issued a single, *Kites*, which did become a chart hit. This was in a different style, psychedelic in the manner of the Beatles, with a pronounced Eastern influence, a mellotron swathe underlining the music, and a spoken word interlude by Chinese actress Jacqui Chan. Although the Shulman brothers had mixed feelings about the song, they eventually disbanded Simon Dupree and the Big Sound and formed the progressive rock group Gentle Giant, whose music had far more in common with *Kites* than with blue-eyed soul.

ALBERT KING BORN UNDER A BAD SIGN

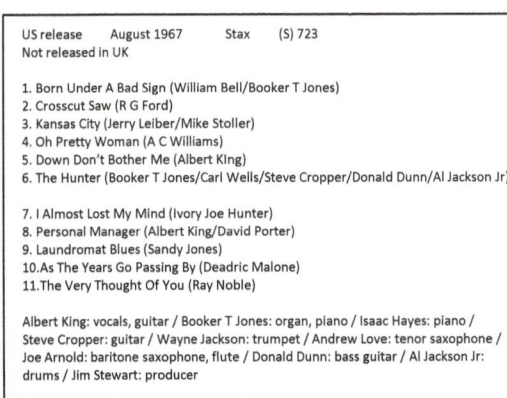

US release August 1967 Stax (S) 723
Not released in UK

1. Born Under A Bad Sign (William Bell/Booker T Jones)
2. Crosscut Saw (R G Ford)
3. Kansas City (Jerry Leiber/Mike Stoller)
4. Oh Pretty Woman (A C Williams)
5. Down Don't Bother Me (Albert King)
6. The Hunter (Booker T Jones/Carl Wells/Steve Cropper/Donald Dunn/Al Jackson Jr)
7. I Almost Lost My Mind (Ivory Joe Hunter)
8. Personal Manager (Albert King/David Porter)
9. Laundromat Blues (Sandy Jones)
10. As The Years Go Passing By (Deadric Malone)
11. The Very Thought Of You (Ray Noble)

Albert King: vocals, guitar / Booker T Jones: organ, piano / Isaac Hayes: piano / Steve Cropper: guitar / Wayne Jackson: trumpet / Andrew Love: tenor saxophone / Joe Arnold: baritone saxophone, flute / Donald Dunn: bass guitar / Al Jackson Jr: drums / Jim Stewart: producer

Left-handed blues guitarist Albert King famously played an upside-down Gibson Flying V, without changing the strings. *Born Under A Bad Sign* is an enhanced compilation of the singles he recorded during the previous eighteen months, with the Stax studio musicians, performing elsewhere as the Mar-Keys, in attendance. The meeting of traditional blues with contemporary R&B is an extremely productive one. King's eloquent lead guitar and heartfelt singing (or perhaps it is the other way round) combine on a vibrant set of songs that could almost make the listener believe that the blues is a newly conceived art-form rather than one that is decades old. Like his namesake B B King, and unlike most of the rock players who incorporated the blues into their music, Albert King prefers to keep his guitar playing simple, concentrating on the message and the tone of his phrases rather than attempting to break speed records. The only real criticism that could be made about the music is that most of the tracks end too soon, fading out while King is still in full flow. Many of the album's songs entered the repertoire of other blues and rock artists, with the title track, famously covered by Eric Clapton and Cream, becoming a very well-known blues standard.

JAMES BROWN COLD SWEAT

US release August 1967 King (KS) 1020
UK release August 1967 Polydor 184100 as **MR SOUL** with different cover

1. Cold Sweat Part 1 (James Brown/Alfred Ellis)
2. Cold Sweat Part 2 (James Brown/Alfred Ellis)
3. Fever (Eddie Cooley/John Davenport)
4. Kansas City (Jerry Leiber/Mike Stoller)
5. Stagger Lee (Harold Logan/Lloyd Price)
6. Good Rockin' Tonight (Roy Brown)
7. Mona Lisa (Jay Livingston/Raymond Evans)
8. I Want To Be Around (Johnny Mercer/Sadie Vimmerstedt)
9. Nature Boy (Eden Ahbez)
10. Come Rain Or Come Shine (Johnny Mercer/Harold Arlen)
11. I Loves You Porgy (George Gershwin/DuBose Heyward)
12. Back Stabbin' (James Brown/Gene Redd)

James Brown: vocals, organ, producer / Waymon Reed: trumpet / Joe Dupars: trumpet / Levi Rasbury: trombone / Alfred 'Pee Wee' Ellis: alto saxophone / Maceo Parker: tenor saxophone / Eldee Williams: tenor saxophone / St Clair Pinckney: baritone saxophone / Jimmy Nolen: guitar / Alphonso Kellum: guitar / Bernard Odum: bass guitar / Clyde Stubblefield: drums / New York Studio Orchestra and Chorus (7,8,9,10)

James Brown continues to make genius singles but poor albums. His song, *Papa's Got A Brand New Bag*, invented funk nearly two years previously. *Cold Sweat*, maintaining a funk beat over a single chord for seven minutes, while Brown directs the rhythm section, crystallises the genre and becomes one of Brown's definitive performances. Sadly, the singer makes no attempt to continue the vitality and innovation of this track throughout the rest of the album. Indeed, the selection of rock 'n' roll and night club standards that fill the vinyl are like the work of another artist altogether – one who certainly has a fine soul voice, but is not at all interested in seeing what can be done with a rhythmic groove. A few of the tracks even abandon the powerhouse backing band altogether and replace it with an orchestra, making the music teeter on the edge of easy listening, of a kind that could have been produced many years earlier. The listener can only puzzle over James Brown's belief that the people who thrilled to the *Cold Sweat* single would be in the least interested in retro music like this.

DIANA ROSS & THE SUPREMES   GREATEST HITS

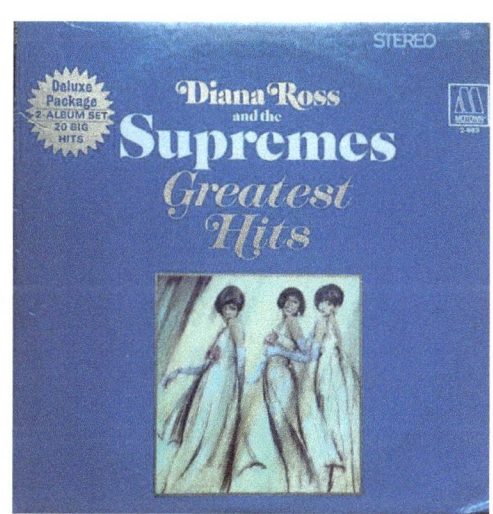

The hit singles and a few B-sides by Motown's most successful group filled a double album of *Greatest Hits* (reduced to a single album in the UK by omitting four tracks). For the first time, Diana Ross is given star billing ahead of the rest of the group in the album credits. By the time the album was released, Florence Ballard had been ousted, to be replaced by Cindy Birdsong, but she sings on all the tracks on the album. It is an impressive collection, with the Holland-Dozier-Holland writing team finding a variety of inventive ways to display Diana Ross's voice to best effect. The album reached number one in both the US and the UK, remaining in both charts for well over a year.

```
US release    August 1967    Motown          MS-2-663
UK release    January 1968   Tamla Motown    (S)TML 11063
16 track single album

1. When The Lovelight Starts Shining Through His Eyes
2. Where Did Our Love Go
3. Ask Any Girl
4. Baby Love
5. Run Run Run

6. Stop! In The Name Of Love
7. Back In My Arms Again
8. Come See About Me
9. Nothing But Heartaches
10. Everything Is Good About You (Eddie Holland/James Dean)

11. I Hear A Symphony
12. Love Is Here And Now You're Gone
13. My World Is Empty Without You
14. Whisper You Love Me Boy
15. The Happening (Holland/Dozier/Holland/Frank DeVol)

16. You Keep Me Hangin' On
17. You Can't Hurry Love
18. Standing At The Crossroads Of Love
19. Love Is Like An Itching In My Heart
20. There's No Stopping Us Now

All compositions by Brian Holland/ Lamont Dozier/Eddie Holland except where stated

Diana Ross: vocals / Mary Wilson: vocals / Florence Ballard: vocals / musicians as on Motown albums listed earlier / Brian Holland: producer / Lamont Dozier: producer
```

THE FOUR TOPS   GREATEST HITS

```
US release    August 1967    Motown          MS/MT 662
UK release    January 1968   Tamla Motown    (S)TML 11061
different cover, 16 tracks

1. Baby I Need Your Loving
2. It's The Same Old Song
3. Reach Out I'll Be There
4. Ask The Lonely (Ivy Jo Hunter/William Stevenson)
5. Standing In The Shadows Of Love
6. Loving You Is Sweeter Than Ever (Ivy Jo Hunter/Stevie Wonder)

7. I Can't Help Myself
8. Without The One You Love
9. 7 Rooms Of Gloom
10. Something About You
11. Bernadette
12. Shake Me, Wake Me (When It's Over)

All compositions by Brian Holland/ Lamont Dozier/Eddie Holland except where stated
```

The Four Tops were formed in 1953 and recorded for Chess through the fifties without any success. Signed to Motown in 1963, the quartet was paired with the same Brian Holland/Lamont Dozier/Eddie Holland songwriting team as employed by the Supremes and was soon enjoying substantial chart hits. Lead singer Levi Stubbs had a particularly striking, moving voice and the songwriters became adept at creating melodies and lyrics with a degree of anguish that suited Stubbs very well. *Greatest Hits* became easily the Four Tops' best selling album, reaching number one in the UK, and earning a gold disc in the US.

THE BYRDS   GREATEST HITS

The Byrds' *Greatest Hits* presents the highlights of the group's career to date and makes clear why its contribution to the music of the mid-sixties is so valuable. This is the definitive folk rock collection by the group that pioneered the genre. All except tracks 2, 3, and 6 were issued as the A sides of singles. It is by far the most successful album

```
US release    August 1967     Columbia    CS 9516 / CL 2716
UK release    October 1967    CBS         (S)BPG 63107

1. Mr Tambourine Man (Bob Dylan)
2. I'll Feel A Whole Lot Better (Gene Clark)
3. The Bells Of Rhymney (Idris Davies/Pete Seeger)
4. Turn! Turn! Turn! (Pete Seeger)
5. All I Really Want To Do (Bob Dylan)
6. Chimes Of Freedom (Bob Dylan)

7. Eight Miles High (David Crosby/Gene Clark/Jim McGuinn)
8. Mr Spaceman (Jim McGuinn)
9. 5D (Fifth Dimension) (Jim McGuinn)
10. So You Want To Be A Rock 'n' Roll Star (Chris Hillman/Jim McGuinn)
11. My Back Pages (Bob Dylan)

Gene Clark: vocals, percussion (1-7) / Jim McGuinn: guitar, vocals / David Crosby: guitar, vocals / Chris Hillman: bass guitar, vocals / Mike Clarke: drums / Jerry Cole: guitar (1) / Leon Russell: piano (1) / Larry Knechtel: bass guitar (1) / Hal Blaine: drums (1) / Van Dyke Parks: organ (9) / Hugh Masekela: trumpet (10) / Terry Melcher: producer (1-6) / Allen Stanton: producer (7-9) / Gary Usher: producer (10,11)
```

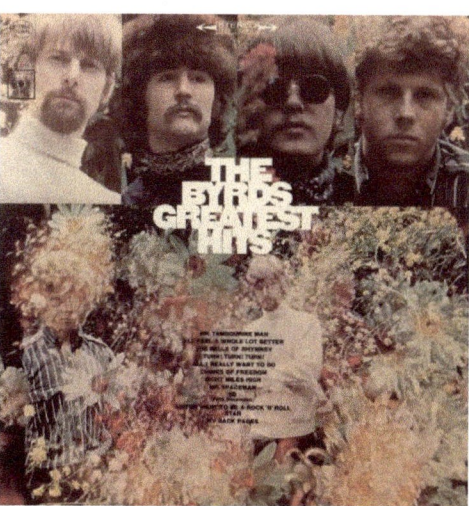

made by the Byrds, achieving platinum status in the US, although, mysteriously, it failed to enter the chart in the UK.

TIM BUCKLEY   GOODBYE AND HELLO

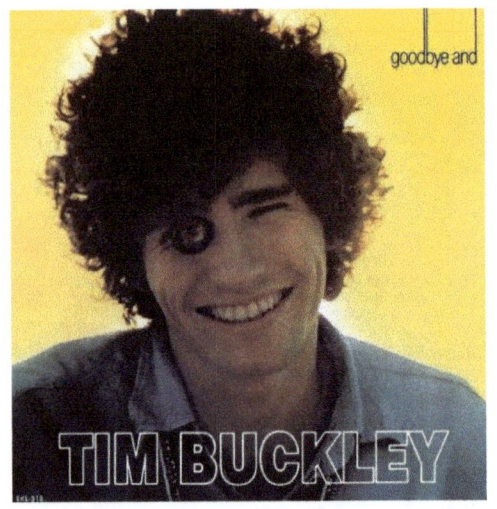

| US release | August 1967 | Elektra | EKS-7318 / EKL-318 |
| UK release | August 1967 | Elektra | EKS 7318 / EKL 318 |

1. No Man Can Find The War
2. Carnival Song
3. Pleasant Street
4. Hallucinations
5. I Never Asked To Be Your Mountain
6. Once I Was
7. Phantasmagoria In Two
8. Knight-Errant
9. Goodbye And Hello
10. Morning Glory

All compositions by Tim Buckley, tracks 1,4,8,8,10 co-written by Larry Beckett

Tim Buckley: vocals, guitar, kalimba, vibraphone / Lee Underwood: guitar / Brian Hartzler: guitar / John Forsha: guitar / Jerry Yester: keyboards, producer / Don Randi: keyboards / Dave Guard: kalimba, percussion / Jim Fielder: bass guitar / Jimmy Bond: bass / Carter C.C. Collins: percussion / Eddie Hoh: drums

With a stronger set of songs than on his first album, *Goodbye And Hello* brings Tim Buckley's extraordinary voice into sharper focus. One song, *Morning Glory,* seems to encapsulate Buckley's art particularly well and it achieved extra resonance when issued as a single. Although it was not a hit, the song attracted the attention of other artists, including Linda Ronstadt with the Stone Poneys, Blood Sweat And Tears, and, in the UK, Fairport Convention. The music throughout the album has an improvisational quality, but Buckley is nevertheless able to create distinctive melodies that are further enhanced by the sympathetic playing of lead guitarist Lee Underwood and the other musicians used. Above all, *Goodbye And Hello* does not sound at all like music that Bob Dylan, or any other singer songwriter, could have produced in 1967.

JOAN BAEZ   JOAN

| US release | August 1967 | Vanguard | VSD-79240/VRS-9240 |
| UK release | August 1967 | Fontana | (S)TFL 6082 |

1. Be Not Too Hard (Christopher Logue/Donovan)
2. Eleanor Rigby (John Lennon/Paul McCartney)
3. Turquoise (Donovan)
4. La Colombe (The Dove) (Jacques Brel/Alasdair Clayre)
5. Dangling Conversation (Paul Simon)
6. The Lady Came From Baltimore (Tim Hardin)
7. North (Joan Baez/Nina Dusheck)
8. Children Of Darkness (Richard Farina)
9. The Greenwood Side (Traditional)
10. If You Were A Carpenter (Tim Hardin)
11. Annabel Lee (Don Dilworth/Edgar Allan Poe)
12. Saigon Bride (Joan Baez/Nina Dusheck)

Joan Baez: vocals, guitar / Peter Schickele: arranger, conductor / Bruce Langhorne: guitar (9) / Richard Romoff: bass (1) / Russ Savakus: bass (9) / Alvin Rogers: drums (1) / Maynard Solomon: producer

For her eighth album, Joan Baez followed the lead of Judy Collins and makes an album of orchestrated songs, mostly written by contemporary singer songwriters. As did Ms Collins before her, Joan Baez chooses a Beatles song as an appropriate inclusion in this company, and she also contributes two rare compositions of her own. As always, the pure beauty of her singing voice makes her own versions of these songs sound as definitive as the originals. *Joan* did much to keep the singer relevant in an age when she was facing intense competition from precisely those performers whose work she was interpreting. The album made a respectable showing in the US album chart, even if UK listeners were less interested.

GLEN CAMPBELL   GENTLE ON MY MIND

Glen Campbell was a busy session guitarist during the sixties, playing on records by Simon and Garfunkel, the Monkees, and the Beach Boys, amongst others. He also played live on several occasions with the Beach Boys, deputising for Brian Wilson, who returned the favour by producing a single for Campbell, *Guess I'm Dumb,* in 1965. Sadly, the record was not a hit, despite displaying all the melodic and arranging strengths of the Beach

Boys' own recordings. Campbell's version of a song by bluegrass performer John Hartford was another matter. *Gentle On My Mind*, which won four Grammy awards the following year, was a modest chart hit, but managed to sell steadily over the years, eventually reaching platinum disc status. The album released around the song became a substantial hit too, something that Campbell's previous five albums had failed to do, thereby launching the solo career of one of country music's most prominent artists. The music on the album is in the same country-pop mode as the single, with Campbell's mellow singing voice taking precedence over his guitar playing and delivering songs that are easy to like.

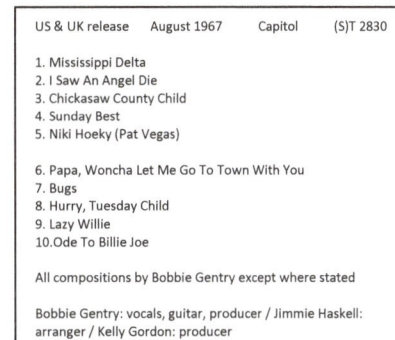

US release   August 1967   Capitol   (S)T 2809
Not released in UK

1. Gentle On My Mind (John Hartford)
2. Catch The Wind (Donovan)
3. It's Over (Jimmie Rodgers)
4. Bowling Green (Terry Slater/Jackie Ertel)
5. Just Another Man (Glen Campbell/Joe Allison)
6. You're My World (Umberto Bindi/Gino Paoli/Carl Sigman)
7. The World I Used To Know (Rod McKuen)
8. Without Her (Harry Nilsson)
9. Mary In The Morning (Michael Lendell/Johnny Cymbal)
10. Love Me As Though There Were No Tomorrow (Jimmy McHugh/Harold Adamson)
11. Cryin' (Roy Orbison/Joe Melson)

Glen Campbell: vocals, guitar / James Burton: guitar / Doug Dillard: banjo / Leon Russell: piano, arranger / Joe Osborn: bass guitar / Jim Gordon: drums / Al De Lory: arranger, producer

BOBBIE GENTRY   ODE TO BILLIE JOE

US & UK release   August 1967   Capitol   (S)T 2830

1. Mississippi Delta
2. I Saw An Angel Die
3. Chickasaw County Child
4. Sunday Best
5. Niki Hoeky (Pat Vegas)
6. Papa, Woncha Let Me Go To Town With You
7. Bugs
8. Hurry, Tuesday Child
9. Lazy Willie
10. Ode To Billie Joe

All compositions by Bobbie Gentry except where stated

Bobbie Gentry: vocals, guitar, producer / Jimmie Haskell: arranger / Kelly Gordon: producer

Occasionally, a new artist emerges with a performance so arresting and so iconic that they become able to sustain a lengthy career on the back of this one song. Such was the case with Bobbie Gentry, whose narrative song *Ode To Billie Joe* was issued as a single in July and became a big hit in both the US and the UK. Gentry's mystery tale, delivered as though by a small-town American family over supper, and with no final answer as to what exactly happened, has all the dramatic impact of a best-selling novel or a film, but artfully compressed into a four minute song. The addition of an eerie underscoring for strings and a minimal double bass part was all that was required to turn Bobbie Gentry's original demo into a finished masterpiece. The rest of the album is attractive enough and proves the singer songwriter's worth, but contains nothing else as remarkable as the title track. Which does not matter at all.

PIERRE HENRY & MICHEL COLOMBIER   MESSE POUR LE TEMPS PRESENT

French release   c. August 1967   Philips   836.893 DSY
UK release   1969   Philips   4FE8004   different cover
US release   1969   Limelight   LS 86065   different cover

1. Messe Pour Le Temps Présent – Prologue
2. Messe Pour Le Temps Présent – Psyché Rock
3. Messe Pour Le Temps Présent – Jérico Jerk
4. Messe Pour Le Temps Présent – Teen Tonic
5. Messe Pour Le Temps Présent – Too Fortiche
6. Le Voyage – Les Divinités Paisibles
7. La Rein Verte – Rock Electronique
8. La Rein Verte – Marche Du Jeune Homme
9. La Rein Verte – Les Insectes
10. La Rein Verte – Eblouissement De La Reine
11. La Rein Verte – Danse Du Jeune Homme
12. Variations Pour Un Porte Et Un Soupir – Fièvre
13. Variations Pour Un Porte Et Un Soupir – Mort

All compositions by Pierre Henry; tracks 1-5 co-composed by Michel Colombier

The music on this album comprises electronic compositions created as ballet music for the choreographer Maurice Béjart between 1962 and 1967. The pieces produced by Pierre Henry on his own comprise electronic pulses and squeaks, together with a little percussion, the sounds being derived from magnetic tape manipulation rather than any kind of synthesizer. For the work composed in collaboration with Michel Colombier, the electronic noises are used as decoration and commentary on some basic rock music riffs and rhythms played by an anonymous studio group. The result marks the first time that an avant garde classical composer had shown any interest in what was going on in the rock music world, although Pierre Henry's daring rather failed to make any impact outside France. The US and UK record companies delayed releasing the album for another two years, which did not help. It was some thirty years later that the dance music clubs in the UK picked up on the second part of the *Messe Pour Le Temps Présent*, subtitled *Psyché Rock*, as they realised that the energetic rock beat was being played with a surprising finesse by the French session musicians. The music was treated to remix versions by Fatboy Slim and others, who did not have to expend very much effort to make the music sound utterly contemporary.

TUBBY HAYES ORCHESTRA   100% PROOF

UK release   August 1967   Fontana   (S)TL 5410
Not released in US

1. 100% Proof (Tubby Hayes)
2. A Night In Tunisia (Dizzy Gillespie/Frank Paparelli)
3. Milestones (Jim Britt/Miles Davis)
4. Sonnymoon For Two (Sonny Rollins)
5. Bluesology (Milt Jackson)
6. Nutty (Thelonious Monk)

Tubby Hayes: tenor saxophone, flute, vibraphone / Ray Warleigh: alto saxophone, flute / Roy Willox: alto saxophone, flute / Harry Klein: baritone Saxophone (1,6) / Ronnie Ross: baritone saxophone, bass clarinet (2-5) / Ronnie Scott: tenor saxophone, clarinet / Bob Efford: tenor saxophone, oboe, flute, bass clarinet / Greg Bowen: trumpet / Ian Hamer: trumpet / Kenny Baker: trumpet / Kenny Wheeler: trumpet   Les Condon: trumpet / Chris Smith: trombone / Johnny Marshall: trombone / Keith Christie: trombone / Nat Peck: trombone / Gordon Beck: piano / Jeff Clyne: bass / Johnny Butts: drums (1,6) / Ronnie Stephenson: drums (2-5) / no producer credited

Edward 'Tubby' Hayes was arguably the most technically adept British tenor saxophonist of his era. During the late fifties he played in a highly regarded modern jazz quintet with fellow saxophonist Ronnie Scott, the Jazz Couriers, and he made many recordings from 1955 onwards. He played as part of the Duke Ellington Orchestra in 1964 when it performed at the Royal Festival Hall in London. *100% Proof* is a big band album, presenting convincing interpretations of some classic hard bop material. The lengthy title track, a Tubby Hayes original, is a showcase for the leader's fluid saxophone, where the rest of the band frequently drops out altogether to give his playing free rein. Elsewhere, Hayes demonstrates his ability on flute and on vibes, as well as playing more tenor saxophone, and he also finds space for some other members of the orchestra to solo, although inevitably nobody gets to play for very long. Overall, the album is a fine addition to the jazz catalogue, even if it is not a startlingly original one.

VARIOUS ARTISTS   CLUB SKA '67

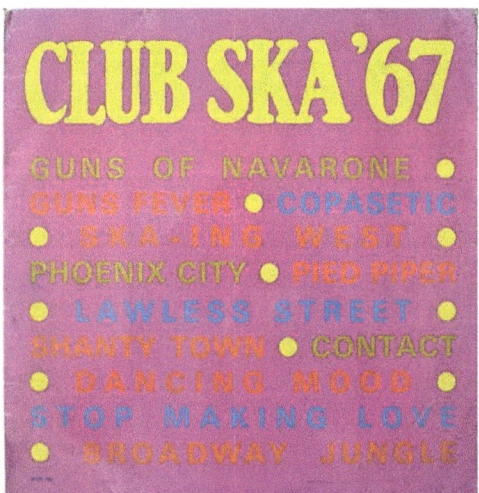

UK release   August 1967   WIRL/Island   LP-948
Not released in US until 1980   Mango   MLPS 9598

1. Guns Of Navarone (The Skatalites)
2. Phoenix City (Roland Alphonso)
3. 007 (Shanty Town) (Desmond Dekker)
4. Broadway Jungle (The Flames [The Maytals])
5. Contact (Roy Richards)
6. Guns Fever (Baba Brooks)
7. Dancing Mood (Delroy Wilson)
8. Stop Making Love (The Gaylads)
9. Pied Piper (Rita Marley)
10. Lawless Street (The Soul Brothers)
11. Ska-ing West (Sir Lord Comic)
12. Copasetic (The Rulers)

All music by the Skatalites – Tommy McCook: tenor saxophone / Roland Alphonso: tenor saxophone / Johnny Moore: trumpet / Lester Sterling: alto saxophone / Baba Brooks: trumpet / Don Drummond: trombone / Jah Jerry Haynes: guitar / Jackie Mittoo: piano, organ / Lloyd Brevett: bass / Lloyd Knibb: drums

or by the Soul Brothers – Ernest Ranglin: guitar / Wallin Cameron: guitar / Harry Haughton: guitar / Hux Brown: guitar / Jackie Mittoo: piano, organ / Roland Alphonso: tenor saxophone / Dennis Campbell: tenor saxophone / Johnny Moore: trumpet / Bobby Ellis: trumpet / Bryan Atkinson: bass guitar / LLoyd Brevett: bass / Bunny Williams: drums / Joe Isaacs: drums

The Maytals are singers Toots Hibbert / Raleigh Gordon / Jerry Mathias   The Gaylads are singers B.B.Seaton / Winston Stewart / Maurice Roberts   Roy Richards plays harmonica
Coxsone Dodd: producer

Club Ska '67 is a compilation of well-known Jamaican ska hits from 1964 to 1966. It was issued on the Jamaican WIRL label, but pressed in the UK under the auspices of Island records and given a catalogue number within that company's album sequence. Ska is distinguished by a stabbing off-beat (or strictly speaking an after-beat – an extra beat inserted in between each beat played in four-four time, giving the music a bouncy, sprung quality). It can be heard on all the tracks included here. The music represents the first influence of Jamaica on the popular music of the UK. Only Georgie Fame made any significant attempt to play the music himself, but it did get played in the clubs and both *Guns Of Navarone* and *007 (Shanty Town)* were minor chart hits. *Club Ska '67* itself sold well enough to enter the lower reaches of the album charts. A decade later, of course, the music was enthusiastically adopted by a number of white and mixed race British groups, including the Specials and Madness.

THE SEEDS   FUTURE

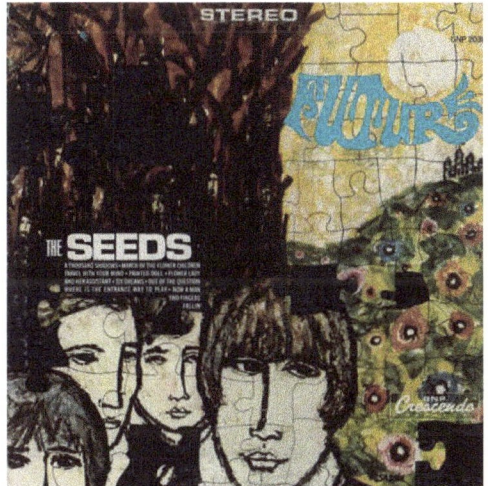

| US release | August 1967 | GNP Crescendo | GNP 2038 |
| UK release | November 1967 | Vocalion | SAV-N 8070 |

1. Introduction (Sky Saxon/Daryl Hooper)
2. March Of The Flower Children (Sky Saxon/Daryl Hooper)
3. Travel With Your Mind (Sky Saxon/Daryl Hooper/Jan Savage)
4. Out Of The Question (Sky Saxon)
5. Painted Doll (Sky Saxon)
6. Flower Lady And Her Assistant (Sky Saxon)
7. Now A Man (Sky Saxon/Daryl Hooper/Jan Savage)

8. A Thousand Shadows (Sky Saxon/Daryl Hooper/Jan Savage)
9. Two Fingers Pointin' On You (Sky Saxon)
10. Where Is The Entrance Way To Play (Sky Saxon)
11. Six Dreams (Sky Saxon)
12. Fallin' (Sky Saxon/Daryl Hooper)

Sky Saxon: vocals, bass guitar, arranger, producer / Jan Savage: guitar, gong, vocals / Daryl Hooper: keyboards, sitar, vocals, arranger / Harvey Sharpe: bass guitar / Rick Andridge: drums, vocals

Realising that his punk music brand was reaching its sell-by date, Sky Saxon decided to recast his songs by adding a range of more or less exotic instruments to his simple chord structures. The result is distinctly uncomfortable and entirely fails to give Saxon his hoped-for respect as a rival to the Beatles. At least, however, it is preferable to his next move, which was to redirect his energies towards making the Seeds into a very unconvincing blues band, even if he did somehow manage to persuade members of the Muddy Waters group to participate.

ERIC BURDON & THE ANIMALS   WINDS OF CHANGE

| US release | September 1967 | MGM | (S)E-4484 |
| UK release | September 1967 | MGM | C(S)-8052 |

1. Winds Of Change
2. Poem By The Sea
3. Paint It Black (Mick Jagger/Keith Richards)
4. The Black Plague
5. Yes I Am Experienced

6. San Franciscan Nights
7. Man – Woman
8. Hotel Hell
9. Good Times
10. Anything
11. It's All Meat

All compositions by Eric Burdon and the Animals

Eric Burdon: vocals / Vic Briggs: guitar, sitar, keyboards, trumpet / John Weider: guitar, violin / Danny McCulloch: bass guitar / Keith Olsen: bass guitar / Barry Jenkins: drums / Tom Wilson: producer

The original Animals disbanded in late 1966 and Eric Burdon relocated to America, where he recorded an uncharacteristic and not very inspired album with a jazz band backing, released (though not in the UK) as *Eric Is Here*. He formed a new band, using British musicians, but he continued to concentrate his energies on the American market. He retained the Animals name, despite the kind of music played being rather different. Clearly besotted with the music dominating the scene in California, Burdon attempted to create his own version of it, although his two guitarists were not really interested in delivering the improvised solos needed to make the style work. John Weider plays the violin more than guitar, overdubbing his parts to create a substantial string section in places. The gentle *San Franciscan Nights* made a surprisingly charming single (once its odd police megaphone introduction has passed) and was a hit in both the US and the UK. *Good Times*, lifted by John Weider's strings, was strong enough for a single too, although it fared less well and was consigned to a B-side in the US. Some of the other songs on the album, however, find Burdon trying rather too hard to convince people how cool he is. He ends up sounding unfortunately embarrassing, such as when he attempts to provide an answer/tribute to Jimi Hendrix, *Yes I Am Experienced,* without incorporating any of the sonic adventure that made Hendrix sound so remarkable, or when he chooses to provide lists of performers he likes, which he does on two of the tracks. One can applaud Eric Burdon for making a serious move in a new musical direction, but realistically, he should have worked on the music a little more before trying to record it.

VAN MORRISON   BLOWIN' YOUR MIND!

With the benefit of hindsight, *Blowin' Your Mind!* can be seen as a transitional album, in which Van Morrison, putting the basic R&B of Them firmly behind him, tries to create his personal interpretation of music delivered straight from the soul. Morrison and his fans have been very dismissive of the album, claiming that the songs were only ever intended as demos, or else that the songs were candidates for single release, but not an album, and that in any case they hate the cover, with its suggestion of a drug reliance that Morrison did not have. The reality is that Morrison had not quite reached a full comprehension of how the music in his head should work in practice. The musicians employed for the session are well able to produce a steady groove, for Morrison to spin his lines over the top, but without the sense of power kept in check and of space and responsiveness, that was to prove so vital for the singer's eventual Caledonian soul. Remarkably, despite Morrison's inability to explain or even understand exactly the kind of musical support he was looking for, the album includes one indisputable classic in *Brown Eyed Girl* – a song that has entered the repertoire of bar bands everywhere.

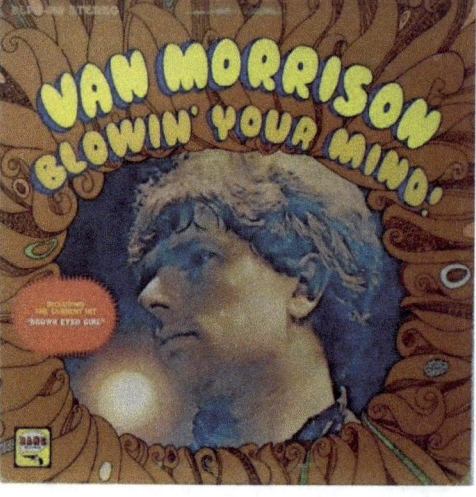

```
US release     September 1967    Bang     BLP(S) 218
UK release     January 1968      London   HAZ 8346

1. Brown Eyed Girl
2. He Ain't Give You None
3. T.B. Sheets

4. Spanish Rose
5. Goodbye Baby (Wes Farrell, Bert Russell)
6. Ro Ro Rosey
7. Who Drove The Red Sports Car?
8. Midnight Special (traditional)

All compositions by Van Morrison except where stated

Van Morrison: vocals, guitar, harmonica / Al Gorgoni: guitar /
Hugh McCracken: guitar / Paul Griffin: piano / Garry Sherman:
organ, arranger / Eric Gale: bass guitar / Russ Savakus: bass
guitar / Gary Chester: drums / The Sweet Inspirations (Cissy
Houston, Sylia Shemwell, Myrna Smith, Estelle Brown): vocals
/ Bert Berns: producer
```

THE KINKS   SOMETHING ELSE

Business as usual for the Kinks. Turning their backs on psychedelia, on Beatles arrangement fantasy too, Ray Davies and his bandmates continue the work of creating memorable songs played within the beat group format. With one song in particular, the approach strikes gold. The astonishingly evocative portrait of London life that is *Waterloo Sunset* provides one of rock music's finest achievements of the mid-sixties and does this with nothing more exotic than guitars, drums, and voices. It is placed as the finale for an album that has already taken the listener through the most consistent set of Kinks songs yet put together. *David Watts,* chosen to open the album, is an addition to Ray Davies' series of finely judged character studies. As musically memorable as the rest, it turns the focus around by aiming the irony at the song's narrator rather than the person named in the title. It would have made a fine single. The momentum that the song sets up is maintained by the music that follows, right through to the deliberately weary *End Of The Season,* which would have provided an obvious ending for the album too, were it not for the necessity of giving pride of place to the magnificent *Waterloo Sunset.* Ray's brother Dave makes three strong songwriting contributions too, one of which, *Death Of A Clown,* was issued as being a solo single by him, although the whole group is actually in attendance. *Waterloo Sunset* was one of the Kinks' biggest hit singles and was closely followed by *Death Of A Clown,* but the *Something Else* album performed much less well than might have been expected. Unfortunately, its success was sabotaged by the Pye record company itself, choosing to release a rival Kinks record, a bargain priced compilation, with the earlier hit, *Sunny Afternoon,* as its selling point, just a few weeks later.

```
UK release     September 1967    Pye       N(S)PL 18193
US release     January 1968      Reprise   R(S) 6279

1. David Watts (Ray Davies)
2. Death Of A Clown (Dave Davies/Ray Davies)
3. Two Sisters (Ray Davies)
4. No Return (Ray Davies)
5. Harry Rag (Ray Davies)
6. Tin Soldier Man (Ray Davies)
7. Situation Vacant (Ray Davies)

8. Love Me Till The Sun Shines (Dave Davies)
9. Lazy Old Sun (Ray Davies)
10. Afternoon Tea (Ray Davies)
11. Funny Face (Dave Davies)
12. End Of The Season (Ray Davies)
13. Waterloo Sunset (Ray Davies)

Ray Davies: vocals, guitar, harmonica, keyboards, tuba, percussion,
producer / Dave Davies: guitar, vocals / Pete Quaife: bass guitar,
vocals / Mick Avory: drums / Nicky Hopkins: keyboards / Rasa Davies:
vocals / Shel Talmy: producer
```

THE BEACH BOYS   SMILEY SMILE

During late 1966 and early 1967, Brian Wilson was working on the production of a suite of songs to be issued under the name of *Smile.* The single, *Good Vibrations,* was released as a highly impressive preview of the album. The combination of the Beach Boys' most sublime harmony singing with the sound produced by a precisely controlled version of the electronic instrument known as the theremin made for a particularly inspiring piece of music. Unfortunately, Brian Wilson's increasingly fragile mental tate, together with an ongoing dispute between the group and its record company, resulted in

```
US release      September 1967    Brother    (S)T 9001
UK release      September 1967    Capitol    (S)T 9001

1. Heroes And Villains (Brian Wilson/Van Dyke Parks)
2. Vegetables (Brian Wilson/Van Dyke Parks)
3. Fall Breaks And Back To Winter (W.Woodpecker Symphony) (Brian
                                                           Wilson)
4. She's Goin' Bald (Brian Wilson/Mike Love/Van Dyke Parks)
5. Little Pad (Brian Wilson)

6. Good Vibrations (Brian Wilson/Mike Love)
7. With Me Tonight (Brian Wilson)
8. Wind Chimes (Brian Wilson)
9. Gettin' Hungry (Brian Wilson/Mike Love)
10. Wonderful (Brian Wilson)
11. Whistle In (Brian Wilson)

Mike Love: vocals / Brian Wilson: vocals, keyboards, bass guitar / Carl
Wilson: vocals, guitar / Al Jardine: vocals, guitar / Dennis Wilson: vocals,
drums / session musicians / The Beach Boys: producer
```

Wilson abandoning the *Smile* project altogether. Some of the music was finished, but much of it was not, with the vocal parts missing from backing tracks that had themselves not been fully signed off. The unexpected release in 2004 of a finished recording of *Smile* in Brian Wilson's name (and using the Wondermints group to deliver all the playing and singing apart from Wilson's own) provided a triumphant vindication of the music ideas that were in Brian Wilson's head and made it clear that if the music had been completed in 1967, then it would have made an album that would certainly have been hailed as one of the most unqualified masterpieces of the decade. The music emerges as a coherent work that is almost symphonic in its ambition, with themes that are developed in different ways through the various sections, linking the songs together. *Smiley Smile* is what was released instead. It includes the original version of *Good Vibrations*, but otherwise comprises some swiftly re-recorded (and simpler) versions of some of the *Smile* songs, alongside some even more swiftly recorded music that struggles to become anything more than filler (on an album that is in any case barely longer than just one side of a typical Beatles UK album). Of course, any record that includes both the magnificent *Good Vibrations* and the equally remarkable *Heroes and Villains* (even when presented in a somewhat stripped-down rendering) cannot fail to impress to some extent, but the fact that *Smiley Smile* is clearly a shadow of what it could have been makes it impossible for the album to be be given much acclaim.

CHAD STUART AND JEREMY CLYDE   OF CABBAGES AND KINGS

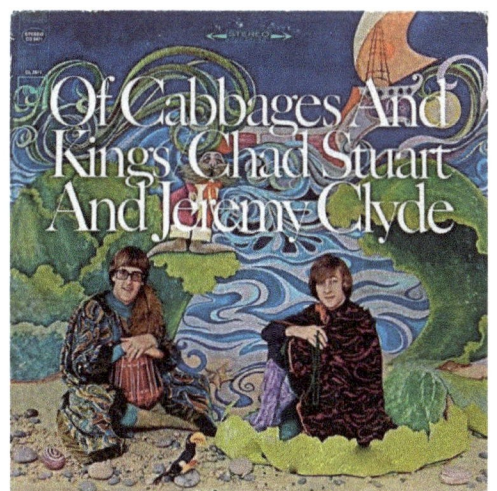

```
US release       September 1967    Columbia   CS 9471/CL 2671
Not released in UK

1. Rest In Peace (Chad Stuart)
2. The Gentle Cold Of Dawn (Jeremy Clyde)
3. Busman's Holiday (Jeremy Clyde)
4. Can I See You (Jeremy Clyde)
5. Family Way (Jeremy Clyde)
6. I'll Get Around To It When And If I Can (James William Guercio)

7. The Progress Suite:
       Prologue (Chad Stuart)
       Decline (Chad Stuart)
       Editorial (Vocal) (Jeremy Clyde)
       Fall (Chad Stuart)
       Epilogue (Vocal) (Jeremy Clyde)

Chad Stuart: vocals, guitar, banjo, ukulele, sitar, keyboards / Jeremy
Clyde: vocals, guitar / James William Guercio: bass guitar / Gary Usher:
producer / various uncredited session musicians   probably including
JIm Gordon: drums
```

Chad Stewart and Jeremy Clyde (previously working as 'Chad and Jeremy') were a British pop-folk duo who managed to achieve far more success in the US than in their home country. *Yesterday's Gone* was a very minor UK hit at the end of 1963, but in the US it became the first of eleven chart hits, including one top ten entry (*A Summer Song*). *Of Cabbages And Kings* was the sixth album to be released by the duo and the first to be made up almost entirely of songs written by themselves. The music is as elaborately arranged, as psychedelic, as any other album from this time, making comparisons with the Beatles *Sgt Pepper* easy, although it is more likely that the main influence on Chad and Jeremy's new direction would have been Donovan and his *Sunshine Superman* and *Mellow Yellow* albums. *Of Cabbages And Kings* is an impressive collection of music, although it was not a huge seller, had no singles taken from it, and was not released at all in the UK, so that it has acquired much less of a long term reputation than other albums from 1967. Regardless, Chad and Jeremy did get to make another record in the same style, *The Ark*, released a year later, although they broke up soon afterwards. Chad Stewart had some success subsequently as a producer, while Jeremy Clyde managed to relaunch himself as an actor.

SCOTT WALKER   SCOTT

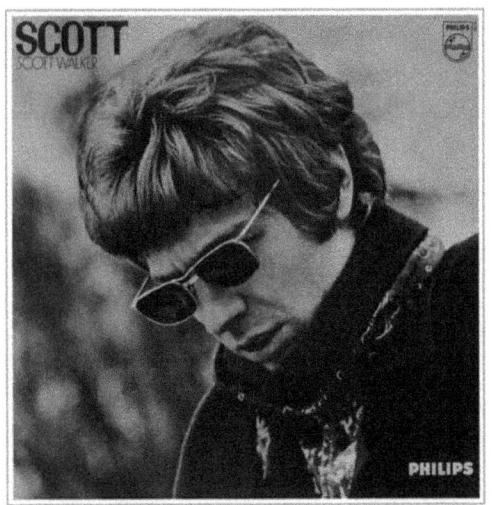

| UK release | September 1967 | Philips | (S)BL 7816 |
| US release | early 1968 | Smash | SRS 67099 / MGS 27099 as |
ALONER

1. Mathilde (Jacques Brel/Gerard Jouannest/Mort Shuman)
2. Montague Terrace (In Blue) (Scott Engel)
3. Angelica (Cynthia Weil/Barry Mann)
4. The Lady Came From Baltimore (Tim Hardin)
5. When Joanna Loved Me (Jack Segal/Robert Wells)
6. My Death (Jacques Brel.Mort Shuman)

7. The Big Hurt (Wayne Shanklin)
8. Such A Small Love (Scott Engel)
9. You're Gonna Hear From Me (André Previn/Dory Previn)
10. Through A Long And Sleepless Night (Mack Gordon/Alfred Newman)
11. Always Coming Back To You (Scott Engel)
12. Amsterdam (Jacques Brel/Mort Shuman)

Scott Walker: vocals / Wally Stott: arranger (1,2,5,7,8) / Reg Guest: arranger (3,4,6,11) / Peter Knight: arranger (9,10) / John Franz: producer

Scott Walker (real name Scott Engel) was a member of the Walker Brothers – two singers and a rather superfluous drummer – who gained nine chart hits in the UK with some undemanding pop material, including two number ones, between 1965 and 1967. The trio, who were not actually brothers, were American, but in a reversal of the usual situation, were much more successful in the UK. The group split following a UK tour in April and Scott launched his solo career with this album. He had a rich, honeyed tenor voice and might have been expected to move even further in an easy listening direction than the Walker Brothers. In fact, his choice of material, including songs written by Jacques Brel and some of his own, digs altogether more deeply. The music is orchestrated, but with arrangements that tend to be unusually constructed, with a touch almost of the avant garde in places. Engelbert Humperdinck employed the same kind of voice on chart topping records like *Release Me* and *The Last Waltz* (which were mainly bought by an older generation). But it is impossible to imagine him ever recording something as unsettling as *Such A Small Love* or *My Death,* or as poetic as *Montague Terrace (In Blue).* Scott Walker was building his own following, however, and his first album entered the top three in the UK album charts.

THE DOORS   STRANGE DAYS

| US release | September 1967 | Elektra | EKS-74014 / EKL-4014 |
| UK release | September 1967 | Elektra | EKS-74014 / EKL-4014 |

1. Strange Days
2. You're Lost Little Girl
3. Love Me Two Times
4. Unhappy Girl
5. Horse Latitudes
6. Moonlight Drive

7. People Are Strange
8. My Eyes Have Seen You
9. I Can't See Your Face In My Mind
10. When The Music's Over

All compositions by the Doors

Jim Morrison: vocals / Robby Krieger: guitar / Ray Manzarek: keyboards, marimba / John Densmore: drums / Doug Lubahn: bass guitar / Paul A. Rothchild: producer

The second album by the Doors consolidates the group's sound and does so with a set of songs almost as strong as those on the first album. There is no *Light My Fire,* but *People Are Strange* and *Love Me Two Times* are serious contenders. They were both issued as singles and were US hits, though not huge ones. The album retains the concept of a marathon, semi-improvised finale: *When The Music's Over* is perhaps more impressive than *The End* and manages to resist including any shocking content. *Strange Days* failed to gain any more UK fans for the group, but it achieved platinum status in the US.

THE CHOCOLATE WATCH BAND   NO WAY OUT

The Chocolate Watch Band was a late arrival in the American punk arena, at a time when its rough and ready sound was already being rapidly superseded by the more sophisticated San Francisco groups. The album cover attempts to pass the group off as a member of the psychedelic vanguard, but the actual music is less convincing, even with occasional touches of sitar (or at least a guitar that sounds like one) or ethereal or distorted organ, and titles like *Dark Side Of The Mushroom.* This track is actually a plodding instrumental where a fuzz-toned guitar tries valiantly to achieve lift-off, but fails. Unnecessary covers of songs by Wilson Pickett and Chuck Berry suggest a problem with finding original material (and half the songs on the album are the work of the production team, not the group). The version of *Come On* is a close copy of the first single by the Rolling Stones, from four years previously, and rather pointless. The energetic opening track, *Let's Talk*

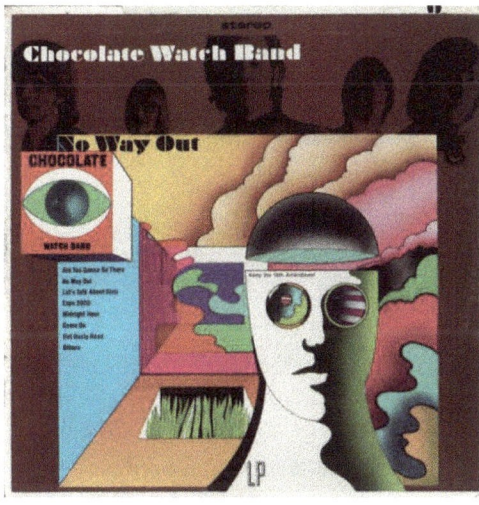

```
US release       September 1967    Tower    (S)T 5096
Not released in UK

1. Let's Talk About Girls (Manny Freiser)
2. In The Midnight Hour (Steve Cropper/Wilson Pickett)
3. Come On (Chuck Berry)
4. Dark Side Of The Mushroom (Bill Cooper/Richard Podolor)
5. Hot Dusty Roads (Steve Stills)

6. Are You Gonna Be There (At The Love-In) (Don Bennett/Ethon McElroy)
7. Gone And Passes By (David Aguilar)
8. No Way Out (Ed Cobb)
9. Expo 2000 (Richard Podolor)
10.Gossamer Wings (Don Bennett/Ethon McElroy)

David Aguilar: vocals, keyboards / Don Bennett: vocals / Mark Loomis:
guitar, keyboards / Sean Tolby: guitar / Bill Flores: bass guitar / Gary
Andrijasevich: drums / Ed Cobb: producer
```

About Girls, however, is instantly memorable and would have made a fine single, although it was the less remarkable *Are You Gonna Be There* that was actually chosen (and did not sell). It is likely that session musicians were used to enhance the Chocolate Watch Band's sound (certainly an uncredited violin player makes a notable appearance) and singer Don Bennett, who carries both *Let's Talk About Girls* and *Are You Gonna Be There,* was not a member of the group.

THE COWSILLS

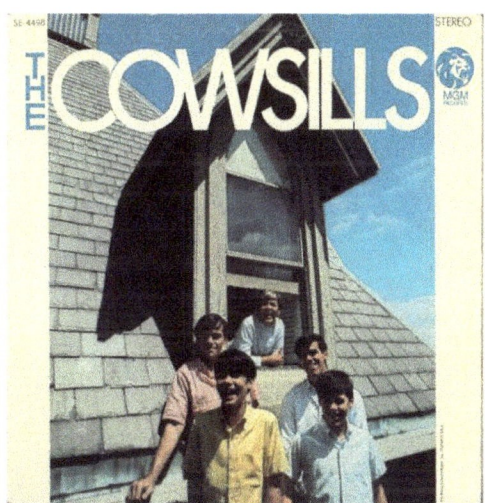

```
US release       September 1967    MGM      (S)E 4498
UK release       September 1967    MGM      MGMC 8059

1. The Rain, The Park And Other Things (Artie Kornfeld/Steve Duboff)
2. Pennies (Artie Kornfeld/Bill Cowsill/Bob Cowsill)
3. La Rue Du Soleil (Artie Kornfeld/Bill Cowsill/Bob Cowsill)
4. Thinkin' About The Other Side (Bill Cowsill/Bob Cowsill)
5. Dreams Of Linda (Artie Kornfeld/Bill Cowsill)
6. River Blue (Artie Kornfeld/Bill Cowsill/Bob Cowsill)

7. Gettin' Into That Sunny, Sunny Feelin' Again (Artie Kornfeld/John Morier)
8. That's My Time Of The Day (Artie Kornfeld/Steve Duboff)
9. Troubled Roses (Richard Keelan)
10.(Stop, Look) Is Anyone There? (Bill Cowsill/Bob Cowsill/Steve Duboff)
11.How Can I Make You See? (Artie Kornfeld/Bill Cowsill/Bob Cowsill)
12.I'm The One You Need (Brian Holland/Lamont Dozier/Eddie Holland)

Barbara Cowsill: vocals / Bill Cowsill: vocals, guitar / Bob Cowsill: guitar,
vocals / Barry Cowsill: bass guitar, vocals / John Cowsill: drums, vocals /
Jimmy Wisner: arranger / Vinnie Bell: guitar / Charles Macy: guitar / Al
Gorgoni: guitar / Artie Butler: organ / Paul Griffin: piano / Gene Bianco:
harp / Buddy Saltzman: drums / Al Rogers: drums / George Devens:
percussion / Artie Kornfeld: producer
```

The Cowsills comprised a mother and four of her sons, the youngest of whom were eleven and thirteen. They performed lightly arranged harmony pop and sounded quite similar to the Mamas and the Papas or a less ambitious Beach Boys. They achieved a big US hit with *The Rain, The Park And Other Things,* which is as memorable as most of the singles by the more established groups, if rather more naive lyrically. It is the stand-out track on the album, its happy sound with a frequently cascading harp helping to define the genre of 'sunshine pop'. In the more inclement UK, however, the Cowsills and indeed their entire genre failed to make much impression.

CLEAR LIGHT

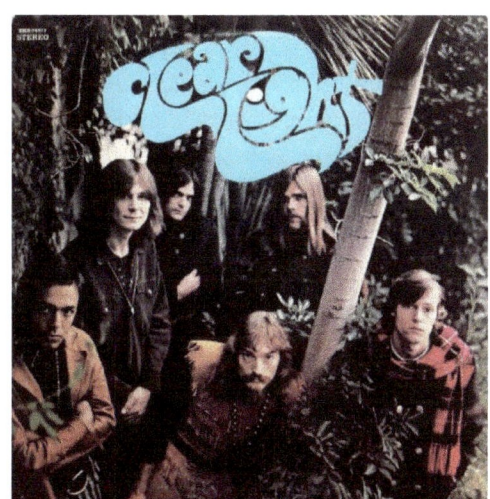

```
US and UK release    September 1967    Elektra    EKS-74011/EKL-4011

1. Black Roses (Clear Light/Wolfgang Dios)
2. Sand (Doug Lubahn)
3. A Child's Smile (Clear Light/Michael Ney)
4. Street Singer (Greg Copeland/Steve Noonan)
5. The Ballad Of Freddie And Larry (Cliff De Young/Ralph Schuckett)
6. With All In Mind (Bob Seal)

7. Mr Blue (Tom Paxton)
8. Think Again (Doug Lubahn)
9. They Who Have Nothing (Bob Seal)
10.How Many Days Have Passed (Bob Seal)
11.Night Sounds Loud (Doug Lubahn)

Cliff De Young: vocals / Bob Seal: guitar, vocals / Ralph Schuckett:
keyboards / Doug Lubahn: bass guitar / Michael Ney: drums,
percussion / Dallas Taylor: drums / Paul A Rothchild: producer
```

The one album completed by Los Angeles group Clear Light is a well played and mildly inventive set of Californian psych-rock by a group that somehow failed to gain the same success as the better known exponents of the same kind of music. This was despite having the same producer and record label as the Doors. The group does not have any member as charismatic as Jim Morrison, although Bob Seal is a frequently inspired lead guitarist, but the real problem lies in the material, which is solid but not particularly memorable. An extended and reworked version of Tom Paxton's song, *Mr Blue,* is satisfyingly ambitious and weird, but not enough on its own to turn the album into a great one. Some of the members subsequently found gainful musical employment elsewhere. Dallas Taylor, one of two drummers playing together here, became a member of Crosby, Stills, Nash, and Young, Ralph Schuckett played with Todd Rundgren in the seventies, and Doug Lubahn played bass guitar on the albums by the Doors.

THE ALAN PRICE SET   A PRICE ON HIS HEAD

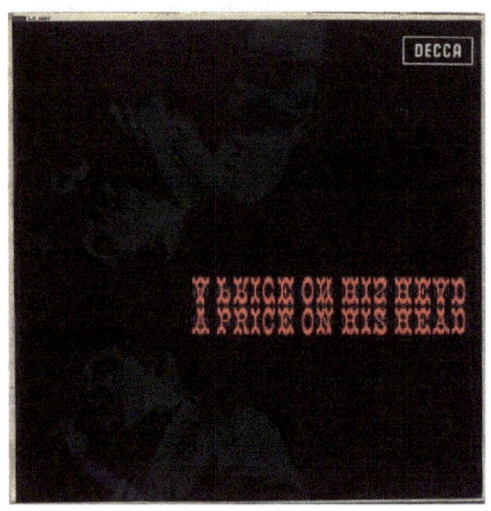

UK release   September 1967   Decca   SKL/LK 4907
Not released in US;   THIS PRICE IS RIGHT   1968
Parrot PAS 71018/ PA 61018 has 7 of the same tracks

1. The House That Jack Built (Alan Price)
2. She's Got Another Pair Of Shoes (Alan Price)
3. Come And Dance With Me (Randy Newman)
4. On This Side Of Goodbye (Gerry Goffin/Carole King)
5. So Long Dad (Randy Newman)
6. No One Ever Hurt So Bad (Randy Newman)
7. Don't Do That Again (Alan Price)

8. Tickle Me (Randy Newman)
9. Grim Fairy Tale (Alan Price)
10. Living Without You (Randy Newman)
11. Happy Land (Randy Newman)
12. To Ramona (Bob Dylan)
13. Biggest Night Of Her Life (Randy Newman)

Alan Price: vocals, keyboards, arranger, producer / Peter Kirtley: guitar / John Walters: trumpet / Clive Burrows: saxophones, flute / Steve Gregory: saxophones, flute / Rod Slade: bass guitar / Ray Mills: drums / Ivor Raymonde: arranger / Mike Leander: arranger

In May 1965, Alan Price left the group he had founded, the Animals, in order to begin a solo career. Initially, he continued to perform the same kind of R&B material as before and the first album he released, in 1966, *The Price To Play*, was in this style. His discovery, however, of the work of American singer songwriter Randy Newman (yet to make an album of his own) caused him to make a surprising change of direction. Seven of the songs on *A Price On His Head* are by Newman, with a further four written by Alan Price himself in the same style. He sticks to piano for the most part and the Set play well but in a rather understated manner, while light orchestral arrangements are added in a few places. The focus is very much on the songs, just as it would have been if this had been an actual Randy Newman album. Issued as a single, *The House That Jack Built* was the last substantial hit that Alan Price enjoyed in the sixties, completing a run of four. The album sold poorly, however, clearly not delivering what fans of the Animals hoped to hear.

SAVOY BROWN BLUES BAND   SHAKE DOWN

UK release   September 1967   Decca   SKL/LK 4883
Not released in US

1. I Ain't Superstitious (Willie Dixon)
2. Let Me Love You Baby (Willie Dixon)
3. Black Night (Jessie Mae Robinson)
4. High Rise (Freddie King/Beverly Bridge/Sonny Thompson)
5. Rock Me Baby (B.B.King/Joe Josea)
6. I Smell Trouble (Don Robey)

7. Oh Pretty Woman (Albert King)
8. Little Girl (Howlin' Wolf)
9. The Doormouse Rides The Rails (Martin Stone)
10. It's My Own Fault (John Lee Hooker)
11. Shake 'Em On Down (Traditional)

Brice Portius: vocals / Martin Stone: guitar / Kim Simmonds: guitar / Bob Hall: piano (1,8,11) / Ray Chappell: bass guitar / Leo Mannings: drums / Mike Vernon: producer

Following the club success of John Mayall and Alexis Korner, the first album by a new British blues group, Savoy Brown Blues Band, provided evidence that the music was beginning to acquire the status of a movement. The band performs convincing versions of an assortment of blues originals, together with one instrumental of their own. It manages to neatly sidestep any accusations of not being sufficiently 'authentic' by featuring a black singer and it is also blessed with two fine guitarists. Neither is quite in the same league as Mayall's players, Eric Clapton and Peter Green, but they both employ the same exciting sound of overdriven Gibson Les Paul guitars and they are certainly fluent enough to make the band sound effective. The album made no impact on the charts, although it did sell well enough to persuade Decca to keep faith with the band.

THE VENTURES   GOLDEN GREATS

The Ventures are the American equivalent of the Shadows, being an instrumental guitar group scoring numerous hits from 1960 onwards. The tracks included on *Golden Greats* date from 1960 to 1964. Curiously, the lead guitar role passed from Bob Boyle to Nokie Edwards in 1963, when the original bass and lead players swapped instruments. The group gamely tried to keep up with rock music developments over the years and their other albums in 1967 included two glorying in the titles *Guitar Freakout* and *Super Psychedelics*, although the actual music changed hardly at all. Sustained by huge success in both the US and Japan, the original Ventures continued to record and perform well into the twenty-first century.

| US release | September 1967 | Liberty | LST-8053/LRP 2053 |
| UK release | September 1967 | Liberty | LBS/LBL 83046 |

1. Telstar (Joe Meek)
2. The Lonely Bull (Sol Lake)
3. Rebel Rouser (Duane Eddy/Lee Hazelwood)
4. Honky Tonk (Bill Doggett/Billy Butler/Clifford Scott/Henry Glover/Shep Shepherd)
5. Let's Go (Lanny Duncan/Robert Duncan)
6. Pipeline (Bob Spickard/Brian Carman)
7. Walk, Don't Run (Johnny Smith)
8. Tequila (Chuck Rio)
9. Apache (Jerry Lordan)
10. Wipe Out (The Surfaris)
11. Memphis (Chuck Berry)
12. Out Of Limits (Michael Gordon)

Nokie Edwards: guitar, bass guitar / Bob Boyle: bass guitar, guitar / Don Wilson: guitar / Howie Johnson: drums (7) / Skip Moore: drums (4) / Mel Taylor: drums / Joe Saraceno: producer

JOHN COLTRANE   EXPRESSION

| US release | September 1967 | Impulse | A(S)-9120 |
| UK release | June 1968 | Impulse | SIPL/MIPL 502 |

1. Ogunde
2. To Be
3. Offering
4. Expression

All compositions by John Coltrane

John Coltrane: tenor saxophone, flute, producer / Pharoah Sanders: piccolo (2) / Alice Coltrane: piano / Jimmy Garrison: bass / Rashied Ali: drums / Bob Thiele: producer

The front cover of *Expression* carries John Coltrane's dates, to make it clear that the saxophonist had died in July. He had succumbed to cancer of the liver at the age of just forty. These are his last recordings. The music gives no indication that Coltrane was ill and it includes some of his most energetic, aggressive playing. Much of *Offering*, in particular, comprises a ferocious duet for tenor saxophone and drums in which the music surges forward without the restraint of either a particular key or a particular pulse. In contrast, the brief opening track, *Ogunde*, provides a peaceful, melodic entry to the album, like a musical Trojan horse. *To Be* is a lengthy work-out for flute, sometimes in collaboration with Pharoah Sanders' piccolo, and is the only occasion when Coltrane featured the instrument in the studio. The album shows that Coltrane had lost none of his questing spirit, despite knowing that he was unlikely to be recording anything else. It is a tribute to a great musician that he was able to ensure that his last album was also one of his most memorable.

MIKE WESTBROOK   CELEBRATION

| UK release | September 1967 | Deram | SML/DML 1013 |
Not released in US

1. Pastoral (Mike Westbrook)
2. Awakening (John Surman)
3. Parade (Mike Westbrook)
4. Echoes And Heroics (Mike Westbrook)
5. A Greeting (Mike Westbrook)
6. Image (John Surman)
7. Dirge (John Surman)
8. Portrait (Mike Westbrook)

Mike Westbrook: piano / Mike Osborne: alto saxophone / Bernie Living: alto saxophone, flute / John Surman: baritone and soprano saxophones, bass clarinet / Dave Chambers: tenor saxophone, clarinet / Dave Holdsworth: trumpet, flugelhorn / Malcolm Griffiths: trombone / Dave Perottet: valve trombone / Tom Bennellick: French horn / George Smith: tuba / Harry Miller: bass / Alan Jackson: drums / Eddie Kramer: producer

British jazz pianist and composer Mike Westbrook managed to maintain a big band, although inevitably all its musicians also found employment elsewhere. He had established his first line-up in 1958 and had moved through several changes in personnel since then, but *Celebration* was the band's first recording. It comprises a shortened version of a two hour work that was performed at a music festival held at Dartington College of Arts in Devon. The music is modern but accessible, clearly influenced by the likes of Charles Mingus, but finding a distinctive voice of its own. In keeping with the album title, the mood of the music is indeed celebratory, with the exception of the accurately titled *Dirge*. Although twelve musicians are involved, they are primarily used to provide colour rather than density and there are numerous passages where only the rhythm section and whoever is soloing can be heard. Fortunately, Westbrook is very well served by his soloists, who include, in John Surman and Mike Oborne, two saxophonists of international standard. *Celebration* is undoubtedly a fine album, but ultimately its primary interest lies in providing a first outing for a band-leader and some individual performers who would go on to make some very great music indeed.

ORNETTE COLEMAN   AN EVENING WITH

UK release   September 1967   Polydor   623 246/247
US release   1975   Arista/Freedom   AL 1900   as
THE GREAT LONDON CONCERT

1. Forms and Sounds for Wind Quintet

2. Sadness
3. Clergyman's Dream

4. Falling Stars
5. Silence

6. Happy Fool
7. Ballad
8. Dough Nuts

All compositions by Ornette Coleman

Ornette Coleman: alto saxophone, violin (4), trumpet (4) / David Izenzon: bass / Charles Moffett: drums / track 1: The Virtuoso Ensemble – Cecil James: bassoon / Sidney Fell: clarinet / Edward Walker: flute / John Burden: horn / Derek Wickens: oboe / Alan Bates: producer

This double album, issued in a box, presents the music played at a concert in south London in August 1965. *Forms And Sounds for Wind Quintet*, which occupies the whole of side one, is not jazz at all, but a composed work in an austere post-Schoenberg classical mode. It helps to enhance Coleman's standing as a composer, but in deliberately avoiding any kind of emotional content, it provides a listening experience that few are likely to want to repeat very often. The performances by Ornette Coleman's trio are another matter altogether, however. This is the same group that appears on the earlier *At The Golden Circle* albums (actually recorded four months after *An Evening With*), although none of the pieces there are repeated on this set. The music, freely improvised around skeletal structures, is varied in mood, frequently very emotional, and a delight throughout. Placed alongside *At The Golden Circle* and *Chappaqua Suite*, the album establishes Ornette Coleman as one of the most vital jazz musicians of his generation. Curiously, the album was not issued in the US until some eight years later, although the music is sufficiently timeless to be able to still make a fresh impact even then.

DAVE DEE, DOZY, BEAKY, MICK & TICH   GOLDEN HITS

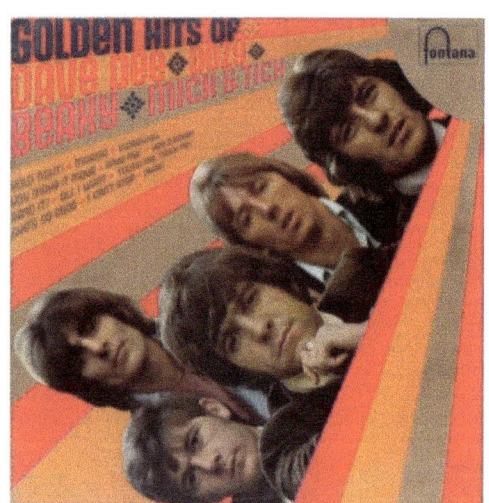

The group with the extraordinary name was adopted by the songwriting team of Ken Howard and Alan Blaikley, previously known for their work with the Honeycombs, and made its first record at the beginning of 1965. *You Make It Move* was a minor UK hit at the end of that year, while *Hold Tight* became the first of eight top ten hits (through to the summer of 1968). The group was much less successful in the US, although Fontana still judged that it was worthwhile to issue a *Greatest Hits* compilation in that country. Always dressed in the height of mod fashion, Dave Dee, Dozy, Beaky, Mick & Tich gave the impression of being at the forefront of pop music development. In truth, although their singles were always very inventive, they were very much aimed at the charts, with cheerful sing-along melodies and catchy choruses. Their original albums failed to convince. Surprisingly, *Golden Hits* was not itself a chart success, but presumably the group's fans had already bought all the singles.

UK release   October 1967
Fontana   (S)TL 5441
US release   October 1967   Fontana SRF 67567/MGF 27567   as   **GREATEST HITS**, 10 tracks, 6 in common

1. Bend It
2. All I Want
3. Touch Me Touch Me
4. She's So Good
5. I Can't Stop
6. Okay!

7. Hold Tight
8. Marina
9. Hideaway
10. You Make It Move
11. Save Me
12. He's A Raver

All compositions by Alan Blaikley/Ken Howard apart from tracks 4,8,12 by Dave Dee, Dozy, Beaky, Mick & Tich

Dave Dee Harman: vocals / Trevor Ward-Davies (Dozy): bass guitar / John Dymond (Beaky): guitar / Mick Wilson: drums / Ian Amey (Tich): guitar / Ken Howard: piano / Steve Rowland: producer

THE YARDBIRDS   THE HITS OF

Canada release   October 1967   Capitol   (D)T 6229
US release   March 1967   Epic   BN 26246/LN 24246   as
GREATEST HITS   different cover and several different tracks

1. Happenings Ten Years Time Ago (Yardbirds)
2. Still I'm Sad (Jim McCarty/Paul Samwell-Smith)
3. My Girl Sloopy (Bert Russell/Wes Farrell)
4. For Your Love (Graham Gouldman)
5. Evil Hearted You (Graham Gouldman)
6. Heart Full Of Soul (Graham Gouldman)
7. I'm A Man (Bo Diddley)
8. Over Under Sideways Down (Yardbirds)
9. Smokestack Lightnin' (Howlin' Wolf)
10. You're A Better Man Than I (Mike Hugg)
11. Shapes Of Things (Keith Relf/Jim McCarty/Paul Samwell-Smith)

Keith Relf: vocals, harmonica / Chris Dreja: guitar, bass guitar (1) / Eric Clapton: guitar (4,9) / Jeff Beck: guitar (except 4,9) / Jimmy Page: guitar (1) / Paul Samwell-Smith: bass guitar (except 1) / Jim McCarty: drums / Brian Auger: harpsichord (4) / Denny Pierce: bongos (4) / Ron Prentice: bass (4) / Giorgio Gomelsky: producer

The chaotic state of the Yardbirds' catalogue is rather emphasised by the fact that a number of countries issued compilations of the group's hits, but with different track listings and different covers. In the UK, no compilation was issued at all. The Canadian version of the album has the most useful selection of songs, certainly rather better than the more well-known US edition, issued a few months earlier. There are one or two strange choices even here (the extended version of the retitled McCoys' hit, *Hang On Sloopy*, was not a single and does little to enhance the Yardbirds' reputation), but for the most part, these are the songs that explain why the Yardbirds continue to be held in high regard. Jeff Beck is a marvel on electric guitar on the majority of the tracks, but he is providing an additional point of interest on songs that are already very distinctive. The album begins and ends, however, with masterpieces of psychedelia on which it is impossible to imagine the music being delivered without the incendiary guitar playing. On *Happening Ten Years Time Ago* this is delivered by two lead guitarists working together, both Jeff Beck and Jimmy Page.

ARLO GUTHRIE   ALICE'S RESTAURANT

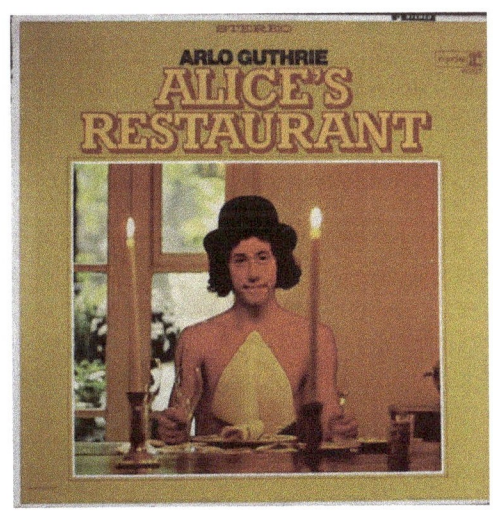

US release   October 1967   Reprise   R(S)-6267
UK release   October 1967   Reprise   R(S)LP 6267

1. Alice's Restaurant Massacree
2. Chilling Of The Evening
3. Ring-Around-A-Rosy Rag
4. Now And Then
5. I'm Going Home
6. The Motorcycle Song
7. Highway In The Wind

All compositions by Arlo Guthrie

Arlo Guthrie: vocals, guitar, banjo / unknown guitar, piano, bass, drums / Fred Hellerman: producer

As the son of iconic folk music pioneer Woody Guthrie, it was not altogether surprising that Arlo chose to follow a folk music career too. He is a decent ragtime acoustic guitarist and he knows how to win over an audience, as he proves on the tongue-in-cheek *Motorcycle Song*, recorded live. The other songs on side two of the album are nothing extraordinary, but fortunately Arlo Guthrie is able to extend the strengths of *The Motorcycle Song* to fill the whole of side one. Also recorded in front of an audience, *Alice's Restaurant Massacree* is essentially a lengthy comedy routine, framed by a memorable chorus, and performed over a guitar accompaniment with a light rhythm section. The tale is funny and bears repeated listening, its success being emphasised by the fact that it served as the inspiration for a film, directed two years later by Arthur Penn and starring Arlo Guthrie himself.

PHIL OCHS   PLEASURES OF THE HARBOR

Phil Ochs was one of the more interesting political folk singers to emerge in the wake of Bob Dylan. His early songs *I Ain't Marching Anymore* and *There But For Fortune* attracted some attention, but overall he failed to gain success anywhere near that achieved by Dylan. *Pleasures Of The Harbor* is his fourth album and the first in which he used a more elaborate accompaniment than just his own acoustic guitar. The result is a distinctly baroque pop sound on many of the tracks, although the concluding song, *The Crucifixion*, makes a startling move towards the avant garde, with dissonant strings surrounding a manic chamber ensemble. *Outside Of A Small Circle Of Friends*, juxtaposing a jaunty honky-tonk piano against barbed lyrics, came close to being a hit and is certainly Phil Ochs' best known song. Sadly, the album's ambitious take on the singer-songwriter genre brought no more record sales than its more straightforward predecessors. Ochs managed to

| US release | October 1967 | A&M | (SP-4)133 |
| UK release | October 1967 | A&M | AML 913 |

1. Cross My Heart
2. Flower Lady
3. Outside Of A Small Circle Of Friends
4. I've Had Her
5. Miranda
6. The Party
7. Pleasures Of The Harbor
8. The Crucifixion

All compositions by Phil Ochs

Phil Ochs: vocals, guitar / Lincoln Mayorga: piano / Warren Zevon: guitar (7) / Ian Freebairn-Smith: arranger / Joseph Byrd: arranger, keyboards (8) / Larry Marks: producer

make three more albums with a similar approach to *Pleasures Of The Harbor,* including a sarcastically titled *Greatest Hits* album, which actually contained entirely new material. The cover was modelled on the one used for Elvis Presley's second *Gold Records* compilation and included the self-deprecating slogan '50 Phil Ochs Fans Can't Be Wrong'. His declining mental state was brought into focus by concerts where he dressed in a gold lamé suit like Elvis and performed sets dominated by cover versions of Elvis Presley, Buddy Holly, and Merle Haggard material. He committed suicide in 1976.

JUDY COLLINS   WILDFLOWERS

| US and UK release | October 1967 | Elektra | EKS 74012/EKL 4012 |

1. Michael From Mountains (Joni Mitchell)
2. Since You Asked (Judy Collins)
3. Sisters Of Mercy (Leonard Cohen)
4. Priests (Leonard Cohen)
5. A Ballata Of Francesco Landini - Lassi! Di Donna
6. Both Sides Now (Joni Mitchell)
7. La Chanson Des Vieux Amants (The Song Of Old Lovers) (Jacques Brel)
8. Sky Fell (Judy Collins)
9. Albatross (Judy Collins)
10. Hey, That's No Way To Say Goodbye (Leonard Cohen)

Judy Collins: vocals, guitar / Joshua Rifkin: keyboards, arranger / Robert Sylvester and Robert Dennis: arrangers on track 4 / Mark Abramson: producer

Wildflowers continues the approach of Judy Collins' previous album, *In My Life,* to even greater effect. Once again, light orchestral arrangements dominate; they are the work of Joshua Rifkin, a man who would soon become well-known in his own right as the pianist responsible for albums of ragtime music composed by Scott Joplin. Ms Collins finds some more songs by Leonard Cohen, as well as two by another new songwriter, Joni Mitchell. Her version of *Both Sides Now* establishes the song as a considerable classic, some two years before Mitchell was able to record her own interpretation. For the first time, Judy Collins also presents three songs of her own, displaying the confidence and expertise of someone who might have been been working as a songwriter for several years. It must have been a source of considerable gratification for Judy Collins when the most impressive artistic statement of her career so far also achieved her greatest commercial success. It reached number five in the US album chart and was eventually awarded a gold disc. Meanwhile *Both Sides Now* was issued as a single and was itself a top ten hit. The single was a hit in the UK too, though not until over two years later.

JOHN MARTYN   LONDON CONVERSATION

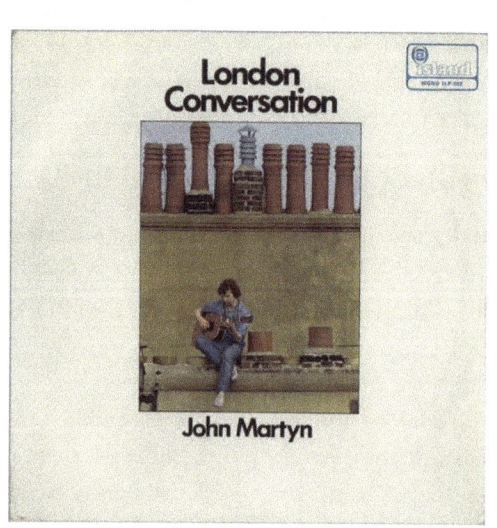

London Conversation is acoustic guitar folk music very much in the style of Bert Jansch, although John Martyn presents all songs here, no instrumentals. Martyn stated that, like Jansch, it was hearing Davy Graham play that inspired him to do the same. Occasionally, a Celtic lilt in Martyn's husky voice is reminiscent of the Incredible String Band, and one track, *Rolling Home,* finds Martyn switching

| UK release | October 1967 | Island | ILP 952 |
| Not released in US | | | |

1. Fairy Tale Lullaby (John Martyn)
2. Sandy Grey (Robin Frederick)
3. London Conversation (John Martyn/Jon Sundell)
4. Ballad Of An Elder Woman (John Martyn)
5. Cocain (Traditional)
6. Run Honey Run (John Martyn)
7. Back To Stay (John Martyn)
8. Rolling Home (John Martyn)
9. Who's Grown Up Now (John Martyn)
10. Golden Girl (John Martyn)
11. This Time (John Martyn)
12. Don't Think Twice It's Alright (Bob Dylan)

John Martyn: vocals, guitar, sitar / uncredited flute on track 8 / Theo Johnson: producer

his guitar for a sitar. Playing in the folk clubs in London, Martyn attracted the attention of record company proprietor Chris Blackwell, who was looking for suitable artists to enable him to expand his Island record label to cover more than just the reggae in which he had hitherto specialised. Overall, *London Conversation* is a competent but not particularly thrilling set, and the Dylan cover with which the record ends is little more than a throw-away. But the album does serve well what turned out to be its main purpose, in introducing a musician who would go on to make a significant contribution to the music of the seventies and beyond.

AL STEWART   BED SITTER IMAGES

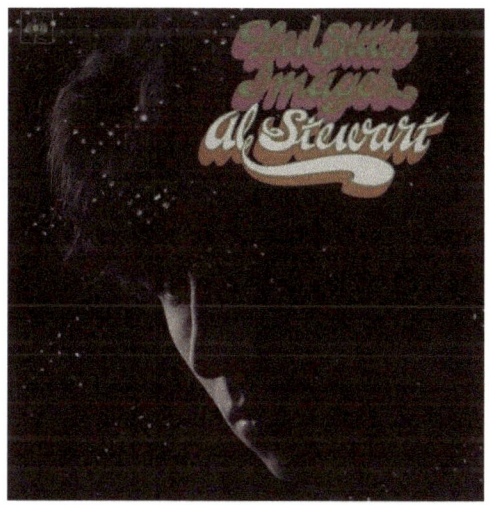

UK release   October 1967   CBS   (S)BPG 63087
Not released in US

1. Bedsitter Images
2. Swiss Cottage Manoeuvres
3. The Carmichaels
4. Scandinavian Girl
5. Pretty Golden Hair
6. Denise At 16
7. Samuel, Oh How You've Changed!
8. Cleave To Me
9. A Long Way Down From Stephanie
10. Ivich
11. Baleeka Doodle Day

All compositions by Al Stewart

Al Stewart: vocals, guitar / Alexander Faris: arranger / Roy Guest: producer

UK singer songwriter Al Stewart had previously issued a pop-folk single for a different label without much success. Signed to CBS, Stewart made an album which fared little better, despite a selection of songs displaying his song writing abilities much more effectively. The music retains the elaborate orchestrated sound of the single, frequently overwhelming Stewart's acoustic guitar playing, although *Denise At 16* and *Ivich* are solo showcases and prove that he is an accomplished performer. Lyrically, Al Stewart mixes intensely personal romantic reminiscing with well-observed descriptions of other people's lives. The former aspect makes him into the first 'confessional' songwriting performer. The orchestrations on recent albums by Judy Collins and Phil Ochs showed how the result can be to greatly enhance the music. For Al Stewart's album, however, these are not done sympathetically and they have the opposite effect. It was significant that CBS chose not to release the album in the US.

BOBBY BARE & THE HILLSIDERS

US release   October 1967   RCA Victor   LSP/LPM-3896
UK release   October 1967   RCA Victor   SF/RD 7918

1. You All Come (Arlie Duff)
2. Find Out What's Happening (Jerry Crutchfield)
3. Love's Gonna Live Here (Buck Owens)
4. I Love You Drops (Bill Anderson)
5. I Washed My Face In The Morning Dew (Tom T. Hall)
6. Goin' Home (Harlan Howard)
7. The Great Snow Man (John D. Loudermilk)
8. Blue Is My Lonely Room (Sid Hill)
9. Release Me (Eddie Miller/W.S. Stevenson)
10. Sweet Dreams (Don Gibson)
11. Six Days On The Road (Carl Montgomery/Earl Green)

Bobby Bare: vocals, guitar / Kenny Johnson: vocals / Brian Hilton: guitar / Frankie Wan: steel guitar / Joe Butler: bass guitar / Noddy Redman: drums / Chet Atkins: producer

Coming from Liverpool, the Hillsiders performed country music rather than beat and did so much more authentically than the Downliners Sect. During 1967 the group was given the chance to play with established country star Bobby Bare and to join the concert bill at the Grand Ole Opry in Nashville, an extraordinary opportunity for a British act. *The English Country Side* is not a spectacular album, but it is not intended to be. Produced by legendary country guitarist Chet Atkins, the music is totally convincing and a tribute to how well the Hillsiders have absorbed an American style that is not rock 'n' roll.

NICO   CHELSEA GIRL

Andy Warhol's singing discovery was included on the first album by the Velvet Underground and three quarters of the group is on hand to support Nico's first solo recording. The singer herself was disappointed at producer Tom Wilson's decision to dispense with a rhythm section and to swaddle many of the songs in strings and flutes. For the rest of us, however, the resulting cool baroque folk sound is something of a delight, with the strings frequently being given a slight touch of dissonance. Nico's ice-maiden singing voice is absolutely perfect in this context and the music should have been something of which she felt very proud, even if much of the outcome was not in her direct control. *Chelsea Girl* also introduces the songwriting of Jackson Browne, a few years before the release of his own first album. He plays in a folk style on many of the tracks, providing the only accompaniment on the concluding *Eulogy To Lenny Bruce*, but he uses an electric guitar to do so.

```
US release      October 1967    Verve   V(6)-5032
UK release      1971            MGM     2353 025

1. The Fairest Of The Seasons (Gregory Copeland/Jackson Browne)
2. These Days (I've Been Out Walking) (Jackson Browne)
3. Little Sister (John Cale/Lou Reed)
4. Winter Song (John Cale)
5. It Was A Pleasure Then (John Cale/Lou Reed/Nico)

6. Chelsea Girls (Lou Reed/Sterling Morrison)
7. I'll Keep It With Mine (Bob Dylan)
8. Somewhere There's A Feather (Jackson Browne)
9. Wrap Your Troubles In Dreams (Lou Reed)
10. Eulogy To Lenny Bruce (Tim Hardin)

Nico: vocals / Jackson Browne: guitar (1,2,7,8,10) / Lou Reed: guitar (3,5,6,9) / Sterling Morrison: guitar (6,9) / John Cale: viola, organ, guitar (3,4,5) / Larry Fallon: arranger / Tom Wilson: producer
```

H.P. LOVECRAFT

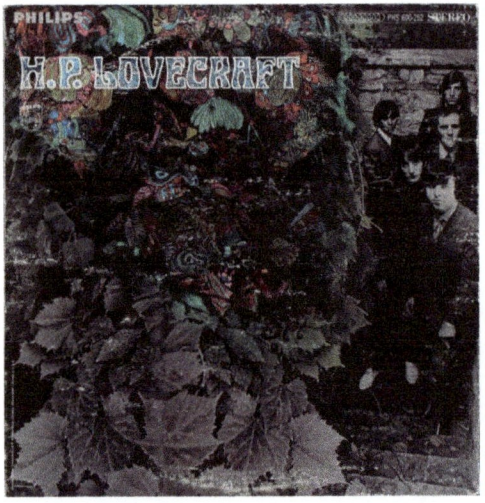

```
US release      October 1967    Philips   PHS-600/PHM-200-252
UK release      October 1967    Philips   (S)BL 7830

1. Wayfaring Stranger (George Edwards)
2. Let's Get Together (Chet Powers)
3. I've Been Wrong Before (Randy Newman)
4. The Drifter (Travis Edmonson)
5. That's The Bag I'm In (Fred Neil)

6. The White Ship (Dave Michaels/George Edwards/Tony Cavallari)
7. Country Boy And Bleeker Street (Fred Neil)
8. The Time Machine (Dave Michaels/George Edwards)
9. That's How Much I Love You Baby (Dave Michaels/George Edwards/Tony Cavallari)
10. Gloria Patria (Traditional)

George Edwards: guitar, bass guitar, vocals / Dave Michaels: keyboards, recorder, vocals / Tony Cavallari: guitar, vocals / Jerry McGeorge: bass guitar, vocals / Michael Tegza: drums, percussion, vocals / Len Druss: clarinet, piccolo, English horn, bass and tenor saxophones / Paul Tervelt: French horn / Jack Henningbaum: French horn / Ralph Craig: trombone / Herb Weiss: trombone / Clyde Bachand: tuba / Eddie Higgins: vibes, arranger / Bill Traut: saxophones, flute, bell, producer
```

H.P. Lovecraft was named after the American fantasy/horror writer and tried to echo his themes in its music. Matching passionate harmony vocals to an ethereal organ sound and occasional confident lead guitar, the group frequently fleshes out its range of timbres on its first album by using a band of session musicians. The group's own instruments always dominate, however. Although half the songs are cover versions, H.P. Lovecraft goes a long way towards making its own versions the definitive ones. But its own songs are actually the strongest on the album. The first song on each side is particularly distinctive – moody and memorable. Two tracks stand out as stylistically different – the appropriately named *Time Machine* takes the band back to the twenties, while the concluding *Gloria Patria* is meditative, unaccompanied choral music performed absolutely straight. The album emerges as commendably varied, well performed, and altogether one of the best debuts in a year full of notably impressive music.

THE WEST COAST POP ART EXPERIMENTAL BAND   VOLUME 2

```
US release      October 1967    Reprise   R(S) 6270
Not released in UK

1. In The Arena (Bob Markley/Danny Harris)
2. Suppose They Give A War And No One Comes (Bob Markley/Roger Bryant)
3. Buddha (Bob Markley/Danny Harris)
4. Smell Of Incense (Bob Markely/Ron Morgan)
5. Overture – WCPAEB Part II (Bob Markley/Danny Harris)

6. Queen Nymphet (Bob Markley/Danny Harris)
7. Unfree Child (Bob Markley/Danny Harris)
8. Carte Blanche (Bob Markley/Danny Harris)
9. Delicate Fawn (Bob Markley/Danny Harris)
10. Tracy Had A Hard Day Sunday (Bob Markley/Danny Harris)

Bob Markley: vocals, producer / Danny Harris: guitar, vocals / Ron Morgan: guitar / Shaun Harris: bass guitar, vocals /John Ware: drums, percussion / Hal Blaine: drums / Jim Gordon: drums / Jimmy Bowen: producer
```

The second major label album by the West Coast Pop Art Experimental Band marks a considerable advance on its predecessor, with music that now justifies the group's name. The music is still very eclectic, but it manages to have a coherence, marking it as the work of an imaginative group creating a style of its own, while trying to be as varied as it can be within the framework of that style. The music has an overall psychedelic ambience without particularly recalling the work of anyone else. Clearly Bob Markley, a man with little musical expertise at the point when he took over the group, has been paying attention to the others and has started to develop a considerable musicality. Markley had reputedly intended the group to become a West Coast equivalent of the influential Velvet Underground and with *Vol.2* this no longer seems like a ridiculous ambition. Impressive.

PEARLS BEFORE SWINE   ONE NATION UNDERGROUND

```
US release    October 1967    ESP-Disk    ESP-1054
UK release    1969            Fontana     STL 5505

1. Another Time (Tom Rapp)
2. Playmate (Saxie Dowell)
3. Ballad To An Amber Lady (Roger Crissinger/Tom Rapp)
4. (Oh Dear) Miss Morse (Tom Rapp)
5. Drop Out! (Tom Rapp)

6. Morning Song (Tom Rapp)
7. Regions Of May (Tom Rapp)
8. Uncle John (Tom Rapp)
9. I Shall Not Care (Roman Tombs/Sara Teasdale/Tom Rapp)
10. The Surrealist Waltz (Lane Lederer/Roger Crissinger)

Tom Rapp: vocals, guitar / Wayne Harley: autoharp, banjo, mandolin, vibes, electronics, vocals / Roger Crissinger: keyboards / Lane Lederer: bass guitar, guitar, vocals, English horn, sarangi, celeste, percussion / Warren Smith: drums / Richard Alderson: producer
```

As fans of the Fugs, Tom Rapp and his friends sent a demo tape to the Fugs' record company and were delighted when ESP-Disk invited them to record an album. *One Nation Underground* is an eccentric folk record with a distinct DIY flavour that fits well into the psychedelic mood of the time, despite featuring electric instruments only sporadically and never doing anything as obvious as rocking out to a driving rhythm. The album has some points of contact with the Incredible String Band, although Tom Rapp does not have any songs as memorable as the best that Mike Heron and Robin Williamson could produce. His songs depend for their effect on the bizarre performances they receive and would not be very interesting without them. The album became one of the best selling records in the ESP-Disk catalogue, although Rapp has stated that neither he nor any of the other members of Pearls Before Swine ever received any payment from the company.

BLOSSOM TOES   WE ARE EVER SO CLEAN

```
UK release    October 1967    Marmalade    608/607 001
Not released in US

1. Look At Me I'm You (Brian Godding/Giorgio Gomelsky)
2. I'll Be Late For Tea (Brian Godding)
3. The Remarkable Saga Of The Frozen Dog (Kevin Westlake)
4. Telegram Tuesday (Brian Godding)
5. Love Is (Brian Godding)
6. What's It For (Jim Cregan)
7. People Of The Royal Parks (Kevin Westlake)

8. What On Earth (Brian Godding)
9. Mrs Murphy's Budgerigar (Jim Cregan/Kevin Westlake)
10. I Will Bring You This And That (Brian Godding)
11. Mister Watchmaker (Brian Godding)
12. When The Alarm Clock Rings (Jim Cregan)
13. The Intrepid Balloonist's Handbook Volume One (Jim Cregan)
14. You (Brian Godding)
15. Track For Speedy Freaks (Or Instant LP Digest)
              (Godding/Gomelski/Cregan/Westlake)

Brian Godding: guitar, keyboards, vocals / Jim Cregan: guitar, vocals / Brian Belshaw: bass guitar, vocals / Kevin Westlake: drums, vocals / David Whittaker: arranger / Richard Hill: arranger / Giorgio Gomelsky: producer
```

Giorgio Gomelsky, the manager of the Yardbirds, started his own record label, Marmalade, in late 1966 and the album by Blossom Toes was the first to be issued, with three of its tracks also released on a single. Neither sold very well at all, but the album remains something of a marvel. The Beatles' *Sgt Pepper* seems like an obvious influence, but Blossom Toes had written all their songs before hearing it. Nevertheless, the combination of inventive songwriting and elaborate arrangements does place the music firmly within the same progressive pop-rock category. Some of the lyrics are very bizarre, but they are performed with such confidence as to make them seem natural! There are also some rather impressive pieces of relatively conventional songwriting, most notably the tear-jerking *Mister Watchmaker*. To emphasise the group's zany approach to music, the last track on the album comprises all the songs, fragmented, speeded up, and compressed into a melange of sound. Sadly, the group found that promoting the album was difficult because the musicians could not easily perform the songs in a live context without the studio tricks and the arrangements, so that Blossom Toes remained an act with only minority appeal, when they deserved so much more.

NIRVANA — THE STORY OF SIMON SIMOPATH

| UK release | October 1967 | Island | ILPS 9059 / ILP 959 |
| US release | early 1968 | Bell | 6015 (S) |

1. Wings Of Love
2. Lonely Boy
3. We Can Help You
4. Satellite Jockey
5. In The Courtyard Of The Stars
6. You Are Just The One
7. Pentecost Hotel
8. I Never Had A Love Like This Before
9. Take This Hand
10. 1999

All compositions by Alex Spyropoulos / Patrick Campbell-Lyons

Alex Spyropoulos: vocals, keyboards / Patrick Campbell-Lyons: vocals, guitar / Ray Singer: guitar / Michael Coe: French horn, viola / Sylvia Schuster: cello / Brian Henderson: bass guitar / Peter Kester: drums / David Preston: drums / Patrick Shanahan: drums / Syd Dale: arranger / Chris Blackwell: producer

The London-based duo responsible for the first pop-rock album issued on the Island label has no connection with the American group that hijacked the Nirvana name some two decades later. *The Story Of Simon Simopath* is a fairly elaborately arranged song cycle with a linking fantasy plot no less silly than many subsequent versions of the genre. The music is often gorgeous, though it has far more in common with the world of the stage musical than any kind of beat music and when it is not gorgeous it tends to wander into a world of twee whimsy, in which the simpering quality of Patrick Campbell-Lyons' singing voice does not help. Clearly the album is an ambitious undertaking and it needed rather more promotion on the part of Nirvana's management and record company than they were prepared to give it. The dramatic *Pentecost Hotel* was issued as a single and as part of the post-*Sgt Pepper* sound world it might have been expected to do well, but this did not happen.

THE BONZO DOG DOO-DAH BAND — GORILLA

| UK release | October 1967 | Liberty | LBS/LBL 83056 |
| US release | October 1967 | Imperial | LP-12370 |

1. Cool Britannia (Traditional/Neil Innes/Vivian Stanshall)
2. The Equestrian Statue (Neil Innes)
3. Jollity Farm (Les Sarony)
4. I Left My Heart In San Francisco (Doug Cross)
5. Look Out, There's A Monster Coming (Vivian Stanshall)
6. Jazz, Delicious Hot, Disgusting Cold (Bonzo Dog Doo-Dah Band)
7. Death Cab For Cutie (Neil Innes/Vivian Stanshall)
8. Narcissus (Ethelbert Nevin)
9. The Intro And The Outro (Vivian Stanshall)
10. Mickey's Son And Daughter (Eddie Lisbonna/Tommie Connor)
11. Big Shot (Vivian Stanshall)
12. Music For The Head Ballet (Neil Innes)
13. Piggy Bank Love (Neil Innes)
14. I'm Bored (Vivian Stanshall)
15. The Sound Of Music (Richard Rogers/Oscar Hammerstein III)

Vivian Stanshall: vocals, trumpet, euphonium, tuba, ukulele / Neil Innes: vocals, keyboards, guitar / Rodney Slater: saxophones, clarinets, trombone / Vernon Dudley Bohay-Nowell: bass guitar, banjo, saxophones, whistle / Sam Spoons: percussion, bass / Legs Larry Smith: drums, tuba, tap dancing / Roger Ruskin Spear: effects / Gerry Bron: producer

The members of the Bonzo Dog Doo-Dah Band viewed themselves as Dada performance artists, in which comedy, traditional jazz, music hall, and pop music of various kinds were all pushed into the blender. It is possible to see in the band's antics the comedy style that was soon to develop into Monty Python's Flying Circus. It is humour that relies on an absurd situation rather than a punchline, such as on the classic *The Intro And The Outro*, where an increasingly unlikely line-up is introduced to the audience ("looking very relaxed, Adolf Hitler on vibes"). *The Equestrian Statue*, which simply imagines the title item galloping round the town and being appreciated, comes closest to being a piece of sixties pop and was released as a single, but failed to become a hit. Overall, *Gorilla* is something of a comedy classic and bears repeated listening, which is quite an achievement in itself.

SLY & THE FAMILY STONE — A WHOLE NEW THING

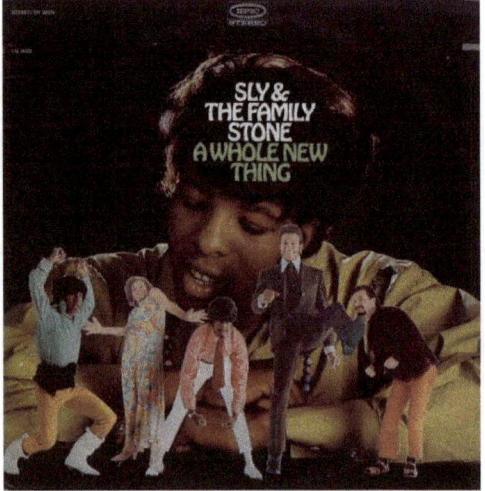

Sly Stewart had worked as house producer for Autumn records before forming his own band in 1966. *A Whole New Thing* is Sly and the Family Stone's first album. The music is dynamic, uptempo soul, driven by a particularly dominant and funky rhythm section, with powerful brass.

The sheer energy of the record makes it an obvious blueprint for the brass rock groups that were to follow a couple of years later, far more so than the more emotional approach of Otis Redding, using the same instrumentation. Whether this is enough to justify the claim that this was "a whole new thing" is debatable. Certainly the album sold poorly, although this might have had something to do with the fact that none of the songs is particularly distinctive melodically.

McCOY TYNER   THE REAL McCOY

US release   October 1967   Epic   BN26324/LN 24324
Not released in UK

1. Underdog
2. If This Room Could Talk
3. Run Run Run
4. Turn Me Loose
5. Let Me Hear It From You
6. Advice

7. I Cannot Make It
8. Trip To Your Heart
9. I Hate To Love Her
10. Bad Risk
11. That Kind Of Person
12. Dog

All compositions by Sly Stewart

Sly Stone (Stewart): vocals, guitar, keyboards, harmonica, producer / Freddie Stone: guitar, vocals / Larry Graham: bass guitar, vocals / Cynthia Robinson: trumpet, voice / Jerry Martini: tenor saxophone / Greg Errico: drums / Vet Stone: vocals / Mary McCreary: vocals / Elva Mouton: vocals

US release   October 1967   Blue Note   BST8/BLP 4264
Not released in UK

1. Passion Dance
2. Contemplation
3. Four By Five
4. Search For Peace
5. Blues On The Corner

All compositions by McCoy Tyner

McCoy Tyner: piano / Joe Henderson: tenor saxophone / Ron Carter: bass / Elvin Jones: drums / Alfred Lion: producer

McCoy Tyner left the John Coltrane Quartet at the end of 1965 and was signed to Blue Note as a bandleader in his own right. Tyner took Coltrane's music as his starting point and *The Real McCoy* also includes the drummer from the Quartet, Elvin Jones, who had left to go on his own as well. Understandably, the piano dominates more than previously and Tyner plays substantial solos on every track. Joe Henderson is a fine tenor saxophonist, though a little more tied to bop procedures than Coltrane had become. His greater precision, however, helps to make Tyner's music discover its own voice. *The Real McCoy* does not convey the sensation of barriers being pushed forwards or broken in the way that John Coltrane's music always did, and it even includes a straightforward blues performance, but it is a very fine modern jazz album nevertheless.

MILES DAVIS   SORCERER

US release   October 1967   Columbia   CS 9532/CL 2732
UK release   October 1967   CBS   (S)BPG 63097

1. Prince Of Darkness (Wayne Shorter)
2. Pee Wee (Tony Williams)
3. Masqualero (Wayne Shorter)
4. The Sorcerer (Herbie Hancock)

5. Limbo (Wayne Shorter)
6. Vonetta (Wayne Shorter)
7. Nothing Like You (Bob Dorough/Fran Landesman)

Miles Davis: trumpet / Wayne Shorter: tenor saxophone / Teo Macero: producer / tracks 1-6: Herbie Hancock: piano / Ron Carter: bass / Tony Williams: drums / track 7: Bob Dorough: vocals / Frank Rehak: trombone / Paul Chambers: bass / Jimmy Cobb: drums / Willie Bobo: percussion / Gil Evans: arranger

For the third album by his quintet, Miles Davis continues to develop the 'time, no changes' approach. There is a confidence about the compositions contributed by members of the band and what they are able to do with them that suggests they know their position at the forefront of sixties jazz is unassailable. Miles is quite content to give his musicians free rein and he does not play at all on *Pee Wee*, knowing that they will stay true to his vision. In general, Miles considered these studio adventures to be complete in themselves and he did not attempt to add them to his live set, which still relied on material the group had played for a long time. *Masqualero* was an exception, however, and the quintet frequently improvised on the tune after this first recording was made. The final track on the album is very much an oddity. It was recorded five years earlier than the other material and with a largely different line-up. This includes singer Bob Dorough who provides the natural focus as he delivers his own composition. Miles, who does not solo, is effectively taking the role of sideman on his own session here.

TEN YEARS AFTER

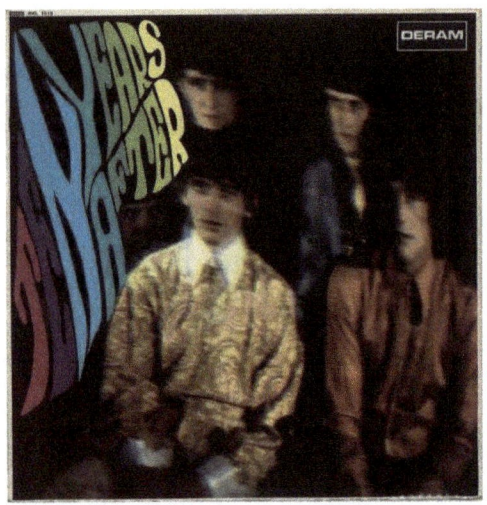

```
UK release    October 1967    Deram    SML/DML 1015
US release    October 1967    Deram    DES 18009/DE 16009

1. I Want To Know (Sheila McLeod)
2. I Can't Keep From Crying Sometimes (Al Kooper)
3. Adventures Of A Young Organ (Alvin Lee/Chick Churchill)
4. Spoonful (Willie Dixon)
5. Losing The Dogs (Alvin Lee/Gus Dudgeon)

6. Feel If For Me (Alvin Lee)
7. Love Until I Die (Alvin Lee)
8. Don't Want You Woman (Alvin Lee)
9. Help Me (Ralph Bass/Sonny Boy Williamson)

Alvin Lee: vocals, guitar / Chick Churchill: organ / Leo Lyons: bass guitar /
Ric Lee: drums / Mike Vernon: producer
```

Another new British group fascinated by the blues, and including an impressive guitarist. Ten Years After, named in honour of the first recordings by Elvis Presley that kick-started rock 'n' roll, were signed to Decca's subsidiary label and allowed to make an album without releasing any singles first, let alone having a hit. Alvin Lee glories in being a very flashy guitarist, albeit one that is only lightly amplified, and he is seldom content to play one note when six will do. Most of the solo work is his. He also handles the lead vocals, so that the other musicians very much appear to function as his backing group. Even the jazzy instrumental, *Adventures Of A Young Organ,* devotes as much solo space to the guitar as it does to Chick Churchill's playing. Half the album is made up of Alvin Lee's songs, which do what they have to do, even if they would not win any prizes for originality. *Love Until I Die,* for example, borrows the riff from Robert Johnson's *Crossroads,* as frequently performed by Eric Clapton, in its entirety. Overall, however, the eponymous album by Ten Years After is an encouraging first outing for a band that would manage to sustain a lengthy career.

DAVID McWILLIAMS   VOLUME 2

```
UK release    October 1967    Major Minor
                                         S/M MLP 10
US release    October 1967    Kapp  KS-3547

1. Days Of Pearly Spencer
2. Can I Get There By Candlelight
3. For Josephine
4. How Can I Be Free
5. Brown Eyed Gal
6. Marlena

7. For A Little Girl
8. Lady Helen Of The Laughing Eyes
9. Time Will Not Wait
10. What's The Matter With Me
11. There's No Lock Upon My Door
12. Tomorrow's Like Today

All compositions by David McWilliams

David McWilliams: vocals, guitar / Mike Leander:
arranger, producer
```

Convinced that he had a major star on his hands, Phil Solomon, the owner of Major Minor records, persuaded David McWilliams to record and release three albums in less than a year. In truth, he was a much less interesting singer songwriter than Solomon hoped and the rush of material meant that little of it was developed in the recording studio as much as it could have been. Just one song was given an elaborate treatment and it really stands out. *Days Of Pearly Spencer* was released as a single and received extensive promotion, but this did not include being played on the BBC, which refused to co-operate due to Solomon's involvement with the pirate Radio Caroline. As a result, the record was not a hit, but it remains a classic of the period (which was recognised several years later when Marc Almond recorded a cover version of it). The song is swept along by a surging string arrangement and given a touch of psychedelia by having McWilliams sing the chorus on the other end of a telephone line, something that even the Beatles had not thought of doing. Curiously the song was originally intended to be the B-side, with the much less striking *Harlem Lady* on the reverse. *Days Of Pearly Spencer* did become a big hit in many European countries, however, and ultimately sold a million copies altogether.

BUFFALO SPRINGFIELD   AGAIN

For the astonishing second album by Buffalo Springfield, the group is no longer playing folk rock. Instead it is delivering ambitious and varied music in the manner of the Beatles' *Sgt Pepper,* albeit rooted more obviously in rock concerns. The three songwriters are pulling in different directions, which would ultimately end in the break-up of the group, but it is what gives this album its impressive variety. The Neil Young songs *Expecting To Fly* and *Broken Arrow* are the obvious tour de force productions, incorporating subtle string arrangements woven into the mix and kaleidoscopic sound structures. Richie

US release	October 1967	Atco	(SD) 33-226
UK release	October 1967	Atlantic	588/587 091

1. Mr Soul (Neil Young)
2. A Child's Claim To Fame (Richie Furay)
3. Everydays (Steve Stills)
4. Expecting To Fly (Neil Young)
5. Bluebird (Steve Stills)

6. Hung Upside Down (Steve Stills)
7. Sad Memory (Richie Furay)
8. Good Time Boy (Richie Furay)
9. Rock And Roll Woman (Steve Stills)
10. Broken Arrow (Neil Young)

Steve Stills: vocals, guitar, piano, organ, producer (3,5,6,9) / Neil Young: vocals, guitar, producer (4,9,10) / Richie Furay: vocals, guitar, producer (2,7,8) / Bruce Palmer: bass guitar / Dewey Martin: drums, vocals, producer (8) / Jim Fielder: bass guitar (3) / Bobby West: bass guitar (5) / James Burton: dobro (2) / Don Randi: piano (4,10) / Jack Nitzsche: electric piano (4), arranger (4), producer (4) / Charlie Chin: banjo (5) / American Soul Train (probably the Memphis Horns): horns (8) / Chris Sarns: guitar (10) / Jim Horn: clarinet (10) / Charles Greene: producer (1) / Brian Stone: producer (1) / Ahmet Ertegun: producer (5)

Furay's songs are the polar opposite in their simplicity, with *Sad Memory* being a duo performance for Furay's acoustic guitar and mournful vocals and Neil Young's shimmering electric guitar. Steve Stills sits somewhere in between. *Everydays* is particularly striking with its jazzy piano offset against electric guitar sustain. *Bluebird* is more of a blueprint for Stills' next group (Crosby, Stills, and Nash), but surprises by dissolving into a banjo-led finale. The track loses some of its extra impact, however, by the decision to edit down the original nine-minute recording to cut out most of the guitar soloing. The song was cut down even further for release as the first of thee singles taken from the album. They were not big US hits, although they did make respectable showings in the Hot Hundred, and the album itself achieved a moderate chart placing.

THE SOPWITH CAMEL

US release	November 1967	Kama Sutra	KLP(S) 8060
Not released in UK			

1. Hello Hello (Peter Kraemer/Terry MacNeil)
2. Frantic Desolation (Peter Kraemer/Terry MacNeil)
3. Saga Of The Low Down Let Down (William Sievers)
4. Little Orphan Annie (Peter Kraemer/Terry MacNeil)
5. You Always Tell Me Baby (Peter Kraemer/Terry MacNeil)
6. Maybe In A Dream (Peter Kraemer/Terry MacNeil)

7. Cellophane Woman (William Sievers)
8. The Things That I Could Do With You (Peter Kraemer/Terry MacNeil)
9. Walk In The Park (William Sievers)
10. The Great Morpheum (Peter Kraemer/Terry MacNeil)
11. Postcard From Jamaica (Peter Kraemer/Terry MacNeil)

Peter Kraemer: vocals / Terry MacNeil: piano, guitar / William Sievers: guitar / Martin Beard: bass guitar / Norman Mayell: drums / Erik Jacobsen: producer

The Sopwith Camel scored a US hit in January 1967 with the jaunty *Hello Hello*, sounding like the Lovin' Spoonful with added honky-tonk piano. It was the first top forty hit by a San Francisco band. As it happened, the two groups shared a producer, Erik Jacobsen. The Sopwith Camel struggled to record enough material for an album and by the time that the eponymous record was released, the group had disbanded. The resemblance with the Lovin' Spoonful continues throughout the album. There are, however, occasional touches of psychedelic guitar, which is more in the style expected of a group from San Francisco. But given the wealth of adventurous music by other artists to have appeared since the success of *Hello Hello*, the album delivers rather too little too late.

JEFFERSON AIRPLANE   AFTER BATHING AT BAXTER'S

US release	November 1967	RCA Victor	LSO/LOP-1511
UK release	November 1967	RCA Victor	SF/RD 7926

1. Streetmasse – The Ballad Of You & Me & Pooneil (Paul Kantner)
2. Streetmasse – A Small Package Of Value Will Come To You Shortly (Bill Thompson/ Gary Blackman/Spencer Dryden)
3. Streetmasse – Young Girl Sunday Blues (Marty Balin/Paul Kantner)
4. The War Is Over – Martha (Paul Kantner)
5. The War Is Over – Wild Tyme (H) (Paul Kantner)
6. Hymn To An Older Generation – The Last Wall Of The Castle (Jorma Kaukonen)
7. Hymn To An Older Generation – Rejoyce (Grace Slick)

8. How Suite It Is – Watch Her Ride (Paul Kantner)
9. How Suite It Is – Spare Chaynge (Jack Casady/Jorma Kaukonen/Spencer Dryden)
10. Shizoforest Love Suite – Two Heads (Grace Slick)
11. Shizoforest Love Suite – Won't You Try / Saturday Afternoon (Paul Kantner)

Grace Slick: vocals, keyboards, recorder / Marty Balin: vocals, guitar / Paul Kantner: vocals, guitar / Jorma Kaukonen: guitar, sitar, vocals / Jack Casady: bass guitar / Spencer Dryden: drums, percussion, arranger (7) / Gary Blackman: voice (2) / Bill Thompson: voice (2) / Al Schmitt: producer

For the group's third album, Jefferson Airplane was determined to be adventurous and experimental, even if the result was not particularly commercial. Accordingly, the music was pieced together from assorted recordings made over a period of four months. Al

Schmitt was credited as the producer, but in fact he had little to do with how the album turned out. The songs are grouped together into five suites, playing continuously within each one. Paul Kantner's songs are the most conventional, although *Won't You Try/Saturday Afternoon,* unusually but successfully, merges two songs into one. The others would have fitted easily into the group's previous album, but they are distinguished here by the increased fire in the playing and singing of all concerned, with the guitar of Jorma Kaukonen and the bass guitar of Jack Casady being particularly revelatory. These two are given space to really show what they can do on the lengthy instrumental, *Spare Chaynge,* which is presumably entirely improvised. The two songs by Grace Slick are notably more complicated than Kantner's and give her the chance to remind the listener what an exceptional instrument her voice is. Meanwhile, a track by drummer Spencer Dryden presents a sound collage of both tuned and untuned percussion and jabbering voices, placed as the second track on the album where it can make the necessary statement of intent early (and following the startling guitar feedback already heard framing the opening track). The title of *After Bathing At Baxter's* is a veiled suggestion that much of this music was inspired by the group's drug-taking, but it remains perhaps the most remarkable and durable product of the San Francisco sound.

COUNTRY JOE AND THE FISH   I-FEEL-LIKE-I'M-FIXIN'-TO-DIE

| US release | November 1967 | Vanguard | VSD7/VRS 9266 |
| UK release | November 1967 | Fontana | (S)TFL 6087 |

1. The Fish Cheer / I-Feel-Like-I'm-Fixin'-To-Die (Joe McDonald)
2. Who Am I (Joe McDonald)
3. Pat's Song (Joe McDonald)
4. Rock Coast Blues (Joe McDonald)
5. Magoo (Joe McDonald)
6. Janis (Joe McDonald)
7. Thought Dream (Joe McDonald)
8. Thursday (David Cohen/Chicken Hirsh)
9. Eastern Jam (The Fish)
10. Colors For Susan (Joe McDonald)

Joe McDonald: vocals, guitar, organ / Barry Melton: guitar, vocals, kazoo / David Cohen: guitar, keyboards, bells, vocals / Bruce Barthol: bass guitar, harmonica, vocals / Chicken Hirsh: drums, percussion / Samuel Charters: producer

The second album by Country Joe and the Fish shows a similar advance on the first as was also evident on the two most recent albums by Jefferson Airplane. Kicking off with a sanitised version of the four letter cheer that the group delighted in getting audiences to yell at their concerts, the album moves through a varied programme of folk, rock, and psychedelic moods. There is much electric music for the mind and body, as on the first album, but several of the tracks prefer to employ acoustic guitars and a more gentle ambience. *Eastern Jam* is the Fish equivalent of the Airplane's improvised *Spare Chaynge,* with two guitarists ready to show what they can do. The title track, *I-Feel-Like-I'm-Fixin'-To-Die* is a savage attack on the American war in Vietnam, dressed in a jolly disguise, while *Magoo* and *Colors For Susan* are impressionist pieces of great sensitivity (not withstanding the thunder claps on the first of these!). While not quite scaling the heights of *After Bathing At Baxter's,* the Country Joe and the Fish album succeeds very well in acting as a primer for demonstrating the concerns and the sounds of the San Francisco music scene.

LOVE   FOREVER CHANGES

| US and UK release | November 1967 | Elektra | EKS7/EKL 4013# |

1. Alone Again Or (Bryan Maclean)
2. A House Is Not A Motel (Arthur Lee)
3. Andmoreagain (Arthur Lee)
4. The Daily Planet (Arthur Lee)
5. Old Man (Bryan Maclean)
6. The Red Telephone (Arthur Lee)
7. Maybe The People Would Be The Times Or Between Clark And Hilldale (Arthur Lee)
8. Live And Let Live (Arthur Lee)
9. The Good Humor Man He Sees Everything Like This (Arthur Lee)
10. Bummer In The Summer (Arthur Lee)
11. You Set The Scene (Arthur Lee)

Arthur Lee: vocals, guitar, producer / Bryan Maclean: vocals, guitar / John Echols: guitar / Ken Forssi: bass guitar / Michael Stuart: percussion / Billy Strange: guitar (3,4) / Don Randi: piano (3,4) / Carol Kaye: bass guitar (3,4) / Hal Blaine: drums (3,4) / David Angel: arranger / Arnold Belnick, Darrel Terwilliger, James Getzoff, Marshall Sosson, Robert Barene: strings / Jesse Ehrlich: viola / Norman Botnick: violin / Bud Brisbois: trumpet / Roy Caton: trumpet / Ollie Mitchell: trumpet / Richard Leith: trombone / Chuck Berghofer: bass / Bruce Botnick: producer

Love was a third established band to raise its game in the last months of 1967. *Forever Changes* is a collection of imaginative and frequently inspired songs given arrangements and group performances to tip them into greatness. None more so than the opening *Alone Again Or*, one of just two tracks not written by Arthur Lee. The listener is left in doubt as to whether love is being celebrated or lamented and the minor key acoustic guitar plus mariachi trumpet solo does not resolve the confusion. Generally, the album moves Love's music in a folk direction and away from anything that rocks, although *A House Is Not A Motel* and *Live And Let Live* do manage to find space for urgent electric guitar solos. *Forever Changes* provides an impressive American response to the musical possibilities opened up by the Beatles' *Sgt Pepper*, although it has to contend with the similar approaches of the albums *Triangle* by the Beau Brummels and *Buffalo Springfield Again* for the top accolade. At the time, the album was not a commercial success, although it fared a little better in the UK than in the US, reaching number twenty-four in the album chart.

13th FLOOR ELEVATORS   EASTER EVERYWHERE

It is obvious that the 13th Floor Elevators are trying hard to adopt a more ambitious approach on their second album, in line with what the foremost US groups were doing during 1967. Sadly, they have elected to retain the demented chicken sound that they seem to consider as being their trademark. It serves as an annoying distraction, obscuring the fact that the songs are actually more distinctive and well-written than before (apart from the ill advised Bob Dylan cover, which the Elevators drench in electric guitars to no very positive effect). To this extent the group has indeed found a way to move forward, but the limitations in the musician's playing abilities are starting to become apparent. In particular, Stacy Sutherland, whose lead guitar dominates the proceedings, is clearly no match for the guitarists playing on the recent albums by Jefferson Airplane or Country Joe and the Fish or Buffalo Springfield. Sometimes musical simplicity can be refreshing, but sometimes it merely reflects a lack of imagination. Compared to the competition at this time, *Easter Everywhere* is not refreshing.

THE KINKS   SUNNY AFTERNOON

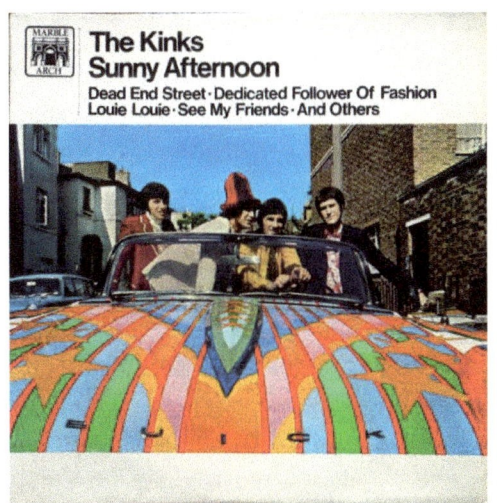

Sunny Afternoon is a bargain priced compilation, issued as a follow-up to the earlier *Well Respected Kinks*, also on the Marble Arch label. As before, it mainly comprises a selection of single A and B sides, going back as far as 1964, and for the most part not included on the group's original albums. Inevitably, the result is a strong selection and the album did well in the charts, in fact considerably better than the recently released *Something Else* album.

THE MOODY BLUES   DAYS OF FUTURE PASSED

Disenchanted by the group's failure to achieve much success after the single *Go Now* reached number one at the beginning of 1965, bass player Clint Warwick and singer/guitarist Denny Laine left the Moody Blues during 1966. They were replaced by John Lodge, a school-friend of Ray Thomas, and Justin Hayward, a former backing musician for Marty Wilde. There was no immediate improvement in the group's fortunes, but in September 1967, the struggling Moody Blues were

| UK release | November 1967 | Deram | SML/DML 707 |
| US release | November 1967 | Deram | DES 18012/DE 16012 |

1. The Day Begins (Peter Knight/Graeme Edge)
2. Dawn Is A Feeling (Mike Pinder)
3. Another Morning (Ray Thomas)
4. Peak Hour (John Lodge)
5. Forever Afternoon (Tuesday?) (Justin Hayward) / Time To Get Away (John Lodge)
6. The Sunset (Mike Pinder) / Twilight Time (Ray Thomas)
7. Nights In White Satin (Justin Hayward) / Late Lament (Graeme Edge/Peter Knight)

Justin Hayward: vocals, guitar, sitar, piano / Mike Pinder: vocals, mellotron, piano, tamboura, percussion / Ray Thomas: vocals, flute, piano, percussion / John Lodge: vocals, bass guitar / Graeme Edge: drums, vocals / Peter Knight: arranger / The London Festival Orchestra / Tony Clarke: producer / Michael Dacre-Barclay: producer

asked by their record company, Decca, to consider recording a rock version of Dvorak's *New World Symphony*, with an orchestra. Later recordings by the likes of Louis Clark *(Hooked On Classics)* suggest that this might not have turned out very well, but in the event the Moody Blues decided to use the allotted studio time to record their own songs, with arranger Peter Knight agreeing to provide orchestral accompaniment and linking material. Decca, which had been thinking in terms of a demonstration record to highlight the quality of its improved stereo recording (which it branded 'Deramic Sound System') decided to release the record anyway – with a mono version issued too, despite this rather making a mockery of the whole project. The concept of combining popular music with an orchestra was hardly new and neither did the presence of an orchestra make the songs have anything to do with classical music. Some of the songs on *Days Of Future Passed* are rather good, but the orchestral links threaten to turn the whole thing into the soundtrack for a TV soap. Nevertheless, the album has managed to acquire the kudos of a landmark recording regardless and a significant element in the birth of progressive rock, a genre influenced by classical music. The key track, *Nights In White Satin,* was a much smaller hit in the UK than people remember (it reached no higher than number 19 in the charts, although a reissue five years later, when the Moody Blues had become big stars, and following the record's belated climb to the top of the US charts, did a little better at number 9). The songwriting credits on the original album fail to mention the individual members of the Moody Blues involved, but instead conjure the name 'Redwave' as a catch-all for the whole band, placed alongside that of Peter Knight.

KALEIDOSCOPE   TANGERINE DREAM

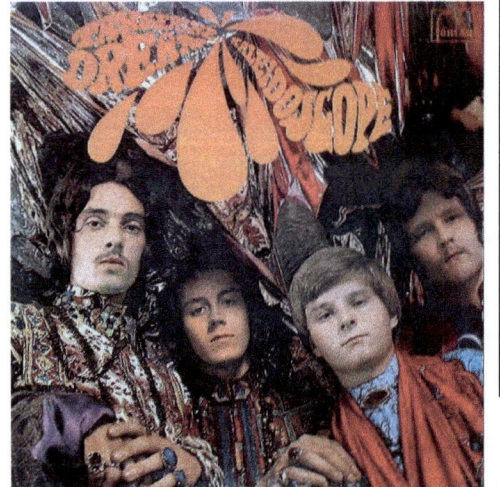

| UK release | November 1967 | Fontana | (S)TL 5448 |

Not released in US

1. Kaleidoscope
2. Please Excuse My Face
3. Dive Into Yesterday
4. Mr Small, The Watch Repairer Man
5. Flight From Ashiya
6. The Murder Of Lewis Tollani
7. (Further Reflections) In The Room Of Percussion
8. Dear Nellie Goodrich
9. Holidaymaker
10. A Lesson Perhaps
11. The Sky Children

All compositions by Peter Daltrey/Eddy Pumer

Peter Daltrey: vocals, keyboards / Eddy Pumer: guitar, keyboards / Steve Clark: bass guitar, flute / Dan Bridgman: drums / Dick Leahy: producer

Tangerine Dream is the first album by a London band calling itself Kaleidoscope and has nothing to do with the established US band with the same name (or with a later band copying the album title, for that matter). *Flight From Ashiya* was issued as a single in advance of the album, but was not a hit. The music is inventive pop-rock, very reminiscent of the early songs by Pink Floyd, though without the lengthy instrumental forays. Indeed Kaleidoscope avoids solo playing altogether, preferring to concentrate on the songs themselves. The single is particularly striking and deserved to have been a huge seller. Sadly, the album fared no better, selling so few copies that with the dawn of sixties record collecting in the UK a couple of decades later, *Tangerine Dream* became one of the first rare records to reach a three figure value.

THE HOLLIES   BUTTERFLY

Butterfly extends the *Sgt Pepper* approach of arranging the songs imaginatively enough to make them all sound different and distinct to the point where the album could well have been titled *Lance Corporal Pepper's Lonely Hearts Club Band*. The instruments played by the Hollies themselves are very often enhanced by string or brass or woodwind arrangements. Although there are no songs as powerful as the best of those by the Beatles, the level of the songwriting is high and most of the tracks would have made perfectly satisfactory singles (indeed *Dear Eloise* was issued as a single in the US). The addition of the hit *King Midas In Reverse* to the US version of the album makes little difference to its impact. Remarkably, the album that stands as the finest made by the Hollies did not do well in the charts.

```
UK release    November 1967    Parlophone    PCS/PMC 7039
US release    November 1967    Epic BN 26344/LN 24344
as DEAR ELOISE/KING MIDAS IN REVERSE with different cover and some
different tracks

1. Dear Eloise
2. Away, Away, Away
3. Maker
4. Pegasus
5. Would You Believe
6. Wish You A Wish

7. Postcard
8. Charlie And Fred
9. Try It
10. Elevated Observations?
11. Step Inside
12. Butterfly

All compositions by Allan Clarke/Tony Hicks/Graham Nash

Allan Clarke: vocals, harmonica / Graham Nash: guitar, vocals, harmonium
/ Tony Hicks: guitar, vocals, sitar / Bernie Calvert: bass guitar, keyboards /
Bobby Elliott: drums / John Scott: arranger / Ron Richards: producer
```

THE MONKEES
PISCES, AQUARIUS, CAPRICORN & JONES LTD.

Pisces, Aquarius, Capricorn & Jones Ltd is the fourth album by the Monkees, released only just over a year since the first. It does not present anything startlingly different from its predecessors and it makes few concessions at all to the psychedelia so prevalent in the other albums being issued at this time. Two tracks, however, do include prominent sounds generated by the newly available Moog synthesizer – Micky Dolenz being one of its first customers. There are, perhaps, fewer top quality songs than on the earlier albums, with only *Pleasant Valley Sunday,* which was issued as a single, really standing out. This suggests that the Monkees or their producer were trying less hard to make the best album that they could. The market was secure.

```
US release    November 1967    Colgems      COS/COM-104
UK release    November 1967    RCA Victor   SF/RD 7912

1. Salesman (Craig Smith)
2. She Hangs Out (Jeff Barry)
3. The Door Into Summer (Bill Martin/Chip Douglas)
4. Love Is Only Sleeping (Barry Mann/Cynthis Weil)
5. Cuddly Toy (Harry Nilsson)
6. Words (Tommy Boyce/Bobby Hart)

7. Hard To Believe (Davy Jones/Eddie Brick/Kim Capli)
8. What Am I Doing Hangin' Round? (Boomer Clarke/Travis Lewis)
9. Peter Percival Patterson's Pet Pig Porky (Peter Tork) /
10. Pleasant Valley Sunday (Gerry Goffin/Carole King)
11. Daily Nightly (Mike Nesmith)
12. Don't Call On Me (John London/Mike Nesmith)
13. Star Collector (Gerry Goffin/Carole King)

Davy Jones: vocals, percussion / Mike Nesmith: vocals, guitar / Peter
Tork: vocals, guitar, keyboards / Micky Dolenz: vocals, drums, guitar,
synthesizer / Douglas Dillard: banjo (8) / Bill Martin: keyboards / Chip
Douglas: keyboards, bass guitar, producer / Eddie Hoe: drums / Kim
Capli: drums, percussion, guitar, bass guitar, piano (7) / Paul Beaver:
synthesizer (13) / Pete Candoli, Robert Helfer, Al Porcino,Manuel
Stevens: trumpets (2) / Richard Noel: trombone (2) / Richard Leith, Philip
Teele: bass trombones (2) / Shorty Rogers: arranger (2) / Bill Chadwick:
effects (4) / Edgar Lustgarten: cello (5) / Ted Nash, Tom Scott, Bud
Shank: woodwinds (5) / Leonard Atkins, Arnold Belnick, Nathan Kaproff,
Wilbert Nuttycombe, Jerome Resiler, Darrel Terwilliger: violins (7) /
Oliver Mitchell, Anthony Terran: flugelhorns (7) / Vincent DeRosa: French
horn (7) / Jim Horn: baritone saxophone (7) / Robert Knight: bass
trombone (7) / Roger Farris: arranger (7) / George Tipton: orchestrator
(7) / Robert Rafelson: piano (12)
```

THE STRAWBERRY ALARM CLOCK   INCENSE AND PEPPERMINTS

```
US release    November 1967    UNI    (7)3014
UK release    November 1967    Pye    NPL 28106

1. The World's On Fire (Strawberry Alarm Clock)
2. Birds In My Tree (George Bunnell/Steve Bartek)
3. Lose To Live (Mark Weitz/Strawberry Alarm Clock)
4. Strawberries Mean Love (George Bunnell/Steve Bartek)

5. Rainy Day Mushroom Pillow (George Bunnell/Steve Bartek)
6. Paxton's Back Street Carnival (George Bunnell/Steve Bartek)
7. Hummin Happy (George Bunnell/Randy Seol)
8. Pass Time With The SAC (Strawberry Alarm Clock)
9. Incense And Peppermints (John Carter/Tim Gilbert)
10. Unwind With The Clock (Lee Freeman/Ed King)

Mark Weitz: keyboards, vocals / Ed King: guitar, vocals / Lee
Freeman: guitar, bass guitar, harmonica, drums, woodwinds,
vocals / George Bunnell: bass guitar, guitar, vocals / Gary
Lovetro: bass guitar, vocals / Randy Seol: drums, vibraphone,
percussion, vocals / Steve Bartek: flute / Greg Munford: vocals
(9) / Frank Slay: producer / Bill Holmes: producer
```

The uplifting *Incense And Peppermints*, floating harmony vocals on a sustained electric guitar and a fizzing electric organ, was a well-deserved number one in the US in November 1967 – six months after its release. The album built around the hit struggles to find other songs with the same appeal, although the dreamy *Rainy Day Mushroom Pillow* comes close, and the lengthy the lengthy opening track, *The World's On Fire,* improves on the Doors by adding a flute, even if the band lacks a dynamic lead singer.

The album is certainly engaging and sounds like an ideal accompaniment to the summer of love, except that it was released too late.

VAN DYKE PARKS   SONG CYCLE

Van Dyke Parks is an unusual figure to be working in popular music. He dislikes most rock music, including that of the Beatles, yet he is best known for working with Brian Wilson on the Beach Boys' most remarkable songs – those making up the *Smile* project. *Song Cycle* is Parks' own first album. The man's quirkiness is emphasised by his opening the album with an uncredited snippet of the folk/country singer Steve Young, performing a traditional song, and later by including a mirrored musical pair – a song he calls *Van Dyke Parks* with a 'Public Domain' credit (because it is actually an inventive rendering of the hymn *Nearer My God To Thee*) followed by a song of his own, titled *Public Domain*. One track, *Laurel Canyon Blvd,* is presented in two separate fragments, yet even when when taken together they still seem like an excerpt from a longer work. Throughout the album the music is truly kaleidoscopic in its complexity, with dense, continually changing arrangements. There are passing resemblances to music hall, ragtime, country, classical, cartoon soundtrack music, and the avant garde, but none of it sounds remotely like rock music. It is noticeable that despite a smattering of guitars and percussion in the musician credits, there is no bass guitar. *Song Cycle* sold very poorly, much to the chagrin of Warner Bros, which had allowed Parks to spend a record-breaking amount of money on the recording, expecting a product that would be a big seller. It is, however, as much a masterpiece as *Sgt Pepper,* the album that Van Dyke Parks' music has most in common with (despite being largely produced before the release of that particular record), if one could imagine all remaining traces of rock music being expunged from the Beatles songs.

```
US release    November 1967    Warner Bros    W(S) 1727
UK release    early 1968       Warner Bros    WS 1727

1. Black Jack Davy (Traditional) / Vine Street (Randy Newman)
2. Palm Desert (Van Dyke Parks)
3. Widow's Walk (Van Dyke Parks)
4. Laurel Canyon Blvd (Van Dyke Parks)
5. The All Golden (Van Dyke Parks)
6. Van Dyke Parks (Nearer My God To Thee) (Public Domain)

7. Public Domain (Van Dyke Parks)
8. Donovan's Colours (Donovan Leitch)
9. The Attic (Van Dyke Parks)
10. Laurel Canyon Blvd (Van Dyke Parks)
11. By The People (Van Dyke Parks)
12. Pot Pourri (Van Dyke Parks)

Van Dyke Parks: vocals, piano / Randy Newman: piano (1) / Dick Rosmini: guitar / Ron Elliott: guitar / Steve Young: vocals, guitar (1) / Gayle Levant: harp / Carl Fortina: accordion / Allan Reuss, Leon Stewart, Nicolai Bolin, Thomas Tedesco, Vasil Crienica, William Nadel: balalaikas / Arthur Briegleb, Richard Hyde, Richard Perissi, Thomas Shepard, Vincent De Rosa: brass / George Fields, Jay Migliori, James Horn, Norman Benno, Ted Nash, Thomas Morgan, Thomas Scott, William Green: woodwinds and reeds / Virginia Majewski: viola / Misha Goodatieff: violin / Armand Kaproff, Charles Berghofer, Darrel Terwilliger, Dennis Budimer, Donald Bagley, Frederick Seykora, Gregory Bemko, Harry Bluestone, Jerry Reisler, Jesse Erlich, Joseph Ditullio, Joseph Saxon, Leonard Malarsky, Leonard Selic, Lyle Ritz, Nathan Gershman, Philip Goldberg, Ralph Schaffer, Robert West, Samuel Boghossian, Trefoni Rizzi, William Kurasch: strings / Red Rhodes: pedal steel guitar / Jack Glaser: effects / Earl Palmer, Gary Coleman, Hal Blaine, James Gordon: percussion / Billie J Barnum, Durrie Parks, Gaile Parks, Gerri Engemann, James Hendricks, Julia E Rinker, Karen Gunderson, Nick Woods, Paul Jay Robbins, Vanessa Hendricks: choir / Kirby Johnson: conductor / Leonard Waronker: producer
```

MIRIAM MAKEBA   PATA PATA

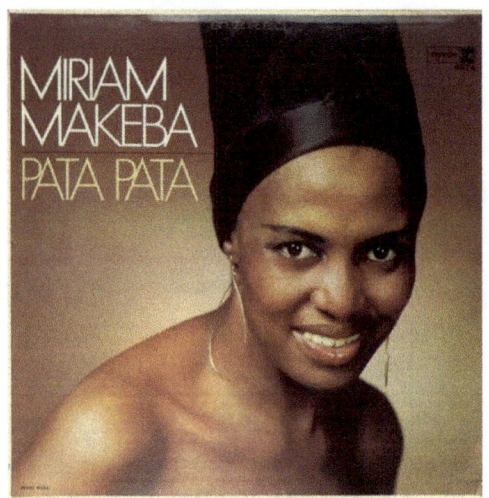

```
US release    November 1967    Reprise    R(S) 6274
UK release    November 1967    Reprise    RSLP 6274

1. Pata Pata (Jerry Ragovoy/Miriam Makeba)
2. Ha Po Zamani (Dorothy Masuka)
3. What Is Love (Jerry Ragovoy)
4. Maria Fulo (Severino Dias De Oliveira)
5. Yetentu Tizaleny (M.A. Betresidk)
6. Click Song Number One (Miriam Makeba)

7. Ring Bell, Ring Bell (George Weiss/Jerry Ragovoy)
8. Jol'inkomo (Gibson Kente/Letta Mbulu)
9. West Wind (Caiphus Semenia/William Salter)
10. Saduva (Miriam Makeba)
11. A Piece Of Ground (Jeremy Taylor)

Miriam Makeba: vocals / Jerry Ragovoy, Jimmy Wisner, Luchi De Jesus, Severino Dias De Oliveira: arrangers, producers
```

South African singer Miriam Makeba moved to the US in 1959, a little before the jazz musicians Hugh Masekela and Dollar Brand. She made numerous recordings through the sixties and beyond, employing a style that was crammed full of references and influences from her home country. She became in the process the first African international music star. Her last studio recording was in 2004 – she died four years later at the age of seventy-six. *Pata Pata* is her best known song and a hit in many countries, though not in either the US or the UK. She had first recorded the song in the fifties, when, of course, producer Jerry Ragovoy's name was not included in the credits. Shortly after the release of this album, she married black power activist Stokely Carmichael and for the crime of wanting fair treatment for black people was banned, for the next twenty years, from continuing to live in the US.

RAVI SHANKAR — AT THE MONTEREY POP FESTIVAL

US release	November 1967	World Pacific	WPS-21442
UK release	November 1967	Columbia	S(C)X 6273

1. Raga Bhimpalasi (Traditional)
2. Tabla Solo In Ektal (Traditional)
3. Dhun (Dadra And Fast Teental) (Traditional)

Ravi Shankar: sitar / Kamala Chakravarty: tamboura / Alla Rakha: tabla / Richard Bock: producer

Master sitar player Ravi Shankar first toured in the UK, Germany, and the US in 1956, and recorded his first LP, *Three Ragas*. Due to the growing interest in the sitar within rock music, after its introduction by George Harrison, Shankar was invited to perform at the Monterey Pop Festival in June 1967. He was the only artist to be paid for his appearance and played a much longer set than anyone else, on the last afternoon of the festival. As always, he performed his interpretations of traditional Indian concert music. The album souvenir of the occasion contains just part of what he played. It sold well enough to enter the album chart in the US. It is interesting to note that an album featuring Ravi Shankar playing with violinist Yehudi Menuhin was released in the US during the same month as the Monterey Festival. *West Meets East* proceeded to dominate the classical music chart until the beginning of the next year and even managed to scrape into the general album chart, though much lower down than *At The Monterey Pop Festival*.

JOHN FAHEY — REQUIA

US release	November 1967	Vanguard	VSD7/VRS-9259
UK release	early 1969	Vanguard	SVRL 19055

1. Requiem For John Hurt
2. Requiem For Russell Blaine Cooper
3. When The Catfish Is In Bloom
4. Requiem For Molly Parts 1-4
5. Fight On Christians, Fight On

All compositions by John Fahey

John Fahey: guitar, effects / Barry Hansen: effects / Samuel Charters: effects

For his first album for a major label, John Fahey tries an experiment with his own version of musique concrète, to set alongside his familiar bluesy instrumentals. The four pieces making up the *Requiem For Molly* find the acoustic guitar battling against a collage of processed orchestral and found sound samples. The collage provides some very interesting effects, but they do not appear to have anything to do with what the guitar is playing, which continues to sound very conventional. It would appear at this point as though Fahey is unsure as to what kind of artist he now wants to be. He is trying to be a melodic player of blues and ragtime guitar at the same time as being an avant garde pioneer, but he needed to make a choice. To be fair, Fahey has since stated that the experiment was a good learning experience, but one that he no longer likes.

GLEN CAMPBELL — BY THE TIME I GET TO PHOENIX

By The Time I Get To Phoenix, the song, is an evocative portrait of the end of a relationship, set to a highly memorable melody, and it was the first collaboration between Glen Campbell and songwriter Jimmy Webb. It was originally recorded by Johnny Rivers a year earlier, but it was Campbell who had the hit (not in the UK, although the song

US release	November 1967	Capitol	(S)T 2851
UK release	early 1968	Ember	NR 5041 extra track

1. By The Time I Get To Phoenix (Jimmy Webb)
2. Homeward Bound (Paul Simon)
3. Tomorrow Never Comes (Ernest Tubb/Johnny Bond)
4. Cold December (In Your Heart) (Alex Hassilev)
5. My Baby's Gone (Hazel Houser)
6. Back In The Race (Glen Campbell/Vic Dana)
7. Hey Little One (Dorsey Burnette)
8. Bad Seed (Bill Anderson)
9. I'll Be Lucky Someday (Bob Wills/Dickie McBride/Lee Martin)
10. You're Young And You'll Forget (Jerry Reed)
11. Love Is A Lonesome River (Glen Campbell)

Glen Campbell: vocals, guitar / James Burton: guitar / Joe Osborn: bass guitar / Jim Gordon: drums / Al De Lory: arranger, producer / Nick Venet: producer (3) / Mort Garson: arranger (4,8) / Leon Russell: arranger (5) / Jimmie Haskell: arranger (3)

became well-known there regardless). Propelled by its hit single, the album became Campbell's second platinum seller in the US and the following year it became the first country record to win the Grammy award for album of the year.

GARY BURTON QUARTET   LOFTY FAKE ANAGRAM

| US release | November 1967 | RCA Victor | LSP/LPM 3901 |
| UK release | November 1967 | RCA Victor | SF/RD 7923 |

1. June the 15 1967 (Mike Gibbs)
2. Feelings And Things (Mike Gibbs)
3. Fleurette Africaine (Duke Ellington)
4. I'm Your Pal (Steve Swallow)
5. Lines (Gary Burton)
6. The Beach (Gary Burton)
7. Mother Of The Dead Man (Carla Bley)
8. Good Citizen Swallow (Gary Burton)
9. General Mojo Cuts Up (Steve Swallow)

Gary Burton: vibraphone / Larry Coryell: guitar / Steve Swallow: bass / Bob Moses: drums / Brad McCuen: producer / Darol Rice: producer

Gary Burton is a virtuoso vibraphone player, capable of playing with three mallets in each hand simultaneously, and formerly a member of the band led by saxophonist Stan Getz. *Lofty Fake Anagram* is the second album made by his quartet – *Duster* was released earlier in the same year. Burton makes a point of choosing the work of up-and-coming young jazz composers. Mike Gibbs and Carla Bley (and indeed Burton himself and his bass player, Steve Swallow) write interesting, modern pieces with a similar approach to Wayne Shorter and Herbie Hancock, working with Miles Davis. This gives Burton's group a modern sound, even if he is not really at the cutting edge. Nevertheless, guitarist Larry Coryell thrives in this environment, far more so than he did with Chico Hamilton or the Free Spirits. He tries hard to make his tone innovative, even if it is hardly in the same league as Jeff Beck or Jimi Hendrix. He does, however, manage to coax his instrument into emitting a burst of controlled feedback, on *General Mojo Cuts Up*. This is the first time that feedback has been used on a jazz record. This does not, of course, mean that *Lofty Fake Anagram* can be considered as any kind of fusion jazz precursor. The rhythms are very much jazz rhythms, with nothing in the way of a rock backbeat, while Steve Swallow is still using a double bass at this point, not a bass guitar, and he is not playing riffs. The best this writer can come up with in regard to the anagram mentioned in the album title is that it stands for 'Key Of (A) Flat'.

THE ELECTRIC FLAG   THE TRIP

| US release | November 1967 | Sidewalk | (S)T5908 |
Not released in UK

1. Peter's Trip
2. Joint Passing
3. Psyche Soap
4. M-23
5. Synesthesia
6. A Little Head
7. Hobbit
8. Inner Pocket
9. Fewghh
10. Green And Gold
11. The Other Ed Norton
12. Flash, Bam, Pow
13. Home Room
14. Peter Gets Off
15. Practice Music
16. Fine Jung Thing
17. Senior Citizen
18. Gettin' Hard

All compositions by the Electric Flag

Mike Bloomfield: guitar / Nick Gravenites: vocals, guitar / Peter Strazza: tenor saxophone / Marcus Doubleday: trumpet, flugelhorn / Bob Notkoff: violin / Barry Goldberg: keyboards / Harvey Brooks: bass guitar / Buddy Miles: drums / Paul Beaver: synthesizer / John Court: producer

Mike Bloomfield left the Paul Butterfield Blues Band early in 1967 and formed a rock band with a brass section, intending to play "American music", by which he primarily meant blues and soul. The first recording by the Electric Flag was the soundtrack to a film centred around the taking of LSD, written by a young Jack Nicholson and starring Peter Fonda. *The Trip* did well in the US, but was prevented by the censor from being shown in the UK, so that the soundtrack album was not released there either. As a showcase for the music of Bloomfield's new band, the album is less than ideal, as most of the tracks are little more than short fragments and many of them are designed as ambient sound portraits of a drug experience. *Fine Jung Thing*, however, is a lengthy blues instrumental including a fine, extended guitar solo from Mike Bloomfield himself, although without any brass.

THE BOX TOPS   THE LETTER/NEON RAINBOW

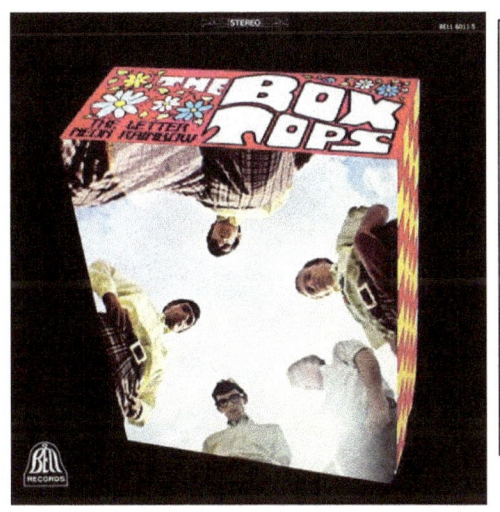

| US release | November 1967 | Bell | BELL 6011(-S) |
| UK release | November 1967 | Stateside | (S)SL 10218 |

1. The Letter (Wayne Carson Thompson)
2. She Knows How (Wayne Carson Thompson)
3. Trains And Boats And Planes (Burt Bacharach/Hal David)
4. Break My Mind (John D Loudermilk)
5. Whiter Shade Of Pale (Gary Brooker/Keith Reid)
6. Everything I Am (Dan Penn/Spooner Oldham)
7. Neon Rainbow (Wayne Carson Thompson)
8. People Make The World (Bobby Womack)
9. I'm Your Puppet (Dan Penn/Spooner Oldham)
10. Happy Times (Dan Penn/Spooner Oldham)
11. Gonna Find Somebody (Bobby Womack)
12. I Pray For Rain (Dan Penn/Spooner Oldham)

Alex Chilton: vocals, guitar / Gary Talley: guitar, vocals / John Evans: keyboards / Bill Cunningham: bass guitar / Danny Smythe: drums / Dan Penn: vocals, producer / Reggie Young: guitar / Bobby Womack: guitar / Bobby Emmons: keyboards / Tommy Cogbill: bass guitar / Gene Chrisman: drums / Mike Leach: arranger / Richard Malone: guitar (1) / Russ Caccamisi: bass guitar (1)

The Letter was recorded by Memphis group, the DeVilles, closely following a demo submitted by the songwriter. The record was released as by the Box Tops and proceeded to reach number one in the US chart. It was a top ten hit in the UK too – sixteen-year-old Alex Chilton's gritty, soulful voice combined with a memorable melody proving to be irresistible. Much of the album that followed was recorded using session musicians. It is a very straightforward light pop/soul affair, centering on Chilton's voice and without any of the guitar histrionics or psychedelic effects distinguishing the other albums made at this time. Sporadic gentle orchestration helps to make the music sound attractive, so that *The Letter/Neon Rainbow* emerges as an unspectacular but highly listenable set of songs. Alex Chilton's voice gave his group a few more hits, most notably *Cry Like A Baby* in 1968 and *Soul Deep* in 1969, but the group broke up in 1970.

THE AMBOY DUKES

| US release | November 1967 | Mainstream | S/6104 / 56104 |
| UK release | November 1967 | Fontana | (S)TL 5468 |

1. Baby Please Don't Go (Joe Williams)
2. I Feel Free (Jack Bruce/Pete Brown)
3. Young Love (Steve Farmer/Ted Nugent)
4. Psalms Of Aftermath (Steve Farmer/Ted Nugent)
5. Colors (Bill White/Rick Lober/Steve Farmer/Ted Nugent)
6. Let's Go Get Stoned (Nickolas Ashford/Valerie Simpson/Jo Armstead)
7. Down On The Philips Escalator (Steve Farmer/Ted Nugent)
8. The Lovely Lady (Steve Farmer)
9. Night Time (Steve Farmer/Ted Nugent)
10. It's Not True (Pete Townshend)
11. Gimme Love (Steve Farmer/Ted Nugent)

John Drake: vocals / Ted Nugent: guitar, sitar (4) / Steve Farmer: guitar / Rick Lober: keyboards / Bill White: bass guitar / Dave Palmer: drums / Bob Shad: producer

The Amboy Dukes, named after a teenage gang in a novel by Irving Shulman, were a showcase for the flamboyant playing of the guitarist, Ted Nugent. The album is not all about heavy guitar excess: *Young Love* and *The Lovely Lady* are in waltz time, with Nugent showing amazing restraint, while *Psalms Of Aftermath* is a psychedelic period piece, with Nugent switching to sitar. Elsewhere, there are harmony vocals in places, and some strong melodies. But it is the overdriven lead guitar that ultimately gives the Amboy Dukes their point. The album opens with a version of *Baby Please Don't Go* that takes the recording made by Van Morrison's Them as its starting point, but allows the lead guitar to extend the underlying riff with sustained playing that just fails to turn the song into a chaotic disaster. In its own way, this is rather magnificent.

HAPSHASH AND THE COLOURED COAT   FEATURING THE HUMAN HOST AND THE HEAVY METAL KIDS

| UK release | November 1967 | Minit | MLS/MLL 40001 | red vinyl |
| US release | November 1967 | Imperial | LP-12377/LP-9377 | |

1. H-O-P-P-Why?
2. A Mind Blown Is A Mind Shown
3. The New Messiah Coming 1985
4. Aoum
5. Empires Of The Sun

All compositions by Michael English/Nigel Waymouth/Guy Stevens

Michael English: vocals, percussion / Nigel Waymouth: vocals, percussion / Amanda Lear: vocals / Brian Jones: piano, harmonica, guitar / John Pearse: violin / Luther Grosvenor: guitar / Greg Ridley: bass guitar / Mike Kellie: drums, percussion / Guy Stevens: producer

Hapshash And The Coloured Coat was a design company run by graphic artists Michael English and Nigel Waymouth, who produced elaborate, psychedelic posters for rock concerts. The album issued in their name is a recording of a 'happening', in which Brian Jones of the Rolling Stones, members of the group Art, and a few friends (none of them being given any credit on the album sleeve) jam rather aimlessly, as though trying to convince the listener that they are really not very talented musically. As a period piece, giving some insight into the hippy mindset, the album is mildly interesting, but perhaps the most notable thing about it is its very early use of the phrase 'heavy metal', borrowed from the writing of William Burroughs, where it is a metaphor for addictive drugs, rather than music. That and the fact that the album is pressed on red vinyl instead of the usual black.

JULIE DRISCOLL, BRIAN AUGER & THE TRINITY   OPEN

| UK release | November 1967 | Marmalade 609/607 002 |
| US release | May 1968 | ATCO SD 33-258 |

1. In And Out (Wes Montgomery)
2. Isola Natale (Brian Auger)
3. Black Cat (Brian Auger)
4. Lament For Miss Baker (Brian Auger)
5. Goodbye Jungle Telegraph (Brian Auger)
6. Tramp (Jimmy McCracklin/Lowell Fulsom)
7. Why (Am I Treated So Bad) (Mavis Staples)
8. A Kind Of Love In (Brian Auger/Julie Driscoll)
9. Break It Up (Brian Auger/Roger Sutton)
10. Season Of The Witch (Donovan Leitch)

Julie Driscoll: vocals (6-10) / Brian Auger: organ, piano, vocals (3) / Dave Ambrose: bass guitar / Clive Thacker: drums / Gary Boyle: guitar (1,2) / prob. Alan Skidmore: tenor saxophone (5,6) / uncredited brass on tracks 3,6,7,8) / Giorgio Gomelsky: producer

Hammond organist Brian Auger led a highly regarded UK R&B band from 1965, Steampacket, featuring a rotating troupe of three singers – Long John Baldry, Julie Driscoll, and Rod Stewart. The band made no records and eventually Auger slimmed the band down to a trio, with the addition of just one singer, Julie Driscoll. Although Ms Driscoll, blessed with model looks and a striking, fluid voice like a more mellow Grace Slick, was a considerable asset for the group, Brian Auger seemed uncertain as to whether he really wanted her to take the spotlight away from himself. Accordingly, she only gets to perform on one side of the debut album, *Open*, while Auger devotes the other side to a selection of jazzy instrumentals. It is the extended, improvised reading of *Season Of The Witch*, with Julie Driscoll in particularly fine form, that shows what this group is really capable of and how the album could have sounded if only Brian Auger had given up his futile longing to be Jimmy Smith.

JOHN MAYALL   THE BLUES ALONE

| UK release | November 1967 | Decca Ace Of Clubs | SCL/ACL 1243 |
| US release | November 1967 | London | PS 534 |

1. Brand New Start
2. Please Don't Tell
3. Down The Line
4. Sonny Boy Blow
5. Marsha's Mood
6. No More Tears
7. Catch That Train
8. Cancelling Out
9. Harp Man
10. Brown Sugar
11. Broken Wings
12. Don't Kick Me

All compositions by John Mayall

John Mayall: vocals, harmonica, keyboards, guitar, bass guitar, drums / Keef Hartley: drums (2,4,6,8-12) / Mike Vernon: producer

Disbanding his latest edition of the Bluesbreakers, John Mayall went into the recording studio to make a solo album. Drummer Keef Hartley was retained for eight tracks, but everything else was played by Mayall himself, overdubbing successive parts to make the music sound as though it is being played by a band. If the intention was to demonstrate that Mayall was capable of creating a good album without the help of any of his star lead guitarists, then the result is a resounding success. The feel is a little different from his other records, but his songwriting, aimed at showing how varied music based on simple blues chord changes can be, is very much on form. The moody *Broken Wings* and the fiery *Don't Kick Me* are particularly strong, probably the best songs in Mayall's career to date. Decca, perhaps not entirely convinced that Mayall could generate sales on his own, put the album on its bargain priced Ace of Clubs label. But radio DJ John Peel, already a significant celebrity, was commissioned to write the sleeve notes, to make it clear that *The Blues Alone* was to be taken seriously.

CREAM   DISRAELI GEARS

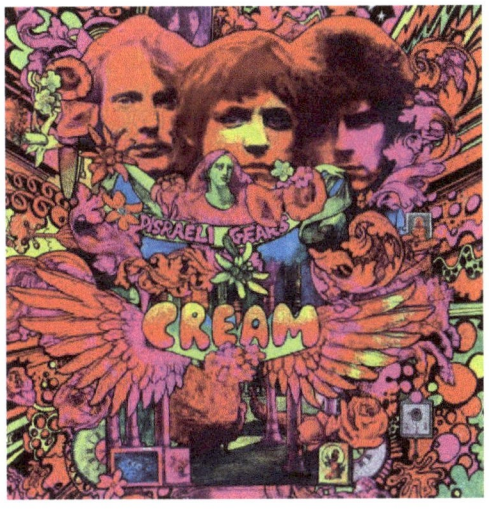

UK release	November 1967	Reaction	594/593 003
US release	November 1967	ATCO	SD 33-232

1. Strange Brew (Eric Clapton/Felix Pappalardi/Gail Collins)
2. Sunshine Of Your Love (Eric Clapton/Jack Bruce/Pete Brown)
3. World Of Pain (Felix Pappalardi/Gail Collins)
4. Dance The Night Away (Jack Bruce/Pete Brown)
5. Blue Condition (Ginger Baker)
6. Tales Of Brave Ulysses (Eric Clapton/Martin Sharp)
7. Swlabr (Jack Bruce/Pete Brown)
8. We're Going Wrong (Jack Bruce)
9. Outside Woman Blues (Blind Joe Reynolds)
10. Take It Back (Jack Bruce/Pete Brown)
11. Mother's Lament (Traditional)

Eric Clapton: vocals, guitar / Jack Bruce: vocals, bass guitar, piano, harmonica / Ginger Baker: drums, vocals / Felix Pappalardi: producer

The second album by Cream is an altogether more sophisticated affair than the debut. There is one blues cover, but *Outside Woman Blues* stands out because the other songs are not blues based. Even *Strange Brew*, which started life as a blues called *Lawdy Mama* and still retains the traditional chord changes (as well as a guitar solo borrowed from Albert King), is transformed into something else by its defiantly non-traditional lyrics. *Sunshine Of Your Love* introduces the concept of a hard rock song based on a riff, but its companions are a remarkably varied selection, showing how flexible the guitar-bass-drums format can be when applied to inspired songwriting. Eric Clapton tries hard to make his guitar stand out from the competition, both in terms of the sheer virtuosity of his lines and by the use of unexpected tones. He turns his guitar into a supercharged mandolin on *Dance The Night Away*, introduces what was to become his hugely influential sustaining 'woman tone' on *Swlabr* (she was like a bearded rainbow), and showcases the newly invented wah-wah pedal on *Tales Of Brave Ulysses*. This song had already been unleashed back in June, as the B-side to the single issue of *Strange Brew*. On many of the tracks, his solos, always kept short, are delivered by two intertwining guitars, by means of studio overdubbing. Meanwhile, Jack Bruce and Ginger Baker function as far more than just a rhythm section, crafting lines and beats that become integral parts of the songs. The album's conclusion is designed to show that Cream, despite its delight in turning rock music into art, did not always take itself completely seriously – it is a rendering of a silly piece of music hall, delivered as if in a London pub by the inebriated clientele gathered around the piano. The album title itself is based on a deliberate mis-hearing of the name given to the gearing system widely used on bicycles.

THE CHAMBERS BROTHERS   THE TIME HAS COME

US release	November 1967	Columbia	CS 9522
UK release	November 1967	Direction	863407

1. All Strung Out Over You (Rudy Clark)
2. People Get Ready (Curtis Mayfield)
3. I Can't Stand It (Lester Chambers)
4. Romeo And Juliet (Lester Chambers)
5. In The Midnight Hour (Steve Cropper/Wilson Pickett)
6. So Tired (Andre Goodwin/Chambers Brothers)
7. Uptown (Betty Mabry)
8. Please Don't Leave Me (George Chambers)
9. What The World Needs Now Is Love (Burt Bacharach/Hal David)
10. The Time Has Come Today (Joseph & Willie Chambers)

Lester Chambers: vocals, harmonica / Willie Chambers: guitar, vocals / Joseph Chambers: guitar, vocals / George Chambers: bass guitar / Brian Keenan: drums / Gary Sherman: arranger / David Rubinson: producer

The Chambers Brothers attempt to amalgamate soul and rock music, much as Sly and the Family Stone were doing, and ignoring the fact that blue-eyed soul groups like the Small Faces and the Spencer Davis Group had already achieved spectacular results in this direction. The climax of the album, and a hit in its own right, is the lengthy *The Time Has Come Today*. The song utilises echo effects, most notably on the percussion sound intended to emulate a ticking clock, and features a long fuzz guitar solo. It is fortunate that drummer Brian Keenan chooses to deliver a virtuoso drum performance at the same time, because it is clear that whichever Chambers brother is responsible for the lead guitar is not much of a soloist. Nevertheless, the music is quite effective in giving substance to the singer's claim that his soul has become "psychedelicized" and it helps to compensate for the hatchet-job the group carries out on its cover of Wilson Pickett's *In The Midnight Hour* on the other side of the album, as well as the unnecessary plagiarising of Willie Cobb's *You Don't Love Me* under the guise of a song called *Please Don't Leave Me*.

ENNIO MORRICONE THE GOOD, THE BAD AND THE UGLY SOUNDTRACK

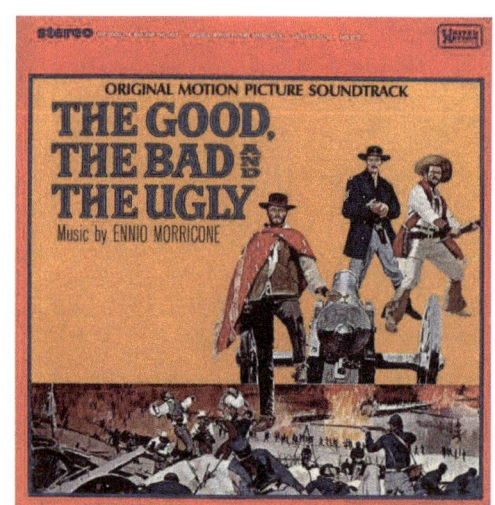

| US release | December 1967 | United Artists | UAS/UAL 4172 |
| UK release | October 1968 | United Artists | (S)ULP 1197 |

1. Main Title
2. The Sundown
3. The Strong
4. The Desert
5. The Carriage Of The Spirits
6. Marcia
7. The Story Of A Soldier
8. Marcia Without Hope
9. The Death Of A Soldier
10. The Ecstasy Of Gold
11. The Trio – Main Title

All compositions by Ennio Morricone

Unione Musicisti di Roma / I Cantore Moderni di Alessandroni / Bruno Nicolai: conductor / Franco De Gemini: harmonica / Nicola Samale: flute / E.Wolf Ferrari: English horn / Michele Lacerenza: trumpet / Francesco Catania: trumpet / Italo Cammarota: occarina / Pino Rucher: electric guitar / Bruno Battisti D'Amario: guitar / Alessandro Alessandroni: whistling / Pierino Munari: percussion / Edda Dell'Orso, Franco Cosacchi, Nino Dei, Enzo Gioieni, Gianna Spagnulo: vocals / Ennio Morricone: producer

Italian composer Ennio Morricone was commissioned to write soundtrack music for a number of Western films made in Italy by director Sergio Leone. *The Good, The Bad And The Ugly* is one of the most celebrated of these and the soundtrack album was a major chart hit in both the US and the UK. Morricone's avant garde background is not particularly apparent beyond his frequent use of acidic harmonies, most notable in his writing for the strings, but he has another technique to make the music sound distinctive. Following the lead set by Maurice Jarre, Morricone incorporates a number of unusual and ethnic instrumental timbres within his orchestra and these dominate the most memorable parts of the music. The arresting *Main Title* is constructed around the sounds of harmonica, electric guitar, and Native American chanting and became a chart hit in its own right – a faithful interpretation by Hugo Montenegro reaching number one in the UK and number two in the US.

THE JIMI HENDRIX EXPERIENCE AXIS: BOLD AS LOVE

| UK release | December 1967 | Track | 613/612 003 |
| US release | January 1968 | Reprise | R(S) 6281 |

1. EXP
2. Up From The Skies
3. Spanish Castle Magic
4. Wait Until Tomorrow
5. Ain't No Telling
6. Little Wing
7. If Six Was Nine
8. You've Got Me Floating
9. Castles Made Of Sand
10. She's So Fine (Noel Redding)
11. One Rainy Wish
12. Little Miss Lover
13. Bold As Love

All compositions by Jimi Hendrix except track 10

Jimi Hendrix: guitar, vocals, piano, glockenspiel, recorder / Noel Redding: bass guitar, vocals, foot stomping (7) / Mitch Mitchell: drums, vocals / Graham Nash: foot stomping (7), vocals (8) / Gary Leeds: foot stomping (7) / Trevor Burton: vocals (8) / Roy Wood: vocals (8) / Chas Chandler: producer

The second album by the Jimi Hendrix Experience presents just as much virtuoso guitar playing as before, but it does so in a rather more subtle manner. The music is no longer rooted in the blues and has much more of a pop sensibility, although the opening *EXP* is an excuse for Hendrix to be as noisy as possible, with multiple overdubbed guitars, all of them feeding back. The track is considerably longer on the stereo album than on the mono. *Bold As Love* ends the album with Hendrix's most majestic guitar playing, drenched in phasing, a whooshing effect that had only just been discovered (on the Small Faces single, *Itchycoo Park,* issued in August). In between, the songs are very varied, ranging from the positively gentle *Little Wing* to the riff-based flight of fancy that is *If Six Was Nine*. Taken together, the contrasting musics of the two albums, *Are You Experienced* and *Axis: Bold As Love,* confirm Jimi Hendrix's status as the most remarkable electric guitarist of his generation.

ART SUPERNATURAL FAIRY TALES

The British R&B group, the V.I.Ps, which had been playing since late 1963 and had released a number of singles, changed its name to Art to indicate a new musical direction. By the time that the album was released, however, the band had added an extra member and had changed its name again, to

Spooky Tooth, so that promotion of *Supernatural Fairy Tales* was abandoned. It is, however, rather a fine album – and who could resist a set that opens with such a delightful title, *I Think I'm Going Weird?* Driven by Greg Ridley's thunderous bass guitar and Luther Grosvenor's fuzz chords and riffs, this is as heavy as rock music gets in the days before heavy metal. There are hardly any instrumental solos, since the keyboards and guitar are too busy keeping the storm going. On the title track there is heavy-handed phasing too. It adds the appropriate supernatural quality.

```
UK release    December 1967    Island    ILP 967
Not released in US

1. I Think I'm Going Weird
2. What's That Sound (For What It's Worth) (Steve Stills)
3. African Thing
4. Room With A View
5. Flying Anchors
6. Supernatural Fairy Tale

7. Love Is Real
8. Come On Up (The Young Rascals)
9. Brothers, Dads And Mothers
10.Talkin' To Myself
11.Alive Not Dead
12.Rome Take Away Three

All compositions by Art except where stated

Mike Harrison: vocals,keyboards / Luther Grosvenor: guitar, vocals / Greg Ridley: bass guitar / Mike Kellie: drums / Guy Stevens: producer
```

PROCOL HARUM

```
UK release    December 1967    Regal Zonophone    (S)LRZ 1001
US release    September 1967   Deram             DES18008/DE 16008
       A Whiter Shade Of Pale added, Good Captain Clack omitted

1. Conquistador
2. She Wandered Through The Garden Fence
3. Something Following Me
4. Mabel
5. Cerdes (Outside The Gates Of)

6. A Christmas Camel
7. Kaleidoscope
8. Salad Days (Are Here Again)
9. Good Captain Clack
10.Repent Walpurgis (Matthew Fisher)

All compositions by Keith Reid/Gary Brooker except track 10

Gary Brooker: vocals, piano / Matthew Fisher: organ / Robin Trower: guitar / David Knights: bass guitar / B.J. Wilson: drums / Denny Cordell: producer
```

A Whiter Shade Of Pale, matching obscure, poetic lyrics to an organ part inspired by Bach, was released in May and proceeded to become one of the best-selling singles ever, with over ten million copies sold. The UK album that eventually followed was on a different label and with a new guitarist and drummer for the group, Procol Harum, but the hit song was notably absent. The American version of the album does include the single and is stronger for it. The album tracks do, however, prove that the songwriting success of *A Whiter Shade Of Pale* was not a lucky fluke. The music press was critical of Procol Harum for not dancing around on stage as pop stars were supposed to do, but the group believed that its music (and perhaps its colourful clothing too) was enough. On the album, the combination of Keith Reid's Dylanesque lyrics with Gary Brooker's imaginative way with a melody and Matthew Fisher's classically inclined organ playing certainly is enough. Robin Trower's guitar has much less to do than on most rock records, but when it does sound, as with the gritty sustain he adds to *Cerdes (Outside The Gates Of),* his contribution is vital. The music gives the impression of being on the verge of something very new and in retrospect we can hear that Procol Harum is anticipating, as much as did the Beatles' *Sgt Pepper,* the sound and the methods of progressive rock, even if the song structures remain straightforward. Six months later, the American *Billboard* magazine used the phrase 'progressive rock' (for the first time in print) to describe the most recent development and Procol Harum was one of three groups (along with the Crazy World of Arthur Brown and the Who) specifically mentioned.

TRAFFIC   MR FANTASY

```
UK release    December 1967    Island          ILPS 9061/ILP 961
US release    December 1967    United Artists  UAS 6651/UAL 3651
        as HEAVEN IS IN YOUR MIND, different cover and several different tracks

1. Heaven Is In Your Mind (Chris Wood/Jim Capaldi/Steve Winwood)
2. Berkshire Poppies (Chris Wood/Jim Capaldi/Steve Winwood)
3. House For Everyone (Dave Mason)
4. No Face, No Name And No Number (Jim Capaldi/Steve Winwood)
5. Dear Mr Fantasy (Chris Wood/Jim Capaldi/Steve Winwood)

6. Dealer (Jim Capldi)
7. Utterly Simple (Dave Mason)
8. Coloured Rain (Chris Wood/Jim Capaldi/Steve Winwood)
9. Hope I Never Find Me There (Dave Mason)
10.Giving To You (Chris Wood/Dave Mason/Jim Capaldi/Steve Winwood)

Steve Winwood: vocals, keyboards, guitar, bass guitar, percussion / Dave Mason: vocals, guitar, sitar, bass guitar, mellotron, tambura / Chris Wood: flute, tenor saxophone, organ, vocals / Jim Capaldi: drums, percussion, vocals / Jimmy Miller: producer
```

Steve Winwood left the hit-making Spencer Davis Group in April 1967 in order to create more wide-ranging music with musicians he had met jamming in a Birmingham club called The Elbow Room. The quartet rented a cottage in Berkshire to rehearse, thereby establishing one of rock music's great clichés ('getting it together in the country'). Three fascinating singles, in different styles, were released and became hits in the UK; *Paper Sun, Hole In My Shoe,* and

Here We Go Round The Mulberry Bush, the third being the title song from a film directed by Clive Donner. The first two songs were included on the US version of the album, although they had not been chart hits there. The music on the album is extremely varied, with the four musicians each playing several instruments to make the sound palette as extensive as possible. Two songs, the first and last on side one, incorporate improvised guitar solos (played completely differently on the mono and stereo versions of the album), while *Giving To You* is a jazzy instrumental. The songwriting, helped by the fact that the band splits into two camps, Dave Mason vs the rest, is at an extremely high level, with no track capable of being considered mere filler. In short, *Mr Fantasy* takes its place as one of the half dozen or so iconic records to be issued during December 1967.

THE SPENCER DAVIS GROUP   THE BEST OF

UK release   December 1967   Island   ILPS 9070/ILP 970
Not issued in US   US **GREATEST HITS** with only 10 tracks and just 4 in common   early 1968   United Artists   UAS 6641/UAL 3641

1. I'm A Man (Jimmy Miller/Steve Winwood)
2. Gimme Some Lovin' (Muff Winwood/Spencer Davis/Steve Winwood)
3. Every Little Bit Hurts (Ed Cobb)
4. This Hammer (Spencer Davis Group)
5. Back Into My Life Again (Jackie Edwards/Jimmy Miller)
6. Waltz For Lumumba (Steve Winwood)
7. Together Till The End Of Time (Frank Wilson)

8. Keep On Running (Jackie Edwards)
9. Trampoline (Steve Winwood)
10. When I Come Home (Jackie Edwards/Steve Winwood)
11. Strong Love (Deadric Malone/Edward Silvers/Mary M Brown)
12. Somebody Help Me (Jackie Edwards)
13. She Put The Hurt On Me (Lawrence Nelson)
14. Goodbye Stevie (Spencer Davis Group)

Spencer Davis: guitar, vocals / Steve Winwood: vocals, keyboards, guitar, harmonica / Muff Winwood: bass guitar / Pete York: drums / Jimmy Miller: producer (1,11) / Chris Blackwell: producer

Island chose to issue to issue a compilation of the hits by the group that Steve Winwood had just left during the same month as the first album by his new group, hoping that the publicity would help sales of both albums. The Spencer Davis Group had always been much more convincing as a singles concern, putting more effort into those than the albums. As a result, this really is *The Best Of The Spencer Davis Group*. The run of five UK hits, *Keep On Running, Somebody Help Me, When I Come Home, Gimme Some Lovin',* and *I'm A Man,* (the last two being big hits in the US too), are the equal of any R&B band operating in the mid-sixties and very much better than most. With Steve Winwood being the natural focus for the group and dominating the records with his singing and playing on both keyboards and guitar, it was inevitable that he would eventually want to go his own way. But these early recordings provide an impressive grounding for his subsequent career.

THE BEATLES   MAGICAL MYSTERY TOUR Double EP

Magical Mystery Tour, a film made by the Beatles for television, attracted some criticism from people who did not want to watch what seemed like a dodgy home movie, but there is no gainsaying the quality of the music (and viewed as a very early collection of music videos, the film is no worse than other examples of the genre and considerably more interesting than most). The music is a continuation of the style and approach applied to the *Sgt Pepper* album. *I Am The Walrus* is another experimental John Lennon extravaganza to set alongside *Strawberry Fields Forever* and *A Day In The Life; The Fool On The Hill* is one of the most charming of Paul McCartney's compelling melodies; *Blue Jay Way* is a particularly successful example of George Harrison's ongoing project of amalgamating Indian music with Western pop-rock. The Beatles chose to issue these most recent recordings in the form of a double EP package, although arguably it might have been better to wait until they had enough for a proper album. In the US, the songs were used to fill half an album, which was completed by adding the songs released as singles during the past months, including

UK release   December 1967   Parlophone   (S)MMT-1
US release   December 1967   Capitol   (S)MAL 2835
as LP with different cover and 5 extra tracks

1. Magical Mystery Tour (John Lennon/Paul McCartney)
2. Your Mother Should Know (John Lennon/Paul McCartney)
3. I Am The Walrus (John Lennon/Paul McCartney)
4. The Fool On The Hill (John Lennon/Paul McCartney)
5. Flying (John Lennon/Paul McCartney/George Harrison/Ringo Starr)
6. Blue Jay Way (George Harrison)

John Lennon: vocals, guitar, keyboards, bass harmonica, banjo, percussion / Paul McCartney: vocals, bass guitar, guitar, keyboards, recorder, percussion / George Harrison: vocals, guitar, organ, bass harmonica, swarmandal, violin, percussion / Ringo Starr: drums, percussion, vocals / David Mason, Elgar Howarth, Roy Copestake, John Wilbraham: trumpets (1) / Mal Evans, Neil Aspinall: percussion (1) / Sidney Sax, Jack Rothstein, Ralph Elman, Andrew McGee, Jack Greene, Louis Stevens, John Jezzard, Jack Richards: violins (3) / Lionel Ross, Eldon Fox, Brian Martin, Terry Weil: cellos (3) / Neill Sanders, Tony Tunstall, Morris Miller: horns (3) / Mike Sammes Singers (3) / Christopher Taylor, Richard Taylor, Jack Ellory: flutes (4) / unknown cello (6) / George Martin: producer

both *Penny Lane* and *Strawberry Fields Forever*. The result is a particularly satisfying record, even if it is not one that the Beatles themselves had planned to release.

THE ROLLING STONES   THEIR SATANIC MAJESTIES REQUEST

```
UK release       December 1967    Decca      TXS/TXL 103
US release       December 1967    London     NP(S)-2

1. Sing This All Together
2. Citadel
3. In Another Land (Bill Wyman)
4. 2000 Man
5. Sing This All Together (See What Happens)

6. She's A Rainbow
7. The Lantern
8. Gomper
9. 2000 Light Years From Home
10. On With The Show

All compositions by Mick Jagger/Keith Richards except track 3

Mick Jagger: vocals, percussion, glockenspiel / Keith Richards:
guitar, bass guitar, vocals / Brian Jones: mellotron, organ,
guitar, dulcimer, flute, tenor saxophone, vibraphone,
theremin, brass, recorder, harp, sarod, percussion, effects / Bill
Wyman: bass guitar, keyboards, percussion, oscillator, vocals /
Charlie Watts: drums, percussion / Nicky Hopkins: keyboards /
John Paul Jones: string arrangement (6) / Ronnie Lane: vocals
(3) / Steve Marriott: vocals (3) / Eddie Kramer: percussion (9) /
The Rolling Stones: producers
```

While retaining a significant r&b influence and generally making music with a harder edge than the Beatles, the Rolling Stones had nevertheless been moving in the same direction as their rivals. Their songs had been getting more sophisticated and more innovative. It was not altogether surprising, therefore, that in late 1967, the Stones should have created an album sharing many of the same characteristics as the Beatles' *Sgt Pepper*. Employing to the full Brian Jones' ability to make sensible music out of any instrument he picked up, *Their Satanic Majesties Request* presents songs suffused with an astonishing variety of tones and timbres. At the same time, many of them have a jam session ambience, most notably the sprawling second version of *Sing This All Together* and the Eastern-flavoured instrumental *Gomper*. Even without the imaginative instrumentation, the songs are amongst the most interesting that Mick Jagger and Keith Richards had written and are very varied in mood and theme. They include *She's A Rainbow*, a remarkably delicate, even beautiful composition, and one of the first pieces of musical science-fiction, the intensely atmospheric *2000 Light Years From Home*. The album is contained within a cover as striking as the one employed by the Beatles, a gatefold creation with a 3D lenticular image filling most of the front. *Their Satanic Majesties Request* has been the subject of much unfair criticism in more recent times by people who feel that this kind of proto-progressive rock is not what the Rolling Stones should be about. The fact that the group has never returned to this style of music has much to do with the ending of the competition with the Beatles, together with the fact that Brian Jones is sadly no longer around to provide the necessary impetus. As a demonstration, however, of what sixties music-making could achieve, regardless of who produced it, the album stands proud.

THE WHO   SELL OUT

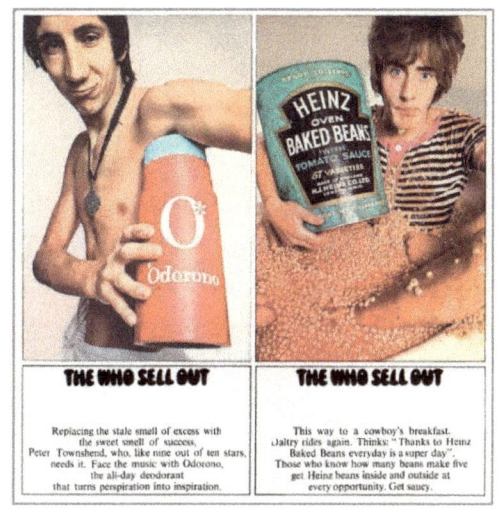

```
UK release       December 1967    Track      613/612 002
US release       December 1967    Decca      DL (7)4950

1. Armenia City In The Sky (Speedy Keene)
2. Heinz Baked Beans (John Entwistle)
3. Mary Anne With The Shaky Hand (Pete Townshend)
4. Odorono (Pete Townshend)
5. Tattoo (Pete Townshend)
6. Our Love Was (Pete Townshend)
7. I Can See For Miles (Pete Townshend)

8. Can't Reach You (Pete Townshend)
9. Medac (John Entwistle)
10. Relax (Pete Townshend)
11. Silas Stingy (John Entwistle)
12. Sunrise (Pete Townshend)
13. Rael (1 and 2) (Pete Townshend)

Roger Daltrey: vocals / Pete Townshend: guitar, vocals / John Entwistle:
organ (13) / Speedy Keene: vocals (1) / Kit Lambert: producer
```

The third album by the Who is loosely based around the theme of advertising. As the cover suggests, the treatment is distinctly satirical. The album is structured as if it was a pirate radio broadcast, with some real station jingles being used in between some of the tracks, although there is no DJ speaking. Given that the offshore pirate radio stations in the UK had been made illegal in August, the album serves as a very timely tribute to them. Some of the Who's songs are also constructed as though they are advertisements, although most of them are not and are unrelated to the overall advertising concept. They include some of Pete Townshend's most effective compositions to date, in the same league as contemporaneous songs by John Lennon and Paul McCartney. The thunderous *I Can See For Miles,* released as a single, is arguably the group's greatest of all and certainly one of the classic recordings broadly counted as being psychedelic. The opening *Armenia City In The Sky,* driven by eerie backwards recorded horns, is very powerful too, but this is written by a friend, Speedy Keene, who would later achieve some brief fame as a member of the group Thunderclap Newman. Pete Townshend was obviously particularly fond of the chord patterns he uses during the second half of *Rael 1,* because he recycled them as part of *Tommy,* the Who's next album project.

THE BEACH BOYS   WILD HONEY

```
US release     December 1967    Capitol    (S)T 2859
UK release     March 1968       Capitol    (S)T 2859

1. Wild Honey
2. Aren't You Glad
3. I Was Made To Love Her (Henry Cosby/Lula Hardaway/Stevie Wonder/Sylvia Moy)
4. Country Air
5. A Thing Or Two
6. Darlin'
7. I'd Love Just Once To See You
8. Here Comes The Night
9. Let The Wind Blow
10. How She Boogalooed It (Al Jardine/Bruce Johnston/Carl Wilson/Mike Love)
11. Mama Says

All compositions by Brian Wilson/Mike Love except tracks 3 and 10

Mike Love: vocals / Brian Wilson: vocals, keyboards, percussion, bass guitar (5) / Carl Wilson: vocals, guitar, bass guitar (2,4,9), percussion / Bruce Johnston: vocals, organ (1,10), bass guitar (1) / Al Jardine: vocals, guitar (7) / Dennis Wilson: vocals, drums, percussion / Hal Blaine: drums (6) / Ron Brown: bass guitar (3,6,8) / Paul Tanner: electro-theremin (1) / unknown brass / Beach Boys: producer
```

There was still pressure on Brian Wilson to finish *Smile* and release it, but instead the Beach Boys completed an entirely new album, for which Wilson composed the majority of the music. It marks a return to the simpler approach of the group's early days, with hardly any session musicians being employed. In retrospect, it is possible to argue that the Beach Boys are simply anticipating the similar scaling down in ambition to be shown a little later by both the Beatles and the Rolling Stones, but that does little to assuage the feelings of regret in listeners who know that the group is capable of so much more than this. Three tracks on side two go some way to ease the pain: *Darlin'* (issued as a single), *Here Comes The Night,* and *Let The Wind Blow* are memorable performances carrying hints of the vocal brilliance that makes *Smile* so great. But *Mama Says* is a reworking of a section from the original recording of *Vegetables,* left off the version that was included on the *Smiley Smile* album. In this new context, the song seems like something of a musical giving the finger.

THE LOVIN' SPOONFUL   EVERYTHING PLAYING

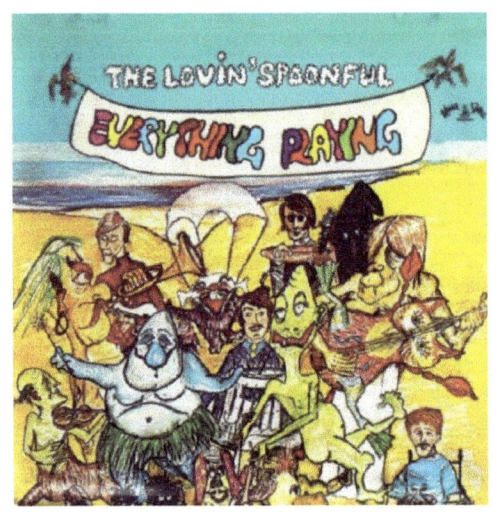

```
US release     December 1967    Kama Sutra    KLP(S) 8061
UK release     December 1967    Kama Sutra    KLP 404

1. She Is Still A Mystery (John Sebastian)
2. Priscilla Millionaira (John Sebastian)
3. Boredom (John Sebastian)
4. Six O'Clock (John Sebastian)
5. Forever (Steve Boone)
6. Younger Generation (John Sebastian)
7. Money (John Sebastian)
8. Old Folks (Joe Butler)
9. Only Pretty, What A Pity (Jerry Yester/Joe Butler)
10. Try A Little Bit (John Sebastian)
11. Close Your Eyes (Jerry Yester/John Sebastian)

John Sebastian: vocals, guitar / Jerry Yester: guitar, banjo, keyboards, vocals, orchestration / Zalman Yanovsky: guitar (4) / Steve Boone: bass guitar, vocals / Joe Butler: drums, vocals / Joe Wissert: producer
```

With the departure of guitarist Zalman Yanovsky, some of the soul seemed to go out of the Lovin' Spoonful. He was fired following his becoming an informer during a drug bust, which upset most of the musical community of which the group was a part. There are some John Sebastian songs on *Everything Playing* that are the equal of his previous output, but taken as a whole, the album is a little lacking in inspiration. Released as singles, *Six O'Clock* and *She Is Still A Mystery* were moderate US hits, but it was not entirely surprising when John Sebastian left his own band in early 1968.

DIONNE WARWICK   GOLDEN HITS – PART ONE

The combination of songwriting by Burt Bacharach and Hal David with Dionne Warwick's smooth, soulful voice produced some sublime orchestrated pop music through the sixties. She scored several US hits with the songs and some were hits in the UK as well, although she faced competition from local artists recording their own cover versions, recognising a good thing when they heard it. Scepter took rather a long time to release a compilation of the hits – the songs on this album date from 1962 to 1964 – but the company released a second volume two years later to bring the story up to date. The songs have none of the gospel influence that characterises soul music, although Ms Warwick brings considerable passion and emotion to her interpretations, revealing the quality and power of the writing in a way that a lesser singer might not have.

```
US release    December 1967   Scepter   SPS 565
UK release    May 1970        Wand      WNC 1

1.  Don't Make Me Over
2.  Anyone Who Had A Heart
3.  Make It Easy On Yourself
4.  I Smiled Yesterday
5.  Wishin' And Hopin'
6.  Walk On By
7.  Reach Out To Me
8.  You'll Never Get To Heaven (If You Break My Heart)
9.  This Empty Place
10. It's Love That Really Counts
11. (There's) Always Something There To Remind Me
12. Any Old Time Of Day

All compositions by Burt Bacharach/Hal David

Dionne Warwick: vocals / Burt Bacharach: arranger, producer / Hal David: producer
```

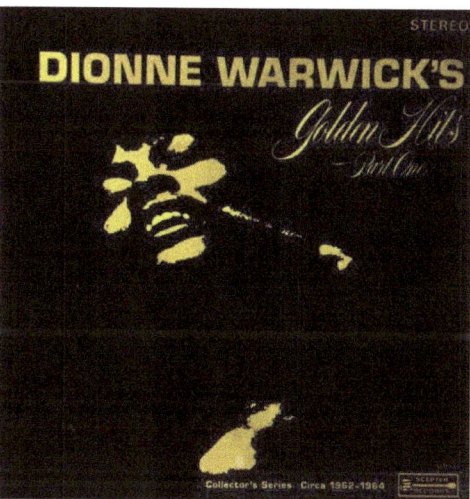

THE BUTTERFIELD BLUES BAND
THE RESURRECTION OF PIGBOY CRABSHAW

```
US and UK release   December 1967   Elektra   EKS 74015/EKL 4015

1. One More Heartache (Smokey Robinson and Miracles)
2. Driftin' And Driftin' (Charles Brown/Eddie Williams/Johnny Moore)
3. Pity The Fool (Deadric Malone)
4. Born Under A Bad Sign (Booker T Jones/William Bell)
5. Run Out Of Time (Gene Dinwiddie/Kathy Peterson/Paul Butterfield)
6. Double Trouble (Otis Rush)
7. Drivin' Wheel (Roosevelt Sykes)
8. Droppin' Out (Paul Butterfield/Tucker Zimmerman)
9. Tollin' Bells (Traditional)

Paul Butterfield: vocals, harmonica / Elvin Bishop: guitar / Mark Naftalin: keyboards / Bugsy Maugh: bass guitar, vocals / Phil Wilson: drums / David Sanborn: alto saxophone / Gene Dinwiddie: tenor saxophone / Keith Johnson: trumpet / John Court: producer
```

Mike Bloomfield left the Butterfield Blues Band earlier in the year to form his own band, the Electric Flag. Without him, Paul Butterfield suffered some of the same problems as had faced the Lovin' Spoonful. Leaving Elvin Bishop to handle all the guitar playing, Butterfield employed a new rhythm section and added brass instruments to the line-up. Despite the fact that some of the new members were skilled jazz players, the band on *The Resurrection Of Pigboy Crabshaw* largely abandons the improvisational approach of *East West* and concentrates on performing straightforward rhythm and blues material with much efficiency but not a huge amount of inspiration. No doubt Elvin Bishop relished the new challenge (the 'Pigboy Crabshaw' reference is to him) and his playing is good enough to cope, but his solos are kept very short. David Sanborn, who would emerge as a considerable jazz star just a few years later, is given hardly any chance at all to show what he can do. Paul Butterfield kept his band going for another four years, but it is clear that from this point on, his music was no longer playing a significant role.

THE PEANUT BUTTER CONSPIRACY   THE GREAT CONSPIRACY

```
US release   December 1967   Columbia   CS 9590/CL 2790
UK release   December 1967   CBS        (S) 63277

1.  Turn On A Friend (Al Brackett)
2.  Lonely Leaf (John Merrill)
3.  Pleasure (John Merrill)
4.  Too Many Do (Al Brackett)
5.  Living, Loving Life (Al Brackett)
6.  Invasion Of The Poppy People (John Merrill)
7.  Captain Sandwich (John Merrill)
8.  Living Dream (Al Brackett)
9.  Ecstacy (John Merrill)
10. Time Is After You (Al Brackett)
11. Wonderment (John Merrill)

Sandi Robison: vocals / Bill Wolff: guitar / John Merrill: guitar / Al Brackett: bass guitar / Jim Voigt: drums / Gary Usher: producer
```

The Peanut Butter Conspiracy was allowed to make a second album for Columbia, but it fared little better than the first, despite having the same bright, attractive sound and quality songs. *Turn On A Friend* must have gained friends for the group due to its inclusion on the Columbia sampler album, *The Rock Machine Turns You On*, but they sadly did not feel the need to explore any further what the group had to offer. The core members of the Peanut Butter Conspiracy, Sandi Robison, John Merrill, and Al Brackett, managed to record one more album, two years later, for a different label, but with the group finding no improvement in its fortunes, it disbanded not long afterwards.

SCOTT McKENZIE   THE VOICE OF

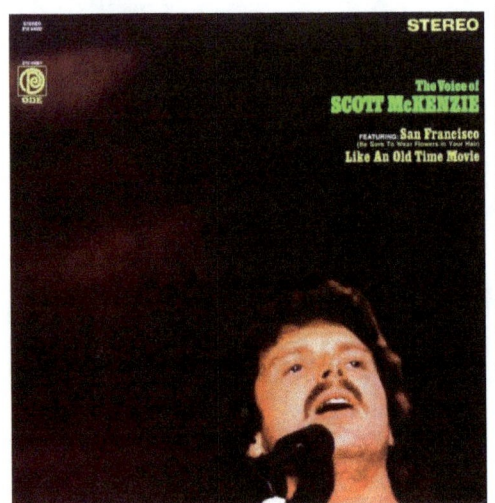

| US release | December 1967 | Ode | Z12 44002/1 |
| UK release | December 1967 | CBS | (S) BPG 63157 |

1. San Francisco (Be Sure To Wear Flowers In Your Hair) (John Phillips)
2. Celeste (Donovan Leitch)
3. It's Not Time Now (John Sebastian/Zalman Yanovsky)
4. What's The Difference (Chapter II) (Scott McKenzie)
5. Reason To Believe (Tim Hardin)
6. Like An Old Time Movie (John Phillips)
7. No, No, No, No, No (Geoff Stephens/Michel Polnareff)
8. Don't Make Promises (Tim Hardin)
9. Twelve-Thirty (John Phillips)
10. Rooms (John Phillips)
11. What's The Difference (Chapter I) (Scott McKenzie)

Scott MacKenzie: vocals / John Phillips: guitar, producer / Gary L Coleman: bells / Joe Osborn: bass guitar / Hal Blaine: drums / Lou Adler: producer

San Francisco (Be Sure To Wear Flowers In Your Hair) was the anthem of the summer of love. Written and produced by John Phillips of the Mamas and Papas and performed by Scott McKenzie (who had originally been invited to become a founder member of Phillips' group), the record was released in May in the US, reaching number four in the chart, and in July in the UK, reaching number one. Unfortunately, McKenzie's record company waited until the end of the year before releasing an album featuring the song. It was no longer summer and the mood was changing. For the most part, McKenzie performs songs that are already fairly well known. His high tenor voice is ideal for bringing the necessary haunting quality to the songs he has chosen and the album emerges as a rather fine example of the interpretive singer's art, but one that did little to set up a long-term career for the singer. He retired from professional music during the seventies, although in 1986 he did become a member of a revived version of the Mamas and Papas.

TIM ROSE

| US release | December 1967 | Columbia | CS 9577/CL 2777 |
| UK release | December 1967 | CBS | (S)BPG 63618 |

1. I Got A Loneliness (Tim Rose)
2. I'm Gonna Be Strong (Barry Mann/Cynthia Weil)
3. I Gotta Do Things My Way (Tim Rose/Richard Hussan)
4. Fare Thee Well (Tim Rose)
5. Eat, Drink And Be Merry (Ferguson/Ferguson)
6. Hey Joe (Billy Roberts)
7. Morning Dew (Bonnie Dobson/Tim Rose)
8. Where Was I? (Norman Martin)
9. You're Slipping Away From Me (Tim Rose)
10. Long Time Man (Tim Rose)
11. Come Away, Melinda (Fred Hellerman/Fran Minkoff)
12. King Lonely The Blue (Pomme/Andriani)

Tim Rose: vocals, guitar, arranger / Jay Berliner: guitar (1,4,7,8,11) / Hugh McCracken: guitar (2,5,7,9,10) / Stuart Scharf: guitar (11) / Art Butler: keyboards (1,2,,8,9) / Charles Smalls: keyboards (3,5,12) / Joey Scott: keyboards (7) / Patti Bown: keyboards (5,10) / Ernest Hayes: keyboards (11) / Charles McCracken: cello (11) / Richard Hussan: bass guitar (1,3,4,5,8,12) / Felix Pappalardi: bass guitar (2,7,9) / Chuck Rainey: bass guitar (5) / Eric Weissberg: bass guitar (11) / Bernard Purdie: drums (1,3,4,5,7,8,12) / Richard Killgore: drums (11) / Jim Fischoff: percussion (2,7,9) / Joey Scott: arranger (2,9) / David Rubinson: producer

Tim Rose was a member of a folk trio, the Big 3, with Cass Elliot, who became one of the Mamas and Papas. His self-titled album is his first as a solo artist. His rough, powerful voice is unusual for a folk singer and helps to make his music stand out. In essence, however, the album's success hinges on just three of its songs, ironically none of them written by Tim Rose himself. Rose's version of *Hey Joe* is inevitably different from that of Jimi Hendrix, and it has no instrumental break, but Rose's voice and twelve-string acoustic guitar make it almost as effective. *Come Away, Melinda* is a powerfully moving anti-war song, previously recorded by Judy Collins some four years earlier, but better suited to Rose's voice and his more sombre interpretation. It was chosen to represent Tim Rose on the CBS sampler album, *The Rock Machine Turns You On*. *Morning Dew* is a subtler anti-war song and the one that has come to be most clearly associated with Rose, although he borrowed the song from its original composer, Canadian folk singer Bonnie Dobson, and added his name to the credit without her permission. Tim Rose continued to perform and make records until the end of his life (he died in 2002), but it is the first album that remains his most essential recording.

LEONARD COHEN   SONGS OF

Published Canadian poet Leonard Cohen began to expand his activities to include songwriting during 1966 and was persuaded by Judy Collins to begin performing his songs himself. He has a very limited singing voice, yet is able to make a considerable emotional impact with the songs on his debut album. Members of the American group Kaleidoscope provide much of the backing, but without bass guitar or drums, the music has no real rock element. Although Cohen made many albums after this one, these songs, and particularly *Suzanne, So Long Marianne,* and *Hey That's No Way To Say Goodbye,* are the ones that cemented his reputation. For some the music is a relentless dirge, for others it is rather beautiful. *Songs Of Leonard Cohen* sold better in Europe than in the US, where it made just a small impact on the album charts – in the UK it reached no higher than number thirteen, but remained in the chart for nearly eighteen months.

```
US release    December 1967   Columbia   CS 9533/CL2733
UK release    December 1967   CBS        (S)BPG 63241

1. Suzanne
2. Master Song
3. Winter Lady
4. The Stranger Song
5. Sisters Of Mercy

6. So Long, Marianne
7. Hey, That's No Way To Say Goodbye
8. Stories Of The Street
9. Teachers
10.One Of Us Cannot Be Wrong

All compositions by Leonard Cohen

Leonard Cohen: vocals, guitar / Willy Ruff: bass (6,8) Jimmy
Lovelace: drums (6) / Nancy Priddy: vocals  (1,6,7) / Fenrus Epp,
Chris Darrow, Solomon Feldthouse,David Lindley: flute and
assorted stringed instruments / Joe Simon: arranger, producer
```

ROY HARPER   COME OUT FIGHTING GHENGIS SMITH

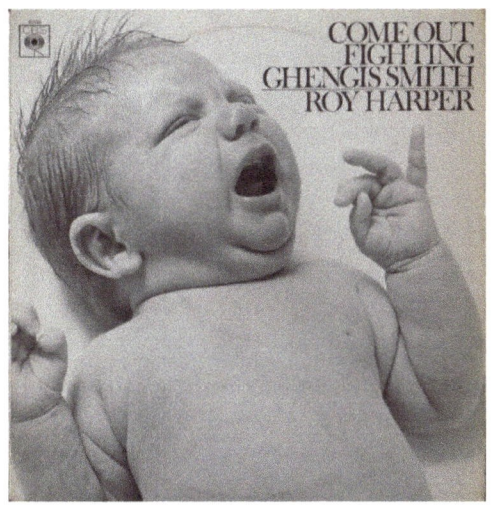

```
UK release   December 1967   CBS    (S)BPG
63184
Not released in US

1. Freak Street
2. You Don't Need Money
3. Ageing Raver
4. In A Beautiful Rambling Mess
5. All You Need Is
6. What You Have

7. Circle
8. Highgate Cemetary
9. Come Out Fighting Ghengis Smith

All compositions by Roy Harper

Roy Harper: vocals, guitar / Laurie Allan:drums / Keith
Mansfield: arranger / Shel Talmy: producer
```

Roy Harper's second album finds him signed to a major label and handed over to the care of the producer of the Kinks and the Who; even if CBS did not bother to promote the record in the US. *You Don't Need Money* soon became familiar through its inclusion on the CBS sampler, *The Rock Machine Turns You On,* where it was renamed *Nobody's Got Any Money In The Summer.* With a light rhythm section underscoring Harper's own playing and singing, the song is attractively eccentric and a very good introduction to the singer songwriter's sound world. Occasionally Harper's singing is reminiscent of his label-mate Al Stewart, but his song structures are much more unpredictable and there is always a slightly manic edge. The arrangements are much more subtle on *Come Out Fighting Ghengis Smith,* allowing Roy Harper's voice to dominate the music as it should. The lengthy *Circle* has a surprising spoken section in the middle, like a dramatised monologue, and later on it has an equally surprising instrumental section in which a minimal guitar battles a small string section. The title track, almost as long, also includes a spoken section, delivered with exaggerated mannerisms and occupying the final third of the song. In between, *Highgate Cemetary* is an acapella performance with the voice treated to a considerable echo and taking on the quality of a mantra. Touches like these emphasise that Roy Harper is a singer songwriter not quite like other people working within the same genre.

VARIOUS COMPOSERS
NEW SOUNDS IN ELECTRONIC MUSIC

The primary focus of interest in this compilation of electronic works is the first recorded piece by Steve Reich, who would become one of the major exponents of the genre of composed music known as minimalism. *Come Out* takes a brief phrase spoken by one of the six black American youths to be beaten up in a Harlem police station in 1964. Reich plays two recordings of the phrase simultaneously on machines running at very slightly different speeds. The interaction between them then generates a rhythmic effect that increasingly takes on the characteristic of music as the piece proceeds, intelligible words eventually disappearing altogether. Richard Maxfield's piece is created from the interaction between an oscilloscope and a tape recorder. The resulting electronic warbles are reminiscent of the sounds made by birds and insects in the jungle at night, which is the reason for the piece being called *Night Music*. The Pauline Oliveros piece is the one that best stands repeated listening. Twelve electronic tones are connected to a keyboard which is then able to play them, live, in a coherent manner, with the sounds being sent to two tape recorders set up to create overlapping

UK release	December 1967	Odyssey	32 16 0160
Not released in UK			

1. Night Music (Richard Maxfield)
2. Come Out (Steve Reich)
3. I Of IV (Pauline Oliveros)

Richard Maxfield, David Tudor, George Engfer: prepared tape (1) / Daniel Hamm: voice (2) / Steve Reich: tape manipulation (2) / Pauline Oliveros: keyboards, electronics (3) / David Behrman: producer

sound loops of different durations. The result sounds like a precursor of the electronic music produced by rock groups like Tangerine Dream in the seventies, using synthesizers. The album is very valuable for the documentation it provides of some pioneering and vital electronic work, even if its music is not of a kind to appeal much to the emotions.

ELLIOTT CARTER / MICHAEL COLGRASS   PIANO CONCERTO / AS QUIET AS

US release	December 1967	RCA Victor Red Seal	LSC/LM-3001
UK release	December 1967	RCA Victor Red Seal	SB/RB 6756

1. Piano Concerto (Elliott Carter)
2. As Quiet As (Michael Colgrass)

Jacob Lateiner: piano / Erich Leinsdorf: conductor / Boston Symphony Orchestra / Howard Scott: producer

Elliott Carter was one of America's most eminent twentieth century classical composers, completing his last work three months before his death in 2012, just short of his one hundred and fourth birthday. Although his music is based on a more traditional approach to melody and harmony than most other composers working alongside him, it is nevertheless ferociously complex in structure, with multiple rhythms being employed simultaneously. His *Piano Concerto* was composed during 1964 to 1965 and this is a recording of its first performance. It includes up to seventy-two different parts within the orchestra playing at the same time, constructed around as many as eight separate rhythmic layers. The music is not exactly accessible, but it does have a compelling grandeur to keep the listener engrossed throughout its two movements, lasting around twenty-six minutes. Michael Colgrass is not in the same league, although his music is rather easier to listen to. *As Quiet As,* composed in 1966, presents seven short impressionistic sketches of things that are quiet, ranging from *A Leaf Turning Colors* to *The First Star Coming Out*. The music is attractive, but not really of any great depth.

THE DON ELLIS ORCHESTRA   ELECTRIC BATH

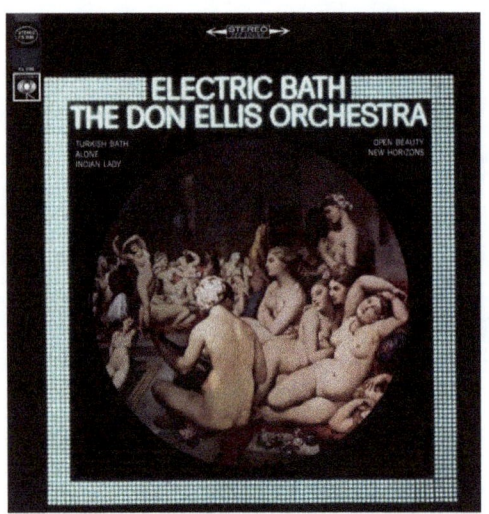

US release	December 1967	Columbia	CS 9585/CL 2785
UK release	December 1967	CBS	(S)BPG 63230

1. Indian Lady (Don Ellis)
2. Alone (Hank Levy)
3. Turkish Bath (Ron Myers)
4. Open Beauty (Don Ellis)
5. New Horizons (Don Ellis)

Don Ellis: trumpet / Alan Weight, Bob Harmon, Ed Warren, Glenn Stuart: trumpets / Dave Sanchez, Ron Myers, Terry Woodson: trombones / Joe Roccisano: alto and soprano saxophones, flute / Ruben Leon: alto and soprano saxophones, flute / Ron Starr: tenor saxophone, clarinet, flute / Ira Schulman: tenor saxophone, clarinet, flute, piccolo / Mike Lang: keyboards / Ray Neapolitan: bass, sitar / Dave Parlato: bass / Frank De La Rosa: bass / Steve Bohannon: drums / Chino Valdes: percussion / Alan Estes: percussion / Mark Stevens: percussion, vibraphone / John Hammond: producer

Don Ellis had an academic background — a degree in music composition followed by postgraduate music study — and practical experience too. He played in an army band, then worked with Maynard Ferguson, Charles Mingus, and others. His decision to form a big band of his own was something of a financial gamble, but it enabled him to put into practice his ideas of combining aspects of Indian and contemporary classical musics with jazz. *Electric Bath* was the third to be recorded by the Orchestra (it was preceded by two live albums), and attracted considerable attention. It was nominated for a Grammy award, although it did not win, and was voted album of the year by readers of the premier American jazz magazine, *Downbeat*. Ellis uses a custom made trumpet with four valves, which enables him to play quarter-tones, and he also treats his instrument electronically on occasion. His playing on *Open Beauty* uses a looped delay effect to enable him to solo against himself. Keyboard player Mike Lang uses an electric piano with echo and delay effects as well. These elements help to give the music a frame of reference for rock audiences, even if the rhythms played are not rock rhythms and the bass players are using the stand-up instruments, not bass guitars. Ellis is fond of using unusual and complex time signatures – *Indian Lady* and *Alone* are both performed in five-four time, while *New Horizons* is constructed around an outlandish cycle of seventeen beats, helpfully divided into two bars of five-four and one of seven-four time. The band is able to play these pieces so effortlessly, that the unusual numbers of beats in the bar are hardly noticed. *Electric Bath* announces the arrival of a major new player in the jazz arena. It had taken Don Ellis about ten years to get there.

ALBERT AYLER   IN GREENWICH VILLAGE

US release   December 1967   Impulse   A(S)-9155
Not released in UK

1. For John Coltrane (Albert Ayler)
2. Change Has Come (Albert Ayler)
3. Truth Is Marching In (Albert Ayler)
4. Our Prayer (Donald Ayler)

Albert Ayler: tenor and alto saxophones / Donald Ayler: trumpet (2,3,4) / Michel Sampson: violin (1,2,3,4) / Joel Freedman: cello (1,2) / Alan Silva: bass (1,2) / Henry Grimes: bass (3,4) / Bill Folwell: bass / Beaver Harris: drums / Bob Thiele: producer

In Greenwich Village is a live album, recorded on two different occasions, at the Village Theatre and the Village Vanguard in New York, and with partly different line-ups. Albert Ayler's music here is made from the same outpouring of the soul as on his earlier recordings, but perhaps it no longer sounds quite so startling. Nevertheless, there are now six or seven musicians improvising simultaneously, with the sounds of violin and cello being added to the mix, so that the music becomes very dense at times, although it remains utterly exhilarating. The first track is dedicated to John Coltrane, and with his ongoing influence no longer present, it is clear that Albert Ayler's group are major contenders for taking over his position at the cutting edge of the jazz avant garde.

WILSON PICKETT   THE BEST OF

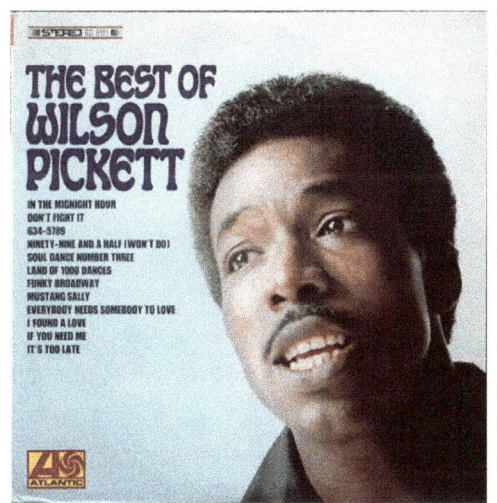

US release   December 1967   Atlantic   (SD) 8151
UK release   December 1967   Atlantic   588/587 092

1. In The Midnight Hour (Steve Cropper/Wilson Pickett)
2. I Found A Love (Robert West/Willie Schofield/Wilson Pickett)
3. 634-5789 (Eddie Floyd/Steve Cropper)
4. If You Need Me (Robert Bateman/Sonny Sanders/Wilson Pickett)
5. Mustang Sally (Bonny Rice)
6. Don't Fight It (Steve Cropper/Wilson Pickett)
7. Everybody Needs Somebody To Love (Bert Berns/Jerry Wexler/Solomon Burke)
8. It's Too Late (Wilson Pickett)
9. Ninety-Nine And A Half (Won't Do) (Steve Cropper/Wilson Pickett)
10. Funky Broadway (Lester Christian)
11. Soul Dance Number Three (Jerry Wexler/Wilson Pickett)
12. Land Of 1000 Dances (Fats Domino/Chris Kenner)

Wilson Pickett: vocals / Steve Cropper: guitar, producer / Jimmy Johnson: guitar / Chips Moman: guitar / Joe Hall: keyboards / Isaac Hayes: keyboards / Spooner Oldham: keyboards / Wayne Jackson: trumpet / Gene Miller: trumpet / Charles Axton: tenor saxophone / Andrew Love: tenor saxophone / Charles Chalmers: tenor saxophone / Floyd Newman: baritone saxophone / Donald Dunn: bass guitar / Tommy Cogbill: bass guitar / Al Jackson: drums / Roger Hawkins: drums / Eddie Floyd: vocals (2) / Mack Rice: vocals (2) / Jerry Wexler: producer

Wilson Pickett's first album made clear what an exciting singer he was and it included four of his biggest hits, also here. *Mustang Sally, Don't Fight It,* and *Funky Broadway* were equally successful – the first named track has since become the most frequently covered song by semi-professional bands playing in bars and clubs, thanks to Pickett's hit version. *If You Need Me* is Pickett's first single, from 1963. It is a decent soul ballad, but lacks the drive of the singer's later work, although it was a small hit in the US. *I Found A Love* is even earlier, being a 1962 hit by a doo-wop group, the Falcons, for which Wilson Pickett was the lead singer. Pickett made many more records after 1967 and scored several more big hits, including a soulful rendering of the Beatles' *Hey Jude,* but his reputation rests on the seminal recordings included on *The Best Of Wilson Pickett.*

JIMI HENDRIX & CURTIS KNIGHT   GET THAT FEELING

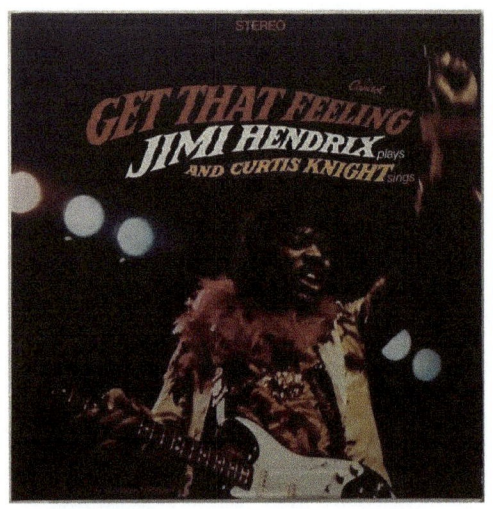

US release   December 1967   Capitol   (S)T-2856
UK release   February 1968   London   SH/HA 8349
only three tracks in common

1. How Would You Feel (Curtis Knight)
2. Simon Says (Curtis Knight)
3. Get That Feeling (Curtis Knight/Ed Gregory)

4. Hush Now (Curtis Knight)
5. Welcome Home (Curtis Knight)
6. Gotta Have A New Dress (Curtis Knight)
7. No Business (Curtis Knight)
8. Strange Things (Curtis Knight)

Curtis Knight: vocals / Jimi Hendrix: guitar, bass guitar / Nathaniel Edmonds: keyboards / Ed Gregory: bass guitar / Hank Anderson: bass guitar / Marion Booker: drums / Ray Lucas: drums / Ed Chalpin: producer

The exploitation of Jimi Hendrix's music begins here. Prior to his discovery by Chas Chandler and his subsequent rise to stardom, Jimi Hendrix worked wherever he could in the US, backing a number of R&B artists. It was while performing as a member of singer Curtis Knight's group, that Hendrix was signed to a management contract with producer Ed Chalpin. Discovering that his client had now become rather famous, Chalpin was keen to get some benefit, despite the fact that he had not actually done anything to advance Jimi Hendrix's career. In an attempt to solve the problem, Hendrix met up with Ed Chalpin and Curtis Knight in the summer of 1967 and completed a little half-hearted recording, playing bass guitar for the most part. *Get That Feeling* is the first of several albums issued by Chalpin, in which he surrounds the new recordings (*No Business, Gloomy Monday,* and *Ballad Of Jimi*) with songs produced one or two years earlier, when Hendrix was playing no more than Curtis Knight wanted him to. To try to make the album seem more than it really is, a recent photograph, of Hendrix performing at Monterey, is used for the cover. Curiously, the British version of the album has a largely different selection of tracks, including *No Business* and *Ballad Of Jimi* (not on the US album), but not including the title track, *Get That Feeling*! The albums are not entirely musically worthless, but they shed no light on Jimi Hendrix's abilities as an artist and are irrelevant to the music on which his reputation rests.

THE DAVID   ANOTHER DAY, ANOTHER LIFETIME

US release   December 1967   VMC   VS 124
Not released in UK

1. Another Day, Another Lifetime / I Would Like To Know
2. I'm Not Alone
3. Sweet December
4. Tell Me More
5. Now To You

6. Professor Crawford
7. Time M
8. So Much More
9. Mirrors Of Wood
10. Of Our Other Days

All compositions by Warren Hansen

Warren Hansen: vocals, keyboards, plasmatar / Mark Bird: guitar / Chuck Spieth: bass guitar / Tim Harrison: drums / Gene Page: arranger / Steven Vail: producer

The David is one of the more obscure California groups, completing just one album for its manager's own record company before breaking up in the early seventies. Some of the songs are given extravagant orchestral arrangements by Gene Page, whose work can be found on a large number of albums in the following years, most notably those by soul singer Barry White. Many, however, manage perfectly well without this assistance, being driven by some outstanding playing from the whole group. Mark Bird, in particular, proves himself to be a very fine guitarist, who well knows his way round a fuzzbox, even if he is only given short solos to play. On the opening medley and *Mirrors Of Wood,* singer and songwriter Warren Hansen plays an instrument of his own invention. The plasmatar has some tonal similarities with an electric sitar on the first track, with an electric cello on the second, but it consists of a wooden frame strung with piano wires and played with a guitar slide. Throughout the album, the songs are interesting and distinctive and *Another Day, Another Lifetime* might have done very well indeed if only it had been taken up by a major record company.

HARPERS BIZARRE   ANYTHING GOES

The American group, Harpers Bizarre, with a name derived from a pun (on the fashion magazine *Harper's Bazaar*), specialised in performing an unlikely mixture of songs by contemporary singer songwriters and classic show tunes, all delivered by multiple voices singing in intricate close harmony, using soft, breathy timbres. The very distinctive, cheerful sound that results gave the group a substantial hit earlier in the year with a version of the Simon and Garfunkel song, *The*

US and UK release	December 1967 Warner Bros W(S) 1716

1. This Is Only The Beginning (Harold Arlen/Ted Koehler)
2. Anything Goes (Cole Porter)
3. Two Little Babes In The Woods (Cole Porter)
4. The Biggest Night Of Her Life (Randy Newman)
5. Pocketful Of Miracles (Sammy Cahn/Jimmy Van Heusen)
6. Snow (Randy Newman)
7. Chattanooga Choo Choo (Harry Warren/Mack Gordon)
8. Hey You In The Crowd (Dick Scoppettone/Ted Templeman)
9. Louisiana Man (Doug Kershaw)
10. Milord (Georges Moustaki/Marguerite Monnot)
11. Virginia City (Dick Scoppettone/Ted Templeman)
12. Jessie (James Griffin/Michael Gordon)
13. You Need A Change (David Blue)
14. High Coin (Van Dyke Parks)

Dick Scoppettone: vocals, guitar, bass guitar / Ted Templeman: vocals, guitar, drums / Eddy James: guitar / Dick Yount: vocals, bass guitar / John Petersen: vocals, drums, percussion / Jack Glaser: effects / Van Dyke Parks: piano, arranger / Bobby Bruce: violin / Joe Bergman: recitation / Perry Botkin Jr: arranger / Nick DeCaro: arranger / Bob Thompson: arranger / Ron Elliott: arranger / Lenny Waronker: producer

59th Street Bridge Song (Feelin' Groovy). It was included on the group's first album, but *Anything Goes*, the second album, finds Harpers Bizarre honing its style with greater élan and generally more satisfying results. The title track and *Chattanooga Choo Choo* were both issued as singles and became hits, though sold less well than the debut. The group did not survive the sixties, breaking up after recording just one more album, but Ted Templeman achieved considerable success as a producer during the seventies and beyond.

NILSSON   PANDEMONIUM SHADOW SHOW

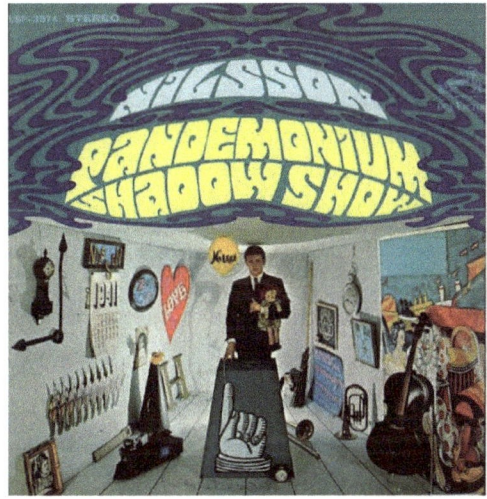

US release	December 1967	RCA Victor	LSP/LPM 3874
UK release	December 1967	RCA Victor	SF/RD 7928

1. Ten Little Indians (Harry Nilsson)
2. 1941 (Harry Nilsson)
3. Cuddly Toy (Harry Nilsson)
4. She Sang Hymns Out Of Tune (Jesse Lee Kincaid)
5. You Can't Do That (John Lennon/Paul McCartney)
6. Sleep Late, My Lady Friend (Harry Nilsson)
7. She's Leaving Home (John Lennon/Paul McCartney)
8. There Will Never Be (Perry Botkin Jr/Gil Garfield)
9. Without Her (Harry Nilsson)
10. Freckles (Cliff Hess/Howard Johnson/Milton Ager)
11. It's Been So Long (Harry Nilsson)
12. River Deep - Mountain High (Phil Spector/Jeff Barry/Ellie Greenwich)

Harry Nilsson: vocals / Perry Botkin Jr: arranger (10,11) / George Tipton: arranger / Rick Jarrard: producer

During the early sixties, Harry Nilsson had some success as a songwriter, including work with Phil Spector. He released four singles himself on the Tower label, which were compiled on an album, *Spotlight On Nilsson*, although sales of the singles and the album were very small. Nevertheless, he was signed to RCA, which issued his first album proper, *Pandemonium Shadow Show* (a title taken from a description in a novel by Ray Bradbury). The music is reminiscent of that performed by Van Dyke Parks on his album, *Song Cycle*, and it has the same disdain for the methods of rock music, albeit with rather less of Parks' ambition. Nilsson chooses to record as many songs by other writers as by himself and they include two by the Beatles. *She's Leaving Home* adds little to the original, but for his version of *You Can't Do That*, Nilsson includes numerous counterpoint lines taken from other Beatles songs, which is rather cleverly done. His rendering of Phil Spector's masterpiece, *River Deep - Mountain High*, keeps close to Spector's own arrangement and is a little pointless, but much of the rest of the album is very interesting. This is particularly true of his own song, *Without Her*, in which an unusual melody is highlighted by an arrangement that gradually gets busier as the song progresses.

THE HOLY MODAL ROUNDERS   INDIAN WAR WHOOP

US release	December 1967	ESP-Disk	ESP 1068
Not released in UK			

1. Indian War Whoop (Traditional)
2. Sweet Apple Cider (Traditional)
3. Soldier's Joy (Traditional)
4. Cocaine Blues (Luke Jordan)
5. Sky Divers (Steve Weber)
6. Radar Blues (Michael Hurley)
7. The I.W.W. Song (Peter Stampfel/Steve Weber)
8. Football Blues (Antonia Duren/Peter Stampfel)
9. Bay Rum Blues (Traditional)
10. Morning Glory (Michael Hurley)

Peter Stampfel: violin, banjo, vocals / Steve Weber: guitar, vocals / Earle Crabtree: keyboards / Sam Shepard: drums / Antonia Duren: vocals / Barbara: vocals / Wendy: vocals / Dr Jackson Illusion: producer

The music of the Holy Modal Rounders, a kind of free-wheeling psychedelic folk, essentially sounds like the work of a small group of musicians too stoned to play properly but insisting on performing anyway. *Indian War Whoop* is the group's third album. There is a pronounced seam of humour running through the music, although it is clear that Peter Stampfel and Steve Weber, the core members, are much more adept at their instruments than first impressions suggest. Too idiosyncratic to be much of an influence, the Holy Modal Rounders have continued to play in one form or another well into the twenty-first century, although Steve Weber died in 2020 at the age of seventy-six.

BOB DYLAN   JOHN WESLEY HARDING

```
US release      December 1967    Columbia    CS 9604/CL 2804
UK release      February 1968    CBS         (S)BPG 63252

1. John Wesley Harding
2. As I Went Out One Morning
3. I Dreamed I Saw St. Augustine
4. All Along The Watchtower
5. The Ballad Of Frankie Lee And Judas Priest
6. Drifter's Escape

7. Dear Landlord
8. I Am A Lonesome Hobo
9. I Pity The Poor Immigrant
10. The Wicked Messenger
11. Down Along The Cove
12. I'll Be Your Baby Tonight

All compositions by Bob Dylan

Bob Dylan: vocals, guitar, harmonica, piano / Charles McCoy: bass guitar / Kenny Buttrey: drums / Pete Drake: pedal steel guitar (11,12) / Bob Johnston: producer
```

It had been eighteen months since the release of Bob Dylan's previous album, *Blonde On Blonde,* yet it seemed much longer. There had been many rumours as to what he had been up to in the intervening time, including the report that he had been involved in a serious motorbike accident, which had left him with a broken neck. The fact that Dylan's voice had apparently changed on the new album, had become more mellow, added weight to that particular theory. Certainly, Dylan had been glad to escape from the weight of expectation heaped upon him, tired too of the controversy dogging his live performances ever since he made the decision to play with an electric rock band. The music on *John Wesley Harding* is simpler, with lyrics that are less extravagant than before, if sometimes just as difficult to fully understand. The lead electric guitar and keyboards are gone, to be replaced by a low-key country-folk style, in which, with the exception of two tracks where a pedal steel guitar is added, Bob Dylan's own playing is supported by nothing more than a bass guitar and lightly tapped drums. It is the general mood that counts – the individual songs are for the most part not the kind of thing to drill very far into the listener's memory, although *All Along The Watchtower,* with its particularly intriguing time-loop lyrics, would soon become a rock music standard. In chart terms, *John Wesley Harding* became Bob Dylan's most successful album since *Bringing It All Back Home.* Artistically, listeners and critics were entitled to feel a little more guarded, although most were so pleased to have Bob Dylan back, that they would have been prepared to acclaim anything.

1968

THE KINKS   LIVE AT KELVIN HALL

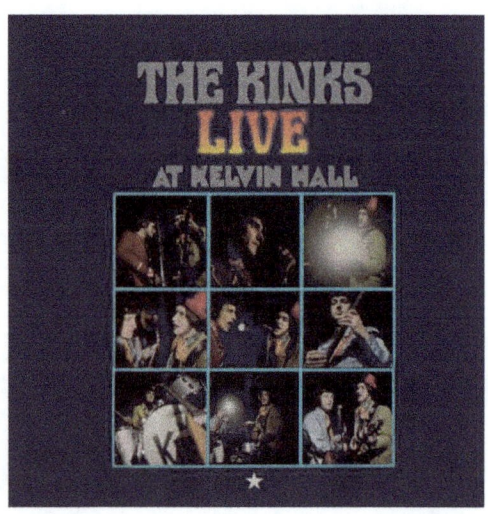

It was a curious decision to release a live album by the Kinks at this time. The recording quality is not very good, and giving a pronounced emphasis to the screaming and applause of the fans seems to tie the Kinks to an era and a musical approach that was fast disappearing. The Kinks perform well enough, and Pete Quaife's bass playing is something of a revelation, but some

```
UK release    January 1968    Pye        N(S)PL 18191
US release    August 1967     Reprise    R(S) 6260

1. Till The End Of The Day
2. A Well Respected Man
3. You're Lookin' Fine
4. Sunny Afternoon
5. Dandy

6. I'm On An Island
7. Come On Now
8. You Really Got Me
9. Medley – Milk Cow Blues (John Estes)/Batman Theme (Neil Hefti)/Tired Of Waiting For You

All compositions by Ray Davies except where stated

Ray Davies: vocals, guitar, producer / Dave Davies: guitar, vocals / Pete Quaife: bass guitar / Mick Avory: drums
```

of the songs chosen are not among the group's best and the routine interpretations they all receive add nothing to the original versions. Live performances of beat material should add an extra layer of excitement to the music, but this does not really happen here. Clearly the group's fans thought so too, because *Live At Kelvin Hall* was easily the worst selling album of the Kinks' career thus far.

THE BYRDS   THE NOTORIOUS BYRD BROTHERS

David Crosby left the Byrds during the recording of *The Notorious Byrd Brothers,* and Michael Clarke was not much involved either, yet the album manages to be the undoubted highlight of the group's career. A large number of session musicians are employed to make all the songs stand out, while the members of the Byrds themselves deliver some exceptional and varied songwriting and surround the melodies with their most delicious, rich harmony singing. There is some very effective playing with the new Moog synthesizer, most notably on *Dolphins Smile,* where it is used to create an exaggerated facsimile of the sounds made by real dolphins. The Byrds have taken to heart the Beatles' principle of giving each song a distinctive musical colour, so that the album becomes the group's own equivalent of *Sgt Pepper,* and is almost as remarkable a body of work, even if it could not hope to compete in terms of record sales.

```
US release      January 1968    Columbia    CS 9575/CL 2775
UK release      January 1968    CBS         (S)BPG 63169

1. Artificial Energy (Chris Hillman/Michael Clarke/Roger McGuinn)
2. Goin' Back (Gerry Goffin/Carole King)
3. Natural Harmony (Chris Hillman)
4. Draft Morning (Chris Hillman/David Crosby/Roger McGuinn)
5. Wasn't Born To Follow (Gerry Goffin/Carole King)
6. Get To You (Chris Hillman/Roger McGuinn)
7. Change Is Now (Chris Hillman/Roger McGuinn)
8. Old John Robertson (Chris Hillman/Roger McGuinn)
9. Tribal Gathering (Chris Hillman/David Crosby)
10. Dolphins Smile (Chris Hillman/David Crosby/Roger McGuinn)
11. Space Odyssey (Robert J Hippard/Roger McGuinn)

Roger McGuinn: vocals, guitar, synthesizer / David Crosby: vocals, guitar (4,7,9,10), bass guitar (8) / Chris Hillman: vocals, bass guitar, guitar (8), mandolin (4) / Michael Clarke: drums (1,4,8,9,10) / Gene Clark: vocals (2) / James Burton: guitar / Clarence White: guitar / Paul Beaver: piano, synthesizer / Terry Trotter: piano / Barry Goldberg: organ / Dennis McCarthy: celeste / Hal Blaine: drums (6,7) / Jim Gordon: drums (2,3,5) / Curt Boettcher: vocals / William Armstrong: violin / Victor Sazer: violin / Carl West: violin / Paul Bergstrom: cello / Lester Harris: cello / Raymond Kelley: cello / Jacqueline Lustgarten: cello / Alfred McKibbon: bass / Ann Stockton: harp / Richard Hyde: trombone / Roy Caton: trumpet / Virgil Fums: trumpet / Gary Weber: trumpet / Jay Migliori: tenor saxophone / Dennis Faust: percussion / Firesign Theatre (Peter Bergman, Philip Proctor, Phil Austin, David Ossman): sound effects (4) / Gary Usher: producer, synthesizer, percussion, vocals
```

JOHN MAYALL   THE DIARY OF A BAND VOLS 1-2

```
UK release    January 1968        Decca      SKL/LK 4918/9
US release    February 1970/April 1971    London    PS 570 / PS 589

1. Blood On The Night (John Mayall)
2. Edmonton – Cooks Ferry Inn    speech impromptu
3. I Can't Quit You Baby (Willie Dixon)
4. Keef Hartley & John Mayall interviews / Anzio Annie / Snowy Wood /
        The Lesson excerpts (Mick Taylor/John Mayall)
5. My Own Fault (John Mayall)
6. God Save The Queen (John Bull)
7. Gimme Some Lovin' (extract) (Muff and Steve Winwood/Spencer Davis)
8. The Train (John Mayall)
9. Crying Shame (John Mayall)
10. Local Boy Makes Good    speech impromptu
11. Help Me (Ralph Bass/Willie Dixon)
12. Blues In B flat (John Mayall)
13. Soul Of A Short Fat Man excerpt (Keef Hartley/John Mayall)

John Mayall: vocals, keyboards, harmonica / Mick Taylor: guitar / Dick Heckstall-Smith: tenor and soprano saxophones / Chris Mercer: tenor and baritone saxophones / Paul Williams: bass guitar, voice (1,2) / Keith Tillman: bass guitar / Keef Hartley: drums / Mike Vernon: producer
```

During the previous two months or so, John Mayall had been recording his group's live performances using a reel-to-reel machine placed on top of his Hammond organ. *The Diary Of A Band,* a double album with the two records issued separately, presents some of the highlights and reveals the sound quality to be remarkably good. For the most part, the music comprises lengthy blues improvisations by the band, proving what fine musicians they all are. *The Train,* complete with outstanding solos from Dick Heckstall-Smith and Mick Taylor, is worth the price of admission on its own. In addition, there are a number of pieces of on-stage banter, to give a flavour of what the complete performances would have been like. Sometimes these have musical extracts included, such as the opening bars from *Gimme Some Lovin'*, in recognition of the fact that the Spencer Davis Group was on the same bill, and the slightly bizarre rendition of the National Anthem performed in response to an unexpected club rule. The opening *Blood On The Night* is a totally improvised musical protest at the beating-up of bass player Paul Williams just before he had to go on stage (although he still plays). At the start of side two, interviews with Keef Hartley and John Mayall by a member of the audience are interleaved with guitar solos from Mick Taylor, to make the point that he had developed very rapidly into a hugely imaginative and gifted player. In a magazine interview several years later, John Mayall claimed that the guitarist on *The Lesson* is actually Jimi Hendrix. The playing does not sound like him, but then he would have been using Mick Taylor's equipment, including a Gibson Les Paul in place of his accustomed Fender Stratocaster, and a much lower volume than he normally employed. It certainly explains why the track is titled *The Lesson*.

CANNED HEAT   BOOGIE WITH

| US release | January 1968 | Liberty | LST 7541/LRP 3541 |
| UK release | January 1968 | Liberty | LBS/LBL 83103 |

1. Evil Woman (Larry Weiss)
2. My Crime (Canned Heat)
3. On The Road Again (Jim Oden)
4. World In A Jug (Bob Hite)
5. Turpentine Moan (Canned Heat)
6. Whiskey Headed Woman No.2 (Canned Heat)
7. Amphetamine Annie (Canned Heat)
8. An Owl Song (Alan Wilson)
9. Marie Laveau (Henry Vestine)
10. Fried Hockey Boogie (Larry Taylor)

Bob Hite: vocals / Alan Wilson: vocals, harmonica, slide guitar / Henry Vestine: guitar / Larry Taylor: bass guitar / Fito De La Parra: drums / Sunnyland Slim: piano (6) / Dr John: piano, arranger (9) / Dallas Smith: producer

The cover of the second album by Canned Heat makes it look as though the music is going to be a psychedelic extravaganza. In fact, the group is playing the blues as before, except that guitarist Henry Vestine has discovered the delights of high volume distortion and delivers supercharged playing throughout, in a manner not found on the records of the blues masters that the members of Canned Heat revere. In the process, he gives the record a distinction that makes it a particularly compelling example of its genre. The majority of the songs are written by the group, but they employ traditional themes and lyric phrases to keep contact with the music's roots. The album includes a lengthy jam session, *Fried Hockey Boogie*, in which each member is given a chance to show what he can do as a soloist. *On The Road Again* was issued as a single and was a chart hit in both the US and the UK. Its distinctive rhythm became the group's trademark, or at least until it was hijacked at the end of 1969 by Norman Greenbaum, for his single, *Spirit In The Sky*.

DR JOHN   GRIS-GRIS

| US release | January 1968 | Atco | (SD) 33-234 |
| UK release | January 1968 | Atlantic | 588 147 |

1. Gris-Gris Gumbo Ya Ya (Dr John)
2. Danse Kalinda Ba Doom (Dr John/Harold Battiste)
3. Mama Roux (Dr John/Jessie Hill)
4. Danse Fambeaux (Dr John)
5. Croker Courtbullion (Harold Battiste)
6. Jump Sturdy (Dr John)
7. I Walk On Guilded Splinters (Dr John)

Dr John (Mac Rebennack): vocals, keyboards, percussion / Steve Mann: slide guitar, banjo / Ernest McLean: guitar, mandolin / Plas Johnson: tenor saxophone / Lonnie Boulden: flute / Bob West: bass guitar / John Boudreaux: drums / Dido Pedido: percussion / Richard Washington: percussion / Joni Jonz, Prince Ella Johnson, Shirley Goodman, Sonny Ray Durden, Tami Lynn: vocals / Harold Battiste: bass, clarinet, clarinet, percussion, producer

As a teenager, Mac Rebennack was a working musician in New Orleans and co-wrote the rock 'n' roll classic, *Lights Out*, recorded by Jerry Byrne. An injury to a finger on his left hand forced him to give up the guitar and instead he became a pianist. During the sixties he was a busy session player in Los Angeles. Inspired by psychedelia, he came up with the idea of a music style that would combine references to voodoo and mysticism with New Orleans R&B and a general trippy ambience. The result was issued as the album *Gris-Gris*, with Rebennack transformed into a witch-doctor figure called Dr John Creaux, the Night Tripper. The music hybrid is very effective, with the opening *Gris-Gris Gumbo Ya Ya* and the closing *I Walk On Guilded Splinters* being particularly striking, drawing the listener into a mood of general weirdness. Dr John's growling vocals are little removed from speech, like an early version of rapping, except that his drawling is far too laid back and lazy. In contrast, *Mama Roux* is almost a straightforward piece of R&B. It was issued as a single, but made no more impression on the charts than did the parent album itself. *I Walk On Guilded Splinters*, however, has been recorded by many other artists over the years. A version by Marsha Hunt was almost a UK hit in May 1969.

MILES DAVIS   NEFERTITI

| US release | January 1968 | Columbia | CS 9594 |
| UK release | January 1968 | CBS | (S) 63248 |

1. Nefertiti (Wayne Shorter)
2. Fall (Wayne Shorter)
3. Hand Jive (Tony Williams)
4. Madness (Herbie Hancock)
5. Riot (Herbie Hancock)
6. Pinocchio (Wayne Shorter)

Miles Davis: trumpet / Wayne Shorter: tenor saxophone / Herbie Hancock: piano / Ron Carter: bass / Tony Williams: drums / Teo Macero: producer (1-3) / Howard A. Roberts: producer (4-6)

The fact that *Nefertiti* was released just three months after the previous Miles Davis album is indicative of the high level of creativity being felt by all the members of the Quintet. As it happens, the new album is very much the group's masterpiece, with the three composing members delivering some particularly inspiring material, giving *Nefertiti* the edge over its predecessors. The most startling innovation is provided by the title track, where the horns play the theme repeatedly, moving slightly out of phase with each other at times, but not otherwise improvising. Instead, the focus is handed over to Tony Williams, who effectively plays a solo throughout the piece, turning it into a kind of drum concerto. Alternate, earlier takes of the tracks have subsequently been issued and reveal that the group experimented with different tempos and time signatures for them. It is clear, however, that in every case Miles Davis and his producer selected the most effective version for release.

SPIRIT

| US release | January 1968 | Ode | Z12 44004/44003 |
| UK release | January 1968 | CBS | (S) 63278 |

1. Fresh Garbage (Jay Ferguson)
2. Uncle Jack (Jay Ferguson)
3. Mechanical World (Jay Ferguson/Mark Andes)
4. Taurus (Randy California)
5. Girl In Your Eye (Jay Ferguson)
6. Straight Arrow (Jay Ferguson)
7. Topanga Windows (Jay Ferguson)
8. Gramophone Man (Spirit)
9. Water Woman (Jay Ferguson)
10. The Great Canyon Fire In General (Jay Ferguson)
11. Elijah (John Locke)

Jay Ferguson: vocals, percussion / Randy California: guitar, vocals / John Locke: keyboards / Mark Andes: bass guitar, vocals / Ed Cassidy: drums / Marty Paich: arranger / Lou Adler: producer

Spirit is a rock group with jazz leanings: Randy California's keening lead guitar lines meeting Ed Cassidy's jazz drums (a generation older than the others, he had performed with people like Gerry Mulligan and Roland Kirk), while pianist John Locke and bass player Mark Andes play a little of both and act as a bridge between them. As a result, Spirit have a lighter, more polished sound than most other groups. A couple of tracks benefit from ethereal orchestral arrangements that fade into the background, but for the most part the group's own carefully balanced parts are enough to make the interesting songwriting sound special. *Mechanical World* was chosen for release as a single, although its stop-start rhythm makes it less immediately attractive than the smoothly melodic *Fresh Garbage* or *Uncle Jack*. It did not fare very well, but the parent album entered the US album chart regardless and stayed there for several months.

THE VELVET UNDERGROUND   WHITE LIGHT/WHITE HEAT

Without Nico, the Velvet Underground produce music that is harder and more relentless. The lyrics are mostly designed to shock (*The Gift* and *Lady Godiva's Operation* both have macabre tales to tell; elsewhere there are clear sexual and drug references). There is nothing resembling a ballad, no beauty, but there is much guitar feedback and monotonous, pile-driver rhythms. The album very much glories in the noise that it makes. *Sister Ray* is an improvised jam lasting well over a quarter of an hour, but there is no jazz influence and nothing that could be described as a coherent solo. There is no individual track as strikingly artistic as *Venus In Furs* on the previous album, but the cumulative effect of the music on *White Light/White Heat* is much more powerful, more overwhelming than its predecessor. Sales were poor, but the album's influence on seventies punk and much of the music that followed it is obvious.

| US release | January 1968 | Verve | V(6)-5046 |
| UK release | January 1968 | Verve | (S)VLP 9201 |

1. White Light/White Heat (Lou Reed)
2. The Gift (Velvet Underground)
3. Lady Godiva's Operation (Lou Reed)
4. There She Comes Now (Velvet Underground)
5. I Heard Her Call My Name (Lou Reed)
6. Sister Ray (Velvet Underground)

Lou Reed: vocals, guitar, piano / John Cale: vocals, viola, organ, bass guitar / Sterling Morrison: vocals, guitar, bass guitar / Maureen Tucker: drums / Tom Wilson: producer

KALEIDOSCOPE   A BEACON FROM MARS

This is the second album by the American Kaleidoscope. The group continues its fascination with exotic stringed instruments and with its attempts to find common ground between the folk musics of America and the Middle East, even while infusing both of them with the rhythmic drive and the amplification of rock music. This time, each side of the album climaxes with an extended improvisation, although they have rather different characters. *Taxim*, derived from a Turkish piece, builds up a considerable momentum, but with acoustic instruments, no drum kit, and little connection at all with rock 'n' roll. *A Beacon From Mars*, however, employs electric guitar feedback fairly extensively and captures the mood of a Grateful Dead live performance at a time when that group had yet to produce a recording like this. *I Found Out* was released as a single, although it was no more successful than the album. It is particularly striking, although its use of a dobro to deliver the decorative lead lines and its waltz time rhythm help to make the song sound a little odd compared to the music dominating the charts.

| US release | January 1968 | Epic | BN 26333/LN 24333 |
| Not released in UK | | | |

1. I Found Out (Earl Shakelford)
2. Greenwood Sidee (Traditional)
3. Life Will Pass You By (Chris Darrow)
4. Taxim (Kaleidoscope)
5. Baldheaded End Of A Broom (Traditional)
6. Louisiana Man (Doug Kershaw)
7. You Don't Love Me (Willie Cobbs)
8. Beacon From Mars (Kaleidoscope)

Solomon Feldthouse: vocals, sax, bouzouki, dobro, vina, oud, doumbek, dulcimer, violin, guitar / David Lindley: guitar, banjo, violin, mandolin / Fenrus Epp: violin, viola, bass guitar, organ, piano, harmonica / Chris Darrow: bass guitar, guitar, mandolin, vocals / John Vidican: drums, percussion / Mike Goldberg: producer / Stu Eisen: producer

SIMON & GARFUNKEL   THE GRADUATE SOUNDTRACK

| US release | January 1968 | Columbia | OS 3180 |
| UK release | January 1968 | CBS | (S) 70042 |

1. The Sounds Of Silence (Paul Simon)
2. The Singleman Party Foxtrot (Dave Grusin)
3. Mrs Robinson (Paul Simon)
4. Sunporch Cha-Cha-Cha (Dave Grusin)
5. Scarborough Fair/Canticle (Interlude) (Traditional/Paul Simon)
6. On The Strip (Dave Grusin)
7. April Come She Will (Paul Simon)
8. The Folks (Dave Grusin)
9. Scarborough Fair/Canticle (Traditional/Paul Simon)
10. A Great Effect (Dave Grusin)
11. The Big Bright Green Pleasure Machine (Paul Simon)
12. Whew (Dave Grusin)
13. Mrs Robinson (Paul Simon)
14. The Sounds Of Silence (Paul Simon)

Paul Simon: vocals, guitar / Art Garfunkel: vocals / other musicians as credited on earlier albums / Dave Grusin: piano, arranger / Teo Macero: producer

The Graduate, released at the end of 1967, was a hugely successful film, directed by Mike Nichols, and starring Dustin Hoffman in his first major role. Although Simon and Garfunkel were already doing very well, the inclusion of some of their music in the soundtrack helped to push them to a new level of popularity. In truth, there was only one song used that had not already been released on the duo's own records, but it was a particularly memorable one. *Mrs Robinson* is presented here in two short recordings, neither of them the same as the completed version later released on Simon and

Garfunkel's *Bookends* album. The pieces of music by David Grusin do what they have to do in a vaguely jazzy sort of way, but are not the reason that people bought the soundtrack album. This became a very big seller, particularly in the US, where it was eventually awarded a double platinum disc, for two million sales.

ARETHA FRANKLIN   LADY SOUL

| US release | January 1968 | Atlantic | (SD) 8176 |
| UK release | January 1968 | Atlantic | 588/587 099 |

1. Chain Of Fools (Don Covay)
2. Money Won't Change You (James Brown/Nat Jones)
3. People Get Ready (Curtis Mayfield)
4. Niki Hoeky (Jim Ford/Lolly Vegas/Pat Vegas)
5. (You Make Me Feel Like) A Natural Woman (Gerry Goffin/Carole King/Jerry Wexler)

6. Since You've Been Gone Sweet Sweet Baby) (Aretha Franklin/Ted White)
7. Good To Me As I Am To You (Aretha Franklin/Ted White)
8. Come Back Baby (Ray Charles)
9. Groovin' (Eddie Brigati/Felix Cavaliere)
10. Ain't No Way (Carolyn Franklin)

Aretha Franklin: vocals, piano / Bobby Womack: guitar / Jimmy Johnson: guitar / Joe South: guitar / Eric Clapton: guitar (7) / Spooner Oldham: keyboards / Bernie Glow: trumpet / Joe Newman: trumpet / Mel Lastie: trumpet / King Curtis: tenor saxophone / Frank Wess: tenor saxophone, flute / Seldon Powell: tenor saxophone, flute / Haywood Henry: baritone saxophone / Tony Studd: bass trombone / Warren Smith: vibraphone / Tom Cogbill: bass guitar / Roger Hawkins: drums / Carolyn Franklin: vocals / The Sweet Inspirations – Cissy Houston, Sylvia Shemwell, Myrna Smith, Estelle Brown: vocals / Arif Mardin: arranger / Tom Dowd: arranger / Jerry Wexler: producer

Aretha Franklin's third hit Atlantic album shines brighter than its immediate predecessor, if only because it includes three of her biggest singles; the two listed on the cover sticker and *(You Make Me Feel Like) A Natural Woman*. She is confident enough of her abilities to tackle a James Brown song, *Money Won't Change You*, and she effortlessly makes the song her own. She does the same with Curtis Mayfield's *People Get Ready*, although her version of the Young Rascals' *Groovin'*, soulful though it is, loses the delightful summer laziness of the original. One track, *Good To Me As I Am To You*, includes what the cover rather smugly refers to as a 'guitar obbligato' by Eric Clapton. It is a hugely sympathetic guitar counterpoint to Aretha's powerful slow blues performance, adding to the song's effectiveness, but without taking the attention away from the singer. Aretha Franklin's singing throughout the album entirely justifies its title: she proves that she is the foremost soul singer of the time.

IRON BUTTERFLY   HEAVY

| US release | January 1968 | Atco | (SD) 33-227 |
| UK release | late 1970 | Atco | 2465-015 |

1. Posession (Doug Ingle)
2. Unconscious Power (Doug Ingle/Danny Weis/Ron Bushy)
3. Get Out Of My Life, Woman (Allen Toussaint)
4. Gentle As It May Seem (Danny Weis/Darryl DeLoach)
5. You Can't Win (Danny Weis/Darryl DeLoach)

6. So-Lo (Doug Ingle/Darryl DeLoach)
7. Look For The Sun (Doug Ingle/Danny Weis/Darryl DeLoach)
8. Fields Of Sun (Doug Ingle/Darryl DeLoach)
9. Stamped Ideas (Doug Ingle/Darryl DeLoach)
10. Iron Butterfly Theme (Doug Ingle)

Darryl DeLoach: vocals, percussion / Danny Weis: guitar / Doug Ingle: organ, vocals / Jerry Penrod: bass guitar, vocals / Ron Bushy: drums / Brian Stone: producer / Charles Greene: producer

The first album by Californian band, Iron Butterfly, is the first in which the music is explicitly described as being 'heavy'. Unfortunately, next to the music of Cream or the Jimi Hendrix Experience, *Heavy* barely qualifies. The bass playing is restrained and mixed to the back of the soundstage, while the guitarist tries to disguise his lack of expertise by relying on a fuzzbox to make his lead lines seem exciting. Only on the concluding *Iron Butterfly Theme* does he investigate what might be achieved by overloading his amplifier, and by then it is too late. Perhaps the group members realised that the music they were offering lacked any strong distinguishing features, because three of them left before the album was even released. The organ player, Doug Ingle, and the drummer, Ron Bushy, were left to find new musicians to play with them in order for Iron Butterfly to continue. The structure pictured on the album sleeve is intended to look like a human ear, but is hardly more convincing in this than the music is in sounding heavy.

STEPPENWOLF

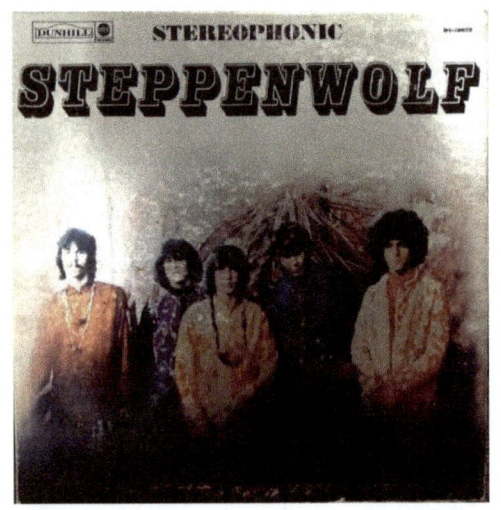

US release	January 1968	Dunhill	DS-50029
UK release	January 1968	RCA Victor	RD 7974

1. Sookie Sookie (Don Covay)
2. Everybody's Next One (Gabriel Mekler/John Kay)
3. Berry Rides Again (John Kay)
4. Hootchie Kootchie Man (Willie Dixon)
5. Born To Be Wild (Mars Bonfire)
6. Your Wall's Too High (John Kay)

7. Desperation (John Kay)
8. The Pusher (Hoyt Axton)
9. A Girl I Knew (John Kay/Morgan A Cavett)
10. Take What You Need (Gabriel Mekler/John Kay)
11. The Ostrich (John Kay)

John Kay: vocals, guitar, harmonica / Michael Monarch: guitar, vocals / Goldy McJohn: keyboards / Rushton Moreve: bass guitar, vocals / Jerry Edmonton: drums, vocals / Gabriel Mekler: producer

Hard rock band Steppenwolf managed to maintain a career through several albums, following the impact it made with just two songs, neither of them written by members of the band. They are both on this debut album. *The Pusher* is a harsh, unsettling complaint aimed at attacking the use of mind-altering drugs and adopting, therefore, an opposite position to that of the majority of Steppenwolf's contemporaries. *Born To Be Wild* is driving and uplifting; a paean to the lifestyle of the biker. The song's lyrics just happen to use the phrase "heavy metal thunder", which some listeners have found significant, but it refers to the motorbikes and not to the music. *Born To Be Wild* was a number two hit in the US singles chart, but both of these songs made a greater impact when included in the soundtrack to the influential film, *Easy Rider,* some eighteen months later.

BLUE CHEER   VINCEBUS ERUPTUM

US release	January 1968	Philips	PHS/PHM 600-264
UK release	January 1968	Philips	(S)BL 7839

1. Summertime Blues (Eddie Cochran/Jerry Capehart)
2. Rock Me Baby (B.B.King/Joe Josea)
3. Doctor Please (Dickie Peterson)

4. Out Of Focus (Dickie Peterson)
5. Parchment Farm (Mose Allison)
6. Second Time Around (Dickie Peterson)

Dickie Peterson: vocals, bass guitar / Leigh Stevens: guitar / Paul Whaley: drums / Voco Kesh: producer

The debut album by the Californian band Blue Cheer is more deserving of the *Heavy* title than was Iron Butterfly, but instead it settles for a Latin title that is supposed to mean something like 'breaking out of chains', except that it gets the words wrong. It would be possible to argue that the group similarly gets the style of the Jimi Hendrix Experience wrong. In truth, Blue Cheer does try very hard to replicate the sound of the simpler tracks on *Are You Experienced,* but its failure to convincingly achieve this is purely the consequence of the musicians not having the skills of the Experience members. To suggest, as some have, that Blue Cheer's updating of the Eddie Cochran rock 'n' roll standard, *Summertime Blues,* by overdriving the electric guitar, creates the first piece of heavy metal is to vastly over-rate the group's influence, especially since Jimi Hendrix's music is so much more forceful and original. *Purple Haze* and *Foxy Lady* both appeared before *Summertime Blues* and are far more deserving of the proto-heavy metal appellation. Blue Cheer's own songs are more distinctive than the cover versions that fill half the album, but ultimately the group is doing no more than plugging the gap before the next album by Jimi Hendrix can appear – or the next album by Cream, another guitar trio with far more power, combined with musical expertise, than Blue Cheer can manage. The group went on to make several more even less distinguished albums than this one, although guitarist Leigh Stevens only stayed around for one of them.

THE ELECTRIC PRUNES   MASS IN F MINOR

The management of the Electric Prunes agreed with their record company that the group's third album would be a rock mass, composed by David Axelrod. The group members had little or no say in the matter and when it became apparent that some of them were unhappy at devoting a whole album to the project, they were unceremoniously replaced in the recording studio. The combination of chanting male vocals (largely created by overdubbing James Lowe's voice) with spirited rock music actually works rather well – as the Yardbirds had already demonstrated three years earlier with their single, *Still I'm Sad.* Or at least it does on the first side of the album. On the second side, the concept starts to wear a little thin, especially when the replacement lead guitarist is much less interesting than the Electric Prunes' own Ken Williams. This rather gives the lie to the official line that Williams and Mike Gannon had been elbowed aside because they could not play the music. David Axelrod actually tries too hard to keep the music simple, based on the two or three chords he believes are sufficient for rock-based music, yet he fails to provide enough melodic invention to compensate. An orchestra is added in places, but in a rather half-hearted manner. The *Mass in F Minor* is a bold experiment, but perhaps one that could have been made to work rather better if the Electric Prunes had been allowed a greater input.

| US release | January 1968 | Reprise | R(S) 6275 |
| UK release | January 1968 | Reprise | RLP 6275 |

1. Kyrie Eleison
2. Gloria
3. Credo
4. Sanctus
5. Benedictus
6. Agnus Dei

All compositions by David Axelrod

James Lowe: vocals / Mark Tulin: bass guitar, keyboards / Quint Weakley: drums / Ken Williams: guitar (1-3) / Mike Gannon: guitar (1-3) / Richie Podolor: guitar (4-6) / Bill Henderson: guitar, vocals (4-6) / Claire Lawrence: keyboards, vocals (4-6) / Don Randi: keyboards (4-6) / David Axelrod: arranger / David Hassinger: producer

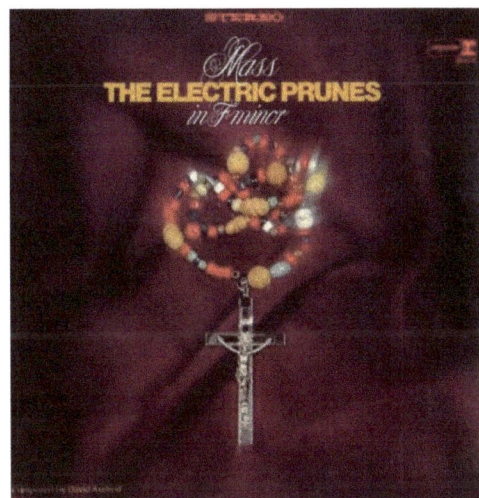

ULTIMATE SPINACH

| US release | January 1968 | MGM | SE 4518 |
| UK release | January 1968 | MGM | C(S) 8071 |

1. Ego Trip
2. Sacrifice Of The Moon (In Four Parts)
3. Plastic Raincoats / Hung-Up Minds
4. (Ballad Of The) Hip Death Goddess
5. Your Head Is Reeling
6. Dove In Hawk's Clothing
7. Baroque #1
8. Funny Freak Parade
9. Pamela

All compositions by Ian Bruce-Douglas

Geoffrey Winthrop: vocals, guitar, sitar / Barbara Hudson: vocals, guitar, kazoo / Ian Bruce-Douglas: vocals, keyboards, guitar, sitar, harmonica, flute, theremin / Richard Nese: bass guitar / Keith Lahteinen: vocals, drums, percussion / Ian Lorber: producer

In an attempt to turn attention away from California, a significant marketing campaign tried to promote 'the Boston sound' as the next big thing, but in the event only Ultimate Spinach managed to make much commercial headway. The music has all the familiar trappings of psychedelia, but with less improvisational content and a greater reliance on unusual instrumental timbres. The group does not have one of the new synthesizers, but manages to do very well with guitar effects, applied with considerable imagination, a selection of different keyboards, and a theremin. *Dove In Hawk's Clothing* is an anti-war song somewhat in the manner of Country Joe and the Fish, the group that Ultimate Spinach most resembles in general, although for the most part, with the help of some little classical touches, it manages to deliver a sound that is its own. There is no obvious single, and none was released, but the album did well in the US charts regardless. A worthy follow-up, *Behold & See*, was released later in the year, but made less impact, and the band did not survive the sixties.

EDDIE HARRIS   THE ELECTRIFYING

The Electrifying Eddie Harris would be a decent but unexceptional jazz album, in a mixture of hard bop and Latin jazz styles, were it not for the fact that Harris chooses to play his instrument through an electronic device called a varitone. The resulting electric saxophone is hardly a revolutionary leap of Jimi Hendrix proportions, but it is certainly an intriguing novelty. The varitone creates a second saxophone line, an octave lower than the one played by the performer, so that Eddie Harris sounds as though he is being shadowed by a musical

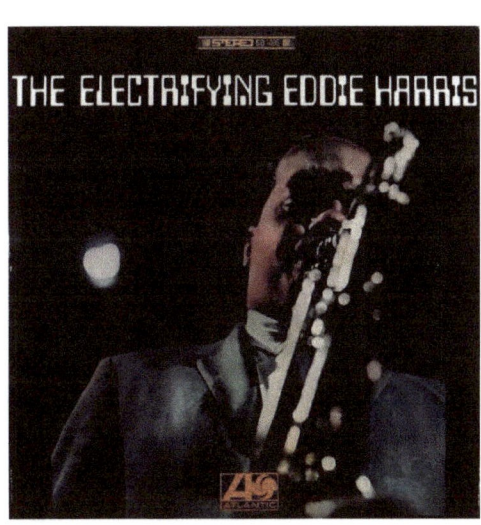

| US release | January 1968 | Atlantic | SD 1495 |
| Not released in UK |

1. Theme In Search Of A Movie (Charles Stepney)
2. Listen Here (Eddie Harris)
3. Judie's Theme (Melvin Jackson)
4. Sham Time (Eddie Harris)
5. Spanish Bull (Eddie Harris)
6. I Don't Want No One But You (Eddie Harris)

Eddie Harris: tenor saxophone / Jodie Christian: piano / Melvin Jackson: bass / Richard Smith: drums / strings (1) / Ray Barretto, Joe Wohletz: percussion (2,4,5) / Melvin Lastie, Joe Newman: trumpet (4) / King Curtis: tenor saxophone (4) / David Newman: tenor saxophone (4) / Haywood Henry: baritone saxophone (4) / Arif Mardin: arranger (1,4), producer

doppelganger. This was enough, however, on his second album to employ the device, to give a Harris a substantial US chart hit and for a single taken from it, *Listen Here*, to become a hit as well.

PRINCE BUSTER   FABULOUS GREATEST HITS

UK release   c.January 1968   Fab / Melodisc   MS 1

1. Earthquake
2. Texas Hold-Up
3. Freezing Up Orange Street
4. Free Love
5. Julie (R.Mellon)
6. Take It Easy
7. Judge Dread
8. Too Hot
9. Ghost Dance
10. Ten Commandments
11. Al Capone
12. Barrister Pardon

All compositions by Cecil (Prince Buster) Campbell except track 5

Prince Buster: vocals, producer / musicians include Ernest Ranglin: guitar, bass guitar / Jah Jerry Haynes: guitar / Gladstone Anderson: piano / Arland Drumbago Parks: drums / Dennis Campbell, Val Bennett: tenor saxophone / Raymond Harper, Baba Brooks: trumpet / Junior Nelson: trombone

Prince Buster was a Jamaican singer and producer, responsible for a large number of ska hits in the country during the sixties. He was one of the main people responsible for the way that the music developed and when ska gave way to the slightly slower rock steady towards the end of the decade, Buster continued to be successful. *Al Capone* was a considerable club hit in the UK in 1967 and entered the singles chart too, some three years after its release in Jamaica. As a prime representative of the Jamican 'rude boy' culture, the song was enormously influential and Prince Buster's spoken inserts were repeated by the Specials when they initiated a British ska revival with their song *Gangsters*.

RICHIE HAVENS   SOMETHING ELSE AGAIN

US release   January 1968   Verve Forecast   FT(S) 3034
UK release   January 1968   Verve Forecast   (S)VLP 6005

1. No Opportunity Necessary, No Experience Needed (Richie Havens)
2. Inside Of Him (Richie Havens)
3. The Klan (Alan Arkin/David Arkin)
4. Sugarplums (John Court)
5. Don't Listen To Me (Richie Havens)
6. From The Prison (Jerry Merrick)
7. Maggie's Farm (Bob Dylan)
8. Somethin' Else Again (Richie Havens)
9. New City (John Court/Richie Havens)
10. Run, Shaker Life (Traditional)

Richie Havens: vocals, guitar, sitar, tamboura, percussion / Adrian Guillery: guitar / Paul Williams: guitar, vocals (10) / Warren Bernhardt: keyboards / Jeremy Steig: flute / John Blair: violin (2) / Don Payne: bass guitar / Denny Gerrard: bass guitar (10) / Eddie Gomez: bass / Donald MacDonald: drums / Skip Prokop: drums (10) / Daniel Ben Zebulon: percussion, vocals (10) / John Court: producer

Richie Havens refines the style he introduced on the previous *Mixed Bag* and delivers a very fine album indeed. He alternates songs based on his furiously strummed acoustic guitar with more delicate performances and, on the appropriately named title track, he plays an instrumental employing the sitar shown on the album cover. The musicians working on most tracks on the album performed their own jazz-flavoured music as Jeremy and the Satyrs and released their own album in January. It is clear, however, that Richie Havens is controlling the group's sound on his own album, using the musician's abilities to enhance his own vision. There is nothing on the Jeremy and the Satyrs album as vital and as exhilarating as *No Opportunity Necessary, No Experience Needed*. *Something Else Again* made a tiny showing in the US album chart, but set Richie Havens further along the road to being considered a major artist.

THE GOLDEN DAWN   POWER PLANT

The album made by Texan band, the Golden Dawn, was released many months after it was recorded because the independent record company International Artists was concentrating its limited resources on promoting the more successful 13th Floor Elevators. As it happens, however, *Power Plant* is rather impressive – and, thankfully, there is no trace of any sound made by a jug. Certainly the music is more roughly recorded than other albums released at this time, but the confident playing of the two guitarists, together with occasional imaginative touches, like the wind chimes sounding throughout *Evolution*, the gargling guitar effect on *Every Day*, and the cavernous harmonica sound on *I'll Be Around*, easily compensate. The music is close to its American punk roots, but the quality of the song-writing and the sparkling playing by all the musicians goes a long way to transcend the limitations of the style. It is a considerable shame that the Golden Dawn did not get the chance to make a follow-up, although George Kinney did manage to record some worthwhile music with many of the same people nearly forty years later.

```
US release    January 1968    International Artists    IA-LP-4
Not released in UK

1.  Evolution (George Kinney/Bobby Rector)
2.  This Way Please (George Kinney/Tom Ramsey)
3.  Starvation (George Kinney/Tom Ramsey)
4.  I'll Be Around (George Kinney/Tom Ramsey)
5.  Seeing Is Believing (George Kinney/Tom Ramsey)

6.  My Time (George Kinney/Bill Hallmark/Jimmy Bird)
7.  A Nice Surprise (George Kinney/Bill Hallmark/Bobby Rector)
8.  Every Day (George Kinney/Tom Ramsey)
9.  Tell Me Why (George Kinney/Tom Ramsey)
10. Reaching Out To You George Kinney/Bill Hallmark)

George Kinney: vocals / Tom Ramsey: guitar / Jimmy Bird: guitar
/ Bill Hallmark: bass guitar / Bobby Rector: drums / Lelan Rogers:
producer
```

TOMORROW

```
UK release    January 1968     Parlophone    PCS/PMC 7042
US release    February 1968    Sire          SES 97012

1.  My White Bicycle (Keith West/Ken Burgess)
2.  Colonel Brown (Keith West/Ken Burgess)
3.  Real Life Permanent Dream (Keith West)
4.  Shy Boy (Keith West/Ken Burgess)
5.  Revolution (Keith West/Steve Howe)

6.  The Incredible Journey Of Timothy Chase (Keith West)
7.  Auntie Mary's Dress Shop (Keith West/Ken Burgess)
8.  Strawberry Fields Forever (John Lennon/Paul McCartney)
9.  Three Jolly Little Dwarfs (Keith West/Ken Burgess)
10. Now Your Time Has Come (Keith West)
11. Hallucinations (Keith West/Ken Burgess)

Keith West: vocals / Steve Howe: guitar, sitar / Junior Wood: bass
guitar / Twink Alder: drums / Mark P. Wirtz: keyboards, producer
```

During 1967, the band formerly known as the In-Crowd, attracted some attention with two psychedelic singles, *My White Bicycle* and *Revolution*. They are virtuoso productions, with reversed tape sections, abrupt rhythm changes, and some rather fine guitar playing, with and without a wah-wah pedal. The records were not hits, unfortunately, but they act as the main draw on the group's album. The other songs have not received as much care and production imagination as the singles, although they include several memorable moments. Tomorrow tackles the Beatles *Strawberry Fields Forever* as a straightforward group performance without recording effects, as if to demonstrate how the Beatles could have performed the song if they were still playing live, although realistically, Steve Howe's ability to combine two different guitar parts played simultaneously is crucial. A few of the tracks on the album were intended for producer Mark Wirtz's aborted rock opera. The group was involved in a hit single the previous August, credited to singer Keith West. *Excerpt From A Teenage Opera* sounded just as its title suggested it should, with several melodic pieces slotted together and a children's choir joining in the chorus. Created by Mark Wirtz, it gave the impression that a full work was on its way, but this never appeared. A compilation of various songs that might have been included in the complete opera was released in 1996. They were performed by various artists, including Tomorrow. The result is a tantalising impression of a work that Mark Wirtz never did finish properly.

TAJ MAHAL

Henry Saint Clair Fredericks, who performs as Taj Mahal, formed a confident and distinctive R&B band with Ry Cooder in 1964, the Rising Sons, and recorded enough material for an album, although this was not released until many years later. Ry Cooder is retained for Taj Mahal's first solo album, which preserves the strengths of the old band. Both musicians have an archivist's interest in the blues, but at the same time Taj Mahal does not feel the need to closely reproduce the style of the original versions. The result is an album full of

```
US release    January 1968    Columbia     CS/CL 9579
UK release    January 1968    Direction    (S) 8-63279

1. Leaving Trunk (Sleepy John Estes)
2. Statesboro Blues (Blind Willie McTell)
3. Checkin' Up On My Baby (Sonny Boy Williamson)
4. Everybody's Got To Change Sometime (Sleepy John Estes)

5. E Z Rider (Traditional)
6. Dust My Broom (Robert Johnson)
7. Diving Duck Blues (Sleepy John Estes)
8. The Celebrated Walkin' Blues (Traditional)

Taj Mahal: vocals, guitar, harmonica / Jesse Ed Davis: guitar / Ry
Cooder: guitar, mandolin / Bill Boatman: guitar / James Thomas:
bass guitar / Gary Gilmore: bass guitar / Sanford Konikoff: drums /
Chuck Blackwell: drums / David Rubinson: producer
```

traditional blues tunes, but one that makes the music sound fresh and modern. It acts as a very effective reference primer for the blues-rock groups of the time seeking to interpret the music for themselves. *Statesboro Blues* was chosen to preview the album on the CBS sampler *The Rock Machine Turns You On*, where Jesse Ed Davis' sparkling slide guitar lead helps to make the song really stand out.

FLEETWOOD MAC   PETER GREEN'S FLEETWOOD MAC

| UK release | February 1968 | Blue Horizon | (S) 7-63200 |
| US release | February 1968 | Epic | BN 26402 |

1. My Heart Beat Like A Hammer (Jeremy Spencer)
2. Merry Go Round (Peter Green)
3. Long Grey Mare (Peter Green)
4. Hellhound On My Trail (Traditional)
5. Shake Your Moneymaker (Elmore James)
6. Looking For Somebody (Peter Green)
7. No Place To Go (Howlin' Wolf)
8. My Baby's Good To Me (Jeremy Spencer)
9. I Loved Another Woman (Peter Green)
10. Cold Black Night (Jeremy Spencer)
11. The World Keep On Turning (Peter Green)
12. Got To Move (Homesick James Williamson)

Peter Green: vocals, guitar, harmonica / Jeremy Spencer: vocals, guitar, piano / John McVie: bass guitar / Bob Brunning: bass guitar (3) / Mick Fleetwood: drums / Mike Vernon: producer

In June 1967, guitarist Peter Green made his last recording with John Mayall's Bluesbreakers, the single *Double Trouble/It Hurts Me Too*. The rhythm section at that time comprised John McVie on bass guitar and Mick Fleetwood on drums. Green had already made the decision to leave and form his own group and he asked McVie and Fleetwood to join with him. In the event, McVie hesitated, reluctant to give up the guaranteed wage he had with the Bluesbreakers, so Bob Brunning performed with Green's new band for a few weeks. Quite sure, however, that John McVie could be persuaded, Peter Green named his new band in honour of his chosen rhythm section, Fleetwood Mac. Curiously, Green seemed to lack confidence in his own abilities, so asked a second guitarist, Jeremy Spencer, to join the group as well. Spencer, who specialised in slide guitar and was a huge fan of the Chicago blues player Elmore James, acted as an alternative group leader. The first album released by Fleetwood Mac divides its focus equally between Green and Spencer and, with Green determined to make the music as varied as he can manage within the blues format, the man renowned for the sensitivity of his lead guitar playing provides further examples of it on just two tracks. All of this does, however, result in an album that is indeed commendably varied. Despite the members of Fleetwood Mac being from London and having what some would say is the wrong skin colour for the blues, their album bears close comparison with the album by Taj Mahal. Both records manage to stay true to the blues tradition while simultaneously making the music sound totally contemporary. Perhaps surprisingly, *Peter Green's Fleetwood Mac* (the name on the record labels, though not on the cover) was a big hit in the UK, although it sold poorly in the US.

BLOOD SWEAT & TEARS   CHILD IS FATHER TO THE MAN

| US release | February 1968 | Columbia | CS 9619 |
| UK release | February 1968 | CBS | (S) 63296 |

1. Overture (Al Kooper)
2. I Love You More Than You'll Ever Know (Al Kooper)
3. Morning Glory (Larry Beckett/Tim Buckley)
4. My Days Are Numbered (Al Kooper)
5. Without Her (Harry Nilsson)
6. Just One Smile (Randy Newman)
7. I Can't Quit Her (Irwin Levine)
8. Meagan's Gypsy Eyes (Steve Katz)
9. Somethin' Goin' On (Al Kooper)
10. House In The Country (Al Kooper)
11. The Modern Adventures Of Plato, Diogenes And Freud (Al Kooper)
12. So Much Love / Underture (Gerry Goffin/Carole King)

Al Kooper: vocals, keyboards / Steve Katz: guitar, lute, vocals / Fred Lipsius: alto saxophone, piano / Jerry Weiss: trumpet, flugelhorn / Randy Brecker: trumpet, flugelhorn / Dick Halligan: trombone / Jim Fielder: bass guitar / Bobby Colomby: drums, vocals / Anahid Ajemian, Paul Gershman, Manny Green, Julie Held, Harry Katzman, Leo Kruczek, Harry Lookofsky, Gene Orloff : violins / Harold Coletta: viola / Charles McCracken, Alan Schulman: cellos / Al Gorgoni: organ, guitar, vocals / Melba Moorman, Valerie Simpson: vocals / Doug James: percussion / Fred Catero: sound effects / John Simon: producer, organ, piano, percussion

Al Kooper left the Blues Project in early 1967 and formed Blood, Sweat and Tears, initially as a quartet (with guitarist Steve Katz, also from the Blues Project), but gradually adding members until there were eight musicians involved, including a brass section. For the album, a string section is added too, which has the effect of minimising the jazz influence on the music. The strings open the album on their own (apart from someone's maniacal laughter), playing an *Overture* that introduces the main themes of Al Kooper's songs, and they make a major return on the oddly titled *The Modern Adventures Of Plato, Diogenes and Freud*. There is barely any blues influence in Kooper's new music either: instead the band plays intelligent, melodic rock, in which the large range of instrumental timbres available allows the music to be arranged to considerable effect. There are several particularly nice touches included, such as the backwards guitar soloing on both *My Days Are Numbered* and *I Can't Quit Her* (and the missing beats on the outro of that second song), the combination of honky-tonk piano with sedate organ on the version of Tim Buckley's *Morning Glory*, the stuttering fairy-chime keyboard and final ondioline playing on *Meagan's Gypsy Eyes*, and the assorted sound effects on *House In The Country*. *Child Is Father To The Man* is a fine album by an impressive band and further confirmation of the enviable musicianship that Al Kooper had already demonstrated in his work with the Blues Project and Bob Dylan.

THE HERD   PARADISE LOST

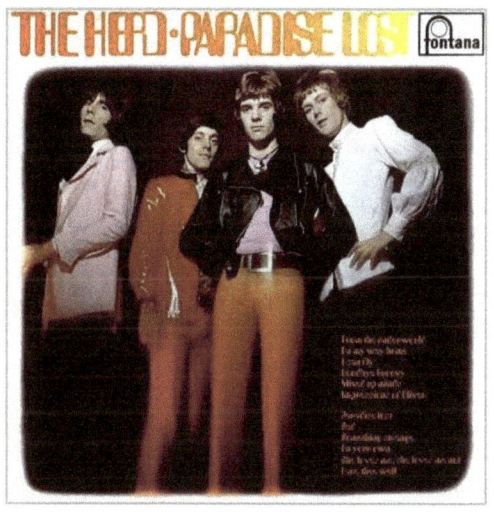

UK release   February 1968   Fontana   (S)TL 5458
Not released in US   5 tracks included on **LOOKIN' THRU YOU** later in year   Fontana SRF 67579

1. From The Underworld (Ken Howard/Alan Blaikley)
2. On My Way Home (Andy Bown/Peter Frampton)
3. I Can Fly (Ken Howard/Alan Blaikley)
4. Goodbye Groovy (Ken Howard/Alan Blaikley)
5. Mixed Up Minds (Andy Bown/Peter Frampton)
6. Impressions Of Oliver (Andy Bown/Peter Frampton)

7. Paradise Lost (Ken Howard/Alan Blaikley)
8. Sad (Ken Howard/Alan Blaikley)
9. Something Strange (Ken Howard/Alan Blaikley)
10. On Your Own (Peter Frampton)
11. She Loves Me, She Loves Me Not (Andy Bown/Peter Frampton)
12. Fare Thee Well (Andrew Steele)

Peter Frampton: vocals, guitar / Andy Bown: keyboards, vocals / Gary Taylor: bass guitar, vocals / Andrew Steele: drums / Mike Leander: arranger (1) / Reg Tilsley: arranger / Steve Rowland: producer

The Herd's striking hit singles in 1967 were yet more evidence of the commercial skills of songwriters Ken Howard and Alan Blaikley, already responsible for several hits by the Honeycombs and Dave Dee, Dozy, Beaky, Mick And Tich. The music media, however, were far more interested in the photogenic looks of the group's sixteen-year-old frontman, Peter Frampton. Half of the group's album is written by Frampton, with keyboards player Andy Bown, and the pair show that they are rapidly learning from Howard and Blaikley. The songs are attractive pop of no great depth, but with occasional evidence that Peter Frampton is also a decent guitarist. The group's period of success was short and Frampton jumped ship to become a founder member of the much more hard rocking Humble Pie. He also managed to release one of the best selling albums of the seventies, *Frampton Comes Alive*. Meanwhile, Andy Bown found himself a secure future as the keyboards player with Status Quo, even if he was never entirely accepted as a full member.

THE BEE GEES   HORIZONTAL

UK release   February 1968   Polydor   583/582 020
US release   February 1968   Atco   (SD) 33-233

1. World
2. And The Sun Will Shine
3. Lemons Never Forget
4. Really And Sincerely
5. Birdie Told Me
6. With The Sun In My Eyes

7. Massachusetts
8. Harry Braff
9. Day Time Girl
10. The Earnest Of Being George
11. The Change Is Made
12. Horizontal

All compositions by Barry, Robin, and Maurice Gibb

Barry Gibb: vocals, guitar / Robin Gibb: vocals, organ / Maurice Gibb: vocals, bass guitar, keyboards, guitar / Vince Melouney: guitar / Colin Petersen: drums / Bill Shepherd: arranger / Robert Stigwood, the Bee Gees: producer

Horizontal provides continuing evidence of the Gibb brothers' skills as songwriters and it includes the group's first major international hit, *Massachusetts*, and its successful follow-up, *World*. The album is, however, a much more straightforward pop affair than its predecessor and it lacks the imaginative arrangement details that gave *Bee Gees First* qualification for membership of the *Sgt Pepper's Lonely Hearts* Club. There is some evidence that the Bee Gees have, in Vince Melouney, a fine guitarist, but his appearances are mostly half-buried in the mix or else missing altogether. His timely interjections are what make *World* so effective and they prevent the group, if only for a moment, from descending into easy-listening balladry.

THE INTERNATIONAL SUBMARINE BAND   SAFE AT HOME

US release   February (mono)/April (stereo) 1968   LHI Records   (S) 12001
Not released in UK until 1985 on Statik Records

1. Blue Eyes (Gram Parsons)
2. I Must Be Somebody Else You've Known (Merle Haggard)
3. A Satisfied Mind (Jack Rhodes/Joe Hayes)
4. Folsom Prison Blues/That's All Right (Johnny Cash/Arthur Crudup)
5. Miller's Cave (Jack Clement)
6. I Still Miss Someone (Johnny Cash)
7. Luxury Liner (Gram Parsons)
8. Strong Boy (Gram Parsons)
9. Do You Know How It Feels To Be Lonesome? (Gram Parsons/Barry Goldberg)

Gram Parsons: vocals, guitar / Bob Buchanan: guitar, vocals / John Nuese: guitar / Chris Ethridge: bass guitar / Jon Corneal: drums, vocals / Earl Ball: piano / Jay Dee Maness: pedal steel guitar / Joe Osborn: bass guitar (1,7) / Suzi Jane Hokom: producer, vocals (9)

If we ignore the fact that rock 'n' rollers like Elvis Presley, Carl Perkins, and the Everly Brothers were country singers deciding to add a little R&B beat, then *Safe At Home* by the International Submarine Band can be considered to be the first country-rock album. Formed by Gram Parsons and his college friends John Nuese and Bob Buchanan, the band was signed to Lee Hazlewood's LHI label, but had already ceased to function by the time the album was released, following Gram Parsons' invitation to join the Byrds. The key track on *Safe At Home* is the medley of *Folsom Prison Blues* and *That's All Right*, a combination that reaffirms Elvis Presley's belief that there is little musical difference between country and the blues, but which also drives the whole thing along with a powerful, funky rhythm quite unlike the usual country approach. The rest of the album is straightforward country, albeit with more energy than many Nashville products could manage, with session player Jay Dee Maness dominating the proceedings with his skilful pedal steel guitar. Ultimately, it is the fact that the record was made in Los Angeles and not Tennessee that is most significant.

THE RASCALS   ONCE UPON A DREAM

Dropping the 'Young' from their name, the Rascals continue with the intelligent pop approach of the previous *Groovin'* album. Much attention is devoted to the arrangements of the songs, helping to make each one stand out, although none is as distinctive as *Groovin'* itself. The album still managed to do well in the US album chart, however, and *It's Wonderful* was a moderate chart hit in advance of the album release (and still used the Young Rascals credit). It is, however, a textbook example of a fairly undistinguished song being definitely salvaged by the psychedelic ambience and effects included in the arrangement.

US release   February 1968   Atlantic   (SD) 8169
UK release   February 1968   Atlantic   588/587 098

1. Intro / Easy Rollin'
2. Rainy Day
3. Please Love Me
4. Sound Effect
5. It's Wonderful
6. I'm Gonna Love You (Gene Cornish)
7. Dave & Eddie
8. My Hawaii
9. My World
10. Silly Girl
11. Singin' The Blues Too Long
12. Bells
13. Sattva
14. Finale: Once Upon A Dream

All compositions by Felix Cavaliere and Eddie Brigati except track 6

Felix Cavaliere: vocals, keyboards, sitar / Eddie Brigati: vocals, percussion, tamboura / Gene Cornish: vocals, guitar / Dino Danelli: drums, percussion / Chuck Rainey: bass guitar / Ron Carter: bass / Richard Davis: bass / King Curtis: tenor saxophone / Steve Marcus: soprano saxophone / Hubert Laws: flute / Melvin Lastie: trumpet / Buddy Lucas: harmonica / David Brigati: vocals / Gene Orloff: arranger / Adrian Barber: sound effects / Arif Mardin: arranger, producer

VANILLA FUDGE   THE BEAT GOES ON

Producer Shadow Morton employed the Vanilla Fudge for a project of his own, which was then released as the group's second album. Taking Sonny Bono's song, *The Beat Goes On,* as a recurring linking piece, Morton attempts an overview of five hundred years of music and history in an ill-assorted medley where the only real link is the extravagant organ playing of Mark Stein and some pretentious vocalising. Carmine Appice has since described the album as being one that even the heavy-handed comedy group, Spinal

US release   February 1968   Atco   (SD) 33-237
UK release   February 1968   Atlantic   588/587 100

1. Sketch (Vanilla Fudge)
2. The Beat Goes On (Sonny Bono)
    including: Variations on a Theme by Mozart (Wolfgang Amadeus Mozart)
    Old Black Joe (Stephen Foster)
    Don't Fence Me In (Cole Porter)
    12th Street Rag (Euday Bowman)
    In The Mood (Joe Garland/Andy Razaf)
    Hound Dog (Jerry Leiber/Mike Soller)
    Beatles Medley (John Lennon/Paul McCartney)
    Für Elise/Moonlight Sonata (Ludwig Van Beethoven)
3. The Beat Goes On (Sonny Bono)
    including: Voices In Time
        Merchant (Vanilla Fudge) / The Game Is Over
            (Jean-Pierre Bourtayre/Jean Bouchety)

Mark Stein: vocals, keyboards / Vince Martell: guitar, vocals / Tim Bogert: bass guitar, vocals / Carmine Appice: drums, vocals / Shadow Morton: producer / John Linde: producer

Tap, would have been wary of making, which seems like an accurate assessment. *The Beat Goes On* is hugely ambitious, but the result does not justify the effort that must have been made to create it.

OTIS REDDING   THE DOCK OF THE BAY

Otis Redding and all but one member of his backing group, the Bar-Kays, were killed in a plane crash in December 1967. The album, *The Dock Of The Bay*, which collects together a motley assortment of songs, some of which were released as singles, and includes his big posthumous hit, the title track, serves as his memorial. Both the album and single were Otis Redding's most successful records, which is a little ironic since the song itself, *(Sittin' On) The Dock Of The Bay*, a gentle ballad of great charm, is so far removed from Redding's usual strident soul style that Stax did not not originally want to release it at all. The album also includes Otis Redding's duet with Carla Thomas, *Tramp*, despite the song already being included on a joint album, *King & Queen*, but it is something of a classic and can stand the exposure.

```
US release    February 1968   Volt    (S) 419
UK release    May 1968        Stax    231/230 001   different cover

1. (Sittin' On) The Dock Of The Bay (Otis Redding/Steve Cropper)
2. I Love You More Than Words Can Say (Booker T Jones/Eddie Floyd)
3. Let Me Come On Home (Booker T Jones/Otis Redding)
4. Open The Door (Otis Redding)
5. Don't Mess With Cupid (Deanie Parker/Eddie Floyd/Steve Cropper)
6. The Glory Of Love (Billy Hill)
7. I'm Coming Home (Otis Redding)
8. Tramp (James McCracklin/Lowell Fulsom)
9. The Huckle-Buck (Andy Gibson/Roy Alfred)
10. Nobody Knows You (When You're Down And Out) (Jimmie Cox)
11. Ole Man Trouble (Otis Redding)

Otis Redding: vocals, producer / Booker T Jones: keyboards / Isaac Hayes: keyboards / Steve Cropper: guitar / Donald Dunn: bass guitar / Al Jackson: drums / Wayne Jackson: trumpet / Joe Arnold: tenor saxophone / Carla Thomas: vocals (8)
```

JOHN RENBOURN   SIR JOHN ALOT OF MERRIE ENGLANDES MUSYK THYNG & YE GRENE KNYGHTE

```
UK release    February 1968   Transatlantic   TRA 167
US release    February 1968   Reprise         RS 6344

1. The Earle Of Salisbury (William Byrd)
2. The Trees They Do Grow High (Traditional)
3. Lady Goes To Church (John Renbourn)
4. Morgana (John Renbourn)
5. Transfusion (Charles Lloyd)
6. Forty-Eight (John Renbourn/Terry Cox)
7. My Dear Boy (John Renbourn)
8. White Fishes (John Renbourn/Ray Warleigh)
9. Sweet Potato (Booker T Jones)
10. Seven Up (John Renbourn/Terry Cox)

John Renbourn: guitar / Ray Warleigh: flute / Terry Cox: percussion, glockenspiel / Nathan Joseph: producer
```

John Renbourn attempts to widen the basis of his music with *Sir John Alot Of...* It is an instrumental album, but only half of it is traditional or traditional-sounding music of a kind to be conjured up by the album title. Side one comprises delicate chamber pieces for flute, acoustic guitar, and percussion, with a distinct medieval flavour. The pieces on side two, however, use the same instrumentation to deliver a set of bluesy performances of a much more modern character. This combination of musical interests is probably unique to John Renbourn, but it has the effect of producing a rather delightful album. The use of extra musicians to a much greater extent than on his previous recordings indicates his ambition to become part of a group, which would be soon realised.

RALPH McTELL   EIGHT FRAMES A SECOND

Transatlantic Records seemed to be on the lookout for skilled acoustic guitarists, following its success with Bert Jansch and John Renbourn. Ralph McTell is a fine ragtime player and he also happens to be a very good songwriter, most notably on the evocative title track of his debut album. The arranger of the sympathetic string part is Tony Visconti, on his first major job here, but later acclaimed for his work with David Bowie. *Eight Frames A Second* is a pleasant album rather than an exciting one and lacks a killer song to make it more than that. But such a song would soon come.

| UK release | February 1968 | Transatlantic | TRA 165 |
| US release | 1969 | Capitol | ST-240 |

1. Nanna's Song
2. The Mermaid And The Seagull
3. Hesitation Blues (Traditional)
4. Are You Receiving Me?
5. Morning Dew (Bonnie Dobson)
6. Sleepytime Blues
7. Eight Frames A Second
8. Willoughby's Farm
9. Louise
10. Blind Blake's Rag (Traditional)
11. I'm Sorry – I Must Leave
12. Too Tight Drag (Blind Blake)
13. Granny Takes A Trip (Geoff Boyer/Joe Beard)

All compositions by Ralph McTell except where stated

Ralph McTell: vocals, guitar / Mac McGann: guitar / Bob Strawbridge: mandolin / Mick Bennett: washboard / Mick Bartlett (Henry VIII): jug / Tony Visconti: arranger / Gus Dudgeon: producer

ROTARY CONNECTION

| US release | February 1968 | Cadet Concept | LPS 312 |
| UK release | February 1968 | Chess | CRL 4538 |

1. Amen (Charles Stepney/Marshall Paul)
2. Rapid Transit (Charles Stepney/Marshall Paul)
3. Turn Me On (Sidney Barnes/Greg Perry)
4. Pink Noise (Charles Stepney/Marshall Paul)
5. Lady Jane (Mick Jagger/Keith Richards)
6. Like A Rolling Stone (Bob Dylan)
7. Soul Man (Isaac Hayes/David Porter)
8. Sarsum Mentes (Charles Stepney/Marshall Paul)
9. Didn't Want To Have To Do It (John Sebastian)
10. Black Noise (Charles Stepney/Marshall Paul)
11. Memory Band (Richard Rudolph/Charles Stepney)
12. Ruby Tuesday (Mick Jagger/Keith Richards)
13. Rotary Connection (Charles Stepney/Marshall Paul)

Sidney Barnes: vocals / Minnie Riperton: vocals / Judy Hauff: vocals / Bobby Simms: guitar / Mitch Aliotta: bass guitar / Kenny Venegas: drums / Charles Stepney: arranger, producer, keyboards / Marshall Chess: producer, theremin / Bobby Christian: guitar / Pete Cosey: guitar / Louis Satterfield: bass guitar / Phil Upchurch: bass guitar / Morris Jennings: drums / Bill Bradley: electronics / Chuck Barksdale: vocals

A rock trio called the Proper Strangers was amalgamated with a group of soul singers and placed under the supervision of arranger Charles Stepney. He is given free reign to create arrangements that are both lush and eccentric and it is these that define the album as much as the sound of the three singers performing together. Marshall Chess made some of his best session musicians available to complete the album, but they have relatively little to do. *Rotary Connection's* blend of soul and rock sensibilities creates a pleasingly innovative sounding record. There are some rather over-familiar songs chosen for the cover version treatment, but even they are so cleverly arranged that they are made to sound as fresh as the rest of the music. The Rotary Connection concept (for Charles Stepney's project is hardly a functioning band) was retained for five more albums, although this first one inevitably made the most impact. Minnie Riperton enjoyed a brief career as a successful solo singer, although she is not given much priority here.

ETTA JAMES   TELL MAMA

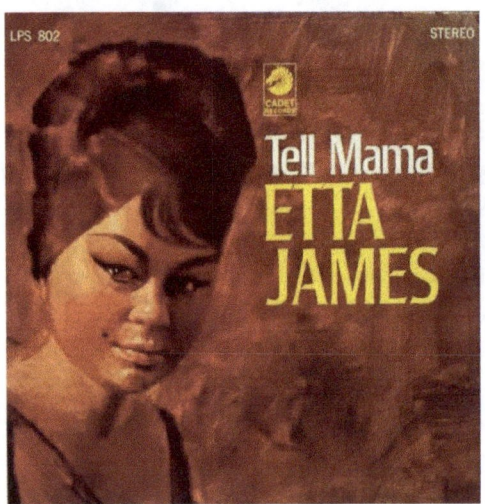

| US release | February 1968 | Cadet | LP(S) 802 |
| UK relesae | February 1968 | Chess | CRL 4536 |

1. Tell Mama (Clarence Carter/Marcus Daniel/Wilbur Terrell)
2. I'd Rather Go Blind (Billy Foster/Ellington Jordan/Etta James)
3. Watch Dog (Don Covay)
4. The Love Of My Man (Ed Townsend)
5. I'm Gonna Take What He's Got (Don Covay)
6. The Same Rope (Leonard Caston Jr/Lloyd Webster)
7. Security (Otis Redding)
8. Steal Away (Jimmy Hughes)
9. My Mother-In-Law (George David/Lee Diamond)
10. Don't Lose Your Good Thing (Rick Hall/Spooner Oldham)
11. It Hurts Me So Much (Charles Chalmers)
12. Just A Little Bit (Rosco Gordon)

Etta James: vocals / Gene Miller: trumpet / James Mitchell: tenor saxophone / Aaron Varnell: tenor saxophone / Floyd Newman: baritone saxophone / Jimmy Ray Jenkins: guitar / Albert Lowe: guitar / George Davis, Spooner Oldham, Carl Banks, Barry Beckett, Marvell Thomas: keyboards / David Hood: bass guitar / Roger Hawkins: drums / Charles Chalmers; vocals / Rick Hall: producer

Etta James made her first records in the early fifties, as a protegée of R&B band leader Johnny Otis. In 1968, she was thirty and the experience she has, compared with the other artists making soul records at the time, shows in the strength and grittiness of her voice. She became a major influence on Janis Joplin and the tracks on her eighth and most successful album make it clear why this was. The title track was her biggest US hit single, while the powerful soul ballad, *I'd Rather Go Blind,* became a rhythm and blues standard in the wake of her recording, becoming a big hit when covered by Christine Perfect (McVie) in the UK. Personal problems prevented Ms James from being able to fully benefit from the impact made by the *Tell Mama* album, although she did manage to make many more records after this one, even if the music-buying public appeared to be largely disinterested.

THE ELECTRIC FLAG   A LONG TIME COMIN'

```
US release      March 1968      Columbia    CS 9597
UK release      March 1968      CBS         (S) 63294

1. Killing Floor (Howlin' Wolf)
2. Groovin' Is Easy (Ron Polte)
3. Over-Lovin' You (Barry Goldberg/Mike Bloomfield)
4. She Should Have Just (Ron Polte)
5. Wine (Traditional)

6. Texas (Buddy Miles/Mike Bloomfield)
7. Sittin' In Circles (Barry Goldberg)
8. You Don't Realise (Mike Bloomfield)
9. Another Country (Ron Polte)
10. Easy Rider (Mike Bloomfield)

Mike Bloomfield: guitar, vocals / Nick Gravenites: vocals / Barry Goldberg: keyboards / Michael Fonfara: keyboards / Herbie Rich: baritone saxophone, organ, guitar / Marcus Doubleday: trumpet / Stemzie Hunter: alto saxophone / Peter Strazza: tenor saxophone / Harvey Brooks: bass guitar / Buddy Miles: drums, vocals / Richie Havens: sitar, percussion / Sivuca: guitar, percussion / Paul Beaver: synthesizer / Leo Daruckzek, Charles McCracken, Bobby Notkoff, Julius Held, George Brown: violins / Cass Elliot: vocals (2) / Joe Church: producer, percussion / John Court: percussion, vocals, producer
```

The proper first album by Mike Bloomfield's Electric Flag is not quite a five-star record, but still a much better demonstration of the band's strengths than *The Trip*. The first track, a brass-rock version of the Howlin' Wolf blues, *Killing Floor*, is an outstanding album opener, pure dynamite. But the rest of *A Long Time Comin'* makes little attempt to extend the style of this powerful start, trying instead to prove how versatile the Electric Flag can be. Some of the tracks attempt to take on the mantle of the late Otis Redding, but neither Nick Gravenites nor Buddy Miles has a voice to match his so that the songs fall a little flat. The lengthy *Another Country*, however, is an ambitious tour de force of intricate arranging and the kind of impressive guitar solo one would expect from Mike Bloomfield. His playing also acts as effective icing on the distinctive rock songs, *Groovin' Is Easy* and *Sittin' In Circles*, while the slow big-band blues, *Texas*, is very much designed as a guitar showcase. It would be helpful to describe the album as a very promising opening salvo for a band going on to produce some really great music, but unfortunately Mike Bloomfield decided to abandon his own project just a few months later and it became sadly apparent that, whether or not he was soloing, his presence in the band was vital.

JAMES BROWN   I CAN'T STAND MYSELF WHEN YOU TOUCH ME

```
US release      March 1968      King        1030
UK release      March 1968      Polydor     184 136    different cover, slightly different track listing

1. I Can't Stand Myself (When You Touch Me) Part 1 (James Brown)
2. There Was A Time (Bud Hobgood/James Brown)
3. Get It Together Part 1 (Alfred Ellis/James Brown/Bud Hobgood)
4. Baby, Baby, Baby, Baby (Bud Hobgood/James Brown/James Crawford)
5. Time After Time (Jule Styne/Sammy Cahn)
6. The Soul Of J.B. (Bud Hobgood/Gladys Knochelman/James Brown)

7. I Can't Stand Myself (When You Touch Me) Part 2 (James Brown)
8. Get It Together Part 2 (Alfred Ellis/James Brown/Bud Hobgood)
9. Why Did You Take Your Love Away From Me (Bud Hobgood/James Brown)
10. Need Your Love So Bad (Little Willie John)
11. You've Got To Change Your Mind (Bobby Byrd/Gene Redd/James Brown/Ron Lenhoff)
12. Funky Soul #1 (Bud Hobgood/James Brown/James Crawford)

James Brown: vocals, organ, producer / Tracks 1,7: Fat Eddie Setser: guitar / Tim Hedding: organ / Tim Drummond: bass guitar / William Bowman: drums // Tracks 3,8: Waymond Reed: trumpet / Joe Dupars: trumpet / Levi Rasbury: trombone / Pee Wee Ellis: alto saxophone / Maceo Parker: tenor saxophone / Eldee Williams: tenor saxophone / St Clair Pinckney: baritone saxophone / Jimmy Nolen: guitar / Alphonso Kellum: guitar / Bernard Odum: bass guitar / Jabo Starks: drums
```

James Brown continues to make half a dozen albums each year, padding out the hit singles with quickly recorded filler and with unused material from his extensive archive. *I Can't Stand Myself When You Touch Me* is one of Brown's best selling albums and starts well, with three prime pieces of funk, all of them issued as singles. Two are reprised on side two, although these Part 2 versions would have been better served by reuniting them with the Part 1 recordings, taking advantage of the album format. The rest of the album, however, is forgettable, with Brown either singing medium tempo soul ballads with far less energy and conviction than Otis Redding or Aretha Franklin, or else proving again that he is an indifferent organ player. His revival of Little Willie John's *Need Your Love So Bad* is completely outclassed by the interpretation released by Fleetwood Mac a few months later, an eclipse that should not have happened.

LAURA NYRO   ELI AND THE 13TH CONFESSION

| US release | March 1968 | Columbia | CS 9626 |
| UK release | March 1968 | CBS | (S) 63346 |

1. Luckie
2. Lu
3. Sweet Blindness
4. Poverty Train
5. Lonely Women
6. Eli's Coming

7. Timer
8. Stoned Soul Picnic
9. Emmie
10. Woman's Blues
11. Once It Was Alright Now (Farmer Joe)
12. December's Boudoir
13. The Confession

All compositions by Laura Nyro

Laura Nyro: vocals, piano / Paul Griffin: piano (6,11) / Hugh McCracken: guitar / Ralph Casale: guitar / Chet Amsterdam: guitar, bass guitar / Bernie Glow: trumpet / Pat Calello: trumpet / Ernie Royal: trumpet / Wayne Andre: trombone / Jimmy Cleveland: trombone / Ray DeSio: trombone / Joe Farrell: tenor saxophone, flute / Zoot Sims: tenor saxophone / George Young: tenor saxophone / Chuck Rainey: bass guitar / Buddy Saltzman: drums / Artie Schroeck: drums, vibraphone / Charlie Calello: arranger, producer

Laura Nyro raises her level of ambition and performance considerably with her second album, presenting a suite of songs that provides a totally immersive experience. She sings in a very emotional manner: when she is happy, as on *Luckie* or *Eli's Coming*, she lifts the listener's spirits along with her own. Conversely, when describing a desperate situation, as on *Poverty Train*, she is capable of moving the listener to tears. *Eli And The 13th Confession* is a soul album, with its roots clearly placed within gospel, even if its variable rhythms are not really aimed at dancers. The album scraped into the US album charts, but was a greater influence on other musicians than this might suggest. As before, some of its songs were taken into the singles charts by other performers, notably Three Dog Night and the Fifth Dimension.

JONI MITCHELL   SONG TO A SEAGULL

| US release | March 1968 | Reprise | RS 6293 |
| UK release | March 1968 | Reprise | RSLP 6293 |

1. I Had A King
2. Michael From Mountains
3. Night In The City
4. Marcie
5. Nathan La Franeer

6. Sistowbell Lane
7. The Dawntreader
8. The Pirate Of Penance
9. Song To A Seagull
10. Cactus Tree

All compositions by Joni Mitchell

Joni Mitchell: vocals, guitar, piano, banshee / Stephen Stills: bass guitar (3) / Lee Keefer: banshee (5) / David Crosby: producer

The first album by Joni Mitchell has a simple sound, with only *Night In The City* departing from the formula of a woman singing in a lovely soprano voice to the accompaniment of her acoustic guitar playing. David Crosby was nominally the producer, but he made the decision to simply let Joni Mitchell get on with it. The link with the early albums of Joan Baez is obvious, except that Joni is playing her own songs exclusively and they have little connection with the world of traditional music. The songs are an equal partnership between intricate melodies, driven by a guitar tuned in a variety of unusual ways, and beautiful, carefully worked out lyrics, capable of being read on their own as poetry. *Night In The City* stands out musically due to Joni switching to an accomplished honky tonk piano and Stephen Stills underscoring the music with a driving electric bass part. There are, however, several other imaginative touches on different songs, such as the banshee wail on *Nathan La Franeer* and the vocal counterpoint on *The Pirate Of Penance*. The album sides are separately subtitled 'I Came To The City' and 'Out Of The City And Down To The Seaside' in an attempt to provide some kind of programme for the songs, but the majority are complete narrative vignettes in their own right. *Marcie* is perhaps the perfect product of Joni Mitchell's art, maintaining a clever red-green series of metaphors through the song, while presenting an intriguing young female character who may or may not be based on Joni Mitchell herself.

THE INCREDIBLE STRING BAND   THE HANGMAN'S BEAUTIFUL DAUGHTER

The Hangman's Beautiful Daughter is the Incredible String Band's best selling album, although in the US this does not mean very much, as the group remained a minority appeal act. The music still sounds delightfully eccentric, but it is rather more densely arranged than previously, with Mike Heron and Robin Williamson overdubbing extra instrumental parts as well as

UK release	March 1968	Elektra	EUK(S7)258
US release	March 1968	Elektra	EKS 74021

1. Koeeoaddi There (Robin Williamson)
2. The Minotaur's Song (Robin Williamson)
3. Witches Hat (Robin Williamson)
4. A Very Cellular Song (Mike Heron)
5. Mercy I Cry City (Mike Heron)
6. Waltz Of The New Moon (Robin Williamson)
7. The Water Song (Robin Williamson)
8. Three Is A Green Crown (Robin Williamson)
9. Swift As The Wind (Mike Heron)
10. Nightfall (Robin Williamson)

Mike Heron: vocals, guitar, sitar, hammered dulcimer, keyboards / Robin Williamson: vocals. guitar, gimbri, oud, mandolin, penny whistle, pan pipes, chahanai, piano, water harp, harmonica, percussion / Lirorice McKechnie: vocals, percussion / Dolly Collins: keyboards / David Snell: harp / Richard Thompson: vocals (2) / Judy Dyble: vocals (2) / Joe Boyd: producer

calling on a small number of friends. The band's name is starting to seem less appropriate, as there are several wind and keyboard derived sounds to be heard, but the music retains its folk character and there is no rock rhythm section. *The Minotaur's Song* takes a surprising detour into Gilbert and Sullivan territory, while the very lengthy *A Very Cellular Song* is something of a musical adventure, incorporating an extract from Joseph Spence and the Pinder Family's *We Bid You Goodnight* (from *The Real Bahamas* album) amidst its wanderings.

STEFAN GROSSMAN   AUNT MOLLY'S MURRAY FARM

UK release	March 1968	Fontana	(S)TL 5463
Not released in US			

1. Aunt Molly's Murray Farm (Stefan Grossman)
2. Foregone Conclusion (Stefan Grossman)
3. Religious Trainfare Blues (Steve Mann)
4. See See Rider (Ma Rainey)
5. Delia (Elizabeth Cotton)
6. Sideways Nowhere Bound (Stefan Grossman)
7. Special Rider Blues (Skip James)
8. Wall Hollow Blues (Stefan Grossman)
9. Cow Cow's 4/4 Waltz (Steve Mann)
10. Dallas Rag (Traditional)
11. All My Friends Are Gone (Rev. Gary Davis/Steve Grosmman)
12. Number One (Steve Grossman)
13. Money's All Gone (Traditional)
14. Big Road Blues (Traditional)
15. Roberta (Steve Grossman)

Steve Grossman: guitar, vocals / Terry Brown: producer

Stefan Grossman is a skilled American acoustic guitarist, who has maintained a lengthy career with a large number of record releases, yet has somehow failed to attract the acclaim and kudos gained by the likes of John Fahey and John Renbourn. His first album was intended as a tutorial, *How To Play Blues Guitar,* which achieved what it was supposed to do, although it left Grossman exposed to accusations of arrogance. *Aunt Molly's Murray Farm,* the follow-up, was recorded in the UK and comprises a set of assorted guitar and vocal performances, some blues and some not. Grossman can certainly play, but at this point he has to contend with many other guitarists doing the same thing. He cannot match John Renbourn's sheer virtuosity nor John Fahey's sense of adventure and fun and this is perhaps his problem.

THE MOVE   MOVE

UK release	March 1968	Regal Zonophone	(S)LRZ 1002
Not released in US			

1. Yellow Rainbow
2. Kilroy Was Here
3. (Here We Go Round) The Lemon Tree
4. Weekend (Bill Post/Doree Post)
5. Walk Upon The Water
6. Flowers In The Rain
7. Hey Grandma (Jerry Miller/Don Stevenson)
8. Useless Information
9. Zing! Went The Strings Of My Heart (James F.Hanley)
10. The Girl Outside
11. Fire Brigade
12. Mist On A Monday Morning
13. Cherry Blossom Clinic

All compositions by Roy Wood except where stated

Carl Wayne: vocals / Roy Wood: guitar. vocals / Trevor Burton: guitar, vocals / Ace Kefford: bass guitar, vocals / Bev Bevan: drums, vocals / Nicky Hopkins: keyboards / Tony Visconti: arranger / Denny Cordell: producer

The Move, intended to be a Birmingham equivalent of the Who, and the group's manager, Tony Secunda, embarked on a promotional campaign designed to shock. The group would destroy televisions on stage with an axe and signed its contract with producer Denny Cordell on the naked back of a model. The campaign backfired, however, when Secunda circulated a cartoon showing prime minister

Harold Wilson in bed with his secretary. Wilson sued and the Move lost both the case and a considerable sum of money. Secunda was duly fired. Meanwhile, however, the group scored three top ten hits during 1967 (and two more, including a number one with *Blackberry Way*, during 1968). Two of the singles, *Flowers In The Rain* and *Fire Brigade*, are included on the group's debut album; the first of these had the much-vaunted distinction of being the first song, not including the programme theme, to be played at the launch of BBC's Radio One at the end of September, 1967. The Move's music is bright, guitar-based pop, rather like that of Dave Dee, Dozy, Beaky, Mick And Tich, and the album is a strong collection of songs, if not one that has much compositional depth. The three cover versions included are of songs associated with Eddie Cochran, Moby Grape, and Phil Spector, an eclectic selection that emphasises the extent to which Roy Wood, as the Move's songwriter and effective leader, was well aware of the kind of beat music that worked.

FEVER TREE

```
US release      March 1968    UNI    73024
UK release      March 1968    UNI    UNL 102

1. Imitation Situation 1 (Toccata And Fugue (J.S.Bach/Rob Landes/Scott & Vivian Holtzman)
2. Where Do You Go? (Michael Knust/Scott & Vivian Holtzman)
3. San Francisco Girls (Return Of The Native) (Michael Knust/Scott & Vivian Holtzman)
4. Ninety-Nine And A Half (Steve Cropper/Wilson Pickett)
5. Man Who Paints The Pictures (Michael Knust/Scott & Vivian Holtzman)
6. Filigree And Shadow (Scott & Vivian Holtzman)

7. The Sun Also Rises (Rob Landes/Scott & Vivian Holtzman)
8. Day Tripper/We Can Work It Out (John Lennon/Paul McCartney)
9. Nowadays Clancy Can't Even Sing (Neil Young)
10. Unlock My Door (Rob Landes/Scott & Vivian Hotlzman)
11. Come With Me (Rainsong) (Rob Landes/Scott & Vivian Holtzman)

Dennis Keller: vocals / Michael Knust: guitar / Rob Landes: keyboards, harp, flute, recorder, cello / E.E.Wolfe III: bass guitar / John Tuttle: drums / David Angel: arranger (1,6) / Gene Page: arranger (7-11) / Scott & Vivian Holtzman: producers
```

San Francisco Girls (Return Of The Native) is an anthem for the city even more effective than the one sung by Scott McKenzie, albeit not a big hit and not so well known. This is evident not least because it includes a superb guitar part, employing Eric Clapton's favourite sustained 'woman tone'. Only one other track on Fever Tree's album is in the same style, the powerful *Man Who Paints The Pictures*, which is unfortunate, because an album sounding like this throughout would have been extremely effective. The fact that the group is floundering in its attempt to find a distinctive sound is emphasised by the inclusion of three mismatched cover versions. For the most part, however, Fever Tree attempts an uncomfortable fusion of rock with classical music. This is an early innovation, but one that was managed much more effectively by other groups a little later. Meanwhile, the inclusion of *San Francisco Girls* is almost enough to seal the album's greatness on its own.

THE UNITED STATES OF AMERICA

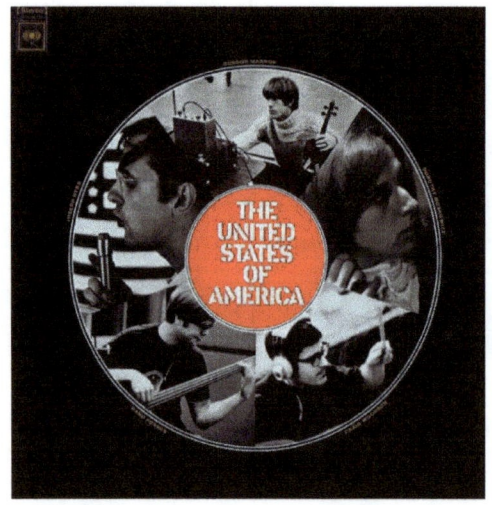

```
US release      March 1968    Columbia    CS 9614
UK release      March 1968    CBS         (S) 63340

1. The American Metaphysical Circus (Joseph Byrd)
2. Hard Coming Love (Joseph Byrd/Dorothy Moskowitz)
3. Cloud Song (Joseph Byrd/Dorothy Moskowitz)
4. The Garden Of Earthly Delights (Joseph Byrd/Dorothy Moskowitz)
5. I Won't Leave My Wooden Wife For You, Sugar (Joseph Byrd/Dorothy Moskowitz)

6. Where Is Yesterday (Gordon Marron/Ed Bogas/Dorothy Moskowitz)
7. Coming Down (Joseph Byrd/Dorothy Moskowitz)
8. Love Song For The Dead Ché (Joseph Byrd)
9. Stranded In Time Gordon Marron/Ed Bogas)
10. The American Way Of Love (Joseph Byrd/The United States of America)

Dorothy Moskowitz: vocals / Joseph Byrd: keyboards, electronics, vocals / Gordon Marron: violin, electronics, vocals / Rand Forbes: bass guitar / Craig Woodson: drums / Ed Bogas: keyboards / Don Ellis: trumpet (5) / David Rubinson: producer
```

The album by Joseph Byrd's United States Of America is a brave attempt to create rock music using the electronic effects employed by modern classical composers before synthesizers became widely available. There is no electric guitar but Rand Forbes plays one of the first fretless bass guitars. Craig Woodson is credited with playing electric drums and primitive drum machines could indeed be obtained at this time, but the aural evidence is that Woodson is actually using a conventional drum kit. Nevertheless, the range of electronic sounds that Byrd and his colleagues are able to create is impressive, whether being used to produce a dense melange of textures or music that is more spacious and atmospheric. The track that was used on the CBS sampler, *The Rock Machine Turns You On*, is not typical of the album as a whole. *I Won't*

Leave My Wooden Wife For You, Sugar is an electronic pop song with lyrics unashamedly stolen from a poem by Adrian Henri (*Song Of Affluence* – published in 1967 as part of *Penguin Modern Poets 10*) and not credited.

FIFTY FOOT HOSE   CAULDRON

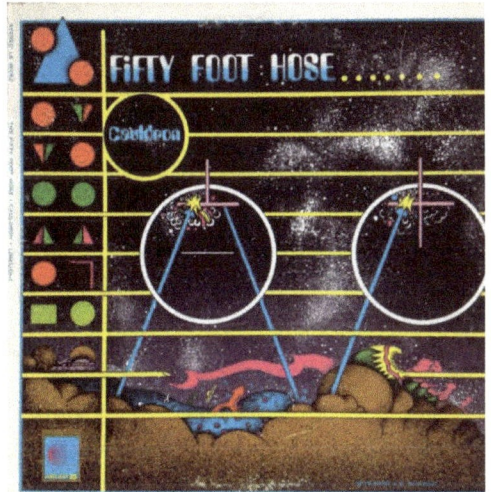

US release   March 1968   Limelight   LS 86062
UK release   1969   Mercury   SLML 4030

1. And After (Cork Marcheschi)
2. If Not This Time (David Blossom)
3. Opus 777 (Cork Marcheschi)
4. The Things That Concern You (Larry Evans)
5. Opus 11 (Cork Marcheschi)
6. Red The Sign Post (David Blossom/Ted Roswicky)
7. For Paula (Cork Marcheschi)
8. Rose (David Blossom)
9. Fantasy (David Blossom)
10. God Bless The Child (Billie Holiday)
11. Cauldron (Cork Marcheschi/David Blossom/Kim Kimsey)

Nancy Blossom: vocals / Cork Marcheschi: theremin, electronics / Larry Evans: guitar, vocals / David Blossom: guitar, piano, kalimba / Terry Hansley: bass guitar / Kim Kimsey: drums / Dan Healy: producer

Fifty Foot Hose was working in the same territory as The United States Of America, creating a rock music that incorporates electronics, but because it did not have the mighty Columbia record company working for it, the band did not even manage the limited fame and reputation enjoyed by its rival. Many of the pieces included on *Cauldron* are exclusively electronic. In between are unabashed rock songs, complete with strident electric guitars, but also including sounds generated by entirely electronic means. The band is rather more inclined to use dissonance than the United States of America and has a clear liking for the avant garde. Like the Columbia band, Fifty Foot Hose does not have access to an expensive Moog synthesizer, but is able to manage very well without one. Neither band survived the sixties, although Cork Marcheschi attempted a revival of Fifty Foot Hose in the nineties. Clearly, however, its time had passed.

THE BEACON STREET UNION   THE EYES OF

The Beacon Street Union is a less celebrated member of the 'Boston sound' than Ultimate Spinach, although the group's first album did manage to make a brief appearance in the US album chart. The approach of the group and its chief songwriter, bass player Wayne Ulaky, is to try a little bit of everything in the hope that at least some of it will stick.

US release   March 1968   MGM   SE 4517
UK release   March 1968   MGM   CS 8069

1. My Love Is (Wayne Ulaky)
2. Beautiful Delilah (Chuck Berry)
3. Sportin' Life (Traditional)
4. Four Hundred And Five (Beacon Street Union/Wes Farrell)
5. Mystic Mourning (Richard Weisberg/Robert Rhodes/Wayne Ulaky)
6. Sadie Said No (John Wright/Wayne Ulaky)
7. Speed Kills (John Wright/Wayne Ulaky)
8. Blue Avenue (Wayne Ulaky)
9. South End Incident (I'm Afraid) (Wayne Ulaky)
10. Green Destroys The Gold (Wayne Ulaky)
11. The Prophet (John Wright/Wayne Ulaky)

John Wright: vocals / Paul Tartachny: guitar, vocals / Robert Rhodes: keyboards / Wayne Ulaky: bass guitar, vocals / Richard Weisberg: drums / Tom Wilson: voice / Wes Farrell: producer

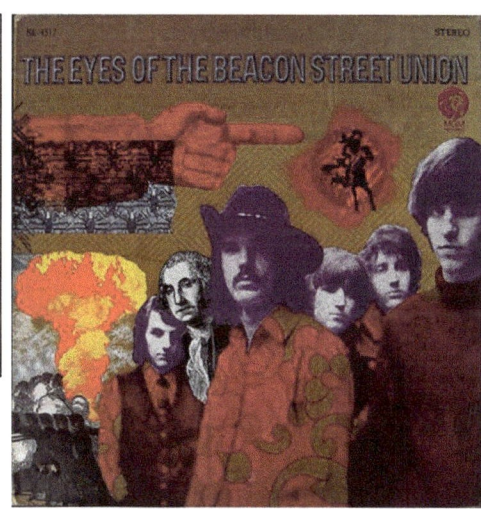

There is some psychedelia certainly, but it is made to share space with the blues, with satire (for how else is the cover of *Beautiful Delilah* to be interpreted, performed as if the intention is to mock the Kinks?), and even some really good songwriting. And all of it is performed expertly by a group in total control of what it wants to achieve. The album's opening track, with brief passages of lush harmony singing and stabbing rhythm guitar, provides a compelling example of how good the Beacon Street Union can be.

THE MOTHERS ON INVENTION   WE'RE ONLY IN IT FOR THE MONEY

Nothing was immune from Frank Zappa's barbed wit on the third album by his Mothers of Invention, least of all the hippies, who might have been expected to be his best customers, or the Beatles, whose *Sgt Pepper Lonely Hearts Club Band* cover is ruthlessly parodied for *We're Only In It For The Money*. The music is a masterpiece of tape manipulation and editing, as Zappa joins together numerous short recordings into a seamless suite of songs. It includes one of the first examples of sampling on a rock record, as Zappa includes a few seconds of one of his own early recordings, originally issued as being by the Rotations. There are a few edits that Zappa supposedly did not really want to make, such as the removal of controversial wording from one or two tracks, although he was happy to use the result to gain publicity for the record. The

process includes the addition of an excised verse from the track *Mother People* to the end of side one, with the music reversed and edited into a short passage of processed whispering. This is actually referred to on the sleeve, so the edit must have been done before the album's artwork was finalised. Zappa intended that the music on *We're Only In It For The Money* should be considered at the same time as that on the subsequent *Lumpy Gravy* and *Uncle Meat* albums, so that the combined effect of them all is as a single work. This could have been edited differently in detail, Zappa suggests, with an alternate selection of tracks appearing in the albums, compared to the one that was actually chosen for release. This is the beginning of Zappa's much discussed 'conceptual continuity', whereby all his music can be interpreted as being inter-related, as being aspects of one huge many-faceted work. Meanwhile, the music on the third Mothers Of Invention album provides as much listening substance as any of its contemporaries, including the Beatles, with songs that manage to combine styles as diverse as fifties doo-wop and the avant garde within a remarkably listenable whole.

```
US release    March 1968    Verve    V6-5045X
UK release    March 1968    Verve    (S)VLP 9199
```

1. Are You Hung Up
2. Who Needs The Peace Corps
3. Concentration Moon
4. Mom & Dad
5. Bow Tie Daddy
6. Harry, You're A Beast
7. What's The Ugliest Part Of Your Body?
8. Absolutely Free
9. Flower Punk
10. Hot Poop

11. Nasal Retentive Calliope Music
12. Let's Make The Water Turn Black
13. The Idiot Bastard Son
14. Lonely Little Girl
15. Take Your Clothes Off When You Dance
16. What's The Ugliest Part Of Your Body? (Reprise)
17. Mother People
18. The Chrome Plated Megaphone of Destiny

All compositions by Frank Zappa

Frank Zappa: guitar, piano, vocals, producer / Ian Underwood: keyboards, woodwinds / Bunk Gardner: woodwinds, voice / Euclid James Motorhead Sherwood: baritone and soprano saxophones / Roy Estrada: bass guitar, vocals / Billy Mundi: drums, vocals / Jimmy Carl Black: drums, trumpet, vocals / Pamela Zarubica (Suzy Creamcheese): vocals / Dick Barber: noises / Eric Clapton, Gary Kellgren, Spider Barbour, Dick Kunc, Vicki Kellgren, Ronnie Williams : voice / Sid Sharp: conductorl

THE GREAT SOCIETY   CONSPICUOUS ONLY IN ITS ABSENCE

```
US release    March 1968    Columbia    CS 9624
UK release    March 1968    CBS         (S) 63476
```

1. Sally Go Round The Roses (Lona Stevens/Zelma Sanders)
2. Didn't Think So (Grace Slick)
3. Grimly Forming (Peter Vandergelder)
4. Somebody To Love (Darby Slick)
5. Father Bruce (Darby, Grace, Jerry Slick/David Miner)
6. Outlaw Blues (Bob Dylan)
7. Often As I May (Grace Slick)
8. Arbitration (Peter Vandergelder)
9. White Rabbit (Grace Slick)

Grace Slick: vocals, keyboards, bass guitar / Darby Slick: guitar / David Miner: guitar / Peter Vandergelder: bass guitar, soprano saxophone / Jerry Slick: drums / Peter Abram: producer

The Great Society was one of the pioneering San Francisco bands, incorporating improvisation into its performances of folk-rock material. It was offered a recording contract with Columbia, but before it could make an album, singer Grace Slick accepted an offer to join Jefferson Airplane. Without her, the remaining members of the Great Society, which included Grace's husband Jerry and his brother Darby, decided to disband. *Conspicuous Only In Its Absence* is an ironically titled live album, recorded at the Matrix in San Francisco some two years before its release. It is clear that the band would have become one of the genre's big names. The concert has not been professionally recorded, but the result is to make the music sound exactly as groups did sound when playing in clubs at the time, when using a decent p.a. system to enable the vocals to be heard properly. Interest naturally focuses on the two songs that Grace Slick took with her when becoming Jefferson Airplane's lead singer. *Somebody To Love* is much less energetic than the well known Airplane version, but still manages to make a strong impression. In some ways, *White Rabbit* is more interesting than its later incarnation, because the Great Society uses the song as the climax for a lengthy modal improvisation in which Peter Vandergelder hands his bass guitar to Grace Slick and holds forth on soprano saxophone. The members of the band must have been extremely disappointed to see their dreams of stardom shattered, but we do at least have this live recording as a memento of a band that had an important part to play in the rock music of the mid-sixties and not just as the original home of Jefferson Airplane's famous singer.

THE DRIFTERS   GOLDEN HITS

| US release | March 1968 | Atlantic | SD 8153 |
| UK release | May 1968 | Atlantic | 588/587 103 |

1. There Goes My Baby (Ben E King/George Treadwell/Lover Patterson)
2. True Love, True Love (Doc Pomus/Mort Shuman)
3. Dance With Me (Elmo Glick/George Treadwell/Irving Nahan/Lewis Lebish)
4. This Magic Moment (Doc Pomus/Mort Shuman)
5. Save The Last Dance For Me (Doc Pomus/Mort Shuman)
6. I Count The Tears (Doc Pomus/Mart Shuman)
7. Some Kind Of Wonderful (Gerry Goffin/Carole King)
8. Up On The Roof (Gerry Goffin/Carole King)
9. On Broadway (Jerry Leiber/Mike Stoller/Cynthia Weil/Barry Mann)
10. Under The Boardwalk (Arthur Resnick/Kenny Young)
11. I've Got Sand In My Shoes (Arthur Resnick/Kenny Young)
12. Saturday Night At The Movies (Barry Mann/Cynthia Weil)

Ben E King (1,3,4,5,6), Johnny Lee Williams (2), Rudy Lewis (7,8,9), Johnny Moore (10,11,12), Charlie Thomas, Dock Green (1-7), Eugene Pearson (8-12), Elsbeary Hobbs (1-3), Tommy Evans (4-8), Johnny Terry (9-12): vocals / Abdul Samad: guitar / Stan Applebaum: arranger (1-6) / Ray Ellis: arranger (7) / Gary Sherman: arranger (8-10) / Teacho Wilshire: arranger (11,12) / Jerry Leiber, Mike Stoller: producer (1-9) / Bert Berns: producer (10-12)

The golden hits included on the album of the same name date from 1959 until 1964, when a succession of different lead singers (primarily Ben E King, Rudy Lewis, and Johnny Moore) delivered some classy pop material with considerable success in both the US and the UK. The original Drifters sang doo-wop in the fifties, but the entire line-up was replaced towards the end of the decade, to perform with a smoother vocal group sound, just as doo-wop began to lose its popularity. The new Drifters became the main influence on the vocal groups recorded by Berry Gordy on his Tamla and Motown labels, although Ben E King and his colleagues were not given much of a dance beat to work with. The harmony pop favoured by the Drifters was distinctly out of place next to the music styles making an impact in 1968, yet *Golden Hits* sold well in the US and the UK and the group did manage to gain a few more chart hits during the seventies.

SCOTT WALKER   SCOTT 2

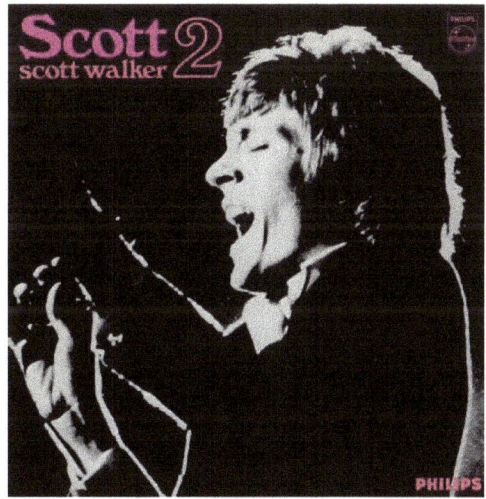

| UK release | April 1968 | Philips | (S)BL 7840 |
| US release | April 1968 | Smash | SRS-67106 |

1. Jackie (Jacques Brel/Gérard Jouannest/Mort Shuman)
2. Best Of Both Worlds (Don Black/Mark London)
3. Black Sheep Boy (Tim Hardin)
4. The Amorous Humphrey Plugg (Scott Walker)
5. Next (Jacques Brel/Mort Shuman)
6. The Girls From The Streets (Scott Walker)
7. Plastic Palace People (Scott Walker)
8. Wait Until Dark (Henry Mancini/Jay Livingston/Raymond Evans)
9. The Girls And The Dogs (Jacques Brel/Gérard Jouannest/Mort Shuman)
10. Windows Of The World (Burt Bacharach/Hal David)
11. The Bridge (Scott Walker)
12. Come Next Spring (Lenny Adelson/Max Steiner)

Scott Walker: vocals / Peter Knight: arranger (6,10) / Reg Guest: arranger (3,4,9) / Wally Stott: arranger (1,2,12) / John Franz: producer

Scott Walker's second solo album continues the style of the first and reached number one in the UK album chart. *Jackie* was issued as a single and was a small hit, but prevented from doing better by a BBC ban, due to its controversial lyrics. Walker finds another set of dramatic, emotional songs to cover, including four more by Jacques Brel, although the most interesting performances are, once again, the songs that he composed himself. The evocative *Plastic Palace People*, composed with a repeating structure of three linked melodic sections, is particularly striking. *Scott 2* confirms Scott Walker as a maverick artist, combining the roles of singer songwriter and interpretive singer in a profoundly unusual manner, at least as far as rock music is concerned.

THE MONKEES   THE BIRDS THE BEES & THE MONKEES

The fifth album by the Monkees reverts to the original idea of providing music relating to the television series rather than to a real group and only one track, *Daydream Believer*, features all four Monkees. Even then, most of the instruments are played by session musicians. This is the only track on which Peter Tork appears at all. *The Birds The Bees & The Monkees* was the least successful Monkees album thus far, and did not appear in the UK album chart, but it still sold a million copies. *Daydream Believer* and *Valleri*, which are easily the best tracks on the album, were issued as singles and were both hits.

| US release | April 1968 | Colgems | COS/COM-109 |
| UK release | April 1968 | RCA Victor | SF/RD 7948 |

1. Dream World (Davy Jones/Steve Pitts)
2. Auntie's Municipal Court (Mike Nesmith)
3. We Were Made For Each Other (Carole Bayer/George Fischoff)
4. Tapioca Tundra (Mike Nesmith)
5. Daydream Believer (John Stewart)
6. Writing Wrongs (Mike Nesmith)
7. I'll Be Back Up On My Feet (Denny Randell/Sandy Linzer)
8. The Poster (Davy Jones/Steve Pitts)
9. P.O. Box 9847 (Tommy Boyce/Bobby Hart)
10. Magnolia Simms (Mike Nesmith)
11. Valleri (Tommy Boyce/Bobby Hart)
12. Zor And Sam (John and Bill Chadwick)

Davy Jones: vocals (1,3,5,8,11) / Micky Dolenz: vocals, percussion (2,5,7,9,12) / Peter Tork: piano (5) / Mike Nesmith: vocals, guitar. percussion, keyboards (2,4,5,6,10) / Michael Deasy: guitar (1,3,7,8) / Al Hendrickson: guitar (1,3) / Jerry McGee: guitar (1,3,9,11) / Keith Allison: guitar (2,12) / Bill Chadwick (2,12) / James Burton: guitar (3) / Al Casey: guitar (7,8) / Dennis Budimir: guitar (7) / Howard Roberts: guitar (8) / Louie Shelton: guitar (9,11) / Don Randi: keyboards (1,8) / Michael Melvoin: keyboards (3,7,12) / Bobby Hart: keyboards (9) / Paul T.Smith: keyboards (10) / Max Bennett: bass guitar (1,3,7,8,10,12) / Richard Dey: bass guitar (2,6,12) / Chip Douglas: producer, bass guitar (5,12) / Lyle Ritz: bass guitar (8) / Joe Osborn: bass guitar (9,11) / Earl Palmer: drums (1,3,7,10) / Eddie Hoh: drums (2,4,5,6,12) / Hal Blaine: drums (8,12) / Billy Lewis: drums (9,11) / strings, brass, percussion

THE JIMI HENDRIX EXPERIENCE SMASH HITS

| UK release | April 1968 | Track | 613/612 004 |
| US release | July 1969 | Reprise | MS 2025 some different tracks |

1. Purple Haze
2. Fire
3. The Wind Cries Mary
4. Can You See Me
5. 51st Anniversary
6. Hey Joe (Billy Roberts)
7. Stone Free
8. The Stars That Play With Laughing Sam's Dice
9. Manic Depression
10. Highway Chile
11. The Burning Of The Midnight Lamp
12. Foxy Lady

All compositions by Jim Hendrix except where stated

Jimi Hendrix: guitar, vocals , harpsichord (11) / Noel Redding: bass guitar / Mitch Mitchell: drums / The Breakaways: vocals (6) / The Sweet Inspirations (Cissy Houston, Sylvia Shermwell, Estelle Brown, Myrna Smith): vocals (11) / Chas Chandler: producer

With Jimi Hendrix having produced four hit singles, but not apparently planning to make any more, Track decided to issue a compilation album, including both sides of the singles and filling up the space with four tracks from *Are You Experienced*. Several months after first being issued, the singles no longer have the power to shock, but they remain outstanding demonstrations of what Jimi Hendrix can do with an electric guitar. The US edition of the album was released over a year later and is an inferior selection. It has only one B-side (*Stone Free*) and both sides of the fourth UK single *(The Burning Of The Midnight Lamp)* are missing altogether, although the album does have a previously unreleased alternative version of *Red House*.

McGOUGH & McGEAR

| UK release | April 1968 | Parlophone | PCS/PMC 7047 |

Not released in US

1. So Much In Love (Roger McGough/Mike McGear)
2. Little Bit Of Heaven (Roger McGough)
3. Basement Flat (Roger McGough/Mike McGear)
4. From Frink, A Life In The Day Of and Summer With Monica (Andy Roberts/Roger McGough); including Anji (Davy Graham) and Moanin' (Bobby Timmons)
5. Come Close And Sleep Now (Roger McGough)
6. Yellow Book (Roger McGough/Mike McGear)
7. House In My Hear (Roger McGough/Mike McGear)
8. Mr Tickle (Mike McGear)
9. Living Room (Mike McGear)
10. Do You Remember (Roger McGough/Mike McGear)
11. Please Don't Run Too Fast (Mike McGear)
12. Ex Art Student (Roger McGough/Mike McGear)

Roger McGough: vocals / Mike McGear: vocals / Andy Roberts: guitar (4,5) / Jimi Hendrix: guitar (1) / Paul McCartney: vocals, piano, drums, producer / Jane Asher: vocals / Noel Redding: bass guitar (1,12) / Mitch Mitchell: drums (1,12) / Graham Nash: vocals (1) / Dave Mason: sitar (12) / Wib Bennett: flute (12) / prob. Mike Evans: tenor saxophone

Paul McCartney produced this album by his brother Mike McGear and poet Roger McGough, with very occasional help from a few of his famous friends. *So Much In Love* and *Ex Art Student* are completed songs, with the Jimi Hendrix Experience and Traffic's Dave Mason very much in evidence, and they make the first track at least into something rather memorable. The rest consists of poems by Roger McGough or ideas by Mike McGear with minimal support by Andy Roberts and Paul McCartney himself and an occasional unnamed saxophonist. The album is essentially a dry run for the better rehearsed Scaffold records, the work of a comedy and poetry trio in which McGough and McGear were joined by John Gorman. It provides an early commercial outlet for Roger McGough, who was to develop into arguably Britain's finest poet, but he is rather better served by the first album credited to the Liverpool Scene or else the later albums by Grimms.

THE ZOMBIES   ODESSEY AND ORACLE

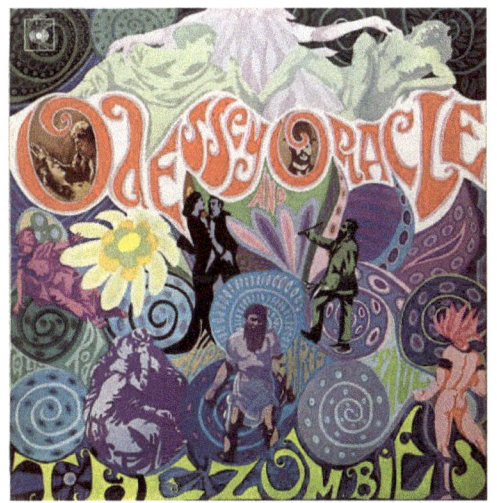

```
UK release       April 1968       CBS        (S) 63280
US release       April 1968       Columbia   TES 4013

1. Care Of Cell 44 (Rod Argent)
2. A Rose For Emily (Rod Argent)
3. Maybe After He's Gone (Chris White)
4. Beechwood Park (Chris White)
5. Brief Candles (Chris White)
6. Hung Up On A Dream (Rod Argent)

7. Changes (Chris White)
8. I Want Her She Wants Me (Rod Argent)
9. This Will Be Our Year (Chris White)
10. Butcher's Tale (Western Front 1914) (Chris White)
11. Friends Of Mine (Chris White)
12. Time Of The Season (Rod Argent)

Colin Blunstone: vocals / Rod Argent: keyboards, vocals / Paul
Atkinson: guitar, vocals / Chris White: bass guitar, vocals / Hugh
Grundy: drums, vocals / The Zombies, Ken Jones: producer
```

The Zombies were unable to achieve any chart success after their initial hit, *She's Not There*, but a new record company signed them anyway and allowed the group to make a second album. *Odessey And Oracle* (the spelling mistake is the fault of the sleeve designer) is a much greater album than anyone outside of the group itself might have expected. Chris White and Rod Argent have developed into world-class songwriters and between them create a set of songs in a post-*Sgt Pepper* style that sounds to be the strongest to have been issued by anyone since the Beatles themselves. Rod Argent is able to coax a huge range of sounds from his various keyboard instruments, which include a mellotron, here used more extensively than on any album so far produced. As a result, there are hardly any session musicians, although horns are added to *This Will Be Our Year*. The atypical *Time Of The Season*, sounding like a seventies rock song, was issued as a single and eventually became a very big US hit, but not until a year later. By this time, the Zombies had disbanded and were no longer in a position to gain any further success on the back of their hit. Rod Argent, however, formed a new band named after himself to make music in the style of *Time Of The Season*, while Colin Blunstone achieved some headway as a solo performer.

DONOVAN   A GIFT FROM A FLOWER TO A GARDEN

```
UK release       April 1968       Pye       N(S)PL 20000
US release       December 1967    Epic      L2N 6071/B2N 171    also issued as two separate LPs.
                                            WEAR YOUR LOVE LIKE HEAVEN and FOR LITTLE ONES

1. Wear Your Love Like Heaven              11. Song Of The Naturalist's Wife
2. Mad John's Escape                       12. The Enchanted Gypsy
3. Skip-a-long Sam                         13. Voyage Into The Golden Screen
4. Sun                                     14. Isle Of Islay
5. There Was A Time                        15. The Mandolin Man And His Secret
6. Oh Gosh                                 16. Lay Of The Last Tinker
7. Little Boy In Corduroy                  17. The Tinker And The Crab
8. Under The Greenwood Tree (words by William Shakespeare)   18. Widow With Shawl (A Portrait)
9. The Land Of Doesn't Have To Be          19. The Lullaby Of Spring
10. Someone Singing                        20. The Magpie
                                           21. Starfish-on-the-Toast
                                           22. Epistle To Derroll

All compositions by Donovan Leitch

Donovan: vocals, guitar, harmonica / Eric Leese: guitar / Mike O'Neill: keyboards / Harold McNair: flute / Mike Carr:
vibraphone / Cliff Barton: bass guitar / Jack Bruce: bass guitar (10) / Ken Baldock: bass / Keith Webb: drums /
Tony Carr: drums, percussion / Candy John Carr: percussion / Mickie Most: producer
```

Having established himself as a successful pop artist, no longer bound by whatever constraints the world of folk music might impose, Donovan released an extravagant double album, housed within a box. In the US, the boxed set was also released as two separate records, but this was not done in the UK. Donovan has not lost the inspiration he showed on *Sunshine Superman* and *Mellow Yellow* and delivers twenty-two songs full of his accustomed charm and melodic appeal. Most of the music is produced by Donovan himself, despite the Mickie Most credit. The two albums do indeed have different characters: the first disc has its music presented as if played by an established group, while its companion is simpler, with Donovan singing and playing his acoustic guitar with only a minimal support from Harold McNair's flute and a little percussion. His singles released during this time are not included, but *A Gift From A Flower To A Garden* manages to be thoroughly impressive even without them.

SIMON & GARFUNKEL   BOOKENDS

| US release | April 1968 | Columbia | KCS 9529 |
| UK release | April 1968 | CBS | (S) 63101 |

1. Bookends Theme
2. Save The Life Of My Child
3. America
4. Overs
5. Voices Of Old People
6. Old Friends
7. Bookends Theme

8. Fakin' It
9. Punky's Dilemma
10. Mrs Robinson
11. A Hazy Shade Of Winter
12. At The Zoo

All compositions by Paul Simon

Paul Simon: vocals, guitar, producer / Art Garfunkel: vocals, percussion, producer / Larry Knechtel: keyboards, bass guitar (10) / John Simon: synthesizer (2) / Joe Osborn: bass guitar / Hal Blaine: drums / Jimmie Haskell: arranger / Roy Halee: producer

Bookends would be a great album simply for including Paul Simon's most sublime song, but *America* is surrounded by other songs that are almost as good. For the most part, Simon's acoustic guitar is still the dominant instrument, but *Save The Life Of My Child* is underscored by a dense synthesizer part and a gospel choir that takes the song somewhere else altogether. *Fakin' It* utilises as its launch point the musical train simulation that ends the Beatles' *Strawberry Fields Forever* so that the two songs could easily be pasted together to make a single work. Whether the use of an obvious quote to preface a song called *Fakin' It* is significant is not clear. Meanwhile, *Voices of Old People* is exactly what it says and not a song at all, but it dovetails beautifully with the song *Old Friends* and has been carefully arranged to withstand repeated listening. *Old Friends* itself incorporates a chamber orchestral section, lurching into dissonance and out again with considerable effectiveness. The duo was rewarded for a particularly fine piece of musical art by its biggest sales success yet.

MOBY GRAPE   WOW/GRAPE JAM

| US release | April 1968 | Columbia | CS9613/CXS3 |
| UK release (WOW only) | April 1968 | CBS | (S)63271 |

1. The Place And The Time (Jerry Miller/Don Stevenson)
2. Murder In My Heart For The Judge (Jerry Miller/Don Stevenson)
3. Bitter Wind (Bob Mosley)
4. Can't Be So Bad (Jerry Miller/Don Stevenson)
5. Just Like Gene Autry: A Foxtrot (Skip Spence)

6. He (Peter Lewis)
7. Motorcycle Irene (Skip Spence)
8. Three-Four (Jerry Miller/Skip Spence)
9. Funky-Tunk (Skip Spence)
10. Rose Colored Eyes (Bob Mosley)
11. Miller's Blues (Jerry Miller)
12. Naked, If I Want To (Jerry Miller)

13. Never (Bob Mosley)
14. Boysenberry Jam
15. Black Currant Jam

16. Marmalade
17. The Lake (Michael Hayworth, Moby Grape)

Jerry Miller: guitar, vocals / Peter Lewis: guitar, vocals / Skip Spence: guitar, vocals, piano / Bob Mosley: bass guitar, vocals / Don Stevenson: drums, vocals / Al Kooper: piano (15) / Mike Bloomfield: piano (16) / Michael Hayworth: vocals (17) / David Rubinson: arranger, producer

The second album by Moby Grape does not quite reach the heights of the first, but it still includes some fine songs. *Can't Be So Bad* adds a horn arrangement to the supercharged guitar sound that was a major feature of the first album, while *Murder In My Heart For The Judge* employs a plunging guitar to underscore its verse and *He* adds a poignant string part to a folk ballad to great effect. The album finishes with a brief reference to a track from the first album, now transformed with a fuzz guitar. As before, however, the group is close to being overwhelmed by the level of hype applied to its promotion. The first album was almost entirely issued on a set of singles; this time there is a bonus record containing a set of rather uninspired jam sessions. One is an exercise in frustration – having gained the attention of one of the premier American guitarists of the time, Mike Bloomfield, the group sticks him in front of a piano, while Jerry Miller, a man with half his talent, struts around on guitar. The slow blues, *Never,* has some lyric phrases that Robert Plant borrowed for Led Zeppelin's *Since I've Been Loving You,* but the song structures are different and it is likely that the phrases are being borrowed by Bob Mosley too from an earlier blues performance. On the main album, the last track on side one requires the listener to change the speed of the record deck to 78 rpm for a song that attempts, somewhat pointlessly, to capture the ambience of a much older era.

SLY & THE FAMILY STONE   DANCE TO THE MUSIC

```
US release    April 1968      Epic         BN 26371/LN 24371
UK release    August 1968     Direction    8-63412        different
cover

1. Dance To The Music
2. Higher
3. I Ain't Got Nobody (For Real)
4. Dance To The Medley

5. Ride The Rhythm
6. Color Me True
7. Are You Ready
8. Don't Burn Baby
9. Never Will I Fall In Love Again

All compositions by Sylvester Stewart (Sly Stone)

Sly Stone: vocals, keyboards, guitar, harmonica, producer / Freddie
Stone: guitar, vocals / Rose Stone: keyboards, vocals / Cynthia
Robinson: trumpet, vocals / Jerry Martini: tenor saxophone / Larry
Graham: bass guitar, vocals / Greg Errico: drums / Vet Stone, Mary
McCreary, Elva Mouton: vocals
```

Dance To The Music was the first big hit by Sly and the Family Stone, a deliberately commercial song intended to make an impact. It is, however, by far the weakest track on the album named after it, and is not improved by being extended into a marathon on the track entitled *Dance To The Medley*. The rest of the album, however, employs driving rhythms and an urgent brass section, achieving the same kind of result as in the music of the Electric Flag, albeit without the guitar solos. This is not funk, as defined by the music of James Brown, but as a fusion of soul music with rock it works very well.

ARS NOVA

```
US release    April 1968      Elektra      EKS-74020
UK release    April 1968      Elektra      EKS 74020/EKL 4020

1.  Pavan For My Lady (Wyatt Day)
2.  General Clover Ends A War (Gregory Copeland/Wyatt Day)
         Entracte: Le Messe Notre Dame (Guillaume De Machaut)
3.  And How Am I To Know (Wyatt Day)
         Entracte: Dancer (Maury Baker)
4.  Album In Your Mind (Jon Pierson/Wyatt Day)
5.  Zarathustra (Richard Strauss/Maury Baker)

6.  Fields Of People (Jon Pierson/Wyatt Day)
         Entracte: Vita De L'Alma Mia (Claudio Monteverdi)
7.  Automatic Love (Wyatt Day)
         Entracte: A Thought (Jon Pierson/Jonathan Raskin)
8.  I Wrapped Her In Ribbons (Gregory Copeland/Wyatt Day)
         Entracte: Ada Wulff November 12 1956 (Wyatt Day)
9.  Song To The City (Gregory Copeland/Wyatt Day)
         Entracte: Aquel Cabellero (Anonymous)
10. March Of The Mad Duke's Circus (Gregory Copeland/Wyatt Day)

Jon Pierson: vocals, trombone / Wyatt Day: vocals, guitar, keyboards /
Giovanni Papalia: guitar / Maury Baker: drums, percussion, organ / Bill
Folwell: vocals, trumpet, bass / Jonathan Raskin: vocals, guitar, bass
guitar / Paul A Rothchild: producer
```

Two members of Ars Nova play brass instruments, played in a formal manner without any jazz influence, and these have a considerable presence in the group's music, giving it a very distinctive sound. They dominate the medieval bits and pieces that the group incorporates within its own songs, often in the form of concluding sections referred to as *Entractes*. A more modern classical influence is displayed on *Zarathustra*, which presents a rock instrumental loosely based on the Richard Strauss introduction used so effectively within the soundtrack to the film 2001: A Space Odyssey. This line-up of Ars Nova fell apart following a disastrous performance supporting the Doors, the shame of which is that the group's intricate, imaginative music is far more interesting than that of the more famous group, even if it does not have any member able to match the charisma of Jim Morrison. *Fields Of People* was subsequently recorded by the Move, whose members recognised a good song when they heard it.

QUICKSILVER MESSENGER SERVICE

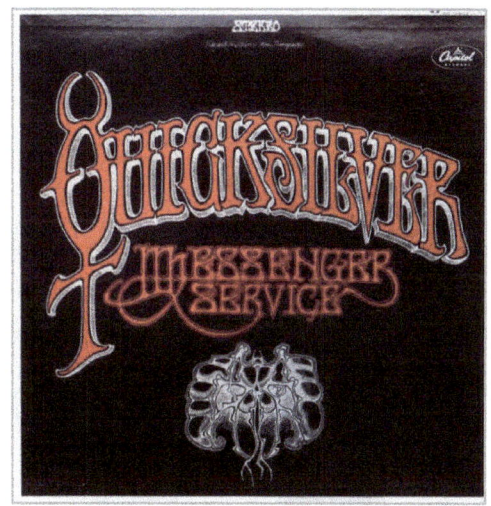

The first album by Californian group Quicksilver Messenger Service sounds like the missing link between Jefferson Airplane and the Grateful Dead. Although the group does not have a singer to compete with Grace Slick or Marty Balin, its instrumental playing is a match for anyone in the rival groups. Quicksilver Messenger Service has two skilled guitarists, who frequently play together to create a double lead effect. One of them, John Cipollina, uses a wide finger vibrato that makes his playing immediately identifiable. The lengthy *The Fool* is what gives the album its greatness. David Freiberg overdubs his viola at the beginning and end of the track, which has some of the character of a jam except that it is clearly structured to make the music varied and continually compelling. The album has little of the avant garde innovation that helps to make the albums *After Bathing At Baxters* and *Anthem Of The Sun* (soon to be released at this point) so vital, but it remains a triumphant vindication of San Francisco's claim to be a centre of musical excellence.

| US release | May 1968 | Capitol | ST-2904 |
| UK release | May 1968 | Capitol | (S)T 2904 |

1. Pride Of Man (Hamilton Camp)
2. Light Your Windows (David Freiberg/Gary Duncan)
3. Dino's Song (Dino Valenti)
4. Gold And Silver (Gary Duncan/Steve Schuster)
5. It's Been Too Long (Ron Polte)
6. The Fool (David Freiberg/Gary Duncan)

Gary Duncan: guitar, vocals / John Cipollina: guitar / David Freiberg: bass guitar, viola, vocals / Greg Elmore: drums / Nick Gravenites, Harvey Brooks, Pete Welding: producer

THE WEST COAST POP ART EXPERIMENTAL BAND
VOL.3 A CHILD'S GUIDE TO GOOD & EVIL

| US release | May 1968 | Reprise | RS 6298 |
| UK release | May 1968 | Reprise | RSLP 6298 |

1. Eighteen Is Over The Hill (Bob Markley/Ron Morgan)
2. In The Country (Bob Markley/Shaun Harris)
3. Ritual #1 (Bob Markley/Shaun Harris/John Ware)
4. Our Drummer Always Plays In The Nude (Bob Markley/Shaun Harris)
5. As The World Rises And Falls (Bob Markley/Ron Morgan)
6. Until The Poorest People Have Money To Spend (Bob Markley/Shaun Harris)
7. Watch Yourself (Buddy Guy/Robert Yaezel)
8. A Child's Guide To Good And Evil (Bob Markley/Shaun Harris)
9. Ritual #2 (Bob Markley/Shaun Harris)
10. A Child Of A Few Hours Is Burning To Death (Bob Markley/Ron Morgan)
11. As Kind As Summer (Bob Markley/Shaun Harris/Roger Bryant)
12. Anniversary Of Wotld War III (Bob Markley)

Bob Markley: percussion, vocals, producer / Shaun Harris: vocals, bass guitar / Ron Morgan: guitar, sitar, vocals / Hal Blaine: drums / Jimmy Bowen: producer

There is not much going on here that could really be described as experimental and there is no question of making any comparison with the work of the Velvet Underground (as the group hoped), but the third volume of the West Coast Pop Art Experimental Band's series of albums is nevertheless a very fine psychedelic folk-rock record. The song titles seem designed to give the group an intellectual depth that it does not always have, but the final track, titled *Anniversary of World War III* and completely silent, does make a very effective point with regard to the probable state of the world after a nuclear war. The record is undoubtedly the most durable of the group's albums, with songs that are made to sound very attractive with lush group harmonies, and it ultimately proves that by sheer persistence, the West Coast Pop Art Experimental Band has very definitely learned its craft.

CREEDENCE CLEARWATER REVIVAL

| US release | May 1968 | Fantasy | 8382 |
| UK release | May 1968 | Liberty | LBS 83259 |

1. I Put A Spell On You (Herb Slotkin/Screamin' Jay Hawkins)
2. The Working Man (John Fogerty)
3. Suzie Q (Dale Hawkins/Eleanor Broadwater/Stanley Lewis)
4. Ninety-Nine And A Half (Won't Do) (Steve Cropper/Wilson Pickett)
5. Get Down Woman (John Fogerty)
6. Porterville (John Fogerty)
7. Gloomy (John Fogerty)
8. Walk On The Water (John and Tom Fogerty)

John Fogerty: vocals, guitar, percussion / Tom Fogerty: guitar, vocals / Stu Cook: bass guitar, vocals / Doug Clifford: drums, vocals / Saul Zaentz: producer

The group formerly known as the Golliwogs changed its name and promptly scored chart successes with the *Suzie Q* single and this accompanying album. Having 'Revival' as part of its title seems appropriate because the group represents a return to a simpler kind of rock music than that being played by the San Francisco musicians or else by those still in thrall to the sounds and methods of *Sgt Pepper's Lonely Hearts Club Band*. Even John Fogerty's delight in playing long guitar solos and the consequent splitting of *Suzie Q* in two to enable it to be accommodated on a single does not take very much away from the group's liking for straight-ahead rhythms and a basic guitar-bass-drums sound. The fact that the album includes new versions of two songs from the fifties might suggest that Creedence Clearwater Revival is really attempting a return to the original rock 'n' roll style, but the group manages to sound considerably removed from that, if only due to the guitar soloing. It is not immediately apparent that Creedence Clearwater Revival would become one of the most successful groups of the late sixties, but that was nevertheless what happened.

ARCHIE SHEPP   THE MAGIC OF JU-JU

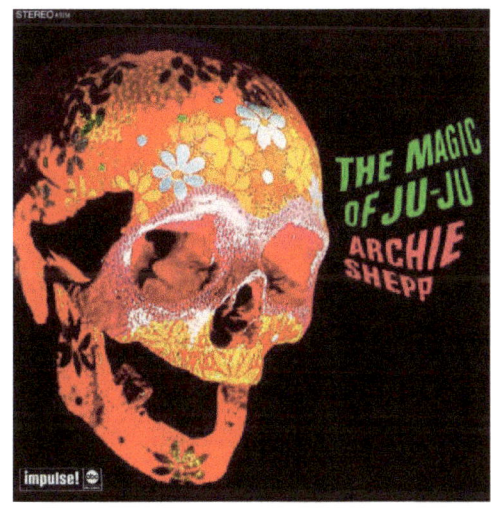

| US release | May 1968 | Impulse | AS-9154 |
| UK release | May 1968 | Impulse | IMPL 8030 |

1. The Magic Of Ju-Ju
2. You're What This Day Is All About
3. Shazam!
4. Sorry 'Bout That

All compositions by Archie Shepp

Archie Shepp: tenor saxophone / Martin Banks: trumpet, flugelhorn / Mike Zwerin: trombone / Reggie Workman: bass / Norman Connors: drums / Beaver Harris: drums / Frank Charles, Dennis Charles, Ed Blackwell: percussion / Bob Thiele: producer

The two sides of *The Magic Of Ju-Ju* are a little different in character, although they are united by the emotional, virtuoso playing of the tenor saxophone by Archie Shepp, who is the only soloist. The title track, occupying the whole of side one, establishes an African rhythm, complete with traditional talking drums, over which Shepp treats the listener to a frenzied and highly emotional outpouring. Eventually the bass and the kit drums join in, which has the effect of increasing the rhythmic density. The other horns contribute a repetitive riff for just the last minute. By comparison, the pieces on side two sound almost conventional, like soul jazz with slightly more ragged playing than the genre is used to. They provide an effective balance for the album as a whole, although the African flavour of the first side is what gives the album its point and its purpose.

GARY BURTON / CARLA BLEY   A GENUINE TONG FUNERAL

| US release | May 1968 | RCA Victor | LSP-3988 |
| UK release | February 1969 | RCA Victor | SF 8015 |

1. The Opening / Interlude: Shovels / The Survivors / Grave Train
2. Death Rolls
3. Morning Part One
4. Interlude: Lament / Intermission Music
5. Silent Spring
6. Fanfare / Mother Of The Dead Man
7. Some Dirge
8. Morning Part Two
9. The New Funeral March
10. The New National Anthem / The Survivors

All compositions by Carla Bley

Gary Burton: vibraphone / Larry Coryell: guitar / Steve Swallow: bass / Bob Moses: drums / Steve Lacy: soprano saxophone / Mike Mantler: trumpet / Gato Barbieri: tenor saxophone / Jimmy Knepper: trombone / Howard Johnson: tuba, baritone saxophone / Carla Bley: piano, organ, conductor / Brad McCuen: producer

A Genuine Tong Funeral is an extended work by Carla Bley, described by her as "a dark opera without words". Given the sombre brass chords that open the proceedings and the minor key writing that follows, with the eloquent solos played by the various musicians acting as the statements of characters, one can understand what she means. The music skilfully interweaves the composed and improvised elements to the extent that it is difficult to tell which is which, although the outstanding solo work by all concerned is presumably improvised. It is remarkable that Gary Burton is prepared to hand over control of an album issued in his own name to someone else, especially when his own playing features comparatively infrequently. In retrospect, however, it is clear that he knew he was participating in a genuinely great piece of art. Carla Bley's career was given a tremendous boost by having an established and acclaimed jazz performer becoming involved, but equally Gary Burton's own standing was enhanced by his key role in the first major work by someone who turned out to be one of the greatest composers working in jazz. Drummer Bob Moses fell out with Carla Bley during the recording and is credited as 'Lonesome Dragon' on the album sleeve, but has since expressed his great admiration for Ms Bley and her music.

JOHNNY CASH   AT FOLSOM PRISON

Johnny Cash scored a hit in 1956 with *I Walk The Line*, that could be taken for rockabilly, but he very quickly reverted to being a pure country performer. Carl Perkins, who had been more influential as a rock 'n' roll artist (he wrote *Blue Suede Shoes*, after all) was content to work as the lead guitarist in Johnny Cash's band. Cash's career as a country singer was given a huge boost by his performance for the long-term inmates at the maximum security Folsom Prison in California and the subsequent chart success of the album of his concert. It is easy to see why Cash went down well at the prison, with his tough, macho persona and an already well-known song, *Folsom Prison Blues*, sympathising with the prison inmates. Cash and his band perform their songs in a very straightforward manner, with no concessions to rock or any other music that is not country, and he avoids too the sweetening effect that would have been produced by using a pedal steel guitar. Carried by the positive publicity, the album eventually achieved three million sales in the US, though without reaching any higher than number thirteen in the album chart, and it even managed half a million sales in the UK.

```
US release       May 1968    Columbia    CS 9639
UK release       May 1968    CBS         (S)63308
```

1. Folsom Prison Blues (Johnny Cash)
2. Dark As The Dungeon (Merle Travis)
3. I Still Miss Someone (Johnny Cash/Roy Cash Jr)
4. Cocaine Blues (T.J.Arnall)
5. 25 Minutes To Go (Shel Silverstein)
6. Orange Blossom Special (Ervin Rouse)
7. The Long Back Veil (Danny Dill/Marijohn Wilkin)
8. Send A Picture Of Mother (Johnny Cash)
9. The Wall (Harlan Howard)
10. Dirty Old Egg-Sucking Dog (Jack Clement)
11. Flushed From The Bathroom Of Your Heart (Jack Clement)
12. Jackson (Billy Ed Wheeler/Gaby Rodgers)
13. Give My Love To Rose (Johnny Cash)
14. I Got Stripes (Charlie Williams/Johnny Cash)
15. Green, Green Grass Of Home (Curly Putnam)
16. Greystone Chapel (Glen Sherley)

Johnny Cash: vocals, guitar, harmonica / June Carter: vocals / Carl Perkins: guitar, vocals / Luther Perkins: guitar / Marshall Grant: bass guitar / W.S.Holland: drums / The Statler Brothers – Lew DeWitt, Don Reid, Harold Reid, Phil Balsley: vocals / Bob Johnston: producer

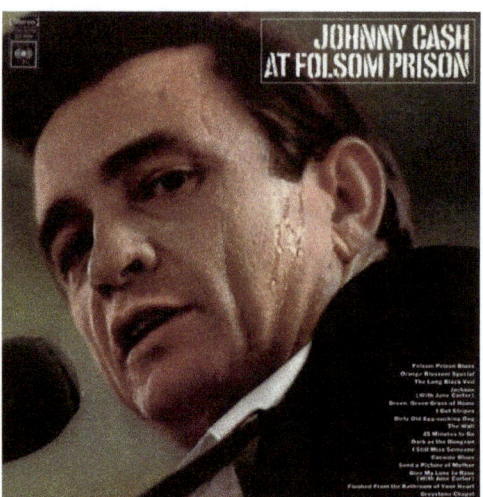

FRANK ZAPPA   LUMPY GRAVY

```
US release       May 1968    Verve    V6-8741
UK release       May 1968    Verve    (S)VLP 9223
```

1. Lumpy Gravy Part I
2. Lumpy Gravy Part II

Composed and produced by Frank Zappa

Paul Smith, Mike Lang, Lincoln Mayorga, Pete Jolly: keyboards / Jim Haynes, Tommy Tedesco, Tony Rizzi, Al Viola, Dennis Budimir: guitar / Bob West, John Balkin, Jimmy Bond, Lyle Ritz, Chuck Berghofer: bass guitar / John Guerin, Frankie Capp, Shelly Manne: drums / Emil Richards, Gene Estes, Alan Estes, Victor Feldman: percussion / Jimmy Zito: trumpet / Kenneth Shroyer: trombone / Arthur Maebe, Vincent De Rosa, Richard Parisi: French horn / Ted Nash, Jules Jacob, John Rotella, Bunk Gardner, Don Christlieb, Gene Cipriano: woodwinds / Alexander Koltun, Tibor Zelig, Ralph Schaeffer, Bernard Kundell, William Kurasch, James Getzoff, Phillip Goldberg, Leonard Selic, Arnold Belnick, Leonard Malarsky, Harold Ayres, Jerome J.Reisler, Harry Hyams, Joseph DiFlore, Jerome A.Kessler, Raymond J.Kelly, Joseph Saxon, Jessa Ehrlich, Harold G.Bemko: strings

Lumpy Gravy is the first of Frank Zappa's composed orchestral works to be given a major label release and it was recorded a little before the sessions that produced the Mothers of Invention album, *We're Only In It For The Money*. Blithely ignoring the fact that he was contracted to MGM records, Zappa had intended *Lumpy Gravy* to be issued by Capitol a year earlier, but, not surprisingly, MGM objected. This, however, gave Zappa time to rewrite and improve the work. It is very much a cross-genre affair, with cheerful pop-rock instrumentals sandwiching a continually changing soundscape incorporating speech fragments, more pop-rock elements, and some ferociously avant garde orchestral and percussive writing. It is as though it was composed as the soundtrack to a fast moving cartoon film. Recent CD reissues of *Lumpy Gravy* break the work down into more than twenty sections, each with its own title, which emphasises the way in which the music ricochets around from minute to minute, changing its style each time. It is reported that the musicians involved had assumed they would be playing music of doubtful quality by a dodgy rock guitarist they did not know, but were left with some respect for Frank Zappa after discovering what was actually involved. One of the musicians, Bunk Gardner, is a member of the Mothers of Invention, but presumably the others did not discuss the matter with him. Frank Zappa used the name Abnuceals Emuukha Electric Symphony Orchestra for the ensemble he had hired, but the significance of the name is obscure.

ERIC BURDON & THE ANIMALS   THE TWAIN SHALL MEET

```
US release       May 1968    MGM    SE 4537
UK release       May 1968    MGM    CS 8074
```

1. Monterey
2. Just The Thought (The Animals/Hilton Valentine)
3. Closer To The Truth
4. No Self Pity
5. Orange And Red Beams (Danny McCulloch)
6. Sky Pilot
7. We Love You Lil
8. All Is One

All compositions by the Animals except where stated

Eric Burdon: vocals / Vic Briggs: guitar, sitar / John Weider: guitar, violin / Danny McCulloch: bass guiitar, vocals / Barry Jenkins: drums / unknown horns, woodwinds, strings / Tom Wilson: producer

On the opening *Monterey*, Eric Burdon is still reciting lists of the people he likes, but the rhythmic drive achieved by the bass guitar and the electric sitar playing over everything is terrific. The track is an encouraging start for an album that turns out to be greatly superior to the earlier *Winds Of Change*. Part of the reason might be because Burdon is inclined to let the band play without him. He surrenders the lead vocal to Danny McCulloch on a couple of tracks, while *We Love You Lil* is entirely instrumental. The album continues to be festooned with the trappings of psychedelia, which are starting to sound a little clichéd, but someone is becoming rather good at thinking of novel arrangements to give the band's skills extra focus. This is particularly apparent on *All Is One,* where the momentum is deliberately broken in places by intriguing flute and orchestral string inserts.

THE SMALL FACES   OGDEN'S NUT GONE FLAKE

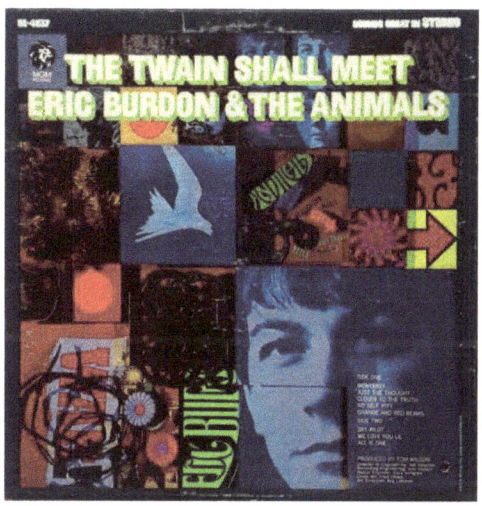

Ogden's Nut Gone Flake, named after a brand of tobacco, is housed in a round cardboard sleeve, opening out into joined circles, easily torn but very effective visually. The gimmick is compounded by having 'Professor' Stanley Unwin do his characteristic gobbledygook narration in between the tracks on side two. Happily, the songs are rather good, so the novelties cannot be accused of trying to divert attention from poor quality music. The title track is an instrumental version of the earlier single, *I've Got Mine,* with added orchestral flourishes, and it functions well as a prologue to the album. The music that follows is part heavy rock and part whimsical cockney humour, a blend that works very well in the creation of a fascinating musical programme. The Small Faces are demonstrating that they have acquired an excellent understanding of the LP medium. *Afterglow* and *Lazy Sunday* were issued as singles, with the latter being idiosyncratic and laced through with the humour, yet one of the group's biggest hits. The album itself went to a well-deserved number one in the UK album charts.

UK release	May 1968	Immediate	IMSP 012
US release	June 1968	Immediate	Z12 52008

1. Ogden's Nut Gone Flake (Small Faces)
2. Afterglow (Ronnie Lane/Steve Marriott)
3. Long Agos And Worlds Apart (Ian McLagan)
4. Rene (Ronnie Lane/Steve Marriott)
5. Song Of A Baker (Ronnie Lane/Steve Marriott)
6. Lazy Sunday (Ronnie Lane/Steve Marriott)
7. Happiness Stan (Ronnie Lane/Steve Marriott)
8. Rollin' Over (Lane/Marriott)
9. The Hungry Intruder (Ian McLagan/Ronnie Lane/Steve Marriott)
10. The Journey (Small Faces)
11. Mad John (Ronnie Lane/Steve Marriott)
12. Happydaystoytown (Small Faces)

Steve Marriott: vocals, guitar, harmonica, keyboards, bass guitar, producer / Ronnie Lane: vocals, bass guitar, guitar, bass, producer / Ian McLagan: keyboards, vocals, guitar, bass guitar / Kenney Jones: drums / Stanley Unwin: narration

P.P.ARNOLD   THE FIRST LADY OF IMMEDIATE

UK release	May 1968	Immediate	IMSP 011
Not released in US			

1. If You Think You're Groovy (Ronnie Lane/Steve Marriott)
2. Something Beautiful Happened (Paul Korda)
3. Born To Be Together (Barry Mann/Cynthia Weil/Phil Spector)
4. Am I Still Dreaming (P.P.Arnold)
5. Though It Hurts Me Badly (P.P.Arnold)
6. The First Cut Is The Deepest (Cat Stevens)
7. Everything Is Gonna Be Alright (Andrew Oldham/David Skinner)
8. Treat Me Like A Lady (P.P.Arnold)
9. Would You Believe (Jeremy Paul)
10. Life Is But Nothing (Andrew Rose/David Skinner)
11. Speak To Me (Andrew Oldham/Mike Hurst)
12. The Time Has Come (Paul Korda)

P.P.Arnold: vocals / musicians include members of the Small Faces (Steve Marriott: vocals, guitar / Ronnie Lane: bass guitar / Ian McLagan: keyboards / Kenney Jones: drums) and the Nice (Keith Emerson: keyboards / David O'List: guitar / Lee Jackson: bass guitar / Ian Hague:drums) / Producers – Steve Marriott and Ronnie Lane (1) / Mike Hurst (2,3,6,9,11,12) / Mick Jagger (4,5,8) / Andrew Oldham (7,10)

Pat Arnold was one of the Ikettes, backing Ike and Tina Turner, but following a tour of the UK in late 1966 she decided to try to establish a solo career as part of the British beat scene. The friendship she had started with Mick Jagger while touring with the Rolling Stones led to a recording contract with the Immediate label belonging to the Stones' manager, Andrew Loog Oldham. During 1968, P.P.Arnold made two albums. *Kafunta* has a much more striking cover, but *The First Lady Of Immediate* has generally better songs. Her dynamic soul voice works very well with a rock music backing from the likes of the Small Faces and the Nice, even with the inevitable addition of orchestral instruments. *The First Cut Is The Deepest, The Time Has Come,* and *If You Think You're Groovy* were issued as singles and were small chart hits in the UK, as was *Angel Of The Morning,* included on *Kafunta. Everything Is Gonna Be Alright* became a significant club hit, although P.P.Arnold gained rather more mainstream kudos from her prominent contribution to the Small Faces hit, *Tin Soldier.*

THE PENTANGLE

| UK release | May 1968 | Transatlantic | TRA 162 |
| US release | May 1968 | Reprise | RS 6315 |

1. Let No Man Steal Your Thyme (Traditional)
2. Bells (Pentangle)
3. Hear My Call (Staple Singers)
4. Pentangling (Pentangle)
5. Mirage (Bert Jansch)
6. Way Behind The Sun (Traditional)
7. Bruton Town (Traditional)
8. Waltz (Pentangle)

Jacqui McShee: vocals / Bert Jansch: guitar, vocals / John Renbourn: guitar / Danny Thompson: bass / Terry Cox: drums / Shel Talmy: producer

Having played and recorded together on several occasions, the decision by Bert Jansch and John Renbourn to join permanently in a group was both sensible and inevitable. The rhythm section was taken from Alexis Korner's most recent Blues Incorporated line-up and the group was completed by singer Jacqui McShee, who was discovered by Renbourn and has a particularly lovely and distinctive voice. The music on the group's first album is a blend of folk with jazz, even without the presence of horns or a piano. The rhythms played by Danny Thompson and Terry Cox swing, they do not rock. Bert Jansch and John Renbourn are both playing the acoustic guitars for which they are known and because they are used to playing with each other, they dovetail extremely well. Essentially, Jansch acts like a rhythm guitarist and Renbourn more like a lead player. It is Jacqui McShee's singing that gives the music an extra dimension, although the group rations her performances. *Bells* and *Waltz* are instrumentals and *Pentangling* is almost so, but this makes her voice sound all the sweeter when it does appear.

VARIOUS ARTISTS   THE ROCK MACHINE TURNS YOU ON

By 1968, Columbia records had signed several particularly noteworthy artists, all people who were helping to guide the course of rock music. Its executives realised that this could be used as the central theme of a very effective marketing campaign, under the general title of 'The Rock Machine'. A sampler album, including key tracks from each of fourteen crucial albums, was issued in the UK and several other countries, though

| UK release | May 1968 | CBS | (S)PR 22 |
| Not released in US | | | |

1. I'll Be Your Baby Tonight: Bob Dylan
2. Can't Be So Bad: Moby Grape
3. Fresh Garbage: Spirit
4. I Won't Leave My Wooden Wife For You Sugar: The United States Of America
5. Time Of The Season: The Zombies
6. Turn On A Friend: The Peanut Butter Conspiracy
7. Sisters Of Mercy: Leonard Cohen
8. My Days Are Numbered: Blood Sweat And Tears
9. Dolphins Smile: The Byrds
10. Scarborough Fair/Canticle: Simon and Garfunkel
11. Statesboro Blues: Taj Mahal
12. Nobody's Got Any Money In The Summer: Roy Harper
13. Come Away Melinda: Tim Rose
14. Flames: Elmer Gantry's Velvet Opera

Personnel as on the original albums / Elmer Gantry's Velvet Opera are: Dave Terry: vocals, songwriter / Colin Forster: guitar / John Ford: bass guitar, vocals / Richard Hudson: drums, vocals / Barry Kingston: producer

not, for some reason, the US. The price was set at half the usual selling amount for an album. The campaign was extremely successful. Columbia picked the right tracks for inclusion in the sampler and watched while both the original albums and *The Rock Machine Turns You On* itself entered the charts. All the original albums are included in this book, with the exception of the record by Elmer Gantry's Velvet Opera. The *Flames* track made a brilliant, exciting single, although it managed to avoid becoming a hit, but the rest of the group's album is not in the same league.

VARIOUS ARTISTS   LISTEN HERE!

The British label specialising in folk music, Transatlantic, had the same idea as CBS and issued a bargain priced sampler album. It was less successful than *The Rock Machine Turns You On* and it concentrated on artists rather than their latest albums, so that some of the tracks were singles. It does, however, provide an excellent taster for what the label had to offer. In amongst the familiar folk names there are some newcomers destined to make a name for themselves later on. Skilled guitarist Gordon Giltrap is one; the gentle teenage brother and sister duo calling itself the Sallangie is another. She is Sally Oldfield, later a significant recording artist in her own right, while her brother Mike would soon become a very big name indeed. Ron Geesin is an avant garde performer who is playing a free-form improvisation for banjo here – later he would be responsible for a soundtrack recording with Roger Waters of Pink Floyd. The Purple Gang would ultimately be overtaken by their own song: the delightful *Granny Takes A Trip* miraculously failed to take the charts by storm, but it gave much publicity to a Chelsea clothes boutique whose name the song had borrowed.

UK release   May 1968   Transatlantic   TRASAM 2
Not released in US

1. Travellin' Song (Bert Jansch): The Pentangle
2. Eight Frames A Second (Ralph McTell): Ralph McTell
3. In Love With A Stranger (Gordon Giltrap): Gordon Giltrap
4. Tic Tocative (Bert Jansch/John Renbourn): Bert Jansch and John Renbourn
5. Song (John Donne/John Renbourn): John Renbourn
6. The Circle Game (Joni Mitchell): The Ian Campbell Group
7. Urge For Going (Joni Mitchell): The Johnstons
8. Harvest Your Thoughts Of Love (Bert Jansch): Baert Jansch
9. Love In Ice Crystals (Sally and Mike Oldfield): The Sallyangie
10. Blues For Dominique (Bob Bunting): Bob Bunting
11. Certainly Random (Ron Geesin): Ron Geesin
12. Granny Takes A Trip (Christopher Beard/Geoffrey Bowyer): The Purple Gang

1: Bert Jansch: vocals, guitar / Jacqui McShee: vocals / John Renbourn: guitar / Danny Thompson: bass / Terry Cox: drums / Shel Talmy: producer   2: Ralph McTell: vocals, guitar / Tony Visconti: arranger / Gus Dudgeon: producer   3: Gordon Giltrap: vocals, guitar / Bill Leader: producer   4: Bert Jansch: guitar / John Renbourn: guitar / Bill Leader: producer   5: John Renbourn: vocals, guitar / Nathan Joseph: producer   6: Ian Campbell: guitar, vocals / Lorna Campbell: vocals / Brian Clark: guitar, vocals / John Dunkerley: guitar / George Watts: flute / Dave Pegg: bass / Rick Storey: arranger   7: Adrienne Johnston: vocals / Lucy Johnston: vocals / Mike Moloney: vocals / Paul Brady: vocals, guitar / Darrell Runswick: bass / David Palmer: arranger / Nathan Joseph: producer   8: Bert Jansch: vocals, guitar / Nathan Joseph, Bill Leader: producer   9. Sally Oldfield: vocals / Mike Oldfield: vocals, guitar / Nathan Joseph: producer   10: Bob Bunting: vocals, guitar / Tony Visconti: arranger / Nathan Joseph: producer   11. Ron Geesin: banjo / Nathan Joseph: producer   12: Peter Walker: vocals / Geoffrey Bowyer: piano / Christopher Beard: guitar / Dee Jay Robinson: mandolin / Tony Moss: bass / Joe Boyd: producer

GRAHAM GOULDMAN
THE GRAHAM GOULDMAN THING

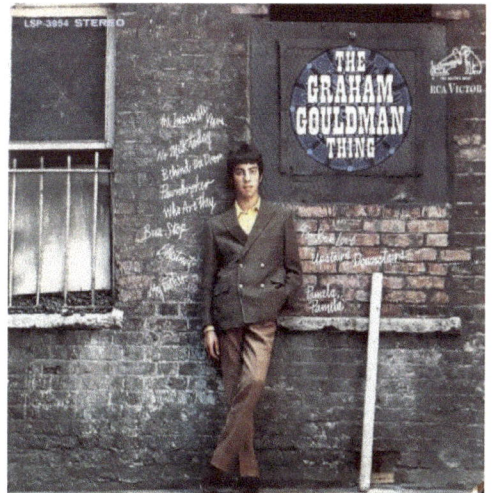

US release   May 1968   RCA Victor   LSP 3954
Not released in UK

1. The Impossible Years
2. Bus Stop
3. Behind The Door
4. Pawnbroker
5. Who Are They
6. My Father
7. No Milk Today
8. Upstairs Downstairs
9. For Your Love
10. Pamela, Pamela
11. Chestnut

Graham Gouldman: vocals, guitar, producer / John Paul Jones: arranger, producer, bass guitar, keyboards / Clem Cattini: drums / Peter Noone: producer

Graham Gouldman was the composer of several hits by the Hollies, Herman's Hermits, Wayne Fontana, and the Yardbirds. Some of these appear on his solo album in versions which add a little more orchestration than was on the originals, but which otherwise keep fairly close to the familiar performances. The new songs make less impact, but could nevertheless have been made into hits if adopted by the groups already using Gouldman songs. The album is pleasant pop-rock, but sounds rather as though it was put together as a set of demos for the songs. Gouldman fails to gain credibility as a significant artist in his own right and it seems unsurprising that the British arm of RCA passed on the chance to release the album. Graham Gouldman did eventually manage to become part of a very successful group in the seventies, 10cc, having learned to perform with an authority that he does not really have here.

RICHARD HARRIS   A TRAMP SHINING

Richard Harris brings his skills as an actor to his role as singer and is able to deliver the songs very effectively despite not technically having a very good singing voice. The record is the first major showcase for the work of Jimmy Webb, who had gained a few hits recorded by other people, but never an entire album. *MacArthur Park,* probably Webb's best-known song, was issued as a single by Harris and became a big hit in both the US and the UK. The song includes several sections with contrasting moods and tempos and has a lyric that has been much misunderstood. The song's central metaphor is of the park in Los Angeles, a place of romantic significance for the singer, yet spoilt since the ending of the romance in question, while having the appearance of an iced cake similarly spoilt, when seen from a distance in the dark. This seemed to present an image too complicated for many listeners

to appreciate. Taking the lyrics literally, they could not understand why anyone would choose to leave a cake outside in the rain. *MacArthur Park* provides a natural focus for the album, but is surrounded by music of such a high standard that it does not dominate. Swathed in lush orchestrations, the music of *A Tramp Shining* confirms Jimmy Webb as a very special songwriter and Richard Harris as an ideal person to put the songs across.

US release	May 1968	Dunhill	DS-50032
UK release	May 1968	RCA Victor	SF/RD 7947

1. Prelude / Didn't We?
2. Interlude / Paper Chase
3. Interlude / Name Of My Sorrow
4. Interlude / Lovers Such As I
5. In The Final Hours
6. MacArthur Park
7. Dancing Girl
8. Interlude / If You Must Leave My Life
9. A Tramp Shining

All compositions by Jimmy Webb

Richard Harris: vocals / Jimmy Webb: producer, arranger / Sid Sharp: arranger / Mike Deasy: guitar / Tommy Tedesco: guitar / Larry Knechtel: keyboards / Jules Chaikin: trumpet / Jim Horn: saxophone / Joe Osborn: bass guitar / Hal Blaine: drums

THE FAMILY TREE   MISS BUTTERS

US release	May 1968	RCA Victor	LSP-3955
Not released in UK			

1. Birthday/Dirgeday
2. Melancholy Vaudeville Man
3. Any Other Baby
4. Sideshow
5. Mrs McPheeny
6. Butter Lament (Bob Segarini/Harry Nilsson)
7. Simple Life
8. Slippin' Thru' My Fingers
9. Nine To Three
10. Lesson Book Life
11. Nickelodeon Music
12. Miss Butters
13. The Underture

All compositions except track 6 by Bob Segarini

Bob Segarini: vocals, guitar / Jimmy DeCocq: keyboards, guitar / Michael Duré: keyboards, guitar, vocals / Vann Slatter: drums / Bill Trochim: bass guitar / George Tipton: arranger / Rick Jarrard: producer

Miss Butters is a narrative song cycle in the manner of the Pretty Things' *SF Sorrow* or the Who's *Tommy*, but predating both of them. The album was recorded at around the same time as Nilsson's *Aerial Ballet* album, not released until July, using the same producer and arranger. It is not surprising, therefore, that it has a very similar sound. One notable addition is some nifty lead guitar playing, presumably from the mastermind behind the entire project, Bob Segriani. Otherwise, however, the music is attractive, melodic, orchestrated pop music, and apart from the inclusion on *Aerial Ballet* of Nilsson's calling-card, *One*, *Miss Butters* has a rather more memorable set of songs. It was Nilsson's album that sold, however, and the Family Tree was not given another chance to make an attempt at pop immortality, although Bob Segriani managed to maintain a low-level career in music for several years.

ALEXIS KORNER   A NEW GENERATION OF BLUES

UK release	May 1968	Liberty	LBS/LBL 83147
Not released in US			

1. Mary Open The Door (Duffy Power)
2. Little Bitty Girl (Traditional)
3. Baby Don't You Love Me (Traditional)
4. Go Down Sunshine (Alexis Korner)
5. The Same For You (Alexis Korner)
6. I'm Tore Down (B.B.King)
7. In The Evening (Traditional)
8. Somethin' You Got (Chris Kenner)
9. New Worried Blues (Alexis Korner)
10. What's That Sound I Hear (Alexis Korner)
11. A Flower (Alexis Korner)

Alexis Korner: vocals, guitar / Ray Warleigh: alto saxophone, flute / Steve Miller: piano / Danny Thompson: bass / Terry Cox: drums / Ian Samwell: producer

By 1968, people were starting to appreciate the contribution made by Alexis Korner to the development of blues-rock in the UK, so that his album with a new record company, *A New Generation Of Blues,* made rather more impact that those he had released previously. Liberty failed to list the musicians on the record sleeve, which was a pity because they were people that record buyers would have known. The rhythm section of Danny Thompson and Terry Cox was even then making an impression with the Pentangle. But the album title, though optimistic, is not really a very accurate description of what is to be found in the grooves, because the music is very much the same as that played by Alexis Korner on his other recent records. Half the songs are the country blues, with Korner accompanied by his acoustic guitar. The rest of the album has a pronounced jazz feel, with only the version of a B.B.King song (*I'm Tore Down*) having the kind of drive craved by rock audiences. *A New Generation Of Blues* is the work of a man who knows how he wants to perform and knows too that he can play this kind of music very well indeed, but it is considerably removed from what the other members of the British blues scene were doing.

THE SPENCER DAVIS GROUP WITH THEIR NEW FACE ON

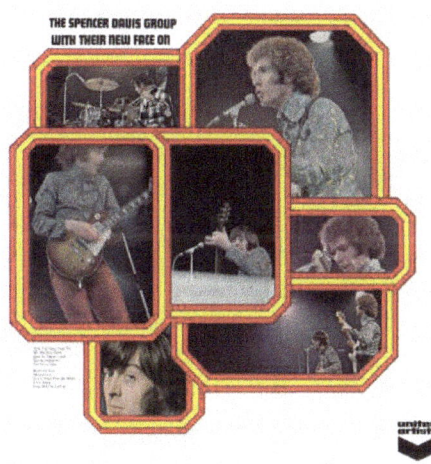

```
UK release      June 1968      United Artists      (S)ULP 1192
US release      June 1968      United Artists      UAS 6652/UAL3652

1. With His New Face On (Eddie Hardin/Spencer Davis)
2. Mr Second Class (Eddie Hardin/Spencer Davis)
3. Alec In Transitland (Eddie Hardin/Kirk Duncan/Pete York/Spencer Davis)
4. Sanity Inspector (Eddie Hardin/Spencer Davis)
5. Feel Your Way (Eddie Hardin/Spencer Davis)
6. Morning Sun (Eddie Hardin/Kirk Duncan/Nicky James/Spencer Davis)
7. Moonshine (Eddie Hardin/Pete York/Spencer Davis)
8. Don't Want You No More (Edde Hardin/Spencer Davis)
9. Time Seller (Eddie Hardin/Spencer Davis)
10. Stop Me, I'm Falling (Eddie Hardin/Spencer Davis)

Eddie Hardin: vocals, organ / Spencer Davis: guitar, bass guitar, vocals / Phil Sawyer: guitar, bass guitar, vocals / Ray Fenwick: guitar, vocals, bass guitar / Kirk Duncan: piano / Pete York: drums / basses and violas on track 9 arranged by Johnny Scott / Mike Hurst: producer / Ron Richards: producer (8,9)
```

The departure of Steve Winwood must have been a considerable blow to the Spencer Davis Group, yet remarkably Davis was able to find a replacement in Eddie Hardin, who had a soulful singing voice quite similar to Winwood's, was a fine player of the Hammond organ, and a talented songwriter as well. To fill out the sound, and apparently not having much confidence in his own guitar playing, Davis successively employed guitarists Phil Sawyer and Ray Fenwick. The group contributed songs to the soundtrack of the Clive Donner film, *Here We Go Round The Mulberry Bush,* and also released two impressive singles, *Time Seller* and *Mr Second Class,* every bit as imaginative as the recent singles with Steve Winwood but unfortunately much less successful. These two songs are included on the album, *With Their New Face On*, although *Time Seller* has an Eddie Hardin vocal replacing the original by the departed Phil Sawyer. The singles are primarily responsible for making the album sound as good as it does, although many of the other songs are excellent too and the album is arguably the best that the group made.

THE MOVE   SOMETHING ELSE EP

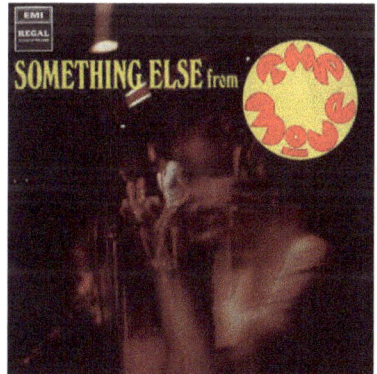

```
UK release      June 1968      Regal Zonophone      TRZ 2001
Not released in US

1. So You Want To Be A Rock 'n' Roll Star (Chris Hillman/Roger McGuinn)
2. Stephanie Knows Who (Arthur Lee)
3. Something Else (Eddie Cochran/Sharon Sheeley)
4. It'll Be Me (Jack Clement)
5. Sunshine Help Me (Gary Wright)

Carl Wayne: vocals, guitar / Roy Wood: guitar, vocals / Trevor Burton: bass guitar / Bev Bevan: drums / Denny Cordell: producer
```

Record companies in the UK became disenchanted with the EP format during 1967. This very late entry to the discography plays at 33 rpm like a miniature LP. The tracks are all cover versions performed by the Move at the Marquee club in London, with the vocals overdubbed afterwards to improve the poor quality captured at the time. Although the group is functioning like a bar band, the interpretations it presents are very superior examples of the genre, with the interplay between Roy Wood's wah-wah lead guitar and Trevor Burton's bass guitar on the extended *Sunshine Help Me* being particularly fine. The Move plays with a huge amount of energy, probably more than would have been displayed by the originators of these songs. On its own, the EP is all the evidence needed to persuade the listener of the Move's greatness.

JOHN MAYALL'S BLUES BREAKERS   BARE WIRES

John Mayall's seventh album in two years finds the largest version of the Bluesbreakers yet, with seven members. The new rhythm section and two of the three brass players are people with jazz backgrounds and they give John Mayall's music on *Bare Wires* a pronounced jazz feel. For the most part, however, Mayall does not present the entire band, but uses smaller groups to highlight different musicians on each of the tracks. The result gives the impression that the band has considerable resources kept in reserve and that the album could have been much longer, a double, and would still have been enormously interesting. Although Mayall sticks rigorously to the blues

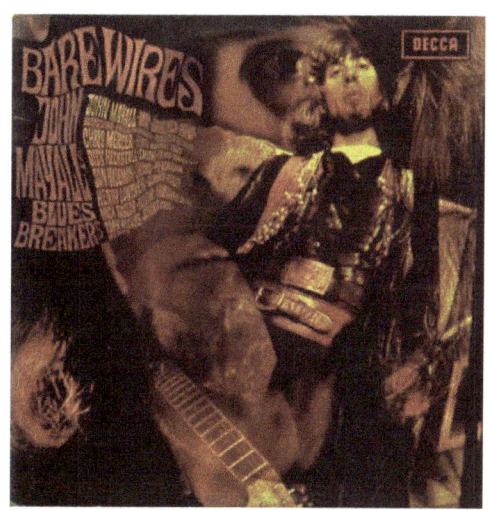

format, he is able to show just how flexible this can be with some outstanding songwriting. The songs on side one of the album are grouped together into a continuous suite, with the vinyl remaining unbanded, although the second side has its songs separated. Mayall would not have admitted to being interested in an album like the Beatles' *Sgt Pepper*, but his *Bare Wires* emerges as very much the blues equivalent. The album reached number three in the UK chart, the best result of Mayall's career, although it did less well in the US.

| UK release | June 1968 | Decca | SKL/LK 4945 |
| US release | June 1968 | London | PS 537 |

1. Bare Wires
2. Where Did I Belong?
3. I Started Walking
4. Open Up A New Door
5. Fire
6. I Know Now
7. Look In The Mirror

8. I'm A Stranger
9. No Reply (John Mayall/Mick Taylor)
10. Hartley Quits (Mick Taylor)
11. Killing Time
12. She's Too Young
13. Sandy

All compositions by John Mayall except where stated

John Mayall: vocals, keyboards, guitar, harmonica, producer / Mick Taylor: guitar, Hawaiian guitar / Henry Lowther: cornet, violin / Chris Mercer: tenor and baritone saxophones / Dick Heckstall-Smith: tenor and soprano saxophones / Tony Reeves: bass, bass guitar / Jon Hiseman: drums / Mike Vernon: producer

VARIOUS ARTISTS   BLUES ANYTIME VOLS 1 & 2

These two LPS, released on the Immediate label, contain some seminal recordings, mostly dating from 1965, by a number of British musicians who went on to rather greater fame. One track, *I'm Your Witchdoctor,* by John Mayall's Bluesbreakers, has rather more import than purely archival interest, because it features the first time that Eric Clapton launched his overdriven guitar tone, thereby inventing the modern electric guitar. *Flapjacks* is a bit of a classic recording too, featuring the early work of a guitarist who never really received the acclaim that was his due – Martin Stone, later featured in the Savoy Brown Blues Band and Mighty Baby. The tracks featuring Eric Clapton and Jimmy Page promise more than they deliver, since there is no twin lead guitar duelling. Jimmy Page sticks to a very basic rhythm guitar to allow Eric Clapton to develop his lead playing on his own. The fact that the rhythm section on some of the tracks comprises members of the Rolling Stones is interesting, but they do not make much of an active contribution.

| UK release | June 1968 | Immediate | IMLP014/ IMCP 015 |
| US release | June 1968 | Immediate | Z12 52006/14 as Anthology of British Blues |

1. I'm Your Witchdoctor (John Mayall): John Mayall's Bluesbreakers
2. Snake Drive (Eric Clapton/Jimmy Page): Eric Clapton and Jimmy Page
3. Ain't Gonna Cry No More (Tony McPhee): T.S. McPhee
4. I Tried (Larry Davis/Don Robey/Joe Scott): Savoy Brown Blues Band
5. Tribute To Elmore (Eric Clapton/Jimmy Page): Eric Clapton and Jimmy Page
6. I Feel So Good (Big Bill Broonzy): Jo-Ann Kelly

7. Telephone Blues (John Mayall): John Mayall's Bluesbreakers
8. You Don't Love Me (Willie Cobbs): T.S. McPhee
9. West Coast Idea (Eric Clapton/Jimmy Page): Eric Clapton and Jimmy Page
10. Ain't Seen No Whisky (Traditional): Jo-Ann Kelly
11. Flapjacks (Stone's Masonry): Stone's Masonry
12. Cold Blooded Woman (Memphis Slim): Savoy Brown Blues Band

13. On Top Of The World (John Mayall): John Mayall's Bluesbreakers
14. Someone To Love Me (Snooky Pryor): T.S. McPhee
15. Can't Quit You Baby (Willie Dixon): Savoy Brown Blues Band
16. Draggin' My Tail (Eric Clapton/Jimmy Page): Eric Clapton and Jimmy Page
17. Dealing With The Devil (Sonny Boy Williamson): Dharma Blues Band
18. Who's Knocking (Jeremy Spencer): Jeremy Spencer

19. Freight Loader (Eric Clapton/Jimmy Page): Eric Clapton and Jimmy Page
20. Look Down At My Woman (Jeremy Spencer): Jeremy Spencer
21. Roll 'Em Pete (Pete Johnson): Dharma Blues Band
22. Choker (Eric Clapton /Jimmy Page): Eric Clapton and Jimmy Page
23. True Blue (Memphis Slim): Savoy Brown Blues Band
24. When You Got A Good Friend (Tony McPhee): T.S. McPhee

1,7,13: John Mayall: vocals, organ / Eric Clapton: guitar / John McVie: bass guitar / Hughie Flint: drums / Jimmy Page: producer // 2,5,9,16,19,22: Eric Clapton: guitar / Jimmy Page: guitar / Mick Jagger: harmonica / Bill Wyman: bass guitar / Ian Stewart: piano / Chris Winters: drums // 3,8,14,24: Tony McPhee: vocals, guitar / Bob Hall: piano / Peter Cruickshank: bass guitar / Dave Boorman: drums // 4,12,15,23: Brice Portius: vocals / Kim Simmonds: guitar / Bob Hall: piano / John O'Leary: harmonica / Ray Chappell: bass guitar / Leo Mannings: drums / 6: Jo-Ann Kelly: vocals / T.S. McPhee band as tracks 3,8,14,24 // 10: Jo-Ann Kelly: vocals / Dave Kelly: guitar // 11: Martin Stone: guitar / Pete Shelley: organ / Keith Tillman: bass guitar / Michael Riley: drums // 17,21: Dave Brock: vocals, guitar / Luke Francis: harmonica / Mike King: piano // 18,20: Jeremy Spencer: vocals, piano / John Charles: bass guitar / Ian Charles: drums

CHICKEN SHACK
40 BLUE FINGERS, FRESHLY PACKED & READY TO SERVE

Chicken Shack was a blues band formed by Stan Webb, a talented guitarist, albeit one who had not played with John Mayall(!) What makes the band stand out, however, is the fact that the spotlight is shared with female singer and keyboard player, Christine Perfect, even

| UK release | June 1968 | Blue Horizon | (S) 7-63203 |
| US release | June 1968 | Epic | BN 26414 |

1. The Letter (Jules Taub/B.B. King)
2. Lonesome Whistle Blues (Rudolph Toombs)
3. When The Train Comes Back (Christine Perfect)
4. San-Ho-Zay (Freddie King/Sonny Thompson)
5. King Of The World (John Lee Hooker)

6. See See Baby (Freddie King/Sonny Thompson)
7. First Time I Met The Blues (Little Brother Montgomery)
8. Webbed Feet (Stan Webb)
9. You Ain't No Good (Christine Perfect)
10. What You Did Last Night (Stan Webb)

Stan Webb: vocals, guitar / Christine Perfect: vocals, piano, organ / Andy Silvester: bass guitar / Dave Bidwell: drums / Alan Ellis: trumpet / Dick Heckstall-Smith: tenor saxophone / Johnny Almond: alto saxophone / Mike Vernon: producer

if Webb is careful to ensure that the balance stays very much in his own favour. Chicken Shack does not strive for the rigid blues authenticity of its label-mate, Fleetwood Mac, but still manages to convince that the musicians have become very familiar with the form. Christine Perfect sings two of the songs, both of which happen to be written by herself, and leaves the listener wishing that she could have sung more. Stan Webb is a less distinguished singer, but lets his eloquent guitar make the loudest statements. He is not in the same league as Eric Clapton or Peter Green or Mick Taylor and has a much less distinctive playing voice of his own, but he certainly knows his way around a fretboard. Horns are added to the group line-up on some of the tracks, but purely to thicken the sound. They get no chance to solo, even though one of them is the Alexis Korner/John Mayall veteran, Dick Heckstall-Smith.

SPOOKY TOOTH   IT'S ALL ABOUT

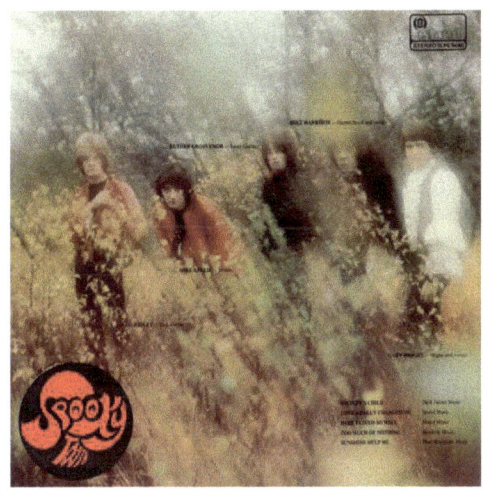

| UK release | June 1968 | Island | ILPS 9080 |
| US release | June 1968 | Bell | BELL 6019 |

1. Society's Child (Janis Ian)
2. Love Really Changed Me (Gary Wright/Jimmy Miller/Luther Grosvenor)
3. Here I Lived So Well (Gary Wright/Jimmy Miller/Luther Grosvenor/Mike Harrison)
4. Too Much Of Nothing (Bob Dylan)
5. Sunshine Help Me (Gary Wright)

6. It's All About A Roundabout (Gary Wright/Jimmy Miller)
7. Tobacco Road (John D. Loudermilk)
8. It Hurts You So (Gary Wright/Jimmy Miller)
9. Forget It, I Got It (Gary Wright/Jimmy Miller)
10. Bubbles (Gary Wright/Luther Grosvenor)

Gary Wright: vocals, organ / Mike Harrison: vocals, piano, harpsichord / Luther Grosvenor: guitar / Greg Ridley: bass guitar / Mike Kellie: drums / Jimmy Miller: producer

Spooky Tooth was formed when the American Gary Wright joined Art, giving the group two keyboard players and two lead singers. It has a very dense, powerful sound, with all the musicians playing at full tilt – none more so than Greg Ridley, whose bass guitar has a thick tone and is positioned well up in the mix. Gary Wright and Mike Harrison sing together much of the time, Wright's soulful tone, often breaking into falsetto, working very effectively against Harrison's grit. *Sunshine Help Me* shows off the group's strengths particularly well. It is a classic performance and it is easy to understand why the Move chose this song to include in its live set. The album was not a big seller, but it did establish Spooky Tooth as a band to watch.

IRON BUTTERFLY   IN-A-GADDA-DA-VIDA

The version of Iron Butterfly playing on the group's second album is different from previously, with a new guitarist and bass guitarist. The title track, supposedly based on a mishearing of the phrase 'in the Garden of Eden', occupies the whole of the second side of the album and is the piece on which Iron Butterfly's reputation ultimately rests.

| US release | June 1968 | Atco | SD 33-250 |
| UK release | June 1968 | Atlantic | 588/587 116 |

1. Most Anything You Want (Doug Ingle)
2. Flowers And Beads (Doug Ingle)
3. My Mirage (Doug Ingle)
4. Termination (Erik Brann/Lee Dorman)
5. Are You Happy (Doug Ingle)

6. In-A-Gadda-Da-Vida (Doug Ingle)

Doug Ingle: vocals, organ / Erik Brann: guitar / Lee Dorman: bass guitar / Ron Bushy: drums / Jim Hilton: producer

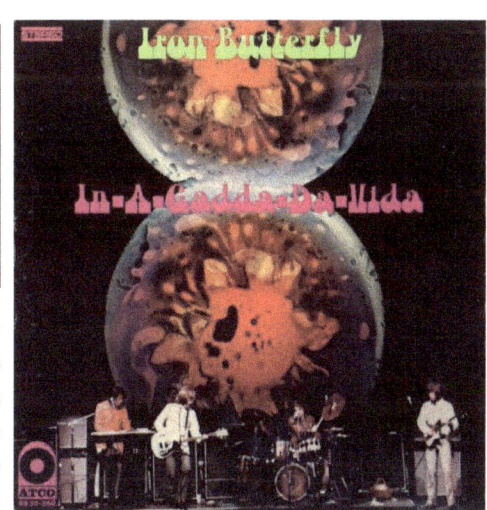

A simple mono-chord riff is repeated over and over as the backcloth for a series of solos by keyboards, guitar, and drums, once the nonsense lyric is dispensed with. There is minimal interaction between the soloists and the rhythm section and since the soloists themselves are not particularly inspired players, the result does become rather tedious. The hard rock songs on the album's first side are more interesting, but not enough that they would have made the album stand out if they were all that was on offer. It is curious that *In-A-Gadda-Da-Vida*, the song, has become so celebrated, because there are many better examples of rock groups improvising at length on record and quite a few of them are earlier than Iron Butterfly. The group has acquired the reputation of being a major influence in the development of hard rock and even heavy metal, which is entirely unjustified.

VANILLA FUDGE   RENAISSANCE

US release	June 1968	Atco	SD 33-244
UK release	June 1968	Atlantic	588/587 110

1. The Sky Cried – When I Was A Boy (Mark Stein/Tim Bogert)
2. Thoughts (Vinnie Martell)
3. Paradise (Carmine Appice/Mark Stein)
4. That's What Makes A Man (Mark Stein)
5. The Spell That Comes After (Essra Mohawk)
6. Faceless People (Carmine Appice)
7. Season Of The Witch (Donovan Leitch)

Mark Stein: vocals, keyboards / Vince Martell: vocals, guitar / Tim Bogert: vocals, bass guitar / Carmine Appice: vocals, drums / Shadow Morton: producer

For its third album, Vanilla Fudge are back on track, performing its own musical vision rather than carrying out a project for the producer, Shadow Morton. There is one epic recasting of a well-known song in the manner that gave Vanilla Fudge its reputation – this time it is Donovan's *Season Of The Witch* that gets the treatment. For most of the album, however, the group performs songs written by its members, playing these with the same full-on heaviness as enjoyed by Spooky Tooth. Although the album does not include a big hit single, as the first album did, *Renaissance* emerges as the most focused record made by the group thus far. Its title, presumably referring to the artistic failure of the previous *The Beat Goes On* album, seems to be entirely appropriate.

THE BEACH BOYS   FRIENDS

US release	June 1968	Capitol	ST 2895
UK release	September 1968	Capitol	ST 2895

1. Meant For You (Brian Wilson?Mike Love)
2. Friends (Brian, Carl, Dennis Wilson/Al Jardine)
3. Wake The World (Brian Wilson/Al Jardine)
4. Be Here In The Mornin' (Brian, Carl, Dennis Wilson/Al Jardine/Mike Love)
5. When A Man Needs A Woman (Brian & Dennis Wilson/Al Jardine/Jon Parks/Steve Korthof)
6. Passing By (Brian Wilson)
7. Anna Lee, The Healer (Brian Wilson/Mike Love)
8. Little Bird (Dennis Wilson/Steve Kalinich)
9. Be Still (Dennis Wilson/Steve Kalinich)
10. Busy Doin' Nothin' (Brian Wilson)
11. Diamond Head (Brian Wilson/Albert Vescovo/James Ackley/Lyle Ritz)
12. Transcendental Meditation (Brian Wilson/Mike Love/Al Jardine)

Mike Love: vocals / Brian Wilson: vocals, keyboards / Carl Wilson: vocals, guitar / Al Jardine: vocals, guitar / Bruce Johnston: vocals, bass guitar / Dennis Wilson: vocals, drums / session musicians / The Beach Boys: producer

With *Friends*, centred on a single that comes close to equalling the group's most remarkable recent songs, the Beach Boys concentrate on what they do best. The songs are very melodic and delivered using lush harmony vocals and low-key arrangements with several session musicians. Brian Wilson is very much involved in the production even if he no longer receives sole credit, but the music is still not managing to match that on the shelved *Smile* project. It is fair to say that the Beach Boys are no longer anywhere near the pop music cutting edge, but *Friends* remains a very worthwhile collection of music. Its sales, however, were disappointing, the lowest in the Beach Boys' career to date.

STEVE MILLER BAND   CHILDREN OF THE FUTURE

The first album by the Steve Miller Band has a large number of innovative ideas. It is made by an American band recording in London, so that it is able to draw on the strengths of both countries' music. The first side comprises a suite of songs, united by the 'Children of the Future' theme that both

US release	June 1968	Capitol	SKAO 2920
UK release	June 1968	Capitol	ST 2920

1. Children Of The Future (Steve Miller)
2. Pushed Me To It (Steve Miller)
3. You've Got The Power (Steve Miller)
4. In My First Mind (Steve Miller/Jim Peterman)
5. The Beauty Of Time Is That It's Snowing (Psychedelic B.B.) (Steve Miller)
6. Baby's Callin' Me Home (Boz Scaggs)
7. Steppin' Stone (Boz Scaggs)
8. Roll With It (Steve Miller)
9. Junior Saw It Happen (Jim Pulte)
10. Fanny Mae (Buster Brown)
11. Key To The Highway (Big Bill Broonzy/Charlie Segar)

Steve Miller: vocals, guitar, harmonica / Boz Scaggs: vocals, guitar / Jim Peterman: keyboards, vocals / Lonnie Turner: bass guitar / Tim Davis: drums, vocals / Glyn Johns: producer

begins and ends the work. Some of the pieces included are very short, in the manner of the better known Beatles album, *Abbey Road*, issued more than a year later. The suite begins with what sounds like an explosion in a guitar factory and ends with ambient found sound, out of which pokes a very accurate B.B.King impersonation. Side two gives clues about the band's origins as a blues group, but Steve Miller and his colleagues continually add touches to take the music away from its roots, such as the harpsichord and acoustic guitar duet that underscores *Baby's Callin' Me Home* or the gospel organ that suffuses a stately version of Big Bill Broonzy's *Key To The Highway*. In between there is some very classy modern rock playing, the kind that would eventually be known as 'classic rock'. Steve Miller would lead various different line-ups of his band through numerous recordings and live performances well into the twenty-first century: *Children Of The Future* provides ample evidence of the fertile music mind that enabled him to do this.

RANDY NEWMAN

After several of his songs were recorded by other artists, and taken into the charts by Alan Price, Randy Newman finally gets to make an album of his own. He largely chooses to ignore the songs that were already well known and, as a result, presents a set that is much less compelling than it could have been. Like Nilsson and Van Dyke Parks before him (Parks being co-producer of the album), he pretends that rock music does not exist and surrounds most of the songs with lush orchestral arrangements. With a singing voice that is close to speech and with his sardonic sense of humour shining through theatrical lyrics, Newman sounds as though he is performing a stage show. His songs would become more precisely focused on his subsequent recordings, but this first album is a very good start. The back of the sleeve has the subtitle 'Randy Newman Creates Something New Under The Sun' which seems like a reasonable boast.

| US release | June 1968 | Reprise | RS 6286 |
| UK release | June 1968 | Reprise | RSLP 6286 |

1. Love Story
2. Bet No One Ever Hurt This Bad
3. Living Without You
4. So Long Dad
5. I Think He's Hiding
6. Linda

7. Laughing Boy
8. Cowboy
9. The Beehive State
10. I Think It's Going To Rain Today
11. Davy The Fat Boy

All compositions by Randy Newman

Randy Newman: vocals, piano, arranger / Ron Elliott : guitar / Victor Sazer: cello / Sal Valentino: guitar, vocals / Jim Gordon: drums / Tom Tedesco: guitar/ Wilbur Schwartz: alto saxophone / Harold Ayres: viola / Israel Baker: violin / Arnold Belnick : violin / Harold Bemko: cello / Joseph Di Fiore: viola / Jesse Ehrlich: cello / James Getzoff: flute / Jan Hlinka: viola / Armand Kaproff: cello / Louis Kievman: viola / William Kurasch: violin / Leonard Malarsky: violin / Lyl e Ritz: bass guitar / Ralph Schaeffer: violin / Leonard Selic: viola / Frederick Seykora: cello / Sidney Sharp: violin / William Weiss: violin / Tibor Zelig: violin / Michael Deasy: guitar / Tommy Morgan: harmonica / Don Lanier: guitar / Hubert Anderson: percussion / Milton Bernhart : trombone / Gene Cipriano: saxophone / James Decker: French horn / Joseph Di Tullio: cello / Herb Ellis: guitar / Carl Fortina: accordion / Gene Garf: keyboards / William Green: saxophone / William Hinshaw: French horn / James Horn: saxophone / Richard Hyde: trombone / Norman Jeffries: drums / Raymond Kelley: cello / Michael Lang: piano / Gayle Levant: harmonica / Lew McCreary: trombone / Sidney Miller: saxophone / Oliver Mitchell: trumpet / Louis Morell: guitar / Ted Nash: saxophone / Gordon Pope: saxophone / James Rowles: piano / Thomas Scott: saxophone / Anthony Terran: trumpet / Nick De Caro: accordion / James Burton: guitar / Al Casey: guitar / Gary Coleman: percussion / Frank De Caro: guitar / Carol Kaye: bass guitar / Donald Bagley: bass guitar / Harry Bluestone: violin / Samuel Boghossian: viola / David Duke: French horn / Elizabeth Ershoff: harp / David Filerman: cello / Joseph Gibbons: guitar / Plas Johnson: saxophone / Larry Knechtel: guitar, bass guitar, keyboards / Robert Knight: trombone / Jay Migliori: saxophone /Richard Perissi: French horn / William Perkins: saxophone / Jerome Reisler: violin / Lenny Waronker: producer / Van Dyke Parks: producer (order of musicians as on LP sleeve)

ARETHA FRANKLIN   ARETHA NOW

Aretha Franklin's fourth album for Atlantic continues her catalogue of inspirational soul songs and became her third gold disc in the US. It is made essential by the inclusion of *I Say A Little Prayer*, in which she takes a pretty song by Dionne Warwick and transforms it into a gospel-soul classic. Released as a single, the song became the ninth in a run of US chart successes and also reached number four in the

| US release | June 1968 | Atlantic | SD 8186 |
| UK release | June 1968 | Atlantic | 588/587 114 |

1. Think (Aretha Franklin/Ted White)
2. I Say A Little Prayer (Burt Bacharach/Hal David)
3. See Saw (Don Covay/Steve Cropper)
4. Night Time Is The Right Time (Lew Herman)
5. You Send Me (Sam Cooke)

6. You're A Sweet Sweet Man (Ronnie Shannon)
7. I Take What I Want (David Porter/Isaac Hayes/Mabob Hodges)
8. Hello Sunshine (King Curtis/Ron Miller)
9. A Change (Clyde Otis/Dorian Burton)
10. I Can't See Myself Leaving You (Ronnie Shannon)

Aretha Franklin: vocals, piano / Jimmy Johnson: guitar / Tommy Cogbill: guitar / Spooner Oldham: keyboards / Wayne Jackson: trumpet / Andrew Love: tenor saxophone / Charles Chalmers: tenor saxophone / Floyd Newman: baritone saxophone / Willie Bridges: baritone Saxophone / Jerry Jemmot: bass guitar / Roger Hawkins: drums / Jerry Wexler: producer

UK, becoming her biggest hit of the sixties. Aretha Franklin's gospel heritage is very close to the surface throughout the album, and it is this element that makes her so unassailable as the premier soul singer of her generation, regardless of gender.

THE SPONTANEOUS MUSIC ENSEMBLE   KARYOBIN

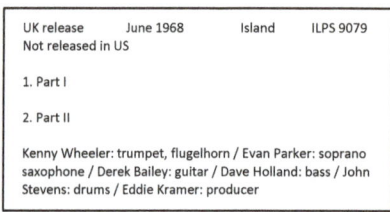

UK release   June 1968   Island   ILPS 9079
Not released in US

1. Part I
2. Part II

Kenny Wheeler: trumpet, flugelhorn / Evan Parker: soprano saxophone / Derek Bailey: guitar / Dave Holland: bass / John Stevens: drums / Eddie Kramer: producer

The Spontaneous Music Ensemble was more an outlet for a number of like-minded British improvising musicians to put their ideas into practice than a regular group, so it is not surprising that its second album has only drummer John Stevens and trumpeter Kenny Wheeler in common with the first. *Karyobin* marks the recording debut of three very significant jazz/ improvised music talents – saxophonist Evan Parker, bass player Dave Holland, and guitarist Derek Bailey. The guitarist later stated that he did not like the album, but that may have something to do with the fact that Island gets his name wrong on the cover. The music is a single continuous performance and, with the album's subtitle relating to imaginary birds living in paradise, the musicians do indeed play in short phrases, calling and responding to each other, like a rather energetic dawn chorus. The most active participant is John Stevens, whose drums are never silent. He delivers a continual stream of percussive sound, even if none of it is intended to establish a pulse. The least active is Derek Bailey, whose guitar is overwhelmed by the range of other tones on offer so that he most often prefers to play nothing at all. The influence of American avant garde jazz has largely disappeared – these musicians are trying, with some success, to create a purely improvised music that is not related to any kind of jazz as normally defined.

PINK FLOYD   A SAUCERFUL OF SECRETS

UK release   June 1968   Columbia   S(C)X 6258
US release   July 1968   Tower   ST 5131

1. Let There Be More Light (Roger Waters)
2. Remember A Day (Rick Wright)
3. Set The Controls For The Heart Of The Sun (Roger Waters)
4. Corporal Clegg (Roger Waters)
5. A Saucerful Of Secrets (David Gilmore/Nick Mason/Rock Wright/Roger Waters)
6. See-Saw (Rick Wright)
7. Jugband Blues (Syd Barrett)

Syd Barrett: guitar, vocals (2,3,7) / David Gilmore: guitar, vocals (1,3-6) / Rick Wright: keyboards, xylophone, vocals / Roger Waters: bass guitar, vocals, percussion / Nick Mason: drums, percussion / Stanley Myers Orchestra (4) / Salvation Army brass section (7) / Norman Smith: producer, drums (2), vocals

Pink Floyd's *A Saucerful Of Secrets* is a transitional album in terms of personnel. Syd Barrett was becoming increasingly unreliable and left the band during the recording sessions. Only one of his songs is used and he contributes to only two other tracks. David Gilmour had already been recruited to provide guitar support for Barrett and the album is completed by him. Both guitarists play on *Set The Controls For The Heart Of The Sun*. The result of all this is that there is a shift away from the concise, quirky pop-song approach that was Syd Barrett's speciality and towards an atmospheric, ambient sound with a pronounced science-fiction flavour. There was an element of this on the group's first album, most notably on the improvisational piece, *Interstellar Overdrive*, but now the approach is extended to cover virtually all the music. The range of tones and effects that Rick Wright is able to coax from his keyboards is crucial in making the music work. The music is psychedelic in the wide sense of being concerned with exotic sounds, but it is looking forward to more innovative approaches rather than blindly following a trend. The long title piece has the character of a soundtrack recording. It is instrumental and divided into three distinct sections, culminating in a sequence of drawn-out chords rather like a piece of church music. Although this final section is beautiful, it does sound relatively conventional after the maelstrom of electronic and percussive sounds that precede it, so that what is intended to serve as a climax actually falls a little flat. This is no more than a minor disappointment, however, on an album whose display of imagination and innovation is otherwise very evident.

THE CRAZY WORLD OF ARTHUR BROWN

UK release	June 1968	Track	613/612 005
US release	September 1968	Track	SD 8198

1. Prelude – Nightmare (Arthur Brown)
2. Fanfare – Fire Poem (Arthur Brown/Vincent Crane)
3. Fire (Arthur Brown/Vincent Crane/Mike Finesilver/Peter Ker)
4. Come And Buy (Arthur Brown/Vincent Crane)
5. Time (Arthur Brown)
6. Confusion (Vincent Crane)

7. I Put A Spell On You (Screamin' Jay Hawkins)
8. Spontaneous Apple Creation (Arthur Brown/Vincent Crane)
9. Rest Cure (Arthur Brown/Vincent Crane)
10. I've Got Money (James Brown)
11. Child Of My Kingdom (Arthur Brown/Vincent Crane)

Arthur Brown: vocals / Vincent Crane: organ, piano, vibraphone, arranger / Nick Greenwood: bass guitar / Drachen Theaker: drums / John Marshall: drums (7,11) / Jon Hiseman: drums (3) / Kit Lambert: producer / Pete Townshend: producer

During the previous year, while the Crazy World Of Arthur Brown was building a following with live performances, the singer made a big impression with a stage act that included wearing a literally flaming head-dress and black and white face paint. He also possessed a remarkable, rich singing voice, capable of ascending into a shrieking falsetto. Unusually, the band had no guitarist, but relied on the virtuoso playing of organist Vincent Crane to complement Arthur Brown's singing. *Fire* was released as a single alongside the album and seemed to embody the stage act within its dramatic music. It rose quickly to number one in the UK chart. On the group's album, *Fire* forms part of a suite of songs occupying the whole of the first side and although it serves as a focus and high point, the entire suite is extremely compelling. The group's strengths continue through to the album's second side, where Arthur Brown includes a couple of covers. He is able to perform a definitive version of *I Put A Spell On You* (completely outclassing the novelty approach of the song's writer, Screamin' Jay Hawkins) as well as a James Brown song, where, unlike all other such attempts, the singer has the voice to properly do justice to the original. The album has an orchestral brass section added to the mix in places, although Vincent Crane's organ playing is so satisfying on its own that this hardly seems necessary. The lack of a guitarist gives the music a generally smooth character, albeit one possessing considerable force when required, and this helps to make the album sound very distinctive.

SILVER APPLES

US release	June 1968	Kapp	KS-3562
Not released in UK			

1. Oscillations (Simeon/Danny Taylor/Stanley Warren)
2. Seagreen Serenades (Simeon/Taylor/Warren)
3. Lovefingers (Simeon/Taylor/Warren)
4. Program (Simeon/Taylor/Warren)
5. Velvet Cave (Simeon/Taylor/Warren)

6. Whirly-Bird (Simeon/Taylor/Warren)
7. Dust (Simeon/Taylor/Warren)
8. Dancing Gods (Traditional Navajo)
9. Misty Mountain (Simeon/Taylor/Eileen Lewellen)

Dan Taylor: vocals, drums / Simeon (Coxe III): electronics, flute, vocals / Barry Bryant: producer

Silver Apples was a New York duo playing music propelled only by drumming and electronics. Without being able to afford one of the new synthesizers, Simeon made an assembly of several linked oscillators in order to produce simple patterns of squeaky tones. Because there is no instrument to provide any harmonic support, the songs are modal in structure, sounding as though Dan Taylor is improvising his melodies over the rhythm, using lyrics written for the most part by poet Stanley Warren. The decision to employ only electronics and percussion, rather than integrate the playing into music produced by a wider range of instruments, as was being done by several other groups, was forced on Silver Apples by an original larger number of musicians disliking having to perform with electronics that were not capable of providing much interesting timbre. But it certainly gives the duo a unique sound. Music so stark was never likely to gain much support at the time, although some fifteen years later groups of this kind had become more commonplace.

OS MUTANTES

The first album by the trio, Os Mutantes, frequently appears on lists of the most remarkable albums of the sixties, yet it would have been unknown and unheard by most music fans in the US and UK, because it was only issued in Brazil. Although the group's music has some contact with the greats of Brazilian music, Gilberto Gil and Jorge Ben, it is nothing

Brazil release	June 1968	Polydor	LPNG 44.018

Not released in UK or US

1. Panis Et Circensis (Caetano Veloso, Gilberto Gil)
2. A Minha Menina (Jorge Ben)
3. O Relogio (Os Mutantes)
4. Adeus Maria Fulo (Humberto Teixeira/Sivuca)
5. Baby (Caetano Veloso)
6. Senhor F (Os Mutantes)
7. Bat Macumba (Caetano Veloso, Gilberto Gil)
8. Le Premier Bonheur Du Jour (Franck Gerald/Jean Renard)
9. Trem Fantasma (Caetano Veloso, Os Mutantes)
10. Tempo No Tempo (Once Was A Time I Thought) (John Phillips/Os Mutantes)
11. Ave Gengis Khan (Os Mutantes)

Rita Lee: vocals, recorder, autoharp, percussion / Sergio Dias: vocals, guitar / Arnaldo Baptista: vocals, keyboards, bass guitar / Dirceu: drums / Jorge Ben: vocals, guitar (2) / Dr Cesar Baptista: vocals (11) / Clarisse Leite: piano (6) / Claudio Baptista: electronics / Gilberto Gil: percussion (7) / Rogerio Duprat: arranger / Manoel Barenbein: producer

like the rhythmic Latin music generally heard in Brazil. It seems probable that the primary influence is Frank Zappa's Mothers Of Invention, because that is what it sounds like. As with Zappa, the music is complex and multi-layered, but with an accessible core that makes the music easy to appreciate. It is apparent that although the music fits in well with the psychedelic approach of the time, the members of Os Mutantes are well aware of what they should be doing. They are not simply piling on effect after effect, but have a clear idea of the artistic direction they are following. It is a shame that the group's efforts were not much heard at the time because the album is indeed a rather impressive piece of work.

SOUNDTRACK   2001: A SPACE ODYSSEY

US release	June 1968	MGM	S1E-13 ST X
UK release	June 1968	MGM	CS 8078

1. Also Sprach Zarathustra (Introducion) (Richard Strauss)
2. Requiem (excerpt) (György Ligeti)
3. Lux Aeterna (excerpt) (György Ligeti)
4. The Blue Danube (excerpt) (Johann Strauss)
5. Gayane Ballet Suite (Adagio) (Aram Khachaturian)
6. Atmospheres (György Ligeti)
7. The Blue Danube (excerpt) (Johann Strauss)
8. Also Sprach Zarathustra (Introduction) (Richard Strauss)

Berlin Philharmonic Orchestra conducted by Karl Böhm (1,8) / Bavarian Radio Orchestra conducted by Francis Travis (2) / Stuttgart Schola Cantorum conducted by Clytus Gottwald (3) / Berlin Philharmonic Orchestra conducted by Herbert Von Karajan (4,7) / Leningrad Philharmonic Orchestra conducted by Gennadi Rozhdestvensky (5) / Sudwestfunk Orchestra conducted by Ernest Bour (6)

Stanley Kubrick, the director of the acclaimed science fiction film, *2001: A Space Odyssey*, commissioned Alex North to compose the music, but eventually decided to use the established classical pieces that he had originally used as a temporary soundtrack. The opening section of *Also Sprach Zarathustra*, composed by Richard Strauss in 1896, is ideal for the purpose it now has, as a beginning for the film. It is dramatic and seems complete – indeed the music that follows in the full work (not included here) is a distinct anticlimax. The three pieces by contemporary Hungarian composer György Ligeti provide music that most explicitly fits the science fiction theme, although Kubrick neglected to ask Ligeti's permission for the music to be used. The pieces all have a similar structure in which long drawn-out notes with closely adjacent frequencies are piled on top of each other to create an intensely atmospheric soundscape. The music creates a powerful mood without actually delivering a melody. By virtue of being included on a big-selling soundtrack album, Ligeti acts as a populariser for modern avant garde orchestral and choral music whether or not he actually wants to be. His music acquires a significance rather greater than simply being effective mood music.

FAIRPORT CONVENTION

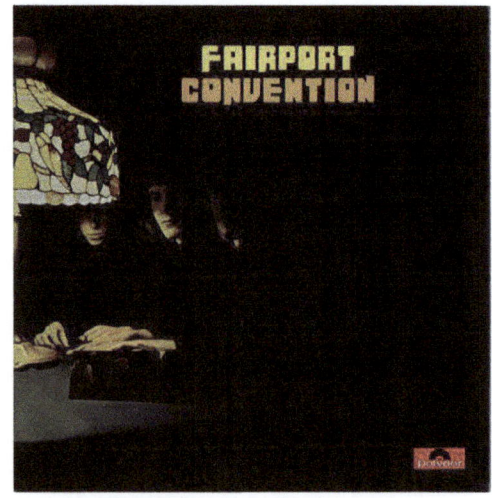

The first album by a new British group, Fairport Convention, contains American-inspired folk-rock, very much in the style of Jefferson Airplane or the Peanut Butter Conspiracy. There is a similar balance of male and female lead vocals, even if Judy Dyble and Iain Matthews do not make much attempt to integrate their singing. The music is played with enormous confidence and expertise, as though the group had indeed benefited from any nights playing to appreciative audiences at the Avalon Ballroom. The first track, one of several cover versions apparently chosen for their exclusivity, reveals some devastating playing by the group's lead guitarist, Richard Thompson, aged just nineteen. Even then, he sounds like no other guitarist. There are two songs by Joni Mitchell, still not recorded by her at the time, and both of them are treated with the kind of loving respect that they deserve. The group's own songs are equally distinctive, whether delivered as storming rock music (*It's Alright Ma, It's Only Witchcraft*, with more incendiary playing from Richard Thompson to match the title) or else caressing, sensitive balladry *(Decameron, Sun Shade)*. We know now that Judy Dyble was unceremoniously dumped even before the album was released and that Fairport Convention did not long pursue this particular musical approach, but that may be because in one album, the group shows how it has completely mastered it.

| UK release | June 1968 | Polydor | 583/582 035 |
| US release | 1970 | Cotillion | SD 9024 |

1. Time Will Show The Wiser (Emitt Rhodes)
2. I Don't Know Where I Stand (Joni Mitchell)
3. If (Stomp) (Iain Matthews/Richard Thompson)
4. Decameron (Richard Thompson/Paul Ghosh/Andrew Horvitch)
5. Jack O'Diamonds (Bob Dylan/Ben Carruthers)
6. Portfolio (Judy Dyble/Tyger Hutchings)

7. Chelsea Morning (Joni Mitchell)
8. Sun Shade (Richard Thompson/Paul Ghosh/Andrew Horvitch)
9. The Lobster (Richard Thompson/Tyger Hutchings/George Painter)
10. It's Alright Ma, It's Only Witchcraft (Richard Thompson/Tyger Hutchings)
11. One Sure Thing (Harvey Brooks/Jim Glover)
12. M1 Breakdown (Tyger Hutchings/Simon Nicol)

Judy Dyble: vocals, autoharp, recorder, piano / Iain Matthews: vocals / Simon Nicol: guitar, vocals / Richard Thompson: guitar, mandolin, vocals / Tyger Hutchings: bass guitar, bass, jug / Martin Lamble: drums, violin / Claire Lowther: cello (6) / Joe Boyd: producer / Tod Lloyd: producer

ILL WIND   FLASHES

| US release | June 1968 | ABC | ABCS-641 |
Not released in UK

1. Walkin' And Singin' (Ken and Tom Frankel)
2. People Of The Night (Ken and Tom Frankel)
3. Little Man (Ken and Tom Frankel)
4. Dark World (Ken and Tom Frankel)
5. L.A.P.D. (Richard Griggs)

6. High Flying Bird (Bill Edd Wheeler)
7. Hung Up Chick (Ken and Tom Frankel)
8. Sleep (Ken and Tom Frankel)
9. Full Cycle (Ken and Tom Frankel)

Connie Devanney: vocals / Richard Griggs: guitar, vocals / Ken Frankel: guitar, banjo / Carey Mann: bass guitar, vocals / David Kinsman: drums / Tom Wilson: producer

The Massachusetts band Ill Wind was one of the first to be taken on by producer Tom Wilson's own company, but it failed to achieve the national success that the members had hoped for. *Flashes* presents a set of inventive and well-played folk rock, suffused with the spirit of San Francisco, despite the band never having been there. Connie Devanney is an outstanding lead singer with a beautiful, smooth voice, albeit lacking the emotional grit of Grace Slick. Essentially, however, Ill Wind create a convincing illusion of what the Great Society might have sounded like two years further on, if Grace had never left. The band manages to breathe fresh life into the counter-culture anthem *High Flying Bird* and its own songs are well-written, even if there is no single track to make the same kind of impact as *Somebody To Love* or *White Rabbit*. It seems likely that if Ill Wind had actually been based in California, then it would have become a major name, but sadly the band fell apart after making just the one album.

FAMILY   MUSIC IN A DOLL'S HOUSE

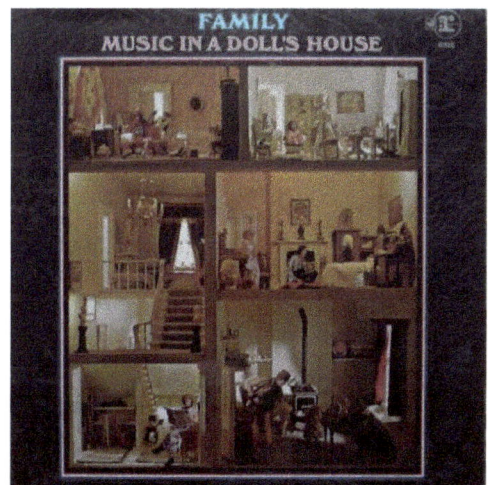

| UK release | July 1968 | Reprise | R(S)LP 6312 |
| US release | July 1968 | Reprise | RS 6312 |

1. The Chase
2. Mellowing Grey
3. Never Like This (Dave Mason)
4. Me My Friend
5. Variation On A Theme Of Hey Mr Policeman (Charlie Whitney)
6. Winter
7. Old Songs, New Songs
8. Variation On A Theme Of The Breeze (Charlie Whitney)

9. Hey Mr Policeman (Charlie Whitney/Ric Grech/Roger Chapman)
10. See Through Windows
11. Variation On A Theme Of Me My Friend (Charlie Whitney)
12. Peace Of Mind
13. Voyage
14. The Breeze
15. 3 X Time

All compositions by Roger Chapman/ Charlie Whitney except where stated

Roger Chapman: vocals, harmonica, tenor saxophone / Charlie Whitney: guitar, sitar / Jim King: tenor and soprano saxophones, harmonica, vocals / Ric Grech: bass guitar, violin, cello, vocals / Rob Townsend: drums / Tubby Hayes: tenor saxophone (7) / Mike Batt: arranger / Dave Mason: producer, mellotron / Jimmy Miller: producer (12,14)

The first album by Family, like a mutant offspring of *Sgt Pepper* and Traffic's *Dear Mr Fantasy*, was produced by a member of the latter group, Dave Mason. He cannot resist getting Family to include one of his own songs, but *Never Like This* does fit in perfectly with the group's own songs – probably the reason that Mason wanted to work with Family in the first place. It is an interesting idea to include brief instrumental references to three of the album's songs, using different arrangements (the *Variation* tracks), and it has the effect of helping to bind the songs into what seems like a continuous suite. Lead singer Roger Chapman has an extraordinary and unique voice, as though he is singing through a tremolo effect circuit, and he gives the songs a unifying character, which is necessary because they are otherwise a remarkably varied collection. It seems that the songs come first and the group uses its considerable resources to ensure that each one makes its maximum impact, rather than trying to impress the listener with flashy displays of personal virtuosity – like the Beatles, in fact. As a first album by a new group, *Music In A Doll's House* is an astonishingly accomplished piece of work and it was rewarded by a placing in the UK album charts, even if it was not a huge seller.

THE MOODY BLUES   IN SEARCH OF THE LOST CHORD

```
UK release    July 1968    Deram    SML/DML 711
US release    July 1968    Deram    DES 18017

1.  Departure (Graeme Edge)
2.  Ride My See-Saw (John Lodge)
3.  Dr Livingstone, I Presume (Ray Thomas)
4.  House Of Four Doors (John Lodge)
5.  Legend Of A Mind (Ray Thomas)
6.  House Of Four Doors Part 2 (John Lodge)

7.  Voices In The Sky (Justin Hayward)
8.  The Best Way To Travel (Mike Pinder)
9.  Visions Of Paradise (Justin Hayward/Ray Thomas)
10. The Actor (Justin Hayward)
11. The Word (Graeme Edge)
12. Om (Mike Pinder)

Justin Hayward: vocals, guitar, sitar, keyboards, bass guitar, percussion / Mike Pinder: vocals, keyboards, cello, guitar, bass guitar, autoharp, tambura / Ray Thomas: vocals, flute, soprano saxophone / John Lodge: vocals, bass guitar, cello, guitar, percussion / Graeme Edge: vocals, drums, percussion, piano / Tony Clarke: producer
```

Encouraged by the unexpected success of the *Days Of Future Passed* album, the Moody Blues set about creating a set of new songs for a follow-up. This time there is no orchestra in attendance, and instead the group members rely on their own considerable skills on several instruments to create a varied panoply of timbres to make the songs sound as impressive as possible. Mike Pinder's mellotron is a dominant ingredient, but it is by no means the only instrumental texture on offer. The songs are linked together so that each one segues smoothly into the next and a tremendous amount of imagination is applied to the details of the arrangements. One particularly good example of the care being taken is the monotone flute part played over the second half of *The Best Way To Travel*. Heard through headphones in stereo, the flute can be heard to be circling around the head of the listener. The technology to achieve this effect had supposedly not yet been invented, but the Moody Blues manage to do it anyway. All the members of the group contribute songs and for the most part the songwriter delivers the lead vocal. In the case of Graeme Edge, this means that he recites poems over the sounds produced by the other musicians. Justin Hayward has arguably the most expressive voice, but the fact that his vocals are rationed means that they make all the more impact whenever he does sing. *In Search Of The Lost Chord*, with a title suggesting a concept of sorts, is a hugely impressive work and succeeds in giving the Moody Blues credibility as perhaps the most powerful producers of inventive pop-rock material after the Beatles.

THE NICE   THE THOUGHTS OF EMERLIST DAVJACK

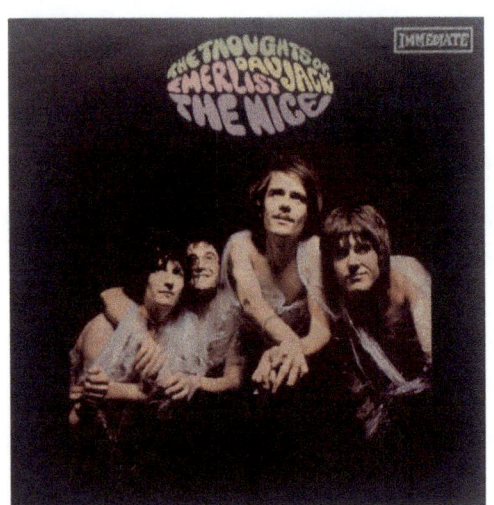

```
UK release    July 1968    Immediate    IMSP/IMLP 016
US release    July 1968    Immediate    Z12 52004

1.  Flower King Of Flies (Keith Emerson/Lee Jackson)
2.  The Thoughts Of Emerlist Davjack (Keith Emerson/David O'List)
3.  Bonnie K (Lee Jackson/David O'List)
4.  Rondo (Dave Brubeck/The Nice)

5.  War And Peace (The Nice)
6.  Tantalising Maggie (Keith Emerson/Lee Jackson)
7.  Dawn (Brian Davison/Keith Emerson/Lee Jackson)
8.  The Cry Of Eugene (Keith Emerson/Lee Jackson/David O'List)

Keith Emerson: keyboards, vocals / David O'List: guitar, trumpet, vocals / Lee Jackson: bass guitar, percussion, vocals / Brian Davison: drums, percussion / Billy Nicholls: vocals (2) / Produced by the Nice
```

Initially formed as a backing group for singer P.P.Arnold, the Nice soon began to tour on its own. Perhaps feeling that the album was not as strong as it could be, Immediate held it back for several months and eventually released it in the wake of the band's chart success with a single, a rock instrumental version of *America* from the musical *West Side Story*. As it happens, however, the album is an interesting debut. Although David O'List's fuzz-toned guitar plays a substantial part, the music on the album is dominated by Keith Emerson's skilful playing on organ and other keyboard instruments.

Between them, these two are able to give the songs a wealth of fascinating lines and textures. The fact that none of the group's members can sing very well is frequently disguised by processing the vocals or else adopting a barking tone with no attempt to hit precise notes. Meanwhile, *Rondo, War And Peace,* and most of *Dawn* are instrumentals. *The Thoughts Of Emerlist Davjack* (the name derived from a cute amalgamation of the group members' surnames) is evidence of a set of fertile musical imaginations at play, although the Nice and Keith Emerson would manage to create more acclaimed material a little later.

SKIP BIFFERTY

UK release   July 1968   RCA Victor   SF/RD 7941
Not released in US

1. Money Man (Skip Bifferty)
2. Jeremy Carabine (Graham Bell/John Turnbull/Colin Gibson)
3. When She Comes To Stay (Graham Bell/John Turnbull)
4. Guru (John Turnbull/Colin Gibson)
5. Come Around (Graham Bell/John Turnbull/Mick Gallagher)
6. Time Track (Graham Bell/John Turnbull/Colin Gibson)
7. Gas Board Under Dog Part 1 (John Turnbull/Mick Gallagher)

8. Inside The Secret (Graham Bell)
9. Orange Lace (Graham Bell/John Turnbull)
10. Planting Bad Seeds (Graham Bell/John Turnbull/Mick Gallagher/Vic Smith)
11. Yours For At Least 24 (Graham Bell/John Turnbull/Mick Gallagher/Colin Gibson)
12. Follow The Path Of The Stars (Graham Bell/Mick Gallgher/Vic Smith)
13. Prince Of Germany The First (John Turnbull/Colin Gibson)
14. Clearway 51 (Graham Bell/Colin Gibson/Mick Gallagher)

Graham Bell: vocals / John Turnbull: guitar, vocals / Mick Gallagher: keyboards / Colin Gibson: bass guitar / Tommy Jackman: drums / Vic Smith: producer

Newcastle group Skip Bifferty recorded a fine single during 1967, *On Love,* complete with sudden changes of mood and instrumentation, and wrapped in a striking raspy guitar riff. It was followed by the more deliberately commercial *Happy Land,* enhanced by a string section. Sadly neither record was a hit and the songs are not included on the group's album, but they would have made it a very much stronger record if they had been. Producer Vic Smith (later to work for the Jam) does the group few favours by delivering a rather muddy recording quality, but it remains the case that the songwriting is not really very distinguished, with only *When She Comes To Stay* leaving much of a lasting impression. Singer Graham Bell has a powerful rock voice and was heard on several other records during the following years, but John Turnbull and Mick Gallagher made rather more impact in the long run, becoming members of Ian Dury's Blockheads.

TYRANNOSAURUS REX — MY PEOPLE WERE FAIR AND HAD SKY IN THEIR HAIR… BUT NOW THEY'RE CONTENT TO WEAR STARS ON THEIR BROWS

UK release   July 1968   Regal Zonophone   (S)LRZ 1003
Not released in US

1. Hot Rod Mama
2. Scenescof
3. Child Star
4. Strange Orchestras
5. Chateau In Virginia Waters
6. Dwarfish Trumpet Blues

7. Mustang Ford
8. Afghan Woman
9. Knight
10. Graceful Fat Sheba
11. Weilder Of Words
12. Frowning Atahualpa (My Inca Love)

All compositions by Marc Bolan

Marc Bolan: vocals, guitar / Steve Peregrine Took: percussion / John Peel: narration (12) / Tony Visconti: producer

After his equipment was repossessed by the group's record company, Marc Bolan, the former guitarist with John's Children, decided to make a virtue of the situation and started to perform cut-down acoustic music, supported only by a percussionist. The songs, suffused throughout by Bolan's mystical, poetic approach, have no connection with traditional folk, but instead represent the kind of thing that amateur hippy musicians would produce when called upon to perform something spontaneous. Bolan's enthusiastic, but primitive guitar playing combines with his high, warbling singing voice and Steve Peregrine Took's clattering percussion to create music that is distinctly weird and yet somehow very compelling. The fact that Stephen Porter had chosen to rename himself after a character in J.R.R.Tolkien's *Lord Of The Rings* and that the pair decided to give their album a title that is probably the longest ever used is entirely in keeping with their image.

THE WIND IN THE WILLOWS

| US release | July 1968 | Capitol | SKAO 2956 |
| UK release | July 1968 | Capitol | (S)T 2956 |

1. Moments Spent (Paul Klein/Steve DePhillips)
2. Uptown Girl (Art Petzal/Paul Klein)
3. So Sad (Don Everly)
4. My Uncle Used To Love Me But She Died (Roger Miller)
5. There Is But One Truth Daddy (Paul Klein/Kenneth Grahame)
6. The Friendly Lion (Paul Klein/Wayne Kirby)
7. Park Ave. Blues (Paul Klein/Steve DePhillips)
8. Djini Judy (Paul Klein/Wayne Kirby)
9. Little People (Paul Klein/Wayne Kirby)
10. She's Fantastic And She's Yours (Paul Klein/Peter Brittain/F.Ruvola)
11. Wheel Of Changes (Paul Klein/Peter Brittain)

Paul Klein: vocals, guitar / Deborah Harry: vocals, percussion, tambura / Peter Brittain: guitar, vocals / Wayne Kirby: keyboards, vibraphone, bass, vocals, arranger/ Ida Andrews: flute, piccolo, bassoon, chimes, vocals / Steve DePhillips: bass guitar, vocals / Anton Carysforth: drums / Artie Kornfeld: producer, percussion

The music played by the Wind in the Willows is, for the most part, gentle, unassuming hippy pop. The songs glide softly by without making much impact and without making many demands on the instrumental abilities that the group members undoubtedly have. One track, *There Is But One Truth Daddy,* incorporates a reading from the Kenneth Grahame book after which the group is named and provides some indication that there is a little ambition here, although it could have been stretched rather further. The album would probably have been long forgotten were it not for the fact that the second singer is Debbie Harry. She is somewhat under-employed and only delivers a lead vocal on one track, *Djini Judy,* but she would eventually achieve super-stardom, as the leader of Blondie.

SAGITTARIUS   PRESENT TENSE

US release   July 1968   Columbia   CS 9644
Not released in UK

1. Another Time (Curt Boettcher)
2. Song To The Magic Frog (Curt Boettcher/Michele O'Malley)
3. You Know I've Found A Way (Curt Boettcher/Lee Mallory)
4. The Keeper Of The Games (Curt Boettcher)
5. Glass (Ernie Sheldon/Larry marks)
6. Would You Like To Go (Curt Boettcher/Gary Alexander)
7. My World Fell Down (Geoff Stephens/John Carter)
8. Hotel Indiscreet (James Griffin/Michael Z.Gordon)
9. I'm Not Living Here (Curt Boecher)
10. Musty Dusty (Curt Boettcher)
11. The Truth Is Not Real (Gary Usher)

Gary Usher: producer, arranger, synthesizer / Curt Boettcher: producer (6,10), arranger, vocals, guitar / Keith Olsen: arranger (5) / Glen Campbell: vocals, guitar / Bruce Johnston: vocals / Terry Melcher: vocals / Jim Bell: vocals, oboe / Michele O'Malley: vocals / Sandy Salisbury: vocals, guitar / Lee Mallory: guitar, vocals / Michael Fennelly: sitar, vocals / Doug Rhodes: keyboards, bass guitar , vocals / Joey Stec: guitar / Ron Edgar: drums / Dave Burgess: guitar / Hal Blaine: drums

The album by Sagittarius is not the music of a real band, but rather a studio project masterminded by producer Gary Usher, well known for his work with the Byrds, the Beach Boys, Chad and Jeremy, and the Peanut Butter Conspiracy. Usher favours an orchestrated pop approach, with lush harmony vocals and a generally happy sound. *Present Tense* is a prime example of what has become known as 'sunshine pop'. Essentially the music is like a meeting between the Beach Boys and the Mamas and Papas, if this had taken place a couple of years earlier, albeit with songs that do not quite have the impact of the best material created by those groups. The exception is the memorable *My World Fell Down,* which would have made a good single for the Mamas and Papas. It was indeed issued as a single, under the Sagittarius name, and was a modest US hit, but the album itself was not very successful.

THE MILLENNIUM   BEGIN

The album credited to the Millennium is a companion to the one by Sagittarius. It is the work of Curt Boettcher, hired by Gary Usher to arrange the vocals and other parts on *Present Tense,* and it employs the same set of musicians. Although smooth harmony vocals are again the central focus, in general the music of *Begin* relies much more on its propulsive rhythm section and is too energetic to fulfil the requirements of sunshine pop. There is no single track as memorable as *My World Fell Down,* but the greater reliance on psychedelic textures and effects, combined with the sheer exuberance of the performances, makes a much more impressive album. Sadly, *Begin* did not make much commercial headway and Curt Boettcher abandoned a planned follow-up. Clearly feeling unable to include The Millennium within its Rock Machine promotion package (as the music is neither folk-rock nor a vehicle for electric guitar solos), Columbia did not make much effort to get behind the record. It becomes something of a lost classic of the era as a result.

US release	July 1968	Columbia	CS 9663
Not released in UK			

1. Prelude (Ron Edgar/Doug Rhodes)
2. To Claudia On Thursday (Michael Fennelly/Joey Stec)
3. I Just want To Be Your Friend (Curt Boettcher)
4. 5 a.m. (Sandy Salisbury)
5. I'm With You (Lee Mallory)
6. The Island (Curt Boettcher)
7. Sing To Me (Lee Mallory)
8. It's You (Michael Fennelly/Joey Stec)
9. Some Sunny Day (Lee Mallory)
10. It Won't Always Be The Same (Michael Fennelly/Joey Stec)
11. The Know It All (Curt Boettcher)
12. Karmic Dream Sequence #1 (Curt Boettcher/Lee Mallory)
13. There Is Nothing More To Say (Curt Boettcher/Michael Fennelly/Lee Mallory)
14. Anthem (Begin) (Curt Boettcher/Lee Mallory)

Curt Boettcher: producer, vocals, guitar / Keith Olsen: producer / Lee Mallory: vocals, guitar / Sandy Salisbury: vocals, guitar / Joey Stec: vocals, guitar / Michael Fennelly: vocals, guitar / Doug Rhodes: bass guitar, keyboards / Ron Edgar: drums

NILSSON   AERIAL BALLET

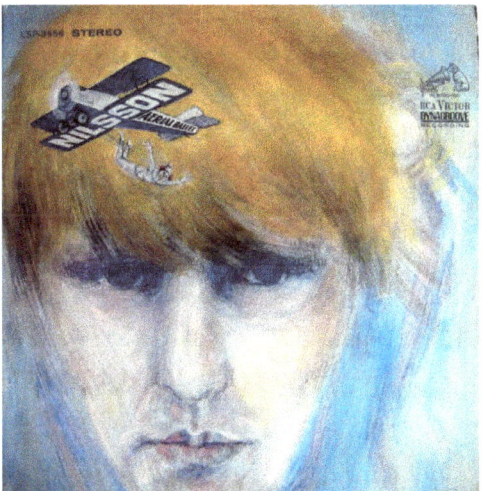

Nilsson continues to display his prowess as a singer and songwriter and this time he chooses to use his own material almost entirely. The exception, a cover of Fred Neil's *Everybody's Talkin'*, became the album's most famous track after it was used as the title music for John Schlesinger's Oscar-winning film, *Midnight Cowboy*. It is rivalled by Nilsson's own song, *One*, however, which became a big hit in the US in a version recorded by Three Dog Night. It has been covered by many other artists since then. Nilsson visited the Beatles in London immediately prior to the release of *Aerial Ballet,* since John Lennon in particular had become a big fan of the previous album. The friendship between the two was cemented when Lennon heard a demo of *One* and decided to take the lyrics personally. The similarity between the music of Nilsson and that of Curt Boettcher (as displayed on the Sagittarius and Millennium albums) is very close, but Nilsson managed to achieve far greater recognition.

US release	July 1968	RCA Victor	LSP-3956
UK release	July 1968	RCA Victor	SF/RD 7973

1. Daddy's Song (only on first issues)
2. Good Old Desk
3. Don't Leave Me
4. Mr Richland's Favorite Song
5. Little Cowboy
6. Together
7. Everybody's Talkin' (Fred Neil)
8. I Said Goodbye To Me
9. Little Cowboy (Reprise)
10. Mr Tinker
11. One
12. The Wailing Of The Willow Harry Nilsson/Ian Freebairn Smith)
13. Bath

All compositions except tracks 7 and 12 by Harry Nilsson

Harry Nilsson: vocals / George Tipton: arranger / Michael Melvoin: keyboards / Larry Knechtel: keyboards, bass guitar / Lyle Ritz: bass / Alvin Casey: guitar / Dennis Budimir: guitar / Jim Gordon: drums / Rick Jarrard: producer

THE DOORS   WAITING FOR THE SUN

US and UK release	July 1968	Elektra	EKS 74024/EKL 4024

1. Hello, I Love You
2. Love Street
3. Not To Touch The Earth
4. Summer's Almost Gone
5. Wintertime Love
6. The Unknown Soldier
7. Spanish Caravan
8. My Wild Love
9. We Could Be So Good Together
10. Yes, The River Knows
11. Five To One

All compositions by the Doors

Jim Morrison: vocals / Ray Manzarek: keyboards / Robby Krieger: guitar / John Densmore: drums / Douglas Lubahn: bass guitar / Kerry Magness: bass guitar (6) / Leroy Vinnegar: bass (7) / Paul A. Rothchild: producer

For the Doors' third album, Jim Morrison had wanted to include another lengthy extemporisation, *The Celebration Of The Lizard,* but was over-ruled. Instead we get the strutting *Five To One*, dominated by Robby Krieger's fiery guitar playing; we get more Krieger, delivering a passable imitation of flamenco guitar in a depiction of a *Spanish Caravan* taken literally; and we get a powerful anti-war diatribe, complete with a dramatised firing squad, in *The Unknown Soldier*. We also get a blatant rip-off of the Kinks, with *Hello, I Love You,* but the song is so catchy that we are inclined to forgive the perpetrators. Clearly the Doors are trying hard to impress, while staying true to their signature sound, and the group was rewarded with the biggest sales of any of its albums.

THE COLLECTORS

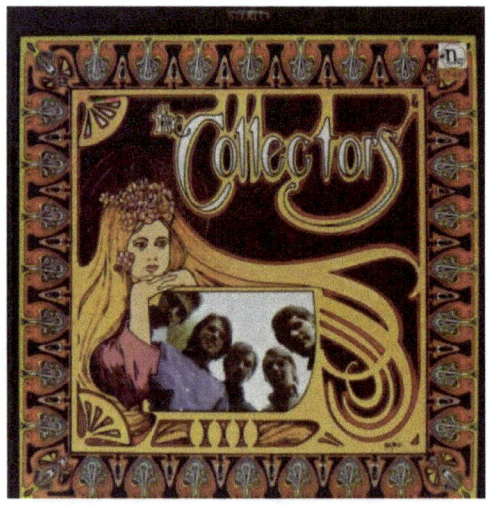

US release   July 1968   Warner Bros   WS 1746
Not released in UK

1. What Is Love
2. She (Will-O-The-Wind)
3. Howard Christman's Older
4. Lydia Purple (Don Dunn/Tony McCashen)
5. One Act Play
6. What Love (Suite)

All compositions by the Collectors except track 4

Howie Vickers: vocals / Bill Henderson: guitar, recorder, vocals / Claire Lawrence: organ, tenor saxophone, flute, recorder, vocals / Glenn Miller: bass guitar, vocals / Ross Turney: drums / Jesse Erlich: cello (4) / Larry Knechtel: keyboards (4) / Norm Jeffries: vibraphone (4) / Dave Hassinger: producer

By the time that it released its first album, Canadian group the Collectors had been performing for seven years and the music does indeed sound like the work of seasoned musicians well used to working together. They manage to make the familiar sound of a powerful lead singer with harmony backing vocals and a robust rhythm section sound fresh and exciting. Like the Beatles, the group adds a particular instrumental sound to each track, whether this is the spacious keyboards of *What Is Love*, the Jethro Tull-style flute of *She (Will-O-The-Wind)*, or the cello and harpsichord combination of *Lydia Purple*. The second side of the album is given over to just one track, described as a suite, although it is clearly a single, albeit multi-faceted, work – and it sticks firmly to the same key throughout. The song is commendably ambitious, although it is eclipsed by some other long rock compositions of the time, most notably *1983…A Merman I Should Turn To Be*, released three months later by Jimi Hendrix. The Collectors were able to keep a career in music going well into the twenty-first century, although the departure of singer Howie Vickers towards the end of 1969 persuaded the remaining members to change the name of the group, to Chilliwack.

THE GRATEFUL DEAD   ANTHEM OF THE SUN

US and UK release   July 1968   Warner Bros   WS 1749

1. That's It For The Other One (Garcia/Kreutzmann/Lesh/ McKernan / Weir/ Constanten)
2. New Potato Caboose (Phil Lesh/Robert Petersen)
3. Born Cross-Eyed (Bob Weir)
4. Alligator (Phil Lesh/Pigpen McKernan/Robert Hunter)
5. Caution (Do Not Stop On Tracks) (Garcia/Kreutzmann/Lesh/McKernan/Weir)

Bob Weir: guitar, vocals / Jerry Garcia: guitar, vocals / Pigpen McKernan: keyboards, vocals / Phil Lesh: bass guitar, trumpet, keyboards, percussion, vocals / Bill Kreutzmann: drums, percussion / Mickey Hart: drums, percussion / Tom Constanten: keyboards / David Hassinger: producer

For its second album, the Grateful Dead attempts to translate the incendiary impact of its live performances on to vinyl with considerable success. The music is seamlessly pieced together from several different live and studio recordings, but retains the sense of a group of musicians taking considerable risks with improvised rock music and refusing to simply repeat what has worked before. The apparently telepathic interplay that would sustain the group through a thirty-year career is clearly already in place. The addition of a second drummer, Mickey Hart, to the line-up is to enable a much greater rhythmic subtlety rather than increased drive. *Born Cross Eyed* was released as a single, though with a noisy feedback-driven finale that is omitted here. The track is the group's only venture into proper psychedelia and includes Phil Lesh demonstrating his prowess on the trumpet he studied first. Through the rest of the album, the music is not about inventive song-writing, in the manner of the Grateful Dead's peers, Jefferson Airplane or County Joe and the Fish, but is devoted to the joy of simply playing. It is a feeling that is conveyed very well indeed.

AL KOOPER / MIKE BLOOMFIELD / STEVE STILLS   SUPER SESSION

Already bored with his rock big band, Blood, Sweat & Tears, Al Kooper invited guitarist Mike Bloomfield to take part in a jam session in a recording studio. Like Kooper, Bloomfield was also on the point of leaving his own band, the Electric Flag. Presented as the rock equivalent of an after-hours jazz performance, the resulting *Super Session* album is clearly making the point that rock's best musicians are now as worthy of attention as the best jazz players. *Albert's Shuffle* and *Really* allow Mike Bloomfield free reign to do what he likes best, which is to play the blues, but *Stop* and *His Holy Modal*

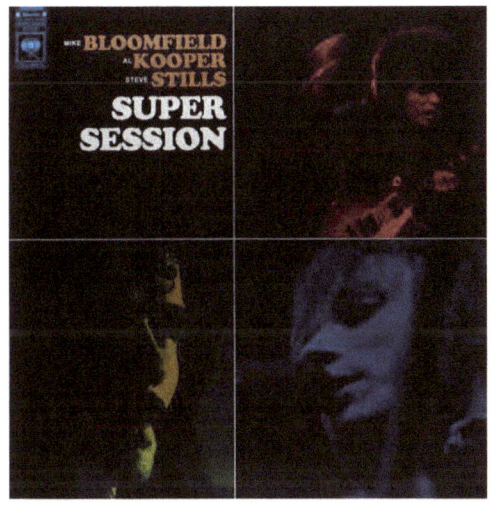

| US release | July 1968 | Columbia | CS 9701 |
| UK release | July 1968 | CBS | S 63396 |

1. Albert's Shuffle (Al Kooper/Mike Bloomfield)
2. Stop (Jerry Ragovoy/Mort Shuman)
3. Man's Temptation (Curtis Mayfield)
4. His Holy Modal Majesty (Al Kooper/Mike Bloomfield)
5. Really (Al Kooper/Mike Bloomfield)

6. It Takes A Lot To Laugh, It Takes A Train To Cry (Bob Dylan)
7. Season Of The Witch (Donovan)
8. You Don't Love Me (Willie Cobb)
9. Harvey's Tune (Harvey Brooks)

Al Kooper: keyboards, vocals, guitar, arranger, producer / Mike Bloomfield: guitar (1-5) / Steve Stills: guitar, vocals (6-9) / Barry Goldberg: piano (1,2) / Harvey Brooks: bass guitar / Eddie Hoh: drums / Joe Scott: arranger

Majesty are a little more ambitious, with the latter track being named in honour of John Coltrane and played as though it is indeed a piece by him. Kooper solos on an electronic keyboard instrument called an ondioline, whose tone is very similar to Coltrane's soprano saxophone. Mike Bloomfield failed to show for the planned second evening of recording (he was rather more interested in pursuing his love of heroin at the time) so Kooper contacted another guitarist, also in the throes of leaving a collapsing band, Steve Stills of Buffalo Springfield. Stills' musical interests are not centred on the blues like Mike Bloomfield, so that side two of the album has a rather different character to side one. The long interpretation of Donovan's *Season Of The Witch* relies very much on improvised playing, however, with Stills showing how the wah-wah pedal is capable of being played with much more gentleness than had previously been employed by Jimi Hendrix or Eric Clapton. After the recording was finished, Al Kooper hired an uncredited brass section to fill in gaps in the pieces produced during both days, or even, in the case of the short *Harvey's Tune*, to provide the entire melodic interest. *Super Session* turned out to be a surprisingly big selling album, the most successful of Al Kooper's career thus far.

THE BUTTERFIELD BLUES BAND   IN MY OWN DREAM

| US and UK release | July 1968 | Elektra EKS 74025 / EKL 4025 |

1. Last Hope's Gone (David Sanborn/Jim Hayne/Paul Butterfield)
2. Mine To Love (Bugsy Maugh)
3. Get Yourself Together (Bugsy Maugh)
4. Just To Be With You (Bernie Roth)

5. Morning Blues (Bugsy Maugh)
6. Drunk Again (Elvin Bishop)
7. In My Own Dream (Paul Butterfield)

Paul Butterfield: vocals, harmonica, guitar / Elvin Bishop: guitar, vocals / Mark Naftalin: keyboards / David Sanborn: soprano, alto, baritone saxophones / Gene Dinwiddie: tenor saxophone, flute, percussion, mandolin, vocals / Keith Johnson: trumpet, piano / Bugsy Maugh: bass guitar, vocals / Phillip Wilson: drums, percussion, vocals / Al Kooper: organ (4,6) / John Court: producer, vocals

This is the second Paul Butterfield album to feature jazz musicians as part of the line-up. The band finally realises that this is the case and creates a thoroughly satisfying fusion of jazz and blues techniques. David Sanborn's alto saxophone is given as much prominence as Elvin Bishop's guitar as a solo instrument and the rhythms played by drummer Phillip Wilson are fluid and make the group swing. There is no trace of a steady rock backbeat. Paul Butterfield's own presence is minimised – a harmonica player in a jazz group would not appear to have much of a role and Butterfield rather proves this to be true. Realistically, *In My Own Dream* does not have the innovative power of the earlier *East West* album, but it is undoubtedly the work of a formerly great band trying very hard, with some considerable success, to prove that it is still relevant.

BUFFALO SPRINGFIELD   LAST TIME AROUND

The last album by Buffalo Springfield comprises an assortment of hurriedly completed ideas and out-takes by a band that had already ceased to function. The result is a considerable come-down from the near perfection of the previous album, but there is still much here to appreciate. Neil Young clearly has his mind on other projects, but Richie Furay himself to be very adept at creating an atmospheric ballad, while Steve Stills is clearly bursting with creative ideas, even if he does not seem to have the patience at this time to finish anything off properly. Furay's *The Hour Of Not Quite Rain* has lyrics written by the winner of a competition, but it emerges as the most satisfying song on the album. *Last Time Around* is not really the best way to remember a group that was often great, although if produced by anyone else, the music would doubtless be considered to be very much worth listening to.

THE BAND   MUSIC FROM BIG PINK

```
US release    July 1968    Atco     SD 33-256
UK release    1969         Atco     228 024

1.  On The Way Home (Neil Young)
2.  It's So Hard To Wait (Richie Furay/Neil Young)
3.  Pretty Girl Why (Steve Stills)
4.  Four Days Gone (Steve Stills)
5.  Carefree Country Day (Jim Messina)
6.  Special Care (Steve Stills)
7.  The Hour Of Not Quite Rain (Richie Furay/Micki Callen)
8.  Questions (Steve Stills)
9.  I Am A Child (Neil Young)
10. Merry-Go-Round (Richie Furay)
11. Uno Mundo (Steve Stills)
12. Kind Woman (Richie Furay)

Steve Stills: vocals, guitar, keyboards, bass guitar, percussion /
Neil Young: vocals, guitar, harmonica, piano / Richie Furay:
vocals, guitar / Jim Messina: bass guitar, vocals, producer /
Bruce Palmer: bass guitar (1) / Jim Fielder: bass guitar (3) /
Gary Marker: bass guitar (9) / Richard Davis: bass (12) / Dewey
Martin: drums / Buddy Miles: drums (6) / Jimmy Karstein:
drums (8,10) / Jeremy Stuart: keyboards (10) / Rusty Young:
pedal steel guitar (12) / other musicians unknown
```

```
US release    July 1968    Capitol    SKAO 2955
UK release    July 1968    Capitol    ST 2955

1.  Tears Of Rage (Bob Dylan/Richard Manuel)
2.  To Kingdom Come (Robbie Robertson)
3.  In A Station (Richard Manuel)
4.  Caledonia Mission (Robbie Robertson)
5.  The Weight (Robbie Robertson)
6.  We Can Talk (Richard Manuel)
7.  Long Black Veil (Danny Dill/Marijohn Wilkin)
8.  Chest Fever (Robbie Robertson)
9.  Lonesome Suzie (Richard Manuel)
10. This Wheel's On Fire (Bob Dylan/Rick Danko)
11. I Shall Be Released (Bob Dylan)

Robbie Robertson: guitar, vocals / Richard Manuel:
keyboards, vocals / Garth Hudson: keyboards, soprano and
tenor saxophones / Rick Danko: bass guitar, vocals, violin /
Levon Helm: drums, vocals
```

During 1967, while supposedly recovering from a motorbike accident, Bob Dylan spent some time recording at a pink-painted house in New York State with the musicians who had recently accompanied him during his stage performances. The results were not officially released until 1975, but in the interim, the musicians, who had originally played as the Hawks, having backed rock 'n' roll singer Ronnie Hawkins since 1958, made an album of songs inspired by the Bob Dylan sessions, though not actually recorded at the pink house. *Music From Big Pink* was released as being simply by 'the Band'. Stylistically, the music is a blend of country with rock, albeit with relatively obscure lyrics, but performed as though the singers were interpreting soul or gospel. The result has a freshness and an exhilarating quality that served as a considerable inspiration for many other artists (notably Eric Clapton) and sold well to the general public too, although it was not a huge hit. Bob Dylan painted the picture used for the album cover and was happy to let the Band record three of his recent songs, but he is not otherwise involved in the music. *The Weight*, issued as a single, is an obvious highlight and emphasises how well the group's songwriters had absorbed Bob Dylan's influence. Robbie Robertson was doubtless well aware of the religious interpretation that would be inspired by the reference to Nazareth in the first line, although he was actually intending to refer to the town in Pennsylvania where Martin guitars were made.

SAVOY BROWN   GETTING TO THE POINT

```
UK release    July 1968    Decca     KL/LK 4935
US release    July 1968    Parrot    PAS 71024    different cover

1.  Flood In Houston (Chris Youlden/Kim Simmonds)
2.  Stay With Me Baby (Chris Youlden/Dave Peverett/Kim Simmonds)
3.  Honey Bee (Muddy Waters)
4.  The Incredible Gnome Meets Jaxman (Kim Simmonds)
5.  Give Me A Penny (Traditional)
6.  Mr Downchild (Chris Youlden/Kim Simmonds)
7.  Getting To The Point (Kim Simmonds)
8.  Big City Lights (Bob Hall/Chris Youlden)
9.  You Need Love (Willie Dixon)

Chris Youlden: vocals / Kim Simmonds: guitar / Dave Peverett: guitar /
Rivers Jobe: bass guitar / Roger Earle: drums / Bob Hall: piano / Mike
Vernon: producer
```

The Savoy Brown Blues Band continues to suffer drastic changes in personnel and for its second album presents a line-up in which only guitarist Kim Simmonds remains from the debut (although pianist Bob Hall makes guest appearances as before). He chooses to drop the 'Blues Band' part of the name too, although the music is the same British blues interpretation as previously. Simmonds seems very concerned to make it clear that the band is his (it is his picture alone that graces the front cover) and his lead guitar playing dominates the music throughout, including two instrumentals. New guitarist Dave Peverett has to be content with a very subsidiary role. Singer Chris Youlden is a considerable find, as he has an immediately recognisable sound of his own and serves as a good foil for the lead guitar. *Getting To The Point* is a worthy addition to the British blues discography, although it does lack the authenticity of the earlier John Mayall or Fleetwood Mac recordings, without offering anything new in the way that Mayall's *Bare Wires* does. It is to the band's credit, however, that it is able to include a considerably rearranged version of the Muddy Waters song, *You Need Love,* without, as Led Zeppelin later did, trying to pretend that it is a group composition.

RAINBOW FFOLLY   SALLIES FFORTH

```
UK release       July 1968      Parlophone      PCS/PMC 7050
Not released in US

1.  She's Alright
2.  I'm So Happy
3.  Montgolfier '67
4.  Drive My Car
5.  Goodbye
6.  Hey You
7.  Sun Sing

8.  Sun And Sand (Jonathan Dunsterville/Stewart Osborn/Roger Newell)
9.  Labour Exchange
10. They'm
11. No (Roger Newell/Jonathan Dunsterville)
12. Sighing Game (Roger Newell/Jonathan Dunsterville)
13. Come On Go

All compositions by Jonathan Dunsterville except where stated

Jonathan Dunsterville: vocals, guitar / Richard Dunsterville: vocals, guitar / Roger Newell: vocals, bass guitar / Stewart Osborn: vocals, drums / John Jackson, Malcolm Jackson: producer
```

The one album made by Rainbow Ffolly owes much to the Beatles' *Sgt Pepper,* but the songs have a pronounced whimsical streak and a lightness of touch that makes the group sound distinctive as well as being enormously attractive. The music was recorded in an independent studio in order to produce a demo to send to record companies. It was Parlophone that signed the group and declared the recordings perfectly good enough for release as they were. *Drive My Car* was chosen for a single, but sadly both it and the album were judged to be too idiosyncratic by the market-place and they did not sell. It had been intended that the album would be issued in a round cover, which might have generated some more interest, but the idea was abandoned when the Small Faces beat the Rainbow Ffolly to the record shops.

MILES DAVIS   MILES IN THE SKY

```
US release    July 1968    Columbia    CS 9628
UK release    July 1968    CBS         (S) 63352

1. Stuff (Miles Davis)
2. Paraphernalia (Wayne Shorter)
3. Black Comedy (Tony Williams)
4. Country Son (Miles Davis)

Miles Davis: trumpet, cornet / Wayne Shorter: tenor saxophone / Herbie Hancock: piano, electric piano / Ron Carter: bass, bass guitar / Tony Williams: drums / George Benson: guitar (2) / Teo Macero: producer
```

George Benson is added to the quintet for *Paraphernalia,* one of a few Miles Davis tracks recorded with a guitarist at this time, although this was the only one to be released until much later. The really revolutionary move, however, is the adoption of electric piano and bass guitar on *Stuff* and the use of a rhythm that is funky and straight ahead, like something that might have appeared on an Otis Redding recording. This is not a rock influence specifically and one cannot imagine a group like the Rolling Stones employing a beat rather far removed from a rock 'n' roll four-four, but it does mark the beginning of the development that would soon lead to the invention of fully-fledged jazz fusion. Miles and Wayne Shorter deliver their customary melodic soloing over the top, well-used to the enormous energy of the different rhythms put together by drummer Tony Williams.

HERBIE HANCOCK   SPEAK LIKE A CHILD

Restricted to a somewhat subsidiary role on the recordings of Miles Davis, Herbie Hancock relishes the opportunity to stretch out on his own *Speak Like A Child* album. Although a trio of wind instruments appears on four of the tracks, it is only there to provide a little colour and the musicians do not play any solos. Hancock's approach is very much the melodic free improvisation in rhythm of his main employer and he provides new interpretations of two tracks already recorded with the Quintet, but the emphasis on piano gives the music a different feel. Mickey Roker is not as skilled at finding unusual ways of implying the beat as Tony Williams, but his playing is good enough on a set of songs that is really all about Herbie Hancock alone.

```
US release      August 1968       Blue Note    BST 84279
Not released in UK

1. Riot (Herbie Hancock)
2. Speak Like A Child (Herbie Hancock)
3. First Trip (Ron Carter)
4. Toys (Herbie Hancock)
5. Goodbye To Childhood (Herbie Hancock)
6. The Sorcerer (Herbie Hancock)

Herbie Hancock: piano/ Jerry Dodgion: flute / Thad Jones:
flugelhorn / Peter Phillips: bass trombone / Ron Carter: bass /
Mickey Roker: drums / Duke Pearson: producer
```

ALICE COLTRANE   A MONASTIC TRIO

```
US release     c.August 1968    Impulse    AS-9156
UK release     1976             Impulse    IMPL 8031

1. Ohnedaruth
2. Gospel Trane
3. I Want To See You
4. Lovely Sky Boat
5. Oceanic Beloved
6. Atmic Peace

All compositions by Alice Coltrane

Alice Coltrane: piano, harp, producer / Jimmy Garrison: bass
/ Ben Riley: drums (1) / Rashied Ali: drums (2-6) / Pharoah
Sanders: bass clarinet (1)
```

Alice Coltrane's first album in her own name is a moving tribute to her late husband. She reveals herself to be a talented harp player as well as a pianist and she uses the instrument throughout the album's second side. She likes to create a lush carpet of sound and the harp is ideal to enable her to do this. The music has no obvious pulse, despite Rashied Ali playing a busy drum part, but successfully manages to be gloriously meditative even without being at all quiet. The two tracks that are different are both on the first side, with Alice Coltrane playing piano. *Ohnedaruth* sounds like something left over from a John Coltrane session and the fact that Pharoah Sanders delivers a short and characteristically frenetic solo helps to complete the illusion. *Gospel Train* is exactly what the title promises – a straightforward piece of soul jazz.

DON ELLIS   SHOCK TREATMENT

```
US release     August 1968    Columbia    CS 9668
UK release     August 1968    CBS         S 63356

1.  A New Kind Of Country (Hank Levy)
2.  Mercy Maybe Mercy (Hank Levy)
3.  Opus 5 (Howlett Smith)
4.  Beat Me Daddy, Seven To The Bar (Don Ellis)
5.  The Tihai (Don Ellis)
6.  Milo's Theme (Don Ellis)
7.  Star Children (Don Ellis)
8.  Homecoming (Don Ellis)
9.  Seven Up (Howlett Smith)
10. Zim (John Magruder)

Don Ellis: trumpet, arranger / Alan Weight, Ed Warren, Glenn
Stuart, Bob Harmon: trumpet / Vince Diaz, Ron Myers, Dave
Sanchez: trombone / Terry Woodson: bass trombone / Ruben
Leon, Joe Lopez, Joe Roccisano: alto and soprano saxophone,
flute / Ira Shulman: tenor saxophone, flute, piccolo, clarinet /
Ron Starr: tenor saxophone, flute, clarinet / John Magruder:
baritone saxophone, flute, clarinet, bass clarinet / Mike Lang:
keyboards / Frank DelaRosa, Dave Parlato: bass / Ray
Neapolitan: bass, sitar / Steve Bohannon: drums / Alan Estes,
Carlos Valdes, Chino Valdes, Mark Stevens, Ralph Humphrey:
percussion / John Hammond: producer
```

The follow-up to Don Ellis's acclaimed *Electric Bath* album is again the work of a big band, performing pieces that are often written in unusual time signatures. The music has tremendous energy and Don Ellis applies electronic effects to his trumpet in places, but the real shock, implied by the album title, is the presence of an angel choir on two tracks, although this rather has the effect of reducing the impact of the music, which cannot have been Ellis's intention. Don Ellis is still hoping for a breakthrough of rock music proportions, although his music sounds too cautious, too close to mainstream jazz to achieve this, when compared, for example, to *Miles In The Sky*, released the previous month.

MARVIN GAYE   IN THE GROOVE

Marvin Gaye was signed to the Tamla label by Berry Gordy in 1960 and made a number of records in different styles with some success, though without achieving the degree of stardom enjoyed by many of his label mates. *I Heard It Through The Grapevine* changed this state of affairs when it was released as a single and became an enormous hit in both the US and the UK. Neither Gaye nor Gordy had much faith in the song and initially resisted producer Norman Whitfield's insistence that

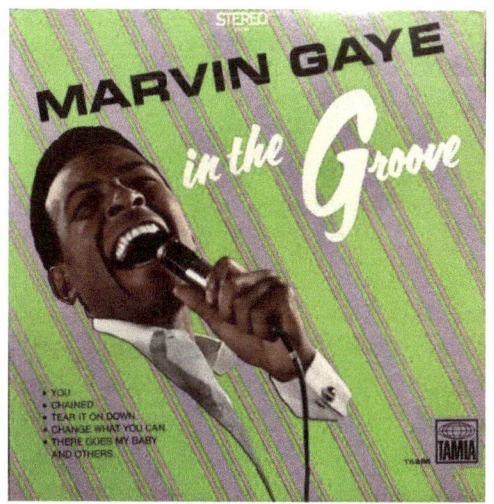

| US release | August 1968 | Tamla | TS 285 |
| UK release | August 1968 | Tamla Motown | (S)TML 11091 |

1. You (Jeffrey Bowen/Jack Goga/Ivy Jo Hunter)
2. Tear It On Down (Nickolas Ashford/Valerie Simpson)
3. Chained (Frank Wilson)
4. I Heard It Through The Grapevine (Barrett Strong/Norman Whitfield)
5. At Last (I Found A Love) (Marvin Gaye/Anna Gaye/Elgie Stover)
6. Some Kind Of Wonderful (Gerry Goffin/Carole King)
7. Loving You Is Sweeter Than Ever (Ivy Jo Hunter/Stevie Wonder)
8. Change What You Can (Marvin Gaye/Anna Gaye/ Elgie Stover)
9. It's Love I Need (Stephen Bowden/Ivy Jo Hunter)
10. Every Now And Then (Eddie Holland/Frank Wilson)
11. You're What's Happening (George Gordy/Robert Gordy/Allen Story)
12. There Goes My Baby (Benjamin Nelson/Lover Patterson/George Treadwell)

Personnel similar to that on other Tamla Motown albums / The Andantes - Jackie Hicks, Marlene Barrow, Louvain Demps; The Originals - Freddie Gorman, Walter Gaines, C.P.Spencer, Hank Dixon; Gladys Knight & The Pips - Gladys Knight, Merald Knight, William Guest, Edward Patten; Telma Hopkins; Joyce Vincent Wilson; Pamela Vincent: vocals / Norman Whitfield, Ivy Jo Hunter, Frank Wilson: producer

it should be a single. Afterwards, however, they were happy for the album *In The Groove* to be retitled *I Heard It Through The Grapevine*. The song plays effortlessly to Marvin Gaye's strengths as a singer – his ability to float a lyric over the rhythm with an easy, relaxed delivery, yet managing to sound passionate and soulful at the same time. The cool electric piano intro is also a key factor, drawing the listener into the song and giving the music a touch of modernity that is only matched by one other song on the album – *Chained*, whose underlying guitar figure and brass riffing makes the music sound like a candidate for a Sly Stone or Electric Flag album. *In The Groove* provides an eminently listenable set of songs, but it lacks the sense of overall artistry, of a singer in charge of his own music, that would come on his later albums.

JAMES BROWN   LIVE AT THE APOLLO VOLUME II

| US release | August 1968 | King | KS-12-1022 |
| UK release | 1969 | Polydor | 583 729/730 |

1. Think (Lowman Pauling)
2. I Wanna Be Around (Sadie Vimmerstedt/Johnny Mercer)
3. That's Life (Dean Kay/Kelly Gordon)
4. Kansas City (Jerry Leiber/Mike Stoller)
5. Let Yourself Go (James Brown)
6. There Was A Time (James Brown)
7. I Feel All Right (James Brown)
8. Cold Sweat (James Brown/Pee Wee Ellis)
9. Maybe The Last Time (James Brown)
10. I Got You (James Brown)
11. Prisoner Of Love (Russ Columbo/Clarence Gaskill/Leo Robin)
12. Out Of Sight (James Brown)
13. Try Me (James Brown)
14. Bring It Up (James Brown/Nat Jones)
15. It's A Man's Man's Man's World (James Brown/Betty Jean Newsome)
16. Lost Someone Medley (James Brown/Bobby Byrd/Lloyd Stallworth)
17. Please Please Please (James Brown/Johnny Terry)

James Brown: vocals, producer / Pee Wee Ellis: organ, alto saxophone / Maceo Parker: tenor saxophone / Eldee Williams: tenor saxophone / St.Clair Pinckney: baritone saxophone / Waymon Reed: trumpet / Joe Dupars: trumpet / Levi Rasbury: valve trombone / Jimmy Nolen: guitar / Alphonso Kellum: guitar / Bernard Odum: bass guitar / Jabo Starks: drums / Clyde Stubblefield: drums / Ronald Selico: percussion / Marva Whitney: vocals (1) / Bobby Byrd: vocals / Bobby Bennett: vocals / Sylvia Medford, Marilyn Jones, Richard Jones: violins

When the original *Live At The Apollo* was released, James Brown was able to use the album as proof that he was the premier soul singer of the time. He is still trying to do this with the second volume, recorded during 1967, apparently unaware that the rules of the music have changed considerably and that the man responsible for this is himself. Side two of the album presents James Brown, the inventor of funk, and is very fine indeed. For the rest of the set, however, he is still performing the same material as five years previously, happy to provide a nostalgic tour through his early hits for the benefit of fans old enough to connect with them. He sings them well; he is still the premier soul singer of the time, but he is far too important an artist to be content with this kind of coasting. Curiously, another major innovator of black music behaved in the same way: Miles Davis was developing fusion jazz on record during 1968-70 yet played live sets that largely ignored this fact and relied on music from several years earlier in his career. As it happens, the nature of James Brown's live shows would indeed change during the next couple of years (as did that of Miles Davis). For the moment, although *Live At The Apollo Volume II* is greatly superior to the half-hearted studio albums that James Brown continued to churn out, it is a much less valuable live presentation than it might have been.

BIG BROTHER & THE HOLDING CO.   CHEAP THRILLS

The difference between the extraordinarily powerful *Cheap Thrills* and the first album by Big Brother and the Holding Company is in the guitar playing. All three of the musicians involved in delivering substantial guitar parts have discovered how to make their instruments feed back, how to deliver an overdriven, distorted tone, how to sound exciting. Most

| US release | August 1968 | Columbia | KCS 9700 |
| UK release | August 1968 | CBS | (S) 63392 |

1. Combination Of The Two (Sam Andrew)
2. I Need A Man To Love (Janis Joplin/Sam Andrew)
3. Summertime (George & Ira Gershwin/DuBose Heyward)
4. Piece Of My Heart (Bert Berns/Jerry Ragovoy)
5. Turtle Blues (Janis Joplin)
6. Oh Sweet Mary (Janis Joplin/Peter Albin)
7. Ball And Chain (Big Mama Thornton)

Janis Joplin: vocals / James Gurley: guitar / Sam Andrew: guitar, bass guitar / Peter Albin: bass guitar, guitar / Dave Getz: drums / John Simon: piano (5), producer

impressive of all is the maelstrom that James Gurley unleashes on *Ball And Chain*. This is a live recording, although the other tracks are made to sound live too by the overdubbing of crowd noise. It can be no coincidence that during the months since the group's debut was recorded, both Jimi Hendrix and Cream had toured the USA, demonstrating what the electric guitar could be like. With this supercharged sound behind her, Janis Joplin rises to the challenge and is superb. John Peel played *Combination Of The Two* on his radio programme in the UK, making the comment that he wished all soul singers sounded like this, clearly believing that Ms Joplin was black. But that is what *Cheap Thrills* is, soul music with a raucous rock guitar backing, and the combination of the two works extremely well. Janis Joplin left the band after this, because she did not like having to share the spotlight with the other musicians, but the truth is that she never sounded so totally involved in the music as she does here.

CREAM   WHEELS OF FIRE

| UK release | August 1968 | Polydor | 583/582 031/2 |
| US release | August 1968 | Atco | SD 2-700 |

1. White Room (Jack Bruce/Pete Brown)
2. Sitting On Top Of The World (Howlin' Wolf)
3. Passing The Time (Ginger Baker/Mike Taylor)
4. As You Said (Jack Bruce/Pete Brown)
5. Pressed Rat And Warthog (Ginger Baker/Mike Taylor)
6. Politician (Jack Bruce/Pete Brown)
7. Those Were The Days (Ginger Baker/Mike Taylor)
8. Born Under A Bad Sign (Booker T Jones/William Bell)
9. Deserted Cities Of The Heart (Jack Bruce/Pete Brown)
10. Crossroads (Robert Johnson)
11. Spoonful (Willie Dixon)
12. Traintime (Jack Bruce)
13. Toad (Ginger Baker)

Eric Clapton: guitar, vocals / Jack Bruce: bass guitar, vocals, cello, guitar, harmonica, recorder, keyboards / Ginger Baker: drums, percussion, vocals/ Felix Pappalardi: producer, viola, keyboards, trumpet, tonette, bells

The third album by Cream is a double record enclosed in a printed silver foil-covered sleeve, with the two records also issued separately as *Wheels Of Fire In The Studio* and *Wheels Of Fire Live At The Fillmore*. The studio sides continue the style established by the previous *Disraeli Gears,* mixing blues performances with more ambitious hard-rock recordings, combining poetic lyrics with virtuoso playing from all three musicians. There are two songwriting pairs at work here: Pete Brown creating words to fit the contours of Jack Bruce's music and Ginger Baker working together with jazz pianist Mike Taylor. The live sides, with *Toad* recorded at the Fillmore, but the rest actually recorded at an alternative San Francisco venue, the Winterland, have a rather different character. *Traintime* is a feature for Jack Bruce's harmonica playing, reprised from his days with the Graham Bond Organisation, while *Toad* sets up a very long Ginger Baker drum solo. Arguably, these tracks, which might have worked well on the stage, do not make for happy repeated listening on record, but the remaining two live tracks provide more than adequate compensation. The band plays its interpretation of Robert Johnson's *Crossroads* very fast and Eric Clapton delivers two solos which, together, provide a masterclass in how to improvise with melodic distinction at speed over the blues chord changes. Clapton has claimed his dissatisfaction with the soloing here, because he believes himself to be a beat out of step with the bass and drums, but for everyone else, this is precisely what gives the playing its tension and excitement. *Spoonful* is a long modal adventure for the whole band, in which Cream soon leaves the song structure behind and performs an astonishing free improvisation in time. This is the approach that led Ginger Baker to explain that when Cream played live it modelled itself on the jazz of the Ornette Coleman Trio, even if Eric Clapton was unaware of the fact! Taken as a whole, *Wheels Of Fire* is an astonishing showcase for the work of a very great and important rock group. This would have been the case even if the album had not been a big seller, but in fact it reached the top three in the album charts of both the US and the UK and sold enough in both countries to be given a pair of platinum disc awards.

JEFF BECK   TRUTH

UK release	August 1968	Columbia	S(C)X 6293
US release	August 1968	Epic	BN 26413

1. Shapes Of Things (Jim McCarty/Keith Relf/Paul Samwell-Smith)
2. Let Me Love You (Jeff Beck/Rod Stewart)
3. Morning Dew (Bonnie Dobson)
4. You Shook Me (Willie Dixon)
5. Ol' Man River (Jerome Kern/Oscar Hammerstein II)
6. Greensleeves (Traditional)
7. Rock My Plimsoul (Jeff Beck/Rod Stewart)
8. Beck's Bolero (Jimmy Page)
9. Blues De Luxe (Jeff Beck/Rod Stewart)
10. I Ain't Superstitious (Willie Dixon)

Jeff Beck: guitar, bass guitar (5) / Rod Stewart: vocals / Ron Wood: bass guitar / Micky Waller: drums / John Paul Jones: bass guitar (8), organ (4,5) / Nicky Hopkins: piano (3,4,8,9) / Keith Moon: drums (4,8) / Jimmy Page: guitar (8) / Micky Most: producer

For his first solo album since leaving the Yardbirds, Jeff Beck assembled a crack band including a struggling singer, Rod Stewart, with a small number of singles to his name, but no great success. Much of the music consists of blues interpretations, in which Jeff Beck makes clear that he is a player capable of inventing very original lines. *I Ain't Superstitious* is a particular showcase for his guitar expertise, playing interesting games with both a wah-wah pedal and the moving of the music back and forth across the stereo image. He opens the album with a reminder of his previous greatest hit, the new version of *Shapes Of Things* being rather different to the Yardbirds' original, yet just as dynamic. To provide contrast, there are four tracks that are defiantly not related to the blues, including a well-played acoustic guitar rendering of the traditional *Greensleeves*. There is also an instrumental piece constructed over a twelve-string guitar rhythm played by Jimmy Page and with the rhythm section provided by John Paul Jones and the Who's Keith Moon. The presence of two members of the future Led Zeppelin emphasises the fact that Jeff Beck very much invents this group's sound with *Truth*, although his unsympathetic management and his own mercurial temper prevented him from building the fanbase enjoyed by Led Zeppelin.

FLEETWOOD MAC   MR. WONDERFUL

UK release	August 1968	Blue Horizon	(S) 7-63205

Not released in US

1. Stop Messin' Round (Peter Green/Clifford Davis)
2. I've Lost My Baby (Jeremy Spencer)
3. Rollin' Man (Peter Green/Clifford Davis)
4. Dust My Broom (Elmore James/Robert Johnson)
5. Love That Burns (Peter Green/Clifford Davis)
6. Doctor Brown (J.T.Brown/Buster Brown)
7. Need Your Love Tonight (Jeremy Spencer)
8. If You Be My Baby (Peter Green/Clifford Davis)
9. Evenin' Boogie (Jeremy Spencer)
10. Lazy Poker Blues (Peter Green/Clifford Davis)
11. Coming Home (Elmore James)
12. Trying So Hard To Forget (Peter Green/Clifford Davis)

Peter Green: vocals, guitar, harmonica / Jeremy Spencer: vocals, guitar / John McVie: bass guitar / Mick Fleetwood: drums / Christine Perfect: piano / Duster Bennett: harmonica / Steve Gregory: alto saxophone / Dave Howard: alto saxophone / Johnny Almond: tenor saxophone / Roland Vaughan: tenor saxophone / Mike Vernon: producer

The second album by Fleetwood Mac is a frustrating affair, combining on one record some sublime Peter Green guitar in a modern blues setting, with four differently titled versions of the same song (*Dust My Blues*) played by Jeremy Spencer, who is clearly running out of inspiration. Peter Green's accommodating personality allows these performances to spoil his album and he also does not do anything about manager Clifford Davis muscling in on his compositions and demanding co-writing credits on all of Green's songs. Apart from the concluding *Trying So Hard To Forget*, a mournful and rather moving country blues, Green's songs benefit from an added brass section, which gives them some needed extra drive, given that Jeremy Spencer is not interested in providing any rhythm guitar support. There is also some apposite piano from Chicken Shack's Christine Perfect on some tracks, although this is pushed way back in the mix. Had the Spencer tracks been replaced by the splendid performances issued by the group as singles: *Black Magic Woman, Need Your Love So Bad,* and just three months later, *Albatross,* then *Mr Wonderful* would have lived up to its boasting name. As it is, the image of Mick Fleetwood's scrawny frame provides an irony that is all too appropriate.

TEN YEARS AFTER   UNDEAD

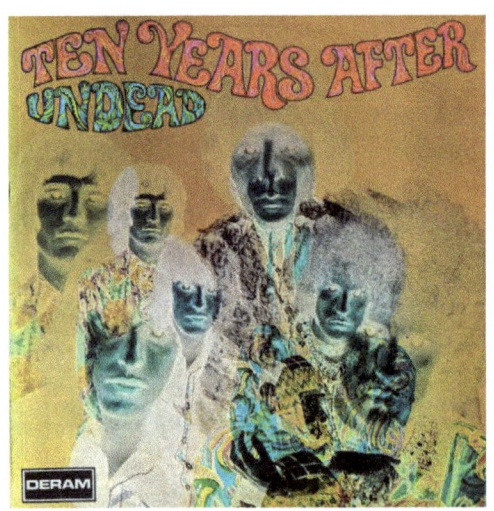

| UK release | August 1968 | Deram | SML/DML 1023 |
| US release | August 1968 | Deram | DES 18016 |

1. I May Be Wrong, But I Won't Be Wrong Always (Alvin Lee)
2. Woodchopper's Ball (Woody Herman/Joe Bishop)
3. Spider In My Web (Alvin Lee)
4. Summertime (George & Ira Gershwin/DuBose Heyward) / Shantung Cabbage (Ric Lee)
5. I'm Going Home (Alvin Lee)

Alvin Lee: vocals, guitar / Chick Churchill: organ / Leo Lyons: bass guitar / Ric Lee: drums / Mike Vernon: producer

Someone decided that it would be amusing to title a live album by Ten Years After *Undead*. The music is played at a small club in London, Klook's Kleek, and recorded at the studio that happened to be located next door. Perhaps wanting to obtain as clear a recording as possible, the band plays quietly and Alvin Lee uses very little sustain on his guitar, giving him a tone much closer to that of a jazz guitarist than that of his British blues peers. Ten Years After plays a version of the Woody Herman big band signature tune, *Woodchopper's Ball*, to emphasise the group's affinity with jazz. Plans were mooted to stage a concert in which Ten Years After would play with the Woody Herman Orchestra, but these were abandoned when it was realised that the two versions were at different tempos and in different keys. An instrumental performance of *Summertime* is used to set up a drum solo by Ric Lee, but the rest of the set comprises the blues, which the band plays confidently if with no great originality. *I'm Going Home* is a relatively short rendering of a song that became a marathon feature of Ten Years After's stage set, allowing Alvin Lee to demonstrate his facility at speed as well as quote from several rock 'n' roll classics in acknowledgement of the group being named in honour of Elvis Presley's first hits.

ERIC BURDON & THE ANIMALS   EVERY ONE OF US

| US release | August 1968 | MGM | SE-4553 |
Not released in UK

1. White Houses (Eric Burdon)
2. Uppers And Downers (Eric Burdon)
3. Serenade To A Sweet Lady (John Weider)
4. The Immigrant Lad (Eric Burdon)
5. Year Of The Guru (Eric Burdon)
6. St. James Infirmary (Traditional)
7. New York 1963 – America 1968 (Eric Burdon/ Zoot Money)

Eric Burdon: vocals / Vic Briggs: guitar, bass guitar / John Weider: guitar, celeste / Danny McCulloch: bass guitar, guitar, vocals / Zoot Money: keyboards, vocals / Barry Jenkins: drums / Eric Burdon and the Animals: producer

Eric Burdon continues to squander his talent. His band has become very good indeed, but Burdon continually wrecks the proceedings with his dull lyrics and little attempt to deliver the soulful singing of which he is more than capable. There are many fine musical moments on *Every One Of Us*: the rhythm section cooks and there is some stunning lead guitar playing. John Weider's *Serenade To A Sweet Lady* is a delightful instrumental, gentle but compelling. Keyboard player Zoot Money, fresh from the failure of his own band, is added to the line-up to considerable benefit. But none of this has anything to do with Burdon himself, who ranges from being ineffective to being embarrassing. It is such a shame.

COUNTRY JOE AND THE FISH   TOGETHER

Country Joe McDonald plays a much smaller role in his own group for the third album, leaving the other members to compose much of the material and not performing at all on some of the tracks. Perhaps as a result, the album does appear less interesting than its predecessors, even if some individual tracks (most notably *Waltzing In The Moonlight* and *Untitled Protest*) are very fine indeed. The last track, little more than a vocal complaint accompanied by a harmonium drone, stands out as different from anything

else recorded in the group's name. For the most part, however, *Together* finds Country Joe and the Fish trying very hard to sound like itself, without attempting any of the innovation that made the first two albums so satisfying.

JULY

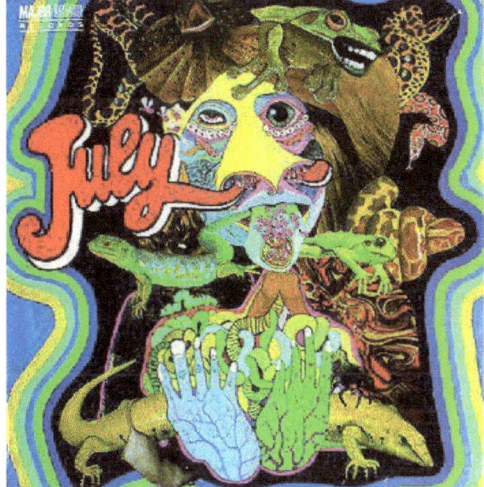

UK release	August 1968	Major Minor MMLP 29
US release	August 1968	Epic BN 26416

1. My Clown
2. Dandelion Seeds
3. Jolly Mary
4. Hallo To Me
5. You Missed It All
6. The Way
7. To Be Free
8. Move On Sweet Flower
9. Crying Is For Writers (Chris Jackson)
10. I See
11. Friendly Man
12. A Bird Lived

All compositions except track 9 by Tom Newman

Tom Newman: vocals, guitar, producer / Tony Duhig: guitar, organ / Jon Field: flute, organ, vocals / Alan James: bass guitar / Chris Jackson: drums, organ / Tommy Scott: producer

US release	August 1968	Vanguard	VSD-79277
UK release	August 1968	Vanguard	SVRL 19006

1. Rock And Soul Music (Country Joe and the Fish)
2. Susan (Chicken Hirsh)
3. Mojo Navigator (Barry Melton/Joe McDonald/Ed Denson)
4. Bright Suburban Mr & Mrs Clean Machine (Chicken Hirsh, Barry Melton)
5. Good Guys Bad Guys Cheer/The Streets Of Your Town (Barry Melton)
6. The Fish Moan
7. The Harlem Song (Joe McDonald)
8. Waltzing In The Moonlight (Chicken Hirsh/Barry Melton)
9. Away Bounce My Bubbles (Chicken Hirsh)
10. Cetacean (Bruce Barthol)
11. An Untitled Protest (Joe McDonald)

Joe McDonald: vocals, guitar / Barry Melton: guitar, vocals / David Cohen: keyboards, guitar, vocals / Bruce Barthol: bass guitar, guitar, organ, vocals / Chicken Hirsh: drums, percussion, vocals / Robin McDonald: percussion (11) / Samuel Charters: producer

July is the first album to feature Tom Newman, later a solo performer and producer/studio manager for Richard Branson's fledgling Virgin record company. It is a pity that the album was effectively issued a month late and that Major Minor could not manage to finance a stereo version, although in the US, where mono albums were only being made for radio station promotion, it was released in stereo. The album is something of a psychedelic extravaganza, with every available studio effect being utilised to the full, and the songs having a typically episodic structure. Clearly feeling that this approach had already been fulfilled by other artists to the point of nausea, reviewer Fred Dellar described the album as the worst he had ever heard, but in fact it seems more like a fascinating summary of the genre's possibilities. It is easy to see why Tom Newman was able to sustain his subsequent career.

ECLECTION

UK release	August 1968	EKS 74023/EKL 4023
US release	August 1968	EKS 74023

1. In Her Mind (Georg Hultgreen)
2. Nevertheless (Michael Rosen)
3. Violet Dew (Georg Hultgreen)
4. Will Tomorrow Be The Same (Georg Hultgreen)
5. Still I Can See (Georg Hultgreen)
6. In The Early Days (Georg Hultgreen)
7. Another Time Another Place (Georg Hultgreen)
8. Morning Of Yesterday (Georg Hultgreen)
9. Betty Brown (Georg Hultgreen)
10. St.Georg and The Dragon (Michael Rosen)
11. Confusion (Michael Rosen)

Kerilee Male: vocals / Michael Rosen: vocals, guitar, trumpet / Georg Hultgreen: vocals, guitar / Trevor Lucas: vocals, bass guitar / Gerry Conway: drums, vocals / Phil Dennys: arranger / Ossie Byrne: producer

Eclection plays folk rock, very much in the same style as to be found on the first album by Fairport Convention, although with slightly less impressive songs. Curiously, the most striking track that Eclection recorded, *Mark Time,* was consigned to the B-side of the *Nevertheless* single and not included on the album. *Eclection* is delightful all the same and failed to achieve the success of Fairport Convention mainly because the group did not put in the necessary promotional work. Singer Kerilee Male, possessed of a highly attractive singing voice, decided that she did not enjoy working in the music business and returned to her native Australia. Although Dorris Henderson, veteran of an album with John Renbourn, was recruited as a fine replacement, the group's momentum was destroyed and it broke up at the end of 1969 without making another album. Ironically, both Trevor Lucas and Gerry Conway were later members of Fairport Convention.

THE BYRDS   SWEETHEART OF THE RODEO

With the departure of both David Crosby and Michael Clarke, the Byrds were left with only two original members. New recruit Gram Parsons was allowed to divert the group's sound towards country-rock, in the manner of his own previous album with the International Submarine Band. Roger McGuinn abandoned both his trademark twelve-string guitar and the

THE GOLDEN AGE OF ROCK Volume One 1963-1968

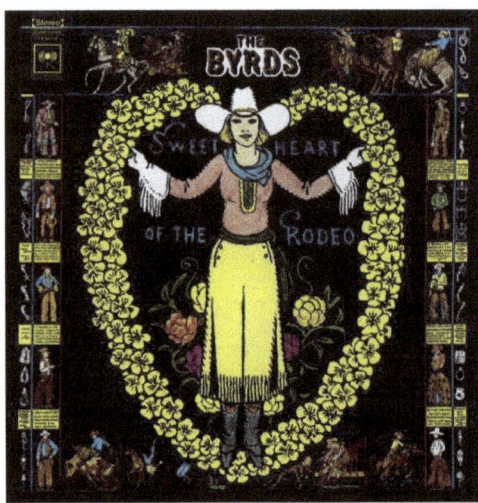

| US release | August 1968 | Columbia | CS 9670 |
| UK release | August 1968 | CBS | (S) 63353 |

1. You Ain't Goin' Nowhere (Bob Dylan)
2. I Am A Pilgrim (Traditional)
3. The Christian Life (Charles & Ira Louvin)
4. You Don't Miss Your Water (William Bell)
5. You're Still On My Mind (Luke McDaniel)
6. Pretty Boy Floyd (Woody Guthrie)
7. Hickory Wind (Gram Parsons/Bob Buchanan)
8. One Hundred Years From Now (Gram Parsons)
9. Blue Canadian Rockies (Cindy Walker)
10. Life In Prison (Merle Haggard/Jelly Sanders)
11. Nothing Was Delivered (Bob Dylan)

Gram Parsons: vocals, guitar, keyboards / Roger McGuinn: guitar, vocals / Chris Hillman: bass guitar, mandolin, guitar, vocals / Kevin Kelley: drums / Lloyd Green: pedal steel guitar / JayDee Maness: pedal steel guitar / Clarence White: guitar / John Hartford: banjo, violin, guitar / Earl P.Ball: piano / Barry Goldberg: piano / Roy Husky: bass / Gary Usher: producer

inventive ambition of *The Notorious Byrd Brothers*, and the Byrds' harmony vocals were downgraded, if not dispensed with altogether. What is effectively a Gram Parsons album, albeit a good one, had the result of interrupting the Byrds' forward momentum and ensured that, after Parsons left the group, it never again made a significant studio album. Attempting to move fully into the country music arena, the Byrds accepted a booking to appear at the Grand Ol' Opry, the bastion of country music, but they did not go down well. Meanwhile, *Sweetheart Of The Rodeo* became very much the least successful album in the group's career thus far.

JIMMY WEBB   JIM WEBB SINGS JIM WEBB

| US release | August 1968 | Epic | BN 26401 |
| UK release | August 1968 | CBS | 63355 |

1. You're So Young
2. Run, Run, Run
3. I Can Do It On My Own
4. I'll Be Back
5. I'm In Need
6. I Keep It Hid
7. Life Is Hard
8. Our Time Is Running Out
9. I Need You
10. Then

All compositions by Jimmy Webb

Jimmy Webb: vocals, piano, arranger / Hank Levine: producer, arranger / Skip Mosher, Jim Stotler, Greg Waitman: vocals

Disappointingly, Jimmy Webb's first solo album does not include versions of any of the songs that had become well-known through hits by other people. That is because the record is made up of early demos, orchestrated without any participation or approval by Webb himself. There is no indication as to when the recordings were made, but the simple structure of the songs and the basic group sound beneath the orchestrations suggests that they must be from around three years before the album's release date. Jimmy Webb is not much of a singer, but then he never became any better on the later albums that he did sanction. He disowned *Jim Webb Sings Jim Webb* and claimed that its release set back his career as a recording artist, although for the insight it provides into the formative work of a truly great songwriter its value is nevertheless considerable.

THE HOLLIES   GREATEST

Taken together, the hit singles on *Greatest* prove the Hollies to be one of the most impressive groups of the sixties, even if success in the US was much more limited. Initially making compelling versions of songs written, and often recorded, by other people, the Hollies started to write their own material and these later hits became

| UK release | August 1968 | Parlophone | PCS/PMC 7057 |
| Not released in US |

1. I Can't Let Go (Al Gorgoni/Chip Taylor)
2. Bus Stop (Graham Gouldman)
3. We're Through (Allan Clarke/Tony Hicks/Graham Nash)
4. Carrie Anne (Allan Clarke/Tony Hicks/Graham Nash)
5. Here I Go Again (Clive Westlake/Mort Shuman)
6. King Midas In Reverse (Allan Clarke/Tony Hicks/Graham Nash)
7. Yes I Will (Gerry Goffin/Russ Titelman)
8. I'm Alive (Clint Ballard Jr)
9. Just One Look (Doris Payne/Gregory Carroll)
10. On A Carousel (Allan Clarke/Tony Hicks/Graham Nash)
11. Stay (Maurice Williams)
12. Look Through Any Window (Charles Silverman/Graham Gouldman)
13. Stop Stop Stop (Allan Clarke/Tony Hicks/Graham Nash)
14. Jennifer Eccles (Allan Clarke/Graham Nash)

Allan Clarke: vocals, harmonica / Graham Nash: vocals, guitar / Tony Hicks: guitar, vocals / Eric Haydock: bass guitar (1,3,5,7,8,9,11,12) / Bernie Calvert: bass guitar (2,4,6,10,13,14) / Bobby Elliott: drums / Ron Richards: producer

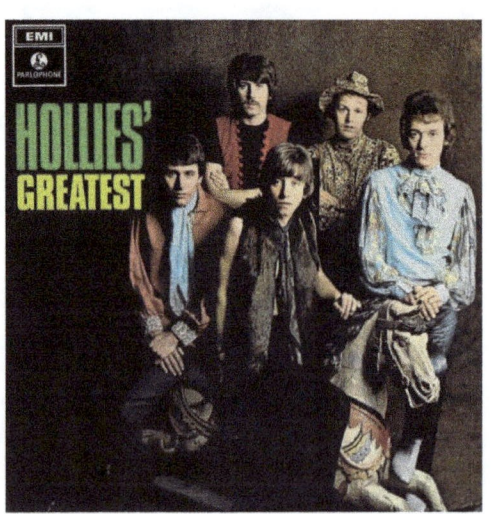

increasingly imaginative, in line with the progress being achieved by the group's contemporaries. *Greatest* does not present the singles in chronological order, but the Hollies were skilled musicians from the outset so that there is little change in the playing quality to make the order of songs seem jarring. Graham Nash left the group after the last hit, *Jennifer Eccles*, and although the Hollies did achieve a few more chart entries, including a number two hit in 1974 with *The Air That I Breathe*, they ceased to be the market leaders they had been up to that point.

THE GODS   GENESIS

UK release   August 1968   Columbia   S(C)X 6286
Not released in US

1. Towards The Skies (Joe Konas)
2. Candles Getting Shorter (Joe Konas/Ken Hensley)
3. You're My Life (Joe Konas/Lee Kerslake)
4. Looking Glass (Joe Konas/Ken Hensley)
5. Misleading Colours (Joe Konas/Lee Kerslake)
6. Radio Show (Harold Robertson/Paul Sugarman)
7. Plastic Horizon (Harold Robertson/Paul Sugarman)
8. Farthing Man (Joe Konas)
9. I Never Knew (Joe Konas/Ken Hensley)
10. Time And Eternity (Joe Konas/Lee Kerslake)

Joe Konas: guitar, vocals / Ken Hensley: keyboards, guitar, percussion, vocals / John Glascock: bass guitar, vocals / Lee Kerslake: drums / David A. Paramor: producer

The Gods originally included young guitarist Mick Taylor in the line-up, but by the time the group got to make an album, Taylor had departed to join John Mayall's Bluesbreakers. *Genesis* is the work of musicians who have successfully found a way to move on from playing the blues and have developed a robust hard rock sound, very like that of fellow EMI outfit, Deep Purple. The vocals are delivered by three members of the band singing in close harmony, but as a way of increasing the impact rather than making a sweet sound. Behind them, the organ and guitar work as equal partners to keep the momentum going. It is a sound that gave Deep Purple considerable success – the Gods were less fortunate, largely because the group's songs are not as distinctive. But Ken Hensley and Lee Kerslake did well with their next band, Uriah Heep, while John Glascock worked for a few years as bass player with the Kinks.

DONOVAN   IN CONCERT

UK release   September 1968   Pye   N(S)PL 18237
US release   August 1968   Epic   BN 26386

1. Introduction
2. Isle Of Islay
3. Young Girl Blues
4. There Is A Mountain
5. Poor Cow
6. Celeste
7. The Fat Angel
8. Guinevere
9. Widow With Shawl (A Portrait)
10. Preachin' Love
11. The Lullaby Of Spring
12. Writer In The Sun
13. Pebble And The Man
14. Rules And Regulations
15. Mellow Yellow

All compositions by Donovan Leitch

Donovan: vocals, guitar, harmonica / Harold McNair: flute, alto saxophone / Lorin Newkirk: piano, organ / David Troncoso: bass / Tony Carr: drums, percussion / Candy John Carr: percussion / The Flower Quartet / Mickie Most: producer

Donovan's live album quickly becomes embarrassing at the start, although this is not the singer's fault, but rather that of his announcers, whose introductions are painfully over the top. The actual concert is a good one, in which Donovan proves that his songs are memorable, even when shorn of the arrangements they receive on the original records. Many of the songs are accompanied by nothing more than Donovan's acoustic guitar; others add a flute and some percussion; while just a few have a full group, although it is one that plays jazz rather than folk-rock. In this way, Donovan manages to vary the mood of the music he is playing and proves himself, if such a proof were even needed, to be an artist in admirable control of his art.

DEEP PURPLE   SHADES OF DEEP PURPLE

Deep Purple was originally put together by the former drummer with the Searchers, Chris Curtis, but had left him behind by the time the group made its first album. Jon Lord had previously been a member of the Artwoods, while Ritchie Blackmore had been in the Outlaws and had worked as a successful session guitarist. The 1963 hit by Heinz, *Just Like Eddie*, features his playing. Kicked off by some extraordinary effects-laden organ playing from Jon Lord, *Shades Of Deep Purple* presents the work of a supremely confident and skilled set of musicians. The music is inventive hard rock, whose character is well summarised by the way the group manages to breathe new life into the much-covered *Hey Joe*. It is already obvious that Deep Purple is going to be a group with an illustrious career.

```
UK release     September 1968    Parlophone       PCS/PMC 7055
US release     July 1968         Tetragrammaton   T-102

1.  And The Address (Ritchie Blackmore/Jon Lord)
2.  Hush (Joe South)
3.  One More Rainy Day (Jon Lord/Rod Evans)
4.  Prelude: Happiness (Deep Purple) / I'm So Glad (Skip James)
5.  Mandrake Root (Ritchie Blackmore/Jon Lord/Rod Evans)
6.  Help (John Lennon/Paul McCartney)
7.  Love Help Me (Ritchie Blackmore/Rod Evans)
8.  Hey Joe (Billy Roberts)

Rod Evans: vocals / Ritchie Blackmore: guitar / Jon Lord: organ, vocals / Nick Simper: bass guitar, vocals / Ian Paice: drums / Derek Lawrence: producer
```

STATUS QUO   PICTURESQUE MATCHSTICKABLE MESSAGES

Status Quo had been attempting to find single success for a couple of years, as the Spectres and as Traffic Jam, but *Pictures Of Matchstick Men* was the one that achieved it, entering the top echelons of the charts in both the UK and the US in early 1968. The hit song's melodic pop-rock, with enough guitar effects and phasing to make it sound psychedelic, was repeated throughout the clumsily titled album released in its wake.

```
UK release        September 1968    Pye             N(S)PL 18220
US release        September 1968    Cadet Concept   LPS 315
different cover, 2 tracks missing

1.  Black Veils Of Melancholy (Francis Rossi)
2.  When My Mind Is Not Live (Francis Rossi/Rick Parfitt)
3.  Ice In The Sun (Marty Wilde/Ronnie Scott)
4.  Elizabethan Dreams (Marty Wilde/Ronnie Scott)
5.  Gentleman Joe's Sidewalk Café (Kenny Young)
6.  Paradise Flat (Marty Wilde/Ronniw Scott)
7.  Technicolour Dreams (Anthony King)
8.  Spicks And Specks (Barry Gibb)
9.  Sheila (Tommy Roe)
10. Sunny Cellophane Skies (Alan Lancaster)
11. Green Tambourine (Paul Leka/Shelley Pinz)
12. Pictures Of Matchstick Men (Francis Rossi)

Francis Rossi: guitar, vocals / Rick Parfitt: guitar, vocals / Roy Lynes: organ, vocals / Alan Lancaster: bass guitar / John Coghlan: drums / John Schroeder: producer
```

The music is pleasant enough but has little depth or expertise and it is impossible to imagine that it would serve as the first landmark in a music career lasting over half a century and still counting. It has to be emphasised, however, that this is not the style that would sustain the group through that time. *Ice In The Sun,* composed to be reminiscent of *Pictures Of Matchstick Men*. was a hit, but two other singles released from the album were not and the album itself did not sell very well either.

PROCOL HARUM   SHINE ON BRIGHTLY

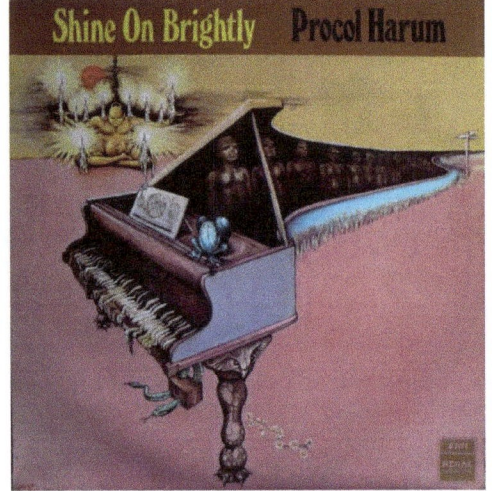

```
UK release    September 1968    Regal Zonophone   (S)LRZ 1004
US release    September 1968    A&M               SP 4151  different cover

1.  Quite Rightly So (Gary Brooker/Matthew Fisher/Keith Reid)
2.  Shine On Brightly (Gary Brooker/Keith Reid)
3.  Skip Softly (My Moonbeams) (Gary Brooker/Keith Reid)
4.  Wish Me Well (Gary Brooker/Keith Reid)
5.  Rambling On (Gary Brooker/Keith Reid)
6.  Magdalene (My Regal Zonophone) (Gary Brooker/Keith Reid)
7.  In Held 'Twas In I (Gary Brooker/Matthew Fisher/Keith Reid)

Gary Brooker: vocals, piano / Robin Trower: guitar, sitar, vocals / Matthew Fisher: organ, piano, harpsichord, vocals / Dave Knights: bass guitar / B.J.Wilson: drums / Denny Cordell: producer / Tony Visconti: producer
```

Shine On Brightly finds Procol Harum trying to forge a signature sound as the natural development of its definitive *A White Shade Of Pale* and achieving this with rather more distinction than on the first album. Every track on *Shine On Brightly* has a memorable melody. Robin Trower's thick, sustained guitar has now moved centre stage and is paired with a piano or an organ that almost always sounds influenced by classical music. The contrast works very well and it seems as though Procol Harum has succeeded in creating a surrealistic music to match the surrealistic imagery of the song lyrics. The long *In Held 'Twas In I* that occupies most of the album's second side is made up of a series of linked pieces and is effectively a medley. The fact that it is cast as a single work, however, makes it very much a forerunner for the procedures of progressive rock. Although *Quite Rightly So* did not fare very well in the chart as a single, the album sold rather better than its predecessor and quite rightly so!

GILES, GILES AND FRIPP — THE CHEERFUL INSANITY OF

UK release	September 1968	Deram	SML/DML 1022
US release	September 1968	Deram	DES 18019

1. The Saga Of Rodney Toady (Robert Fripp)
2. North Meadow (Peter Giles)
3. Newly-weds (Peter Giles)
4. One In A Million (Michael Giles)
5. Call Tomorrow (Peter Giles)
6. Digging My Lawn (Peter Giles)
7. Little Children (Robert Fripp)
8. The Crukster (Michael Giles)
9. Thursday Morning (Michael Giles)
10. Just George (Michael Giles)
11. How Do They Know (Michael Giles)
12. Elephant Song (Michael Giles)
13. The Sun Is Shining (Michael Giles)
14. Suite No.1 (Robert Fripp)
15. Erudite Eyes (Robert Fripp)

Robert Fripp: guitar, mellotron, vocals / Peter Giles: bass guitar, vocals / Michael Giles: drums, vocals/ Mike Hill, Nicky Hopkins: keyboards / Ted Barker, Cliff Hardy: trombone / Ivor Raymonde: arrangements / Raymond Cohen, Gerry Fields, Kelly Isaacs, Boris Pecker, William Reid, G.Salisbury: violin / John Coulling, Rebecca Patten: viola / Alan Ford, Charles Tunnell: cello / The Breakaways (Margot Quantrell, Barbara Moore, Jean Ryder, Betty Prescott): vocals / Wayne Bickerton: producer

The album by Giles, Giles and Fripp is a very odd affair, comprising songs that are intended to be funny, but mostly fail to hit the mark, combined with three or four tracks that aim to be innovative and inventive and do have some rather fine electric guitar playing. Their impact is reduced, however, by the songs with which they have to share vinyl space. It is surprising that such a determinedly uncommercial set was ever considered a good bet for release by a major record company and it did indeed sell extremely poorly. The reason for including the album here, however, is that the unlikely trio metamorphosed within just a few months into King Crimson, the group responsible for the first album to fully justify being called 'progressive rock'. Logically, the catalyst for the surprising development was multi-instrumentalist Ian McDonald, who joined the trio shortly after the album was released, along with his girlfriend, Judy Dyble, who had previously been the lead singer with Fairport Convention. Some recordings made by the expanded line-up have since been released and are very much more interesting than the contents of *The Cheerful Insanity*.

BLUES PROJECT — PLANNED OBSOLESCENCE

US release	September 1968	Verve Forecast	FTS-3046

Not released in UK

1. If You Got To Make A Fool Of Someone (Rudy Clark)
2. Calypso (Andy Kulberg/Jim Roberts)
3. Frank 'n' Curt: Incensed (John Gregory)
4. Turtle Dove (Andy Kulberg)
5. Mojo Hannah (Andre Williams/Barbara Paul/Clarence Paul)
6. Niartaes Hornpipe (John Gregory)
7. Endless Sleep (Dolores Mance/Jody Reynolds)
8. She Raised Her Hand (Andy Kulberg/Jim Roberts)
9. Dakota Recollection (Blues Project)

John Gregory: guitar, vocals / Richard Greene: violin / Donald Kretmar: saxophone, bass guitar / Andy Kulberg: flute, bass guitar, piano / Roy Blumenfeld: drums / Produced by Blues Project/Seatrain

With the departure of Al Kooper, Danny Kalb, and Steve Katz, the remaining two members of The Blues Project recruited new musicians and carried on. Abandoning music having anything to do with the blues, however, and moving flute and violin to the foreground, *Planned Obsolescence* was effectively the work of a new band. Subsequent albums were released as being by Seatrain and indeed this name was also used for the production credit on this record's labels, as well as being flimsily disguised on one of the track titles. Making violin a lead instrument, but without adopting much influence at all from country music, was a bold move and the music of *Planned Obsolescence* is refreshing and attractive. But tying it to the Blues Project name did it few favours and the group struggled to make a place for itself in a crowded marketplace. Beginning the album with a song associated with Freddie and the Dreamers was not the best idea either, especially as it was never a great composition. The rest of the album is rather fine, however, and deserved to make a much bigger impression than it did.

JEFFERSON AIRPLANE — CROWN OF CREATION

Crown Of Creation is more tightly arranged and has a more distinguished set of songs than any of Jefferson Airplane's previous albums, as impressive as these were. There is no obvious improvisational content, although both Jorma Kaukonen and Jack Casady play with such freshness and imagination as to confirm the mastery of their instruments. The short solo that Jorma Kaukonen interpolates into *Share A Little Joke*, in particular, manages to be both unusually phrased

| US release | September 1968 | RCA Victor | LSP 4058 |
| UK release | September 1968 | RCA Victor | SF/RD 7976 |

1. Lather (Grace Slick)
2. In Time (Marty Balin/Paul Kantner)
3. Triad (David Crosby)
4. Star Track (Jorma Kaukonen)
5. Share A Little Joke (Marty Balin)
6. Chushingura (Spencer Dryden)
7. If You Feel (Gary Blackman/Marty Balin)
8. Crown Of Creation (Paul Kantner)
9. Ice Cream Phoenix (Charles Cockey/Jorma Kaukonen)
10. Greasy Heart (Grace Slick)
11. The House At Pooneil Corners (Marty Balin/Paul Kantner)

Grace Slick: vocals, keyboards / Marty Balin: vocals, guitar / Paul Kantner: guitar, vocals / Jorma Kaukonen: guitar, vocals / Jack Casady: bass guitar / Spencer Dryden: drums, keyboards, vocals / Gary Blackman: nose (1) / Al Schmitt: producer

and exhilarating. Meanwhile Grace Slick proves her ability to deliver strong lyrics with a huge amount of emotional resonance. The opening *Lather* is a striking case in point. David Crosby's song, *Triad,* is included because Crosby was a friend and his own group, the Byrds, was unwilling to put it on an album of their own (the group did record it, for possible inclusion on *The Notorious Byrd Brothers).* Happily, the controversial lyrics do sound more startling when delivered by a female voice, especially when that voice belongs to Grace Slick. *Crown Of Creation* is an obvious candidate for the finest album to have emerged from the entire San Francisco phenomenon and it confirms Jefferson Airplane as a very important group.

DAVID ACKLES

| US release | September 1968 | Elektra | EKS 74022 |
| UK release | September 1968 | Elektra | EKS 74022/EKL 4022 |

1. The Road To Cairo
2. When Love Is Gone
3. Sonny Come Home
4. Blue Ribbons
5. What A Happy Day
6. Down River
7. Laissez-Faire
8. Lotus Man
9. His Name Is Andrew
10. Be My Friend

All compositions by David Ackles

David Ackles: vocals, piano / Douglas Hastings: guitar / Danny Weis: guitar / Michael Fonfara: organ / Jerry Penrod: bass guitar / John Keliehor: percussion / David Anderle: producer / Russ Miller: producer

David Ackles is a singer songwriter who composes and performs with a piano, rather than the ubiquitous guitar, and as a result, his songs are more complex and theatrical than those of most of his peers. With their sophisticated melodies and lyrics, the songs recall the work of the composers responsible for the Great American Songbook of the forties and fifties, rather than anything to do with folk music. They certainly impressed some of David Ackles' contemporaries: Julie Driscoll recorded *The Road To Cairo* with the Brian Auger Trinity, while Spooky Tooth and the Hollies presented their own versions of *Down River*. The musicians used to accompany Ackles on the album are members of the band Rhinoceros (two had originally been in Iron Butterfly) and are seemingly playing well outside their comfort zone, although they rise to the occasion very well indeed. The album was not a commercial success, but Elektra stayed true to its signing long enough for him to make two more albums.

DUSTER BENNETT   SMILING LKE I'M HAPPY

British blues artist Tony Bennett, who used the nickname 'Duster' to avoid a rather obvious confusion, performed as a one-man band, with a bass drum strapped to his back and struck with a mallet attached to his elbow, a hi-hat cymbal clashed with a foot pedal, a harmonica held in a holder fastened round his

| UK release | September 1968 | Blue Horizon | (S) 7-63208 |
| US release | September 1968 | Blue Horizon | BH 7701 |

1. Worried Mind (Duster Bennett)
2. Life Is A Dirty Deal (Juke Boy Bonner)
3. Country Jam (Duster Bennett)
4. Trying To Paint It In The Sky (Duster Bennett)
5. Times Like These (Duster Bennett/Stella Sutton)
6. My Lucky Day (Duster Bennett)
7. Got A Tongue In Your Head (Duster Bennett)
8. Jumping At Shadows (Duster Bennett)
9. 40 Minutes From Town (Duster Bennett)
10. Shame Shame Shame (Bob Geddins/Jimmy McCracklin)
11. My Love Is Your Love (Magic Sam)
12. Shady Little Lady (Duster Bennett)

Duster Bennett: vocals, guitar, harmonica, percussion / Stella Sutton: vocals / Peter Green: guitar / Ham Richmond: piano / Mick Fleetwood: drums / Mike Vernon: producer

neck, and an electric guitar in his hands. Purely for the sake of a little variety on record, a small number of other musicians make occasional appearances (including master guitarist Peter Green), but Duster Bennett is perfectly capable of carrying the proceedings on his own. *Smiling Like I'm Happy* is an unusual but very worthwhile addition to the British blues catalogue. It is the most satisfying of four albums that Bennett issued on the Blue Horizon label. He maintained an active career until 1976, when he was sadly killed in a road accident. During 1970 he was actually included as a member of John Mayall's Bluesbreakers. Although the title of his first album implies a certain mournfulness, Duster Bennett's music is better represented by the sheer exhilaration of *My Lucky Day*, which easily demonstrates the strengths of his one-man band approach.

PETER BRÖTZMANN OCTET   MACHINE GUN

German release   c. September 1968   Brö   BRÖ 2
Not released in UK or US

1. Machine Gun (Peter Brötzmann)
2. Responsible (Fred Van Hove)
3. Music For Han Bennink (Willem Breuker)

Peter Brötzmann: tenor saxophone, baritone saxophone, producer / Evan Parker: tenor saxophone / Willem Breuker: tenor saxophone / Fred Van Hove: piano / Buschi Niebergall: bass / Peter Kowald: bass / Han Bennink: drums / Sven-Ake Johansson: drums

To match its album title, the music by the German Peter Brötzmann Octet is very aggressive free jazz. Brötzmann himself plays the saxophone as though he is trying to blow the building down with the force of his breath and the rest of the group is swiftly persuaded to adopt the same approach. In the hands and mouths of black American free jazz musicians, it is apparent that the anger of the music is often directed at the social situation in which they find themselves. Peter Brötzmann does not have or need this excuse: he just loves the sound of music played like this. *Machine Gun* is the second album to be released under the Brötzmann name, but it is the one that first attracted attention to his extraordinary playing. He has since appeared on over a hundred more, including half a dozen as a member of Last Exit, the band that took jazz fusion during the late eighties to places it had not anticipated. The music of *Machine Gun* is the same as the most extreme moments of Jimi Hendrix's playing, albeit delivered entirely without electric enhancement, and performed without the benefit of any tranquil, melodic release.

TERRY RILEY   IN C

US release   September 1968   Columbia Masterworks   MS 7178
UK release   1971   CBS   S 64565

1. In C   part one
2. In C   part two

Terry Riley: soprano saxophone / Darlene Reynard: bassoon / Jerry Kirkbride: clarinet / David Shostac: flute / Jan Williams: marimba / Lawrence Singer: oboe / Margaret Hassell: piano / Stuart Dempster: trombone / Jon Hassell: trumpet / Edward Burnham: vibraphone / David Rosenboom: viola / David Behrman: producer

This is the first recording of a piece composed in 1964 and it represents the beginning of the modern classical music genre known as minimalism. Framed by a repeated high C on the piano, creating a pulse, the music has no melody but instead decorates the C note with other instruments, slowly changing the texture of the music and including other notes, but always using the C as a reference, as though a simple modal improvisation is taking place. The music is static yet manages to be compelling at the same time. Terry Riley clearly felt that he was on to something significant and several other composers did too, because during the following years many other works were created in which very slow evolution in texture or note order took place, but with little or no explicit melody. Minimalism.

DONOVAN   HURDY GURDY MAN

US release   September 1968   Epic   BN 26420
Not released in UK

1. Hurdy Gurdy Man
2. Peregrine
3. The Entertaining Of A Shy Girl
4. As I Recall It
5. Get Thy Bearings
6. Hi It's Been A Long Time
7. West Indian Lady

8. Jennifer Juniper
9. The River Song
10. Tangier
11. A Sunny Day
12. The Sun Is A Very Magic Fellow
13. Teas

All compositions by Donovan Leitch

Donovan: vocals, guitar, tambura / Alan Parker: guitar / Clem Cattini: drums / John Paul Jones: bass guitar / other musicians unknown / Mickie Most: producer

Close behind his live album comes another strong Donovan studio set, but it was only issued in the US. *Hurdy Gurdy Man* was named after a hit single, one of the most striking that Donovan made. The song is dominated by a raucous sustained electric guitar, which is very much the kind of thing that Jimmy Page was playing, so that several sources claim that he is the guitarist. Others are equally insistent that it is Allan Holdsworth, although he was not a session player and did not appear on record with his own group, 'Igginbottom, until the following year. In 1968, nobody would have known who he was, although the rumour is a good example of the power of wishful thinking. Clem Cattini, the drummer on the session, was sure that the guitarist was actually Alan Parker. Another Donovan single, the charming *Jennifer Juniper,* is also included on the album, along with a jazz performance, *Get Thy Bearings,* featuring a confident saxophonist who is probably Harold McNair. This song was later borrowed by King Crimson for inclusion in the band's live set.

H.P. LOVECRAFT   II

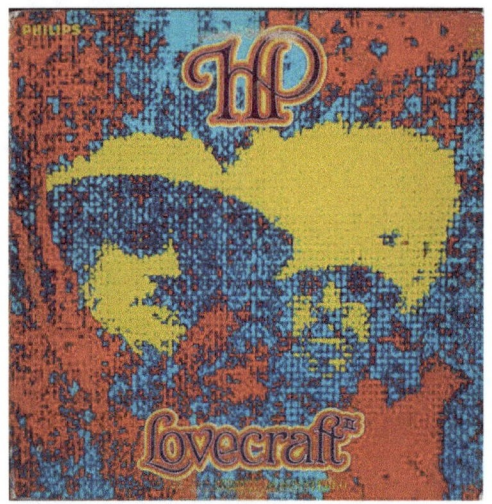

US release   September 1968   Philips   PHS 600-279
UK release   September 1968   Philips   SBL 7872

1. Spin Spin Spin (Kent Foreman)
2. It's About Time (Kent Foreman/Lydia Wood)
3. Blue Jack Of Diamonds (Jeff Boyan)
4. Electrallentando (George Edwards)
5. At The Mountains Of Madness (George Edwards/Dave Michaels/Tony Cavallari)
6. Mobius Trip (George Edwards)
7. High Flying Bird (Billy Ed Wheeler)
8. Nothing's Boy (Ken Nordine)
9. Keeper Of The Keys (Mike Brewer/Tom Shipley)

George Edwards: vocals, guitar, bass guitar / Tony Cavallari: guitar, vocals / Dave Michaels: vocals, keyboards, arranger / Jeff Boyan: bass guitar, vocals / Michael Tegza: drums, vocals / Ken Nordine: voice / George Badonsky: producer

As impressive as the first album by H.P.Lovecraft is, it is entirely eclipsed by the second. A combination of interlocking soulful voices with acoustic guitar and thoughtful one-handed keyboard playing provides a solid basis for the application of some very inventive production and arranging touches. Orchestral instruments are added in places, but only for short passages; the same is true of echo effects. Veteran wordsmith Ken Nordine is employed to have his speech surrounded by vocal effects, but for less then a minute. The group completely understands that less can sometimes bring a result that is very much more. A few months earlier, the music on *H.P.Lovecraft II* would have been described as psychedelic, even with a complete absence of distorted lead electric guitars, but now the music seems to be simply the result of applying a huge amount of imagination in order to bring out the best of some rather good songs.

McCOY TYNER   TENDER MOMENTS

Tender Moments implies an album full of ballads, but in fact only one track, *All My Yesterdays,* qualifies. McCoy Tyner, however, is starting to establish his own jazz style, drawing on the music he played with John Coltrane to some extent, but shying away from anything too discordant. Rather like much of the music on the album released by Archie Shepp a few months earlier, Tyner is creating an updated version of soul jazz in which the musicians can sound utterly contemporary but still very accessible. It is significant that both Bennie Maupin and Julian Priester would later be involved in the early fusion experiments of Herbie Hancock, who adopted much the same philosophy as McCoy Tyner, albeit within a context that revelled in what could be done with electric amplification. Tyner gives himself the major share of the solo space on *Tender Moments* and entirely justifies this by continuing to be a masterful piano soloist. For him the possibilities of the acoustic instrument have not at all been exhausted.

```
US release     September 1968    Blue Note    BST 84275
Not released in UK

1.  Mode To John
2.  Man From Tanganyika
3.  The High Priest
4.  Utopia
5.  All My Yesterdays
6.  Lee Plus Three

All compositions by McCoy Tyner

McCoy Tyner: piano / Lee Morgan: trumpet / James Spaulding:
alto saxophone, flute / Bennie Maupin: tenor saxophone / Julian
Priester: trombone / Bob Northern: French horn / Howard
Johnson: tuba / Herbie Lewis: bass / Joe Chambers: drums /
Francis Wolff: producer
```

J.K. & Co.   SUDDENLY ONE SUMMER

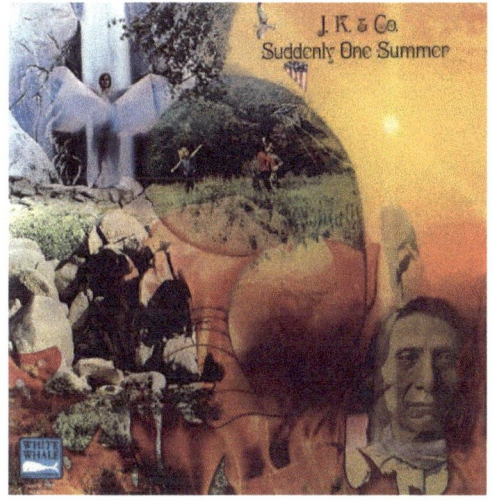

```
US release    c. September 1968    White Whale    WWS 7117
Not released in UK

1.  Break Of Dawn
2.  Fly
3.  Little Children
4.  Christine Speed
5.  Crystal Ball
6.  Nobody

7.  O.D.
8.  Land Of Sensations And Delights
9.  The Times
10. Magical Fingers Of Minerva
11. Dead

All compositions by Jay Kaye

Jay Kaye: vocals, guitar / Bob Buckley: arranger / musicians
include Charlie Failkner: bass guitar, Hugh Lochhead: drums,
Roger Law: guitar / Robin Spurgin: producer
```

Fifteen year-old Jay Kaye recorded his only album in Vancouver, although he lived in Los Angeles. *Suddenly One Summer* is an astonishingly accomplished set of songs, crammed full of inventive arrangements that make the album seem to fit into the general psychedelic approach of the time, although it does not resemble the work of any other artist in particular. As has been pointed out elsewhere, however, *Fly* could be included in any record by Radiohead and it would not sound out of place. Unfortunately, White Whale chose the opening piece of electronica, *Break Of Dawn*, for release as a single, hoping to attract attention for the shortest single ever produced. The music lasts just thirty-two seconds, but it really functions as an introduction to *Fly* and is atmospheric rather than melodic. Kaye made no more records and *Suddenly One Summer* is not at all well known, but arranger Bob Buckley, who is responsible for much of the album's musical success, has maintained a busy career since then, including arranging for stars such as Bryan Adams and Celine Dion, and composing orchestral works of his own.

HARVEY MANDEL   CRISTO REDENTOR

```
US release    September 1968    Philips    PHS 600-281
UK release    September 1968    Philips    SBL 7873

1.  Cristo Redentor (Duke Pearson)
2.  Before Six (Larry Frazier)
3.  The Lark (Harvey Mandel/Abe Kesh)
4.  Snake (Harvey Mandel)
5.  Long Wait (Harvey Mandel/Barry Goldberg)

6.  Wade In The Water (Sam Cooke)
7.  Lights Out (Harvey Mandel)
8.  Bradley's Barn (Harvey Mandel)
9.  You Can't Tell Me (Harvey Mandel/Dino Valenti)
10. Nashville 1a.m. (Harvey Mandel/Abe Kesh)

Harvey Mandel: guitar / Chip Martin: guitar / Bob Jones: guitar (4,7)
/ Pete Drake: pedal steel guitar / Steve Miller: keyboards (1,2,6) /
Barry Goldberg: keyboards (3,5) / Graham Bond: piano (9) /
Catherine Gotthoffer: harp (1) / Larry Easter: tenor saxophone (2) /
Charlie Musselwhite: harmonica (3,5) / Art Stavro: bass guitar / Bob
Moore: bass guitar / Eddie Hoh: drums / Kenny Buttrey: drums /
Carter Collins: percussion (2) / Armando Peraza: percussion (6) /
Jacqueline May Allen, Carolyn Willis, Edna Wright, Julia Tillman:
vocals (1) / Nick De Caro: piano (1), arranger / Abe Kesh: producer
```

Cristo Redentor is an instrumental album by the former guitarist with the Charlie Musselwhite Blues Band, although none of the tracks is a blues. Mandel is a true virtuoso, with more of a country influence than most electric guitarists playing rock, but otherwise adopting a similar imaginative approach to that of Jeff Beck. The album is extremely varied, with Mandel finding a new way to play his guitar on every track. He can be remarkably self-effacing, with both the evocative title piece and *The Lark* having no lead guitar soloing at all, although the train impersonation that Mandel keeps going through the latter track is what holds the music together. Elsewhere, however, he dazzles with his fluency and his choice of notes, and he easily incorporates the range of studio effects currently available, including lines heard backwards and jumping from side to side in stereo. Harvey Mandel later played with John Mayall's Bluesbreakers and with Canned Heat, returning to playing the blues, although he did not really manage to repeat with those groups the daring expertise he displays on *Cristo Redentor*.

MUDDY WATERS   ELECTRIC MUD

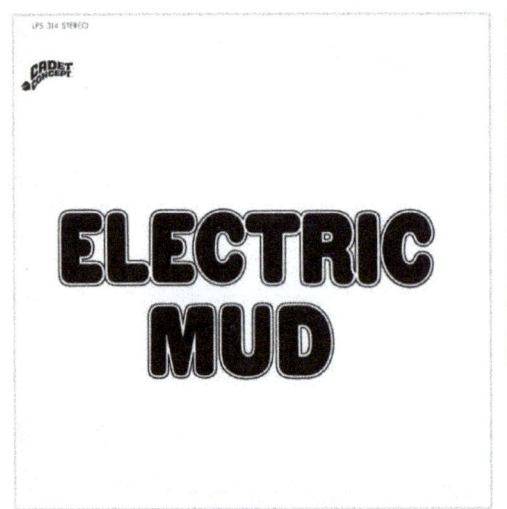

| US release | October 1968 | Cadet Concept | LPS 314 |
| UK release | October 1968 | Chess | CRLS 4542 |

1. I Just Want To Make Love To You (Willie Dixon)
2. Hoochie Coochie Man (Willie Dixon)
3. Let's Spend The Night Together (Mick Jagger/Keith Richards)
4. She's All Right (Muddy Waters)
5. I'm A Man (Mannish Boy) (Muddy Waters)
6. Herbert Harpers Free Press (Robert Lee Thurston/Sidney Barnes)
7. Tom Cat (Charles Williams)
8. Same Thing (Willie Dixon)

Muddy Waters: vocals / Pete Cosey: guitar / Phil Upchurch: guitar / Roland Faulkner: guitar / Gene Barge: soprano saxophone, harmonica, producer / Louis Satterfield: bass guitar / Morris Jennings: drums / Charles Stepney: keyboards, arranger, producer / Marshall Chess: producer

Encouraged by their success with the Rotary Connection album, Charles Stepney and Marshall Chess came up with the idea of recording blues veteran Muddy Waters with the Chess session musicians, who were encouraged to make the music sound as contemporary as possible. At the age of fifty-five Muddy was not very open to having his music altered in this way and he did not like what he was hearing from the backing musicians. The guitarists use sustain and wah-wah on everything they play and to Muddy's ears the blues emotion disappears. Nevertheless, he sings his songs with all the passion he can muster, even when one of them is by the Rolling Stones. *Electric Mud* is not a great blues album and Muddy Waters is probably quite right about the playing of the guitarists. Jimi Hendrix was in the process of demonstrating how it was very possible to play the blues with an overdriven guitar equipped with effects and next to him, the Chess guitarists do sound deficient (even if one of them is the great Pete Cosey, later to be a member of Miles Davis's improvised funk band). But *Electric Mud* represents a bold experiment that was worth trying and it has enough that is interesting to justify the attempt.

THE JIMI HENDRIX EXPERIENCE   ELECTRIC LADYLAND

Electric Ladyland is a double album (also issued as two separate single albums) during the course of which Jimi Hendrix demonstrates exactly why he must be considered the most influential electric guitarist of his generation. It is an extremely varied record. *Voodoo Chile* is a blues, or almost. It is derived from Muddy Waters' *Catfish Blues*, with Jimi Hendrix working his accustomed magic on the electric guitar, yet it manages to convey more blues artistry and emotion than the whole of *Electric Mud*. It is the only blues performance, even if much of the rest of the album is at least influenced by the music. But the opening *And The Gods Made Love* is an electronic piece, with all the sounds generated by the guitar, while the long *1983... A Merman I Should Turn To Be* is fully-fledged progressive rock, at a time when the genre was not yet defined, created in the studio out of several different sections and with multiple layers of sound throughout. The *Moon Turn The Tides...* segment, mostly comprising gentle electronic whooshing in stereo, is given its own title but is realistically the final part of *1983*. There is nothing else in the Jimi Hendrix oeuvre like this, even if the guitarist builds his music on this album with

| UK release | October 1968 | Track | 613008/9 |
| US release | October 1968 | Reprise | 2 RS 6307 |

1. And The Gods Made Love
2. Have You Ever Been (To Electric Ladyland)
3. Cross Town Traffic
4. Voodoo Chile
5. Little Miss Strange (Noel Redding)
6. Long Hot Summer Night
7. Come On (Earl King)
8. Gypsy Eyes
9. The Burning Of The Midnight Lamp
10. Rainy Day, Dream Away
11. 1983... A Merman I Should Turn To Be
12. Moon, Turn The Tides... Gently, Gently Away
13. Still, Raining, Still Dreaming
14. House Burning Down
15. All Along The Watchtower (Bob Dylan)
16. Voodoo Chile (Slight Return)

All compositions by Jimi Hendrix apart from where stated

Jimi Hendrix: guitar, vocals, harpsichord, bass guitar, producer / Noel Redding: bass guitar, vocals / Mitch Mitchell: drums, vocals / Dave Mason: vocals (3), guitar (15) / Jack Casady: bass guitar (4) / Steve Winwood: organ (4) / Al Kooper: piano (6) / Freddie Smith: tenor saxophone (10) / Mike Finnigan: organ (10,13) / Buddy Miles: drums (10,13) / Larry Faucette: percussion (10,13) / Chris Wood: flute (11) / Brian Jones: percussion (15) / The Sweet Inspirations (Cissy Houston, Myrna Smith, Estelle Brown, Sylvia Shemwell): vocals (9)

numerous different guitar parts on every track, apart from the minimal *Gypsy Eyes*. *Rainy Day, Dream Away* and *Still Raining, Still Dreaming* are two halves of the same piece, a semi-improvised shuffle for the most part, but split so that the extraordinary burst of talking wah-wah guitar that comes in the middle can be heard twice. The album is concluded by two tracks which seem to embody Jimi Hendrix's art particularly well. He manages to transform Bob Dylan's skeletal *All Along The Watchtower* into a rock interpretation so definitive that Dylan himself started to play the song in live performance more like this. The guitarist's solo in the piece is a masterclass in how to make an improvisation interesting, employing a different approach and sound during each of the verse repeats. *Voodoo Chile (Slight Return)* shares its lyrical theme with the earlier *Voodoo Chile*, but not its music, as Hendrix creates a structured rock song with an authoritative wah-wah introduction. This was the one track from the album that Jimi Hendrix chose to feature within his stage set. There are several guest musicians to be heard on the album. Some, like Traffic's Dave Mason or Al Kooper, were simply glad to be allowed to play a part on what must have been obvious was going to be a very special record. Steve Winwood, however, is able to make his organ playing an essential ingredient of *Voodoo Chile*, while Chris Wood adds some effective flute playing to *1983… A Merman I Should Turn To Be*. For this listener, *Electric Ladyland* vies with *Sgt Pepper's Lonely Hearts Club Band* for the distinction of quintessential sixties album, to be played to anyone wanting to understand the artistic heights of which the music of the decade was capable.

TRAFFIC

| UK release | October 1968 | Island | ILPS 9081T |
| US release | October 1968 | United Artists | UAS 6676 |

1. You Can All Join In (Dave Mason)
2. Pearly Queen (Jim Capaldi/Steve Winwood)
3. Don't Be Sad (Dave Mason)
4. Who Knows What Tomorrow Will Bring (Jim Capaldi/Steve Winwood)
5. Feelin' Alright? (Dave Mason)
6. Vagabond Virgin (Dave Mason/Jim Capaldi)
7. Forty Thousand Headmen (Jim Capaldi/Steve Winwood)
8. Cryin' To Be Heard (Dave Mason)
9. No Time To Live (Jim Capaldi/Steve Winwood)
10. Means To An End (Jim Capaldi/Steve Winwood)

Steve Winwood: vocals, keyboards, guitar / Dave Mason: vocals, guitar, bass guitar / Chris Wood: flute, tenor saxophone / Jim Capaldi: drums, vocals / Jimmy Miller: producer

The second album by Traffic is a touch more sophisticated than the first, with the songwriting even more refined, and the traces of psychedelia and general weirdness stripped out (with the possible exception of the lyrics to *Forty Thousand Headmen*). The divide between Dave Mason and the rest still remains, but it is clearly being used to push each side into delivering the best it can manage. The songs are tighter, with little room left for solo improvisation, but the members of the band are still very much concerned with creating as much textural variation as possible. Chris Wood emerges as the musician rising most effectively to the challenge of advancing from the high standard set by the first album, with his filigree additions on saxophone and flute enhancing the music whenever they occur. The group was no longer bothering to issue singles at this point, but the album performed well in the charts in both the UK and the US.

JETHRO TULL   THIS WAS

Jethro Tull built up a following during club and festival performances in the summer of 1968 by taking liberties with the blues format, adding a flute to the usual line-up. The extraordinary stage antics of the flute player, Ian Anderson, who was also the lead singer, increased the group's impact. The first album shows why the group was so acclaimed. The flute is given an extra focus by the inclusion of an instrumental borrowed from jazz player Roland Kirk.

| UK release | October 1968 | Island | ILPS 9085/ILP 985 |
| US release | February 1969 | Reprise | RS 6336 |

1. My Sunday Feeling (Ian Anderson)
2. Some Day The Sun Won't Shine For You (Ian Anderson)
3. Beggar's Farm (Mick Abrahams/Ian Anderson)
4. Move On Alone (Mick Abrahams)
5. Serenade To A Cuckoo (Roland Kirk)
6. Dharma For One (Ian Anderson, Clive Bunker)
7. It's Breaking Me Up (Ian Anderson)
8. Cat's Squirrel (Traditional)
9. A Song For Jeffrey (Ian Anderson)
10. Round (Jethro Tull, Terry Ellis)

Ian Anderson: vocals, flute, harmonica, claghorn, piano / Mick Abrahams: guitar, vocals / Glenn Cornick: bass guitar / Clive Bunker: drums / David Palmer: arranger / Terry Ellis: producer

Anderson uses Kirk's unorthodox techniques, including singing through the flute while playing it. *A Song For Jeffrey* adds an extra novelty by distorting Anderson's singing voice so that the track sounds like something that Captain Beefheart might have produced. The album cover shows the group members made to look like old men, but the title, *This Was*, refers to the fact that guitarist Mick Abrahams had already left the group, giving the usual excuse of 'musical differences'.

CAPTAIN BEEFHEART & HIS MAGIC BAND   STRICTLY PERSONAL

US release   October 1968   Blue Thumb   BTS 1
UK release   October 1968   Liberty   LBS/LBL 83172

1. Ah Feel Like Ahcid
2. Safe As Milk
3. Trust Us
4. Son Of Mirror Man – Mere Man

5. On Tomorrow
6. Beatle Bones 'n' Smokin' Stones
7. Gimme Dat Harp Boy
8. Kandy Korn

All compositions by Don Van Vliet

Captain Beefheart (Don Van Vliet): vocals, harmonica / Alex St.Clair: guitar / Jeff Cotton: guitar / Jerry Handley: bass guitar / John French: drums / Bob Krasnow: producer

For Captain Beefheart's second album, the music is still rooted in the blues, but with a much heavier, more beefy (!) sound than previously. John French likes to lock his drum patterns into the jagged riffs played by the two guitarists, rather than providing an obvious beat for the others to play against, which has the effect of making the rhythm sound lumpy and idiosyncratic. At the same time, the guitarists, neither of which is taking on the established rhythm guitar role, are playing different lines, while the bass guitarist, using a very deep, smeared note selection, adds a third line to the mixture. They are fighting each other's rhythms, yet manage, seemingly against the odds, to integrate regardless. With Captain Beefheart delivering his Howlin' Wolf growl and holler over the top, the Magic Band have a sound like no other. Producer Bob Krasnow is very heavy-handed with his use of phasing, something that Beefheart later decided he did not like, but it helps to emphasise the unique character of the music and suits it very well indeed. *Strictly Personal* is made to appear quite straightforward by the Beefheart albums that followed it, but compared to any other band it is nothing of the kind.

RHINOCEROS

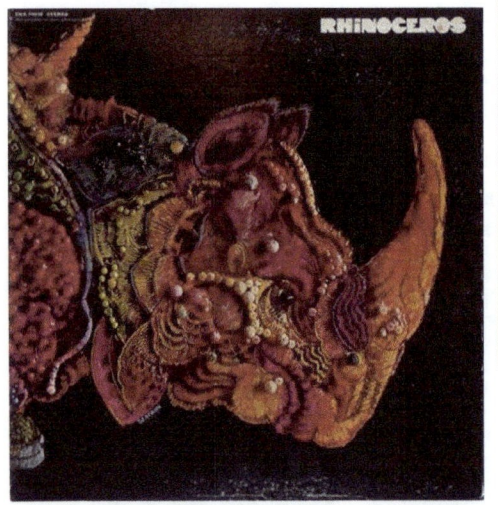

US release   October 1968   Elektra   EKS-74030
UK release   October 1968   Elektra   EKS 74030/EKL 4030

1. When You Say You're Sorry (Alan Gerber)
2. Same Old Way (John Finley)
3. Apricot Brandy (Danny Weis/Michael Fonfara)
4. That Time Of The Year (Alan Gerber)
5. You're My Girl (Beth Beatty/Dick Cooper/Ernie Shelby)

6. I Need Love (Larry Williams)
7. I've Been There (Alan Gerber/John Finley)
8. Belbuekus (Danny Weis/John Finley)
9. Along Comes Tomorrow (Alan Gerber)
10. I Will Serenade You (John Finley)

John Finley: vocals / Alan Gerber: vocals, piano / Danny Weis: guitar, piano / Doug Hastings: guitar / Michael Fonfara: organ / Jerry Penrod: bass guitar / Billy Mundi: drums / Paul A.Rothchild: producer

Rhinoceros was put together by the Elektra record company and included a few musicians who had previously played in other groups. Danny Weis and Jerry Penrod had been members of Iron Butterfly, Michael Fonfara played with the Electric Flag, and Billy Mundi was with the Mothers of Invention. The instrumental *Apricot Brandy* did well as a single: its funky guitar hook makes it absolutely irresistible. Sadly the rest of the album is not in the same league. It is superbly well played but it is rather anonymous. Its songs have the right rock sound and are intelligently constructed, but struggle to stay in the listener's memory even after a few plays. A couple of them were covered by other artists regardless, but the album sales did not match the record company's expectations.

THE STEVE MILLER BAND   SAILOR

The second album by the Steve Miller Band expands on the promise of the first and includes two particularly remarkable tracks. *Living In The U.S.A.* is exciting and extremely catchy, although for some reason it failed to become a big hit single. *Song For Our Ancestors* is an evocative instrumental, with guitars managing to emulate the imagined cries of dinosaurs before a gentle momentum is established. The result sounds like something that might have been included on a Pink Floyd album.

| US release | October 1968 | Capitol | ST 2984 |
| UK release | October 1968 | Capitol | ST/T 2984 |

1. Song For Our Ancestors (Steve Miller)
2. Dear Mary (Steve Miller)
3. My Friend (Boz Scaggs/Tim Davis)
4. Living In The U.S.A. (Steve Miller)
5. Quicksilver Girl (Steve Miller)
6. Lucky Man (Jimmy Peterman)
7. Gangster Of Love (John Watson)
8. You're So Fine (Jimmy Reed)
9. Overdrive (Boz Scaggs)
10. Dime-A-Dance Romance (Boz Scaggs)

Steve Miller: vocals, guitar, harmonica / Boz Scaggs: guitar, vocals / Jim Peterman: keyboards, vocals / Lonnie Turner: bass guitar, vocals / Tim Davis: drums, vocals / Glyn Johns: producer

The rest of the album does not sound like this and is informed by the blues, but the band is so varied in its approach to the material that *Sailor* does not at all come across as a blues album. Although the record was recorded in the US this time, the British producer Glyn Johns is retained and he encourages Steve Miller and his colleagues to pay more attention to the methods of *Sgt Pepper*. This ensures that every track has a distinguishing feature to make it stand out. *Sailor* is a very impressive album and it did well in the US chart, although it was ignored by the UK audience.

DAVID AXELROD   SONG OF INNOCENCE

| US and UK release | October 1968 | Capitol | ST 2982 |

1. Urizen
2. Holy Thursday
3. The Smile
4. A Dream
5. Song Of Innocence
6. Merlin's Prophecy
7. The Mental Traveler

All music composed by David Axelrod

David Axelrod: arranger, producer / Don Randi: conductor, keyboards / Al Casey: guitar / Howard Roberts: guitar / Pete Wyant: guitar / Carol Kaye: bass guitar / Earl Palmer: drums / Gene Estes: percussion / Gary Coleman: percussion / Allen Di Rienzo: trumpet / Freddie Hill: trumpet / Ollie Mitchell: trumpet / Tony Terran: trumpet / Lew McCreary: trombone / Richard Leith: trombone / Arthur Maebe: French horn / Henry Sigismonti: French horn / Vincent de Rosa: French horn / Bill Hinshaw: French horn / Arnold Belnick: violin / Benjamin Barrett: violin / Bobby Bruce: violin / Harry Bluestone: violin / Henry Roth: violin / Jack Shulman: violin / Leonard Malarsky: violin / Marshall Sosson: violin / Nathan Ross: violin / Sid Sharp: violin / Tibor Zelig: violin / Alvin Dinkin: viola / Gareth Nuttycombe: viola / Harry Hyams: viola / Myron Sandler: viola / Anne Goodman: cello / Douglas Davis: cello / Harold Schneier: cello / Raphael Kramer: cello

The producer of the Electric Prunes' *Mass In F Minor* makes no pretence this time that the album is anything other than his own work. The combination of orchestral players with electric guitars and a rock rhythm section is less interesting than it might have been because Axelrod prefers to set a mood rather than create any melodic development. The result is like the soundtrack for an unseen film or else background music in which even the fiery guitar solos which play from time to time fail to particularly engage with the listener. Axelrod claimed that his musical background was in jazz (and he did indeed produce albums for Cannonball Adderley), but the static rhythms he employs here have no jazz content and Song Of Innocence has no bearing on the development of fusion jazz as has been claimed by some. The music is supposed to be inspired by the poems of William Blake, but with no vocals present it is hard to distinguish what this influence might be. David Axelrod was allowed to make several more albums similar to this one, including another that purported to be by the Electric Prunes, but they are all the result of too much ambition being coupled with too little musical expertise. The fact that Axelrod did not benefit from any kind of formal musical training remained a problem throughout his surprisingly long career.

WALTER CARLOS   SWITCHED-ON BACH

Designed to show the capabilities of the newly available Moog synthesizer, *Switched-On Bach*, an album of Bach pieces played entirely on the instrument, became a surprise hit, selling over a million copies in the US alone. As the Moog synthesizer could only play one note at a time, the album took a long time to make, spent carrying out a huge amount of overdubbing. Reproducing the precise music of Bach was not actually an ideal situation in which to demonstrate the various effects and tones the Moog synthesizer

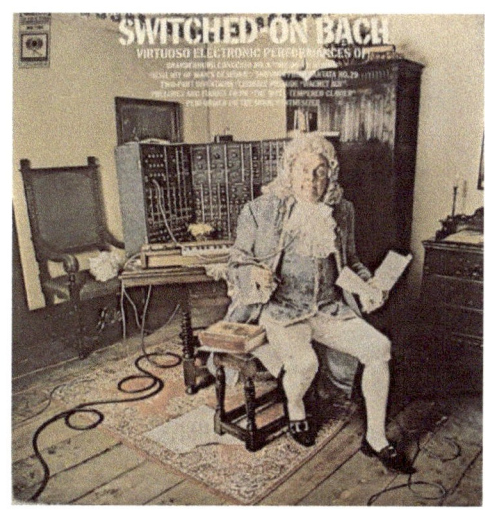

could produce, although the fact that the music could be played at all was impressive. The second movement of the third Brandenburg Concerto, however, provides an opportunity for Carlos to really let rip. Written by Bach as just two chords, it is commonly suggested that these are intended to provide the inspiration for an improvised passage, and this is exactly what Carlos plays. It is worth noting that modern reissues of the album credit Wendy Carlos, who is the same person.

```
US release    October 1968    Columbia Masterworks    MS 7194
UK release    October 1968    CBS            S/M 63501

1.  Sinfonia To Cantata No.29
2.  Air On A G String
3.  Two Part Invention In F Major
4.  Two Part Invention In B flat Minor
5.  Two Part Invention In D Minor
6.  Jesu, Joy Of Man's Desiring
7.  Prelude And Fugue No.7 In E flat Major

8.  Prelude And Fugue No.2 In C Minor
9.  Chorale Prelude Wachet Auf
10. Brandenburg Concerto No.3 First Movement
11. Brandenburg Concerto No.3 Second Movement
12. Brandenburg Concerto No.3 Third Movement

All compositions by Johannes Sebastian Bach

Walter Carlos: synthesizer / Benjamin Folkman: synthesizer / Rachel Elkind: producer
```

CARAVAN

```
UK release October 1968  Verve Forecast  (S)VLP 6011
US release   October 1968  Verve Forecast  FST 3066

1.  Place Of My Own
2.  Ride
3.  Policeman
4.  Love Song With Flute
5.  Cecil Rons

6.  Magic Man
7.  Grandma's Lawn
8.  Where But For Caravan Would I? (Caravan/
                                    Brian Hopper)

all compositions except track 8 by Caravan

Pye Hastings: vocals, guitar, bass guitar / David Sinclair: organ, vocals / Richard Sinclair: bass guitar, guitar, vocals / Richard Coughlan: drums / Jimmy Hastings: flute (4) / Tony Cox: producer
```

Caravan was one of two groups to have evolved from a Canterbury band by the name of Wilde Flowers – the other being Soft Machine. The music places the organ to the forefront, with the guitar being restricted to a rhythm role and often placed well back in the mix. The two lead singers have very different voices – Richard Sinclair is a smooth tenor, while Pye Hastings has what might be described as a strangled, squeaky whisper, except that it manages to convey considerable emotional impact regardless. Caravan has created some highly melodic, memorable material, with occasional psychedelic touches, but essentially not displaying a strong influence from any other group. The songs are very varied and include a lengthy exploration of the possibilities of using eleven-four time (*Where But For Caravan Would I?*). David Sinclair is an inventive organist, with a good ear for different tones and capable of delivering well-constructed solos. One other solo voice is heard, when Pye Hastings' older brother Jimmy, an accomplished jazz performer, is drafted in to play flute on the appropriately titled *Love Song With Flute*. Caravan was able to sustain a long career from this auspicious start, although the use of tightly arranged material here gives the album a markedly different character from its successors.

THE IDLE RACE   BIRTHDAY PARTY

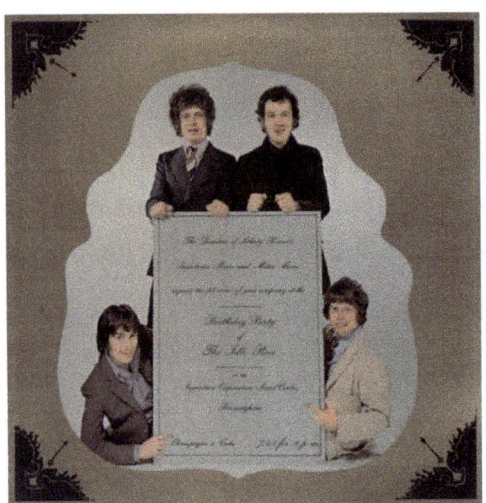

```
UK release    October 1968    Liberty    LBS/LBL 83132E
US release    October 1968    Liberty    LST-7603

1.  Skeleton And The Roundabout
2.  Happy Birthday (Patty Hill/Mildred J.Hill)
3.  The Birthday
4.  I Like My Toys
5.  Morning Sunshine
6.  Follow Me Follow
7.  Sitting In My Tree

8.  On With The Show
9.  Lucky Man
10. Don't Put Your Boys In The Army, Mrs Ward
11. Pie In The Sky (Dave Pritchard)
12. The Lady Who said She Could Fly
13. End Of The Road

All compositions by Jeff Lynne except where stated

Jeff Lynne: vocals, guitar, piano / Dave Pritchard: guitar, vocals / Greg Masters: bass guitar, vocals / Roger Spencer: drums, vocals / Cy Payne: arranger / Eddie Offord: producer / Gerald Chevin: producer
```

The first album to feature the work of Jeff Lynne comprises attractive, inventive pop, clearly influenced by the Beatles, though without sounding very much like them. The previous year the Idle Race had issued a single, *Imposters Of Life's Magazine,* which is something of a psychedelic masterpiece, sounding as though the group members believed this might be their only record and were determined to include as much in it as possible. Nothing on *Birthday Party* tries as hard as this and it suffers in places from being a little twee, although it is clear that the Idle Race, and Jeff Lynne in particular, is possessed of a huge amount of talent. *Skeleton And The Roundabout* was chosen for release as a single, but its novelty approach did not achieve much in the way of sales.

TYRANNOSAURUS REX   PROPHETS, SEERS & SAGES: THE ANGELS OF THE AGES

UK release   October 1968   Regal Zonophone (S)LRZ 1005
Not issued in US

1. Deboraarobed
2. Stacey Grove
3. Wind Quartets
4. Conesuala
5. Trelawny Lawn
6. Aznageel The Mage
7. The Friends
8. Salamander Palagander
9. Our Wonderful Brownskin Man
10. O Harley (The Saltimbanques)
11. Eastern Spell
12. The Travelling Tragition
13. Juniper Suction
14. Scenescof Dynasty

All compositions by Marc Bolan

Marc Bolan: vocals, guitar / Steve Peregrin Took: percussion, vocals / Tony Visconti: producer

The second album by Tyrannosaurus Rex proves that a format that might be expected to leave Marc Bolan struggling for ideas actually has enough resonance for a record that includes more memorable songs than previously. *Prophets & Sears* begins with a version of a song that was the closest the duo had come to achieving a greatest hit, *Debora*, although the unfortunate decision was taken to reverse the tape for the second half of the track, an effect which rapidly becomes irritating. The album sold less well than its predecessor, forcing Bolan to begin to make changes for subsequent records.

DILLARD & CLARK   THE FANTASTIC EXPEDITION OF

US release   October 1968   A&M   SP 4158
UK release   early 1969   A&M   AMLS 939

1. Out On The Side (Gene Clark)
2. She Darked The Sun (Gene Clark/Bernie Leadon)
3. Don't Come Rollin' (Gene Clark/Doug Dillard/Bernie Leadon)
4. Train Leaves Here This Morning (Gene Clark/Bernie Leadon)
5. With Care From Someone (Gene Clark/Doug Dillard/Bernie Leadon)
6. The Radio Song (Gene Clark/Bernie Leadon)
7. Git It On Brother (Lester Flatt)
8. In The Plan (Gene Ckark/Doug Dillard/Bernie Leadon)
9. Something's Wrong (Gene Clark/Doug Dillard)

Gene Clark: vocals, guitar, harmonica / Doug Dillard: banjo, violin, guitar , vocals / Bernie Leadon: guitar, banjo, vocals / Donald Beck: mandolin, dobro / David Jackson: bass / Andy Belling: harpsichord (5,6,8) / Chris Hillman: mandolin (7,9) / Joel Larson: drums (1) / Larry Marks: producer

Doug Dillard left the bluegrass group that he ran with his brother because he did not like the way they were moving significantly away from the tradition. He was just in time to link up with Gene Clark, who was happy to follow the direction of the music that Doug Dillard loved. *The Fantastic Expedition of Dillard & Clark* strains at the bluegrass tradition too, but it retains the prominent use of banjos, fiddles, and mandolins and apart from the first track there is no drummer. Gene Clark has written some of his most attractive songs and playing them as though they are decades old, but with the sublime close harmony singing that is Gene Clark's trademark, results in music that is an absolute delight. The lack of drums and electric instruments prevents the album from sounding like any kind of country-rock, but in a straight comparison with *Sweetheart Of The Rodeo* by Clark's former employers, the Byrds, it is clear that *The Fantastic Expedition Of Dillard & Clark* contains music that is more durable and profound, even if it sold much less well. The album also includes the work of Bernie Leadon, formerly part of an obscure country-flavoured rock group called Hearts and Flowers, but later a founder member of a similar group that was not at all obscure – the Eagles.

THE YOUNG TRADITION   GALLERIES

The Young Tradition is a vocal trio specialising in performing traditional material. *Galleries* is very much more varied than this description implies, partly because traditional and medieval instruments are added on some of the tracks and partly because the singers are careful to make their interpretations sound different by taking turns to lead the singing or even dropping out entirely to let one of two of the others perform on their own. Peter Bellamy plays concertina on just one track while on one other, he takes up an acoustic guitar in order to render a passable imitation of a Robert Johnson recording, complete with added crackle. Otherwise, the music has no connection with the world of rock, although Traffic would later borrow *John Barleycorn* for a version of their own. Meanwhile, *Galleries* provides a fascinating tour of Britain's old music (and a touch of American), presented as though the listener is indeed passing by a series of audible tableaux in a gallery. It is a thoughtful and ultimately rather impressive album.

| UK release | October 1968 | Transatlantic | TRA 172 |
| US release | October 1968 | Vanguard | VSD-79295 |

1. Intro: Ductia (Anonymous)
2. The Barley Straw (Traditional)
3. What If A Day (Thomas Campion)
4. The Loyal Lover (Traditional)
5. Entrace: Stones In My Passway (Robert Johnson)
6. Idumea (Charles Wesley/Ananias Davisson)
7. The Husbandman And The Servingman (Traditional)
8. The Rolling Of The Stones (Traditional)
9. The Bitter Withy (Traditional)
10. The Banks Of The Nile (Traditional)
11. Wondrous Love (Rev. Robert Seagrave)
12. Medieval Mystery Tour (Anonymous/Bert Jansch/John Renbourn)
13. Divertissement: Upon The Bough (Anonymous)
14. Ratcliff Highway (Traditional)
15. The Brisk Young Widow (Traditional)
16. Interlude (The Pembroke Unique Ensemble)
17. John Barleycorn (Traditional)
18. The Agincourt Carol (Anonymous)

Heather Wood: vocals, whistle / Royston Wood: vocals, percussion / Peter Bellamy: vocals, whistle, guitar, concertina / David Munrow: shawm / Roddy Skeaping: viol / Adam Skeaping: viol / Chris Hogwood: percussion / Dolly Collins: portative organ, arranger / Dave Swarbrick: violin, mandolin / Bill Leader: producer

MICHAEL MANTLER / THE JAZZ COMPOSER'S ORCHESTRA

| US release | c.October 1968 | JCOA | LP 1001/2 |
| UK release | 1974 | JCOA | JD 3001 |

1. Communications #8
2. Communications #9
3. Communications #10
4. Preview
5. Communications #11 Part 1
6. Communications #11 Part 2

Steve Lacy, Al Gibbons, Steve Marcus: soprano saxophone / Gene Hull, Bob Donovan, Frank Wess, Jimmy Lyons: alto saxophone / Gato Barbieri, Lew Tabackin, George Barrow, Pharoah Sanders: tenor saxophone / Charles Davis: baritone saxophone / Don Cherry: cornet / Lloyd Michels, Randy Brecker, Stephen Furtado: flugelhorn / Roswell Rudd, Jimmy Knepper, Jack Jeffers: trombone / Bob Northern, Julius Watkins: French horns / Howard Johnson: tuba / Larry Coryell: guitar / Cecil Taylor, Carla Bley: piano / Steve Swallow, Kent Carter, Ron Carter, Richard Davis, Charlie Haden, Reggie Workman, Eddie Gomez, Bob Cunningham, Alan Silva: bass / Andrew Cyrille, Beaver Harris: drums / Michael Mantler: conductor, producer

The Jazz Composer's Orchestra was founded by Michael Mantler and Carla Bley in 1965 with the intention of composing and performing big band avant garde works. An album was recorded but only released in the Netherlands by Fontana. Undeterred, the pair proceeded to set up their own record company and the Orchestra made a second album, a boxed double, which was released in the US and Germany, and eventually in the UK, France, and Japan. Five compositions by Mantler are presented, ranging in length from under three and a half minutes to well over half an hour, but each one set up to highlight the solo playing of one or two particularly gifted individuals. In order, the soloists are Don Cherry and Gato Barbieri, Larry Coryell, Steve Swallow and Roswell Rudd, Pharoah Sanders, and Cecil Taylor. The music is dense and tumultuous, with strident orchestral chords and flourishes being used to underscore the various soloists as they play. Cecil Taylor particularly impresses with the sheer energy of his ferocious piano playing on the long *Communications #11*, but Larry Coryell is revelatory in the way he decides to use his guitar as a sound source. The photographs included in the booklet accompanying the records shows him holding his guitar close to the amplifier in order to generate feedback, a technique never previously considered by a a guitarist playing jazz. *The Jazz Composer's Orchestra* double album is a considerable landmark within avant garde jazz, both for its music and for its pioneering achievement in managing to show how the private circumvention of established record companies can produce a successful result.

THREE DOG NIGHT

The band that was a one-hit wonder in the UK (*Mama Told Me Not To Come* in August 1970) was responsible for several best selling albums and singles in the US. The group's first album set the formula for its music. Three good rock singers took turns to be the lead voice and presented versions of a variety of songs taken from other artists' albums. The fact that the musician members of the

| US release | October 1968 | ABC/Dunhill | DS-50048 |
| UK release | October 1968 | Stateside | SSL 5006 |

1. One (Nilsson)
2. Nobody (Beth Beatty/Dick Cooper/Ernie Shelby)
3. Heaven Is In Your Mind (Steve Winwood/Jim Capaldi)
4. It's For You (John Lennon/Paul McCartney)
5. Let Me Go (Danny Whitten)
6. Chest Fever (Robbie Robertson)
7. Fine Someone To Love (Johnny Watson)
8. No One Ever Hurt So Bad (Randy Newman)
9. Don't Make Promises (Tim Hardin)
10. The Loner (Neil Young)
11. Try A Little Tenderness (Harry Woods/James Campbell/Reginald Connelly)

Danny Hutton: vocals / Chuck Negron: vocals / Cory Wells: vocals / Michael Allsup: guitar / Jimmy Greenspoon: keyboards / Joe Schermie: bass guitar / Floyd Sneed: drums / Gabriel Meklar: producer

group were very accomplished ensured that the versions were worthwhile. There is no getting away from the fact that Three Dog Night are essentially a superior bar band, but they do make some effort to choose songs that are not immediately obvious. It is not *The Weight* that they take from the Band, but *Chest Fever,* although the song loses something in being made to sound polished. The inevitable Beatles song is one that John Lennon and Paul McCartney gave to Cilla Black rather than recording themselves, enabling Three Dog Night to add an unusual vocal arrangement without upsetting the more famous group's fans. But somehow – and certainly in the context of the fiercely competitive late sixties – it all seems a bit pointless.

THE NAZZ

US release	October 1968	SGC	SD 5001
UK release	October 1968	SGC	221001

1. Open My Eyes
2. Back Of Your Mind
3. See What You Can Be
4. Hello It's Me
5. Wildwood Blues (The Nazz)
6. If That's The Way You Feel
7. When I Get My Plane
8. Lemming Song
9. Crowded (Stewkey Antoni/Thom Mooney)
10. She's Goin' Down

All compositions by Todd Rundgren except where stated

Todd Rundgren: guitar, vocals, arranger / Stewkey Antoni: vocals, keyboards / Carson Van Osten: bass guitar, vocals / Thom Mooney: drums / Bill Traut, Michael Friedman, the Nazz: producer

The first album by studio wizard Todd Rundgren is by his group of the time, the Nazz. *Open My Eyes* is a production masterpiece, combining harmony vocals, fluent guitar playing and a hook riff, surprising changes of rhythm, deep phasing.and, above all, a bright, memorable melody, to create a perfect single for the late sixties. Bizarrely, the record was a commercial failure, although it attracted much attention when it was included on the seventies anthology of American garage and punk music, *Nuggets,* despite the sound of the song, owing more to the Beatles than to the Seeds, meaning that it does not really qualify. The rest of the Nazz album keeps the momentum going after the first track, presenting a succession of expertly produced material in the same lively pop-rock style. The group did not survive the lack of interest shown by the public to three albums in a row, but Todd Rundgren was nevertheless able to build a highly successful solo career of his own. The talent he needed for this is apparent on every track of *Nazz*.

THE BEAU BRUMMELS   BRADLEY'S BARN

US release   October 1968   Warner Bros   WS 1760
Not released in UK

1. Turn Around (Ron Elliott/Robert Durand)
2. An Added Attraction (Come And See Me) (Sal Valentino)
3. Deep Water (Ron Elliott/Sal Valentino)
4. Long Walking Down To Misery (Ron Elliott)
5. Little Bird (Ron Elliott)
6. Cherokee Girl (Ron Elliott/Robert Durand)
7. I'm A Sleeper (Ron Elliott/Sal Valentino)
8. The Loneliest Man In Town (Ron Elliott/Charles Elliott)
9. Love Can Fall A Long Way Down (Ron Elliott/Robert Durand)
10. Jessica (Ron Elliott/Sal Valentino)
11. Bless You California (Randy Newman)

Sal Valentino: vocals / Ron Elliott: guitar, arranger / Harold Bradley: guitar / Jerry Reed: guitar / Wayne Moss: guitar / David Briggs: keyboards / Norbert Putnam: bass, bass guitar / Kenny Buttrey: drums / Lenny Waronker: producer

Reduced by the draft to just two members, the remaining Beau Brummels, Sal Valentino and Ron Elliott, decided to emphasise the country element of the previous *Triangle* for an entire album, with the help of some well-known session musicians. The group's approach to country rock is highly distinctive, with songs that strain the genre's conventions and are inclined to add such non-standard sounds as marimbas and double basses played with bows. The songs are kept short and have no instrumental solo work at all, yet they manage to make a considerable impact. A couple of the tracks are orchestrated, but this is done with considerable subtlety, so that the restrained ambience of the music is not upset. The Beau Brummels would reconvene, original members included, in the mid-seventies, but *Bradley's Barn* is effectively an impressive swansong for one of America's most high profile groups during the sixties.

NEIL YOUNG

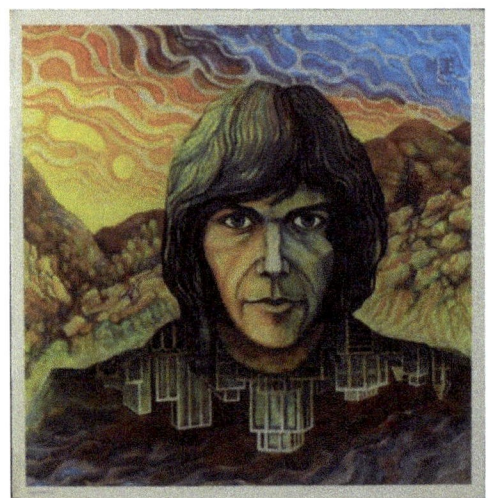

| US release | November 1968 | Reprise | RS 6317 |
| UK release | January 1969 | Reprise | RSLP 6317 |

1. The Emperor Of Wyoming
2. The Loner
3. If I Could Have Her Tonight
4. I've Been waiting For You
5. The Old Laughing Lady

6. String Quartet From Whiskey Boot Hill (Jack Nitzsche)
7. Here We Are In The Years
8. What Did You Do To My Life?
9. I've Loved Her So Long
10. The Last Trip To Tulsa

All compositions by Neil Young except where stated

Neil Young: vocals, guitar, keyboards, producer / Ry Cooder: guitar, producer / Jack Nitzsche: piano, arranger, producer / Jim Messina: bass guitar / Carol Kaye: bass guitar / George Grantham: drums / Earl Palmer: drums / Merry Clayton, Brenda Holloway, Patrice Holloway, Gloria Jones, Sherlie Matthews, Gracia Nitzsche: vocals / David Briggs: producer

Neil Young is the first member of Buffalo Springfield to release a solo record and the album reveals that he is still a very creative songwriter. There are seven new songs here that would have been an asset for an album by the group and they are delivered in an engaging soft rock style, with just a touch of country. Each side of the album starts with an instrumental – *The Emperor Of Wyoming* has the same approach as the songs that follow, but *String Quartet From Whiskey Boot Hill* is exactly what its title says. Assisted by the occasional use of strings on other songs, the track manages to match the mood of the album even without any rock element being present. *The Last Trip To Tulsa* concludes the set in a very low-key manner, as Neil Young delivers a halting, stream of consciousness narrative, accompanied only by his acoustic guitar. Young remixed the album and re-released it a year later, feeling that his vocals were rather buried in the arrangements, but the new version makes only a marginal difference to music that cannot help being decidedly introverted, wherever the vocals are placed.

GEORGE HARRISON WONDERWALL MUSIC

| UK release | November 1968 | Apple | (S)APCOR 1 |
| US release | November 1968 | Apple | ST-3350 |

1. Microbes
2. Red Lady Too
3. Tabla And Pakavaj
4. In The Park
5. Drilling A Home
6. Guru Vandana
7. Greasy Legs
8. Ski-ing
9. Gat Kirwani
10. Dream Scene
11. Party Seacombe
12. Love Scene
13. Crying
14. Cowboy Music
15. Fantasy Sequins
16. On The Bed
17. Glass Box
18. Wonderwall To Be Here
19. Singing Om

All compositions by George Harrison

George Harrison: arranger, producer, keyboards, guitar / Indril Bhattacharya: sitar / Shambu-Das: sitar / Chandra Shakher: bass sitar / Ashish Kahn: sarod / Shiv Kumar Shermar: santoor / Sharad Kumar: shehnai / Hanuman Jadev: shehnai / S.R.Kenkare: bansuri / Vinayak Vora: tar shehnai / Mahapurush Misra: percussion / Shankar Ghosh: percussion / Rijram Desad: harmonium, percussion / John Barham: keyboards, flugelhorn, arranger / Tony Ashton: keyboards / Colin Manley: guitar / Philip Rogers: bass guitar / Big Jim Sullivan: bass guitar / Roy Dyke: drums / Tommy Reilly: harmonica / Eric Clapton: guitar (8) / Ringo Starr: drums (8)

Wonderwall Music comprises nineteen short instrumental pieces composed by George Harrison for use as the soundtrack of a low budget film directed by Joe Massot. There is a little rock music included, but for the most part Harrison writes for Indian instruments, occasionally interacting with the rock but more often presented on their own. The music serves its primary purpose very well, although as an album it is all a little inconsequential. It does make clear, however, that George Harrison has made enormous progress and should now be taken very seriously as a songwriter, even if he still suffers from being in the shadow of John Lennon and Paul McCartney and is unlikely to be given much space to shine on records by the Beatles. *Wonderwall Music* is the first album to be released on Apple, the Beatles' own record label.

THE ASSOCIATION GREATEST HITS!

The Association achieved five top ten US hits during 1966-1968 with a blend of harmony vocals and beat, making the group a precursor of the sunshine pop genre. Surprisingly, the classic songs *Never My Love, Along*

Comes Mary, Cherish, and *Windy* were not hits in the UK, despite getting extensive radio play. They have managed to wriggle their way into the remembered sixties soundtrack regardless. During this period, the group made four albums, but it largely retained is best efforts for the hit singles, so that *Greatest Hits* becomes by far its strongest collection. Jim Yester is the brother of Jerry Yester, producer, solo artist, and eventual member of the Lovin' Spoonful.

US release	November 1968	Warner Bros	WS 1767
UK release	November 1968	Warner Bros	W(S) 1757

1. The Time It Is Today (Russ Giguere)
2. Everything That Touches You (Terry Kirkman)
3. Like Always (Bob Alcivar/Larry Ramos/Tony Ortega)
4. Never My Love (Don & Dick Addrisi)
5. Requiem For The Masses (Terry Kirkman)
6. Along Comes Mary (Tandyn Almer)
7. Enter The Young (Terry Kirkman)
8. No Fair At All (Jim Yester)
9. Time For Livin' (Don & Dick Addrisi)
10. We Love (Ted Bluechel)
11. Cherish (Terry Kirkman)
12. Windy (Ruthann Friedman)
13. Six Man Band (Terry Kirkman)

Terry Kirkman: vocals, flute, saxophone, percussion / Jules Alexander: guitar, vocals (6,8,11) / Larry Ramos: guitar, vocals (1-5,7,9,10,12,13) / Russ Giguere: guitar, vocals, percussion / Jim Yester: guitar, keyboards, vocals / Brian Cole: bass guitar, vocals, flute / Ted Bluechel: drums, guitar, bass guitar, vocals / Bones Howe: producer (1-5,9,10,12) / Curt Boettcher: producer (6,11) / Jerry Yester: producer (8) / The Association: producer (7,13)

SRC

US release	November 1968	Capitol	ST 2991
UK release	November 1968	Capitol	(S)T 2991

1. Black Sheep
2. Daystar
3. Exile
4. Marionette
5. Onesimpletask
6. Paragon Council
7. Refugeve
8. Interval

All compositions by SRC

Scott Richardson: vocals / Gary Quackenbush: guitar / Steve Lyman: guitar, vocals / Glenn Quackenbush: organ / Robin Dale: bass guitar, vocals / E.G. Clawson: drums / John Rhys: producer

Standing for Scott Richard Case, after the lead singer, SRC played a hugely attractive combination of effete teen vocals with atmospheric organ and dominant, sustained guitar, and the group deserved to achieve enormous record sales. There is much in common between the sound of the American SRC and that of the British Procol Harum, except that the delightfully named Gary Quackenbush is allowed to be a much more pervasive player than Robin Trower. The group does not have a *Whiter Shade Of Pale,* but its songs are nevertheless very distinctive. *Black Sheep* was issued as a strong single, but was not a hit, although the group did manage to make two more albums after its debut. The third was by a changed line-up with a different lead guitarist.

CANNED HEAT   LIVING THE BLUES

US release	November 1968	Liberty	LST-27200
UK release	November 1968	Liberty	LDS/LDL 84001E

1. Pony Blues (Charlie Patton)
2. My Mistake (Alan Wilson)
3. Sandy's Blues (Bob Hite)
4. Going Up The Country (Alan Wilson)
5. Walking By Myself (Jimmy Rogers)
6. Boogie Music (Skip Taylor)
7. One Kind Favor (Blind Lemon Jefferson)
8. Parthenogenesis (Canned Heat)
9. Refried Boogie Part I (Canned Heat)
10. Refried Boogie Part II (Canned Heat)

Bob Hite: vocals / Alan Wilson: guitar, vocals, harmonica / Henry Vestine: guitar / Larry Taylor: bass guitar, percussion / Fito de la Parra: drums / Mac Rebennack: piano, arranger (6) / Miles Grayson: arranger (3) / John Fahey: guitar (8) / John Mayall: piano (5,8) / Jim Horn: flute (4) / Joe Sample: piano (3) / Skip Taylor: producer

Perhaps borrowing an idea from Cream's *Wheels Of Fire* album, the third album by Canned Heat is a double, the first consisting of studio recordings, while the second is live. The live performance is a long version of the track that concluded the previous album, *Fried Hockey Boogie,* where each member of the band delivered a long solo over a boogie rhythm based on a single chord. Expanded to half an LP side for each musician, the music becomes boring in the extreme, because although Henry Vestine can stand the exposure, the rest are simply not sufficiently interesting improvisers to justify the length of their solos. The studio tracks are much better and include a fascinating medley, *Parthenogenesis,* in which an assortment of blues bits and pieces, using different combinations of instruments, is bolted together to considerable cumulative effect. *Going Up The Country,* with an Alan Wilson lead vocal in his distinctive falsetto style and a flute part to provide a hook, was issued as a single and became a hit in both the US and the UK. It was subsequently chosen as one of the pieces used as mood music at the start of the film about the Woodstock music festival. *Living The Blues* is undoubtedly an indulgent album and it could only have been made by a group enjoying a peak of popularity. Realistically, the only way onwards from that point was down.

JOHN MAYALL   BLUES FROM LAUREL CANYON

| UK release | November 1968 | Decca | SKL/LK 4972 |
| US release | November 1968 | London | PS 545 |

1. Vacation
2. Walking On Sunset
3. Laurel Canyon Home
4. 2401
5. Ready To Ride
6. Medicine Man
7. Somebody's Acting Like A Child
8. The Bear
9. Miss James
10. First Time Alone
11. Long Gone Midnight
12. Fly Tomorrow

John Mayall: vocals, keyboard, guitar, harmonica, producer / Mick Taylor: guitar / Peter Green: guitar (10) / Stephen Thompson: bass guitar / Colin Allen: drums / Mike Vernon: producer

After just a few months, John Mayall abandoned his expanded line-up and his flirtation with jazz, slimming down to his original quartet format and retaining only guitarist Mick Taylor from before. The songs on *Blues From Laurel Canyon* are linked together physically and tell the story of John Mayall's holiday in the Laurel Canyon area of Los Angeles. With regard to the standard of his songwriting, Mayall is still on the same roll as with *Bare Wires* and is managing to create an astonishing variety of material from the one basic blues structure. The band rises to the challenge and Mick Taylor in particular plays with a fire and an inspiration to eclipse what he has played previously. The first and last tracks on the album are little more than jams and provide an excellent showcase for Taylor's abilities. For just one track, *First Time Alone*, Peter Green is recalled to the band for the sake of the sensitive ambience that only he can provide. Meanwhile, *The Bear* quotes Canned Heat's signature boogie riff for a tribute to the band, with whom Mayall stayed while in Laurel Canyon (Canned Heat returns the favour by having Mayall play piano on its own recent album). Between them, *Blues From Laurel Canyon* and *Bare Wires* represent the pinnacle of this era's British fascination with the blues. And at the start of *Blues From Laurel Canyon* an aeroplane flies across the stereo, which is magnificent!

ALBERT COLLINS   LOVE CAN BE FOUND ANYWHERE (EVEN IN A GUITAR)

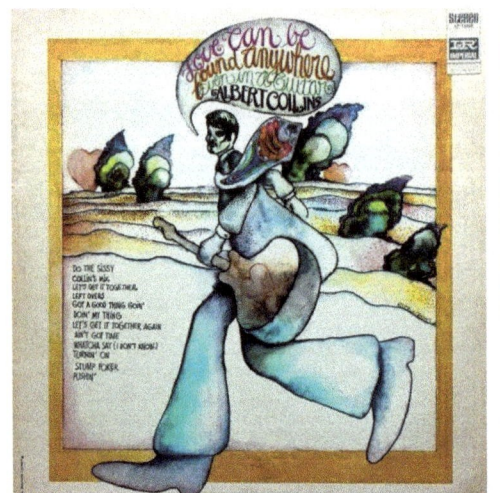

| US release | November 1968 | Imperial | LP-12428 |
| UK release | November 1968 | Liberty | LBS 83238 |

1. Do The Sissy (Stephen Hollister)
2. Collin's Mix (Albert Collins)
3. Let's Get It Together (Albert Collins)
4. Got A Good Thing Goin' (Albert Collins)
5. Left Overs (Albert Collins)
6. Doin' My Thing (Jim Mulloy)
7. Let's Get It Together Again (Albert Collins)
8. Ain't Got Time (Stephen Hollister)
9. Turnin' On (Stephen Hollister)
10. Whatcha Say (I Don't Know) (Albert Collins)
11. Pushin' (Stephen Hollister)
12. Stump Poker (Bill Rice/Jerry Foster)

Albert Collins: guitar, vocals / Bill Hall: producer, arranger / band uncredited but possibly: Alan Batts: keyboards / Larry Burton: guitar / Aron Burton: bass guitar / Casey Jones: drums / A.C. Reed: tenor saxophone / Chuck Smith: baritone saxophone

Blues guitarist Albert Collins made a few singles during the fifties without much success, but his career was revitalised in 1968, when Canned Heat arranged for him to sign a recording contract with Imperial Records. The title of his first album with the company, *Love Can Be Found Anywhere (Even In A Guitar)*, is taken from a line recited by Canned Heat's singer, Bob Hite, during the group's recording of *Fried Hockey Boogie*. Bob Hite also wrote the album's sleeve notes. The music consists almost entirely of funky blues instrumentals, allowing Albert Collins to display his credentials. He has a particularly piercing tone, albeit without much sustain, and is instantly recognisable as soon as he starts to play. Unusually, he uses a capo half way up the neck of his guitar, forcing him to play high notes, and he uses his fingers to strike the strings, not a plectrum. Although he never became a big star, he did manage to maintain a substantial career playing nothing but blues guitar.

THE NEW TWEEDY BROTHERS

```
US release      c.November 1968    Ridon    SLP 234
Not released in UK

1.  Somebody's Peepin' (Steve Ekman)
2.  I Can See It (Steve Ekman)
3.  I'd Go Anywhere (Dan & Fred Lackaff)
4.  Danny's Song (Dan Lackaff)
5.  Wheels Of Fortune (Dan Lackaff)

6.  I See You're Looking Fine (Steve Ekman)
7.  What's Wrong With That (Fred Lackaff)
8.  Someone Just Passed By (Steve Ekman)
9.  Her Darkness In December (Fred Lackaff)
10. Lazy Livin' (Dennis Fagaly)

Steve Ekman: guitar, vocals / Fred Lackaff: guitar, vocals /
Dave McClure: bass guitar / Danny Lackaff: drums, vocals /
Rick Keefer: producer
```

Newcomers to the San Francisco scene, the New Tweedy Brothers were not offered a contract with a record company and had to pay for their own privately pressed album. It was issued in a unique hexagonal sleeve, simulating the appearance of a cube, which must surely have attracted attention, although less than a thousand copies were made. Broadly similar to Quicksilver Messenger Service or Mad River, the music of the New Tweedy Brothers very much deserves to have been given greater exposure. *I Can See It* and *Her Darkness In December* are particularly memorable songs, but all are distinguished by sparkling playing and efficient, if rough toned, close-harmony singing. Given the generally upbeat nature of the music, the singing gives it a flavour of sunshine pop, unexpected but welcome in this context. The record's private production origins are betrayed by a lack of recording sophistication, although the group still manages to include some effective reversed guitar and what sounds like some unusual violin playing in places, although it is not clear who was responsible for this.

SECOND HAND (THE MOVING FINGER)   REALITY

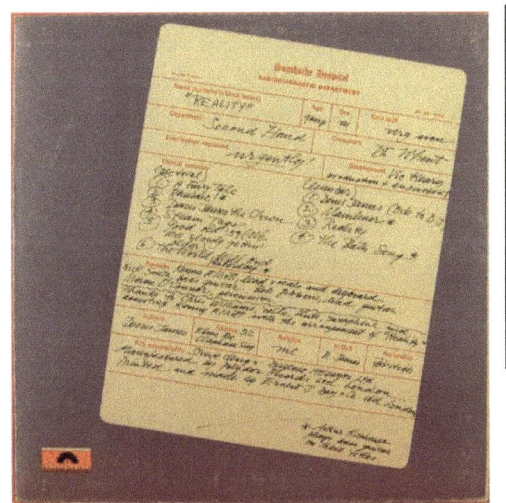

```
UK release      November 1968    Polydor    583 045
Not released in UK

1.  A Fairy Tale (Ken Elliott)
2.  Rhubarb! (Ken Elliott/Bob Gibbons)
3.  Denis James The Clown (Arthur Kitchener)
4.  Steam Tugs (Ken Elliott)
5.  Good Old '59 (We Are Slowly Gettin' Older) (Ken Elliott)
6.  The World Will End Yesterday (Ken Elliott/Bob Gibbons)

7.  Denis James The Clown (Ode To D.J.) (Ken Elliott/Arthur Kitchener)
8.  Mainliner (Ken Elliott)
9.  Reality (Ken Elliott/Bob Gibbons)
10. The Bath Song (Ken Elliott)

Ken Elliott: vocals, keyboards, arranger / Bob Gibbons: guitar / Arthur
Kitchener: bass guitar / Nick South: bass guitar / Kieran O'Connor: drums,
percussion / Chris Williams: cello, flute, saxophone, arranger / Vic Keary:
producer
```

British proto-progressive rock from a group that has much in common with the original Nice, though with a greater fondness for musical chaos. There are many occasions when the music dissolves into free-form noise. Strings are added from time to time, but these are used to provide the kind of abrasive texture that a chamber group can deliver, not to give any kind of lush sweetening. The record labels refer to the group as the Moving Finger, although the cover is clear that it is Second Hand, and this is the name that was used for the belated follow-up album. This lack of concern on the part of the Polydor record company was emphasised by the lack of promotion given to the album, which failed to make much impact at all as a result. In truth, however, although the combination of rock and free improvisation is very innovative, the songs lack the melodic distinction needed to make a real breakthrough.

THE BUDDY MILES EXPRESS   EXPRESSWAY TO YOUR SKULL

With the demise of the Electric Flag, drummer Buddy Miles formed a new band with much the same sound and using some of the same musicians. For the duration of the first track, *Train*, on the album by the Buddy Miles Express, it seems that Miles has succeeded in capturing the qualities that sometimes made the Electric Flag great. The music is powerful and exciting and it is clear that in Jim McCarty (formerly a member of blue-eyed soul specialist Mitch Ryder's Detroit Wheels), Miles has found a guitarist inspired enough to replace the inimitable Mike Bloomfield. For much of the rest of the album, however, Buddy Miles would clearly like to be Otis Redding, singing with the Markeys, and it has to be admitted that Redding did this style of music better. There are still moments when the Buddy Miles Express sounds as revelatory as it does on *Train*, but overall the album comes across as a missed opportunity. The cover includes an enthusiastic testimonial from Jimi Hendrix and we know from subsequent events that the guitarist much admired Buddy Miles' drumming, but it has to be significant that Hendrix did not choose to emulate the approach of the band.

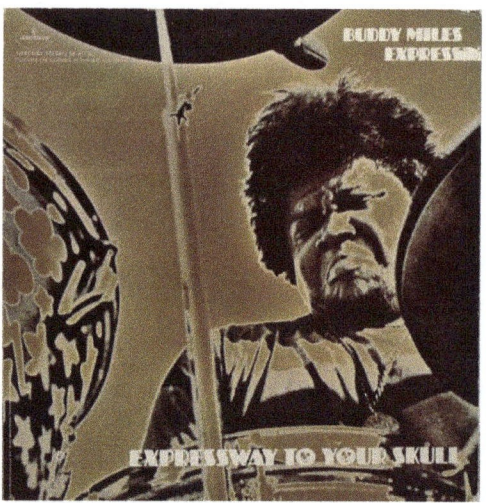

US release	November 1968	Mercury	SR-61196
UK release	November 1968	Mercury	20137 SMCL

1. Train (Buddy Miles/Herbie Rich)
2. Let Your Lovelight Shine (Buddy Miles/Herbie Rich)
3. Don't Mess With Cupid (Otis Redding/Steve Cropper)
4. Funky Mule (M.Holmes)
5. You're The One (That I Adore) (D.Malone)
6. Wrap It Up (Isaac Hayes/Dave Porter)
7. Spot On The Wall (Buddy Miles/Herbie Rich)

Buddy Miles: drums, vocals, guitar, organ, bass guitar / Jim McCarty: guitar / Herbie Rich: organ, tenor saxophone / Terrence Clements: tenor saxophone / Bill McPherson: tenor and soprano saxophones, flute / Marcus Doubleday: trumpet, flugelhorn / Bill Rich: bass guitar / Ron Woods: drums / Lou Reizner: producer

THE AYNSLEY DUNBAR RETALIATION DOCTOR DUNBAR'S PRESCRIPTION

UK release	November 1968	Liberty	LBS/LBL 83177
US release	January 1969	Blue Thumb	BTS 6

1. The Fugitive (Victor Brox)
2. Till Your Lovin' Makes Me Blue (Victor Brox)
3. Now That I've Lost You (B.B.King)
4. I Tried (Don Robey/Joseph Scott/Larry Davis)
5. Change Your Lowdown Ways (Aynsley Dunbar Retaliation)
6. Call My Woman (John Moorshead)
7. The Devil Drives (Victor Brox)
8. Low Gear Man (Victor Brox)
9. Tuesday's Blues (Victor Brox)
10. Mean Old World (Walter Jacobs)

Aynsley Dunbar: drums / Victor Brox: vocals, organ, guitar, cornet / John Moorshead: guitar, vocals / Alex Dmochowski: bass guitar / Ian Samwell: producer

Drummer Aynsley Dunbar formed his own band after leaving John Mayall's Bluesbreakers and released four albums during the next couple of years. Although Dunbar had managed to find some talented musicians to play with him, especially singer and multi-instrumentalist Victor Brox, the Aynsley Dunbar Retaliation struggled to find a place within an increasingly crowded British blues scene. *Doctor Dunbar's Prescription*, the second album to be released, is the most satisfying, but even this is a little anonymous. It has neither the authority of Fleetwood Mac's first album nor the spirit of adventure apparent in the albums made by John Mayall during 1968. It provides a perfectly acceptable listening experience, but it is easy to understand why the group never became particularly successful. In the long run, Aynsley Dunbar realised that his skills as a drummer were always likely to provide him with worthwhile employment and he had no need to be a bandleader in his own right. His list of recordings through to the twenty-first century is impressive and includes stints with such luminaries as Frank Zappa, Journey, Jefferson Starship, and Whitesnake.

THE GROUNDHOGS   SCRATCHING THE SURFACE

UK release	November 1968	Liberty	LBS/LBL 83199
US release	January 1969	World Pacific	WPS-21892

1. Rocking Chair (Tony McPhee)
2. Early In The Morning (Sonny Boy Williamson)
3. Waking Blues (Tony McPhee)
4. Married Men (Tony McPhee)
5. No More Doggin' (Traditional)
6. Man Trouble (Tony McPhee)
7. Come Back Baby (Tony McPhee)
8. You Don't Love Me (Willie Cobbs)
9. Still A Fool (Muddy Waters)

Tony McPhee: guitar, vocals / Steve Rye: vocals, harmonica / Peter Cruickshank: bass guitar / Ken Pustelnik: drums / Mike Batt: producer

Guitarist Tony McPhee formed his band the Groundhogs in 1963 and backed John Lee Hooker on a UK tour in 1964. The group's first album did not appear until four years after that, produced by the unlikely figure of Mike Batt, later known for his work with the Wombles. The group's history gives it a certain authority, especially since McPhee is a very accomplished player, but this did not stop harmonica player Steve Rye from claiming in the record credits that his features, *Early In The Morning* and *You Don't Love Me,* were his own compositions. It is a pity that the Groundhogs' first album was so delayed, because at the end of 1968, the group is facing the same problem as Aynsley Dunbar's Retaliation. *Scratching The Surface* is a good blues album, well played and with an appropriately gritty sound, but ultimately it is not particularly memorable. The problem caused by trying to sound distinctive while playing nothing but the blues is one that Tony McPhee would tackle in the seventies.

THE BONZO DOG BAND — THE DOUGHNUT IN GRANNY'S GREENHOUSE

UK release   November 1968   Liberty   LBS/LBL 83158E
Not released in US

1. We Are Normal (Neil Innes/Vivian Stanshall)
2. Postcard (Neil Innes/Vivian Stanshall)
3. Beautiful Zelda (Neil Innes)
4. Can Blue Men Sing The Whites (Vivian Stanshall)
5. Hello Mabel (Neil Innes)
6. Kama Sutra (Neil Innes/Vivian Stanshall)
7. Humanoid Boogie (Neil Innes)
8. The Trouser Press (Roger Ruskin Spear)
9. My Pink Half Of The Drainpipe (Vivian Stanshall)
10. Rockaliser Baby (Neil Innes/Vivian Stanshall)
11. Rhinocratic Oaths (Neil Innes/Vivian Stanshall)
12. Eleven Mustachioed Daughters (Vivian Stanshall)

Vivian Stanshall: vocals, percussion, trumpet, tuba, euphonium, violin / Neil Innes: vocals, guitar, keyboards, accordion, vibraphone, percussion / Roger Ruskin Spear: guitar, trumpet, clarinet, accordion, percussion / Rodney Slater: saxophone, oboe, trumpet, trombone / Legs Larry Smith: drums, percussion, vocals / Joel Druckman: bass guitar / Gerry Bron: producer / Gus Dudgeon: producer

Although presented as a music and comedy record, the second album by the newly streamlined Bonzo Dog Band is full of wit and cleverness rather than outright laughter. It is also, in contrast to the jazz and music-hall emphasis of the first album, very much a set of pop-rock music, in the post-*Sgt Pepper* mode, where the group tries hard to make the music as varied and as full of interesting detail as possible. *Postcard* and *My Pink Half Of The Drainpipe* (a reference that would have been meaningless to an American audience if the album had been released there) are works of particular genius, encompassing a kaleidoscope of changing musical elements. *The Trouser Press*, complete with a solo played on the device, is more zany and slapstick, while *Can Blue Men Sing The Whites* clothes a serious question, about what would doubtless be called 'cultural appropriation' today, in comedy disguise. The squeezing of some very diverse and considerable individual talents into one band would ultimately cause it to split apart, but in late 1968 this is responsible for an exceptional album.

THE INCREDIBLE STRING BAND — WEE TAM & THE BIG HUGE

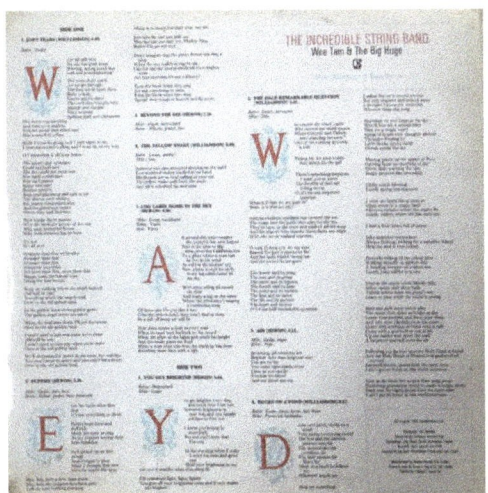

UK release   November 1968   Elektra   EKS 74036/7 / EKL 4036/7
also issued as two separate albums; only issued like this in US

1. Job's Tears (Robin Williamson)
2. Puppies (Mike Heron)
3. Beyond The See (Mike Heron)
4. The Yellow Snake (Robin Williamson)
5. Log Cabin Home In The Sky (Mike Heron)
6. You Get Brighter (Mike Heron)
7. The Half-Remarkable Question (Robin Williamson)
8. Air (Mike Heron)
9. Ducks On A Pond (Robin Williamson)
10. Maya (Robin Williamson)
11. Greatest Friend (Mike Heron)
12. The Son Of Noah's Brother (Robin Williamson)
13. Lordly Nightshade (Robin Williamson)
14. The Mountain Of God (Robin Williamson)
15. Cousin Caterpillar (Mike Heron)
16. The iron Stone (Robin Williamson)
17. Douglas Traherne Harding (Mike Heron)
18. The Circle Is Unbroken (Traditional)

Mike Heron: vocals, guitar, sitar, bass guitar, keyboards, harmonica, percussion / Robin Williamson: vocals, guitar, bass guitar, gimbri, sarangi, violin, keyboards, flute, harmonica, Irish harp, percussion / Rose Simpson: vocals, violin, percussion / Licorice McKechnie: vocals, percussion, Irish harp / Joe Boyd: producer

The Incredible String Band was permitted the indulgence of a double album, although its music is not really sufficiently varied to justify such a long display of its most recent studio efforts. For the most part, the duo remembers the 'string band' part of its name and backs away from the more elaborate approach of much of the previous *Hangman's Beautiful Daughter*, with just a couple of tracks relying on a keyboard drone to underlie the singing. The Incredible String Band still sounds utterly distinctive, but it is the cumulative effect of the material that matters this time, rather than any reliance on individual outstanding songs. After this, the contribution from the duo's girlfriends would increase and a lesson would be taken from *Wee Tam and The Big Huge* that it was time to start introducing a more conventional, rock approach.

THE PENTANGLE — SWEET CHILD

The Pentangle released a double album too, this one coupling a live recording with a studio set. The group members are still very inspired by the novelty of working together and this shows in the performances. The group's blend of jazz with different kinds of traditional material (including blues, spiritual, and medieval dance music, as well as British folk song) works incredibly well and ensures that the group has a very distinctive sound of its own. The fact that they are all such gifted players (and singers) ensures the music's success. To emphasise this, they are each given the chance to demonstrate their solo talents – the bass variations on *Haitian Fight Song* and Jacqi McShee's acapella performance of *So Early In The Spring* stand out. Only the audience applause on the first disc (recorded at the Royal Festival Hall) makes it possible to distinguish the live from the studio recordings, so flawless is the group's playing in both settings. As a manifesto for the group, demonstrating what makes the Pentangle so special, *Sweet Child* is perfect.

| UK release | November 1968 | Transatlantic | TRA 178 |
| US release | November 1968 | Reprise | 2RS 6334 |

1. Market Song (Pentangle)
2. No More My Lord (Traditional)
3. Turn Your Money Green (Furry Lewis)
4. Haitian Fight Song (Charles Mingus)
5. A Woman Like You (Bert Jansch)
6. Goodbye Pork Pie Hat (Charles Mingus)
7. Three Dances: Brentzel Gay (Claude Gervais)/La Rotta (Traditional)/The Earle Of Salisbury (William Byrd)
8. Watch The Stars (Traditional)
9. So Early In The Spring (Traditional)
10. No Exit (Bert Jansch/John Renbourn)
11. The Time Has Come (Ann Briggs)
12. Bruton Town (Traditional)
13. Sweet Child (Pentangle)
14. I Loved A Lass (Traditional)
15. Three Part Thing (Bert Jansch/Danny Thompson/John Renbourn)
16. Sovay (Traditional)
17. In Time (Bert Jansch/Danny Thompson/John Renbourn/Terry Cox)
18. In Your Mind (Pentangle)
19. I've Got A Feeling (Pentangle)
20. The Trees They Do Grow High (Traditional)
21. Moon Dog (Terry Cox)
22. Hole In My Coal (Ewan MacColl)

Jacqui McShee: vocals / Bert Jansch: guitar, vocals / John Renbourn: guitar, vocals / Danny Thompson: bass / Terry Cox: drums, glockenspiel, percussion, vocals / Shel Talmy: producer

JERRY BUTLER — THE ICE MAN COMETH

| US release | November 1968 | Mercury | SR-61198 |
| UK release | November 1968 | Mercury | 20154 SMCL |

1. Hey Western Union Man (Jerry Butler/Kenny Gamble/Leon Huff)
2. Can't Forget About You Baby (Jerry Butler/Billy Butler/Kenny Gamble)
3. Only The Strong Survive (Jerry Butler/Kenny Gamble/Leon Huff)
4. How Can I Get In Touch With You (Jerry Butler/Kenny Gamble/Leon Huff)
5. Just Because I Really Love You (Jerry Butler/Kenny Gamble/Mikki Farrow/Thom Bell)
6. Lost (Jerry Butler/Kenny Gamble/Leon Huff)
7. Never Give You Up (Jerry Butler/Kenny Gamble/Leon Huff)
8. Are You Happy (Jerry Butler/Kenny Gamble/Thom Bell)
9. (Strange) I Still Love You (Jerry Butler/Mikki Farrow/Norman Harris)
10. Go Away Find Yourself (Jerry Butler/Kenny Gamble/Thom Bell)
11. I Stop By Heaven (Jerry Butler/Kenny Gamble/Leon Huff)

Jerry Butler: vocals / Bobby Martin: arranger / Thom Bell: arranger / Kenny Gamble: producer / Leon Huff: producer

Jerry Butler was the original lead singer with the Impressions, the group of which Curtis Mayfield was also a member. While achieving moderate chart success in the US through the sixties, he did particularly well with *Hey Western Union Man* and *Only The Strong Survive*, both of which are included on the album, *The Ice Man Cometh*. The description of Butler as the 'ice man' is supposed to refer to his cool, unemotional demeanour, but his singing is as warm and as soulful as any of his star contemporaries. His music is shaped by the songwriting and production team of Kenny Gamble and Leon Huff, who like the contrast between a strong bass line and shimmering strings. The music is slower and lacks the insistent dance beat of Tamla Motown, but this enables Butler to make all the more impact with his voice. Like Motown, Jerry Butler is more concerned with getting hit singles than extending himself for an album, but *The Ice Man Cometh* works well and was a substantial US album hit in its own right.

NICO — THE MARBLE INDEX

Nico's *The Marble Index* is quite different from her previous album. There is no rhythmic pulse and no rock instrumentation. Instead Nico intones songs that do not have a verse and chorus structure over a discordant background made

| US release | November 1968 | Elektra | EKS-74029 |
| UK release | November 1968 | Elektra | EKS 74029/EKL 4029 |

1. Prelude
2. Lawns Of Dawns
3. No One Is There
4. Ari's Song
5. Facing The Wind
6. Julius Caesar (Memento Hodie)
7. Frozen Warnings
8. Evening Of Light

All compositions by Nico

Nico: vocals, harmonium / John Cale: arranger / Frazier Mohawk: producer

up of her own sparse harmonium playing, and atonal chamber string arrangements provided by her former colleague in the Velvet Underground, John Cale. The avant garde, arty result makes *The Marble Index* stand out from everything else produced at this time and it does not make comfortable listening, despite being something of a creative milestone.

VARIOUS COMPOSERS
CYBERNETIC SERENDIPITY MUSIC

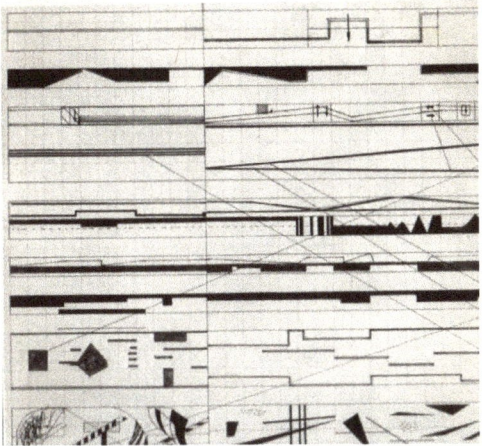

Peter Zinovieff, the inventor of the VCS3 synthesizer, put together a compilation LP called *Cybernetic Serendipity Music*, designed to advertise the concept of music produced by computer. It was originally released to accompany an exhibition at the ICA in London with the same title. The first track was *Illiac Suite (Experiment 4)*, a 1957 piece for string quartet where, for the first time, the actual composition was completely carried out by a computer. It was programmed by Lajaren Hiller and Leonard Isaacson, who get the composing credit on the record. Curiously, the music sounds far more conventional than many purely human string quartets being produced at the time. *Composition 3* by Gerald Strang, produced in 1966 and also included on the LP, was both composed and performed by a computer and sounds much more satisfyingly bizarre, although it is barely more than two minutes long. *Infraudibles*, by Herbert Brün, is performed by a group of musicians more accustomed to working within the realm of free improvisation, which is exactly what the piece sounds like, despite being composed by a computer. Peter Zinovieff himself, who had long been interested in the use of computers for producing music and who also has a piece included on the LP, presented a concert at the Queen Elizabeth Hall in January 1968, where a computer was left alone on the stage to play music it was inventing itself (*Partita For Unattended Computer*).

```
UK release      November 1968      ICA      ICA 01
Not released in US

1.  Illiac Suite (Experiment 4) (Lejaren Hiller and Leonard Isaacson)
2.  Cartridge Music (excerpt) (John Cage)
3.  Strategie (excerpt) (Iannis Xenakis)
4.  Experiment Quatro-Due (Wilhelm Fucks)
5.  Mudgett (excerpt) (J.K.Randall)
6.  Composition 3 (Gerald Strang)
7.  Bit Music (excerpt) (Haruki Tsuchiya)
8.  Enneadic Selections (T.H.O'Beirne)
9.  January Tensions (Peter Zinovieff)
10. Infraudibles (Herbert Brün)

Illinois Composition String Quartet (1) / David Tudor, John Cage (2) / Yomiuri Nippon Symphony Orchestra conducted by Seiji Ozawa (3) / Margot Pinter: piano (4) / Melinda Kassler: vocals (5) / Bernard Rands: cimbalom (10) / Gavin Bryars: bass (10) / Derek Bailey: guitar / Richard Howe: French horn (10) / Evan Parker: soprano saxophone (10)
```

THE NICE   ARS LONGA VITA BREVIS

```
UK release   November 1968   Immediate   IMSP 020
US release   early 1969      Immediate   Z12 52020

1.  Daddy Where Did I Come From (Keith Emerson/Lee Jackson)
2.  Little Arabella (Keith Emerson/Lee Jackson)
3.  Happy Freuds (Keith Emerson/Lee Jackson)
4.  Intermezzo From The Karelia Suite (Jean Sibelius)
5.  Don Edito El Gruva (The Nice)
6.  Ars Longa Vita Brevis – Symphony For Group And Orchestra (The Nice)

Keith Emerson: keyboards, vocals / Lee Jackson: bass guitar, vocals / Brian Davison: drums / Robert Stewart: arranger, conductor / Malcolm Langstaff: guitar (6) / the Nice: producer
```

The second album by the Nice finds the group reduced to a trio following the departure of guitarist David O'List. Keith Emerson has decided to rely much more on his classical music training and the group not only produces a rock version of a piece by Sibelius, but constructs an entire rock symphony to fill the album's second side. One movement of this uses a theme borrowed from one of Bach's *Brandenburg Concertos* (it was issued as a single under the name of *Brandenburger*) but the music is otherwise composed by Keith Emerson, with a little help from the rest of the band, in a classical style. An orchestra is employed to add to the group's own contributions in places. As the first major attempt to amalgamate rock and classical musics in a work of this kind, *Ars Longa Vita Brevis* is rather successful. It is a compelling piece, even if its musical language is based on an approach that is at least a century old and ignores the more recent developments to have taken place in classical music. The album is completed by a few songs in the idiosyncratic style of the group's first album and the combination of the two approaches makes the record a more satisfying set of music than its predecessor, even without the benefit of a guitarist.

SOUNDTRACK   HAIR ORIGINAL BROADWAY CAST RECORDING

| US release | November 1968 | RCA Victor | LSO 1150 |
| UK release | November 1968 | RCA Victor | SF/RD 7959 |

1. Aquarius
2. Donna/Hashish
3. Sodomy
4. Colored Spade
5. Manchester England
6. I'm Black/Ain't Got No
7. Air
8. Initials
9. I Got Life
10. Hair
11. My Conviction
12. Don't Put It Down
13. Frank Mills
14. Be-In
15. Where Do I Go?
16. Black Boys/White Boys
17. Easy To Be Hard
18. Walking In Space
19. Abie Baby
20. Three-Five-Zero-Zero/What A Piece Of Work Is Man
21. Good Morning Starshine
22. The Flesh Failures (Let The Sunshine In)

All compositions by Gerome Ragni/James Rado/Galt MacDermot

Alan Fontaine: guitar / Steve Gillette: guitar / Galt MacDermot: piano / Donald Leight: trumpet / Eddy Williams: trumpet / Zane Paul: woodwinds / Warren Chiasson: vibraphone, percussion / Jimmy Lewis: bass guitar / Idris Muhammad: drums / Donnie Burks, Steve Curry, Lorrie Davis, Ronald Dyson, Sally Eaton, Leata Galloway, Steve Gamet, Walter Harris, Paul Jabara, Diane Keaton, Hiram Keller, Lynn Kellogg, Jonathan Kramer, Marjorie LiPari, Emmaretta Marks, Melba Moore, Mike Moran, Natalie Mosco, Suzannah Norstrand, Shelley Plimpton, James Rado, Gerome Ragni, Robert Rubinsky, Lamont Washington: vocals / Brian Drutman, Denis McNamara, Norrie Paramor, Andy Wisell: producer

Hair is a celebration of the sixties hippy counter-culture transferred to the Broadway stage. As far as the history of musical theatre is concerned, *Hair* is revolutionary, both in its subject matter, including references to recreational drug taking and promiscuity, its use of nudity (albeit in a rather contrived tableau vivant), and the incorporation of a considerable rock emphasis within its music. Of course, as far as the members of the actual counter-culture were concerned, the fact that it was being used as the basis for a Broadway show meant that *Hair* is at best a pastiche of something whose value is being downgraded. Not at all coincidentally, The Death of the Hippie had taken place in San Francisco's Haight-Ashbury district on 6 October 1967. The matter became confused a little when some established performers realised that *Hair* did include some rather memorable songs. Many cover versions of these were recorded and released and although the majority could be dismissed as being by easy-listening artists, the same could not be said for Julie Driscoll or Nina Simone. A recording of the London stage version of *Hair* was released not long after the New York one. Its cast included Paul Nicholas, Marsha Hunt, and Sonja Kristina, while guitarist Alex Harvey was one of the musicians.

JUDY COLLINS   WHO KNOWS WHERE THE TIME GOES

| US release | November 1968 | Elektra | EKS-74033 |
| UK release | November 1968 | Elektra | EKS 74033/EKL 4033 |

1. Hello, Hooray (Rolf Kempf)
2. Story Of Isaac (Leonard Cohen)
3. My Father (Judy Collins)
4. Someday Soon (Ian Tyson)
5. Who Knows Where The Time Goes (Sandy Denny)
6. Poor Immigrant (Bob Dylan)
7. First Boy I Loved (Robin Williamson)
8. Bird On The Wire (Leonard Cohen)
9. Pretty Polly (Traditional)

Judy Collins: vocals, guitar, piano / Stephen Stills: guitar, bass guitar / James Burton: guitar / Buddy Emmons: pedal steel guitar / Mike Melvoin: piano / Van Dyke Parks: piano / Michael Sahl: keyboards / Chris Ethridge: bass guitar / Jim Gordon: drums / David Anderle: producer

Who Knows Where The Time Goes has a different character to that of Judy Collins' previous two albums, as it dispenses with the orchestrations in favour of a full-blooded folk-rock sound. Stephen Stills, late of Buffalo Springfield and as well-known for his contribution to Al Kooper's successful *Super Session* album, is a major contributor. As before, Judy Collins champions up-and-coming songwriters and this time they include Robin Williamson of the Incredible String Band, whose *First Girl I Loved* undergoes a change of gender and is revealed as the achingly beautiful song that it always was. Meanwhile, Ms Collins presents a song found on a publisher's demo, by a songwriter shortly to become much better known as a member of Fairport Convention, Sandy Denny. *Who Knows Where The Time Goes* is the album's highlight and was chosen, absolutely appropriately, as the title. The album fared a little less well in the US chart than its predecessor, but still managed to qualify for a gold record award a year later.

THE DILLARDS   WHEATSTRAW SUITE

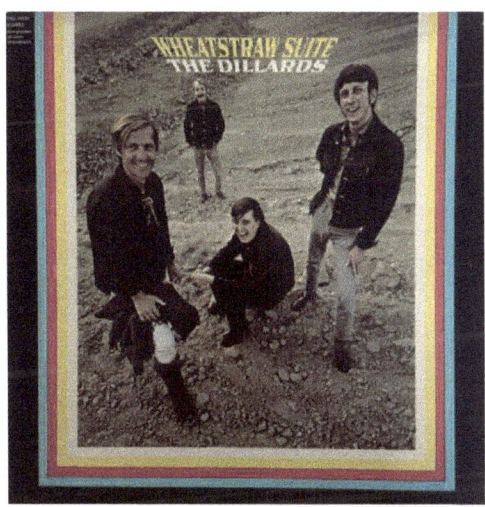

| US release | November 1968 | Elektra | EKS-74035 |
| UK release | November 1968 | Elektra | EKS 74035/EKL 4035 |

1. I'll Fly Away (Albert E.Brumley)
2. Nobody Knows (Mitch Jayne/Rodney Dillard)
3. Hey Boys (The Dillards)
4. The Biggest Whatever (Mitch Jayne/Rodney Dillard)
5. Listen To The Sound (Herb Pedersen/Mitch Jayne)
6. Little Pete (Herb Petersen)
7. Reason To Believe (Tim Hardin)
8. Single Saddle (Arthur Altman/Hal David)
9. I've Just Seen A Face (John Lennon/Paul McCartney)
10. Lemon Chimes (Bill Martin/Rodney Dillard)
11. Don't You Cry (The Dillards)
12. Bending The Strings (Allen Shelton)
13. She Sang Hymns Out Of Tune (Jesse Lee Kincaid)

Rodney Dillard: vocals, guitar, pedal steel guitar, producer / Herb Pedersen: vocals, guitar, banjo / Dean Webb: mandolin / Mitch Jayne: bass / Buddy Emmons: pedal steel guitar / Joe Osborn: bass guitar / Toxey French: drums / Jim Gordon: drums

The Dillards were an American bluegrass band formed by brothers Rodney and Douglas in the late fifties. *Wheatstraw Suite* is the fourth album and the first to be made after the departure of Douglas, who did not like the fact that the others wanted to move away from the traditional bluegrass sound. A little discreet orchestration is added in places, along with lightly played drums, and the songs include some from unlikely sources such as Tim Hardin and the Beatles (although *I've Just Seen A Face* always did have a breath of country air about it). Douglas was right – the music on *Wheatstraw Suite* does not have much bluegrass flavour at all. But it is a captivating set of music all the same and sits well with the records like the Byrds' *Sweetheart Of The Rodeo* attempting to push rock and country back together, even if there is still very little rock in the music of the Dillards.

THE KINKS   ARE THE VILLAGE GREEN PRESERVATION SOCIETY

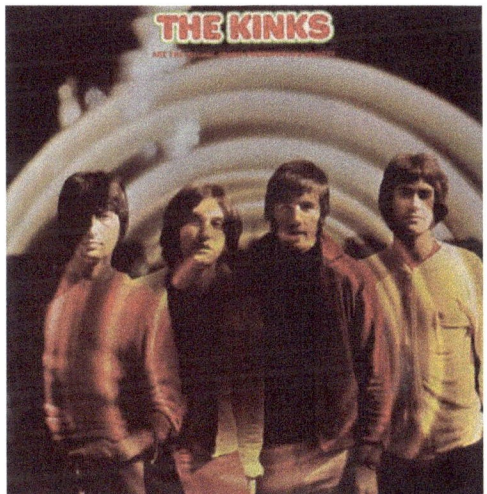

| UK release | November 1968 | Pye | N(S)PL 18233 |
| US release | November 1968 | Reprise | RS 6327 |

1. The Village Green Preservation Society
2. Do You Remember Walter?
3. Picture Book
4. Johnny Thunder
5. Last Of The Steam-Powered Trains
6. Big Sky
7. Sitting By The Riverside
8. Animal Farm
9. Village Green
10. Starstruck
11. Phenomenal Cat
12. All Of My Friends Were There
13. Wicked Annabella
14. Monica
15. People Take Pictures Of Each Other

All compositions by Ray Davies

Ray Davies: vocals, guitar, keyboards, harmonica, producer / Dave Davies: guitar, vocals / Pete Quaife: bass guitar, vocals / Mick Avory: drums / Nicky Hopkins: keyboards / Rasa Davies: vocals

The Kinks Are The Village Green Preservation Society is a collection of songs loosely celebrating the British way of life, as viewed with the benefit of rose-tinted nostalgia. Without doing anything differently from what has become his established way of working, Ray Davies has managed to create a flawless Kinks album, one without any weak tracks at all. There are no songs released as singles and in chart terms the album performed poorly – it took fifty years before it managed to qualify for a gold disc in the UK. In 1968, of course, the Kinks are out of step with the majority of their contemporaries. The music bears no trace of psychedelia and it has none of the arrangement elaboration that is considered essential on the records made by everyone else. The group has an old single B side that expresses its position – *I'm Not Like Everybody Else*. And thank goodness they are not, because Ray Davies and his group's wilful, selfish way with the music produces one of the quintessential albums of its time.

JOHN LENNON AND YOKO ONO   UNFINISHED MUSIC No.1: TWO VIRGINS

| UK release | November 1968 | Apple | (S)APCOR 2 |
| US release | November 1968 | Apple/Tetragrammaton T-5001 |

1. Two Virgins Nos. 1-5 including Together performed by Guy Lombardo and his Royal Canadians
2. Two Virgins Nos. 6-10 including Hushabye Hushabye performed by Fred Douglas and his Orchestra

John Lennon: vocals, effects, keyboards, guitar, percussion, producer / Yoko Ono: vocals, effects, piano, percussion, producer / Pete Shotton: effects

John Lennon met performance artist Yoko Ono in November 1966 and the album, *Unfinished Music No.1: Two Virgins* is the first result of her artistic influence on him. The pair made two further albums like this one, *Unfinished Music No.2: Life With The Lions,* released in May 1969, and *Wedding Album,* released in October/November 1969. All three are characterised by a mixture of speech, found sound, and assorted sound effects, producing a listening experience without enough interesting detail to persuade many listeners to persevere

more than once. But placed against such influential avant garde works as John Cage's *4'33"* or Luc Ferrari's *Presque Rien No.1,* neither of which contains anything at all that might conventionally be described as music, the Lennon-Ono albums are hardly different. (The Cage work is a silent score, intending that any ambient sound should be the focus, while the Ferrari work presents an edited recording of a day at the beach). They all represent valid avant garde efforts to re-assess what counts as music in the first place. What is most surprising about the Lennon-Ono albums is that works so uncompromising, so deliberately avoiding popularity, are presented by a member of the most popular rock group of all and released on that group's own record label. The controversial cover chosen for *Unfinished Music No.1* (and its equally contentious subtitle) proved a little more than the US market could stand and a variety of paper bag coverings was employed to enable the record to be displayed in the shops.

THE BEATLES   (WHITE ALBUM)

The Beatles were faced with a considerable problem with regard to producing a follow-up to *Sgt Pepper's Lonely Hearts Club Band* and it was one that they never really managed to solve. More than ever before, they found themselves in the invidious position of having a reputation to maintain. Audiences had become used to each record being an advance on the previous one

UK release	November 1968	Apple	PCS/PMC 7067/8
US release	November 1968	Apple	SWBO-101

1. Back In The U.S.S.R.
2. Dear Prudence
3. Glass Onion
4. Ob-La-Di, Ob-La-Da
5. Wild Honey Pie
6. The Continuing Story Of Bungalow Bill
7. While My Guitar Gently Weeps (George Harrison)
8. Happiness Is A Warm Gun

9. Martha My Dear
10. I'm So Tired
11. Blackbird
12. Piggies (George Harrison)
13. Rocky Raccoon
14. Don't Pass Me By (Ringo Starr)
15. Why Don't We Do It In The Road?
16. I Will
17. Julia

18. Birthday
19. Yer Blues
20. Mother Nature's Son
21. Everybody's Got Something To Hide Except Me And My Monkey
22. Sexy Sadie
23. Helter Skelter
24. Long, Long, Long (George Harrison)

25. Revolution 1
26. Honey Pie
27. Savoy Truffle (George Harrison)
28. Cry Baby Cry
29. Revolution 9
30. Good Night

All compositions by John Lennon and Paul McCartney except where stated

John Lennon: vocals, guitar, keyboards, bass guitar, harmonica, percussion, effects / George Harrison: vocals, guitar, bass guitar, organ, percussion, effects / Paul McCartney: vocals, bass guitar, keyboards, guitar, percussion, recorder / Ringo Starr: drums, percussion, vocals, piano / Yoko Ono: vocals (6,18), effects (29) / Mal Evans: vocals, percussion (2,18), trumpet (23) / Eric Clapton: guitar (7) / Jack Fallon: violin (14) / Patti Harrison: vocals (18) / Jackie Lomax: vocals (2) / Maureen Starkey: vocals (6) / Chris Thomas: keyboards / assorted session musicians: violin, cellos, horns, saxophones / George Martin: producer, arranger

and were waiting with a collective bated breath for the record that would represent a progression from even *Sgt Pepper*. It became suddenly clear as well that the Beatles were no longer the only artists, or even the best, to be producing records worthy of consideration as works of art. A new generation of rock musicians had been steadily improving their skills and many of these people had developed an instrumental virtuosity, compared to which the Beatles were completely outclassed. There are numerous examples in the previous pages of this book. These players had also been listening hard to other kinds of music – especially the jazz of innovators like John Coltrane – with which the Beatles had no sympathy. It was no accident that the Beatles had earlier recorded the Chuck Berry song, *Rock and Roll Music*, with its declaration of disinterest in modern jazz and symphonic music. Aware of the difficulties involved, they hesitated and eventually let their next recordings be issued in dribs and drabs, wherein their impact was considerably lessened. The music they recorded during the rest of 1967 and early 1968 would have made a formidable LP. *I Am The Walrus, Blue Jay Way, Only A Northern Song,* and *Hello Goodbye* in particular are achievements to rival any of the songs of the previous months, showing precisely the same kind of imagination and detailed sound structure as the earlier songs. The other music, while being on the whole somewhat simpler, nevertheless displays a wide variety of styles and the same assuredness of touch, sufficient to well complement the four more complex pieces. A *Magical Mystery Tour* LP that included the five new *Yellow Submarine* songs held back until January 1969 and *Hello Goodbye*, and segued from one track to the next as on *Sgt Pepper*, would have been a record to rival its predecessor. But we can at least listen to the separate songs.

The LP that did eventually emerge, *The Beatles* (known as *The White Album*), turned out to be not one, but two records – and something of a disappointment. It was acclaimed regardless by many of the critics, but it remains a very inferior collection of songs compared to what had gone before. Gone is the attention to detail and the rich tapestry of sounds. The album does have several redeeming features – not least in George Harrison's *While My Guitar Gently Weeps*, where the guitar seems to do just that (even if Harrison did decide to call on Eric Clapton to play a part he ought to have been quite capable of playing himself); in John Lennon's smouldering *Dear Prudence* and *Cry Baby Cry*, and the madcap, scattershot *Happiness Is A Warm Gun;* and in the powerful *Helter Skelter*, where Paul McCartney sings of climbing up, with a tune that similarly climbs, only to be pulled down again by crashing guitars that remain firmly fixed to the earth. Overall, however, the album provides only a pale shadow of the group's former glory. The fact that it includes a number of tracks whose primary purpose is to act as a pastiche (*Back In The U.S.S.R, Ob-La-Di Ob-La-Da, Yer Blues*) or else a thin joke (*The Continuing Story of Bungalow Bill, Why Don't We Do It In The Road*), is not a good sign. George Harrison songs to rival *While My Guitar Gently Weeps – Not Guilty* and *Sour Milk Sea* – are ignored and replaced by the substandard *Piggies* and *Savoy Truffle*, as though Lennon and McCartney are worried about being upstaged. *Revolution 9* is a superior version of the kind of thing being made by John Lennon and Yoko Ono for their own LPs, but in the context of *The White Album* it merely adds to the messiness with which so many of the songs are presented. At the same time it dabbles with an avant garde experimentation that is not at all apparent on the rest of the album, so that its inclusion seems more annoying than groundbreaking.

It is not hard to find old reviews of the *White Album* that share this author's opinion of it. *Rolling Stone*'s review, preserved on the magazine's website, tries very hard to praise the record, but concludes that it is not as good as *Sgt Pepper*. According to the *White Album Project* website, the magazine's later *Album Guide* states that the record has "loads of self-indulgent filler". Nik Cohn, writing in the *New York Times* in 1968, describes the album as "boring almost beyond belief". Peter Altman, writing in the *Minneapolis Star* at the same time, says that it is "hardly their most exciting or most persuasive album". A contemporary review from the student newspaper of the University of San Francisco, reprinted on *Flashback* magazine's Facebook page in May 2017, states "not the masterpiece one has come to expect from the Beatles". Alan Smith headed his review in *New Musical Express* with "The Brilliant, the Bad, and the Ugly" – two of those adjectives being a remarkable about-turn when applied to the music of a group it was previously considered could do no wrong. The newspaper's *Illustrated Encyclopaedia Of Rock*, published in 1976, refers to the album as "the work of a disintegrating unit", while a year by year guide, published by W.H.Smith in 1980 as *25 Years Of Rock*, makes its opinion clear by omitting any reference to the record altogether. Even as late as 1999, the Parragon *Encyclopaedia Of Albums* was still maintaining that "there was a notable absence of cohesive atmosphere or continuity to this patchy epic". The fact that modern critics are inclined to rate *The White Album* well above *Sgt Pepper* says more about their distrust of experiment and their insistence on cramming everything into predetermined 'genres'. *The White Album* seems easier to relate to because it is closer to modern ideas of what rock music is supposed to sound like – it is, almost by definition, less innovative.

Perhaps the most novel aspect of *The White Album* has turned out to be its cover. The plain white front and back has, as its only identifying feature, the words "The Beatles" embossed off-centre, and also a number, one of a sequence and different for every copy of the album. The minimalism is spoilt a little by the addition of a track listing and a set of pictures inside the gatefold and completely sabotaged by the inclusion of an elaborate poster with a set of the song lyrics and a melange of photographs, like those in a scrapbook, together with four separate large copies of the individual photographs printed in the sleeve. The fact that the white sleeve has acted as a canvas for many of the record's purchasers, who have decided to add their own 'artwork', has been noted by collector Rutherford Chang, who has made it his task to assemble as many used copies of the album as he can manage (2643 as of September 2020). He has also issued a limited edition extreme remix of the *White Album*, produced by simultaneously playing a hundred copies of the original and recording the result. As each side proceeds, the records move out of synchronisation, until by the end, nothing is recognisable, an avant garde treatment that is possibly more interesting than *Revolution 9*. For the cover, Chang has created a collage made from some of his collected copies, combining decorations made by the original owners. Meanwhile, the interest of a different kind of record collector has been piqued by the numbers on the sleeves of *The White Album*. Low numbers have attracted a considerable collectors' premium. In December 2015, the copy with 0000001 on the front was put up for sale at Julien's Auctions in Los Angeles by Ringo Starr. The record sold for $790,000 – the highest price achieved by a commercially released record sold at auction up to that date.

VAN MORRISON   ASTRAL WEEKS

US release	November 1968	Warner Bros	WS 1768
UK release	September 1969	Warner Bros	WS 1768

1. Astral Weeks
2. Beside You
3. Sweet Thing
4. Cyprus Avenue
5. The Way Young Lovers Do
6. Madame George
7. Ballerina
8. Slim Slow Slider

All compositions by Van Morrison

Van Morrison: vocals, guitar / Jay Berliner: guitar / Barry Korfeld: guitar (5) / John Payne: flute, soprano saxophone / Richard Davis: bass / Connie Kay: drums / Warren Smith: vibraphone, percussion / Larry Fallon: harpsichord, strings arranger / Lewis Merenstein: producer

For his second solo album, Van Morrison finds a producer and a set of musicians who understand what he is trying to achieve. The musicians are people used to playing jazz and *Astral Weeks* is constructed like a jazz album, with music that is played with a high degree of improvisation. It presents a unique fusion. Jazz rhythms and instrumentation are combined with folk guitar playing, while Morrison's voice glides over the top, adopting an emotional, freewheeling approach, with lyrics following the Bob Dylan school of poetic surrealism. The result is spiritual and soulful, albeit a kind of soul that has little to do with the sound of Memphis or Detroit. The music has provided the basis for Van Morrison's entire career since, even if he has not really attempted to make a record sounding exactly like this one. *Astral Weeks* is widely considered to be a rock music masterpiece, although its sales are modest. Warner Bros in the UK did not have much confidence that the album would sell and delayed its release by nearly a year.

THE MOTHERS OF INVENTION   CRUISING WITH RUBEN & THE JETS

US release	December 1968	Verve	V6-5055X
UK release	February 1969	Verve	(S)VLP 9237

1. Cheap Thrills
2. Love Of My Life
3. How Could I Be Such A Fool
4. Deseri (Paul Buff/Ray Collins)
5. I'm Not Satisfied
6. Jelly Roll Gum Drop
7. Anything (Ray Collins)
8. Later That Night
9. You Didn't Try To Call Me
10. Fountain Of Love (Frank Zappa/Ray Collins)
11. No No No
12. Anyway The Wind Blows
13. Stuff Up The Cracks

All compositions by Frank Zappa except where stated

Frank Zappa: guitar, vocals, producer / Ray Collins: vocals / Ian Underwood: piano, alto and tenor saxophones / Motorhead Sherwood: baritone saxophone, tambourine / Bunk Gardner: tenor and alto saxophones / Don Preston: piano / Roy Estrada: bass guitar, vocals / Jimmy Carl Black: drums / Arthur Trip III: drums

Pretending, though without much conviction, that this album is the work of somebody else, Frank Zappa includes a slogan on the front cover that reads, "Is this the Mothers of Invention recording under a different name in a last ditch attempt to get their cruddy music on the radio?" Certainly it is not like the other albums by the group, comprising entirely a set of doo-wop recordings, performed very closely to the way such material was played in the fifties. There is a humorous element to what Zappa and his henchmen are doing here, but at the same time it is obvious that they hold this style of music in enormous affection and they play it very well. There is a considerable amount of instrumental expertise going on underneath the singing, most noticeable in the drumming, while Frank Zappa delivers a guitar solo on *You Didn't Try To Call Me* and a much longer one on *Stuff Up The Cracks*. The latter solo is the only time that he breaks from the cover of the music and plays in a completely anachronistic manner, incorporating sustain and using a wah-wah pedal, both of which were unknown in the fifties. *Cruising With Ruben & The Jets* is an interesting album and it provides valuable insight into Frank Zappa's musical mind, although in hindsight it is probably one of the least essential of his many records.

THE ROLLING STONES   BEGGARS BANQUET

The Rolling Stones had followed closely behind the Beatles during the past five years, becoming more adventurous as the Beatles did, even while retaining a slightly harder edge. Just as the Beatles had problems in finding a way to follow *Sgt Pepper*, so the Stones had problems in deciding how to follow their equivalent album, *Their Satanic Majesties Request*. In the

UK release	December 1968	Decca	SKL/LK 4955
US release	December 1968	London	PS 539

1. Sympathy For The Devil
2. No Expectations
3. Dear Doctor
4. Parachute Woman
5. Jig-Saw Puzzle
6. Street Fighting Man
7. Prodigal Son
8. Stray Cat Blues
9. Factory Girl
10. Salt Of The Earth

All compositions by Mick Jagger and Keith Richards

Mick Jagger: vocals, harmonica, percussion / Keith Richards: guitar, bass guitar, vocals / Brian Jones: guitar, harmonica, mellotron, sitar, tambura, vocals / Bill Wyman: bass guitar, bass, vocals, percussion / Charlie Watts: drums, percussion / Nicky Hopkins: keyboards / Rocky Dzidzornu: percussion (1,8,9) / Ric Grech: violin (9) / Dave Mason: percussion (6) / Watts Street Gospel Choir (10) / Anita Pallenberg: vocals (1) / Marianne Faithfull: vocals (1) / Jimmy Miller: producer, vocals (1)

event, the groups found a similar answer, both deciding to rein in the experimentation and the adventure, which in the case of the Stones, meant a return to the bluesier approach of their roots. *Beggars Banquet* is a more coherent work than *The White Album* and it sets out the blues-rock sound that the Rolling Stones have relied on ever since. There are some great songs here, most notably the first track on each side. The rhythm rush and the lyrics of *Sympathy For The Devil* crystallise the Rolling Stones' bad boy image and the song became a staple of the group's stage set until members of the audience took the message rather too seriously (a man was stabbed to death after pulling out a revolver at the Altamont Festival in California a year later, just after the Stones played the song). *Street Fighting Man* is a similar paean to violence and is even more rhythmically propulsive, while finding a way to integrate Brian Jones' sitar playing into a mainstream rock performance. The rest of the album splits the influence equally between the country blues and the harder urban variety and manages to make the music satisfyingly diverse as a result. *Prodigal Son* is a fairly straight copy of *That's No Way To Get Along*, first recorded in 1929 by Robert Wilkins. The credit to Mick Jagger and Keith Richards on the album sleeve and label was excused as a 'mistake' (recent reissues credit Wilkins properly).

THE PRETTY THINGS   S.F.SORROW

UK release	December 1968	Columbia	SCX 6306	
US release	June 1969	Rare Earth	RS 506	different cover

1. S.F.Sorrow Is Born (Phil May/Dick Taylor/Wally Waller)
2. Bracelets Of Fingers (Phil May/Dick Taylor/Wally Waller)
3. She Says Good Morning (May/Taylor/Waller/Twink)
4. Private Sorrow (May/Taylor/Waller/Jon Povey)
5. Balloon Burning (May/Taylor/Waller/Jon Povey)
6. Death (May/Taylor/Waller/Povey/Twink)
7. Baron Saturday (May/Taylor/Waller)
8. The Journey (May/Taylor/Waller/Twink)
9. I See You (May/Taylor/Waller)
10. Well Of Destiny (May/Taylor/Waller/Povey/Twink/Norman Smith)
11. Trust (May/Taylor/Waller)
12. Old Man Going (May/Taylor/Waller/Povey/Twink)
13. Loneliest Person (May?Taylor/Waller/Twink)

Phil May: vocals / Dick Taylor: guitar, vocals / Jon Povey: keyboards, sitar, percussion, vocals / Wally Waller: bass guitar, guitar, wind instruments, piano, vocals / Twink: drums, vocals / Skip Alan: drums / Norman Smith: producer

The Pretty Things signed with Columbia records in September 1967 and proceeded to make two outstanding psychedelic singles, *Defecting Grey* and *Talking About The Good Times*. These are among the most compelling records released at the time, although they were not hits. They were not included on the group's next album, *S.F.Sorrow*, which presents a narrative song cycle in the manner already followed by Nirvana and the Family Tree. As with those albums, the plot is not very well conceived and is ultimately rather depressing, but the music manages to be rather fine. The Pretty Things do not add the orchestrations so prevalent in other albums recorded at the time, but they are able to be extremely inventive and adventurous with the guitars and other instruments that they play themselves. Producer Norman Smith had previously worked as engineer on recording sessions by the Beatles and had produced the first album by Pink Floyd, so he was used to helping his musicians to come up with unusual sounds and approaches to recording. Several of the tracks on *S.F.Sorrow* (and particularly the spooky instrumental *Well Of Destiny*) are as much a demonstration of how to get the most out of a four track studio as was *Sgt Pepper*. Drummer Skip Alan decided to leave the band during the early recording sessions for the album and he was replaced by Twink, the drummer with Tomorrow (although Alan subsequently returned to the Pretty Things). He missed out on the chance to be part of a very special album.

NIRVANA   ALL OF US

| UK release | December 1968 | Island | ILPS 9087 |
| US release | December 1968 | Bell | 6024 |

1. Rainbow Chaser
2. Tiny Goddess
3. The Touchables (All Of Us)
4. Melanie Blue
5. Trapeze
6. The Show Must Go On

7. Girl In The Park
8. Miami Masquerade
9. Frankie The Great
10. You Can Try It
11. Everybody Loves The Clown
12. St John's Wood Affair

All compositions by Patrick Campbell-Lyons and Alex Spyropolous

Patrick Campbell-Lyons: guitar, vocals / Ray Singer: guitar, vocals / Alex Spyropolous: keyboards / uncredited session musicians / Chris Blackwell: producer

The second album by Nirvana presents music that is just as knowingly beautiful as on the first but with a little more reliance on rock rhythms, making the music seem to be more easily accessible. This time there is no linking story although the songs have a unified sound based on the use of lush string arrangements. Essentially, if there is a genre known as progressive pop, as distinct from the progressive rock that became a major feature of the music during the early seventies, then Nirvana's *All Of Us* is it. The heavily phased *Rainbow Chaser*, the only track to use the effect, was issued as a single and was almost a UK hit, but the album sold poorly.

THE SOFT MACHINE

US release   December 1968   Probe   CPLP 4500
Not released in UK

1. Hope For Happiness (Brian Hopper/Kevin Ayers/Mike Ratledge)
2. Joy Of A Toy (Kevin Ayers/Mike Ratledge)
3. Hope For Happiness (Reprise) (B.Hopper/Ayers/Ratledge)
4. Why Am I So Short? (Hugh Hopper/Ayers/Ratledge)
5. So Boot If At All (Ayers/Ratledge/Robert Wyatt)
6. A Certain Kind (Hugh Hopper)

7. Save Yourself (Robert Wyatt)
8. Priscilla (Ayers/Ratledge/Wyatt)
9. Lullabye Letter (Kevin Ayers)
10. We Did It Again (Kevin Ayers)
11. Plus Belle Qu'une Poubelle (Kevin Ayers)
12. Why Are We Sleeping (Ayers/Ratledge/Wyatt)
13. Box 24/5 Lid (Hugh Hopper/Mike Ratledge)

Kevin Ayers: vocals, bass guitar, piano / Mike Ratledge: organ, piano / Robert Wyatt: vocals, drums / Hugh Hopper: bass guitar (13) / The Cake – Jeanette Jacobs, Barbara Morillo, Eleanor Barooshian: vocals (12) / Chas Chandler: producer / Tom Wilson: producer

The other group to have emerged from The Wilde Flowers has music that is much more quirky than Caravan's, although it has the same emphasis on organ playing and a very similar sounding pair of singers. At this stage, Soft Machine does not have a guitarist, having abandoned original member Daevid Allen in France. Mike Ratledge plays a Lowrey organ, when most of his competition relied on Hammonds, so that his playing tone sounds different and very distinctive when he solos. The group likes to run its songs into each other, so that the music on the album comprises three long tracks in effect, with the music on side two being continuous. The album was recorded while the Soft Machine was on tour with Jimi Hendrix in the US and it was not released in the UK, although it was readily obtainable as an import. The cover was a fairly elaborate affair, gatefold, with a rotating piece of extra cardboard to simulate the movement of machinery. The music manages to fulfil very well the expectation that it will be something a little different.

LOTHAR AND THE HAND PEOPLE   PRESENTING

Lothar and the Hand People named themselves in honour of the theremin that they included among their instruments: it was christened Lothar and they, the musicians operating it with their hands, were the Hand People. Unfortunately, the theremin plays a fairly small part in the music on the group's debut album and when it does appear, it is upstaged by the synthesizer that the group is also able to use. *Presenting* starts well with a song already known for the version recorded by Manfred Mann, but fashioned to suit its title by the use of a noisy rhythm track made to sound like the operation of a mechanical device. There is no theremin, however. During the music that follows, the emphasis is on a goofy variety of country rock. Occasionally the electronics intrude, but it is as though the group has been instructed to use them without having much idea as to how they might improve the quality of the songs. Given that the United States of America, Ultimate Spinach, and Silver Apples had already made records in which electronics played a far more crucial role, then any claim that Lothar and the Hand people might have had as electronic pioneers seems to be rather misplaced.

US release   December 1968   Capitol   ST 2997
Not released in UK

1. Machines (Mort Shuman)
2. This Is It
3. This May Be Goodbye
4. That's Another Story
5. Kids Are Little People
6. Ha (Ho)

7. Sex And Violence
8. Bye Bye Love (Felice and Boudleaux Bryant)
9. Milkweed Love
10. You Won't Be Lonely
11. Woody Woodpecker (Ramez Idriss/George Tibbles)
12. It Comes On Anyhow
13. Paul, In Love (Paul Conly)

All compositions by Lothar and the Hand People except where stated

Paul Conly: keyboards, synthesizer / John Emelin: vocals, theremin / Kim King: synthesizer, guitar / Rusty Ford: bass guitar / Tom Flye: drums / Nickolas Venet: producer

THE MONKEES   HEAD

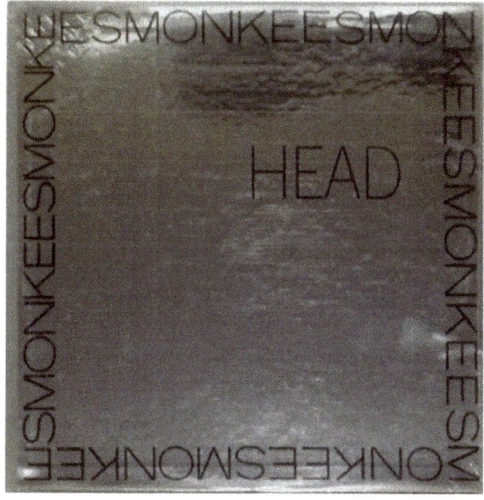

US release   December 1968   Colgems   COSO-5008
UK release   early 1969   RCA Victor   SF/RD 8051

1. dialogue
2. Porpoise Song (Gerry Goffin/Carole King)
3. dialogue
4. Circle Sky (Michael Nesmith)
5. dialogue
6. Can You Dig It? (Peter Tork)
7. dialogue

8. dialogue
9. As We Go Along (Carole King/Toni Stern)
10. dialogue
11. Daddy's Song (Nilsson)
12. dialogue
13. Do I Have To Do This All Over Again (Peter Tork)
14. dialogue/Porpoise Song (Gerry Goffin/Carole King)

Davy Jones: vocals, percussion / Michael Nesmith: vocals, guitar, organ, percussion / Peter Tork: vocals, guitar / Micky Dolenz: vocals / Ken Bloom, Danny Kortchmar, Keith Allison, Bill Chadwick, Ry Cooder, Neil Young, Carole King, Stephen Stills: guitar / Leon Russell, Ralph Shuckett, Michel Rubini: keyboards / Lance Wakely: guitar, bass guitar / Doug Lubahn, Richard Dey, John Gross, Harvey Newmark: bass guitar / Mike Ney, Dewey Martin, Earl Palmer: drums / various strings, horns, percussion / Jack Nitzsche: arranger / Russ Titelman: conductor / The Monkees, Gerry Goffin: producer

Head is the soundtrack album for a rather strange film made by the Monkees earlier in 1968, following the ending of the group's television show. There are only six songs, separated by dialogue taken from the film, but they are good ones. *Porpoise Song*, in particular, is a psychedelic classic with an elaborate production that would sound perfectly placed if included amongst the most adventurous music by the Beatles or the Beach Boys. It has a dreamy ambience as organ and strings drift in and out of the mix and includes the sounds of actual porpoises. *Head* is not really comparable with the other albums by the Monkees, as the inclusion of so much non-musical material makes it a rather different kind of record. But it remains a fascinating artefact, enhanced by the quality of the music that is there, and a perfect archetype of the period. The UK release dispensed with the expensive reflective cover of the American issue, replacing it with a less striking white sleeve.

AL KOOPER & MIKE BLOOMFIELD   LIVE ADVENTURES

US release   December 1968   Columbia   CG 6
UK release   December 1968   CBS   S66216

1. Introduction
2. The 59th Bridge Street Song (Feelin' Groovy) (Paul Simon)
3. I Wonder Who (Ray Charles)
4. Her Holy Modal Highness (Al Kooper/Mike Bloomfield)

5. The Weight (Robbie Robertson)
6. Mary Ann (Ray Charles)
7. Together Till The End Of Time (Frank Wilson)
8. That's All Right (Arthur Crudup)
9. Green Onions (Booker T & the MGs)

10. Introduction
11. Sonny Boy Williamson (Jack Bruce/Paul Jones)
12. No More Lonely Nights (Sonny Boy Williamson)

13. Dear Mr Fantasy (Steve Winwood/Jim Capaldi/Chris Wood)
14. Don't Throw Your Love On Me So Strong (Albert King)
15. Refugee (Al Kooper/Mike Bloomfield)

Al Kooper: vocals, keyboards, producer / Mike Bloomfield: guitar, vocals / John Kahn: bass guitar / Skip Prokop: drums / Paul Simon: vocals (2) / Carlos Santana: guitar (11) / Elvin Bishop: guitar, vocals (12)

Following the success of his *Super Session* album, Al Kooper organised three concerts at the Fillmore in San Francisco to feature his playing with guitarist Mike Bloomfield. The double album issued as *Live Adventures* presents highlights from the concerts, including tracks in which guest artists Carlos Santana and Elvin Bishop are involved. Some vocals from Paul Simon were overdubbed on to the recording of his song, *The 59th*

Bridge Street Song, after the event. Only one piece is reprised from its performance on *Super Session,* the new version of *His Holy Modal Majesty* being given a change of gender despite this rather making a nonsense of the intended reference to John Coltrane. Much of the music comprises the blues and Mike Bloomfield plays with as much fire and inspiration as always, even though he went without sleep for several days before the concerts began. *Sonny Boy Williamson* marks the recording debut of Carlos Santana, playing the blues, although this is not his greatest strength. *No More Lonely Nights* allows Elvin Bishop to demonstrate that he is very nearly the equal of his erstwhile colleague in the Paul Butterfield Blues Band. Although *Live Adventures* has many fine moments, however, it lacks the freshness of the original *Super Session* and it is not altogether surprising that Al Kooper did not repeat the experiment.

BLOOD, SWEAT & TEARS

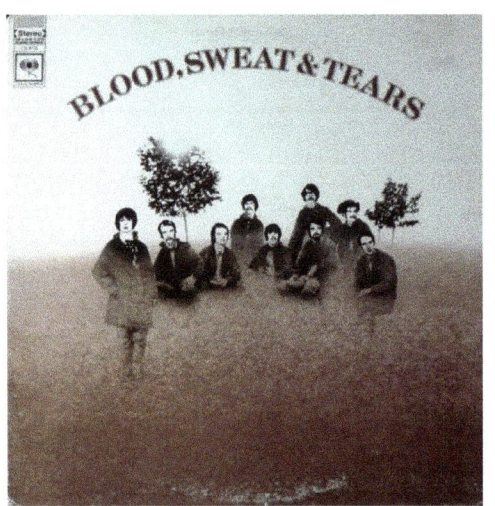

```
US release    December 1968    Columbia    CS 9720
UK release    December 1968    CBS         (S) 63504

1.  Variations On A Theme By Erik Satie
2.  Smiling Phases (Steve Winwood/Jim Capaldi/Chris Wood)
3.  Sometimes In Winter (Steve Katz)
4.  More And More (Don Juan/Pee Vee)
5.  And When I Die (Laura Nyro)
6.  God Bless The Child (Billie Holiday/Arthur Herzog)
7.  Spinning Wheel (David Clayton-Thomas)
8.  You've Made Me So Very Happy (Berry Gordy/Brenda
                    Holloway/Frank Wilson/Patrice Holloway)
9.  Blues Part II (Blood Sweat & Tears)
10. Variation On A Theme By Erik Satie

David Clayton-Thomas: vocals / Steve Katz: guitar, harmonica,
vocals / Dick Halligan: keyboards, flute, trombone, vocals / Lew
Soloff: trumpet, flugelhorn / Chuck Winfield: trumpet,
flugelhorn / Fred Lipsius: alto saxophone, piano / Jerry Hyman:
trombone, recorder / Alan Rubin: trumpet (7) / Jim Fielder: bass
guitar / Bobby Colomby: drums, vocals / James Guercio:
producer
```

With Al Kooper having left his own band, the remaining members found a new singer and a new keyboard player and proceeded to move in much more of a jazz direction. James Guercio, who had been responsible for adding brass instruments to the Buckinghams, was brought in as producer. *Blood, Sweat & Tears* is a very accomplished, sophisticated album that provided the template for many jazz-cabaret bands to follow, although none of those performed with the freshness and excitement of the original, if only because they did not have Bobby Colomby playing the drums. The group is stuffed full of talented improvisers and they all get a chance to solo. The guitarist, however, is granted no more favours than any other member of the band and Steve Katz only gets to make his presence felt on one track, *More And More* (although he sings his own composition, *Sometimes In Winter*). *Blues Part II* is mainly structured as a series of solos that could be added to what is clearly meant to be *Part I,* the track *Somethin' Goin' On,* which can be found on the group's previous album. Al Kooper's ghost is still apparent in that he gets three co-arranging credits, although it seems likely that these are pieces that have been considerably developed since being introduced to the group's repertoire by Kooper. Three singles were taken from the album and all reached number two in the US chart, while the album itself reached number one and was a smaller hit in the UK as well.

DON ELLIS AND HIS ORCHESTRA   AUTUMN

```
US release    December 1968    Columbia    CS 9721
UK release    December 1968    CBS         S/M 63503

1.  Variations For Trumpet (Don Ellis)
2.  Scratt And Fluggs (Don Ellis)
3.  Pussy Wiggle Stomp (Don Ellis)

4.  K.C. Blues (Charlie Parker)
5.  Child Of Ecstacy (Don Ellis)
6.  Indian Lady (Don Ellis)

Don Ellis: trumpet / Glenn Stuart, Bob Harmon, John Rosenberg,
Stu Blumberg: trumpet, flugelhorn / Ernie Carlson, Glenn Ferris,
Terry Woodson: trombone / Don Switzer: bass trombone / Doug
Bixby, Roger Bobo: tuba / Ron Starr: clarinet, soprano and alto
saxophones, flute, piccolo / Sam Falzone: clarinet, soprano and
tenor saxophones, flute / John Magruder: clarinet, bass clarinet,
baritone saxophone / Frank Strozier: alto saxophone / Ira
Schulman: alto saxophone / John Klemmer: clarinet, tenor
saxophone / Pete Robinson: keyboards / Mike Lang: keyboards /
Mark Stevens: vibraphone, percussion / Dave Parlato: bass / Ray
Neapolitan: bass, bass guitar / Ralph Humphrey: drums / Lee
Pastora: percussion / Al Kooper: producer
```

After two years together and continual gigging, Don Ellis felt that his orchestra would be able to tackle a particularly elaborate piece. His *Variations For Trumpet* is a major work, partly improvised and partly composed, and including sections with ferociously complex beat structures. The orchestra copes with the music flawlessly and Don Ellis himself shows what a superb soloist he is. The *Autumn* album including this also has two live tracks, an orchestrated Charlie Parker blues and a reworking of Ellis's *Indian Lady*, demonstrating how energetic the piece has become in live performance. The album is produced by Al Kooper, although one suspects that he did not actually have to do very much. Probably he was really hoping to transmit a message to Blood Sweat and Tears as to what cutting edge big band jazz, styled so that it might be appreciated by rock audiences, could really sound like. *Autumn* is a spectacular album and a thoroughly convincing manifesto for Don Ellis's approach to jazz. It is also, as it happens, a very long album, with sides that are nearly half an hour and the same duration, therefore, as many complete albums issued by rock artists in the US. The suggestion that long sides produce a degradation in sound quality is effortlessly disproved in this case.

CHARLES MINGUS   MINGUS AT MONTEREY

US release	December 1968	Jazz Workshop	JWS 001/2
UK release	1969	Liberty	LDS 84002

1. Duke Ellington Medley (Duke Ellington)
2. Orange Was The Color Of Her Dress, Then Blue Silk (Charles Mingus)
3. Meditations On Integration (Charles Mingus)

Track 1 split over sides 1 &2. Track 2 split over sides 2 & 3. Track 3 split over sides 3 & 4.

Charles Mingus: bass / Charlie McPherson: alto saxophone / Buddy Collette: alto saxophone, flute, piccolo / Jack Nimitz: baritone saxophone, bass clarinet / John Handy III: tenor saxophone / Bobby Bryant: trumpet / Lonnie Hillyer: trumpet / Melvin Moore: trumpet / Lou Blackburn: trombone / Red Callender: tuba / Jaki Byard: piano / Dannie Richmond: drums

Charles Mingus and his band performed at the Monterey Jazz Festival on 20 September 1964. He issued the recording of his set on his own Jazz Workshop label as a mail order item in 1965, but in 1968 was able to achieve proper distribution into record shops and the following year Liberty took over the release for the UK. As far as the music is concerned, the delay matters not at all. The music must have been astonishing to the audience at Monterey and it keeps its impact over four years later. The opening *Duke Ellington Medley* starts with Mingus playing the bass on his own and then, as the concert progresses, more and more musicians are added. *Orange Was The Color Of Her Dress, Then Blue Silk* is a new arrangement, for a larger number of musicians, of a piece that Mingus had been playing for some time with a sextet. Essentially this is a blues, but made more complicated with extra lines and unexpected harmonies, and it also has a truly gorgeous melody line. *Meditations On Integration* is a major new work, finally employing all the musicians listed, and managing to combine composed material with improvisation in a seamless and highly impressive manner. It is an undoubted highlight of Charles Mingus's career and is certainly the apex of his work in the sixties (although financial problems prevented him from producing very much at all during the second half of the decade). The recording quality on *Mingus At Monterey* is a little suspect in places, but we are very lucky to have the music at all, and the impact on listening pleasure is minimal.

MIKE WESTBROOK CONCERT BAND   RELEASE

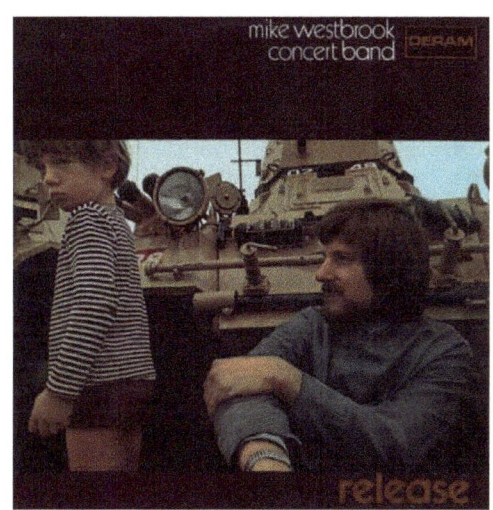

UK release	December 1968	Deram	SML/DML 1031

Not released in US

1. The Few I
2. Forever And A Day / Lover Man (Jimmy Davis/Jimmy Sherman/Roger Ramirez)
3. We Salute You
4. The Few II
5. Folk Song I
6. Flying Home (Benny Goodman/Lionel Hampton/Sid Garis/Sid Robin/Sy Oliver)
7. Sugar (Edna Alexander/Maceo Pinkard/Sidney Mitchell)
8. A Life Of Its Own
9. Take Me Back I
10. Rosie
11. Who's Who
12. Gee Baby, Ain't I Good To You (Andy Razaf/Don Redman)
13. Can't Get It Out Of My Mind
14. The Girl From Ipanema (Antonio Carlos Jobim/Norman Gimbel/Vinicius De Moraes)
15. Folk Song II
16. Take Me Back II

All compositions by Mike Westbrook except where stated

Mike Westbrook: piano / Bernie Living: alto saxophone / Mike Osborne: alto saxophone / Nisar Ahmed (George) Khan: tenor saxophone / John Surman: baritone saxophone / Dave Holdsworth: trumpet, flugelhorn / Malcolm Griffiths: trombone / Paul Rutherford: trombone / Harry Miller: bass / Alan Jackson: drums / Peter Eden: producer

Mike Westbrook acts like a ringmaster here, writing simple themes whose function is to launch the soloists, giving them ideas and inspiration for their exciting forays into what is mostly John Coltrane/Albert Ayler territory. These are impressive musicians, able to dominate the stage with their playing, able to enthral the listener with their energy. The four saxophonists in particular are easily able to demonstrate that they are all world-class players: John Surman making his weighty baritone sound magically light and airy, George Khan and Bernie Living apparently struggling to keep their instruments from exploding, and Mike Osborne bringing the spirit of Bird (Charlie Parker) to life. Mike Westbrook does not solo himself, does not even play very much, secure in the knowledge that he has brought these talented musicians together and enabled them to fly.

MICHAEL GARRICK SEPTET   BLACK MARIGOLDS

UK release   December 1968   Argo   (Z)DA 88
Not released in US

1. Webster's Mood
2. Jazz For Five
3. Good Times
4. Spiders
5. Ursula
6. A Jazz Nativity
7. Black Marigolds
8. What Are Little Girls?
9. Carolling

All compositions by Michael Garrick

Michael Garrick: keyboards / Joe Harriott: alto saxophone / Tony Coe: tenor saxophone / Don Rendell: tenor and soprano saxophones / Ian Carr: trumpet, flugelhorn / Dave Green: bass / Colin Barnes: drums (2,6) / Trevor Tomkins: drums / John Smith: poet (2,6)

Black Marigolds is a more conservative album than Mike Westbrook's *Release*, being much closer to the melodic hard bop that became popular some ten years earlier. There is no problem with that, however, because the soloists that Michael Garrick employs are very fine players of the jazz style indeed, especially Joe Harriott, who forgets his love of Ornette Coleman on this occasion. But Garrick is also able to think of ways to stretch the genre considerably. Two tracks have spoken poetry as a vital ingredient in the jazz improvisation (this captures the attention too firmly to be considered as a mere accompaniment to the poems), while a further three choose to use a harpsichord as the essential instrument, automatically giving a touch of baroque to the jazz. *Black Marigolds* is the most idiosyncratic of the albums made by Michael Garrick so far, but it is also the most interesting.

THE LIVERPOOL SCENE   "AMAZING ADVENTURES OF"

UK release   December 1968   RCA Victor   SF 7995
US release   January 1969   RCA Victor   LSP-4189

1. Tramcar To Frankenstein (Mike Evans/Andy Roberts)
2. The Amazing Adventures Of Che Guevara Part I (Mike Evans)
3. Gliders And Parks (Mike Hart)
4. Burdock River Run (Andy Roberts)
5. The Amazing Adventures Of Che Guevara Part II (Mike Evans)
6. Universes (Adrian Henri/Liverpool Scene)
7. Batpoem (Adrian Henri/Andy Roberts)
8. The Amazing Adventures Of Che Guevara Part III (Mike Evans)
9. Percy Parslow's Hamster Farm (Andy Roberts)
10. Happy Burial Blues (Mike Hart/Mike Evans/Maurice Cockrill)
11. Palms (Mike Hart)
12. The Amazing Adventures Of Che Guevara Part IV (Mike Evans)
13. Love Story (Adrian Henri/Andy Roberts)

Adrian Henri: poet / Mike Evans: poet, tenor saxophone / Andy Roberts: guitar, vocals / Mike Hart: vocals, guitar / Percy Jones: bass guitar / Brian Dodson: drums / John Peel: producer

After the first album credited to the Liverpool Scene, Roger McGough became involved in the more light-hearted Scaffold, while Adrian Henri and Andy Roberts linked up with other musicians and poets. The Liverpool Scene would eventually evolve into a full-blown rock group with poetry, but the *"Amazing Adventures Of"* album is more like the work of a co-operative. Andy Roberts plays acoustic guitar while Adrian Henri recites and Roberts also performs songs of his own as a solo singer songwriter. Mike Hart performs as a solo singer songwriter too, and Mike Evans reads on his own. Just four tracks – *Tramcar To Frankenstein, Universes, Batpoem,* and *Happy Burial Blues* – are the work of a group, but Adrian Henri is only involved in *Universes* and this has music that is like a free-form improvisation rather than a rock group performance. *Tramcar To Frankenstein* is the album's masterpiece, the band managing to play a suitably atmospheric underlay to a poem by Mike Evans before embarking on a furious work-out for saxophone and electric guitar. The album successfully conveys the message that Liverpool, some years after the ending of the Merseybeat phenomenon, is still the home of some extremely creative people, whether poets or musicians. John Peel is credited as producer, but it is likely that he had little real part to play.

TOM RUSH   THE CIRCLE GAME

| US release | December 1968 | Elektra | EKS-74018 |
| UK release | December 1968 | Elektra | EKS 74018 / EKL 4018 |

1. Tin Angel (Joni Mitchell)
2. Something In The Way She Moves (James Taylor)
3. Urge For Going (Joni Mitchell)
4. Sunshine Sunshine (James Taylor)
5. The Glory Of Love (Billy Hill)
6. Shadow Dream Song (Jackson Browne)
7. The Circle Game (Joni Mitchell)
8. So Long (Charlie Rich)
9. Rockport Sunday (Tom Rush)
10. No Regrets (Tom Rush)

Tom Rush: vocals, guitar / Hugh McCracken: guitar / Don Thomas: guitar / Eric Gale: guitar / Jonathan Raskin: guitar, bass guitar / Bruce Langhorne: guitar / Joe Mack: bass guitar / Bob Bushnell: bass guitar / Joe Grimm: saxophone / Buddy Lucas: tenor saxophone / Paul Harris: keyboards, arranger / Herbie Lovelle: drums / Bernard Purdie: drums / Richie Ritz: drums / Arthur Gorson: producer

The sixth album by American folk singer Tom Rush passes pleasantly enough, as he delivers his own versions of songs by his contemporaries in his striking chocolate voice. Whatever distinction these interpretations have, however, has more to do with their careful arrangements than with Rush's singing. Until, that is, the last song on the album is reached. *No Regrets* is his own song and it is absolutely stunning, easily worth the price of the album on its own. He is able to give the words an emotional strength that he simply does not do with the songs written by other people. It is not surprising that *No Regrets* was taken up by many other artists, including the temporarily reunited Walker Brothers, who had a UK hit with the song in 1975, and Midge Ure, who took it back into the charts in 1982.

JAMES TAYLOR

| US release | December 1968 | Apple | SKAO-3352 |
| UK release | December 1968 | Apple | (S)APCOR 3 |

1. Don't Talk Now
2. Something's Wrong
3. Knocking 'Round The Zoo
4. Sunshine Sunshine
5. Taking It In
6. Something In The Way She Moves
7. Carolina In My Mind
8. Brighten Your Night With My Day
9. Night Owl
10. Rainy Day Man
11. Circle Round The Sun (Traditional)
12. The Blues Is Just A Bad Dream

All compositions by James Taylor except where stated

James Taylor: vocals, guitar / Mick Wayne: guitar (7) / Don Shinn: keyboards (1,5,8) / Freddie Redd: organ (7) / Louis Cennamo: bass guitar (1,2,3,5,8,9,10) / Paul McCartney: bass guitar (7) / Bishop O'Brien: drums (2,3,5,7-11) / Peter Asher: vocals, percussion (1,7,10), producer / Skaila Kanga: harp (4) / Amici String Quartet (4) / Richard Hewson: arranger (2,3,4,7,8,9,11,12) / George Harrison: vocals (7)

James Taylor becomes the first person, not a Beatle, to have a record released on the group's own label. He is revealed as being a skilful acoustic guitarist and as having an attractive, slightly vulnerable voice, together with being responsible for at least two classic songs, *Carolina In My Mind* and *Something In The Way She Moves* (a line that George Harrison proceeded to pinch for a song of his own). Most of the songs are given chamber string and keyboard arrangements, which are also frequently used to provide bridging material between the tracks, but although there are many artists for whom these would be a benefit, in James Taylor's case they are more of an unnecessary intrusion, preventing him from fully drawing the listener into his world. The album sold poorly, hampered by Taylor's problems with drug addiction and by the Apple management's inexperience with record promotion.

JOAN BAEZ   ANY DAY NOW

Joan Baez was starting to seem irrelevant, but her decision to make an entire double album of Bob Dylan compositions helped to draw attention back, especially when six of the songs had not been released by the man himself. The musicians that Ms Baez employs include two that played with Dylan on *John Wesley Harding* and *Any Day Now* has the same folk-country flavour as

that album. Some three years earlier, Columbia records had used the slogan "nobody sings Bob Dylan like Bob Dylan" in its advertising, but the truth is that nobody sings Bob Dylan like Joan Baez. The pure beauty of her voice is able to make the most monotone of Dylan's songs into a melodic wonder. She makes no attempt to tackle the rockier Dylan material, but as a compendium of some of his best folk music, *Any Day Now* is hard to beat.

US release	December 1968	Vanguard	VSD-79306/7
UK release	December 1968	Vanguard	SVRL 19037/8

1. Love Minus Zero / No Limit
2. North Country Blues
3. You Ain't Goin' Nowhere
4. Drifter's Escape
5. I Pity The Poor Immigrant
6. Tears Of Rage (Bob Dylan/Richard Manuel)
7. Sad-Eyed Lady Of The Lowlands
8. Love Is Just A Four Letter Word
9. I Dreamed I Saw St. Augustine
10. The Walls Of Redwing
11. Dear Landlord
12. One Too Many Mornings
13. I Shall Be Released
14. Boots Of Spanish Leather
15. Walkin' Down The Line
16. Restless Farewell

All compositions by Bob Dylan except where stated

Joan Baez: vocals, guitar / Jerry Kennedy, Jerry Reed, Harold Bradley, Stephen Stills, Harold Rugg, Grady Martin: guitar / Fred Carter Jr: mandolin / Johnny Gimble, Tommy Jackson, Buddy Spicher: violin / Pete Drake: pedal steel guitar / Hargus Robbins: piano / Roy Huskey Jr: bass guitar / Norbert Putnam: bass guitar / Kenny Buttrey: drums / Maynard Solomon: producer

RICHARD HARRIS
THE YARD WENT ON FOREVER

US release	December 1968	Dunhill	DS-50042
UK release	December 1968	Stateside	SSL 5001

1. The Yard Went On Forever
2. Watermark
3. Interim
4. Gayla
5. The Hymns From The Grand Terrace
6. The Hive
7. Lucky Me
8. That's The Way It Was

All compositions by Jimmy Webb

Richard Harris: vocals / Mike Deasy, Lance Wakely: guitar / Fred Tackett: guitar, trumpet / Larry Knechtel: keyboards / Bud Brisbois, Jules Chaikin: trumpet / Frank Rosolino, Lou Blackburn: trombone / Skip Mosher: flute / Art Maebe, David Duke, George Price, William Henshaw: French horn / Sid Sharp: strings / Joe Osborn: bass guitar / Hal Blaine: drums / Milt Holland, Gary Coleman: percussion / Jimmy Webb: piano, arranger, producer

The Yard Went On Forever is a second volume of songs by Jimmy Webb. There is no *MacArthur Park* this time, but there is a wealth of even more complex and multi-layered material, especially the title track and the lengthy *Hymns From The Grand Terrace*. Delighted in finding a sympathetic interpreter for his music, Webb is pushing his creativity as hard as he can to confirm that he is a songwriter like no other. Different musical ideas pass quickly by the listener and they are densely arranged so that the effect is to make the songs into miniature symphonies. The chorus reprise from the opening of the title track, placed at the end of the first side indicates that the songs are also intended to function as a single work with several parts. As before, Richard Harris demonstrates that his theatricality is ideal for displaying the music to best advantage, even if his pitching is occasionally suspect. There is nothing here with the immediacy of a hit single, but Jimmy Webb's melodic gift continues to be very apparent and there is enough substance to satisfy an inquisitive listener through multiple repeat hearings.

MAD RIVER

US release	December 1968	Capitol	ST 2985
UK release	December 1968	Capitol	(S)T 2985

1. Merciful Monks (Lawrence Hammond)
2. High All The Time (Lawrence Hammond)
3. Amphetamine Gazelle (Lawrence Hammond)
4. Eastern Light (Greg Dewey/Lawrence Hammond)
5. Wind Chimes (Mad River)
6. War Goes On (Lawrence Hammond)
7. Hush Julian (Lawrence Hammond)

Lawrence Hammond: vocals, bass guitar, guitar, recorder, piano / David Robinson: guitar / Rick Bochner: guitar, vocals / Thomas Manning: vocals, bass guitar / Greg Dewey: drums, vocals / Nick Venet: producer

The first album by Californian latecomers Mad River was pressed slightly faster than intended, giving it a manic quality that suits the music very well. This is the sound of the Quicksilver Messenger Service on a permanent amphetamine rush and *Mad River* is quite possibly the most exciting record to have come out of the genre. If this was a mistake, then it was a very fortunate one. The pairing of Lawrence Hammond's anguished singing with David Robinson's abrasive, stinging lead guitar is a match made, if not in heaven, then somewhere very nearby. The Beach Boys' *Wind Chimes* is delicate and beautiful: Mad River's idea of a good piece of music to have the same title is one that is loud and discordant, with a raga solo played on the recorder, which speaks volumes. But it is the following marathon, *War Drags On*, that is the album's masterpiece, complete with a ferocious duet for drums and lead guitar, carrying all the energy of a rocket attack. It is curious that *Mad River* is so little celebrated, when it should by rights be the most well-known West Coast psychedelic album of all.

SPIRIT   THE FAMILY THAT PLAYS TOGETHER

```
US release     December 1968    Ode    Z12 44014
UK release     January 1969     CBS    S/M 63523

1.  I Got A Line On You (Randy California)
2.  It Shall Be (John Locke/Randy California)
3.  Poor Richard (Jay Ferguson)
4.  Silky Sam (Jay Ferguson)
5.  The Drunkard (Jay Ferguson)
6.  Darlin' If (Randy California)

7.  All The Same (Ed Cassidy/Randy California)
8.  Jewish (Randy California)
9.  Dream Within A Dream (Jay Ferguson)
10. She Smiles (Jay Ferguson)
11. Aren't You Glad (Jay Ferguson)

Jay Ferguson: vocals, percussion / Randy California: guitar,
vocals, bass guitar / John Locke: keyboards / Mark Andes:
bass guitar, vocals / Ed Cassidy: drums / Marty Paich:
arranger / Lou Adler: producer
```

The title of the second album by Spirit is a reference to the fact that Ed Cassidy is Randy California's step-father and that the band lived together in a house in Topanga Canyon, California. *The Family That Plays Together* kicks off with a tune that should have been a huge single hit, although miraculously *I Got A Line On You* was nothing of the kind. The album continues with the sophisticated playing familiar from the first album, with some light orchestration in places to enhance the performance. The dissonant strings on *The Drunkard* are particularly striking. The album concludes with guitarist Randy California in an uncharacteristically aggressive mood, but overall the album makes less impact than Spirit's debut, even if it does confirm the band as having an immediately recognisable sound of its own.

THE GUN   GUN

```
UK release     December 1968    CBS    S/M 63552
US release     May 1969         Epic   BN 26468

1.  Race With The Devil
2.  The Sad Saga Of The Boy And The Bee
3.  Rupert's Travels
4.  Yellow Cab Man (Adrian Curtis/Jimmy Parsons)
5.  It Won't Be Long (Heartbeat)

6.  Sunshine
7.  Rat Race
8.  Take Off

All compositions by Adrian Curtis except where stated

Adrian Curtis (Gurvitz): guitar, vocals / Paul Curtis (Gurvitz):
bass guitar / Louis Farrell: drums / Barry St John: vocals /
Sunny Leslie: vocals / John Goodison: producer
```

Race With The Devil, propelled by an urgent rhythm and a distinctive riff from a guitar using the smooth, sustained tone beloved of American groups like SRC, Fever Tree, and Spirit, became a substantial UK hit single in the autumn and an instant hard rock classic. The same guitar sound is all over the group's album, but the single is by far the best track. The group attempts to spice up the hard rock with a few low-key orchestrations and *Take Off* is an attempt to deliver an extended jam, but despite Adrian Curtis overdubbing a second lead guitar part, it mainly succeeds in showing up the guitarist's limitations. The Curtis/Gurvitz brothers managed to make many more albums after this one with different groups, but the single apart, the most interesting aspect of *Gun* is perhaps the fact that the cover is the first to be designed by Roger Dean, later well known for his work with albums by Yes and many other progressive rock bands.

JOHN MARTYN   THE TUMBLER

The first albums by singer songwriters John Martyn and Al Stewart were released in the same month, and Stewart is now responsible for producing Martyn's second. There is accordingly a greater emphasis on the guitar playing. The very first track, *Sing A Song Of Summer*, rushes along at a considerable speed, proving Martyn's enviable ability to construct an intricate accompaniment at the same time as singing a potentially tongue-twisting lyric. Elsewhere, there are two finger-busting instrumentals. The title of the album is presumably a reference to a guitar-playing ability that seems acrobatic! There is a little more emphasis on the blues than before, including two cover songs, which Martyn performs well. *Hello Train* introduces a little studio trickery, as Paul Wheeler's second guitar is made to sound backwards. Harold McNair adds some finely played flute to several tracks, although Al Stewart's inexperience shows by allowing it to be mixed too loudly, fighting rather than enhancing John Martyn's singing voice. *Dusty* was included on Island's sampler album, *You Can All Join In*, and would have made a likely hit single, although this was not to be.

UK release	December 1968	Island	ILPS 9091
Not released in US			

1. Sing A Song Of Summer
2. The River
3. Goin' Down To Memphis
4. The Gardeners (Bill Lyons)
5. A Day At The Sea
6. Fishin' Blues (Henry Thomas)
7. Dusty
8. Hello Train
9. Winding Boy (Jelly Roll Morton)
10. Fly On Home (John Martun/Paul Wheeler)
11. Knuckledy Crunch And Slippledee-Slee Song
12. Seven Black Roses

All compositions by John Martyn except where stated

John Martyn: vocals, guitar / Paul Wheeler: guitar / Harold McNair: flute / David Moses: bass / Al Stewart: producer

RICHIE HAVENS   RICHARD P. HAVENS, 1983

Richie Havens joins the small group of performers confident enough to issue a double album, this one including live material as the last four tracks. He covers several Beatles songs, very effectively performing them in his characteristic style and making them his own. Some of the tracks use a stronger rock arrangement than previously, swamping Havens' acoustic guitar, but his voice ensures that the music still has his own signature. The live recording of *A Little Help From My Friends* is largely devoted to an audience sing-along, in keeping with the song's title, which does not really work on record, but otherwise *Richard P.Havens, 1983* is the singer's most consistently excellent album and easily justifies the lengthy playing time of the double album format.

US release	December 1968	Verve Forecast	FTS-3047-2
UK release	January 1969	Verve Forecast	SVLP 6014

1. Stop Pulling And Pushing Me (Richie Havens)
2. For Haven's Sake (Richie Havens)
3. Strawberry Fields Forever (John Lennon/Paul McCartney)
4. What More Can I Say John? (Richie Havens)
5. I Pity The Poor Immigrant (Bob Dylan)
6. Lady Madonna (John Lennon/Paul McCartney)
7. Priests (Leonard Cohen)
8. Indian Rope Man (Joe Price/Mark Roth/Richie Havens)
9. Cautiously (Maurey Hayden)
10. Just Above My Hobby Horse's Head (Mark Roth/Richie Havens)
11. She's Leaving Home (John Lennon/Paul McCartney)
12. Putting Out The Vibration, And Hoping It Comes Home (Mark Roth/Richie Havens)
13. The Parable Of Ramon (Mark Roth/Richie Havens)
14. A Little Help From My Friends (John Lennon/Paul McCartney)
15. Wear Your Love Like Heaven (Donovan)
16. Run Shaker Life (Traditional) / Do You Feel Good? (Richie Havens)

Richie Havens: vocals, guitar, tambura, keyboards, producer / Teddy Irwin, Paul Williams, Bruce Langhorn: guitar / Weldon Myrick: pedal steel guitar / John Ord, Ken Lauber, Warren Bernhardt, Paul Harris, Charlie Smalls: keyboards / Brad Campbell, Eric Oxendine, Carol Hunter, Stephen Stills, Jymm Fairs : bass guitar / Skip Prokop, Don MacDonald, Paul Humphrey: drum, Arnie Moores / Daniel Ben Zebulon, Bob Chase, Carter Collins: percussion / Jeremy Steig: flute / Colin Walcott: sitar / Diane Comins: harp / Charles Howell: vocals / Mark Roth: producer / John Court: producer (8)

TAJ MAHAL   THE NATCH'L BLUES

US release	December 1968	Columbia	CS 9698	
UK release	December 1968	Direction	(S) 8-63397	different cover

1. Good Morning Miss Brown (Taj Mahal)
2. Corinna (Traditional)
3. I Ain't Gonna Let Nobody Steal My Jellyroll (Taj Mahal)
4. Goin' Up To The Country, Paint My Mailbox Blue (Taj Mahal)
5. Done Changed My Way Of Living (Taj Mahal)
6. She Caught The Katy And Left Me A Mule To Ride (Taj Mahal/Yank Rachell)
7. The Cuckoo (Traditional)
8. You Don't Miss Your Water (William Bell)
9. A Lot Of Love (Homer Banks)

Taj Mahal: vocals, guitar, harmonica / Jesse Ed Davis: guitar, piano, arranger / Al Kooper: keyboards / Gary Gilmore: bass guitar / Chuck Blackwell: drums / Earl Palmer: drums / David Rubinson: producer

For his second album, Taj Mahal continues his ability to make the traditional blues sound like a vibrant, contemporary form. He does not sound much like the British blues bands, however, because for the most part, although he is still using strong rhythms played by drums and electric bass, he is playing an acoustic resonator guitar himself and there are no displays of electric lead guitar virtuosity. Towards the end of the album, Taj Mahal switches to soul music for his inspiration and hardly sounds different at all. His cover of a song by Homer Banks is a timely reminder of where the Spencer Davis Group got its riff for *Gimme Some Lovin'*.

LOVE SCULPTURE   BLUES HELPING

UK release	December 1968	Parlophone	PCS/PMC 7059
US release	June 1969	Rare Earth	RS 505

1. The Stumble (Freddy King/Sonny Thompson)
2. 3 O'Clock Blues (B.B.King/Jules Taub)
3. I Believe To My Soul (Ray Charles)
4. So Unkind (Elmore James/Marshall Sehorn)
5. Summertime (George & Ira Gershwin/Du Bose Heyward)
6. On The Road Again (Floyd Jones/Will Shade)
7. Don't Answer The Door (Jimmy Johnson)
8. Wang Dang Doodle (Willie Dixon)
9. Come Back Baby (Ray Charles)
10. Shake Your Hips (James Moore)
11. Blues Helping (Love Sculpture)

Dave Edmunds: vocals, guitar, keyboards / John Williams: bass guitar, piano, vocals / Bob Congo Jones: drums, vocals / Malcolm Jones: producer / Kingsley Ward: producer

The modishly named Love Sculpture made two singles in 1968. The first, *River To Another Day*, was an attractive pop-rock ballad with a blues B-side that featured a lead guitar sustaining a note through most of the first verse. For the second, Dave Edmunds, the guitarist, dramatically developed his skills in order to present a furious instrumental rendering of a piece by classical composer Aram Khachaturian, *Sabre Dance*. This became a substantial UK chart hit. The group's album, released at the same time as *Sabre Dance*, had obviously been completed rather earlier, because it has nothing like either single, being made up of blues material consisting almost entirely of cover versions. In the light of Dave Edmunds' subsequent career, he was probably playing the blues because it had become popular to do so, rather than as the result of any deeply felt enthusiasm for the genre. To be fair, however, he does a very good job at reproducing the playing style of the likes of Freddy King or B.B.King, even if he cannot match their emotional impact. Significantly, the group's second album, released over a year later, included *Sabre Dance* and no blues playing.

ERIC BURDON & THE ANIMALS   LOVE IS

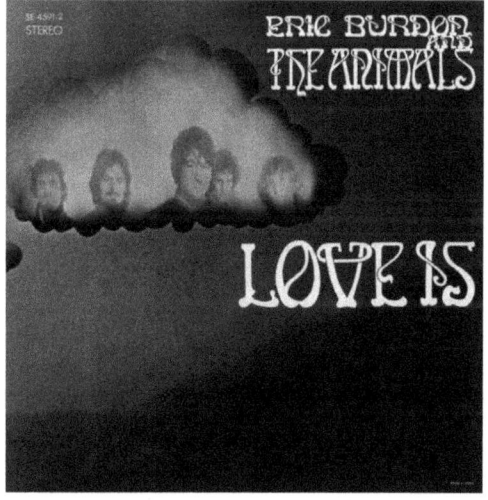

US release	December 1968	MGM	SE-4591-2
UK release	December 1968	MGM	CS 8105 single album only

1. River Deep Mountain High (Phil Spector/Jeff Barry/Ellie Greenwich)
2. I'm An Animal (Sly Stewart)
3. I'm Dying (Or Am I) (Eric Burdon)
4. Ring Of Fire (June Carter/Merle Kilgore)
5. Colored Rain (Steve Winwood/Jim Capaldi/Chris Wood)
6. To Love Somebody (Barry and Robin Gibb)
7. As The Years Go Passing By (Deadric Malone)
8. Gemini (Steve Hammond)/The Madman Running Through The Fields (Zoot Money/Andy Summers)

Eric Burdon: vocals / Andy Summers: guitar, vocals / John Weider: guitar, vocals / Zoot Money: keyboards, bass guitar, vocals /Barry Jenkins: drums, vocals / Robert Wyatt: vocals (1) / the Animals: producer / unknown brass and flute

As before, Eric Burdon is able to produce a decent album because of the quality of his group, which now includes both Zoot Money and Andy Summers from the Big Roll Band/Dantalian's Chariot. He performs a respectable cover of the latter group's classic piece of psychedelia, *The Madman Running Through The Fields*, performed almost identically to the original. Burdon is no longer singing anything resembling R&B, for which his voice continues to be best suited, but at least he is not reciting lists this time. The one song that he has written himself has lyrics of dubious quality, but is musically interesting. He borrows from Van Morrison's vocal approach for *As The Years Go Passing By*, though without attempting any folk-jazz fusion, but Burdon does manage to fly with the music. *Love Is* is probably the best album issued in Burdon's name since the demise of the Animals, although he is stretching the listener's tolerance by making it a double. The UK version reduced it to a manageable single album, but in dropping *As The Years Go Passing By* and the whole of the jamming on side four, the record is considerably weakened.

EYES OF BLUE   CROSSROADS OF TIME

The Eyes Of Blue won the Melody Maker beat group contest in 1966 and recorded two singles for Decca without much success. The group's first album was released by Mercury and comprises keyboard-driven hard rock very much in the style of the recently released albums by the Gods and Deep Purple, but with a little extra jazz and even occasional classical influence. Clearly short of material, the group includes a Beatles cover, presented as Vanilla Fudge might have done, and a song by Love, which is let down by the fact that drummer John Weathers is not really able to deliver the required fury, managing to sound more like a galloping horse. It is not difficult to understand why *Crossroads Of Time* was a commercial failure, although there is enough that is interesting to justify the enthusiasm of more recent record collectors. The group managed to make two more albums and some of the members turned up on several other albums too, most notably Phil Ryan who worked with Man and some of that group's spin-offs.

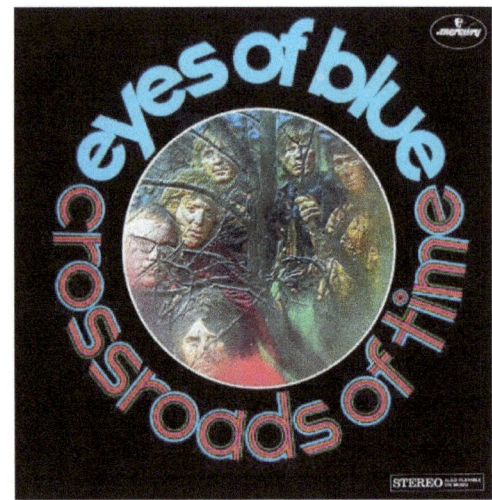

UK release	December 1968	Mercury	20134 SMCL
US release	December 1968	Mercury	SR 61184

1. Crossroads Of Time (Graham Bond)
2. Never Care (Ritchie Francis)
3. I'll Be Your Friend (Ritchie Francis)
4. 7 + 7 Is (Arthur Lee)
5. Prodigal Son (Ritchie Francis)
6. Largo (George Handel)
7. Love is The Law (Graham Bond)
8. Yesterday (John Lennon/Paul McCartney)
9. I Wonder Why (Ritchie Francis)
10. World Of Emotion (Ritchie Francis)
11. Inspiration For A New Day (Ritchie Francis)

Gary Pickford-Hopkins: vocals, guitar / Ritchie Francis: bass guitar, piano, vocals / Phil Ryan: keyboards / Ray Williams: guitar / Wyndham Rees: vocals / John Weathers: drums, vocals / Lou Reizner: producer

ELVIS PRESLEY   ELVIS

On 3 December, NBC in America broadcast a show starring Elvis Presley, commonly referred to since then as the *'68 Comeback Special*. It was the first time that Elvis had been seen performing, other than as a character in a film, for several years. All Elvis had to do was sing some of his greatest hits from nearly ten years previously, wearing black leather for some of them, and the music critics could not wait to celebrate his return from the wilderness. They could apparently ignore the fact that the television programme was pure showbiz nostalgia and had nothing to do with the way rock music was being played at venues like the Fillmore in 1968. Of course Elvis is a magnetic performer and loves being in front of a film camera, but the set, with its songs largely presented in abbreviated versions as part of medleys, is hardly a musical milestone. The show did what it was supposed to do and revitalised the singer's career. This soundtrack album put Elvis back in the charts and allowed him to begin a new approach for the seventies in which he could perform increasingly glitzy music at increasingly glitzy venues. His concerts and his records undoubtedly had a place in the world of music, just not anywhere near its creative cutting edge.

US release	December 1968	RCA Victor	LPM-4088
UK release	January 1969	RCA Victor	RD 8011

1. Trouble (Jerry Leiber/Mike Stoller)
   Guitar Man (Jerry Reed)
2. Lawdy Miss Clawdy (Lloyd Price)
   Baby What You Want Me To Do (Jimmy Reed)
   Heartbreak Hotel (Mae Axton/Tommy Durden)
   Hound Dog (Jerry Leiber/Mike Stoller)
   All Shook Up (Otis Blackwell)
   Can't Help Falling In Love (George Weiss/Hugo Peretti/Luigi Creatore)
   Jailhouse Rock (Jerry Leiber/Mike Stoller)
   Love Me Tender (Vera Matson)
3. Where Could I Go But To The Lord? (J.B.Coats)
   Up Above My Head (Walter Earl Brown)
   Saved (Jerry Leiber/Mike Stoller)
4. Blue Christmas (Billy Hayes/Jay W.Johnson)
   One Night (Dave Bartholomew/Pearl King)
5. Memories (Billy Strange/Mac Davis)
6. Nothingville (Billy Strange/Mac Davis)
   Big Boss Man (Luther Dixon/Al Smith)
   Guitar Man (Jerry Reed)
   Little Egypt (Jerry Leiber/Mike Stoller)
   Trouble (Jerry Leiber/Mike Stoller)
   Guitar Man (Jerry Reed)
7. If I Can Dream (Walter Earl Brown)

Elvis Presley: vocals, guitar / Tracks 2,4 – Scotty Moore: guitar / Charlie Hodge: guitar, vocals / D.J.Fontana, Alan Fortas, Lance LeGault: percussion
Tracks 1,3,5-7 – Mike Deasy, Al Caset, Tommy Tedesco: guitar / Larry Knechtel: keyboards, bass guitar / Don Randi: piano / Tommy Morgan: harmonica / Charles Berghofer: bass / Hal Blaine: drums / John Cyr, Elliot Franks, Frank DeVito: percussion / Billy Goldenberg: conductor / Bones Howe, Steve Binder: producer

ALBERT KING   LIVE WIRE / BLUES POWER

Live Wire / Blues Power is a concert recording from the Fillmore West in San Francisco. The success of groups like Cream had rekindled interest in the guitarists that Eric Clapton and company claimed as an influence. Albert King was one of the most

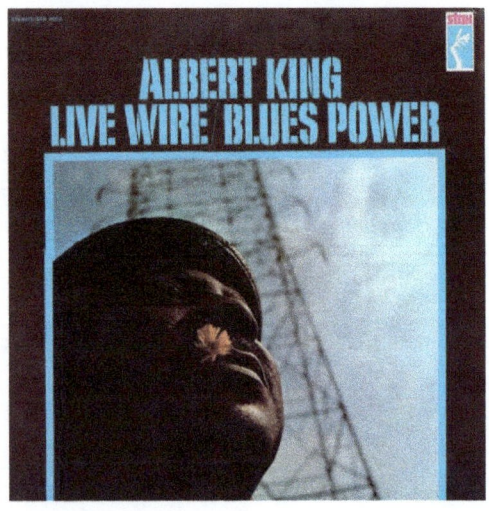

US release	December 1968	Stax	STS 2003
UK release	December 1968	Stax	(S)XATS 1002

1. Watermelon Man (Herbie Hancock)
2. Blues Power (Albert King)
3. Night Stomp (Al Jackson/Albert King)
4. Blues At Sunrise (Albert King)
5. Please Love Me (B.B.King/Jules Taub)
6. Look Out (Albert King)

Albert King: guitar, vocals / Willie James Exon: guitar / James Washington: organ / Roosevelt Pointer: bass guitar / Son Seals: drums / Al Jackson: producer

important of these. His music has the same ingredients as rock, with none of the jazz influence of his namesake B.B.King. He may play a piece by Herbie Hancock, but he turns the jazz original into a fine piece of instrumental rock 'n' roll. Playing live, Albert King is able to extend his solo work so that the problem of his studio recordings seeming to fade out before he has finished is successfully addressed. There is nothing here to match the marathon performances of Cream, but Albert King does solo for several minutes at a time, while the title track, *Blues Power*, provides seven or eight minutes of guitar playing altogether. He tells the audience that he invented blues power and, hearing the muscular, biting tone that he achieves on his guitar, without effects, they could well believe that this was the case.

THE STAPLE SINGERS   SOUL FOLK IN ACTION

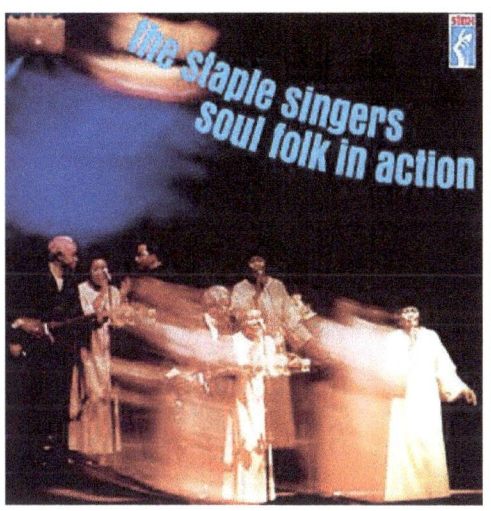

| US release | December 1968 | Stax | STS 2004 |
| UK release | December 1968 | Stax | SXATS 1004 |

1. We've Got To Get Ourselves Together (Bonnie Bramlett/Carl Radle)
2. (Sittin' On) The Dock Of The Bay (Otis Redding/Steve Cropper)
3. Top Of The Mountain (Bettye Crutcher/Marvell Thomas)
4. Slow Train (Steve Cropper/William Bell)
5. The Weight (Robbie Robertson)
6. Long Walk To D.C. (Homer Banks/Marvell Thomas)
7. Got To Be Some Changes Made (Leroy Crume)
8. The Ghetto (Bettye Crutcher/Bonnie Bramlett/Homer Banks)
9. People My People (Homer Banks/Steve Cropper)
10. I See It (James Edwards/Pervis Staples)
11. This Year (Steve Cropper/Tim Riley)

Mavis Staples: vocals / Cleotha Staples: vocals / Pervis Staples: vocals / Roebuck Staples: vocals, guitar / Steve Cropper: guitar, producer / Marvell Thomas: keyboards / Donald Dunn: bass guitar / Al Jackson: drums / Wayne Jackson: trumpet / Andrew Love: tenor saxophone / Joe Arnold: baritone saxophone

Ray Charles and James Brown secularised gospel music during the fifties and invented soul, but gospel continued alongside. The Staple Singers performed in churches and recorded gospel songs, with their first album being issued in 1958. They started to incorporate more mainstream soul during the sixties, although in most cases they chose songs with a social message. Most of the material on the group's first album for the Stax label, *Soul Folk In Action*, is like this, and it includes a slightly oblique tribute to the recently assassinated Martin Luther King, *Long Walk To D.C.* Mavis Staples is an outstanding soul singer and despite the production by Steve Cropper and the presence of the same forceful musicians as recorded with Otis Redding, the music allows the singing to dominate. It is cheerful and uptempo for the most part, but the Staple Singers still manage to evoke the church rather than the disco. This is especially noticeable on the two most familiar songs, where Redding's *The Dock Of The Bay* has added strings and sounds like a paean to the glory of nature rather than a few moments of introspective reflection, and the Band's *The Weight* is revealed as the hymn that it always had the potential to be.

JOHNNIE TAYLOR   WHO'S MAKING LOVE

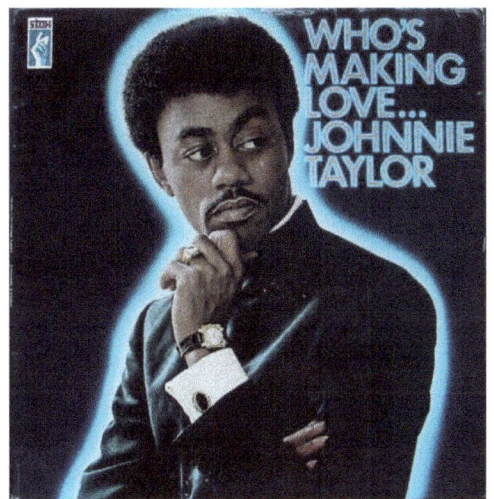

| US release | December 1968 | Stax | STS 2005 |
| UK release | December 1968 | Stax | SXATS 1006 |

1. Who's Making Love (Bettye Crutcher/Don Davis/Homer Banks/Raymond Jackson)
2. I'm Not The Same Person (Homer Banks/James Lately)
3. Hold On This Time (Don Davis/Raymond Jackson)
4. Woman Across The River (Allen A Jones/Bettye Crutcher)
5. Can't Trust Your Neighbor (Isaac Hayes/David Porter)
6. Take Care Of Your Homework (Don Davis/Homer Banks/Thomas Kelly)
7. I'm Trying (Isaac Hayes/David Porter)
8. Poor Make Believer (Don Davis/Homer Banks/James Lately)
9. Payback Hurts (Johnnie Taylor/Steve Cropper)
10. Mr Nobody Is Somebody (Don Davis/Homer Banks/Raymond Jackson)
11. I'd Rather Drink Muddy Water (Eddie Miller)

Johnnie Taylor: vocals / Steve Cropper: guitar / Booker T Jones: keyboards / Isaac Hayes: keyboards / Donald Dunn: bass guitar / Al Jackson: drums, producer / Don Davis: producer

Johnnie Taylor became a considerable star through the seventies and beyond and he was awarded the first platinum single (two million copies sold) for his 1976 hit, *Disco Lady*. His breakthrough was the single, *Who's Making Love*, which was a substantial hit and gold disc winner in 1968. Supported by Booker T and the MGs, Taylor's energetic and rough-toned singing style marks him as the natural successor to the late Otis Redding and the mantle is one that Taylor wears effortlessly and with considerable authority. He manages to cover a lot of ground during the album. As well as keeping true to the established Stax sound, he also links Stax soul with Motown (*Hold On This Time*), recalls Sam Cooke (*Poor Make Believer*), becomes a lounge jazz singer (*I'd Rather Drink Muddy Water*), and pulls the blues into the late sixties (*Woman Across The River*). In short, *Who's Making Love* is an outstanding album.

THE INSECT TRUST

| US release | December 1968 | Capitol | SKAO 109 |
| UK release | December 1968 | Capitol | E-(S)T 109 |

1. The Skin Game (Bill Barth/Nancy Jeffries/Robert Palmer/Trevor Koehler)
2. Miss Fun City (Bill Barth/Nancy Jeffries/Robert Palmer)
3. World War I Song (Joe Callicott)
4. Special Rider Blues (Skip James)
5. Foggy River Bridge Fly (Trevor Koehler)
6. Been Here And Gone So Soon (Bill Barth/Nancy Jeffies/Robert Palmer)
7. Declaration Of Independence (Robert Palmer)
8. Walking On Nails (Gabor Szabo)
9. Brighter Than Day (Bill Barth/Nancy Jeffries/Robert Palmer/Trevor Koehler)
10. Mountain Song (Bill Barth/Nancy Jeffries/Robert Palmer/Trevor Koehler/Luke Faust)
11. Going Home (Bill Barth/Nancy Jeffries)

Nancy Jeffries: vocals, percussion / Bill Barth: guitar, percussion / Bob Palmer: alto saxophone, clarinet, recorder, percussion / Luke Faust: guitar, banjo, percussion, vocals / Trevor Koehler: baritone saxophone, piccolo, piano, percussion, arranger / Hugh McCracken: guitar / Chuck Rainey, Joe Mack: bass guitar / Bernard Purdie, Buddy Salzman: drums / Steve Duboff: percussion, producer

The Insect Trust has a very unusual sound, as if a couple of saxophonists, used to playing in the manner of Albert Ayler, have unexpectedly stumbled into a rehearsal by an acoustic folk blues group and have been invited to stay. There is an anarchic flavour to the Insect Trust's music that nevertheless contrives to remain extremely attractive, if only because of the intensely melodic tones of singer Nancy Jeffries' voice. The group has neither a bass player nor a drummer and frequently manages perfectly well, although session musicians are called on for some of the tracks. It is not surprising that music as original as this did not manage to get anywhere near the charts, although the Insect Trust was allowed to make a second album in 1970.

STEVE REICH   LIVE / ELECTRIC MUSIC

US release   December 1968   Columbia Masterworks   MS 7265
Not released in UK

1. Violin Phase
2. It's Gonna Rain

Both compositions by Steve Reich

Steve Reich: processing / Paul Zukofsky: violin (1) / Brother Walter: voice (2) / David Behrman: producer

The first album entirely devoted to the works of Steve Reich contains two of them, composed in October 1967 and January 1965 respectively. Both pieces explore aspects of Reich's fascination with phase differences, whereby two identical recordings are allowed to gradually go out of synchronisation with each other as they are played back, creating special rhythmic effects. *It's Gonna Rain* takes as its source material a segment from the speech of an evangelist preacher, looped and repeated a huge number of times, until it becomes just a sound, with no readily identifiable words. The piece is divided into two sections, the first using the title phrase, while the second treats a longer speech fragment. There is no melody at all, but that is not the point. *Violin Phase* has a live violinist playing against up to three recordings of himself. Again, phrases are looped and repeated. There is a small amount of melodic interest this time, although the hypnotic effect produced, as before, is not really a function of the actual notes being played. As the piece progresses, a hint of traditional reel playing is recalled, although this is not a deliberate intention. Eventually, Reich (and indeed other composers too) would use the phase effects in more elaborate ways, culminating in what is perhaps Reich's finest work, *Different Trains,* composed in 1988.

KARLHEINZ STOCKHAUSEN   GRUPPEN / CARRÉ

These two works by Karlheinz Stockhausen were composed in the fifties, but this album represents their first release on record. In 1968 they still sound utterly contemporary. Although three or four orchestras are involved, the music does not, for the most part, sound dense or powerful because Stockhausen's concern is the positioning of the musicians and the effect that sounds coming from different directions has on the

German release   December 1968   Deutsche Grammophon   137 002
Not released in UK or US

1. Gruppen fur 3 Orchester
2. Carré fur 4 Orchester und 4 Chöre

Side 1: Kölner Rundfunk-Sinfonie-Orchester conducted by Karlheinz Stockhausen, Bruno Maderna, Michael Gielen
Side 2: Sinfonie-Orchester Des Norddeutschen Rundfunks Hamburg, Chor Des Norddeutschen Rundfunks Hamburg conducted by Stockhausen, Maderna, Gielen, Mauricio Kagel

listener. For *Gruppen (Groups)* the orchestras are placed in front and on either side, for *Carré (Square)* the orchestras are placed all around the listener, one on each side. Inevitably, however, a stereo recording cannot convey all of Stockhausen's intention. The music is not at all melodic, preferring to make a succession of short statements using different timbres and with the pauses having a significant effect on their own. The players of the percussion instruments have the most to do. The result is similar to that produced by free improvisation groups like AMM, only with a much larger number of musicians involved. For anyone used to hearing the Beatles' *Revolution 9*, Stockhausen's works sound familiar and are clearly the product of a similar kind of thought process.

THE MODERN JAZZ QUARTET
UNDER THE JASMIN TREE

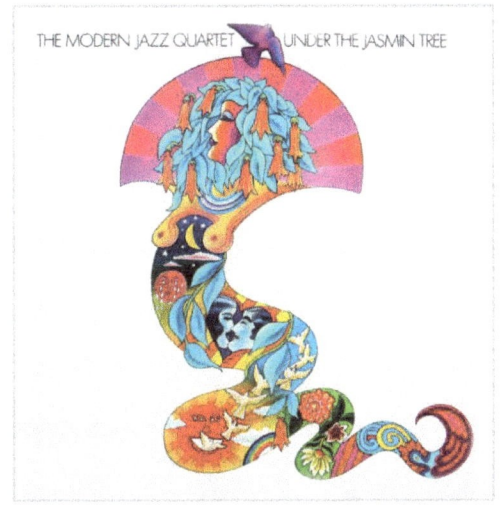

| UK release | December 1968 | Apple | SAPCOR 4 |
| US release | January 1969 | Apple | ST 3353 |

1. The Blue Necklace
2. Three Little Feelings Parts I-III
3. Exposure
4. The Jasmin Tree

All compositions by John Lewis

John Lewis: piano / Milt Jackson: vibraphone / Percy Heath: bass / Connie Kay: drums / no producer credited

The Modern Jazz Quartet was formed in 1952 and kept the same line-up from 1955 onwards. Much of the group's material was composed by pianist John Lewis, who liked to explore the interaction between jazz and classical music, making the group one of the leading exponents of what was later called third stream jazz. By 1968, the group's most successful years were behind it, but it nevertheless became the surprising choice for the fourth album to be released on the Beatles' own Apple label. The cover of *Under The Jasmin Tree* is given an appropriately psychedelic cover, but the music has changed little since the fifties. Having a vibraphone as the lead instrument rather than a saxophone or trumpet, even when played by such a skilled exponent as Milt Jackson, always gave the MJQ a somewhat delicate sound, although drummer Connie Kay frequently tries hard to make the music sound muscular. The opening *The Blue Necklace* has an insistent beat at its start and rattling percussion, perhaps intended to be the shaking of the jewellery in the title, and it continues to sound very forthright when the percussion gives way to regular drumming. *The Jasmin Tree* uses the same rhythm, to give the album an overall structure, but in between it is very much business as usual. *Under The Jasmin Tree*, in essence, is a typical Modern Jazz Quartet album, making no particular advance on its predecessors and making little impact on the music of its time, despite the patronage of the Beatles.

ORNETTE COLEMAN   NEW YORK IS NOW!

For the recordings issued as *New York Is Now!* (and the later *Love Call*) Ornette Coleman invites the classic John Coltrane rhythm section to perform with him. Their reaction is to play in what they feel is the appropriate manner for Coleman's music, so that instead of any rhythm underlay for a modal improvisation, what we get is much closer to the way that Coleman was stretching the conventions of hard bop in the late fifties. As a result, *New York Is Now!* is a more accessible album than the others

| US release | December 1968 | Blue Note | BST 84287 |
| Not released in UK | | | |

1. The Garden Of Souls
2. Toy Dance
3. We Now Interrupt For A Commercial
4. Broad Way Blues
5. Round Trip

All compositions by Ornette Coleman

Ornette Coleman: alto saxophone, trumpet, violin / Dewey Redman: tenor saxophone / Jimmy Garrison: bass / Elvin Jones: drums / Mel Fuhrman: voice (3) / Francis Wolff: producer

issued in recent years. Unless, of course, it is simply a matter of listeners likely to have become accustomed to the sound that the saxophonist makes. Certainly the music he produces from a violin is tumultuous (as on *We Now Interrupt For A Commercial*), but his saxophone playing is much more concise and melodically constructed than the unfettered outpouring of John Coltrane's later music. Coleman's decision to use Dewey Redman as an alternative voice is a good one, because the tenor saxophonist's playing is distinctive, with an unusual breathy tone including an occasional wheezing effect, produced, it must be assumed, by humming through his instrument as he plays.

MILES DAVIS   FILLES DE KILIMANJARO

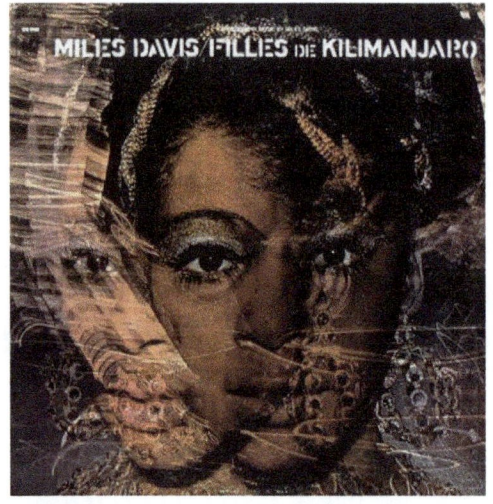

US release	December 1968	Columbia	CS 9750
UK release	December 1968	CBS	S/M 63551

1. Frelon Brun (Miles Davis)
2. Tout de Suite (Miles Davis)
3. Petits Machins (Miles Davis/Gil Evans)
4. Filles de Kilimanjaro (Miles Davis)
5. Mademoiselle Mabry (Miles Davis/Gil Evans)

Miles Davis: trumpet / Wayne Shorter: tenor saxophone / Herbie Hancock: piano (2,3,4) / Chick Corea: piano (1,5) / Ron Carter: bass guitar (2,3,4) / Dave Holland: bass (1,5) / Tony Williams: drums / Teo Macero: producer

Filles De Kilimanjaro catches Miles Davis in the middle of a line-up change to the quintet he has worked with for the past five years, as Herbie Hancock and Ron Carter give way to Chick Corea and Dave Holland. Most of the music recorded employs the electric piano and bass introduced on the previous *Miles In The Sky* album, if not the funky rhythm (although the title track does push pretty hard). Curiously, it is the new players who seem more reluctant to plug in. Dave Holland keeps to an upright bass and Chick Corea, although playing an electric piano, chooses a setting for *Mademoiselle Mabry* that is so close to the sound of a traditional piano that he might as well be using one. That piece is one of two written by Miles Davis in collaboration with Gil Evans, the arranger who produced big band settings for Davis on several occasions previously, although Evans gets no credit on the record sleeve. The music, dedicated to the woman who would become Mrs Betty Davis, incorporates a phrase taken from *The Wind Cries Mary* by Jimi Hendrix. It was reported that Davis had been interested in working with the guitarist until he discovered that Hendrix could not read music notation. The music throughout the *Filles De Kilimanjaro* album takes advantage of the electric piano's greater ability to cut through the horns and Tony Williams' enveloping drumming style by using bluesy riffs to underscore the proceedings, echoed by Ron Carter's bass guitar. Miles Davis and Wayne Shorter are playing much as they have done for several years, but they are made to sound a little different by the newly constructed support. In retrospect, *Filles De Kilimanjaro* seems like a transitional record, linking the quintet work with the birth of fusion jazz represented by Miles Davis's next two albums, *In A Silent Way* and *Bitches Brew*. At the end of 1968, however, the album is merely the next in line in a fascinating journey through Davis's music of the sixties.

ARTIST INDEX

Ackles, David same	278
Adderley, Cannonball Mercy, Mercy, Mercy!	137
Alpert, Herb Tijuana Brass Whipped Cream & Other Delights	45
Amboy Dukes The Amboy Dukes	203
AMM AMMmusic	130
Animals Animal Tracks	48
Animals The Animals	29
Animals The Most Of The Animals	86
Aranbee Pop Symphony Orchestra Today's Pop Symphony	79
Arnold, P.P. The First Lady Of Immediate	247
Ars Nova same	243
Art Supernatural Fairy Tales	206
Artwoods Art Gallery	116
Association Greatest Hits	290
Axelrod, David Song Of Innocence	285
Ayler, Albert In Greenwich Village	215
Ayler, Albert Spirits Rejoice	74
Ayler, Albert Spiritual Unity	34
Baez, Joan 5	29
Baez, Joan Any Day Now	309
Baez, Joan Farewell Angelina	64
Baez, Joan Joan	176
Band Music From Big Pink	266
Barber, Chris Good Mornin' Blues	34
Barock and Roll Ensemble Eine Kleine Beatlemusic EP	46
Beach Boys All Summer Long	23
Beach Boys Best Of The Beach Boys	115
Beach Boys Best Of The Beach Boys Vol.2	163
Beach Boys Friends	254
Beach Boys Pet Sounds	90
Beach Boys Smiley Smile	180
Beach Boys Summer Days (And Summer Nights!)	54
Beach Boys Surfin' USA	4
Beach Boys Today!	38
Beach Boys Wild Honey	210
Beacon Street Union The Eyes Of	237
Beatles Beatles For Sale	30
Beatles A Collection Of Beatles Oldies	119
Beatles A Hard Day's Night	22
Beatles Help!	56
Beatles Long Tall Sally EP	22
Beatles Magical Mystery Tour EP	208
Beatles Please Please Me	3
Beatles Revolver	99
Beatles Rubber Soul	69
Beatles Sgt Pepper's Lonely Hearts Club Band	155
Beatles White Album (The Beatles)	300
Beatles With The Beatles	13
Beatles Yesterday And Today	92
Beau Brummels Bradley's Barn	289
Beau Brummels Introducing	44
Beau Brummels Triangle	168
Beck, Jeff Truth	271
Bee Gees Bee Gees 1st	167
Bee Gees Horizontal	229
Bennett, Duster Smiling Like I'm Happy	278
Berberian, Cathy Beatles Arias	158
Berio, Luciano Circles / Sequenza I, III, V	130
Big Brother & the Holding Company same	172
Big Brother & the Holding Company Cheap Thrills	269
Black, Cilla Cilla	33
Blood Sweat And Tears same	306
Blood Sweat And Tears Child Is Father To The Man	228
Blossom Toes We Are Ever So Clean	191
Blue Cheer Vincebus Eruptum	224
Blues Magoos Psychedelic Lollipop	114
Blues Project Live At The Cafe Au Go Go	83
Blues Project Planned Obsolescence	277
Blues Project Projections	117
Bond, Graham Organization There's A Bond Between Us	72
Bonzo Dog Band The Doughnut In Granny's Greenhouse	295
Bonzo Dog Doo-Dah Band Gorilla	192
Booker T & The MG's Hip Hug-Her	163
Bowie, David David Bowie	157
Box Tops The Letter / Neon Rainbow	203
Brel, Jacques 67	127
Britten, Benjamin War Requiem	7
Brötzmann, Peter Octet Machine Gun	279
Brown, James Cold Sweat	174
Brown, James I Can't Stand Myself When You Touch Me	233
Brown, James Live At The Apollo	5
Brown, James Live At The Apollo Volume II	269
Brown, James Papa's Got A Brand New Bag	62
Brubeck, Dave Quartet At Carnegie Hall	9
Buckinghams Time & Charges	145
Buckley, Tim Goodbye And Hello	176
Buckley, Tim same	109
Buffalo Springfield Again	194
Buffalo Springfield same	123
Buffalo Springfield Last Time Around	265
Burdon, Eric & The Animals Every One Of Us	272
Burdon, Eric & The Animals Love Is	313
Burdon, Eric & The Animals The Twain Shall Meet	246
Burdon, Eric & the Animals Winds Of Change	179
Burke, Solomon The Best Of	55
Kenny Burrell Guitar Forms	53
Burton, Gary and Carla Bley A Genuine Tong Funeral	245
Burton, Gary Quartet Lofty Fake Anagram	202
Butler, Jerry The Ice Man Cometh	296
Butterfield, Paul Blues Band same	63
Butterfield Blues Band East-West	101
Butterfield Blues Band In My Own Dream	265
Butterfield Blues Band Resurrection Of Pigboy Crabshaw	211
Byrds Fifth Dimension	95
Byrds Greatest Hits	175
Byrds Mr Tambourine Man	51
Byrds The Notorious Byrd Brothers	219
Byrds Sweetheart Of The Rodeo	273
Byrds Turn! Turn! Turn!	70
Byrds Younger Than Yesterday	133
Campbell, Glen By The Time I Get To Phoenix	201
Campbell, Glen Gentle On My Mind	176
Canned Heat Boogie With Canned Heat	220
Canned Heat Canned Heat	165
Canned Heat Living The Blues	291
Captain Beefheart & His Magic Band Safe As Milk	158
Captain Beefheart & His Magic Band Strictly Personal	284
Caravan Caravan	286
Carlos, Walter Switched-On Bach	285
Carr, James You Got My Mind Messed Up	141
Carter, Elliott Piano Concerto/Michael Colgrass As Quiet As	214

Carthy, Martin Martin Carthy	73
Cash, Johnny At Folsom Prison	245
Chambers Brothers The Time Has Come	205
Cherry, Don Complete Communion	102
Cherry, Don Symphony For Improvisers	132
Chicken Shack 40 Blue Fingers, Freshly Packed & Ready…	252
Chocolate Watch Band No Way Out	182
Clark, Dave Five Glad All Over	18
Clark, Gene Gene Clark With The Gosdin Brothers	133
Clear Light Clear Light	183
Cline, Patsy Greatest Hits	142
Cohen, Leonard Songs Of Leonard Cohen	212
Coleman, Ornette At The Golden Circle Stockholm Vols 1-2	103
Coleman, Ornette Chappaqua Suite	135
Coleman, Ornette An Evening With	186
Coleman, Ornette New York Is Now!	317
Collectors The Collectors	264
Collier, Graham Deep Dark Blue Centre	148
Collins, Albert Love Can Be Found Anywhere	292
Collins, Judy In My Life	118
Collins, Judy Who Knows Where The Time Goes	298
Collins, Judy Wildflowers	188
Coltrane, Alice A Monastic Trio	268
Coltrane, John Ascension	79
Coltrane, John Expression	185
Coltrane, John Impressions	9
Coltrane, John Kulu Se Mama	128
Coltrane, John Live At The Village Vanguard Again	121
Coltrane, John A Love Supreme	33
Coltrane, John Meditations	105
Cosmic Sounds The Zodiac	150
Country Joe & the Fish Electric Music For The Mind & Body	153
Country Joe & the Fish I-Feel-Like-I'm-Fixin'-To-Die	196
Country Joe & the Fish Together	272
Cowsills The Cowsills	183
Crazy World Of Arthur Brown same	257
Cream Disraeli Gears	205
Cream Fresh Cream	119
Cream Wheels Of Fire	270
Creation We Are Paintermen	173
Creedence Clearwater Revival	244
Dave Dee, Dozy, Beaky, Mick & Tich Golden Hits	186
David Another Day, Another Lifetime	216
Davis, Miles E.S.P.	57
Davis, Miles Filles De Kilimanjaro	317
Davis, Miles Miles In The Sky	267
Davis, Miles Miles Smiles	135
Davis, Miles My Funny Valentine	36
Davis, Miles Nefertiti	221
Davis, Miles Sorcerer	193
Davis, Spencer Group The Best Of	208
Davis, Spencer Group The Second Album	77
Davis, Spencer Group Their First LP	40
Davis, Spencer Group With Their New Face On	251
Deep Psychedelic Moods	112
Deep Purple Shades Of Deep Purple	275
Deviants Ptooff!	149
Dillard & Clark The Fantastic Expedition Of	287
Dillards Wheatstraw Suite	299
Dolphy, Eric Out To Lunch	20
Donovan A Gift From A Flower To A Garden	241
Donovan Hurdy Gurdy Man	280
Donovan In Concert	275
Donovan Mellow Yellow	143
Donovan Sunshine Superman	103
Donovan Sunshine Superman (UK)	161
Donovan Universal Soldier EP	59
Donovan What's Bin Did And What's Bin Hid	46
Doors The Doors	124
Doors Strange Days	182
Doors Waiting For The Sun	263
Downliners Sect The Country Sect	74
Dr John Gris-Gris	220
Drifters Golden Hits	239
Driscoll, Julie, Brian Auger & the Trinity Open	204
Dunbar, Aynsley Retaliation Doctor Dunbar's Prescription	294
Dupree, Simon & the Big Sound Without Reservations	173
Dylan, Bob Another Side Of Bob Dylan	24
Dylan, Bob Blonde On Blonde	95
Dylan, Bob Bringing It All Back Home	39
Dylan, Bob The Freewheelin'	6
Dylan, Bob Greatest Hits	140
Dylan, Bob Highway 61 Revisited	56
Dylan, Bob John Wesley Harding	218
Dylan, Bob The Times They Are A-Changin'	17
Easybeats Good Friday	150
Eclection Eclection	273
Electric Flag A Long Time Comin'	233
Electric Flag The Trip	202
Electric Prunes The Electric Prunes	146
Electric Prunes Mass In F Minor	224
Electric Prunes Underground	172
Ellington, Duke Far East Suite	162
Ellis, Don Orchestra Autumn	306
Ellis, Don Orchestra Electric Bath	214
Ellis, Don Orchestra Shock Treatment	268
Evans, Bill Conversations With Myself	12
Eyes Of Blue Crossroads Of Time	313
Fahey, John Guitar Vol.4	147
Fahey, John Requia	201
Fahey, John The Transfiguration Of Blind Joe Death	129
Fairport Convention Fairport Convention	258
Faithfull, Marianne Come My Way	46
Faithfull, Marianne Marianne Faithfull	46
Fame, Georgie Fame At Last	28
Fame, Georgie Rhythm And Blues At The Flamingo	16
Fame, Georgie Sound Venture	109
Fame, Georgie Sweet Things	88
Family Music In A Doll's House	259
Family Tree Miss Butters	250
Farina, Richard & Mimi Reflections In A Crystal Wind	75
Farlowe, Chris The Art Of Chris Farlowe	116
Fever Tree same	236
Fifth Dimension Up, Up And Away	154
Fifty Foot Hose Cauldron	237
Flatt & Scruggs Greatest Hits	105
Fleetwood Mac Mr Wonderful	271
Fleetwood Mac Peter Green's Fleetwood Mac	228
Floyd, Eddie Knock On Wood	132
Four Seasons Golden Hits	11
Four Tops Greatest Hits	175
Frank, Jackson C. Jackson C, Frank	71
Franklin, Aretha Aretha Now	255
Franklin, Aretha I Never Loved A Man The Way I Love You	141

Franklin, Aretha Lady Soul	223
Free Design Kites Are Fun	146
Free Spirits Out Of Sight And Sound	131
Fugs The Fugs	84
Garrick, Michael Quintet October Woman	35
Garrick, Michael Sextet Black Marigolds	308
Garrick, Michael Sextet Promises	67
Gaye, Marvin In The Groove	268
Gentry, Bobbie Ode To Billie Joe	177
Gerry and the Pacemakers You'll Never Walk Alone EP	15
Getz, Stan Sweet Rain	170
Getz, Stan & Joao Gilberto Getz/Gilberto	18
Giles, Giles And Fripp The Cheerful Insanity Of	277
Gods Genesis	275
Golden Dawn Power Plant	226
Gore, Lesley Golden Hits	50
Gouldman, Graham The Graham Gouldman Thing	249
Graham, Davy Folk, Blues & Beyond	32
Grateful Dead Anthem Of The Sun	264
Grateful Dead same	141
Great Society Conspicuous Only In Its Absence	238
Grossman, Stefan Aunt Molly's Murray Farm	235
Groundhogs Scratching The Surface	294
Gruppo Di Improvvisazione Nuova Consonanza	107
Gun same	311
Guthrie, Arlo Alice's Restaurant	187
H.P.Lovecraft same	190
H.P.Lovecraft H.P.Lovecraft II	280
Hamilton, Chico The Dealer	118
Hancock, Herbie Maiden Voyage	48
Hancock, Herbie Speak Like A Child	267
Handy, John Recorded Live At The Monterey Jazz Festival	91
Hapshash & the Coloured Coat Featuring The Human Host..	203
Hardin, Tim 1	98
Hardin, Tim 2	147
Harper, Roy Come Out Fighting Ghengis Smith	213
Harper, Roy Sophisticated Beggar	131
Harpers Bizarre Anything Goes	216
Harriott, Joe – John Mayer Double Quintet Indo-Jazz Fusions	139
Harriott, Joe – John Mayer Double Quintet Indo-Jazz Suite	86
Harris, Eddie The Electrifying Eddie Harris	225
Harris, Richard A Tramp Shining	249
Harris, Richard The Yard Went On Forever	310
Harrison, George Wonderwall Music	290
Havens, Richie Mixed Bag	138
Havens, Richie Richard P.Havens, 1983	312
Havens, Richie Something Else Again	226
Hayes, Tubby 100% Proof	178
Hendrix, Jimi & Curtis Knight Get That Feeling	216
Hendrix, Jimi Experience Are You Experienced	151
Hendrix, Jimi Experience Axis: Bold As Love	206
Hendrix, Jimi Experience Electric Ladyland	282
Hendrix, Jimi Experience Smash Hits	240
Henry, Pierre Messe Pour Le Temps Present	177
Herd Paradise Lost	229
Herman's Hermits Herman's Hermits	61
Hill, Andrew Point Of Departure	44
Hillsiders Bobby Bare & The Hillsiders	189
Hollies Butterfly	198
Hollies Evolution	157
Hollies For Certain Because	120
Hollies Greatest	274
Hollies Stay With The Hollies	16
Holmes, Jake The Above Ground Sound Of	162
Holy Modal Rounders Indian War Whoop	217
Honeycombs The Honeycombs	26
Idle Race Birthday Party	286
Ill Wind Flashes	259
Impressions Keep On Pushing	21
Impressions People Get Ready	37
Incredible String Band The 5000 Spirits Or The Layers…	169
Incredible String Band The Hangman's Beautiful Daughter	234
Incredible String Band The Incredible String Band	93
Incredible String Band Wee Tam & The Big Huge	295
Insect Trust same	316
International Submarine Band Safe At Home	230
Iron Butterfly Heavy	223
Iron Butterfly In-A-Gadda-Da-Vida	253
J.K. & Co Suddenly One Summer	281
James, Etta Tell Mama	232
Jan & Dean Golden Hits Volume 2	59
Jansch, Bert same	43
Jansch, Bert It Don't Bother Me	71
Jansch, Bert Jack Orion	106
Jansch, Bert Nicola	166
Jansch, Bert & John Renbourn Bert And John	106
Jarre, Maurice Doctor Zhivago Original Soundtrack	75
Jefferson Airplane After Bathing At Baxter's	195
Jefferson Airplane Crown Of Creation	277
Jefferson Airplane Surrealistic Pillow	134
Jefferson Airplane Takes Off	102
Jennings, Waylon Folk – Country	85
Jethro Tull This Was	283
Jones, George The Race Is On	45
Jones, Tom Along Came Jones	49
July July	273
Kaleidoscope (UK) Tangerine Dream	198
Kaleidoscope (US) A Beacon From Mars	222
Kaleidoscope (US) Side Trips	159
Kilroy, Pat Light Of Day	113
King, Albert Born Under A Bad Sign	174
King, Albert Live Wire / Blues Power	314
King, B.B. Blues Is King	129
King, B.B. Live At The Regal	40
Kingsmen In Person Featuring Louie Louie	14
Kinks Face To Face	110
Kinks Kinda Kinks	37
Kinks The Kink Kontroversy	65
Kinks same	27
Kinks Live At Kelvin Hall	218
Kinks Something Else	180
Kinks Sunny Afternoon	197
Kinks Village Green Preservation Society	299
Kinks Well Respected Kinks	104
Kirk, Roland Rip, Rig & Panic	74
Knickerbockers Lies	77
Kooper, Al & Mike Bloomfield Live Adventures	305
Kooper, Al / Mike Bloomfield / Steve Stills Super Session	264
Korner, Alexis A New Generation Of Blues	250
Korner, Alexis Blues Incorporated At The Cavern	28
Korner, Alexis Blues Incorporated Red Hot From Alex	22
Leaves Hey Joe	96
Left Banke Walk Away Renee / Pretty Ballerina	136
Lennon, John & Yoko Ono Unfinished Music 1:Two Virgins	299

Lewis, Gary and the Playboys Golden Greats	112	Modern Jazz Quartet Under The Jasmin Tree	316
Lewis, Ramsey Trio The In Crowd	54	Monk, Thelonious Monk's Dream	5
Litter Distortions	153	Monkees The Birds The Bees And The Monkees	239
Liverpool Scene "Amazing Adventures Of"	308	Monkees Head	305
Liverpool Scene The Incredible New Liverpool Scene	159	Monkees Headquarters	152
Lloyd, Charles Forest Flower	136	Monkees The Monkees	110
Lloyd, Charles Love-In	169	Monkees More Of The Monkees	126
Lothar and the Hand People Presenting	304	Monkees Pisces, Aquarius, Capricorn & Jones Ltd	199
Love Da Capo	117	Monks Black Monk Time	89
Love Forever Changes	196	Moody Blues Days Of Future Passed	197
Love same	81	Moody Blues In Search Of The Lost Chord	260
Love Sculpture Blues Helping	313	Moody Blues The Magnificent Moodies	54
Lovin' Spoonful The Best Of	144	Morricone, Ennio The Good, The Bad And The Ugly	206
Lovin' Spoonful Daydream	83	Morrison, Van Astral Weeks	302
Lovin' Spoonful Do You Believe In Magic	72	Morrison, Van Blowin' Your Mind	179
Lovin' Spoonful Everything Playing	210	Mothers Of Invention Absolutely Free	154
Lovin' Spoonful Hums Of The Lovin' Spoonful	116	Mothers Of Invention Cruising With Ruben & The Jets	302
Lulu Something To Shout About	55	Mothers Of Invention Freak Out!	94
Lynn, Loretta Don't Come Home A Drinkin'	138	Mothers Of Invention We're Only In It For The Money	237
McCartney, Paul The Family Way	128	Move same	235
McCoys Hang On Sloopy	68	Move Something Else EP	251
McGough And McGear McGough and McGear	240	Nazz The Nazz	289
McGuire, Barry Eve Of Destruction	42	Neil, Fred same	122
McKenzie, Scott The Voice Of Scott McKenzie	212	New Jazz Orchestra Western Reunion London 1965	47
McTell, Ralph Eight Frames A Second	231	New Tweedy Brothers The New Tweedy Brothers	293
McWilliams, David Vol.2	194	Newman, Randy Randy Newman	255
Mad River	310	Nice Ars Longa Vita Brevis	297
Mahal, Taj Taj Mahal	227	Nice The Thoughts Of Emerlist Davjack	260
Mahal, Taj The Natch'l Blues	312	Nico Chelsea Girl	189
Makeba, Miriam Pata Pata	200	Nico The Marble Index	296
Mamas And Papas Deliver	137	Nilsson Aerial Ballet	263
Mamas And Papas If You Can Believe Your Eyes And Ears	80	Nilsson Pandemonium Shadow Show	217
Mandel, Harvey Cristo Redentor	281	Nirvana All Of Us	304
Manfred Mann As Is	111	Nirvana The Story Of Simon Simopath	192
Manfred Mann The Five Faces Of	25	Nyro, Laura Eli And The 13th Confession	234
Manfred Mann Instrumental Asylum EP	92	Nyro, Laura More Than A New Discovery	136
Manfred Mann Mann Made	63	Ochs, Phil Pleasures Of The Harbor	187
Manfred Mann Mann Made Hits	104	Os Mutantes same	257
Mantler, Michael The Jazz Composer's Orchestra	288	Owens, Buck Carnegie Hall Concert	99
Martha and the Vandellas Dance Party	44	Parks, Van Dyke Song Cycle	200
Martyn, John London Conversation	188	Parton, Dolly Hello, I'm Dolly	138
Martyn, John The Tumbler	311	Paxton, Tom Ramblin' Boy	23
Mayall, John Bare Wires	251	Peanut Butter Conspiracy The Great Conspiracy	211
Mayall, John The Blues Alone	204	Peanut Butter Conspiracy Is Spreading	143
Mayall, John Blues From Laurel Canyon	292	Pearls Before Swine One Nation Underground	191
Mayall, John Crusade	164	Pentangle The Pentangle	248
Mayall, John The Diary Of A Band Vols 1-2	219	Pentangle Sweet Child	296
Mayall, John A Hard Road	134	Pickett, Wilson The Best Of Wilson Pickett	215
Mayall, John John Mayall Plays John Mayall	39	Pickett, Wilson The Exciting Wilson Pickett	100
Mayall, John with Eric Clapton Blues Breakers	97	Pink Floyd A Piper At The Gates Of Dawn	171
Messiaen, Olivier Et Exspecto Resurrectionem Mortuorum	124	Pink Floyd A Saucerful Of Secrets	256
Miles, Buddy Express Expressway To Your Skull	293	Presley, Elvis Elvis	314
Millennium Begin	262	Presley, Elvis Golden Records Vol 3	10
Miller, Roger The Return Of Roger Miller	35	Presley, Elvis Spinout	112
Miller, Steve Band Children Of The Future	254	Pretty Things Emotions	145
Miller, Steve Band Sailor	284	Pretty Things Get The Picture?	68
Mingus, Charles The Black Saint And The Sinner Lady	6	Pretty Things The Pretty Things	37
Mingus, Charles Mingus At Monterey	307	Pretty Things S.F.Sorrow	303
Mitchell, Joni Song To A Seagull	234	Price, Alan Set A Price On His Head	184
Mitchell, Roscoe Sound	123	Prince Buster Fabulous Greatest Hits	226
Moby Grape same	156	Procol Harum same	207
Moby Grape Wow/Grape Jam	242	Procol Harum Shine On Brightly	276

Artist / Album	Page
Quicksilver Messenger Service same	243
Rainbow Ffolly Sallies Fforth	267
Rascals One Upon A Dream	230
Red Crayola The Parable Of Arable Land	159
Redding, Otis The Dock Of The Bay	231
Redding, Otis Live In Europe	165
Redding, Otis Otis Blue	60
Reich, Steve Live / Electric Music	316
Renbourn, John Another Monday	107
Renbourn, John same	77
Renbourn, John Sir John Alot Of Merrie Englande	231
Rendell, Don / Ian Carr Quintet Dusk Fire	98
Rendell, Don / Ian Carr Quintet Shades Of Blue	47
Revere, Paul & the Raiders Greatest Hits	152
Rhinoceros Rhinoceros	284
Richard, Cliff Cliff's Hit Album	9
Righteous Brothers You've Lost That Lovin' Feelin'	41
Riley, Terry In C	279
Rivers, Johnny Rewind	132
Robinson, Smokey and the Miracles Going To A Go-Go	66
Rockin' Berries In Town	49
Rolling Stones 12 x 5	28
Rolling Stones Aftermath	87
Rolling Stones Beggars Banquet	302
Rolling Stones Between The Buttons	125
Rolling Stones Big Hits (High Tide And Green Grass)	115
Rolling Stones Flowers	160
Rolling Stones Got Live If You Want It!	120
Rolling Stones Got Live If You Want It! EP	52
Rolling Stones Out Of Our Heads	60
Rolling Stones The Rolling Stones	18
Rolling Stones The Rolling Stones EP	17
Rolling Stones The Rolling Stones No.2	31
Rolling Stones Their Satanic Majesties Request	209
Rollins, Sonny East Broadway Run Down	121
Ronettes Presenting The Fabulous Ronettes	30
Rose, Tim Tim Rose	212
Rotary Connection Rotary Connection	232
Rush, Tom The Circle Game	309
Sagittarius Present Tense	262
Sainte Marie, Buffy It's My Way!	20
Sam & Dave Hold On, I'm Comin'	87
Sanders, Pharoah Tauhid	148
Savoy Brown Getting To The Point	266
Savoy Brown Blues Band Shake Down	184
Searchers Meet The Searchers	12
Searchers Smash Hits	118
Second Hand Reality	293
Seeds Future	179
Seeds The Seeds	85
Seeds A Web Of Sound	108
Seeger, Pete We Shall Overcome	13
Serpent Power The Serpent Power	168
Shadows Greatest Hits	8
Shangri-Las Leader Of The Pack	35
Shankar, Ravi At The Monterey Pop Festival	201
Shaw, Sandie The Golden Hits Of	81
Shepp, Archie Fire Music	59
Shepp, Archie Live In San Francisco	97
Shepp, Archie The Magic Of Ju-Ju	245
Shepp, Archie Mama Too Tight	144
Shorter, Wayne Speak No Evil	92
Silver Apples same	257
Silver, Horace Song For My Father	32
Simon and Garfunkel Bookends	242
Simon and Garfunkel The Graduate	222
Simon and Garfunkel Parsley, Sage, Rosemary And Thyme	108
Simon and Garfunkel Sounds Of Silence	78
Simon and Garfunkel Wednesday Morning, 3am	27
Simon, Paul The Paul Simon Songbook	58
Simone, Nina I Put A Spell On You	52
Sinatra, Frank September Of My Years	61
Sinatra, Frank Strangers In The Night	90
Sinatra, Nancy Boots	84
Skip Bifferty same	261
Sly & the Family Stone Dance To The Music	243
Sly & the Family Stone A Whole New Thing	192
Small Faces From The Beginning	156
Small Faces Ogden's Nut Gone Flake	247
Small Faces same (Decca)	88
Small Faces same (Immediate)	160
Smith, Jimmy The Cat	26
Smith, Jimmy Organ Grinder Swing	67
Smoke It's Smoke Time	140
Soft Machine The Soft Machine	304
Sonics Here Are The Sonics	38
Sonny and Cher Look At Us	64
Sopwith Camel The Sopwith Camel	195
Sorrows Take A Heart	68
Soundtrack 2001: A Space Odyssey	258
Soundtrack Blow-Up	166
Soundtrack Hair	298
Soundtrack The Sound Of Music	42
Spector, Phil A Christmas Gift For You From Philles Records	14
Spirit The Family That Plays Together	311
Spirit Spirit	221
Spontaneous Music Ensemble Challenge	94
Spontaneous Music Ensemble Karyobin	256
Spooky Tooth It's All About	253
Springfield, Dusty A Girl Called Dusty	19
Springfield, Dusty Golden Hits	113
SRC SRC	291
Standells Dirty Water	89
Staple Singers Soul Folk In Action	315
Status Quo Picturesque Matchstickable Messages	276
Steppenwolf same	224
Stevens, Cat Matthew & Son	144
Stewart, Al Bed Sitter Images	189
Stockhausen, Karlheinz Gruppen / Carré	316
Stone Poneys Evergreen Vol.2	161
Strawberry Alarm Clock Incense And Peppermints	199
Stuart, Chad & Jeremy Clyde Of Cabbages And Kings	181
Subotnick, Morton Silver Apples Of The Moon	170
Sun Ra The Heliocentric Worlds Of Sun Ra Vol.1	58
Sun Ra The Magic City	80
Supremes A' Go-Go	100
Supremes Greatest Hits	175
Supremes I Hear A Symphony	80
Supremes Where Did Our Love Go	24
Taylor, Cecil Unit Structures	106
Taylor, James same	309
Taylor, Johnnie Who's Making Love	315
Taylor, Mike Quartet Pendulum	93
Taylor, Mike Trio	150

Temptations Temptin'	66
Temptations With A Lot O' Soul	171
Ten Years After same	194
Ten Years After Undead	272
Them Again	78
Them The Angry Young Them	51
Thirteenth Floor Elevators Easter Everywhere	197
Thirteenth Floor Elevators The 13th Floor Elevators	111
Three Dog Night same	288
Tomorrow same	227
Tracey, Stan Quartet Jazz Suite – Under Milk Wood	71
Traffic Mr Fantasy	207
Traffic same	283
Troggs Best Of The Troggs	164
Turner, Ike & Tina River Deep – Mountain High	104
Turtles Happy Together	147
Tyner, McCoy The Real McCoy	193
Tyner, McCoy Tender Moments	280
Tyrannosaurus Rex My People Were Fair And Had Sky…	261
Tyrannosaurus Rex Prophets Sears & Sages…	287
Ultimate Spinach Ultimate Spinach	225
Uncredited Beatlemania	17
Unit 4+2 #1 Featuring Concrete And Clay	50
United States Of America United States Of America	236
Vanilla Fudge The Beat Goes On	230
Vanilla Fudge Renaissance	254
Vanilla Fudge same	172
Various Blues Anytime Vols 1 and 2	252
Various Chicago The Blues Today! Vols 1-3	82
Various Club Ska '67	178
Various A Collection Of 16 Tamla Motown Big Hits	41
Various Cybernetic Serendipity Music	297
Various Listen Here!	248
Various Living legends	126
Various The New Music	139
Various New Sounds In Electronic Music	213
Various R & B	25
Various Raw Blues	125
Various The Real Bahamas	122
Various Rhythm And Blues	21
Various Rhythm & Blues All Stars	21
Various The Rock Machine Turns You On	248
Various What's Shakin'	91
Velvet Underground The Velvet Underground & Nico	142
Velvet Underground White Light/White Heat	221
Ventures Golden Greats	184
Wailers The Wailing Wailers	72
Walker, Scott Scott	182
Walker, Scott Scott 2	239
Warwick, Dionne Golden Hits - Part One	210
Waters, Muddy Electric Mud	282
Watersons Frost And Fire	73
Webb, Jimmy Jim Webb Sings Jim Webb	274
West Coast Pop Art Experimental Band Part One	149
West Coast Pop Art Experimental Band Vol.2	190
West Coast Pop Art Experimental Band Vol.3	244
Westbrook, Mike Celebration	185
Westbrook, Mike Release	307
Who My Generation	70
Who A Quick One	121
Who Ready Steady Who EP	114
Who Sell Out	209
Williamson, Sonny Boy & the Yardbirds	76
Wind In The Willows same	262
Yardbirds Five Live Yardbirds	31
Yardbirds For Your Love	53
Yardbirds Having A Rave Up	65
Yardbirds The Hits Of The Yardbirds	187
Yardbirds Little Games	165
Yardbirds Yardbirds	96
Young Rascals Collections	127
Young Rascals Groovin'	167
Young Rascals The Young Rascals	85
Young Tradition Galleries	287
Young, Larry Unity	101
Young, Neil same	290
Youngbloods The Youngbloods	127
Zappa, Frank Lumpy Gravy	246
Zombies Begin Here	43
Zombies Odessey And Oracle	241

ABOUT THE AUTHOR

The first record that Nick Hamlyn bought with his own money was Chubby Checker's *Let's Twist Again*, just after his tenth birthday. His interest in music grew, proceeding in a very similar manner to the experiences of Harrison Ashby, the hero of Nick's 2015 novel, *Music For A Desert Island*. As a student at UEA, with limited funds, Nick often had to choose between buying records and buying food. He ate a lot of bread and margarine, but his record collection was larger than anyone else's he knew. Some years later, realising that he had thousands of records but was playing only hundreds, he opened a record shop to get rid of the surplus. With his surname, there was only one possibility for the name of the shop. It was *Pied Piper Records*. After twenty-four years, when Nick transferred his energies to the internet, he had to admit that his original strategy had not worked – his personal music collection had become many times larger.

In 1990 he decided to draw on nearly thirty years of music collecting knowledge by publishing his first Collectors' Record Price Guide. During the next decade and a half, the Guide moved through six editions, the later ones published by Penguin Books, and selling well enough to appear, from time to time, in the top ten non-fiction chart (yes, there was one!). During this time he also wrote regular articles for *Music Collector* magazine and contributed to *Vox*. His first appearance in print had come rather earlier than this, when he won second prize in a music writing competition organised by *Melody Maker* in 1980.

Nick has played guitar in several bands over the years. The first, a poetry and music collective called Paris Green (well it was the late sixties) also included the future writing star, Douglas Adams. Much later, Nick was delighted to find himself playing in the same band as a former member of the progressive rock group, Solstice. Another later band, called Four Bop Drop, released a CD of relentlessly uncommercial improvised music on the Slam label in 1997. In live performances on different occasions, this band accompanied trombonist Paul Rutherford and baritone saxophonist George Haslam, alto saxophonist George Khan, and drummer Charles Hayward. More recently, Nick appeared on several occasions in a duo with his sister, Cathy, performing songs written by both of them.

In 2017, Nick published a collection of his short stories, under the title *The Tunnel Of Worlds*. Then, in 2018, he published the book of which he is most proud and which took several years to write, *The First Time: A Book of 20th and 21st Century Music Firsts*. This is a history and discussion of who did what first within the world of music during the last 120 years. He set up his own company, PPR Publishing, in order to produce the book and has since published a small number of books by other people. The company website is www.pprpublishing.co.uk. In 2020 *The First Time* was a finalist in the general non-fiction category of the prestigious Next Generation Indie Book Awards.

His 2020 book, *A Toubab In The Gambia*, is an update of a small privately published book of poems and pictures from 2001, documenting the first of many visits to The Gambia in West Africa.

OTHER BOOKS BY NICK HAMLYN

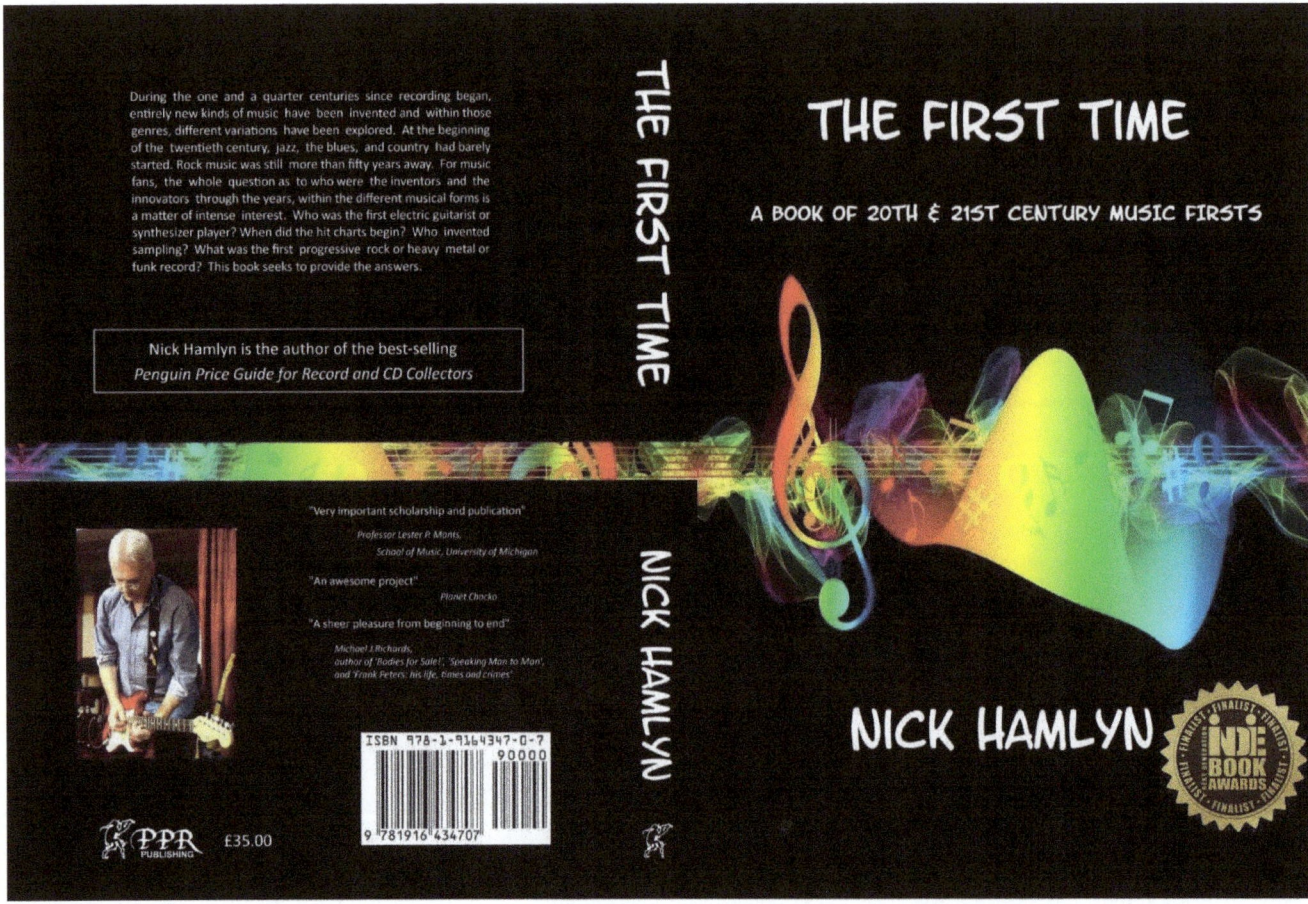

Amazon reviews:

Sam C
5.0 out of 5 stars **Wonderfully comprehensive**
This book provides a lovely overview of approx 150 years of music. It's packed full of information, pictures and interesting asides. I've greatly enjoyed dipping in and out of it and listening to the tracks mentioned, as well as being able to see more clearly which musicians influenced others and how their styles developed. All in all a fantastic book to have for anyone interested in popular music - although I would recommend reading sections that interest you rather than reading it cover to cover as the book is over 400 pages long!

B J Bear
5.0 out of 5 stars **A must for all music lovers**
This book is a must for every library. It is essential for students of music. The facts are amazing and very helpful in answering quiz questions.

dibdob1967
5.0 out of 5 stars **A must for any music enthusiast**
What a fabulous way to dive deep into the world of music & stories of how the music of the 20th century was shaped

A TOUBAB IN THE GAMBIA

Poetry, prose, and pictures

MUSIC FOR A DESERT ISLAND

Novel

Harrison Ashby is a music fan. 'Obsessed' is how his wife Carole would have described him. Born at the start of the nineteen fifties, Harry finds his teenage years underscored by the music of The Beatles and Jimi Hendrix. He also finds his life unexpectedly entwined with that of a successful folk singer by the name of Jed Brandt. As though he were a guest on the long-running BBC radio show, Desert Island Discs, Harry chooses eight pieces of music that seem to represent different areas of his life particularly well and describes how this works for him, as he tells the story of his life. It is an account that is part love story, part teen memoir and coming of age narrative, and part musical discussion. It will interest anyone else who loves music, whether or not they are as overwhelmed by it as much as Harry is, and anyone who remembers the sixties and seventies as he does, or who is drawn to finding out what those decades might have been like for a music fan. In addition, Music For A Desert Island is probably the only novel to include a discography at the end.

THE TUNNEL OF WORLDS

54 short stories

A collection of 53 short stories and one short play by the author of the Penguin Price Guide for Record & CD Collectors and the novel Music for a Desert Island. Like the novel, many of the stories are music based, if only as regards the title. Some are science fiction, many are not; some are happy, some are sad; some are intriguing, a couple try to be scary.

THE PENGUIN PRICE GUIDE FOR RECORD AND CD COLLECTORS

Six editions. No longer available.

FORTHCOMING:

THE GOLDEN AGE OF ROCK   VOLUME TWO   1969-1972

THE GOLDEN AGE OF ROCK   VOLUME THREE   1973-1976

Books available from Amazon or from Nick Hamlyn via piedmusic@gmail.com / www.pprpublishing.co.uk

www.ingramcontent.com/pod-product-compliance
Lightning Source LLC
Chambersburg PA
CBHW051253110526
44588CB00026B/2981